THE HANDBOOK OF SOCIOLOGY AND HUMAN RIGHTS

T0392199

THE HANDBOOK OF SOCIOLOGY AND HUMAN RIGHTS

Edited by

David L. Brunsma
Keri E. Iyall Smith
Brian K. Gran

LONDON AND NEW YORK

First published 2013 by Paradigm Publishers

Published 2016 by Routledge
2 Park Square, Milton Park, Abingdon, Oxon OX14 4RN
711 Third Avenue, New York, NY 10017, USA

Routledge is an imprint of the Taylor & Francis Group, an informa business

Library of Congress Cataloging-in-Publication Data

Handbook of sociology and human rights / edited by David L. Brunsma, Keri E. Iyall Smith,
Brian K. Gran.
   p. cm.
  Includes bibliographical references and index.
  ISBN 978-1-59451-883-6 (pbk : alk. paper)
  1. Sociology—Handbooks, manuals, etc. 2. Human rights—Handbooks, manuals, etc.
I. Brunsma, David L., 1970- II. Iyall Smith, Keri E., 1973- III. Gran, Brian, 1963-
HM585.H363 2012
306.2—dc23

2012024516

ISBN13: 978-1-59451-882-9 (hbk)
ISBN13: 978-1-59451-883-6 (pbk)

Designed and Typeset by Straight Creek Bookmakers.

From Dave:
To Rachel. Forever and a day. I love you.
From Keri:
To True, who has not known life without this book project (literally).
From Brian:
To my family. SDG

Contents

Groups in Society

Institutions in Society

Living Together Locally and Globally

Methodology, Practice, and Theory

FIGURES AND TABLES

Figures

Tables

ACRONYMS

AFL-CIO	American Federation of Labor and Congress of Industrial Organizations
ANT	actor network theory
ASA	American Sociological Association
CA	conversation analysis
CBSM	collective behavior and social movements
CEDAW	Convention on the Elimination of All Forms of Discrimination against Women
CUS	community and urban sociology
DOMA	Defense of Marriage Act
EM	ethnomethodology
EPI	Economic Policy Institute
FGC	female genital cutting
fMRI	functional magnetic resonance imaging
HRW	Human Rights Watch
ICANN	Internet Corporation for Assigned Names and Numbers
ICC	International Criminal Court
ICCPR	International Covenant on Civil and Political Rights
ICESCR	International Covenant on Economic, Social, and Cultural Rights
ICJ	International Court of Justice
ICT	information and communication technology
ICTY	International Criminal Tribunal for the Former Yugoslavia
ILO	International Labour Organization
IMF	International Monetary Fund
INGO	international nongovernmental organization
IRAF	International Association for Religious Freedom
IRLA	International Religious Liberty Association
LGBT	lesbian, gay, bisexual, and transgender
LIS	Luxembourg Income Study
MCA	membership categorization analysis
MSM	men who have sex with men
NAACP	National Association for the Advancement of Colored People
NAFTA	North American Free Trade Agreement
NELP	National Employment Law Project
NGO	nongovernmental organization

NHSL	National Health and Social Life
NIA	National Institute on Aging
NICHD	National Institute of Child Health and Human Development
NSF	National Science Foundation
OECD	Organization for Economic Cooperation and Development
PDHRE	People's Decade for Human Rights Education
PET	positron emission tomography
PISA	Programme for International Student Assessment
SA	sequential analysis
SALC	sociology of age and the life course
SKAT	science, knowledge, and technology
SSP	social structure and personality
STD	sexually transmitted disease
STI	sexually transmitted infection
STS	science and technology studies
SWS	Sociologists for Women in Society
TAN	transnational advocacy network
TANF	Temporary Aid to Needy Families
TINA	there is no alternative
TVA	Tennessee Valley Authority
UDHR	Universal Declaration of Human Rights
UN	United Nations
UNCRC	United Nations Convention on the Rights of the Child
UNESCO	United Nations Educational, Scientific, and Cultural Organization
UNICEF	United Nations International Children's Emergency Fund
WHO	World Health Organization
WSF	World Social Forum
WTO	World Trade Organization
WWII	World War II

PREFACE

Judith R. Blau

Human rights provides a perspective on the world, encourages us to imagine how the world can be a better place, and, indeed, gives us the tools to work with others to make that world a better place. There is no getting around it: hyper-capitalism, especially in the United States, has led to soaring inequalities, hunger, homelessness, disregard for the rights of migrants, and, indirectly, high rates of child abuse and the abuse of women. In contrast, a human rights perspective emphasizes equality, human dignity, and human security (focusing, for instance, on the right to food and housing, labor rights, cultural rights, the rights of LGBT persons and migrants, and the protection of vulnerable groups, such as children). This list is not exhaustive but serves to illustrate how sociology intersects with human rights in a comprehensive way.

United Nations human rights treaties and human rights declarations clarify the particular rights of individuals, but sociologists have the imagination to envision a society that promotes interdependence among human beings and the rights of all individuals. To illustrate, since every child, according to the Convention on the Rights of the Child, has the right to an education, sociologists can help clarify how this right must accompany racial and ethnic inclusion, a comprehensive curriculum that allows each child to find his or her strengths, and the promotion of children's health and nutrition. It is also useful for sociologists to recognize that human rights doctrine has evolved to encompass collective goods, including, for example, cultural pluralism, a healthy environment, universal access to the Internet, and participatory democracy.

It is the case that human rights as a conceptual and practical framework is relatively new. One might date its origins to 1948 (December 10, to be precise), when the fifty-one member states that made up the UN General Assembly approved the Universal Declaration of Human Rights. The prevailing interpretation is that Europeans were so ashamed and humiliated by the horrific acts of genocide committed by the Nazis that they greatly desired to help establish a new world order that advanced peace, human welfare, and a world order grounded in the principle of universal human dignity. These principles were enshrined in the Universal Declaration of Human Rights. Yet in 1948, the imperial powers that dominated the United Nations were crumbling. There were 51 members of the United Nations in 1948; by now the number of member states is 192, and the UN Human Rights Council has nearly as many members as the UN had in 1948, namely 47. In contrast with the 1948 composition of the United Nations, the majority of states represented on the Council are African and Asian. The United States joined the Council in 2009. A remarkable innovation of the Council was to mandate that every country undergo a review of its human rights laws and practices and that nongovernmental organizations (NGOs) be invited to submit reports. In the case of the US review, the US Human Rights Network coordinated submission of reports from twenty-six NGOs.

Have human rights improved in the United States since the nation's review by the Council in fall 2010? Not at all. Whereas the poverty rate declined throughout most of the twentieth century, it rose steadily after 2000 and still increases. The grimmest portrait of poverty in the United States is that 20 percent of American children live in poverty. Poverty is a grim reaper and bodes ill for many other indicators of children's well-being: health, social exclusion by peers, school achievement, and social and emotional adjustment. To put this into perspective, the United States ranks next to last (after the United Kingdom) for all Organization for Economic Cooperation and Development countries on a multidimensional scale of children's well-being. Obviously, the American economic system is not working.

But any economic system depends on political institutions and, most of all, social arrangements and social consensus. This is where sociologists come in. This volume is a cornucopia—or, we might say, a feast—that is rich with theory and applications. It is also an intellectual breakthrough with so many sociologists joining together to shift the sociological paradigm to one that frankly professes—and celebrates—the humanness of human beings.

INTRODUCTION

SOCIOLOGY AND HUMAN RIGHTS

RESITUATING THE DISCIPLINE

David L. Brunsma, Keri E. Iyall Smith, and Brian K. Gran

The roots of the discipline of sociology sink deep into the fertile soils of human rights. While Émile Durkheim seemed unsure of human rights' bases, he helped form the League for the Rights of Man and the Citizen in 1898 (Cotterrell 2007, 117). Max Weber's interest in human rights was tied to his study of expansions in capitalism and bureaucratization (Joas 2005). Karl Marx, famously critical of Bruno Bauer, produced a theory of emancipation in "On the Jewish Question" (1843). In commenting that "human rights are never in such danger as when their only defenders are political institutions and their officers," George Herbert Mead (1915) offered an early recognition of the importance of the struggle for the dignity and self-determination of people and their communities. While using sociological principles and tools to tackle inequalities, W. E. B. Du Bois insisted that ensuring justice is meaningful to everyone.

The foundations of contemporary sociology can be seen in the intellectual traditions of sociology's subdisciplines and their intimate ties to human rights. Contributors to this volume explain how social movements have led to human rights, how our epistemological and theoretical foundations are tethered to human rights, how dignity is a fundamental social-psychological phenomenon, how environmental disasters uncover the structures of human rights (or lack thereof), how organizations could be structured to encourage the development of the human rights of all, how those sociologies that have been marginalized since the founding of the discipline have theorized human rights, as well as how sociology is the discipline centrally poised to develop scholarship devoted to understanding human rights. Sociologists study the globalizing spread of human rights and why human rights look and work differently across societies and time periods. Furthermore, sociologists are concerned with politics and institutions of human rights. They ask whether human rights vary across life courses and localities. Our contributors are setting stages in this volume from whence can emerge a variety of sociologies of human rights and human rights–based sociologies. This is exciting.

Early foundations of the discipline in the American context saw a deep connection between scholarship and activism (e.g., Jane Addams and W. E. B. Du Bois). Such a connection continues to be a subject of discussion within sociology. Although she was not trained as a sociologist, Jane Addams was a charter member of the American Sociological Association. In 1899 Addams published an article in *The American Journal of Sociology* on the benefits of trade unions for society and its improvement. Work she conducted and organized at Hull House continues to be of interest to human rights scholars and sociologists of human rights, including in the areas of labor rights, peace, and making democracy work. W. E. B. Du Bois's early work in Philadelphia and Atlanta, and even in the United Nations from Ghana, was centrally concerned with scholar-activism. Today, groups like Sociologists Without Borders and its members use their research, publications, and intellectual strength to shine bright lights on human rights. The American Sociological Association has taken stands on human rights violations of scholars, urging governments to release scholars and activists. The American Association for the Advancement of Science has established a Science and Human Rights Program, one component of which is devoted to promoting the welfare of scientists, preventing breaches of their rights to research and publish, and, radically, supporting the idea that all human beings have the human right to benefit from science.

Topics at the heart of human rights scholarship are ones that sociologists vigorously research from a range of perspectives. A cornerstone of human rights is the inherent dignity of individuals. For some time, sociologists have studied individuals' basic needs, how they differ across time and space, and whether a hierarchy of needs is universal. A crucial aspect to human life is safety and avoiding violence, whether arising from armed conflict or found in family homes. From their discipline's humble beginnings, sociologists have identified different forms of inequality and its impacts on individuals, families, workplaces, communities, and societies. Why does inequality persist, how can societies reduce it, and why do some individuals and groups prefer it? Sociologists have employed various methodologies to study discrimination; their work has served as evidence in lawsuits seeking to prove and end illegal discrimination. Of course, sociologists are concerned with social change and what factors lead to successful social change or to failures. Sociologists have produced extensive knowledge of how individuals collectively form groups and how these groups can become social movements that produce significant changes in societies. Not surprisingly, sociologists have studied how laws are made and work, as well as whether laws are useful in producing social change. Changes in opinions, beliefs, and values are potent forces for social change. At the same time, social change often has lasting impacts on how people think and live.

Human rights scholars have forcefully argued that human rights are especially useful when governments fail to enforce citizenship rights. Sociologists have studied how communities strive to reach self-determination and how governments may attempt to weaken indigenous cultures. When governments fail to enforce rights—or worse—individuals and families often emigrate from those contexts. Sociologists have identified push factors, including persecution, and pull factors, including expanded opportunities, as reasons why immigrants attempt to reach specific host countries. They have studied the experiences of refugees, including their efforts to secure human rights. Global economic and political change is manifest in the daily lives and struggles of women and other members of communities all over the world. These changes are often hidden from view in analyses of globalization that start from the perspective of multinational corporations, transnational organizations, and international political institutions. Sociology, we believe, is clearly central to studying, understanding, negotiating, and, ultimately, achieving human rights for all.

ENRICHING SOCIOLOGY THROUGH HUMAN RIGHTS

Human rights scholarship requires a careful look at the construction of human-ness—what does it mean to be human? To determine the rights, privileges, and duties of humans, we must conduct empirical and theoretical examinations of humans and their collectivities. Sociological studies of human suffering and vulnerabilities are just beginning to explore this question—and the most promising work is that which takes seriously the question of human rights.

With a deeper understanding of what it means to be human, sociologists must then reexamine community. Under what conditions do people flourish? How does community enable people to enjoy rights and freedoms? What duties must community members carry out to ensure the human rights of others? How can communities create places for the enjoyment of physical and mental health—for all? These are a few questions that will benefit from sociological analysis. Sociologists are experts in the study of community. They can apply their interests in collective human life for the welfare of individuals and communities alike.

Through the study of human rights, sociology will change, giving us a better understanding of relationships between groups in society. Sociologists will uncover another way of exploring points of conflict in both contemporary and historical societies. Analysis of human rights reveals new information about colonialism and resistance. By looking at the beneficiaries of human rights, scholars of human rights uncover new questions about structure and agency that demand sociological exploration.

As sociologists expand the subject of their research to better understand human rights, it is also necessary to think carefully about the ways of doing sociology. The study of human rights makes interdisciplinarity (Frodeman, Klein, and Mitcham 2010) an essential step, as other social science disciplines, the humanities, and legal scholars have undertaken extensive research on human rights. Sociological stud-ies of human rights that ignore this work will provide less relevant and informed knowledge. Similarly, transnational research is essential for understanding human rights collectively. If human rights truly are to reflect the needs of all humans, all voices must be heard to conceptualize human rights. Comparative research allows sociologists to better understand the diversity of ideas about human rights and the accommodations necessary to enjoy human rights. Sociologists will also need to consider the role of lived experience in their research. How do interviews with those who survived the conflict in Darfur, for example, fit into empirical analysis of genocide? Can sociologists examine human rights empirically and engage in advocacy? When is this appropriate, and are there times when it is inappropriate? Advocacy that is informed by knowledge can be a powerful tool in creating the conditions necessary for providing human rights.

Human rights also challenge us as sociologists to honor human rights in our own work as researchers, teachers, and community members. Sociologists are well positioned to consider the place of human rights in doing science. Sociologists can help ensure that, through the process of developing and disseminating knowledge, not only are violations of human rights prevented, but human rights are fully implemented and enjoyed by all. The sociologies to be developed that are most relevant to this goal are those that are attentive (as are the contributors to this volume) to human rights.

The study of human rights offers sociologists the chance to revisit core values of our discipline, especially social justice and peace. American sociology has its early roots in social justice, and over the course of years of strengthening our methods of empirical analysis, it has become easy to forget those roots—and our subject of study (human social life). The study of human rights requires sociologists to reconnect to the history of the discipline and to remember the individuals who make up the N in our studies. Careful consideration of our research subjects (partners) can translate into affirmations of their voices. Thus, the sociological study of human rights can allow sociologists to give voice to their research subjects rather than further objectifying them (and human life). Sociologists examining human rights will also be pushed to consider both the global scope of research and concepts and the contextual-level factors that uniquely impact human rights outcomes.

ENRICHING HUMAN RIGHTS THROUGH SOCIOLOGICAL INQUIRY

Some of sociology's key ideas, theoretical perspectives, and methodological approaches may strengthen human rights scholarship. One key idea sociologists can contribute to human rights scholarship is social construction, the idea that society makes things (categories of people, politics, economics, hierarchies, human rights, etc.); individuals then act toward each other on the basis of the meanings of these things. For instance, sociologists, as well as biologists, contend that race is socially constructed. Studies of the DNA of people belonging to different "racial" categories reveal more similarities across racial categories than within racial categories. Sociologists have demonstrated that some institutions—for instance, mainstream media—help build and maintain these and other social constructions. One common social construction found in mainstream media and elsewhere is vulnerability and the dependence of young people on adults. Sociologists have demonstrated that young people are often not only capable of taking care of themselves but can manage households that include their siblings.

A basic but often impenetrable wall for sociologists is the wall of essentialism; engagement with human rights will purge this. This wall blocks us, epistemologically, from believing in variation and therefore from seeing the evidence of it all around us. Virtually nothing in the social world is essential. Virtually nothing in the social world is an immutable and fixed reality. The notion and reality of diversity is thrilling and constantly changing. Indeed, all we have on the planet is diversity; all we have is variation; we have only glorious, colorful kaleidoscopes of dizzying and amazing variability—end of story. Humankind has been creating this variability since geography and technology allowed it to move great distances. However, our institutions, constitutions, discourses, social constructions, and, yes, sciences seem to do one thing: categorize, limit, bound, silence, mark—and people lose out as a result. Thus, our goal here is to rewrite, renarrate, and reconceptualize our lives, institutions, and interactions in ways that allow all this variation to flourish and remain centered in the experience of itself—human rights helps us focus on this endeavor. The notion and theory of intersectionality (Collins 1990; but also see the brilliant issue of *Gender and Society* 26, no. 1) is the idea that inequality often arises from multiple inequalities, such as those based on differences of race, gender, and class (Collins 1990). Intersectionality is complex (Choo and Ferree 2010) but may provide insights into complicated experiences of inequality that human rights work can tackle.

Social institutions and practices construct groups and foster differences. Political, religious, and legal institutions, for instance, are crucial sites of inquiry into the opportunities and/or constraints of doing human rights. Political institutions and practices rely on categories, such as citizen. Many governments distinguish between citizen and noncitizen. One entitlement of many citizens is the ability to use voting to hold governments accountable. Such a construction means noncitizens cannot hold governments accountable through voting. Instead, if they are to hold a government accountable, noncitizens must use other means. When it comes to voting and other rights, when governments do not enforce citizenship rights, citizens and noncitizens turn to human rights to seek justice and experience socially acceptable living standards, among other rights. In addition, religious institutions often differentiate between adherents and nonadherents. The basis of professions is a distinction between the professional and the nonprofessional. While government supports professions as institutions, government also uses its power to maintain national secrets, as well as what is not secret, what constitutes a military actor versus a contractor, and where the line falls between child abuse and parental discipline. "Law" can be used not only to distinguish between the haves and the have-nots but also to help the haves come out ahead (Galanter 1974). Law can help members of social groups that have historically been in institutionally weak positions. Indeed, rights can indicate membership in a society and that members of a social group are entitled to fair treatment and consideration (Williams 1991). Laws can be, and have been, used to challenge and weaken economic discrimination arising from employment practices, such as in the case of lawsuits brought to end pay inequities and hazardous work practices.

Sociological methodologies may prove useful to studies of human rights. Sociology and other social sciences have developed a considerable ensemble of methodological approaches to studying social phenomena. This ensemble contains qualitative methods, which are especially useful for exploring new phenomena of human rights practices, giving voice to those whose experiences are sometimes ignored, and studying complex processes, such as how human rights practices work in families and communities. Quantitative methods are useful for testing theoretical perspectives of human rights implementation, exploring diversity of human rights implementation, including over time, and attempting to make generalizations about impacts of human rights advances. Sociological comparative and historical methods, which are shared with other social sciences, can be used to study how human rights proponents pursue human rights in different places and times and how notions of human rights have changed. Visual sociology, widely embraced as an innovative approach, is an especially useful means by which to consider frame and reference point. Some visual methods can empower subjects to become research participants.

STICKY ISSUES

Human rights—in practice and in study—are not without controversy. We do not wish to avoid any potential points of controversy or conflict in the study of human rights. Rather, this handbook, with its scope and range, creates an opportunity to reveal, examine, and ask questions that may create a path toward resolving the sticking points. In the end, we truly wish for the forty-four contributions across this volume to speak collectively in whatever myriad ways they might to whoever might read them. We do, however, feel it necessary to highlight some of the issues that scholars get "stuck" on in the process.

There are considerable questions about the role of human rights within the discipline of sociology. Using the concept of social construction, sociologists may be able to conceptualize human rights in new ways and respond to the shifting empirical and theoretical answers to the question, What are human rights? Beyond answering this question, sociologists must also consider the intended and unintended consequences of the changes to these conceptualizations. Sociologists are uniquely equipped to examine how societies can impact social action. Human rights, perhaps a creation of society, and human rights doctrine, clearly a creation of society, have the power to coerce action. Many have noted the extensive work of sociologists cataloging human misery. Thus far, sociologists have not been able to do much work to safeguard against the violation of human rights. But that does not mean that understanding and producing such sociologically grounded safeguards are beyond the scope of sociological research. For instance, sociologists could examine when human rights or human rights doctrine does change action and when it does not. What is the relationship between ethics, human rights, and sociology? What is the relationship between values, human rights, and sociology? Such questions are at the core of scholars' visceral reactions to human rights—yet, that discomfort may prompt sociologists to rethink answers and think about new sociological questions, which certainly is a good thing.

MICRO-LEVEL QUESTIONS

Distinctive questions and concerns are found at the micro level of sociological analysis for the study of human rights. The micro level is uniquely suited to creativity, in both process and outcome. Interpersonal communication (verbal and otherwise) facilitates interactions needed to create and re-create lives based in and supportive of human rights. Such work will inform sociological analyses of rational-choice perspectives of human behavior and institutions, providing insights into how human rights can change what is understood as rational behavior and decisions.

The work of international criminal law, with its focus on the prosecution of individual actors, is cutting-edge when it comes to investigating human rights violations. But we need equally rigorous analysis of human rights affirmations. Symbolic interactionists, ethnomethodologists, sociologists who study communication, mathematical sociologists, and other sociologists are well equipped to conduct this type of analysis. This analysis of micro-level behavior may encourage sociologists to call for changes to legal structures, thereby creating better mechanisms for encouraging rights-affirming behavior and deterring behavior that violates human rights. Scholars studying crime, law, and deviance are able to tell us, for instance, that certainty of punishment is more of a deterrent than severity. Careful analysis of particular social events and organizations, such as tribunals and International Criminal Court trials, may allow sociologists to consider how we are creating new conceptions of human rights violators and practitioners.

Methods used to conduct micro-level analysis will be useful to consider the role of sociologists in human rights research. Qualitative analyses of language, culture, and practices can examine the contexts in which humans practice rights and commit wrongs. Methodology that centers human rights as a part of the everyday will advance both sociology and the study of human rights. Methodologists will push other sociologists to think creatively about forms of both data and analysis. Beyond legal documents, treaties, and conventions, we need to ask what these words on paper mean to people when they interact with each other; does their meaning change behavior or not? Careful investigation using micro-level analysis will be essential to understanding the answer to this question. This research must also recognize that our actions are embedded in distinct local contexts, and sociologists will need to consider carefully how contextual-level factors do or do not impact individual behaviors.

MACRO-LEVEL QUESTIONS

Sociological analysis of institutions in society may further our understanding of barriers and paths to human rights. Some institutions, including technology, the economy, and the criminal justice system (local and global), may present challenges to human rights. While technologies have the potential to protect or violate human rights, it is important to gain a better understanding of how technologies are used and how their use can lead to the distribution of human rights protections or violations. Beyond their intended use, technologies can have unintended consequences for human rights, such as precluding the use of human rights. While failures of technology are normal, oftentimes the impacts of these failures on the environment, distribution of power, and human rights experiences are not readily understood.

A sociological analysis of socioeconomic structures, at all levels of inquiry, is essential to understanding human rights violations and affirmations. Such an analysis will allow for critical restructuring of economic institutions for the purpose of advancing human rights. Sociologists should continue their critical examinations of inequality and how institutions and actors that shape wealth distribution weaken human rights. Critical analyses are essential to identifying new institutional forms that may be useful, perhaps necessary, for affirming human rights. It follows that the political state must also come under the sociologist's microscope, and as the contributions across this volume attest, sociologists are in a central position to add to this conversation.

Just as it is necessary to analyze criminal actions at the individual level, sociologists will be well served to examine how the criminal justice system can contribute to the universalization of human rights. Prosecution of human rights violations is one means by which to define such violations and to identify the value of human rights to various societies. Because there have been relatively few such prosecutions, either via universal jurisdiction or UN courts, many are skeptical about the role of the criminal justice system (local and global) in preventing and stopping human rights violations. A bleak history of prosecutions does not, however, mean that criminal justice systems will forever fail those who lack human rights. Sociological analysis of instances that result in prosecution and those that do not may shed light on how contextual factors influence practices of human rights law. Courts and legal systems that affirm human rights can be powerful apparatuses for securing human rights and halting violations.

The conceptualization of human rights has a history of controversy as old as (or older than) human rights themselves. Are human rights universal? Cultural relativism would urge us to say no. However, researchers have found that cultural diversity has been exaggerated (Glendon 2001 cited in Mahoney 2006), and some call for embracing human rights despite cultural differences (Goonesekere 1994). They find that Confucian, Hindu, Muslim, and European thinkers all agree on basic human rights—that their "arcs" bend toward similar conceptions. These thought traditions share "common convictions," even though they have different ways of teaching and explaining them. Thus, while the universal framework that has been formalized has Western origins, we can in fact find the roots of human rights across cultures and societies. Sociologists should work to discover more similarities among groups of people and expand our understanding of what it means to be a human who is endowed with rights.

As scholars of human rights, we should approach this topic critically. The violation of human rights is systemic: as we write this introduction, ongoing protests in Syria and Egypt are being met by military force with deadly consequences, Haitians are remembering the earthquake that took basic rights of shelter and water now two years ago, Tibetans are enduring decades-long religious persecution, and an oil pipeline that will cross water reservoirs and sacred sites in Canada and the United States is being debated. If we are to contribute to the improvement of human welfare, we must be honest about the state of human rights and the potential to live human rights.

THE HANDBOOK OF SOCIOLOGY AND HUMAN RIGHTS

Representing an exciting moment for sociology to further energize and develop a sociology of human rights (or, more to the point, sociologies of human rights), *The Handbook of Sociology and Human Rights* brings together leading and emergent scholars who seriously engage in revolutionary questions, resituate their substantive concerns within new terrains, and begin mapping the intellectual and practical contours of a human rights sociology. Each chapter responds to two primary questions: (1) How does a human rights perspective change the questions that sociologists ask, the theoretical perspectives and methods that sociologists use, and the implications of sociological inquiry? and (2) How can the sociological enterprise (its epistemologies, theories, methodologies, and results) inform and push human rights theory, discourse, and implementation toward a better world for all humanity?

When we began this project, the American Sociological Association sponsored forty-five sections that support its members' interests in substantive, theoretical, methodological, and applied areas (there are now fifty-one, with human rights being added just after we started this project, followed by sections on altruism, morality, and social solidarity; body and embodiment; global and transnational sociology; inequality, poverty, and mobility; and development). We approached progressive, critical scholars in the hopes they would contribute work to this project that would accomplish several goals. The first objective was to present a brief summary of the state of the area of sociological inquiry and a reckoning of the central concerns and questions that motivate it. The second objective was to give readers a summary of the key findings in the area as well as the most prominent methods its practitioners use. The third objective was to provide readers with a critical discussion of what the human rights paradigm can take from the work in each area, as well as to describe how the human rights paradigm might resituate the area and its constituent questions, methods, theories, and findings and, in turn, reorient readers toward a new set of inquiries, particularly concerning how human rights redefines the research situation and what new questions can and should be asked. Finally, given this, we encouraged the authors to think broadly and critically about doing the work of human rights sociology, to look forward—to raise new questions and new possibilities for both their respective areas and human rights realization.

ONE

GROUPS IN SOCIETY

≈≈

CHAPTER ONE

SEX AND GENDER

Barbara Gurr and Nancy A. Naples

The intellectual history and topics of interest in the sociology of sex and gender are tied intimately to human rights scholarship and activism. The field was generated through the advocacy of activists inside and outside the discipline inspired by the women's movement of the late 1960s and early 1970s (Fox 1995). Recognizing that women's knowledge and experience had been either erased or diminished in importance by a discipline dominated by men and fueled by patriarchal assumptions of what counts as knowledge and who should be the primary conveyers of sociological insights, women sociologists challenged the gendered assumptions of the field (Smith 1987). In 1969, Alice Rossi, who would become one of the first women presidents of the American Sociological Association (ASA) in 1983, presented data at a business meeting demonstrating the underrepresentation of women and the discrimination they faced in the discipline. As a consequence, in 1971, feminist sociologists formed their own association, Sociologists for Women in Society (SWS), and produced a separate journal, *Gender & Society*, which is now one of the leading journals in interdisciplinary gender studies. SWS dedicated itself to establishing the importance of sex and gender research for sociology; ensuring that women's contributions to knowledge and other aspects of social, economic, political, and cultural life were acknowledged in academic literature; challenging sexist language in sociology journals; and increasing women's visibility in the ASA (Fox 1995). The ASA's Sex and Gender Section was formed in 1973 and is now one of the largest sections of the ASA. SWS members hold prominent leadership positions in the ASA, including the presidency. Since the Sex and Gender Section's founding, three new ASA sections have been added that developed directly from the feminist scholarship on sex and gender.

The topics that are prominent in the field of sex and gender are also at the heart of human rights scholarship. They include processes of discrimination and economic inequalities, the roles of social activism and law in challenging gender inequality, the sources of violence against women, and the role of culture in shaping gendered understandings and practices. Sociologists of sex and gender also address the gendered processes of economic development and migration as well as militarization and global capitalism, among other social structural and historical processes (Fukumura and Matsuoka 2002; Mendez 2005; Salzinger 2005). In this regard, sociologists of sex and gender argue that a gender lens offers a powerful tool for uncovering the social dynamics shaping all major institutions (Brush 2003; Coltraine and Adams 2008; Lorber 2002). To capture the diversity of these experiences, sociologists of sex and gender frequently approach their work from an intersectional perspective (Baca Zinn and Dill 1996; Collins 1990; Naples 2009), paying attention to the intersections of gender, race, class, sexuality, age, culture, and other factors that differentially shape social life rather than concentrating on a single dimension.

THE SOCIOLOGY OF SEX AND GENDER

EXAMINING PROCESSES OF DISCRIMINATION AND ECONOMIC INEQUALITIES

Sociologists of sex and gender focus attention on how sex and gender shape structures of inequality and power. Their research addresses structural factors that derive from gender inequality, including the wage gaps between men and women and other forms of discrimination in the labor force (Britton 2003; England 2005); the gender gap in electoral politics (Rossi 1983); and sexist and heteronormative assumptions embedded in law and social policy (Bernstein and Reimann 2001; Naples 1991).

Another dimension of this scholarship relates to understanding the contribution of global economic restructuring for gender dynamics and economic inequalities. Sociologists of sex and gender highlight the fact that globalization is a result of particular actions taken by identifiable actors and that globalization lands in particular places (Sassen 2006, 2007). Rather than view globalization as a process that occurs at a distance from the everyday lives and activities of particular actors, they demonstrate that global economic and political change is manifest in the daily lives and struggles of women and other members of communities in different parts of the world in ways that are often hidden from view in analyses of globalization that start from the perspective of multinational corporations, transnational organizations, and international political institutions (Naples and Desai 2002, vii).

UNDERSTANDING THE ROLE OF SOCIAL ACTIVISM AND LAW FOR CHALLENGING GENDER INEQUALITY

Until sociologists of sex and gender focused attention on women's political activism, especially the important roles they play in their communities, the extent and variety of women's political participation were ignored or unexamined (Naples 1998). Women's community work and activism, when noticed at all by academics, were understood primarily as a natural extension of their caretaking roles and as part of a maternalist politics in which women's engagement in the public sphere was justified through their identities as mothers (Koven and Michel 1993). In contrast to these assessments, women as community activists contribute countless hours of unpaid labor to campaigns to enhance the physical and environmental quality of their communities while tending to the emotional and social needs of other community members. Their approach to community development and leadership often involves collective and empowering strategies that encourage other women and other residents frequently left out of decision-making roles in formal voluntary associations and political parties to increase their political participation (Naples 2011). This scholarship also explores the role of transnational women's, LGBT, and social justice movements that challenge gender oppression, sexual violence, and other human rights violations (Adam, Duyvendak, and Krouwel 1999; Naples and Desai 2002; Tripp and Ferree 2006).

ANALYZING THE SOURCES OF VIOLENCE AGAINST WOMEN IN PUBLIC AND PRIVATE SPHERES

One of the most important issues addressed by sociologists of sex and gender involves analyzing the many ways that women, minority men, and sexually nonconforming men become targets of violence. Studies of domestic violence were noticeably missing in early sociological literature on the family. With the recognition of the ways power inequalities in marital relations contribute to women's risk of violence in the family, as well as how women become targets of sexual harassment at work and in public spaces, sociologists of sex and gender revealed the daily costs associated with gender and sexual inequalities (Baker 2007).

In considering factors that contribute to violence against women, sociologists and other feminist scholars of sex and gender also brought attention to the roles of militarization and global capitalism in increasing risks of violence against women—for example, through the development of coercive sexual labor in military zones and gendered constructions of violence in armed conflict (Enloe 1990, 2000, 2007; Fukumura and Matsuoka 2002); the use of rape as a tool of war (Allen 1996); and the international crisis of sex trafficking and forced marriage, both of which have been centralized by international human rights groups (Gill and Sundari 2011; Zheng 2010).

ASSESSING THE ROLE OF CULTURE AND DIFFERENCE IN SHAPING GENDERED UNDERSTANDINGS AND PRACTICES

A main topic in the sociology of gender focuses on examining how cultural understandings of gender shape the norms of how a feminine or a masculine body should look and act (Connell 2002; Hughs and Witz 1997; Messner 1992; Witz 2000). This contributes to the attention that feminist sociologists have paid to standards of femininity and masculinity as they apply to evaluations of appropriate body size and shape for women and men, stigma attached to those who do not adhere to these standards, and the ways in which early childhood socialization and media serve to enforce these norms (Hesse-Biber and Nagy 2006). Sociologists of sex and gender also use an intersectional approach to explore the power dynamics between women of different racial and ethnic backgrounds (Becker 1994; Kang 2003) and with different abilities (Shakespeare 2006; Zitzelsberger 2005). Feminist scholars also analyze the role of the medical profession, pharmaceutical companies, and new technologies for providing the means by which women and men can reshape their bodies to fit into narrow definitions of appropriate gender and sexuality (Haiken 1999; Loe 2006).

Feminist sociologists of science are especially interested in new reproductive technologies and their ability to challenge the notion of the "natural" mother and father as older, infertile, or same-sex couples access alternative forms of reproduction (Mamo 2007). They point out the inequities in who can access new technologies and the expansion of "reproductive tourism," where wealthy couples travel to poorer countries to purchase reproductive services, including surrogacy arrangements (Purdy 1989). The new field of transgender studies further complicates analysis of the social construction and production of gender as well as the myriad of ways that gender shapes social policy—for example, by challenging hegemonic understandings of gender as a binary system that maps onto bodies that are understood as "male" or "female" (Currah, Juang, and Miner 2007; Valentine 2007).

Sociologists of sex and gender draw insights from postcolonial and third world feminist analysts who emphasize the ways that cultural diversity and other differences, including class, race, ethnicity, country of origin, age, ability, and sexuality, contour the lives of women and men, thus contributing to their different gendered expectations and experiences (Grewal and Caplan 1994, 2000; Alexander and Mohanty 1997; Mohanty, Russo, and Torres 1991). These complexities are particularly salient, for example, when we examine the lives of poor women, who are disproportionately women of color and disproportionately shoulder the burden of the economic and social dislocation resulting from gendered, racialized, and internationalized processes (Buvinic 1998; Sanford 2003; Women's Refugee Commission 2011). This insight relates to an approach that is at the heart of contemporary feminist sociological analyses, namely, intersectionality.

The call for intersectional analyses was first heard from feminists of color who critiqued approaches that constructed women's concerns without attention to the ways that race, class, and sexuality shaped the experiences of women (Baca Zinn and Dill 1996; Collins 1990). The most powerful approaches to intersectionality also include attention to the ways in which these interactions produce contradictions and tensions across these different levels of analysis and dimensions of difference (McCall 2001, 2005; Maynard 1994).

Research Methods for the Study of Sex and Gender

Prior to the intervention of feminist sociologists, when included at all, sex was merely considered as a variable in sociological studies. Feminists first argued for a distinction between the biological category of sex and the social construction of gender, then recognized that the biological category is also socially constructed (Lorber and Moore 2007). Beginning in the 1970s, researchers informed by a feminist call to describe women's experiences and perspectives in their own words began to make women's lives central in ethnographic and other qualitative accounts (Smith 1987). A gendered lens on men's lives and the development of men's studies was inspired by a growing sensitivity to the ways in which femininities and masculinities are coconstituted (Connell 1987, 2005; Kimmel 2005; Pascoe 2007). Since the 1980s, feminist sociologists who are influenced by postmodern analyses of power and knowledge have become particularly concerned with the role of discourse and the myriad of ways power shapes women's lives (Ferguson 1991). Differences in feminist epistemologies of knowledge influence what counts as data and how data should be analyzed; therefore, a postmodern feminist researcher would approach the collection and analysis of interviews differently from a scholar who draws on positivist or symbolic interactionist perspectives (Naples 2003).

Feminist sociologists have been particularly effective in identifying the processes by which power and "relations of ruling" are inherent in disciplinary practices (Smith 1990). Feminist sociologists have raised questions about the ethics of social research, especially as relates to power imbalances in fieldwork and interviewing (Stacey 1991; Wolf 1996). As one strategy, sociologists of sex and gender recommend addressing these inequalities through reflexive practice designed to interrogate how personal and situational factors contribute to power imbalances. For example, Nancy Naples explains that this form of reflexive practice "encourages feminist scholars to examine how gendered and racialized assumptions influence which voices and experiences are privileged in ethnographic encounters" (2003, 22). She also argues that a reflexive "approach also implies the development of more egalitarian and participatory field methods than traditionally utilized in social scientific investigations" (201).

Sociologists of sex and gender employ a number of research methods to better understand the complexities of sex and gender. Small-scale, locally focused studies such as those conducted by Patricia Richards (2005) in Chile and Vincanne Adams (1998) in Tibet often incorporate various interview methods, including in-depth interviews and focus groups, as well as observations of and, occasionally, participation in local communities, nongovernmental organizations, and state-sponsored organizations. Sociologists interested in larger demographic trends such as poverty levels, refugee status, education attainment, and maternal mortality and morbidity frequently employ statistical methods through censuses and surveys (Hafner-Burton 2005; Hafner-Burton and Tsutsui 2005; Spirer 1990). Other quantitative approaches are used to capture aggregate patterns such as wage inequality and gender division of labor in employment across different regions (McCall 2001). Sociologists of sex and gender have also turned to policy and document analysis to better understand the bureaucratic and discursive development of instruments intended to identify and meet women's human rights needs (Merry 2006; Naples 2003; Wotipka and Tsutsui 2008).

HUMAN RIGHTS AND THE SOCIOLOGY OF SEX AND GENDER

SEX AND GENDER IN HUMAN RIGHTS DOCUMENTS

The Universal Declaration of Human Rights (UDHR) affirms the "dignity and rights" of all humankind. However, the near invisibility of sex and gender as specific categories for protection in the UDHR renders addressing the rights of women problematic, particularly in a global or transnational context (Bunch 1990; Freeman 1999; Gaer 1998; Binion 1995). Largely as a result of feminist scholarship and activism, particularly since the mid-1980s, human rights abuses based on or related to sex and gender have become increasingly noted; yet there is still no clear consensus as to how to understand these categories or appropriately address violations of women's and sexual minorities' human rights in an international human rights context. This lack of clarity continues to circumscribe the ability of activists and scholars to adequately frame gender-specific abuses as human rights violations in an international legal framework and also presents challenges to those seeking redress. However, progress has been made toward delineating women's and sexual minorities' human rights and demanding that they be formally recognized and protected. Sociologists of sex and gender contribute to this work through increasingly intersectional analyses of the interactions between gender and the state, citizenship, governance structures, and local and global political economies, among other factors.

Historical Perspective on Sex and Gender in Human Rights Discourse

Attention to sex and gender in human rights discourse and documents can be traced to the late nineteenth century (Lockwood et. al. 1998) and is more evident in the UDHR, which was adopted in 1948. The elaboration of concern for women's rights in particular was further evident in the efforts that resulted from the United Nations Decade for Women (1976–1985), during which women from many different geographical, ethnic, racial, religious, cultural, and class backgrounds took up the task of improving the status of women transnationally. The United Nations sponsored three international women's conferences during this time: in Mexico City in 1975, Copenhagen in 1980, and Nairobi in 1985. Several important human rights documents developed out of these conferences and the efforts of feminist activists and scholars.

The 1976 International Covenant on Civil and Political Rights recognized the equal right of men and women to the enjoyment of all civil and political rights set forth in the covenant (Article 3). This right was further codified in 1979 when the UN General Assembly adopted the Convention on the Elimination of All Forms of Discrimination against Women. Some scholars note that its references to sex include sexual freedom, thereby offering protection to sexual minorities (Mittelstaedt 2008).

In 1990, following decades of concerted effort from feminist activists, organizations, and scholars, Dr. Charlotte Bunch published a foundational call for women's rights as human rights, criticizing the reluctance of states and international structures to address the needs of women and homosexuals from the legal framework of human rights. Three years later, the participants in the World Conference on Human Rights produced the Vienna Declaration and Program of Action, which specified a platform on women's human rights as inalienable from the individual and indivisible from universal human rights, noting that the eradication of sex discrimination is a priority for the international community.

The 1994 International Conference on Population and Development in Cairo featured discussions on sex, sexuality, and sexual health but linked these rights to heterosexual reproduction with no mention of freedom of sexual expression or sexual orientation. At the Fourth World Conference on Women in Beijing in 1995, sponsored by the United Nations, feminist activists finally saw the global emergence of the idea of "women's rights as human rights" (Bunch 1990). Developed by conference participants, the Beijing Platform for Action focused on removing obstacles to women's active participation in all spheres of public and private life through a full and equal share in economic, social, cultural and political decision-making. However, this platform failed to include support for the rights of lesbians and rejected the term "sexual orientation" (Bunch and Fried 1996; see also Baden and Goetz 1997).

KEY AREAS OF CONCERN FOR WOMEN'S HUMAN RIGHTS

Sociologists have identified numerous areas of concern for the development and protection of women's human rights, and they generally understand these areas as linked globally (Naples and Desai 200; Reilly 2009). We offer here three brief illustrations: economic security, gendered violence, and reproductive health.

ECONOMIC SECURITY

The United Nations asserts that women's economic security is at far greater risk than men's globally, and this is particularly true in rural areas that rely heavily on agricultural production (UNFAO 2010). Differential access to employment opportunities continues to reflect and reproduce gendered conceptualizations of women's domestic roles and to inhibit their ability to engage fully in civic life. Further, approximately 75 percent of the world's women are not entitled to property ownership and cannot receive bank loans due to underemployment, unemployment, and insecure employment (Moser 2007). These restrictions impact not only women but families and communities as well (Cagatay 2001).

GENDERED VIOLENCE

Anthropologist Sally Merry points out that "the idea that everyday violence against women is a human rights violation has not been easy to establish" (2006, 2). Part of the difficulty lies in the tensions between global and transnational institutions and local structures. The translation of human rights laws and ideologies between multiple locations is complicated by cultural differences, questions of sovereignty, and access to resources, among other potential impediments (Bunch 1990). In this context, the role of intermediary institutions such as nongovernmental organizations is pivotal. Further complicating the ability of scholars and activists to address gendered violence as a human rights violation is the continuing construction of a public-private dichotomy in which violence against women is framed as a family issue in which state actors are reluctant to intervene (Clapham 2007; Tomasevski 1995). However, there has been some progress toward understanding gendered violence as an issue that transcends public/private dichotomies, particularly when this violence occurs in the context of war. In 2008 the UN Security Council passed Resolution 1820, which formally recognized the particular vulnerabilities of women and girl children to sexual violence during armed conflict and reaffirmed states' obligations to address sexual violence against civilians.

REPRODUCTIVE HEALTH

Maternal and child health continue to be a priority for women's human rights activists in the twenty-first century. Growing attention and increased resources from local, global, and transnational institutions over the last several decades—particularly since the 1994 International Conference on Population and Development explicitly linked the reproductive health and human rights of women to global efforts to reduce poverty—have resulted in important improvements in women's access to adequate health care (WHO 2010). However, globally women experience unequal access to health care. For example, according to the World Health Organization (2000), global maternal mortality and morbidity rates are highest in developing nations.

Guang-zhen Wang and Vijayan Pillai (2001) explain that sociologists have applied two general analytical frames to reproductive health: (1) identifying social-structural factors shaping reproductive health, and (2) examining a rights-based paradigm to elucidate states' obligations to provide reproductive health care. Utilizing these frames has enabled sociologists to offer critical analyses of the interactions between health and social environments that elucidate foundational causes for the disparities in health between sexes, genders, geographic locations, socioeconomic locations, and racial-ethnic identities, among other key factors (Doyal 1995, 2001; Warner-Smith, Bryson, and Byles 2004).

KEY SOCIOLOGICAL QUESTIONS AND INSIGHTS IN THE STUDY OF WOMEN'S HUMAN RIGHTS

A primary question emerging from the feminist sociological study of human rights is, What obstacles challenge universal recognition of women's human rights and prevent a comprehensive consideration of gender within the prevailing human rights frameworks? Findings in response to this question vary but often include the influence of religious groups, social and political constructions of a public-private gendered dichotomy, masculinized notions of citizenship, and the fact that the concept of "universal" human rights tends to mask the multiple dimensions of difference emerging from racial-ethnic, class, and cultural locations, as well as sex and gender differences, and to impose a Western conceptualization of individual rights.

ASSESSING THE INFLUENCE OF RELIGIOUS GROUPS IN
CIRCUMSCRIBING WOMEN'S HUMAN RIGHTS

The lack of women's voices in the development of religious institutions and the concurrent influence of religious doctrine on state practices impose multiple and, at times, severe restrictions on women's freedoms (European Women's Lobby 2006; Winter 2006). For example, at the time of the Beijing Conference for Women, Roman Catholic authorities rejected what they considered the ambiguity of the term "gender" and noted that they understood "gender" to be "grounded in biological sexual identity" (UN Report 1995, 165), thus reinscribing an essentialist role for women that curtails women's opportunities (European Women's Lobby 2006). The role of religious doctrine in determining women's rights is complicated by these essentialist ideas about gender as they intersect with issues of cultural relativism and fundamental human rights (Sunder 2003; Winter 2006). These complications have led many scholars, such as Madhavi Sunder, to assert that "human rights law has a problem with religion" (2003, 1401; see also Reilly 2009).

EXAMINING THE PERSISTENCE OF THE PUBLIC-PRIVATE
DICHOTOMY IN HUMAN RIGHTS DISCOURSE

Sociologists of sex and gender interrogate the social construction of a public-private dichotomy in which some aspects of human lives are conceptualized as occurring or belonging in a public sphere and others are deemed private and thus, in some measure, protected from surveillance or state control (Collins 1994; Okin 1989). Many violations of women's human rights, such as domestic violence, forms of sexual slavery, and child-preference practices that disadvantage girl children, are often considered "private" matters in which global and local states are reluctant to intervene (Bunch 1990; Freeman 1999; MacKinnon 1993). The occurrence of these and similarly gendered phenomena in what is constructed as the "privacy" of family and home constructs boundaries around how these issues are addressed and inhibits the abilities of international systems to intervene in such rights violations.

GENDERING HUMAN RIGHTS DISCOURSE AND PRACTICE

Sociologists of sex and gender point out that the dominant image of the political actor is male (Haney 2000; Bunch 1990; Yuval-Davis 1997), and most human rights institutions are male dominated (Freeman 1999). Therefore, women are largely invisible as human rights institutions deal with human rights violations on a large, public scale (for example, through the institution of democracies, fair housing, and economic security); "it is assumed that women benefit" (Freeman 1999, 515) as members of the larger populace. Failure to specify the needs of women as women presents an obstacle to recognizing the many ways their human rights can be and are violated through an imposed public-private dichotomy (Bunch 1990; MacKinnon 1993). Within this dichotomy, notions of citizenship become conflated with the presumably male political actor (Yuval-Davis 1997), and the human rights of women are subsumed or delegitimized under this rubric of masculinized citizenship.

UNIVERSALIZING NOTIONS OF HUMAN RIGHTS AND OF WOMEN

Citizenship for women is further complicated by political and cultural location, as the women's-rights-as-human-rights frame potentially implies a universalizing notion of women and of rights derived from Western conceptions of citizenship and the state. Sociological perspectives point out the ways in which this runs the risk of further masking local structures and institutions such as diverse family forms, law-enforcement practices, and religious beliefs (Bonnin 1995; Chow 1996; Howard and Allen 1996; Ray and Korteweg 1999). When theoretical space is allotted for the recognition of women outside a Western paradigm, it is often limited in scope. For example, as Chandra Talpade Mohanty argues, "Assumptions of privilege and ethnocentric universality (can) lead to the construction of a ... reductive and homogeneous notion of '... Third World difference'" (2006, 19), wherein third world and postcolonial women and U.S. women of color are produced as a "composite, singular 'Third World Woman'" (Narayan 1997). Women's human rights, therefore, potentially work from a binary framework of "West/not West" as well as "male/not male."

REDEFINING THE HUMAN RIGHTS PARADIGM FROM A FEMINIST PERSPECTIVE

Gender requires a revisioning of human rights as a universal concept as well as a reconstruction of the systems used to create and ensure the sanctity of women's human rights (Staudt 1997; Binion 1995). This includes a blurring of imposed boundaries around "public" and "private" and recognition of the inherently political nature of the "private" lives of women, including domestic lives, religious beliefs and practices, and sexualities. Sociologists recognize that political borders are blurred in the transnational context of global economy, migration, and armed conflict (Freeman 1999; Naples and Desai 2002). Therefore, a feminist and intersectional sociological study of relevant social structures includes, but is not limited to, family and community; local, regional, and global political economies; culture, religion, law, and education; and national and transnational governance, including nongovernmental organizations.

Just as political boundaries are not permanently fixed, a human rights framework is not a static paradigm, as our local and global conceptualizations of what counts as human rights issues and what they require continue to evolve. Feminist sociologists' particular perspective on the intersections of social institutions and structures, such as the family, state, economy, and religion, and individual experiences of power and inequality renders visible the links between the lives of women and sexual minorities, violations of their human rights, and opportunities for protection and redress.

Sociological inquiry into gender and gendered structures and institutions has helped to reveal the ways in which definitions of citizenship; local, national, and transnational institutions and structures; and even the law itself are frequently informed by gendered notions of masculinity that exclude women and their experiences. Sociological analyses of gender thereby offer theoretical tools with which to understand, highlight, and advance an agenda of women's rights as human rights. Emerging emphases in feminist sociological work on the intersections of gender with race, class, sexuality, and other social and political locations (Collins 1994; Richards 2005) provide still greater space for consideration of women's diverse lived experiences under the rubric of human rights, allowing human rights scholars and activists greater opportunity to avoid essentializing women and imposing inadequate Western concepts of "rights."

WHERE DO WE GO FROM HERE?

Recognizing the diversity of women's and men's lives, yet striving to understand "women" and "men" as universal categories, produces a theoretical tension for sociology and for human rights praxis. Women constitute a "group" that exists everywhere; yet they are often differentiated by political, cultural, racial, economic, ethnic, religious, and other considerations. The specific needs of women and non-gender-conforming men for recognition and protection of their human rights share some similarities but vary in many ways. Sensitivity to the differences among women requires nuanced, locally grounded analyses of women's and men's diverse lived experiences; yet, as Gayle Binion asserts, "The facts and conditions of cultural diversity among societies cannot, from a feminist perspective, justify a failure to rectify the conditions in which women live worldwide" (1995, 522), conditions that include gendered violence, economic insecurity, and reproductive health concerns. The international instruments of human rights retain an uncomfortable relationship with culture and gender that requires ongoing reflexive practice and attention to local structures and cultural diversity as well as global economic and political processes that shape everyday life in different parts of the world.

Chapter Two

Aging and the Life Course

Robin Shura and Rachel Bryant

For sociologists, age—like gender, race and ethnicity, social class, and other characteristics typically construed strictly as attributes of individuals—is a feature of social structure that is both external to and coercive of individual experience (Riley, Johnson, and Foner 1972; Kohli 1986). Age carries particular statuses, expectations, and consequences in highly age-conscious societies that influence interaction, regardless of the individual (Chudacoff 1989). Age can also carry with it expectations for human rights. However, the acceptance of human rights instruments (e.g., UDHR, UNCRC) has not had explicitly noticeable effects on scholarship within the sociology of age and the life course (hereafter, SALC), particularly in the United States (Townsend 2006). Indeed, with some exceptions (see Townsend 2006), scholarship in SALC does not include significant explicit conceptual or methodological attention to human rights. This is not due to a lack of considerable sociological scholarship that draws attention to laws and policies and how they relate to age and aging (e.g., Binstock 2007; Rowe et al. 2010; Binstock and Post 1991), including issues of age discrimination (Quadagno and Street 1995), and scholarship on the political economy of age and aging (e.g., Estes et al. 2006). It may reflect the propensity to overlook realities of age segregation and ageism as robust features of social reality that bear on human rights, while being all too aware of the salience of kindred concepts within sociology regarding discriminatory structural segregation and cultural beliefs based on gender, race and ethnicity, or social class. However, attention within SALC to age segregation (Hagestad and Uhlenberg 2005, 2006) and ageism (e.g., Butler 2002 [1972]; Dannefer and Shura 2009) is significant and synergistic with human rights concerns, and debates about generational equity (including rationing health care to "seniors") within SALC are highly relevant (e.g., Binstock and Post 1991; Callahan 1987). These substantive areas speak to the ideological and structural manifestations of prejudices and systematic discriminatory treatment based on age. Yet even this scholarship has generally fallen short of making explicit, formalized scholarly connections to human rights.

This lack of explicit focus on human rights within SALC cannot be understood as due to a failure to make major empirical and theoretical gains or an absence of vigorous scholarship in SALC. "Human rights" largely has not been clarified within SALC scholarship in terms of its conceptual, theoretical, or methodological relevance because this relevance has not, or not yet, been made widely known, articulated, and accessible across sociology. Further, we speculate that the lack of explicit focus on human rights within SALC may be explained by one issue that a diversity of approaches within SALC have in common: a reluctance to make strong and direct claims that social problems exist relevant to their subject matter, in favor of emphasizing descriptive and highly sophisticated analytical approaches using increasingly robust empirical data sources (e.g., see Kohli 2007 or Mayer 2009), or in favor of making refined theoretical contributions to the subfield that allege claims of problems within sociological scholarship itself (Dannefer 2011; Baars et al. 2006; Bengtson et al. 2009a, 2009b). Omission of explicit attention to human rights may be less specific to SALC and more broadly descriptive of perennial disagreements within the field about our roles as sociologists and the proper focus and locus of our work writ large.

The diversity of perspectives and issues within SALC speaks to a deeper, paradigmatic divide within SALC, as both conventional approaches to research and more critical approaches exist within SALC. Dale Dannefer (2011) alleges that the former are more represented than the latter. The dominance of conventional research within SALC in some ways makes understandable the lack of explicit attention to human rights, whereas the significant minority of critical perspectives within SALC unavoidably raises issues that have synergy with human rights concerns—for example, power, ideology, and conflict. And these paradigmatic divides do not touch on debates over whether there is a place for advocacy in sociological scholarship or human rights sociology.

THE SOCIOLOGY OF AGE, AGING, AND THE LIFE COURSE: KEY CONCERNS AND QUESTIONS

The sociology of age and the life course consists of very heterogeneous orientations to research, including subject matter, methodology, and theory. Even inconsistency in the language used to describe its subject matter—older adults versus elders versus the elderly; later life versus later adulthood versus old age; life course versus lifespan—suggests extreme heterogeneity of approaches, including disagreement within the field (Dannefer and Uhlenberg 1999; Thomas 2004; Settersten 2005). Interestingly, SALC includes gerontological approaches (research focused on late life) and research on the life course, which is broadly inclusive of midlife and later life as well as early life events and childhood. However, in part a legacy of section development within the American Sociological Association, and in part reinforced by divisions of major federal funding agencies (e.g., NIA versus NICHD), SALC typically does not subsume scholarship devoted to childhood. SALC research has in the past been accused of being rich in data but lacking in theory (Birren 1959). Perhaps in response to this criticism, several developments have ignited renewed theorizing and attention to theory within SALC.

The life-course perspective within sociology is deceivingly singular, as a plurality of frameworks comprise life-course sociology. In brief, these include seeking to understand how early life experiences or events influence the courses of lives over time (e.g., Elder 1999; Elder et al. 2009; Crosnoe and Elder 2004); how life-course transitions (e.g., transitions from childhood to adulthood, from adulthood to later life/"old age" or retirement) relate to individual and cultural circumstances (e.g., Settersten and Hagestad 1996a, 1996b); how macro-level social structures produce regularity (homogeneity or heterogeneity) in these life-course patterns en masse (e.g., Kohli 1986; Brückner and Mayer 2005); and how these patterns vary over time and place. Through the mid-twentieth century, as cohorts navigated social structures highly regulated and organized by age as a key criterion for role entry and exit, people within these cohorts tended to experience key life transitions (e.g., entry into the workforce, family formation, retirement) at increasingly similar ages. This has created such strong age-linked patterns in human lives that the life course is described as "institutionalized" (Kohli 1986; Kohli and Meyer 1986; Mayer and Müller 1986). Yet shifts in these macro-level structures, as well as new data, raise the question of whether deinstitutionalization of the life course is occurring (Brückner and Mayer 2005; Dannefer and Shura 2007). Some SALC scholars emphasize aging as a process; others criticize a focus on "aging" as reification of the presumption that aging is a "natural" process and prefer to identify age as an influential social construct (Dannefer 1984).

A few substantive areas within SALC include population aging; aging policy and welfare state scholarship; health, ability, and aging (including health changes across the life course, health disparities, caregiving, long-term care, structure and organization of health-care services and aging, chronic illness, end-of-life issues); work and retirement (pensions, retirement policy, later-life employment patterns); intergenerational relationships; later-life migration; cumulating dis/advantage and aging; ageism; quality of life (including ethical issues about medical care and quality of life at the end of life); and gender, race, and social class and their relationships to age. For more robust overviews of substantive, methodological, and theoretical work in SALC, see recent handbooks by Robert H. Binstock and Linda K. George (2006, 2011), Richard A. Settersten Jr. and J. L. Angel (2011), Peter Uhlenberg (2009b), and Dale Dannefer and Chris Phillipson (2010). Additional key SALC areas and findings are elaborated in the following sections.

SUMMARY OF KEY METHODS

There is high value within SALC on quantitative data and sophisticated quantitative analytical techniques, specifically advanced forms of multivariate longitudinal and/or hierarchical modeling that are used to tease out such social patterns as trajectories of age-related trends and changes over time within populations in terms of health, wealth, well-being, and so forth, as well as to tease out cohort and period effects (e.g., Alwin, Hofer, and McCammon 2006). Other methods are also utilized in SALC, with qualitative research generally less represented than quantitative work (for a hallmark exception, see Gubrium 1997), and with participatory and community-building methodologies much less prominent within SALC (for exceptions, see Blair and Minkler 2009; Shura, Siders, and Dannefer 2010). Yet a mainstay of SALC is sophisticated and rich analysis of population-representative data sets. More robust population-representative data sets are becoming available to study processes and patterns related to age and aging, particularly longitudinal data sets (Alwin, Hofer, and McCammon 2006; Kohli 2007). Within SALC, significant portions of strongly data-driven research can be considered social-psychological in orientation, with emphases on individual-level outcomes such as individual health and well-being (Hagestad and Dannefer 2001).

WHAT CAN HUMAN RIGHTS LEARN FROM SOCIOLOGY OF AGE AND THE LIFE COURSE?

Connections between human rights sociology and scholarship within SALC that has salience to human rights remain underdeveloped. Three SALC areas that are promising for integration are explored here: age segregation, ageism, and the extent to which age is an axis of differentiation and discrimination for human rights among groups and individuals across the life course. In relation to these three major areas, population aging, globalization, and debates within SALC about age-linked vulnerability are briefly considered. We present our ideas here not as an exhaustive treatise but as targeted and thought-provoking discussions that we hope may spur further consideration.

For human rights scholarship, inequality is a major concern. A pervasive feature of modernity is the reliance on age as a major basis of social organization across education, work, and other social settings. SALC scholars have examined the social phenomena of age segregation (Hagestad and Uhlenberg 2005, 2006) and ageism (Butler 2002 [1972]; Dannefer and Shura 2009; Hagestad and Uhlenberg 2005); yet there is room for clearer articulation of how these areas of research may intersect with human rights. Age segregation, or the physical and social separation of groups within society based on age, is a systematic and structural feature of "developed" societies. In these societies, norms and expectations linked to age provide an often taken-for-granted guide to "age-appropriate" behavior and social practice, which is not the case in other societies (Rogoff 2003). Based on the rapid rise in age consciousness and the social salience of age as a key meaning-laden status of individuals in the early twentieth century (Achenbaum 1978, 2009; Chudacoff 1989; Rogoff 2003), age segregation is currently a widespread form of social segregation within most major social institutions. This pattern is reinforced by pervasive cultural beliefs that place high social value on some age categories, yet denigrate others. Age during later life is a major and concentrated target of devaluation. Cultural ageism, then, refers to the differential social value and meaning attributed to individuals and groups based on age and has particular salience to the nexus of SALC scholarship and human rights. Ageism and age segregation share a mutually reinforcing relationship in society (Dannefer and Shura 2009; Hagestad and Uhlenberg 2005). This work in SALC has laid the groundwork for potential integration with human rights scholarship: inasmuch as other forms of social segregation and culturally patterned inequalities and prejudices (e.g., racial or ethnic segregation and racism, gender segregation and sexism) are concerns of human rights, there is an opportunity to integrate these important substantive areas within SALC more explicitly with human rights.

Age segregation creates various forms of social vulnerability for many in later life (Hagestad and Uhlenberg 2006; Riley and Riley 1994). Evidence of age segregation within social networks is robust, indicating a large degree of homogeneity of age within people's networks of closest ties (e.g., Uhlenberg and Gierveld 2004), particularly in nonfamily networks (Hagestad and Uhlenberg 2005). Ironically, age segregation endures within a historical period in which the effects of other forms of systematic social segregation (e.g., racial segregation) have been deemed harmful and unjust (Fry 2007), despite assertions that structural opportunities for older people are increasingly mismatched with their capacities (Riley, Kahn, and Foner 1994) and evidence of benefits of age integration for young and old (Hagestad and Uhlenberg 2007; Uhlenberg 2009a; Uhlenberg and Cheuk 2010). Age segregation has placed some elders in particularly vulnerable social positions, especially since many older adults face concentrated loss due to death within their age-homogenous social networks (Dannefer and Shura 2009). This amplifies the probability of social isolation in late life. Issues raised by age segregation and ageism take on special significance as older people are becoming an increasingly large proportion of many countries' populations (e.g., Uhlenberg 2009a). Human rights scholars have an opportunity to build from these SALC findings in ways that frame increased social vulnerability and isolation in later life not as natural problems related to physiological aging processes but rather as socially constructed barriers to full human rights, barriers that limit or obstruct social participation and are reified through ageist social discourse, including ageist discourse within SALC.

An irony of ageism is that, except those who die relatively young, we will all inherit the relatively denigrated status that accompanies older age unless there is a cultural shift. This statement ought to evoke concern and a sense of the importance of tying ageism to broader sociological literatures about human rights that target other "isms" and concomitant forms of social segregation (Hagestad and Uhlenberg 2005). For example, praising others for how "young" they are, or for trying to "stay young" in order to avoid social devaluation, reifies and reproduces ageism: it does not question or undermine the differential value attributed to human beings, human experience, and social reality based on age. It is heuristically informative to develop sociological parallels that make visible the cultural and structural realities of ageism. For instance, is the imperative to "stay young," which is largely celebrated in today's culture, similar to asking a woman to "be manly" or an African American to be "whiter"? Age hegemony, marked by the relative devaluation of oldness and valorization of some aspects of youth, becomes visible through such exercises. Sociologists who link human rights scholarship to age may benefit from considering the ways in which ageism is similar to, or different from, racism and sexism. The connections between dynamics of hegemony and dominance, as well as inferiority and prejudice, as they relate to age and human rights need to be further studied and elucidated.

Human rights scholarship may benefit from a deeper examination of the extent to which age is an axis of differentiation and discrimination for groups and individuals across the life course. Analyses of shared or similar age-linked social vulnerabilities in early and late life, often indicated by "dependency," are needed within human rights scholarship. This includes the need for attention focused on the rights and responsibilities allocated to individuals or groups based on age and the implications for how this changes as individuals grow older. Some basic, starting questions to explore potential linkages between SALC and human rights include the following: Which age groups have which rights? Do any social groups have "special," age-specific rights? Who is responsible for protecting these rights? Which stakeholders (social groups or social institutions) rally against age-specific constructions of rights (e.g., for the old, for institutionalized elders, for adults, for the young) and why? Do some rights turn on or off at specific ages? If so, why? Such questions reframe basic considerations of human rights with a specific emphasis on how age as a social construct may explicitly relate to how human rights are socially constructed. These questions also remind us of the importance of examining power differences according to age: there is a need to consider how social vulnerabilities are shared by both the young and the old in society (e.g., Hagestad 2008; Uhlenberg 2009a).

The concept of the life course can inform human rights scholarship. Rights may change, formally or informally, based on age: a person's rights may look different from different points in his or her life course (Janoski and Gran 2002). SALC may offer conceptual insight and methodological tools to research age-based variations in rights (e.g., voting) by forcing questions of the extent to which age is used to confer and constrain various rights across the life course and why.

Finally, SALC offers strength in terms of its methodological and analytical rigor, as well as some critical theoretical advances. In these areas, SALC might challenge scholars using human rights as a perspective or conceptual framework to hone methods and measures in analyses, identify robust data sources, refine measurement, and employ diverse theoretical perspectives rather than proclaim or reify an ideological line. It is not yet clear within SALC, or not clearly communicated to or by SALC scholars, what human rights sociology entails, what explicit or implicit theoretical premises it employs, what methods it considers primary, upon what forms of data it most heavily relies, and what prominent disagreements or debates may currently exist among scholars who identify as human rights sociologists. Communicating about the tools of human rights sociology, therefore, is a surmountable challenge, as human rights orientations may be seen as too activist and not as mainstream scholarship within SALC without clear theoretical and empirical justification. SALC can challenge human rights perspectives regarding making universal claims and exporting them without nuanced understandings of social-historical contexts that shape experiences and understandings of age.

WHAT CAN SOCIOLOGY OF AGE AND THE LIFE COURSE LEARN FROM HUMAN RIGHTS?

Unlike with some other socially charged and consequential social statuses (e.g., race, gender), unless one dies relatively early, one will experience all ages, replete with more or less social value and potentially with more or fewer rights, different rights, more or less protection of rights, more or fewer responsibilities for protecting others' rights, and even special rights relevant to specific stages of the life course (Bryant and Shura 2009; Foner 1974). Because few SALC scholars are actively engaged in such a perspective, human rights sociologists may make key contributions that will inform this area. Furthermore, age is often presumed to be helpful in determining an individual's competency, a presumption that some SALC scholars heavily critique and that has relevance to human rights. It may be socially acceptable to restrict full participation in specific rights based on presumptions about age-related deficits, even if formally and legally the specific rights in question are conferred irrespective of increased age. There may be a "rising sun" in the life course of human rights, in which various legal rights are not realized until "adulthood" (usually at the arbitrary age of eighteen), and some rights may become informally restricted with greater age (Bryant and Shura 2009). For example, both minor children and adults in late life may experience formal and informal limitations placed on their participation in medical decision-making. Are there counterexamples in which the young and the old possess comparatively stronger rights, or specialized rights, when compared to other age groups? An assessment of the United States suggests that young people benefit more from social rights, such as the right to education, compared to working-age adults, who typically possess weak entitlements to public health insurance unless they can demonstrate financial hardship or enter older age (e.g., Medicare, Medicaid). The contingency and transition, then, of human rights throughout the life course are areas ripe for SALC scholarship, and this research could potentially be bolstered with tools used by human rights sociologists. Further, how potential age-related contingencies that shape the use of human rights intersect with hierarchies of race, class, gender, and health could be fruitful areas to integrate with other sociological research devoted to human rights.

SALC scholars face the challenge of not reproducing ageist assumptions in their work and not taking age segregation or its purported social value for granted in their scholarship. One distinct challenge we pose to SALC scholars is to consider seriously in their scholarship the view of elders as active individuals with continuing capacities to play valued roles within myriad social institutions and in their communities (see, e.g., Shura, Siders, and Dannefer 2010), particularly at a time in history when rapid population aging has led some to recognize that older people may be the world's only expanding natural resource (Freedman 2007). We consider it an important heuristic exercise, and one with relevance to human rights, to pit the ageist assumption as a hypothesis against the hypothesis of "elder as capable," if only to shed light on the extent to which scholars often internalize status quo ageism and age segregation as inevitable, or even desirable, social realities. Prominent messages within mainstream media often perpetuate ageist perceptions, including references to population aging that are almost always negative or even ominous and references to later-life policies that emphasize the social burdens and costs of an aging population rather than potential social benefits. In an increasingly globalized world, one with many rapidly aging populations, SALC and human rights scholars ought to consider the extent to which cultural ageism and the concomitant positive and largely unquestioned value placed on age segregation are being exported globally from the Economic North to the Economic South. Human rights sociology may offer useful insights and tools for meeting these SALC challenges.

The Universal Declaration of Human Rights (UDHR), adopted in 1948 by the United Nations, emphasizes the dignity and rights of all people, which includes people of all ages. SALC scholars give little explicit attention to age as an axis of social differentiation that has real implications for rights. The extent to which beliefs about aging and elders, the lack of prominent and socially valued roles for elders, and other practices and institutions relevant to later life uphold human dignity and rights is another possible perspective through which SALC scholars may benefit from increased attention to human rights. Whenever claims about "rights" and "best interests" are made on behalf of one group by another group, and the target social group does not have a direct, leading role in identifying its own best interests (and it is not clarified how the social division between such groups is justified in the first place), there is fertile ground for analysis from both sociological and human rights perspectives. Upon sociological examination, hegemony and disenfranchisement are likely to be found. Additionally, various substantive areas in SALC are ripe for further consideration of how age explicitly relates to human rights, including end-of-life issues regarding legal and medical decision-making, rights within institutionalized care settings, age-based inequality in social opportunities, debates about later-life policy (e.g., pensions and US Social Security), and specific rights-relevant contexts of midlife experience (e.g., incarceration and disabling conditions), to name just a few avenues of investigation. The sociology of age may be well served by not reifying intergenerational equity debates (e.g., Do children's rights threaten adults' rights? Do elders' rights threaten the idea of rights belonging to adults at midlife and young people?). It is the task of sociology to adopt such questions and social phenomena as subject matter for sociological analysis and to apply appropriate tools of theory, measurement, and analytic rigor in the quest for answers. Combining strengths in SALC with strengths in the sociology of human rights could produce gains in these important areas.

CONCLUSION

The UDHR goal of upholding human dignity and rights, irrespective of age, provides one potential starting point for integration of SALC and human rights scholarship. Approaches to integrated research might begin from analysis of age-segregated and age-pluralistic communities and the value attributed to age therein and, from there, explore how all constituents could be afforded greater opportunities for social participation and positive social value. Rather than raise a flag to rally for "older adults" to become the next social group on behalf of which human rights campaigns are framed, we call sociologists' attention to the need to clarify methods and theories that might allow myriad fruitful substantive areas within SALC to be better integrated with human rights considerations and with pursuits of upholding human dignity across the life course.

Age—a powerful social force and social fact that is coercive of individual experience and organizes social life—may often not be explicitly framed as relevant to human rights by SALC scholars, and it may be overlooked by human rights scholars as a key axis of social differentiation and discrimination. SALC offers rich methodological and theoretical orientations, substantive contributions, and scientific rigor, all of which may be useful tools for research on human rights as they relate to age. SALC may illuminate how people experience human rights over their life courses and how other age-related structures or experiences interface with rights. Finally, SALC is a hugely diverse subdiscipline and can make vast contributions to human rights in regard to policy analysis, population aging, and intergenerational relationships, to name a few. Further communication about, and clearer elaboration of, the tools of human rights research within SALC circles—from clear conceptual definitions of human rights, to elaboration of theories that organize research of human rights, to methods and data in sociology of human rights, to clarification of the respective roles of conventional research, critical research, and advocacy-based sociology within human rights sociology—will most effectively promote increased integration of perspectives. This chapter is intended to suggest thought-provoking, yet limited, substantive ways to further such integration.

CHAPTER THREE

MENTAL HEALTH AND HUMAN RIGHTS

Giedrė Baltrušaitytė

Nearly 54 million people around the world have severe mental disorders such as schizophrenia and bipolar affective disorder (manic-depressive illness). In addition, 154 million people suffer from depression. Mental disorders are increasingly prevalent in developing countries, the consequence of persistent poverty, the demographic transition, military conflicts, and natural disasters (World Health Organization 2007).

Recognition of the effects of social, economic, political, and cultural conditions on mental health and well-being is a current feature of social-policy agendas, with debate increasingly framed in human rights terms. The most significant international effort to protect the rights of those with mental health disorders is UN General Assembly Resolution 46/119 on the Protection of Persons with Mental Illness and the Improvement of Mental Health Care, adopted in 1991. This resolution, while not formally binding, serves as an influential aid in developing human rights–oriented mental-health-care systems and policies. In addition, the World Health Organization (WHO) continues to draw attention to the impacts of human rights violations and refers to social isolation, poor quality of life, stigma, and discrimination as central issues for those with mental disabilities (Lewis 2009a).

Despite the increasing policy attention, sociological attention to the intersection of mental health and human rights remains marginal. While there is a long tradition of sociological research on the phenomenon of mental illness (Goffman 1961; Scheff 1999; Busfield 1996), sociologists have rarely framed their research questions explicitly within the framework of human rights. Analysis of human rights issues and their implications for the situation of people with mental illness, however, is clearly within the sociological terrain.

This chapter provides a summary of key topics and issues in the sociology of mental health and explores the ways in which the sociology of mental health could frame some of its central questions in relation to the paradigm of human rights. I start with the presentation of major sociological ideas about mental illness, psychiatry, and psychiatric care and then provide a summary of the key findings within the field. The subsequent sections cover a discussion of how the sociology of mental health could enrich human rights research as well as redirect its constituent questions toward the human rights paradigm. The chapter concludes with a discussion of the possibilities for a human rights approach to the sociology of mental health.

THE SOCIOLOGY OF MENTAL HEALTH

The sociology of mental health is concerned with several key issues. Scholars in this area of inquiry are interested in a variety of questions in their research, including (1) the linkages between social factors and mental disorders, (2) the ways in which professional discourses and practices shape the phenomenon of mental illness, (3) societal reactions to individuals with mental illness, (4) the effects on the individual of the stigma associated with mental illness, (5) the effects that changes in mental health policy have on mental health care, and (6) the experiences of using mental health services.

SOCIAL FACTORS IN MENTAL ILLNESS

Much of the sociological contribution to our understanding of the onset of mental illnesses is grounded in social epidemiology. Sociologists account for variations in the prevalence of mental illness among various social groups by examining differences in levels of adversity, stressful events, and individual management of stress (Turner, Wheaton, and Lloyd 1995; Pearlin and Schooler 1978; Kessler and McLeod 1984). Pilgrim and Rogers (1999) provide a solid summary of some key assumptions of the sociological research that investigates the links between social factors and mental illness.

According to the scholarship, the probability of mental health problems, particularly severe mental illnesses like schizophrenia, increases as socioeconomic status decreases, with the lowest social classes being clearly disadvantaged. There remains considerable debate about whether poverty increases vulnerability to mental illness or whether individuals, particularly those who are already socially disadvantaged, drift further into poverty because their illness makes them socially incompetent and vulnerable (Kohn 1981; Link, Dohrenwend, and Skodol 1986; Eaton 1980; Miech et al. 1999).

Women are diagnosed as suffering from mental illness more often than men, though most of this difference is accounted for by diagnoses of depression. Men are more likely to have diagnostic labels that refer to and incorporate behavioral threats (e.g., alcoholism, pedophilia). There is still no clear sociological account of these differences, particularly concerning why women are overrepresented in psychiatric populations. Some studies show that gender differences in common mental disorders virtually disappear in the lowest income group (Busfield 1996; Rosenfield 1999; Ridge, Emslie, and White 2011).

The prevalence of mental health problems seems to vary among different ethnic groups, seemingly becoming more common in African-descended rather than European-descended populations. This difference, however, needs to be explained with caution, as there may be methodological problems inherent in such studies. The overrepresentation of minority ethnic groups in psychiatric statistics may reflect continuing disadvantages rooted in slavery, enforced migration, colonialism, and racial discrimination rather than real differences in psychiatric morbidity (Omi and Winant 1986; Brown et al. 1999; Mossakowski 2008; Williams et al. 1997).

Other sociological work has been focused on wider social structures and the capitalist social order as implicated in mental illness. Warner (1994), for instance, attempted to demonstrate that in industrialized societies, recovery rates for schizophrenia are closely linked to fluctuations in state economies and the requirements of the labor market. He concludes that changes in the outcome of schizophrenia reflect changes in the perceived utility for the labor market of those with mental health disorders. Despite the critiques and various methodological problems, the strength of research that investigates the linkages between social factors and mental illness is its focus on the inequalities in mental health among various social groups as related to the social circumstances in which they live.

PROFESSIONAL DISCOURSES AND PRACTICES

Contemporary Western psychiatry is not an internally consistent body of professional knowledge and practice. Despite the variety of conceptual approaches, mental illness in psychiatric discourse is conceptualized as a pathology that, in more severe cases, may affect the ability of the individual to apprehend reality and retain critical insight into his or her health problem (Baltrušaitytė 2010).

By defining those with mental illness as incapable of self-mastery, the psychiatric discourse sustains the need for continuous professional supervision of the patient and legitimates paternalism in psychiatric care. The presumed lack of insight on the part of the affected individual often serves as a ground for the involuntary treatment of people with mental disabilities. Playle and Keeley (1998) have analyzed the notion of treatment nonadherence in psychiatric discourse. They note that nonadherence to treatment is regarded as a symptom of illness. If the patient fails to comply, the presumed lack of critical insight may provide the justification for the professional to diminish the autonomy of the individual by paternalistically imposing compulsory treatment. The close association developed in psychiatric discourse on mental pathology between the notions of mental illness and perceptions of "dangerousness" provides further basis for compulsory psychiatric examination or hospitalization (Dallaire et al. 2000).

Other studies point out that paternalistic health care may, in various ways, inhibit patients' abilities to participate actively in or critically evaluate the medical encounter (Edwards, Staniszweska, and Crichton 2004; Goodyear-Smith and Buetow 2001; Williams 1994). Mead and Copeland (2001) maintain that long-term psychiatric patients may eventually get used to the identities and roles constructed by the psychiatric discourse and imputed to them. These roles and identities often, in turn, alter the relationship of mental patient and caregiver into one of dependence and deference.

Much sociological work has focused on examining the psychiatric conceptualizations of mental illness, noting that categories of mental disorder are socially and culturally relative (Busfield 1996; Warner 1994). An emphasis is often made that mental health and illness are negotiated social concepts and, as such, cannot be understood simply in terms of bodily phenomena. The strength of this sociological work is that it questions the assumed impartiality of psychiatric diagnosis and highlights the socially contingent nature of mental illness. For instance, in D. L. Rosenhan's 1991 study, eight researchers with no history of mental illness or obvious psychiatric problems gained admission to different psychiatric hospitals in the United States by complaining that they heard voices. This study showed how readily psychiatric hospitalization can be achieved, particularly if the patient voluntarily agrees to hospital admission. Rosenhan concluded that it is not possible to distinguish the sane from the insane and that psychiatric diagnoses are not reliable.

The overarching tendency of psychiatry to medicalize social problems is another prominent theme within the sociology of mental health. Sociologists note that the medicalization of life takes away individuals' right to self-determination and creates a dependence on the medical profession. According to Sarbin and Keen (1998), medicalization of mental distress may have even more significant consequences for the affected individual than typically assumed. By relegating mental distress to the realm of neurotransmitters, brain damage, or even psychological processes, the medical model in psychiatry challenges the validity of individual action and agency. All of these ideas, together with other work on professionalization, professional power, and professional practice (Foucault 1995 [1961]; Castel 1988; Scull 1984), have shaped the sociological understanding of psychiatry as an institution of social control that aims at regulating deviant behavior.

STIGMA AND MENTAL ILLNESS

Mental illness is the disability with which the general public seems to feel the least comfortable (Cook and Wright 1995). Public perceptions toward the mentally ill vary by country. The Eurobarometer survey on the self-perceived mental health of European citizens, conducted in 2010, found that, on average, two-thirds (67 percent) of European Union citizens believe they would feel comfortable talking to a person with a significant mental health problem. Notably, the highest prevalence of respondents feeling they would find it difficult to talk to a person with a mental health problem was found among countries that had recently joined the European Union (e.g., Lithuania, Latvia, Bulgaria, Estonia, Poland, Slovakia)—countries sharing long histories of institutionalization of the mentally ill (Eurobarometer 2010). Sociologists continue to investigate the effects of stigma and shame related to mental illness on persons with severe mental disorders and their strategies to cope with perceived devaluation and discrimination (Onken and Slaten 2000; Link et al. 1997; Link and Phelan 2001). According to Onken and Slaten (2000, 101), the ideology of "ableism" that prevails in many societies systematically promotes negative differential and unequal treatment of people because of their apparent or assumed physical, mental, or behavioral differences. Mental health service users know that in the public imagination, they are believed to be unpredictable and dangerous, and this contributes to their own feelings of being rejected and feared (Link and Phelan 2001). This, more often than not, results in their devaluing themselves.

Most persons acquire generalized beliefs that people with mental illness are devalued and discriminated against, but these beliefs do not become personally applicable unless an individual is officially labeled mentally ill. Once such a label is applied, the likelihood increases that a person will devalue him- or herself, fear rejection by others, have a lower income, and become unemployed. Studies show that stigmatization has a dramatic bearing on the distribution of life chances in such areas as earnings, housing, criminal involvement, health, and life itself (Link and Phelan 2001). Employers consistently rank persons with mental disorders last as potential employees, and people suffering from severe mental illness report the difficulties of reentering or staying in the labor market (Schulze and Angermeyer 2003).

CHANGES IN MENTAL HEALTH POLICY AND THE EXPERIENCES OF MENTAL HEALTH SERVICE USERS

In the early 1960s, social researchers noticed that persons who spent long periods in psychiatric hospitals tended to develop "excessive dependence on the institution," which hindered their reintegration into society after they left the hospital (Lamb 1998, 665). Psychiatric hospitals and other custodial institutions where individuals resided for long periods (often involuntarily) became seen as depriving them of their civil rights and reinforcing their stigmatization. Consequently, a policy of deinstitutionalization was introduced in the United States and other Western countries that led to the shift away from large-scale mental hospitals to community-based mental health care, which may include supported housing with full or partial supervision, psychiatric wards of general hospitals, day centers or clubhouses, community mental health centers, and self-help groups for mental health. These services may be provided by government organizations, mental health professionals, or private or charitable organizations.

Today a majority of individuals with mental illness receive community-based mental health services. However, as Fakhoury and Priebe (2002) note, the quality of the community mental care systems varies substantially across countries worldwide. The World Health Organization (2007) notes that in many developing countries, the closing of mental hospitals is not accompanied by the development of community services, leaving a service vacuum. As a result people with mental illness do not receive adequate help. Countries with advanced deinstitutionalization attempt to tackle such issues as confinement of those with dangerous behaviors and successful integration into the community of those with mental illness and their concomitant access to employment and housing. Countries with recent histories of institutionalization, where the development of community mental health care is at its beginnings, face challenges related to the allocation of financial resources, social acceptance of deinstitutionalization, and degrading approaches toward those with mental illness. As a result of these differences, the experience of being a mental health service user may vary significantly across countries and among various social groups.

An early study by Hollingshead and Redlich (1958) examined the links between social class, pathways to treatment, and type of treatment received; it suggested that the lower classes are clearly disadvantaged when it comes to imposing involuntary and restraining treatment. Compared to other social classes, the lowest social class experienced more mental illness, particularly psychosis, and was more likely to enter treatment via courts and official agencies, as well as to receive somatic rather than psychological therapies. Some studies continue to report that members of racial and ethnic minorities receive limited or inadequate mental health services and hold more negative beliefs about the mental health profession. Racial and ethnic minorities are more likely than whites to experience discriminatory treatment and to be restrained (physically or chemically) and secluded, escorted by police, and admitted involuntarily (Cook and Wright 1995).

Furthermore, despite the increasing emphasis in contemporary legal frameworks and professional codes of ethics on patients' autonomy and informed decision-making, some studies show that withholding illness- or treatment-related information from the patient may be common both in inpatient and outpatient settings (Shergill, Barker, and Greenberg 1998). Patients with schizophrenia are less likely to be informed of their diagnosis, and psychiatrists are also more reticent regarding the diagnosis of personality disorders.

THE KEY METHODS UTILIZED IN THE FIELD

Sociologists studying the phenomenon of mental illness utilize a variety of methods. Scholars interested in psychiatric concepts, classifications, and mental-health-related media messages use textual and/or content analysis; sociologists studying professionalization, development of psychiatric care, and mental health policies draw upon archival data. Survey methods are applied in studying users' expectations, needs, and satisfaction with mental health services. Mental health service utilization is assessed by studying patient statistics. Some sociologists have used path models to understand how psychiatric consumers/survivors fare in community settings (Hall and Nelson 1996).

Qualitative research methods are also increasingly used in the field, both by sociologists and by other researchers. Schulze and Angermeyer (2003), for instance, have applied the focus-group method to explore stigma from the subjective perspective of people with schizophrenia. Bradshaw, Roseborough, and Armour (2006) carried out semistructured interviews in their hermeneutic phenomenological study on the lived experience of persons recovering from serious and persistent mental illness.

WHAT THE HUMAN RIGHTS PARADIGM CAN LEARN FROM THE SOCIOLOGICAL WORK ON MENTAL ILLNESS

Human rights scholars can learn from sociological work in the field of mental illness in several ways. First, mental health and illness, as well as treatment options, are unequally distributed among various social groups, with the lowest income groups as well as racial and ethnic minorities being at a clear disadvantage. Experience of social exclusion, discrimination, and poverty (i.e., being denied basic human rights) correlates with vulnerability to mental distress. In turn, socially disadvantaged groups are more likely to experience restrictive and discriminatory psychiatric treatments, resulting in their further stigmatization and social exclusion. Second, health and illness are negotiated social concepts and, as such, cannot be understood simply in terms of bodily phenomena; psychiatric labels are socially contingent. Third, some psychiatric conceptualizations of mental illness (for instance, those emphasizing genetic predisposition to mental pathology) may challenge the individual's right to self-determination and serve as a basis for imposing paternalistic professional practices or compulsory treatment. Finally, paternalism, if structured into mental health care, as well as the stigma of mental illness, may impede individuals' abilities to take a more active and critical stance and prevent realization of their basic rights or questioning of the denial of those rights.

A RESITUATION OF THE SOCIOLOGY OF MENTAL HEALTH WITHIN A HUMAN RIGHTS PARADIGM

Sociologists focus on the various manifestations of discrimination and mistreatment of people with mental disabilities. The resituation of the sociology of mental health within a human rights paradigm encourages us to readdress these issues by exploring more specifically the underlying and sustaining mechanisms of human rights violations in mental illness, as well as the conditions that help people to flourish and enjoy their rights, freedoms, and good mental health.

One potential area for this kind of sociological study is the implementation of mental health policy and law both locally and internationally. There is a long tradition of sociological research on deinstitutionalization policies (Prior 1996; Barham 1992; Scull 1984) and an interest in psychiatric legislation (Dallaire et al. 2000; Carpenter 2000), but this kind of research has not engaged directly with the issue of universal human rights for those with mental illness. Sociologists could start by asking how mental health laws, policies, and programs enhance or limit the rights of people with mental illness. What triggers the implementation of human rights for those with mental illness locally and globally? Who are the key players and interest groups in this process? In his analysis of mental health policy under welfare capitalism, Carpenter (2000) has noted that in some countries, mental health service user movements and the focus on civil liberties have had a significant impact on the development of mental health policies and rights for individuals with mental illness. In other countries, professional groups have been more prominent in debates about procedures and rights in mental health care, leading to more restrictive mental health policy regimes. The peculiarity of the cultural, economic, and political contexts as implicated in mental health policies, initiatives and programs directed toward preserving the mental health of the population, involuntary commitment laws, and their comparative historical analysis might become the starting points for those who wish to get engaged with the human rights issues within mental health.

Sociologists have been actively engaged in exposing the degrading effects of institutional care. The analysis of the nature of psychiatric care in both institutions and community mental-health-care settings remains highly pertinent to the rights-related sociology of mental health. However, if we center the human rights paradigm in our studies, we are prompted to ask not only how psychiatry interferes with the individual's right to self-determination but also how it may enhance the individual's ability to lead an independent and full life. Sociologists have typically rejected the possibility of a genuine concern on the part of psychiatry for the welfare of the mental patient. Are we ready to rethink our position? How should we approach the coercive psychiatric care that seems to be necessary at times?

Furthermore, how do we reconcile the dominant sociological ideas about mental illness with those inherent to the human rights paradigm? Sociologists tend to reject mental illness as a natural, universal phenomenon and prefer to see it as socially constructed. This kind of reasoning has provided a background for much sociological critique of psychiatric care and the unjust social situation of those labeled as "mentally ill," although at the same time it has led to a neglect of the reality of human suffering due to mental illness (Gerhardt 1989). The human rights paradigm, on the contrary, approaches mental illness as a natural phenomenon. One way to solve this apparent problem would be to accept the ontological reality of mental illness but to see it as culturally and socially mediated (Busfield 1996). Then, for instance, the reinforcement or denial of human rights becomes crucial for mental health. Still, these and similar questions remain to be answered.

Finally, if we center the human rights paradigm in our research, we are impelled to focus on the mental health user's life. How do these people fare in the community? How does the experience of mental illness, treatment, or the status of the mental health user itself interact with the opportunity to enjoy other human rights (e.g., an adequate standard of living, the right to work)? How do the answers to these and other pertinent questions change if we introduce socioeconomic status, gender, and ethnicity/race into analysis?

WHAT IS THE FUTURE?

As human beings we possess rights simply because of our humanity. Thus, mental illness by itself provides no justifiable ground for unjust treatment or denial of an individual's autonomy. This approach is advocated by both the sociology of mental health and the human rights paradigm. The sociology of mental health continues to offer a conceptual and theoretical foundation that helps to challenge the negative beliefs and practices related to the phenomenon of mental illness. Human rights scholars assert that people with mental illness need not prove that they deserve certain rights or that they are able to exercise them. Both sociology and the human rights paradigm are interested in social justice and empowerment of socially disadvantaged populations. Thus, a sociology of mental health and human rights could become a powerful tool in fostering positive changes in the situation of people with mental disabilities.

Sociologists have distinctive theoretical tools and a long tradition of empirical research into the phenomenon of mental illness. Sociology goes beyond medical conceptualizations and locates what is often understood as a natural category or a personal tragedy within the broader social context and analysis of social and power relations. By further examining the link between institutional arrangements, societal reactions, professional power, and social control, we can continue to explore and challenge the limitation of rights that may be imposed on those with mental illness.

What about the professional prerogative—which, although restricted, is still preserved—to decide when such limitations are needed? Do there exist ways to challenge this still overly medicalized approach to the rights of people with mental illness? And how about mental health laws and policies shaped by the social construction of violence and mental illness at a sociopolitical level and by the dominant societal perceptions of the mentally ill? Viewing those with mental illness as violent and unpredictable, for instance, may prevent us from acknowledging discriminatory behaviors and practices toward them. As Beresford and Wilson (2002) note, increased claims in favor of restricting the civil and human rights of individuals with mental illness constitute an emerging international development that has also tended to be racialized in its public presentation. The authors argue that these claims are fueled by increasing emphasis in both the media and government policy on the danger, threat, and "otherness" of mental health service users. Such public fears are reinforced by genetic approaches to severe mental illness and mental distress that are gaining increasing power and official legitimacy. These and similar issues should be a focus of a sociology of mental health and human rights.

For a long time, sociologists have devoted relatively little attention to the subjective experience of living with mental illness. Thorne et al. (2002) have analyzed qualitative studies published between 1980 and 1996 that dealt with some aspect of what it is like to live with a chronic illness from the perspective of the individual involved. They noted that studies typically focused on individuals with rheumatic, cardiovascular, or endocrine disorders, and "rarely were persons with chronic psychological or psychiatric disorders related to the physical illness included in these kinds of studies" (Thorne et al. 2002, 443). Cook and Wright (1995, 106) have noted several reasons why a focus on the mentally ill individual has not been very prominent in sociological research. According to them, interaction with people suffering from mental illness is often difficult, as they experience mood swings, tend to withdraw from social contact, or cannot tolerate long survey interviews. Patients in long-term care settings may be inaccessible. Besides, in order to study mental illness, sociologists probably need to be familiar with and understand basic psychiatry. By exploring subjective experience of stigma and discrimination, sociologists might provide useful insights into how people with mental illness themselves define their rights and what impediments they see to realizing them. This would enrich the human rights paradigm from the "bottom-up point of view" (Lewis 2009b).

Finally, what about involving people with mental illness as active participants in our research projects? Participatory action or collaborative research methods have become increasingly used by disability researchers. This kind of research strengthens sociological commitment to social justice and social activism. Indeed, a sociology of mental health and human rights provides a strong reason to redefine our relationship to those we study. By reconstructing people with mental disabilities as credible agents whose views we must respect and take into account when designing legal instruments, implementing mental health policies, and protecting human rights, we could contribute to the empowerment of these people. This is also a way to challenge and reverse negative and stereotypical societal perceptions of mental illness and the mentally ill.

In sum, a sociology of mental health and human rights could contribute to societal and political awareness of the importance of human rights promotion and protection for the mentally ill. The wealth of data produced by our research may in turn serve as a basis for developing legal instruments that would be grounded in sound empirical evidence.

CHAPTER FOUR

RACIAL AND ETHNIC MINORITIES

James M. Thomas and David L. Brunsma

As we slowly make our way through the twenty-first century, the sociological enterprise is rapidly expanding. With more than forty-five sections in the American Sociological Association, an increasing number of doctoral degrees being earned, and more outlets for publishing scholarly works than ever before, the rapid growth of the sociological enterprise has made room for the potential to begin to answer the most pressing social and cultural questions of our time. Problems of the past are not going away; nor are they simply being recycled. They are fundamentally transforming as our social worlds collide with one another, producing new problems (and solutions) in an increasingly transnational world.

The sociological study of racial and ethnic minorities, then, is no different. As the former strengths of national borders begin to give way to corporate power and collective identity movements in various parts of the globe (Sassen 1999), how we think about the relationship between identities and power is shifting—from questions of the local to questions of the global. In this transition, we must not lose sight of one historical and contemporary fact: the study of racial and ethnic minorities must be the study of oppression and resistance. That is, the very definition of the term "minority" refers specifically to a location absent of social power. Starting from here, sociological analysis requires a question that asks how this absence of power has been produced, what mechanisms allow for it to sustain itself, and how this force can be stopped or reversed. Thus, we repeat for effect: the study of racial and ethnic minorities must be the study of oppression and resistance.

In this chapter, we think about one way that the study of racial and ethnic minorities can be reframed, not simply as a struggle for civil rights and social recognition but fundamentally as a struggle for human rights. As we move forward in an era witness to increasing transnational flows of capital, information, and even people, as sociologists we must incorporate a rights-based paradigm to understand the evolution of racial and ethnic minorities, in terms of both their oppressions and their resistances. This is no easy task, however. A rights-based paradigm requires sociologists of racial and ethnic minorities to fundamentally take a moral position through their research agenda. Such a claim to moral authority is not without its problems, and the debate about whether it is our place as social scientists to claim such authority has been a long and complex one. We wish to table this debate until the conclusion for the purposes of reviewing the field of racial and ethnic minority studies. At the end of the chapter, however, we take up this question with great respect and articulate a position in which moral authority becomes a question of sociological analysis and, more importantly, one that deserves a definitive answer.

REVIEW OF THE FIELD

Any review of a field of study requires some sort of organization from which the researcher and the reader can make sense of an otherwise vast and confusing body of knowledge. In a pursuit of such organization, depth is often sacrificed for breadth— ours is no different. By and large, there are currently three general categories into which the majority of sociological scholarship on racial and ethnic minorities can be organized: stratification studies, identity studies, and movement studies. We propose a fourth wave that could center itself in human rights. Within the first three categories, there exists a weak presence of an analytic of rights in general, not to mention human rights specifically. Such discussions are often relegated to secondary analyses or a strongly worded conclusion.

Though there are studies that do not fit these categories, the typology we present here is useful for thinking through the varieties of research in the sociology of racial and ethnic minorities. Such categories are not necessarily separate but often imbricate one another, and scholars often find their work falling within more than one of these categories. For instance, if we take the works of W. E. B. Du Bois, much of his early work documented social ills facing black America during the post-Reconstruction period in the United States. However, if we single out his groundbreaking *The Souls of Black Folks* (1903), then we see an entirely different Du Bois, one devoted to understanding and articulating the mechanisms through which black American identity is structured through the metaphor of the "veil." With this in mind, we wish to proceed by first unpacking what these categories entail and how a rights-based paradigm both contributes to their current scholarship and can also improve upon them.

STRATIFICATION STUDIES

Stratification studies of racial and ethnic minorities stem in large part from the empirically oriented works of the Chicago School, as well as some of the classic sociological theorists. Contemporary works often follow the foundations set forth by many of the giants in this field: Oliver Cox (*Caste, Class, and Race*, 1948), W. E. B. Du Bois (*The Philadelphia Negro*, 2010 [1899]), and Robert E. Park (1914, 1928a, 1928b), who, along with Cox, was influential in developing the Chicago School approach to the study of race and ethnic relations. In these bodies of scholarship, the various ills of racial and ethnic minorities, primarily in the Western context, are exposed through a variety of methodologies, though they are predominantly positivist in their epistemological orientations and lean heavily on the idea that particular methods must be employed in order to document societal ills.

Over time, as sociology has had to respond to the theoretical and methodological critiques of positivism, particularly after the 1950s, stratification studies have become much more diverse in their epistemological and methodological orientations. What has not changed, however, is their primary focus on the documentation and explanation of how particular racial and ethnic minority groups have come to be arranged in relation to the dominant majority. Contemporary works that highlight this particular category of research are Omi and Winant's (1994) influential work on racial formation in the United States and the subsequent revisions to racial formation theory, both in the US context and internationally, that have followed (e.g., Thomas 2010; Bonilla-Silva 2003); Charles Mills's (1997) philosophical treatise on how contemporary race relations were constructed through a racialized social contract during the period of European Enlightenment; and Joe Feagin's research agenda of documenting and problematizing systemic racism in both the US and global contexts (Feagin 2006, 2010). In all instances, these scholars attempt to answer two fundamental questions: how race and ethnicity themselves, as well as the resultant racial social structure, came to be, and what the social, political, and cultural consequences of these hierarchical arrangements are.

The most obvious contribution of stratification studies is the empirical breadth and depth they offer for documenting societal ills and concerns. This is of utmost importance in the current political global climate, where questions of race and ethnicity are often viewed by those in power as a relic of the past. In the Western context, the prevalence of color-blind racism (Bonilla-Silva 2003; Forman and Lewis 2006; Hill 2008) has been well documented and theorized as the overarching contemporary logic behind ethnic and racial stratification. Studies that highlight multiple levels of inequality among racial and ethnic minorities continue to abound, from research on overt discrimination in the European Union (Wrench 2011), to comparisons of rates of success for political incorporation of new immigrants into the US and western European political systems (Mollenkopf and Hoschschild 2010), to documentation of disparate home appreciation between whites and minority groups in the United States (Flippen 2004). Without a doubt, stratification studies continue to serve as a strength of the sociological enterprise in addressing the lack of actualized human rights among racial and ethnic minorities the world over. However, this brings us to questions that still remain for this particular area.

Though stratification studies have their place within the sociological enterprise, particularly concerning the sociological analysis of racial and ethnic minorities, there exists a tendency within these studies to focus strictly on the noticeable presence or absence of inequality, with little or no intellectual debate over remedies for these processes and outcomes. Of course, this is no easy task for sociologists, and there exists within the discipline of sociology an ongoing debate as to whether it is even our job, as academics, to make the case for or against a global human rights agenda as a form of social policy (Sjoberg, Gill, and Williams 2001). This is not to suggest that all stratification studies ignore the merits of advocating for a human rights agenda within the discipline. Such contemporaries as Zuberi and

Bonilla-Silva (2008) and Feagin and Vera (2008) in fact take an explicit stance on the role of human rights in addressing the many inequalities and injustices faced by racial and ethnic minorities around the world. However, simply looking through the recent abstracts of *American Sociological Review, Social Forces,* or *American Journal of Sociology* demonstrates that scholars who study racial and ethnic stratification through a human rights perspective are in the minority.

IDENTITY STUDIES

In addition to the central tendency of sociology to focus on stratification, another realm of inquiry might be called identity studies. Identity studies in the social sciences, particularly those on ethnic and racial identities, derive a large portion of their theoretical strength and empirical foundations from the work of two scholars who shared a similar time period but little else: pragmatist George Herbert Mead and the critical race theorist W. E. B. Du Bois.

Generally speaking, Mead's cornerstone collection of writings, *Mind, Self, and Society* (1967), provides the building blocks for understanding how social scientists talk about the concept of the self and how that concept shares a relationality with social forces external to it. In particular, Mead's (1967) use of the I, the Me, and the Other provides a social explanation of how individuals who belong to particular groups come to recognize their own sense of self and community through an opposition to a generalized other. Over time, various revisions to and iterations of this theory of the self have emerged. In particular, the theoretical strain of symbolic interactionism and its derivatives, especially dramaturgy, were of particular importance in shaping our current understandings of how identities come to be made and reproduced over time (Goffman 1959; Garfinkel 1967).

Currently, identity studies in race and ethnicity that follow this particular theoretical strain are often categorized under the label "performative studies" or "dramaturgical studies" and attempt to respond to questions centered on how identities come to be produced and maintained within particular contexts and in response to certain cultural forces and constraints. For instance, Johnson (2003) explores the contradictory ways in which blackness is put together in American culture. She argues that when blackness as an identity is appropriated to the exclusion of others, it becomes political. More importantly, Johnson's (2003) work questions the notion of an "authentic black self" by problematizing the hypothetical other that would have to exist as its counterpart. Authenticity as an identity configuration for black Americans or any other racialized group of people, according to Johnson, is simply "another trope manipulated for cultural capital" (2003, 3).

Another example of the dramaturgical approach to ethnic and racial studies in sociology would be Picca and Feagin's (2007) work on the Janus-faced nature of whites' attitudes toward race. Here, Picca and Feagin investigate not just how whites code their racial attitudes among peers and coworkers in public spaces (e.g., Bonilla-Silva 2003), but also the various ways in which whites display their attitudes toward race and difference among family, friends, and other whites, or what Goffman (1959) would refer to as the back stage.

The second strain of identity studies within the social sciences concerning race and ethnicity stems from W. E. B. Du Bois and his oft-quoted passage from *The Souls of Black Folks* concerning the metaphor of the veil. Though Du Bois and Mead were contemporaries, they were hardly interlocutors. However, Du Bois's use of the metaphor of the veil to explicate how blacks come to see themselves through both their own eyes and the eyes of others—double consciousness—is dramatically similar to Mead's theorizing of how a generalized other comes to be the referent for the development of the I in social life. In many ways, these two theorists were explaining two sides of the same coin: Mead, how whiteness comes to reproduce itself over time through a constant reference to that which it is not; Du Bois, how the racial and ethnic other comes to recognize that it is not a part of a community through a recognition of its own lack.

Du Bois's illumination of the experience of racialized others in the American context provided much-needed ground for later critical race theorists to stand upon. Further, as Du Bois himself became more global in his travels and writings, his ideas on Pan-Africanism and racism as a global force, rather than an American one, became building blocks for future generations of critical race theorists (Du Bois 1983). Of special importance were the works of the early postcolonial writers, such as Aimé Césaire (2001), Frantz Fanon (2005, 2008), Edward Said (1979), and Stuart Hall (1986). These postcolonial theorists in particular began to advance a theory of race and ethnicity that examined the formation of these othered identities without losing sight of the fact that these identities were born out of a dialectic of struggle and resistance. This particular branch of identity studies has been much more open to interdisciplinary ideas and research, as evidenced by the multiple perspectives that touch, and have been touched by, postcolonialism—from film and narrative studies (Minh-ha 1997), to literature (Kincaid 2000), to cultural theory (Bhabha 2004).

Whether deriving their theoretical and empirical strength from the Meadian tradition or that of Du Bois, identity studies by and large share some common strengths in the study of race and ethnicity, as well as some common weaknesses. First, let us speak to the strengths of this area.

As a whole, these studies provide great insight into the particular mechanisms and technologies through which particular identities come to be expressed. The Meadian emphasis on language, specifically talk (Garfinkel 1967), allows us to understand how race and ethnicity come to be conceptually made and repackaged over time through the production and deployment of language (McIntyre 1997). For example, Ruth Frankenburg's (1993) study on how white women come to make sense of racism and sexism through their lived experiences illustrates how whiteness as a concept is both socially constructed and meaningful in the same ways that otheredness is meaningful to those who experience social life from that perspective (Tatum 2003).

Meanwhile, the emphasis on language, specifically discourse, that arises in part from the tradition of postcolonialism and poststructuralism's influence over the body of literature in the sociological study of racial and ethnic minorities that we call identity studies demonstrates the dialectical nature of identity and the interplay between social forces and social agents, between resistance and oppression. David

Goldberg's (1990) edited volume stands as an exemplar of this model in identity studies, offering essays from such scholars as Kwame Anthony Appiah, Frantz Fanon, Roland Barthes, Paul Gilroy, and Homi Bhabha, among others, to demonstrate the multiple forms and methods through which racism is generated and maintained in philosophy, literature, and social institutions such as politics and law. The connective tissue of these essays, and in most identity studies that begin through a poststructuralist and postcolonial theoretical examination, is that the illumination of these discursive forms of power that create ethnic and racial hierarchies is meant both to reveal and to subvert its multiple manifestations. In this way, the Du Bois tradition of identity studies takes us, as sociologists, to a platform of advocacy, critical questioning, and hope—something that the symbolic interactionist tradition does not necessarily provide with its meticulous attention to explicit forms of language such as conversation, narrative, and conceptual construction (Holstein and Gubrium 1999).

Identity studies, whether in the tradition of Mead or Du Bois, are not without their flaws. Having already spent some time identifying the limits of Meadian analysis, particularly as it concerns a lack of agenda setting for policy-making or critical engagement with social structures and forces, we wish to discuss some concerns we have with the tradition of identity studies stemming from the work of Du Bois and other more critical scholars of race and ethnicity.

Lawrence Grossberg's (1992) examination of popular culture and the formation of conservativism makes the compelling argument that the notion of identity politics is a dead end for a progressive political agenda, in part because the tradition from which identity politics has arisen argues for an essentialized political identity of the other. In a separate but equally important criticism, Grossberg writes that traditional theories of otherness "assume that difference is itself an historically produced economy, imposed in modern structures of power" (1992, 94), rather than seeing difference as fundamentally constitutive. Criticizing Said (1979) specifically, Grossberg argues that Said's form of Orientalism assumes that people who participated in Orientalism traveled to places and cultures that already existed, rather than understanding the Orientalist and Orientalism as a particular logic of difference that, through description of the Oriental other, constituted the very thing it was seeking to describe.

This, then, has been the problem with much of the Du Bois tradition of the racial and ethnic other, as well as contemporary postcolonial theories and writings on the matter. These contemporary studies seek to essentialize the other into a political category, where political agency comes to be defined haphazardly as a politics of resentment. Grossberg's claim, and our critique, is that this limits the possibilities for what subjectivity, agency, and a progressive politics can mean in a world where there is no essential self and where agency is more and more coming to be understood by activity rather than simply by presence.

MOVEMENT STUDIES

The above concern brings us to the third category of scholarship on racial and ethnic minorities: movement studies. The tradition of movement studies, in general, draws its strength from the early works of Karl Marx, in particular his argument that social movements are, for the most part, the end result of historically determined conditions. Movements for social change arise from the collective action of social actors when, in Marx's analysis, they become aware of their social class as a contradiction to the antagonists of those conditions that produced their social class in the first place (Bottomore 1963; Tarrow 1998). Later developments in Marxism reconfigured social-movement theories around the conceptual framework of "resource mobilization" spurred by those in positions of power (Lenin 2007) and later as centered on the need to build consensus through the development of a collective identity (Gramsci 1971).

By the 1960s, however, and influenced heavily by the French student movements, the modern-day civil rights movement in the United States, second-wave feminism, and Black Power, sociology underwent a paradigm shift that emphasized a politically connected view of social movements (Tarrow 1998). Resource mobilization began to take on an entirely different perspective, one spurred forward by political scientists and economists who wanted to understand the rise and success of movements in terms of incentives, sectors, and industries (McCarthy and Zald 1977).

Such an account of social movements did not resonate with many in the discipline of sociology, and by the 1980s an alternative model was being put forward that emphasized culture as a counterparadigm to resource-mobilization theories (Tarrow 1998). This shift in how we understand social movements resulted in a strong emphasis being placed on what was termed "identity politics" and subsequently deemphasized structural approaches to the understanding of social movements and change. The newly placed emphasis on identity formation as part of the social-movement process allowed for culture to play the role of metanarrator in the trajectory of movements and also in how identities come to form a collective around such interactive processes as framing (Goffman 1986), ideological and emotional packaging of grievances (Gamson 1988), and the multiple processes by which social concerns and conditions become social problems (Best 2007).

As relates to the study of racial and ethnic minorities, movement studies scholarship has largely focused on the identity politics paradigm, where the formation of collective politics is emphasized, most typically through the essentializing of racial and ethnic others under a generic political condition they are all assumed to share. For instance, Vermeersch's (2003) study of the active construction of Romani identity within the contemporary Czech and Slovak republics provides a rich analysis of how Romani identity is framed by politically active members and how this framing is tied to explicit political strategies. However, left out of this analysis, and others similar to it (Kuroiwa and Verkuyten 2008; Leibovitz 2007; Nordberg 2006), is the plurality, hybridity, and relationality that is most typical of any ethnic or racial group and how these characteristics constrain and enable any given collective movement.

Also typical of most movement-studies scholarship is the emphasis on social movements among ethnic and racial minorities as they relate to political, cultural, or economic recognition. For instance, much scholarship has been produced on the Black Power movement within contemporary America (Bush 2000; Rojas 2007).

In most of this work, analysis focuses on the movement's goals as they relate to political and economic rights—the right to vote, the right to equal housing and schooling, the right to work, and so forth. Little scholarship, however, focuses on the emphasis of these movements toward recognizing blacks in America as humans worthy of dignity, justice, and other human rights as defined in the Universal Declaration of Human Rights. In fact, there is almost no mention of the influence of such historically significant and, during the 1960s, well-circulated documents on the formation and sustainment of movements that, if we look at the rhetoric of the political leaders of Black Power, was obvious in their speeches, demonstrations, and political platforms. It is from this final point that we can begin to build an agenda for the sociological study of racial and ethnic minorities that incorporates the human rights perspective currently trending within political science, legal studies, and international studies scholarship.

REDEFINING THE FIELD FROM A HUMAN RIGHTS PERSPECTIVE

To return to our opening assertion: the study of ethnic and racial minorities is, and should remain, the study of oppression and resistance. With this statement, we do not declare that sociologists abandon the categorization of scholarship that we presented in the above review. Rather, we demand as scholars and advocates of social justice that sociologists attend to the substantive questions of concern in this twenty-first century—questions of how human rights can be attained for racial and ethnic minorities. Stratification studies must of course continue to document the many instances where groups of ethnic and racial minorities are hierarchically arranged, but must begin to emphasize the effects of such arrangements on the affording and limiting of human rights as acknowledged by international law in the Universal Declaration of Human Rights; the International Covenant on Economic, Social, and Cultural Rights; the International Covenant on Civil and Political Rights; and other human rights instruments ratified by the vast majority of nations the world over since 1948.

Stratification studies, for instance, must begin to examine the effects of the aforementioned human rights instruments on the increasing and decreasing rates of disparity between ethnic and racial minorities and those in power, not just in specific regions but also on a more global scale. And, stratification studies must, from the empirical evidence they find, begin to generate real claims grounded in social-scientific methodology. Sjoberg, Gill, and Williams (2001) contend, as do we, that sociology *necessarily has to* investigate the moral dimension of social life. Citing the works of the philosophers Hilary Putman and John Dewey, Sjoberg, Gill, and Williams (2001) argue that the moral order is neither God-given nor biopsychological in nature. Therefore, it must be sociological at its core. If morality is a product of social and cultural activities, then it deserves sociological attention at the empirical level. Taking it one step further, if morality is accepted as a key component of sociological inquiry, then it follows that we are required as social scientists to explore the nature of moral commitments within our own discipline.

This means, for the purposes of stratification studies, that sociologists begin to not only document social inequalities, but also exert particular moral claims upon those hierarchical arrangements (Brunsma and Overfelt 2007). To maintain an empirical quality, however, these claims must be made at the level of human rights, as these rights are universally recognized among various governing bodies around the world, and are therefore better able to stand the moral position of relativism popular among sociologists of culture and radical constructionism.

For identity studies, a human rights paradigm opens up the possibilities of fostering a politics of community not predicated upon essentialized categories of racial and ethnic difference, but rather a politics of community predicated upon shared experiences and commitments to a shared vision among racial and ethnic minorities. The former is essentially a slippery slope, as a politics of community built upon essentialized categories of difference can only be, in the end, a politics of resentment and a reactionary political platform. What we advocate, however, is a shift toward thinking about ethnic and racial difference as historically grounded in shared experiences, but also oriented toward a progressive future in which commitments among members of oppressed groups are aimed toward achieving a shared vision of hope (Brunsma 2010). The dilemma of intersectional analyses in the social sciences is that, due to the nature of moral relativism that has taken a hold of sociology since the cultural turn in the late 1970s to early 1980s, intersectional analysis has become an "add and stir" form of sociological investigation. Axes of difference have been articulated as being more *problematic* for developing a sense of community and shared visions for a progressive politics because common ground can never truly be found among those who share a racial category but not one of gender, or who have similar class backgrounds but differing sexualities.

We take intersectionality seriously, but through a human rights paradigm in which the rights of all are acknowledged simply because they share the commonality of being human, identity studies can potentially develop a praxis of hope through the investigation of shared commitments toward this hope from those who come from different identity configurations. Rather than an "add and stir" analysis, then, identity studies in the twenty-first century can redirect their focus toward how human rights organizations, instruments, and movements allow those from different ethnic and racial backgrounds to achieve those same rights across the board. Further, identity studies can begin to focus on how human rights themselves are mechanisms for articulating particular identities, including racial and ethnic categories, and what these human rights tools are able to accomplish in the articulation of these identity locations (Brunsma and Delgado 2008).

Last, movement studies in ethnic and racial minority scholarship perhaps have the easiest task of the three categories. A human rights paradigm simply requires a shift in analytical attention—from movements for civil or economic rights to one that centers on movements for human rights. We have already mentioned how a historical sociology could investigate the rhetoric of the Black Power movement, for example, and see it for its articulation of human rights for the black diaspora rather than for political and economic rights for black Americans. Similar measures could be taken in the examination of activist rhetoric among those involved in the movements for indigenous rights among First Nations people in Canada, Aborigines in Australia, the Maori of New Zealand, and American Indians within the United States, both contemporarily and in a historical context. Much of the claims making among these groups has been documented by social scientists as oriented toward achieving political and economic rights, such as reparations (Thomas and Brunsma 2008). However, it would be a relatively simple task for sociologists to examine the ways in which rhetoric that advocated for these various groups' rights was actually a product of a larger human rights paradigm shift in international political movements and legal actions.

CONCLUSION

The human rights paradigm within sociology is both a serious shift in epistemology among sociologists and an evolving field of inquiry. In addition to the growing membership of the Section on Human Rights of the American Sociological Association, an increasing number of publication outlets focus explicitly on illuminating cutting-edge research in the field of human rights and moral inquiry. Further, various organizations around the world with a mission to advance the pursuit and purpose of human rights are seeing a growing number of sociologists enter into their folds, including Sociologists Without Borders (of which we ourselves are members), Human Rights Watch, Amnesty International, and the International Society for Human Rights, to name just a few. The turn toward human rights, then, is not a fad or a passing trend; instead, it should be seen as both a social and a scientific revolution, in the Kuhnian sense (Kuhn 1996). That sociologists are just now beginning to enter into its enterprise in large numbers simply indicates to us that this revolution has been in the making for over sixty years, as indicated by the advancements already made in legal studies and political science, and that our presence as sociologists is necessary for the human rights enterprise to become truly central to both the scientific investigation of social and cultural life and the advancement of a moral inquiry focused on the development, deployment, and achievement of human rights in practice the world over.

CHAPTER FIVE

ASIA AND ASIAN AMERICA

Mary Yu Danico and Phi Hong Su

The Universal Declaration of Human Rights in 1948 argued for the dignity of all human beings and their rights to freedom, justice, and peace. While such sentiments appear straightforward, the constructed meaning of human rights has been heavily swayed by Western thought and ideals about what constitutes dignity and justice. For Asia and Asian America, the human rights paradigm is often contested and questioned for its applicability to people of Asian descent. Does the human rights doctrine assume universality in the reality of the individual lives in particular spaces?

This chapter begins with a discussion of traditional human rights research and paradigms and questions the applicability of a universal human rights paradigm to a world of sovereign states, problematizes whether human rights exist for the stateless or those without a nation or citizenship, and examines the role of "Asian values," including Confucianism, in the evolution of human rights in the diaspora. We then discuss key human rights issues in Asia and Asian America from the past and present and the human rights violations that continue across the globe. We end with a discussion of the limitations of the human rights discourse in its application to Asia and Asian America and frame a critical discussion of what the human rights paradigm can learn from scholarship in Asia, Asian America, and the interstices of states, in order to better enrich human rights research and the reality of human rights for all. We suggest new questions and new possibilities for the study of and advocacy for Asia and Asian America.

HUMAN RIGHTS PARADIGM AND ASIA/ASIAN AMERICA

Are human rights, premised on universal personhood, ultimately universal in their application? It is abundantly clear in the literature on human rights in Asia that this is a persistent concern, posing the following challenges: Do human rights exist outside the West? Can a universalistic paradigm of human rights work in a world of sovereign states? A universal framework is often criticized for Western bias, for cultural blindness to Eastern ways or Asian values, and for being restrictive and assimilative (Kausikan 1995; Zakaria and Lee 1994). While the concept of universality is enticing, does it come at the cost of denying the reality facing individuals and the societies in which they live (Evans 2001b)?

Such problems stem from the fact that the constructed meaning of human rights is not universally shared. Fulfillment of basic survival needs for food and shelter is a human right that may be more pressing for developing Asian countries than broader political and economic concerns. These considerations are embodied by an "Asian values" perspective characterized by collectivism, a strong emphasis on the family and discipline, and denial of the universality of human rights (Hoang 2009; Sen 1999a). From this perspective derive communiqués such as the 1993 Bangkok Declaration, which criticizes human rights universalism. Defense of cultural relativism, however, has in turn been criticized "as a defense against human atrocities, including the suppression of women" (Amirthalingam 2005; Goonesekere 2000).

Human rights is a universal obligation, with allies from around the world subscribing to its tenets. Confucian values, widespread in parts of Asia, for example, have human rights ideals embedded in their philosophy. The key principles of Confucianism promote humanistic philosophy, free conscience, personal dignity, equality before the law, fair punishment, freedom of ideology and speech, patriotism, and a harmonious relationship with the world. Yet, the standard of the West as defender of human rights and the non-West as violator of them persists. Ownership over human rights has conceptually been ascribed to and claimed by the West. While some contend that Western parentage of the notion of human rights is a historical fact (Donnelly 1982), others propose an overhaul of the notion of ownership (Penna and Campbell 1998).

Beyond a state framework, owning human rights is glaringly problematic for those without states, or stateless persons. More than 1 million people are ignored in human rights discourse—these are the noncitizens of the world (Weissbrodt and Collins 2006). The Universal Declaration of Human Rights dictates that everyone has the right to leave and return to his or her homeland. In reality, the concerns of those who escape from ethnic/religious conflict, war, and genocide are not addressed because these individuals often are stateless. People who have been separated by war (e.g., South and North Korea) are denied the right to return to their homes or have only recently been able to do so (as in the case of diasporic Vietnamese); those who are "undocumented," typically as well as their children, are denied human rights because of their stateless status.

CHALLENGING TRADITIONAL HUMAN RIGHTS DISCOURSE

The case of China further evidences the paradoxical boundedness of human rights constructs. Sovereignty is an invaluable virtue in this era of interdependent states, one that exists with as much reverence as, and in contradiction to, a discourse of borderless human rights (Soysal 1994). In problematizing human rights as universal, scholars and activists have addressed the questions of for whom human rights are important and who is responsible for human rights. Consequently, opposition to the perceived imperialist project of universal human rights has manifested in a form of cultural relativism. In Asia's case, this relativism takes the stance of "Asia's different standard" (Cerna 1995). This perspective complicates universalist discourse by noting that rights are conceived differentially across cultures, that the rhetoric of universalism is not useful in implementation, and that universalism confronts and conflicts with the principle of national sovereignty (Kausikan 1995). Engaging this rhetoric of a different standard, Ali Alatas, former Indonesian foreign minister, noted that "in the developing countries we are still struggling to overcome the blights imposed by past colonialism and new exploitation, and by the pervasive effects of an inequitable international order, and consequently, must spend more time on basic needs" (cited by Cerna 1995, 153). Alatas defends the need for developing countries to first secure material conditions for living over and above—perhaps at the expense of—what the West considers pressing human rights concerns. In prioritizing policies that delay the implementation of human rights, these political leaders demonstrate how state sovereignty may present difficulties for a universal pursuit of human rights.

Yet, like its dialectical opposite, relativism is also riddled with problematic implications. The case of *sati*, or Indian ceremonial widow burning based in religious tradition (Stein 1998), drives at the heart of the cultural relativist/universalist debate. How does a relativist approach resolve the problems of practicing human rights? Simply put, perhaps it cannot. That is, cultural relativism is not a panacea for challenges afflicting human rights advocacy. Relativism can foster a dilemma that dictates inaction against atrocities to avoid the charge of cultural chauvinism (Hershock 2000; Turner 2006). From this perspective, relativism invites human tragedy under the guise of difference. In human rights discourse, the debate continues: How do we disentangle this universalist/relativist divide?

While theory, central to sociological work, is borderless, policy and implementation of rights are not. With this in mind, the following section addresses violations of and struggles for human rights in a way that is inclusive of the experiences of individuals and communities. It provides an abridged, and therefore incomplete, portrait of human rights violations in Asia and draws attention to recurring forms of social and political violence.

PORTRAIT OF HUMAN RIGHTS IN ASIA

By the turn of the millennium, media and academic outlets reporting on conditions in Asia decried bleak realities. Tibetans faced forced intermarriages with or sterilization by Chinese to induce cultural genocide (Adams 1998); blogging, protesting, and other forms of political protest continued to be suppressed in Singapore (Rodan 2006). In mainland Southeast Asia, the lack of response toward the spread of HIV/AIDS in Cambodia and Myanmar was noted (Beyrer 1998); the latter state was then also under international scrutiny for the jailing of Nobel laureate Aung San Suu Kyi and for continuing violence against ethnic minorities by the military junta (Hlaing 2005; James 2006). Religious conflict between Buddhists and Muslims and assassinations of police, soldiers, teachers, religious leaders, and other civilians in Thailand led newspapers to condemn the "Crisis of the South" (Albritton 2005).

Less-targeted acts of violence, in the form of public bombings, highway ambushes, and general political unrest and religious persecution, plagued Laos (Thayer 2004).

Examples of human rights violations in Asia span a broad range, from the individual level of a twenty-five-year-old Australian hanged in Singapore for heroin possession (Rodan 2006) to the macro threat of extermination by China confronting Tibetans. Journalists and watchdog groups often bring these issues, posed as violence inflicted against individuals, groups, or societies, to international attention. Notably, violations of rights based on personhood can be intended for collectivities, as demonstrated by the case of Tibet, where the struggle for survival is as much cultural as it is physical (Adams 1998).

Gendered violations of human rights have rightfully received tremendous attention, with much research addressing human trafficking, sex work, bride burnings, and a host of forms of violence against women (Amirthalingam 2005). Asia is particularly susceptible to human trafficking due to endemic poverty coupled with rapid development and a highly stratified social structure. Efforts to address interrelated issues of trafficking, HIV/AIDS, and violence against sex workers often look to conditions in South Asia, where these axes of injustice together result in the trafficking of hundreds of thousands of women, children, and men every year and an atrocious rate of HIV/AIDS second only to South Africa. In Southeast Asia, youth orphaned by the 2005 tsunami were kidnapped and sold into slavery. Innumerable instances of such devastating realities can be recalled; yet even within this discourse, there is division over whether to regard those trafficked as actors with agency or as "victims" (Huda 2006). We cannot hope to expediently resolve issues that are inextricably bound to the structural denigration of women, poverty, exploitation, and abuse without contextualizing these actors' experiences, without being aware, for example, that the resettlement houses for sex workers may be judged as even less hospitable than brothels (Jayasree 2004).

In recognizing the complex causes and implications of human tragedy, we implore scholars to take a more grounded and contextualized approach to studying and advocating for human rights. A holistic approach necessitates looking at flagrant abuses of rights in their institutional and historical contexts. The flouting of habeas corpus and detention of suspected communist sympathizers in Indonesia (van der Kroef 1976), then as now, evidences systemic constraints on political expression within a border. Contextualizing human rights concerns in consideration of political and social structures and historical implications, and in the spirit of solidarity with those who confront violations of their rights, is critical to ushering human rights research beyond its current impasse. Far from proffering a solution, we simply suggest demonstrating more effort in understanding the human condition, beyond the universalist/relativist theoretical divide.

PORTRAIT OF HUMAN RIGHTS IN ASIAN AMERICA

Research and work on human rights in Asian America often adopt the form of civil rights and social justice. However, a human rights framework should and must be applied to the lives of Asian Americans. Since the United States professes a human rights agenda, political and social human rights are taken for granted for Asian Americans in this millennium. This was not always the case. Legal policies have historically hindered rights for Asian Americans. Executive Order 9066, in particular, forced Japanese Americans into concentration camps, stripping them of their basic human rights. Detailed accounts of governmental wrongdoings after the Pearl Harbor attack led to the wrongful internment of Americans of Japanese descent. Michi Weglyn's *Years of Infamy: The Untold Story of America's Concentration Camps,* along with the case of Fred Korematsu, in which Korematsu challenged his internment (323 U.S. 214), highlight the overt and subversive tactics used by the government to disregard basic human rights. Various challenges to these human rights violations led to repatriation.

While glaring institutional violations are not as prevalent today, there are still numerous case studies and reports of discriminatory practices against Asian Americans in areas of hiring, salary, and promotion in private industries, health fields, civil services, and even academic institutions (Jo 1984). Social discrimination also continues to haunt Asian Americans. Anti-immigrant sentiments and racism are realities confronted daily by many Asian Americans (Ancheta 1998). Thus, Asian Americans continue to fight for social justice to gain rights that are due to them.

While citizens of the United States have an easier time finding legal routes to rights, those who are undocumented or trafficked into the US underground economy (e.g., sex workers, sweatshop workers, domestic workers) are exploited and deprived of their basic human rights. Feminist human rights activists have challenged the contradictions of human rights. They push to ensure that the rights of women and girls are seen as an inalienable and integral aspect of human rights (Binion 1995). Along with gender, sexuality is still a shared human rights issue for those living in the United States. With only a limited number of states having legalized civil unions or marriages, continued hate crimes toward lesbian, gay, bisexual, and transgender (LGBT) individuals and enduring legal and social violations highlight the hardship for LGBT communities. There has been a cultural and political shift with the repeal of Don't Ask, Don't Tell in 2010 and the Obama administration's announcement that it would no longer defend the Defense of Marriage Act because it was unconstitutional. Yet, there is still cause to argue that the human rights framing does not address LGBT issues in the United States (Mertus 2007). Asian Americans, women, LGBTs, and those whose identities intersect in dimensions of inequality in race, class, gender, and sexuality continue to face a bigger challenge in gaining justice and rights.

One form through which intersectional issues impacting structural opportunities for Asian Americans are obscured is the myth of the model minority. While the model minority stereotype in itself appears positive and innocuous, the fuel of hostility toward foreigners who are "making it" is evident. During the 1982 US recession, for example, at the peak of anti-Japanese sentiment, Vincent Chin was murdered by two laid-off Detroit autoworkers who saw him as a foreigner responsible for taking jobs from Americans (Kurashige 2002). After 9/11, Sikhs and other South Asians mistaken for Muslims were targeted, and in some cases killed, by those who blamed them for the attacks (Maira 2004). As Tuan (1999) argues, Asian

Americans are perceived as "honorary whites and forever foreigners." Under the human rights framework, every individual should be free to live without fear of violence or death; yet the racialized climate in the United States fosters hostility.

For those without a state or country, the problems are even more glaring, as some individuals face discrimination, assaults, detention without due process, and, in extreme cases, deportation to other countries (Ashar 2003; Paust 2004). The stateless in the United States are most vulnerable and are not offered the human rights protections bestowed upon citizens. Undocumented or stateless people are often homogenized as a single group of criminals. In reality, those who seek refuge in the United States find it is not the safe haven they envisioned.

The climate of intense xenophobia is not new. From the 1940s to the civil rights movement and the 1980s, cities and states across the nation confronted pressure to assimilate at all costs. San Gabriel Valley, California, a suburban community nestled near Los Angeles, faced an influx of affluent Asian immigrants in 1985. As Asian languages popped up in California cities such as Monterey Park, Alhambra, and Arcadia, business owners lobbied their city councils for an "English-only initiative" (Saito 1998). While the United States does not have an official language, various cities, counties, and states have attempted to make English the official language (Arington 1991). These attempts have failed, yet anti-immigrant sentiments continue to haunt various states and cities across the United States.

Much like Asians in Asia, Asian Americans confront structural and social obstacles in obtaining and maintaining basic human rights. Hence, there is a need to rethink and reconstruct a human rights framework that can better adapt to sovereign Asian nations and address issues confronting those in the United States who are perceived to be from another nation.

LESSONS FOR HUMAN RIGHTS FROM THE SOCIOLOGY OF ASIA AND ASIAN AMERICA

The Sociology of Asia and Asian America spans numerous subareas, including ethnic/racial studies, international migration, religious studies, political sociology, and gender and sexuality. Sociological work in and about Asia and Asian America transcends centuries of political and social activism that challenge oppressive governments, organizations, and communities. It is important to recognize that the birth of the human rights framework began in the West; hence, there are cultural barriers that hinder understanding what human rights encompass. When Chinese president Hu Jintao met with President Barack Obama in 2011, he received stern warnings from the US administration about China's human rights policies. President Hu Jintao articulated his commitment to working on human rights in China, but there were concerns that his idea of human rights did not include the political, gender, and religious rights of China's peoples. The work in Asia demonstrates a need for Western activists to learn how best to work in collaboration with governments, communities, and organizations seeking to find ways to avoid human rights violations. Further, the case of China draws attention to just one example of contested territories, including Tibet and Taiwan. In this regard, persisting conflict in Asia also raises questions about how human rights are conceptualized and how violations are avoided.

A human rights paradigm can also learn from the lessons of a century and a half of Asian Americans working toward social justice. Intersecting these efforts with human rights allows for addressing concerns such as the right of ethnic studies to exist as a discipline, realities confronting migrants (Fujiwara 2005), and rights without citizenship (Turner 1993). As Asian American studies programs (and ethnic studies generally) around the nation face potential dismantling, and consequently silencing, by universities, the need for Asian Americans to continue to fight for democracy and to confront oppression is glaring.

Currently, the literature interrogates the conditions under which human rights can be sustainable and whether human rights are universal (Franck 2001; Hoang 2009); there is a continuing discussion of how human rights are applied to Asia (Bell 2000). Less frequently problematized is the question of who violates human rights. Violations of human decency in countries of the West are framed as infringements of civil rights, which somehow appear less insidious. For example, the right to be with family should be inherent to humans, yet border policing in the West results in familial separation. Habitually, it is the developing countries, such as those in Asia, which are riddled with social, economic, and political quandaries, that are condemned as perpetrators of human rights abuses. Efforts undertaken by nongovernmental organizations such as the World Trade Organization have also been decried for degrading human rights and living conditions in the interests of capital (Cohn 2001).

Existing research has suggested ways to rethink and address issues of human rights (Donnelly 2003), including by interjecting a Buddhist framework (Hershock 2000). Yet limited research has accounted for conditions that circumvent or complicate the implementation of human rights, such as those to clean water and fulfillment of basic material needs (Beyrer 1998). This disregard raises an epistemological issue: How do we know what we know? It harkens back to our earlier assertion that allegations of human rights violations are disproportionately levied against developing, not developed, countries.

Studies and contemporary human rights efforts have often taken the form of shaming governments, with few calling the effectiveness of this approach into question (Franklin 2008). Bourgois (1990) also remarks on the constraints of doing human rights work in the academy, noting the need to be mindful of the practical implications of scholarship for the lives of populations being studied. These and other considerations for studying and implementing human rights remain. Short of offering a universal answer to these very pertinent concerns, we celebrate the call to prioritize, as a broader moral imperative of researchers, the ways in which their work incorporates and impacts communities.

CHAPTER SIX

LATINA/O SOCIOLOGY

Rogelio Sáenz, Karen Manges Douglas, and Maria Cristina Morales

Latina/os represent the fastest-growing racial and ethnic group in the United States. Indeed, over the period from 1980 to 2009, the Latina/o population more than tripled—from 14.6 million in 1980 to 48.4 million in 2009—while the overall US population increased by only 36 percent (Sáenz 2010a). Currently, Latina/os account for one of every two persons added to the US population. The rapid growth of the Latina/o population has been fueled by the group's youthfulness, reflected in a median age of twenty-seven compared to forty-one among the white population in 2009.

The variation in the age structures of these two groups will result in an expansion of the Latina/o representation in the United States alongside a declining presence of whites in the coming decades. It is projected that the Latina/o share of the US population is likely to increase from 16 percent in 2010 to 30 percent in 2050, while that of the white population is expected to decline from 65 percent in 2010 to 46 percent in 2050 (US Census Bureau 2008). This divergent demographic future has led to the rise of policy initiatives to halt Latina/o immigration and to apprehend and deport undocumented Latina/os.

The increasingly hostile environment against Latina/os has threatened their basic human rights for US citizens and noncitizens alike. Despite their long presence in the United States, especially in the case of Mexicans and Puerto Ricans, Latina/os continue to be viewed as an invading threat that does not belong in the United States (Chavez 2008). The antagonism against Latina/os is driven by racism and a fear that they are encroaching on the safe and comfortable space where whites have thrived and benefitted from their racial status.

Despite major encroachments on the basic human rights of Latina/os in the United States, human rights concerns continue to be a sidebar in research on Latina/os. Only in the last decade have we seen an increase in research on Latina/os directly addressing matters of human rights. For example, a search of *Sociological Abstracts* using the keywords "Hispanic," "Latino," or "Latina" and "human rights" reveals only twelve entries, all published since 1999, with two-thirds of these published since 2005. The absence of work on human rights related to Latina/os reflects the US practice of granting rights on the basis of citizenship rather than one's being a human being (Turner 2006). Nonetheless, attention to human rights issues affecting Latina/os has increased in the post-9/11 period with the heightened criminalization of immigrants and militarization of the border (Golash-Boza 2009; Sáenz and Murga 2011).

This chapter has several goals. First, we provide an overview of the theoretical perspectives and sociological tool kits that Latina/o scholars have employed in the study of Latina/os. Second, we provide the historical context in which whiteness became an asset for US citizenship along with the racialization of Latina/os. Third, we summarize the contemporary context in which Latina/os live. Finally, we conclude with a discussion of the sociology of Latina/os and its potential linkage to a human rights perspective.

SOCIOLOGICAL TOOL KITS IN THE STUDY OF LATINA/OS

Sociologists who study the Latina/o population use a variety of methodological tools to conduct their research (Rodríguez, Sáenz, and Menjívar 2008; Rodríguez 2008). As scholars try to gain a deep understanding of sociological phenomenon on Latina/os, they tend to rely on qualitative methods including ethnographies, in-depth interviews, and observations (Dunn 2009). In addition, scholars who are interested in historical and legal studies of the Latina/o population tend to make use of historical and legal archives in their research. Court cases, including Supreme Court decisions and dissenting opinions, for instance, are quite revealing of the assumptions undergirding them (López 2006). Moreover, sociologists who are interested in media studies tend to analyze textual, visual, and digital sources. Content analysis of programming content and advertisements, along with newspaper column-width coverage, are all common methodological tools used for studying the media. Furthermore, persons who examine structural forces impacting the behavior of Latina/os tend to rely on quantitative data including census information and large-scale surveys. Additionally, sociologists who examine the transnational aspects of the lives of Latina/os use a variety of methodological approaches, including ethnographies, in-depth interviews, and surveys, in the communities of origin and destination across international borders. Finally, sociologists who study the Latina/o population use a variety of theoretical approaches that capture the inequalities that continue to mark the lives of Latina/os. These approaches include the structural racism (Feagin 2006) and critical race (and LatCrit) (Trucios-Haynes 2001) perspectives.

A HISTORICAL OVERVIEW OF THE RACIALIZATION OF LATINA/OS

Ngai's (2004) concept of Latina/os as alien citizens (or Heyman's [2002] reference to "anticitizens") provides an appropriate point of departure from which to discuss human rights and the US Latina/o population. Alien citizenship ensued from the US legal racialization of people based upon their national origins. Accordingly, the use of racial categories for inclusion and exclusion from the United States dates to the nation's first immigration and naturalization laws of 1790, which limited eligibility for naturalization to free, white aliens (Ngai 2004).

Following the Civil War, naturalization laws were amended to confer citizenship on persons of African descent (former slaves) while continuing the eligibility criterion of white, thereby establishing a black-white color line for the granting of US citizenship (Daniels 2004). The 1924 National Origins Act established a racial hierarchy of the world's inhabitants (Ngai 1999, 2004) in which northern and western Europeans received large quotas, southern and eastern Europeans got small quotas, and Asians were barred from immigrating to the United States.

Western Hemisphere residents (Latin Americans and Canadians) were excluded from the act's quota restrictions, reflecting the political clout of southwestern agricultural interests desiring cheap Mexican labor. Instead the bill established visa requirements for entry into the United States, which resulted in a new category of persons in the racial taxonomy: the "illegal alien" (Bustamante 1972). Although people without proper documentation included all nationalities worldwide, over time the term became synonymous with "Mexican" (Ngai 2004).

The requirement that US citizenship be limited to those defined as either white or black meant that the courts were called upon to make racial determinations. Between 1887 and 1923, the federal courts made more than twenty-five racial determinations (López 2006; Ngai 2004). For the nation's Latina/o population, who per the US black-white citizenship requirements were legally designated white, there are numerous examples of ways the dominant white group defined Latina/os as nonwhite. In the case of *In Re: Rodriguez* (1897), Ricardo Rodriguez, a Mexican-born resident of San Antonio, Texas, was denied naturalization on the grounds that he was not white (De Genova 2005; Sáenz and Murga 2011). However, a district court judge ruled that although Rodriguez was not white, he was nevertheless eligible to become a naturalized citizen because the Texas state constitution recognized Mexicans as citizens of Texas, all citizens of Texas were granted US citizenship when Texas became a US state, and the Treaty of Guadalupe Hidalgo signed in 1848 granted US citizenship to Mexicans living on these lands (De Genova 2005; Sáenz and Murga 2011).

The discomfort of the white population over the Latina/os' default white designation is further reflected in the creation of a "Mexican" racial category for the 1930 census. Due in part to the lobbying efforts of Mexican American leaders who argued that Mexican Americans were white (Snipp 2003, 69), the issue of how to classify the Latina/o population of the United States remained a work in progress. Ironically, whites were quick to view Latina/os as white when *Brown v. Board of Education* pressured the South to desegregate. Accordingly, Texas officials sought to achieve school desegregation by placing Latina/o and black students in the same schools (San Miguel 2005).

The alien citizenship of Latina/os stems from the conquest of the two largest Latina/o groups—Mexicans and Puerto Ricans—characterized by warfare, power, and resource asymmetry between the United States and Latin America (see Bonilla-Silva 2008). US employer demand for cheap Latin American labor (particularly Mexican), supported by legislative initiatives such as the Bracero Program and more recently

NAFTA, continue to pull Latina/os into the United States despite highly racialized immigration and naturalization legislation intent on limiting "undesirables." Policy initiatives in several states (notably Arizona and Alabama) are aimed squarely at the Latina/o undocumented. While individual pieces of legislation have been legally challenged, the racial nature of the efforts, the conflation of legal and illegal, citizen and noncitizen, and the Supreme Court's sanction of racial profiling of "Mexican-looking" people send an unwelcoming message. Further, these types of policy initiatives have intensified over the last few decades as the Latina/o population has grown.

THE CONTEMPORARY CONTEXT

The expanding Latina/o population and its spread to states that have historically not had a significant presence of Latina/os challenge the racial hierarchy and the power monopoly that whites have enjoyed (see Moore 2008). To stem Latina/o encroachment on the existing racial structure, US states have employed a variety of tactics, including highly restrictive immigration laws such as Arizona's Senate Bill (SB) 1070, mobilization of local militias such as the Minutemen to patrol the border, state-mandated abolition of ethnic studies courses (e.g., Arizona's House Bill 2281), passage of English-only legislation and repealing of bilingual education in several states, and local ordinances criminalizing property rental to undocumented immigrants. These efforts have served to set Latina/os once again as a class apart.

At the federal level, revamped immigration laws such as the Illegal Immigrant Reform and Immigrant Responsibility Act of 1996 enhanced border-enforcement activities and loosened deportation criteria. Additionally, the law established a mechanism for partnerships between local law enforcement and federal immigration enforcement via the 287(g) provision. In 2006, the United States passed the Secure Fence Act of 2006 authorizing construction of a US border wall. Further, the Fourteenth Amendment to the US Constitution, which grants citizenship to all persons born in the United States, is at the epicenter of nativists' efforts to overturn the principle as a mechanism to slow the growth of the rapidly expanding US Latina/o population (Wood 1999).

As López (2006) notes, these targeted actions are far from color-blind and share the same highly racial imprimatur of earlier policies that oversaw the internment of Japanese American citizens during World War II and the deportation of Mexican Americans during Operation Wetback in the 1950s. This hostile environment against Latina/os has contributed to citizenship and human rights violations—acceptable collateral damage to maintain white supremacy.

SOCIOLOGY OF LATINA/OS

The sociological study of Latina/os is relatively new, with major developments beginning in the 1970s. However, over the past several decades, the field of the sociology of Latina/os has expanded dramatically. Major substantive areas of study include demography, crime, education, family, gender, health, immigration, inequality, and labor. While much of the research in the area has focused on Latina/os in the United States, research has also addressed the larger transnational context in which Latina/os exist.

Transnationalism describes the processes whereby immigrants maintain ties to the native/sending communities and participate in varying ways in the activities of their communities of origin and destination. In part due to the proximity to Latin American countries, Latina/o immigrants to the United States, particularly more recent arrivals, continue to be linked to their originating communities (Fink 2003; Smith 2005).

Transnationalism impacts both individuals and entire families. Transnational families are created when one or both parents emigrate from the household of origin (Menjívar and Abrego 2009; Parreñas 1998). In the context of the aftermath of 9/11, the "war on drugs," and the global economic recession, crossing borders and maintaining transnational ties has become difficult and dangerous for Latin American migrants. Human rights concerns have escalated along the US-Mexico border due to border-control measures—that is, the erection of a physical and virtual wall, increases in border agents, and the militarization of the border (use of surveillance technology and military personnel) (Dunn 2001). Consequently, what was once a circulatory migrant flow has become increasingly a one-way journey. Sending-community involvement in this migration is constricted, transnational family reunification is hindered, and undocumented immigrants are often "entrapped" along the southern border (Núñez and Heyman 2007).

Particularly alarming is the increase in migrant deaths resulting from the more dangerous and treacherous terrain migrants are forced to travel from Mexico into the United States due to enhanced urban-border enforcement (Eschbach et al. 1999; Massey, Durand, and Malone 2002). Unfortunately, these and other human rights abuses have largely been ignored in the United States. Further, because nation-states maintain power in implementing international human rights, there appears to be little legal recourse for these human rights abuses as the United States refused to sign the International Convention on the Protection of the Rights of All Migrant Workers and Their Families adopted by the UN General Assembly in 1990. This is problematic for Latina/os because many lack citizenship rights afforded by nation-states (see Turner 2006).

Border-control initiatives also create human rights abuses for US-born Latina/os. Heightened border enforcement disrupts the stability of life for all inhabiting this militarized zone. Under the pretext of the "war on drugs," the military is used for domestic policing along the US-Mexico border (Dunn 2001). The militarization that Latina/os are subjected to in the border region parallels other state-sanctioned forms of social control. Border-control operations racially profile all "brown" people regardless of citizenship status (Morales and Bejarano 2009). The Border Network for Human Rights (2003) has documented the extensive use of race as a basis for immigration-related questioning leading to constitutional violations against US citizens and documented immigrants, such as wrongful detentions, searches, confiscation of property, and physical and psychological abuse.

As Latina/os have settled in new destinations (Sáenz, Cready, and Morales 2007), border-control enforcement tactics have followed (Coleman 2007). Turner (2006) notes the increasing need for human rights enforcement in situations where everyone is vulnerable. In this case, all US residents are vulnerable as the militarized state and border-control tactics expand across the country.

No doubt, the historical and contemporary story of the US Latina/o population is far from straightforward. Latina/os encompass a heterogeneous population with differing histories and modes of incorporation into the United States. This heterogeneity makes human rights issues more complex and not neatly encompassed in a single narrative or tradition. Although there are variations, one constant has been the inferior status of Latina/os relative to whites.

WHAT CAN THE HUMAN RIGHTS PARADIGM LEARN FROM THE SOCIOLOGY OF LATINA/OS?

The sociology of Latina/os can expand the human rights paradigm given Latina/os' status as the largest US minority group, their diversity, and their transnational lives, which create a gray area between the human and citizenship rights paradigms. To begin, despite being the nation's largest minority group, Latina/os remain marginally integrated into mainstream institutions. The sociology of Latina/os has been inspired by several societal conditions that Latina/os face, such as precarious employment situations, poverty, educational inequality, injustice in the criminal justice system, a system of rights that does not protect its immigrant community, and other human rights abuses that reflect the group's lack of integration. The human rights abuses that Latina/os confront are not merely associated with the newcomer status of a segment of the population. Indeed, despite their long historical presence in the United States, Mexican Americans continue to occupy the lowest economic positions (Sáenz, Morales, and Ayala 2004) and are largely regarded as "foreigners" (Douglas and Sáenz 2010).

The human rights implications of the extensive social control of Latina/os are reflected in public policies. For instance, SB 1070 made residing in Arizona without legal authorization a crime and conflates the policing of immigration with racial profiling (Heyman 2010; Sáenz and Murga 2011). Arguably, this state-level policy is a response to the threatening Latina/o growth (see Sáenz 2010b) and targets all Latina/os, regardless of citizenship status, who are perceived to be "foreigners" (Heyman 2010). Human rights concerns arise from the exercise of state power to disproportionately target Latina/os, leading to their subjection to extensive social controls, deportation and separation from families, harassment, and criminalization.

The sociology of Latina/os has highlighted Latina/o heterogeneity, which has important implications for the human rights paradigm. Latina/os are stratified by racial identification, skin color, citizenship status, and class (Morales 2009), which increases the complexity of applying the human rights paradigm. The diversity of the Latina/o population, particularly in terms of citizenship status, illustrates a challenge in utilizing the human rights paradigm for the equality, safety, and prosperity of the entire group. The difficult theoretical work of how to grapple with the human rights of Latina/o immigrants—many of whom are outside the umbrella of citizenship rights and simultaneously deprived of human rights given the focus of nation-states—has yet to be done.

Yet, the citizenship diversity among Latino immigrant families has a myriad of human rights implications. There are many "mixed-status families," which consist of members with a variety of statuses, including citizens, visa holders, naturalized citizens, and undocumented individuals. Indeed, Fix and Zimmermann (2001) found that one-tenth of families have mixed status, where one or both parents are noncitizens and the children are citizens. In a study of mixed-status families in the detention/deportation system, Brabeck and Xu (2010) found that parents with higher levels of legal vulnerability experienced greater problems associated with emotional well-being, ability to provide financially, and relationships with their children. In this context, children's emotional stability and academic performance are jeopardized (Brabeck and Xu 2010). Moreover, in the legal system, the onerous requirements to override deportation proceedings create a hurdle few can overcome and one that is nearly insurmountable for undocumented parents of US citizen children (Sutter 2006). Human rights perspectives must consider the cessation of individual deportations in order to maintain "intact" families, a notion that several nations recognize as important (Sutter 2006). Thus, this adds another layer of complexity to the application of human rights when considering whether the locus of protection should be the individual or the family.

INCORPORATING THE HUMAN RIGHTS PARADIGM INTO THE SOCIOLOGY OF LATINA/O RESEARCH

A review of the human rights literature concerning the Latina/o population reveals significant attention to human rights based in Latin America but not in the United States before the 9/11 period. With the rise of human rights abuses in the post-9/11 period, research addressing human rights among Latina/os has shifted toward the United States since 2000. Of the sixteen entries in *Sociological Abstracts* published since 2000, eleven were based in the United States. The research on Latina/os in the United States that has incorporated human rights dimensions includes themes such as the ambiguity of the US-Mexico border (Ortiz 2001), the militarization of the border (Dunn 2001), the US minority rights revolution associated with the civil rights era (Skrentny 2002), abuses against immigrants (Dunn, Aragones, and Shivers 2005; Krieger et al. 2006; Redwood 2008; Vinck et al. 2009), the growth of the prison population (Modic 2008), youth activism and the struggle for human rights associated with the immigrant rights marches of 2006 (Velez et al. 2008), and antigay family policies (Cahill 2009).

Still, the relative dearth of material within the established human rights tradition represents the difficulty the perspective faces in addressing the multiple and continuing human rights violations confronting the US Latina/o population. There are several reasons for this. First, as Dunn (2009) notes, the issue of human rights remains entangled within notions of the nation-state and citizenship. Human rights are conditional on citizenship, which comes with attached rights and duties. Violations (e.g., committing felony acts) can result in the diminishment of citizenship rights (e.g., voter disenfranchisement). Indeed, it is within this tradition that human rights battles for inclusion have occurred in the United States. People of color have challenged their exclusion from the full benefits of US citizenship and sought remedies. However, these remedies are conditioned by citizenship. By definition, the extraterritorial essence of the Latina/o population is a threat to the nation-state. Just as Japanese Americans were viewed during World War II as sympathetic and inextricably linked to Japan, which provided the rationale for their imprisonment, so too, and despite multiple generations of presence in the United States, is there a conflation between Mexican Americans and Mexico. Further complicating the Latina/o human rights story is that significant numbers of the US Latina/o population remain citizens of their countries of origin. Thus, the links to their homelands are still direct and, to many in the United States, threatening.

Second, the narrow framing of human rights conditioned upon citizenship has pitted Latina/o citizen against Latina/o noncitizen. The narrow targeting of, for example, immigration laws on racial grounds has resulted not only in broken families but in an "us-versus-them" mentality that has tolerated human rights violations so long as citizens are not the target (Dunn 2009). As Ngai (2004) argues, this framing of migrants as threats, together with the prolific national discourse surrounding the need to "secure our borders," provides cover for the state to engage in a variety of racist and discriminatory acts that even the Supreme Court acknowledges "would be unacceptable if applied to citizens" (Ngai 2004, 12).

Third, as articulated in the works of LatCrit theorists, the ambiguous racial category that Latinas/os inhabit renders the application of traditional human rights perspectives problematic. Fourteenth Amendment protections are predicated on race, ancestry, or national origin. This leaves most Latina/os who lack a distinct racial category or national origin without a basis for a discrimination claim. As detailed earlier, this is problematic on several fronts, including the fact that some Latina/os are Americans with deep ties to their countries of origin. The effect of both the narrow focus of the equal protection clause and the multidimensional nature of the Latina/o population has allowed for "discrimination to remain remedied" and for "the manipulation of the Latina/o image to exploit racial fears" (Trucios-Haynes 2001, 4).

The human rights perspective offers potential redress to the nation-state/citizenship-rights perspective. This perspective begins with the premise that all human beings have fundamental and inalienable human rights (Blau and Moncada 2005; Sjoberg, Gill, and Williams 2001). These rights are unconditional, universal, and, importantly, transnational. As Turner explains, these individual rights emerge as a result of our "shared vulnerabilities" (2006a, 47). This perspective provides a different frame (outside the citizenship/nation-state divide) from which to evaluate questionable policies despite their legality within the nation-state. Unfortunately, the platform for realizing these rights is relatively narrow. The UN offers a Declaration of Human Rights, but there are only weak enforcement capabilities at the global level. Thus, despite the recognition of inalienable and universal human rights, this perspective has gained little traction.

Further, as Bonilla-Silva (2008) argues, the human rights tradition suffers from its failure to recognize and incorporate race into its analysis. Bonilla-Silva asserts that "the HRT idealizes the autonomous individual who can be located within a universe of abstract rights, devoid of racially constraining social structures" (2008, 11). While the human rights perspective recognizes the inalienable rights of people, it "seems unwilling to temper this view with the fact that there are vast differences of power among individuals as individuals as well as members of social groups or nation-states" (Bonilla-Silva 2008, 12). In short, all people are not the same. Much of the story told, thus far, involves the successful efforts to marginalize the Latina/o population. Immigration laws, including the present-day variations, have been constructed along highly racialized lines with specific racial bogeymen as their target.

THE ROAD FORWARD

Despite the long presence of Latina/os in the United States and the fact that the majority of Latina/os are US born, Latina/os continue to be viewed as "perpetual foreigners" and "anticitizens." Hostilities toward Latina/os have risen over the last several decades as global forces and economic and political linkages between the United States and Latin America have uprooted many Latin Americans who have migrated to the United States. The youthfulness of the Latina/o population also portends a disproportionate growth of Latina/os in the coming decades in this country. Numerous policies have emerged throughout the country, but especially in states bordering Mexico, to stem the entrance of Latina/o immigrants and to roundup and deport those already here. While ostensibly undocumented Latina/os are the target, in reality Latina/o naturalized citizens and US-born Latina/os have also been affected by such policies.

Policies such as Arizona's SB 1070, the vigilantism that has arisen along the border in the form of the Minutemen, the militarization of the border, and the rise of detention centers have made Latina/os, regardless of citizenship status, vulnerable to a wide range of human rights violations. For example, on a daily basis, Latina/o families are being split due to the deportation of family members, while others are questioned or pulled over by law enforcement for looking Latina/o. Moreover, the militarization of the border and governmental efforts to push immigrants to enter through dangerous and treacherous terrains have resulted in the deaths of countless human beings seeking better lives in the United States. Furthermore, the militarization of the border has also occasionally resulted in the killing of Latina/os and Mexican nationals (see Brice 2010). The killing of Esequiel Hernández Jr., an eighteen-year-old high school student who was herding goats in Redford, Texas, at the time of his death at the hands of a US Marine Corps antidrug patrol, best illustrates the vulnerability that Latina/os face along the border as the US government wages war against immigrants and drug traffickers (National Drug Strategy Network 1997). Reverend Mel La Follette, a retired Episcopalian priest in Redford, aptly described the situation: "We were invaded, and one of our sons was slaughtered.... The whole community was violated" (National Drug Strategy Network 1997). Such policies and traumatic events have undone many of the gains Latina/os achieved through civil rights legislation.

Our review of the literature reveals that only recently have we seen the incorporation of human rights concerns into the study of Latina/os. We see this as a much-needed and welcome addition to scholarship on the Latina/o population. Much of the existing literature examining the plight of the Latina/o population has merely alluded to the human rights implications without delving deeply into the human rights consequences of the conditions of the population. However, there is a need to make adjustments in the human rights perspective to better capture the racialized situation of Latina/os in the United States, along with the unequal power relations between the United States and Latin American countries (Bonilla-Silva 2008). Insights from the sociology of Latina/o literature related to the racialization of Latina/os, the heterogeneity of the Latina/o population, the agency that Latina/os possess, and the transnational aspects of the lives of Latina/os are considerations that the human rights perspective must take into account to more fully address the human rights of the Latina/o population.

≈

CHAPTER SEVEN

CHILDREN AND YOUTH

Brian K. Gran

Sociology of children and youth is a vibrant, young area of the discipline. This chapter presents key questions sociologists consider when studying young people, findings from those studies, as well as a discussion of the methods they employ and data they analyze. It then discusses potential contributions sociology of children and youth may make to human rights research and what human rights scholarship may contribute to sociology of children and youth. This chapter concludes by reviewing questions for future research arising from the intersection of human rights and sociology of children and youth.

KEY QUESTIONS

Sociology of children and youth is a young subdiscipline that is experiencing growth all over the world. In 1984, a section on children and youth was established in the Nordic Sociological Association. The American Sociological Association (ASA) Section on Children and Youth was founded in 1991 under the leadership of Professor Gertrud Lenzer, and the section of the German Sociological Association was set up in 1995. Internationally, Research Committee 53, Sociology of Childhood, of the International Sociological Association was established in 1998. Organizations that focus on sociological studies of children and youth are found all over the world, including the European Sociological Association's Research Network 4, Sociology of Children and Childhood.

Sociologists of children and youth research various questions and issues that span the discipline of sociology. One question sociologists ask is how young people's experiences and perspectives have changed over time. An additional question is how young people's experiences vary by location. Does a young person living in one community have different life chances compared to a child living in another community? Are globalization forces reducing or expanding these differences in childhood?

Of course, sociologists want to know why young people's experiences differ across time and space. Do young persons' life chances depend solely on their parents' well-being? What role does community have in how young people fare? Can laws and social-policy programs improve life chances? What factors shape young people's actions and decisions? What encourages young people to participate in their communities? If young people possess rights, what matters to whether a young person exercises those rights?

As is true for all social-science research, sociologists consider how their data-collection approaches shape their findings. A challenge for sociologists of children and youth is ensuring that a young person not only gives informed consent to participate in research but voices opinions about how social-science research is undertaken.

KEY FINDINGS

A starting point for sociology of children and youth is social construction of childhood. Referring to Aries's momentous work, *Centuries of Childhood* (1962), Corsaro (2005) describes how children have come to be seen as different from adults. Nowadays, specializations have been established that are devoted to children, such as psychology of children and sociology of children. Institutions have also developed, including age-organized educational institutions and courts devoted to young people's legal issues. Indeed, conventions on children's rights are widely accepted.

Sociologists of children and youth have demonstrated that young people's experiences have changed, sometimes remarkably, over time. Shorter (1977, 172) contends that mortality levels among young people were so high prior to the Industrial Revolution that parents sometimes did not attend their child's funeral. Turmel (2008) describes how the construction of what came to be considered "normal" changed young people's lives. For instance, public health officials demonstrated that children laboring in factories were typically shorter physically than other children. This information not only led to laws regulating child labor but was used to designate what was normal for a child's development. Across many countries, national laws now restrict young people's paid employment, and international treaties, such as the ILO's Minimum Age Convention (1973), attempt to regulate those governmental efforts.

Sociologists recognize that many factors facing children are frequently out of their control, yet these factors may strongly shape their futures. Low-birth-weight babies receive attention from sociologists because their health has a great deal to do with their parents and the environment in which they were conceived, gestated as fetuses, and now live, rather than anything the children themselves have done. Conley's work not only draws attention to critical factors contributing to births of low-birth-weight babies (Conley, Strully, and Bennett 2003) but has prompted attention to short- and long-term challenges facing these infants (Population Research Bureau 2007).

How young people spend their childhood affects their future paths. Whitbeck (2009) finds that many crucial adolescent experiences are skipped on the way to becoming an adult for young people who are homeless. Furstenberg's (2010) work demonstrates how social class affects a young person's transition to adulthood and, in turn, how those experiences shape his or her long-term experiences. Yeung and Conley's (2008) examination of the Panel Study of Income Dynamics indicates family wealth is a strong predictor of differences in test scores among US black and white students. Employing Bourdieu's ideas, Lareau's (2003) groundbreaking ethnographic study shows how parents cultivate their children's cultural capital. Compared to children from lower-class backgrounds, middle- and upper-middle-class children tend to learn how to express themselves, question authority, and navigate bureaucracy.

Sociologists have paid close attention to how changes in family homes shape young persons' experiences. In a blog posting, Raskoff (2011) notes that evidence exists not only that posttraumatic stress disorder affects many US soldiers but that its consequences are felt in the homes to which they return. She points out that this evidence has not been translated into policy changes that benefit soldiers' families. Sociologists have made significant contributions to what is known about divorces in the United States. In her study of 1998 to 1999 data, Kim (2011) finds that children whose parents have divorced are more likely to experience difficulties in formal schooling and to internalize "problem behaviors." Sociological research on children's rights has informed counseling programs for young people who have been legally separated from their families (Lenzer and Gran 2011).

Corsaro (2005, 67) notes that histories of childhood have often overlooked how children and young people are actors who influence their own circumstances. Adler and Adler (2011) chronicle how self-injury of young people has shifted from individual practice ten years ago to shared experience today. A subculture has emerged of practitioners who share values and vocabulary, partially due to ease of communication via social media.

Sociologists are studying factors leading to child-headed households and how those households fare. While expressing caution regarding their results, Ciganda, Gagnon, and Tenkorang (2010) find evidence that child-headed households in sub-Saharan countries do better in meeting some basic needs than adult-headed households. Edin and Kefalas's (2005) compelling study, *Promises I Can Keep*, shows that rather than stacking odds against themselves, the teenage women they studied made thoughtful decisions in desperate circumstances to become pregnant. Sociologists have asked how a young person comes to terms with his or her sexuality and decides to become sexually active (Myers and Raymond 2010; Regnerus 2007).

Sociologists have examined why some young people appear reluctant to leave home. In their groundbreaking book *Not Quite Adults*, Settersten and Ray (2010) rely on analyses of more than two dozen national data sets and five hundred interviews of young people to tackle how "traditional" US paths to adulthood have dramatically changed. They find that contemporary perceptions of indolent young people may be misperceptions. Instead, some young people opt to live with parents in pursuit of long-term goals, such as saving money to pay off debt and to buy their own homes.

Outside the home, in some societies, many children spend a great deal of time in schools. On the basis of case studies of East Los Angeles, Harlem, and the Bronx, Gaston et al. (2009) demonstrate in *Our Schools Suck* that students are critical of their educational opportunities, yet at the same time strongly desire the benefits they expect from their formal educations. The authors conclude a new civil rights movement is needed to secure equal educational opportunities for all American young people. The importance of education is confirmed by Hao and Pong (2008), whose research demonstrates that upward mobility of first- and second-generation US immigrants is strongly influenced by high school experiences.

In addition to education, government policies can dramatically shape young people's lives in ways that sometimes result in substantially disparate childhoods. In *Divided by Borders*, Dreby (2010) employs ethnography, interviews, and surveys to demonstrate that young people are not passive; rather, the children she studies live on their own, attending school and taking care of themselves, while their parents live and work in another country. Gonzales's (2011) study reminds us that a crucial step for many young people is their change in legal status upon reaching majority. For US "undocumented immigrants," one consequence of reaching majority is a change from legal protection as a young person to needing legal status to participate in society and the economy. Sociologists have shown that illegal status hurts young people's educational engagement and future success, as well as their cognitive development (Preston 2011).

Sociologists have explored what factors contribute to young people's feeling that they are part of their communities. In his groundbreaking study *Fitting In, Standing Out*, Crosnoe (2011) finds that young people who are marginalized experience long-term consequences as adults, including being less likely to attend college. Sociologists (Pugh 2009) have shown that parents purchase consumer goods, like computer games, to bolster their children's feelings of belonging. In *Hanging Out, Messing Around, and Geeking Out*, an innovative collection of twenty-three ethnographic studies, Ito et al. (2009) show how young people use a variety of new media, such as social media, to manage different parts of their lives, from recreation to schooling to romance. A common perception in the United States is that parents are afraid to let their children play outside without adult supervision. In *Adult Supervision Required*, Rutherford (2011) focuses on the contradiction that these days young people enjoy greater autonomy and freedom than their parents did as young people, yet there is greater fear for young people and how they use their freedoms.

In the midst of institutional and structural failures, loss of parents may be especially devastating to young people. In a special issue of *Children, Youth, and Environment*, Babugra (2008) presents her study of physical and emotional stresses young people experience during drought in Botswana. Based on interviews and participatory rural appraisals, Baburga's work shows that during and after disasters, not only do young people need to fulfill physical requirements, but family loss exacerbates their emotional, economic, and educational needs.

Institutions and social structures can not only exert strong pressures but produce conflicts in young people's lives. In his book, *When a Heart Turns Rock Solid*, Black (2010) gives a "sociological storytelling" of three brothers and their friends, whose lives are a struggle to avoid the "pull of the street." Growing up in an impoverished US neighborhood and without English as their primary language, the young men Black studied attempt to overcome weak educations and absent economic opportunities to battle drug addiction and criminal sentencing laws that automatically send people to prison without consideration of mitigating circumstances and failures of government and society. A former gang member, Victor Rios (2010) returned to his neighborhood to shadow forty young men to demonstrate how a culture of punishment pushes these young men into crime.

Young people can be compelled into activities against their will. Government can actively control young people. Margolis (1999) undertook a visual history of forced cultural assimilation among Native American children through public schooling. Other governments have imposed assimilation on indigenous children, including in Australia (van Krieken 1999).

Trafficking in young people truly is global in scope, sometimes in plain sight (Bales and Soodalter 2009). Contributors to a volume arising from a 2009 conference sponsored by the Rutgers Childhood Studies Program considered diverse experiences of children who have been forced to become soldiers and what policies and laws should be established to move to a just society where young people do not participate in armed conflict (Cook and Wall 2011).

Issues of coercion extend to bodily control. Boyle's (2002) groundbreaking work on female genital cutting (FGC) reveals conflicts between international consensuses on human rights, which calls for bans on FGC, national enforcement of those bans, and local practices and beliefs that support FGC practices. Violence against young people is a focus of sociological work that has resulted in steps to prevent and outlaw child abuse. The Family Research Laboratory of the University of New Hampshire and its codirectors, Murray Straus and David Finkelhor, are among the leading sociologists whose work on child abuse has documented significant, long-term harms resulting to children from abuse. Their work has encouraged international calls for national bans on corporal punishment of young people (endcorporalpunishment.org).

As political actors, young people have been collectively involved in producing political change. In the 1960s, young people were involved in the US civil rights movement and other collective behavior. More recently, young people have taken leadership roles in the Arab Spring. In other parts of the world, concerns are expressed about apathy among young people given that they will eventually vote, hold political office, and serve in leadership positions in government and civil society (Tisdall 2008). Sociologists have provided evidence of why young people become engaged and why many turn away from participating in mainstream institutions. Through analyses of three case studies, Rossi (2009) shows that young people make decisions to participate based on institutional characteristics and whether participation will fulfill personal and professional objectives.

Sociologists increasingly focus on how forces of globalization shape young people's lives, while social, political, and economic models and ideas cross national borders. As Western educational policies and practices sweep the world, sociologists ask whether influences of public education will be found elsewhere. A powerful globalizing social force is children's rights. As young people's rights receive greater attention, sociologists are examining whether children's rights are similar everywhere (Gran 2010b). Sociologists are asking how institutions work to advance children's rights (Boyle 2002, 2009; Gran 2011). Thomas, Gran, and Hanson (2011) are undertaking research on organizational features of European independent children's rights institutions and how those features work in practice.

KEY METHODS

No one method is relied upon in sociological studies of children and youth. Qualitative, comparative, historical, visual, and quantitative approaches are prominently used to study young people. Indeed, many sociologists employ multiple methods in studying evidence of social phenomena affecting children and youth.

In *Gender Play*, Thorne (1993) conducted ethnographic research of children at school and on their school playground to show how young people and others are split by gender. In *A Younger Voice: Doing Child-Centered Qualitative Research*, Clark (2010) discusses what she has learned as a qualitative researcher of young people. Taking a child-centered approach, Clark has employed a variety of qualitative approaches in her work, including participant observation, focus groups, interviews, and visual methods. Some sociologists have undertaken multiyear ethnographies to study young people's lives, including Lareau (*Unequal Childhoods*, 2003), Edin and Kafelas (*Promises I Can Keep*, 2005), Pugh (*Longing and Belonging*, 2009), and Black (*When a Heart Turns Rock Solid*, 2010).

Comparative sociology of children and youth often presents useful perspectives on social problems by comparing children's experiences as well as structures shaping their lives. In comparing states in Ethiopia and the Sudan, Jalata (2005) contends that one group, the Tigrayan, make superior educational opportunities available to their young people to ensure those children eventually become leaders instead of Oromo children. Gran and Aliberti (2003) employ qualitative comparative analysis, which is based in Boolean algebra, to explore why some governments and not others have established offices of children's ombudspersons.

Tinkler's (1995) historical study examined how popular magazines shaped the adolescence of women growing up in England from the 1920s to the 1950s. Her book provides insights into how attitudes and concerns of young women were shaped over this three-decade period. In his comparative-historical, quantitative study, Carlton-Ford (2010) finds that young people start life with fewer opportunities if they grow up in countries where major armed conflict has occurred.

For sociologists of children and youth who undertake quantitative research, units of analysis range from individual children to schools to countries. In their analysis of the National Longitudinal Study of Youth for the years 1979 to 1998, Levine, Emery, and Pollack (2007) link data from young people and their mothers to find that teenage childbearing, controlling for background and other factors, has limited impacts on both mother and child. The Luxembourg Income Study (LIS), a database of twenty-five data sets, allows sociologists to compare children's experiences across countries. Contending with definitions of absolute and relative poverty affecting young people, in *Poor Kids in a Rich Country*, Rainwater and Smeeding (2005) compare impacts of income packaging and different kinds of income, for instance, on reducing poverty among young people. An advantage of their study of Australia, Canada, the United States, and twelve European countries is that Rainwater and Smeeding can use the LIS database to examine how one country's income package would work in another country to reduce impacts of income inequality on childhood poverty.

Sociologists employing multilevel modeling have made significant inroads into understanding how context shapes young persons' experiences. Raudenbush and colleagues have used hierarchical linear models to show how classroom size can affect what young people learn at school (Shin and Raudenbush 2011) and how neighborhoods affect young people's verbal abilities, an important predictor of adult success (Sampson, Sharkey, and Raudenbush 2008). Levels, Dronkers, and Kraaykamp (2008) use a double comparative design to distinguish between impacts of an immigrant's sending country and those of the receiving country to study the mathematical performance of 7,403 children who left thirty-five different countries to live in thirteen host countries.

Visual sociologists employ visual evidence to give meanings to young people's contexts and relationships. Clark-Ibáñez (2007) has demonstrated that photo elicitation, the presentation of visual evidence to participants to elicit their viewpoints on social phenomena, empowers young people to use photographs to "teach" researchers about how their home lives affect school experiences. Jon Wagner (1999b) edited a special issue of *Visual Sociology*, "Visual Sociology and Seeing Kids' Worlds," that presented research on how children can use visual narratives to teach their physicians (Rich and Chalfen 1999), how young people understand their contexts (Wagner 1999a), including urban environments (Orrellana 1999), and how video can be used to express young people's points of view (Larson 1999).

As there are various methods, there are several sources of secondary evidence of young people's welfare and rights. Cochaired by Ben-Arieh and Goerge, the International Society for Childhood Indicators (www.childindicators.org) develops standards for data and indicators of children's well-being and rights and publishes the journal *Child Indicators Research*. UNICEF collects data on "the situation of children" and publishes reports about their welfare, including *The State of the World's Children*. It maintains ChildInfo, a website data resource. UNICEF's Innocenti Research Centre is devoted to research on children's rights and welfare and publishes reports and advises different UN agencies. A prominent cross-national database is the Organization for Economic Cooperation and Development's Programme for International Study Assessment, which consists of data from seventy countries about skills and experiences of fifteen-year-old students, particularly their preparation to participate in society as adults.

In the United States, government and nongovernment organizations collect and publish data about children and youth. The Federal Interagency Forum on Child and Family Statistics publishes an annual report, "America's Children." The nongovernmental organization Child Trends regularly updates its DataBank. Kenneth Land coordinates the Child and Youth Well-Being Index Project, a collection of US evidence of the quality of life of American young people. The US Children's Bureau is a resource for state-level data on adoption, child abuse, and general child welfare, among other areas. The Integrated Health Interview Series makes data on child health conditions, health care, and health behaviors publicly available. Many individual states publish state- and county-level data on births, deaths, infant mortality, and low birth weights.

Other organizations tend to focus on particular questions about young people and their well-being. Established in 2009, the International Society for Longitudinal and Life Course Studies will provide a forum for life-course researchers to share data. The American Educational Research Network has set up an Institute on Statistical Analysis for Education Policy, which has the goal of enhancing access to large national and international databases involving education.

Sociologists are striving to develop databases on children's rights. Boyle (2009) was recently awarded a US National Science Foundation (NSF) grant for her study "The Cost of Rights or the Right Cost? The Impact of Global Economic and Human Rights Policies on Child Well-Being since 1989." Gran (2010a) also received NSF support to develop and replicate the Children's Rights Index for the period 1989 to 2009.

What Can Human Rights Scholars Learn from Sociology of Children and Youth?

What can human rights scholars learn from sociology of children and youth? One important contribution is that just as childhood is socially constructed, so is adulthood. Human rights work relies on the dichotomous social construction of adult and child. This dichotomy occasionally invites conflict in human rights. Near-universal ratification of the UN Convention on the Rights of the Child (UNCRC) suggests widespread commitment to special treatment of young people. The Universal Declaration of Human Rights (UDHR) distinguishes between adults and young people in Article 25, where it directs that childhood merits "special assistance." UDHR Article 26 endows parents with the right to choose their child's education. Despite this similarity, the UDHR and UNCRC do conflict in important ways, the most important of which has to do a young person's freedom of conscience. UDHR Article 18 states, "Everyone has the right to freedom of thought, conscience and religion." Article 14 of the UNCRC, however, endows parents with the right to make decisions about a young person's religious beliefs and practices "in a manner consistent with the evolving capacities of the child." This conflict between the UDHR and the UNCRC accentuates the notion that young people are less than human.

Human rights scholars can learn from sociologists about what explains successes of institutions established to advance children's interests, including children's rights. Sociologists can demonstrate means by which the UN Committee on the Rights of the Child and other committees can monitor state implementation of children's rights instruments. Sociologists can offer insights into institutional isomorphism (Hafner-Burton, Tsutsui, and Meyer 2008) of independent institutions for children's rights and how their offices advance young people's rights (Thomas, Gran, and Hanson 2011; Gran 2011).

Human rights scholars can learn from sociologists about how local cultural practices can shape the practice of human rights. Given that adults typically mediate the rights of young people, sociologists can offer information about how human rights work for young people in communities and family homes.

Human rights scholars can learn how sociologists attempt to respect the young people they study. Working with institutions that monitor the interests of human subjects involved in research, sociologists strive to achieve informed consent of young people participating in their research while remaining cautious and aware of young people's interests. Sociologists recognize that young people often cannot and do not make decisions to participate in research.

WHAT CAN SOCIOLOGISTS OF CHILDREN AND YOUTH LEARN FROM HUMAN RIGHTS?

Human rights scholarship can teach many lessons to sociologists of children and youth. One important lesson is that the lives of children and youth take place on a vast playing field. Human rights scholars consider not only human rights treaties and organizations responsible for implementing human rights (and fighting against human rights) but barriers to and catalysts of implementation. Sociologists of young people may learn from human rights scholarship on how social-science evidence is used to monitor young people's rights.

Sociologists can learn from human rights scholars how governments respond to calls for human rights and how those responses vary by political party and form of government. Given that young people's experiences are mediated through manifold institutions, human rights scholars can provide insights into which institutions deserve attention.

Human rights are based on the notion of equality and dignity. Sociologists have examined equal access to education, even calling for a civil right to education as noted above (Gaston et al. 2009). Sociologists can consider other forms of equality important to young people's lives, how those notions of equal rights may change young people's lives, and how those rights may be attained. Important issues will be raised, such as how to implement a child's right to social security that is not based on a relationship with a parent or caretaker. Human rights scholars will provide insights into how human rights will change laws and practices governing young people's experiences with privacy.

Human rights scholars can teach sociologists how to take seriously a young person's dignity. By doing so, a host of research questions will be raised for sociologists. Human rights scholarship will lead to new sociological questions about expectations and norms involving young people, their parents, and schools.

Human rights scholarship can help sociologists rethink other ways young people can participate in research. Human rights scholars may point to new means by which young people can exert formal roles in sociological research, such as assuming council positions in the ASA section on Children and Youth.

IT's NOT *WHAT* BUT *WHO* IS THE FUTURE

At the intersection of human rights and sociology of children and youth can be found many fascinating questions and exciting possibilities. Universal agreements do not exist on what human rights are and what childhood means. Strident disagreements are heard globally over whether young people possess rights. At their core, these differences revolve around what it means to be a child.

Young people may be able to explain what it fundamentally means to be human and to possess rights. Human rights scholars and sociologists will do well to listen to and try to take the perspectives of young people, recognizing their diverse needs, interests, and experiences. Children and youth may teach us about social qualities of human rights and what is necessary to take rights seriously.

CHAPTER EIGHT

RACE, CLASS, AND GENDER

Mary Romero

The traditional sociological lens for analyzing and conceptualizing social inequality has been dominated by class and social class. Over the last century, sociologists have also recognized race and ethnicity as significant in understanding inequality. Most early research was based on a white/black racial binary, classifying all other groups as "ethnic." Gradually scholars conceptualized the ways that legal, economic, political, and social institutional practices racially construct groups. Michael Omi and Howard Winant (1986) presented the conceptualization of racialization as a process in their classic work *Racial Formation in the United States*. Ian Haney López (1993) further developed the legal analysis of race and citizenship in *White by Law* by documenting the legal cases that defined whiteness and the history of allowing persons identified as nonwhite to be citizens. Studies in whiteness contributed an understanding of the social processes involved in categorizing groups previously labeled as nonwhite using white classifications (Roediger 1991; Ignatiev 1995). Apart from these intellectual projects, gender analyses theorized male privilege and gender discrimination. Feminist scholars interrogated the ways that male experiences dominated sociological perspectives that made the experiences of women invisible.

While these different types of social inequality were recognized and flourished as separate fields of study, the analyses of race, class, ethnicity, and gender remained separate from each other. The major consequence was a privileging of certain experiences while hiding or disguising others. Critiques of class analysis pointed to the assumption of white male as the ideal type, race analysis assumed black men, and gender analysis assumed white women (Dill 1983; Baca Zinn et al. 1986). Each of these analyses ignored women of color and assumed their lived experiences were represented by men of color or by white women. Women-of-color scholars challenged this construction of social inequality and social position by arguing that race, class, and gender must be theorized as fluid identities that operate simultaneously with racism, capitalism, and patriarchy rather than as fixed identities (Dill 1983; Baca Zinn et al. 1986; Harris 1990). Theories and research on race, class, and gender emerged from interdisciplinary fields with histories of struggle and with a social-justice agenda, such as African American studies, women's and gender studies, Latino studies, and critical race legal theory. The study of race, class, and gender in sociology continues to have an ongoing connection to interdisciplinary studies.

Race, class, and gender perspectives overlapping with human rights are most likely to turn toward critical race feminism because this intellectual project best illustrates the significance of this sociological lens in developing a human rights analysis and advocacy for women and other marginalized groups. In this chapter, I identify the key concerns and questions in the sociology of race, class, and gender and summarize key findings and methods. I then turn to a critical discussion of the contributions race, class, and gender have made to development of a human rights paradigm. I then resituate race, class, and gender within a human rights paradigm and explore new questions doing so raises. I end the chapter with a brief discussion of these new questions and the potential that resituating the field in a human rights paradigm holds for further developing the field and making contributions to understanding human rights.

KEY CONCERNS AND QUESTIONS

Recalling Sojourner Truth's words from her 1851 speech given at the Women's Convention in Akron, Ohio, "Ain't I a woman?," several women-of-color scholars picked up the mantle and began theorizing a race, class, and gender analysis that was inclusive rather than exclusionary (Dill 1983; Baca Zinn et al. 1986; King 1988; Romero 1988; Segura 1989; Brewer 1993). Theorizing race, class, and gender arose out of the scholarship of women of color who found their voices silenced by a single-axis analysis and instead represented by men of color and white women. Traditional lenses for analyzing social inequality defined women of color in mutually exclusive ways that either completely separated them from men of color and white women or emphasized conflicting agendas and blurred paths toward social justice. Women-of-color scholars turned their inquiry toward explaining how and why individuals located at the juncture of multiple marginalizations were invisible. As sociologists attended to racial formation and to the social construction of race, the fluidity of gendered and class-based racial experiences became visible. Rather than examining social inequality by centering on the lives of relatively privileged individuals as the norm, the focus became the lived experiences of women of color. Incorporating a race, class, and gender analysis challenged previous ways of studying inequality because each no longer could each be treated as a static variable representing all conditions.

Concern that theorizing identities as social identities would lead to essentialism emerged in the interdisciplinary fields of African American studies, Asian Pacific American studies, women's and gender studies, queer studies, disability studies, and other intellectual projects. Alongside political struggles for equal rights, each constituency began to carve out an identity agenda for advocacy and failed to search for points of intersection for coalition building. As each began to encounter more diversity within its group identity, the single axis of oppression was challenged as essentialism and, more importantly, as exclusionary. Identity categories were acknowledged as multidimensional. "Anti-essentialists feared that descriptions of identity often falsely homogenized the experiences of different group members" (Levit 2002, 228). Therefore, not all blacks in the United States are citizens, not all LGBTs are white and middle-class, not all the unemployed are poor workers of color, and not all prisoners convicted for drugs are Latino or black men. To be inclusive of all black people in the United States, fighting racism needs to include immigrants of color. Blacks are not racialized in the same way at different times in history or in different contexts. To be inclusive of black gays and lesbians, racism must also be addressed in developing advocacy programs. Similarly, stereotypes about the sexuality of women are not universal and differ by age, race, ethnicity, and religion. Consequently, sexual harassment cases may not be solely based on gender discrimination and can only be understood by recognizing the multilayered aspects.

Avoiding essentialism involved being inclusive and understanding the complexity of oppression, as well as the privileges that social positions have at certain times and in certain contexts. In analyzing *Degraffenreid v. General Motors*, Kimberlé Crenshaw (1991) described the need for an intersectional approach. White women were hired in the front office, and industrial jobs hired black men. However, no black women were hired in either the front office or industrial jobs. The court found that gender discrimination did not occur because women were hired in the front office and race discrimination did not occur because blacks were hired in industrial jobs. Since the court defined race and gender discrimination as group based and exclusive rather than multifaceted, black women were unable to make a case for either gender or race discrimination. As a result, Crenshaw developed the metaphor of intersectionality to capture analyses that incorporate race, class, and gender. Focusing on power relations, Patricia Hill Collins (1993) introduced the metaphor of interlocking oppressions to highlight the link to structural relations of domination. Other concepts used to capture the complexity of inequality are the matrix of domination (Collins 1990; Baca Zinn and Dill 1994), multiple consciousness (King 1988), interlocking systems of oppression and privilege (Collins 1993), "integrative" (Glenn 1999), race, class, and gender (Pascal 2007), and complex inequality (McCall 2001). Intersectionality aims to address the complexity of social positions as lived experiences rather than static, one-dimensional social conditions. The fluidity of social positions reflects the significance of time and context in analyzing oppression and privilege (King 1988).

Using an inclusive framework for examining social inequalities constantly moves scholars toward identifying additional axes of domination, such as citizenship, age, sexuality, and disability (Glenn 1999; Razack 1998). We might think of intersectionality analysis as akin to working with a Rubik's cube. By turning the axis, we see distinct social locations depending on which position the block is moved to in relationship to the other blocks. After examining a social position as a lived experience (Collins 2000; Jordan-Zachary 2007), the next step is to understand the connection to interlocking oppressions of racism, patriarchy, and capitalism (Collins 2000; Smith 1987; Acker 2006).

KEY FINDINGS

Researchers recognized that individual experiences are concrete and that there are real consequences in the form of privilege and oppression. Race, class, and gender are not static but fluid social positions that take on unique forms of privileges and oppressions in various contexts and in the presence of different social identities. A variety of identities shape and influence social positions, but all are linked to race, class, and gender. Both social and political processes maintain, reinforce, or modify consequences. This is further enhanced by having these processes embedded in the everyday practices of social institutions, such as the law, media, economy, and schools. Structures of power are organized around intersections of race, class, and gender. No single dimension of the axis of domination either captures social reality as experienced by everyone or completely accounts for social inequality. The type of oppression identified may fall under one or more of the following rubrics: exploitation, marginalization, powerlessness, cultural imperialism, or violence (Young 1990). Privilege and oppression are gained or lost in social situations, social institutions, and social structures. Gains or losses in privilege depend on which axis is most salient—race, class, or gender—in a specific context. While race, class, and gender are experienced simultaneously, all three are not necessarily salient in each situation, encounter, or institution.

Rather than essentializing race, class, and gender, intersectional analysis identifies the distinct features in overlapping social positions. Intersectionality avoids an essentialist perspective and does not perceive identities as stable, homogeneous, and undifferentiated. White middle-class feminists identified the home and family as women's work and a universal experience; however, not all women experience care work as unpaid labor or gaining employment outside the home as liberating. A major criticism of essentialism is that the perspective characterizes other cultures as inferior or backward and assumes an evolutionary social process (Narayan 1998; Goodhard 2003).

Intersectionality uses a similar conceptualization as standpoint theory in locating groups' and individuals' position of subordination and/or privilege. Emphasis on lived experiences becomes central in understanding "the relations of ruling" (Smith 1987), as well as moving beyond abstract concepts and understanding real and complex social positions. Identifying the process of power and privilege in social institutions and social interaction is central to understanding how whiteness, maleness, heterosexuality, and middle- and upper-class status are normalized in everyday activities. Recognizing everyday practices that reinforce, maintain, and reproduce privileges based on race, class, and gender illuminates the link between the micro and macro structures. "The form of discrimination experienced by Black women is not related to some 'immutable' characteristic(s) inherent in Black women (skin color for example), but rather, it is a form of discrimination arising because of society's stereotyping of black women, its historical treatment of them" (Aylward 2010, 17). Self-ascriptions are less significant as socially designated labels in understanding processes of subordination and domination (Hulko 2009).

Oppression and privilege are systems that operate in tandem with racism, patriarchy, and capitalism, which mutually reinform each other. Understanding how racism, patriarchy, and capitalism are systems of privilege and oppression that operate in tandem is central to intersectionality.

KEY METHODS

Having an interdisciplinary history that challenged previous scientific knowledge as failing to incorporate race, class, and gender, the field rejects traditional empirical methodology accepted within mainstream sociology. Consequently, a major social science criticism is the emphasis on theorizing lived experiences previously invisible in the prototypes of their respective identity groups (Purdie-Vaughs and Eiback 2008) and the absence of a clearly defined empirical methodology (Nash 2008).

The weakness of intersectionality becomes more obvious when it is applied to empirical analysis: its implications for empirical analysis are, on the one hand, a seemingly insurmountable complexity and, on the other, a fixed notion of differences. This is because the list of differences is endless or even seemingly indefinite. It is impossible to take into account all the differences that are significant at any given moment (Ludvig 2006, 246).

Intersectionality cannot be understood or explained by using an "add-on" approach. The black lesbian experience is not "racism + sexism + homophobia." Instead, an intersectional framework recognizes that various combinations of identities produce substantively distinct experiences. "The facts of identity are 'not additive,' but instead 'indivisible,' operating simultaneously in people's daily experiences" (Levit 2002, 230). Therefore, additional identities are not treated as an accumulated burden or compounded discrimination but recognized as a unique experience produced as a result of various combinations of burdens and discriminations.

Feminist researchers working from an interdisciplinary perspective have primarily used humanistic methodological approaches to avoid the problems arising in past empirical quantitative methodology. They advocate for value-free research, recognizing that all research is influenced by the researcher's questions, conceptual frameworks, and selected methods for collecting and analyzing data. Feminists advocate for socially engaged research in analyzing the intersectionality of race, class, gender, and other structural features. In an effort to avoid essentialism, feminists collect and analyze data about lived experiences. "Everyday life" provides the means to contextualize discrimination and social inequality. In an effort to avoid misrepresenting different cultures, participatory action research is frequently incorporated into the methodology (Harding and Norberg 2005). Recent quantitative research has started to pave the way for new methods for intersectional analyses (Landry 2007).

INTERSECTIONALITY'S CONTRIBUTIONS TO A HUMAN RIGHTS PARADIGM

Intersectionality is fairly absent in human rights with the exception of human rights for women. In response to the criticism that gender is not included, the UN human rights leadership committed to a gender-sensitive perspective, and gender mainstreaming became an accepted practice (UN 2000, 2001, 2009; Riley 2004). This approach called for considering the implications for women and men in all actions, legislation, policy, and programs. For many human rights organizations already working closely with women, the gender-sensitive mandate was interpreted as a call to recognize gender discrimination as impacting other social identities, such as race, class, skin color, age, ethnicity, religion, language, ancestry, sexual orientation, culture, geographic location, and status as citizen, refugee, or migrant (Satterthwaite 2005). Intersectionality is not a one- or two-dimensional approach that privileges certain conditions and denies the existence of others. This interpretation requires a concerted effort to avoid homogeneity of identity or experience by recognizing patterns of "domination and resistance along geopolitical and geoeconomic lines" (Reilly 2004, 83). More recently, time and context have been added to the list of significant features in comprehending interlocking oppressions (Hulko 2009). Intersectionality functions to highlight the way that certain rights are relegated to the margins, particularly when traditional analysis is used and individuals' identities are fragmented into separate categories.

Several human rights documents incorporate an intersectional analysis in articulating a human rights platform. For instance, Point 69 of the declaration of the World Conference against Racism, Racial Discrimination, Xenophobia, and Related Intolerance states,

> We are convinced that racism, racial discrimination, xenophobia and related intolerance reveal themselves in a differentiated manner for women and girls, and can be among the factors leading to a deterioration in their living conditions, poverty, violence, multiple forms of discrimination, and the limitation or denial of their human rights. We recognize the need to integrate a gender perspective into relevant policies, strategies and programmes of action against racism, racial discrimination, xenophobia and related intolerance in order to address multiple forms of discrimination. (2001, 13)

The Committee on the Elimination of Racial Discrimination, General Recommendation 25, Gender Related Dimensions of Racial Discrimination, states,

> The Committee notes that racial discrimination does not always affect women and men equally or in the same way. There are circumstances in which racial discrimination only or primarily affects women, or affects women in a different way, or to a different degree than men. Such racial discrimination will often escape detection if there is no explicit recognition or acknowledgment of the different life experiences of women and men, in areas of both public and private life. (2000)

One of the strongest statements advocating intersectionality in human rights is made by the Association for Women's Rights in Development:

> As a theoretical paradigm, intersectionality allows us to understand oppression, privilege and human rights globally. It helps us to build arguments for

substantive equality from women's histories and community case studies (that is, women writing/speaking from their experiences of specific, interesecting identities) by extracting theoretical statements and overarching principles. This allows us to see that the claims women are making for their equal rights are not merely an instance of a self-interested group promoting its own interests, but instead fundamental to achieving the promise of human rights for all. Interesectionality, therefore, is a tool for building a global culture of human rights from the grassroots to the global level. (Symington 2004, 3)

The Ontario Human Rights Commission refers to an intersectional approach to discrimination as a "contextualized approach":

An intersectional approach takes into account the historical, social and political context and recognizes the unique experience of the individual based on the intersection of all relevant grounds." Applying a contextual analysis involves examining "the discriminatory stereotypes; the purpose of the legislation, regulation or policy; the nature of and or situation of the individual at issue, and the social, political and legal history of the person's treatment in society. (2001, 3)

Incorporating intersectionality into human rights highlights the significance of social, political, and historical context; makes multiple marginalizations visible; and establishes programs and policies that treat social positions as fluid identities operating simultaneously.

Ethnographic research methodology dominates intersectional research and is perceived by many human rights scholars as the most useful tool for obtaining data, particularly in collecting descriptive data. For instance, in her work on women migrant workers, Margaret Satterthwaite advocates ethnography to capture "women's own 'sense of entitlement' concerning their lives, bodies, and futures" (2005, 65) rather than the state's interests. Furthermore, she argues that "human rights advocates could then use an intersectional approach to formulate claims anchored within existing rights standards but which respond to the multiple forms of discrimination making up the limits on women's lives. Moving such claims to the center of advocacy efforts would honor the agency of the women migrant workers whose experiences have so far been described and analyzed only through existing legal norms" (Satterthwaite 2005, 65).

Intersectionality is a recognized tool and conceptual framework for developing advocacy programs and human rights policy because the approach emphasizes the need to identify multiple types of discriminations and to understand how different social locations shape one's access to rights and opportunities. Intersectionality provides an approach for addressing central questions of universalism versus cultural particularism, human nature, and the nature of rationality, to name a few. NGOs advocating for an intersectional approach recognize that narrowly defined laws and human rights statements can only address a single form of discrimination and are not contextualized to address the various economic, social, political, and cultural lived experiences. The approach of understanding antisubordination and privilege involves a participative, dialogic progress engaged in (re)interpretation and (re)definition that is grounded in concrete concerns defined by women's lived experiences (Reilly 2004). Using intersectionality to identify and link organizational power may assist in developing new organizational forms that reduce existing obstacles to human rights and expand our understanding of power dynamics and social reproduction of inequality. Experience has demonstrated that added protection for marginalized groups does not affect the rights of the majority but brings issues facing otherwise isolated groups to the forefront of the global rights agenda.

RESITUATING INTERSECTIONALITY WITHIN A HUMAN RIGHTS PARADIGM

A major challenge of intersectionality is moving beyond the abstract to concrete lived experiences. Too often intersectionality becomes viewed only as a metaphor rather than as lived experience. Identity categories and various concepts such as axis of domination, interlocking oppression, and even intersectionality itself can become blinders to recognizing and analyzing emerging themes. A human rights paradigm may be useful in grounding intersectionality in real issues and problems and assist in further developing an intersectionality-type analysis that includes both the micro and macro. While confusion still arises in the literature over distinctions between identities, social position, intersectionality, and interlocking oppressions, there is growing agreement that there is a distinction between identity categories (race and gender), processes (racialization and gendering), and systems of oppression (racism, patriarchy, and capitalism) (Dhamoon 2010; Hulko 2009). A general consensus exists that there is a "systemic interplay of patriarchal, capitalist, and racist power relations" and a need for intersectionality as "a commitment to cross-boundaries dialogue, networking, and social criticism" (Reilly 2007, 184). Indivisible and interdependent tools are used to facilitate an intersectional analysis in human rights and assist in antiessentialist understanding of the self as complex and dynamic (Crooms 1997). These understandings of intersectionality offer clarity to its use in the field of race, class, and gender.

Several human right scholars have criticized intersectionality as including an endless number of social categories and conflating the structural differences between race, class, and gender (i.e., Butler 1990, 182–183). Others argue that specific historical situations create different social divisions that are meaningful and position groups along economic, political, and social hierarchies. In the case of human rights, the focus of analysis needs to identify the points of intersection for political struggle (Yuval-Davis 2006a). The reflective process is "integral to contesting false universalization and neo-imperialist manifestations of supposedly cosmopolitan values" (Reilly 2004, 86). As Johanna Bond iterates,

> Intersectional analysis provides a vehicle for recognizing all the relevant human rights that are violated in given situation along multiple axes of oppression, rather than merely those rights violations that stem from a singular approach to human rights that focuses on racism or sexism to the exclusion of other identity categories. By recognizing all relevant human rights in a given situation

and the multiple systems of oppression that lead to rights violations, qualified universalism actually promotes the concept of "universal" human rights. International intersectionality provides a more complete picture and analysis of human rights, one that ultimately leads to a more complete or "universal" recognition of human rights. (2003, 156)

Human rights activists recognize both the strength of and the challenges posed by developing a platform based on intersectional analysis.

Critics of intersectional analysis argue that there is an overemphasis on victimization and little if any attention paid to acts of resistance. This is particularly a problem in constructing the "third world" victim because this image is frequently used to justify "imperialist interventions" (Kapur 2002, 2). Focusing on how race, gender, and class interact to create a particular form of discrimination and oppression turns attention to institutional and procedural practices rather than the characteristics of certain groups. Instead of compartmentalizing types of discrimination, intersectionality recognizes that "individuals experience the complex interplay of multiple systems of oppression operating simultaneously in the world" (Bond 2003, 77). This approach empowers instead of reinscribes victimhood, which is significant in rethinking human rights law and policies. Here the questions are not simply framed to understand individual or group oppression; rather, researchers pose questions from the standpoint of organizations in an attempt to understand abuses of organizational power. Margaret Satterthwaite argues that "shifting the focus from only articulating forms of discrimination to also identifying protections" will "uncover human rights norms that already exist, and which could be called upon to fight the subordinating practices made clear through intersectional descriptions of violations" (2005, 12).

Resituating intersectionality within a human rights paradigm pushes the methodological approach to analyze social issues more fully to identify convergences that can be used as effective interventions and that will advocate more inclusive coalition building among groups. Antisubordination analysis redirects efforts to highlight only differences and begins to address questions concerning the ways that individuals and groups are not subordinated by conditions or made dependent. Most intersectionality approaches, including antiracism, aim for the lowest denominator of "tolerance" rather than equal respect and dignity for all. Focusing on the end product of engaging in aid and human rights work may be extremely useful in developing a more clearly defined intersectionality methodology (Yuval-Davis 2006b). Human rights advocates of an intersectional approach strongly recommend moving beyond merely theorizing and applying scholarship to human rights problems (Bond 2003).

LOOKING FORWARD: IDENTIFYING NEW QUESTIONS AND NEW POSSIBILITIES FOR BOTH THE AREA AND HUMAN RIGHTS REALIZATIONS

In analyzing the contributions of international intersectionality to understanding and advocating human rights for women, Bond (2003) points to the need for all laws and policies to embrace intersectionality. The campaign to mainstream gender in human rights laws resulted in an add-on approach that made sure women were included. For many issues not directly identified as gender-specific problems, gender mainstreaming became a "gender-plus" analysis. However, the goal of an international intersectionality approach requires rethinking human problems by considering the salient social categories impacting people's lives in specific situations, which may be age, sexuality, caste, religion, or citizenship. This approach needs to be used to address all populations—migrants, prisoners, refugees, and children. The lack of intersectonality is not only found at the United Nations but common among issue-specific NGOs. If one plays a crucial role as watchdog in representing human rights violations internationally, incorporating an intersectionality approach is central as a human rights practice. Bond notes the inconsistent use of intersectionality in Human Rights Watch (HRW) reports on women. For example, in 1995 HRW produced a report on violence against women in South Africa that identified the role of apartheid in women's decision not to report domestic violence and risk further violence by the state. However, in the case of US prisons, "the report failed to explore the impact of intersecting human rights violations based both on gender and sexual orientation or, in some cases, on race, gender, and sexual orientation" (Bond 2003, 151). As a matter of practice, according to Bond, NGOs need to ask, "How does this type of violation affect different categories of people along multiple axes of oppression, including *inter alia* race, class, ethnicity, gender, religion, and sexual orientation?" (2003, 152). Only through an acceptance of intersectionality in all human rights issues can women or any other group be completely served by laws, policies, and programs.

In my own research, intersectionality is central in framing circumstances Latinos face in an era of nativist anti-immigrant sentiment. Without a recognition of the racialized notions of citizenship and mixed-status families, the range of human rights violations that Latino communities experience during immigration raids and at the hands of law enforcement are minimized. Human rights violations result from militarization of the border, militarized tactics used in immigration raids, indefinite detention of minors and others migrating to the United States, policies that result in migrants' deaths, the terrorizing of low-income Latino communities, conducting raids and using law-enforcement practices without regard for human life or minors' safety, and denial of public services on the basis of race and ethnicity (Romero 2006, 2011).

Bringing human rights and intersectionality together moves us forward in developing an adequate set of universal human rights principles, rights, practices, and methods. Working together by reconceptualizing discourses is a step toward recognizing the legitimacy of more than one agenda and developing an integrated approach that values human dignity as universal. As researchers, we need to move our analysis beyond naming intersections and toward identifying processes for the eradication of discrimination and celebration of diversity. Similarly, researchers and human rights activists can begin to observe ways "in which individuals and communities are engaged in active resistance" (Bond 2003, 159).

≈

Chapter Nine

Sexualities

Mary Bernstein

This chapter addresses two themes in the sociology of sexualities that are relevant to the study of human rights. First, the sociology of sexualities challenges the assumption that sexuality is "essentialist," a property of individuals, something that has its own truth and exists outside social forces, that is somehow presocial and biologically driven or perhaps divinely ordained. In contrast, sexuality is socially constructed. As Gayle Rubin explains, "Desires are not preexisting biological entities, but rather ... they are constituted in the course of historically specific social practices" (1984, 276). Second, sociologists of sexualities theorize the ways in which sexuality serves as an axis of domination and is part of every major social institution. As a result of studying how sexuality both influences and is influenced by major institutions, theorists reconceptualize the concept of power to understand how culture and discourse are constitutive of dominant institutions and produce new forms of knowledge and power that organize and regulate sexuality and provide sites of resistance. Thus, how we understand sexuality, what we define as normal or abnormal, and the types of sexual identities that exist in a given society are influenced by culture and discourse, institutions, and power. Understanding sexuality as an axis of domination and a site of resistance thus expands our study of human rights struggles.

THE SOCIOLOGY OF SEXUALITIES

CHALLENGING ESSENTIALISM: THE BODY, GENDER, AND SEXUALITY

Sociologists of sexualities challenge essentialism by illustrating that our very understandings of what constitutes male and female bodies are socially constructed. Notions of what bodies should look like and the extent to which they should experience pleasure are used to justify regulating and disciplining them. Scholars also find that gender and age structure expectations about what is appropriate sexual activity.

THE BODY

Control over appropriate sexuality is linked to what Ponse termed "the principle of consistency" (1978)—that is, a view that biological sex (genes, genitals, hormones, secondary sex characteristics) is linked to gender (masculinity or femininity) and sexual orientation (whether one is attracted to men or women) in a straightforward manner, so that one is biologically male, masculine, and attracted to women or female, feminine, and attracted to men. Yet, in practice, these do not always align easily, as in the case of gay men, lesbians, bisexuals, and transgender people. Furthermore, control over this alignment starts from birth with the policing of genitals. In the early twentieth century, male circumcision was seen as a way to reduce the male sexual drive. Yet others see circumcision as a means to enhance, rather than reduce, male sexual pleasure (Ross 2009). Jewish rites of male circumcision are tied to men's covenant with god—a patriarchal rite from which women are excluded (Kimmel 2001). In short, views of appropriate genitals for men are bound to views of masculinity, male sexuality, and whether or not sexual pleasure is viewed as problematic, in need of reining in, or in need of enhancement.

Intersexed people who have "ambiguous genitals" are regulated as infants through surgical procedures designed to make their genitals appear to be either male or female (often accompanied later by hormonal treatment). Rather than chromosomes, whether or not a penis is big enough for sexual intercourse determines whether the child is surgically altered. Parents are instructed to socialize their child into the gender that matches the surgically altered genitals. Thus, appropriate views of sexuality and gender are used to justify medically unnecessary surgery on infants in order to support society's sex/gender system (Fausto-Sterling 2000a; Kessler 1990; Preeves 2003).

The desire to control adult sexuality and police gender is also apparent in cultures that practice female genital mutilation. These cultures place a strong value on virginity at marriage and do not believe in a woman's right to sexual agency or sexual pleasure. Thus, with removal of the clitoris and, in some places, the practice of infibulation, girls' bodies are irrevocably altered in ways that ensure they remain virgins and cannot enjoy sexual pleasure as adults (Hosken 1993). While debates over men's bodies concern enhancing male pleasure and sometimes reducing (but never eliminating) it, the assumption is that men will and should enjoy sexuality. Groups simply differ on how best to achieve this goal.

Whereas intersex infants are subjected to surgery without their consent, transgender people who wish to transition surgically are only allowed to do so after receiving a mental-illness diagnosis of gender identity disorder. Although this diagnosis, which is influential globally (GID Reform Advocates 2008), is useful for those whose insurance will pay for hormones and sex-reassignment surgery, others argue that the diagnosis contributes to societal stigma and harms the quest for legal rights and protection. Some transgender activists argue for reform of the diagnosis, facilitating access to surgery and hormones. Others avoid the issue of insurance coverage, advocating removal of the diagnosis coupled with acceptance of "gender-queer" individuals whose gender and physical body may not line up (Burke 2010).

Gendered expectations about sexuality result in a double standard for sexual behavior. Studies of US teenagers illustrate that girls' reputations suffer more damage than boys' due to their having sex and that girls are more likely to be condemned and considered "easy" for carrying a condom than boys are (Hynie and Lydon 1995; Levine 2002; Vanwesenbeeck 1997). In Mexico, González-López (2005) finds that a young woman's virginity provides her with a "capital feminino" that can be exchanged for social status for the family. Research in the United States also finds gendered differences in negotiations around sex. Boys initiate sex far more often than girls. As a result, the responsibility for saying no to sex falls disproportionately on girls. Beneke (1983) argues that this pattern of behavior, where boys are responsible for initiating sex and escalating sexual encounters, results in the development of a rape-like mentality among boys and men, so that boys learn not to listen when girls say no. Both boys and girls believe that a girl risks the loss of her relationship if she refuses to have sex with her boyfriend (Gavey, McPhillips, and Doherty 2001). In addition, boys are far less likely to raise the issue of safer sex than girls are (Holland et al. 1998; Kaiser Family Foundation 2002).

In explaining gendered differences in sexuality, sociologists challenge essentialist explanations. Essentialist models drawing on hormonal studies, brain studies, and sociobiology are methodologically flawed (Schwartz and Rutter 1998; Fausto-Sterling 2000b). Essentialist arguments also make analogies from animal behavior to explain human behavior such as violence, rape, and male dominance. But animals engage in a wide variety of sexual and social behavior, including homosexual behavior, anal and oral sex, and promiscuous sex (Bagemihl 2000), making it problematic to infer what does or does not constitute "normal" sexual behavior in humans. Furthermore, human behavior is based more on learning than on instinct, casting doubt on such analogies.

Instead, sociologists of sexualities posit a combination of factors to account for gender differences in sexuality. For example, fewer women masturbate than men because of the cultural messages they get about what is appropriate sexually for women. As a result, they may not know their bodies. Even for women who know what pleases them sexually, communication between partners may be poor, leading to less satisfaction for women (Schwartz and Rutter 1998). The sexual double standard inhibits women from developing their full sexual potential. Socioeconomic conditions and rural/urban differences also explain sexualized gender inequality (González-López 2005).

Sexualities scholars also study heterosexuality as a social institution that has its own rules and norms that pattern behavior. Heterosexuality as an institution disadvantages heterosexual women, lesbians, and gay men. Ingraham (2008) argues that a romanticized view of heterosexuality symbolized by the big white wedding masks the gendered inequality that takes place within marriage. Others contend that heterosexuality is not only an institution but compulsory. Rich's (1980) concept of compulsory heterosexuality illustrates the ways in which men control female sexuality through physical force, economic inequality, punishment for lesbian sexuality, strictures against masturbation, and stronger punishments for female adultery than for male adultery, which makes women more financially dependent on men, leading women to marry for physical and financial protection (Eisenstein 1983).

SEXUALITY AS AN AXIS OF DOMINATION

Sexualities scholars study the ways in which sexuality is entwined with larger systems of domination. In this section, I examine heteronormativity—that is, "the institutions, structures of understanding and practical orientations that make heterosexuality seem not only coherent—that is, organized as a sexuality—but also privileged" (Berlant and Warner 1998, 548)—through a discussion of sexual orientation, sex education, sexual health, and sex work. I also discuss how colonialism and racial and ethnic inequality are justified through understandings of appropriate (hetero)sexuality and gender.

Sexual Orientation

Psychologists dominate the study of homophobia (Adam 1998), defining it as an irrational fear of lesbians and gay men. These studies find that those who are older, less educated, single, or male tend to be more homophobic than those who are younger, more educated, married, or female (Britton 1990; Yang 1998). The few studies that examine race suggest that African Americans are more homophobic than white Americans (Herek and Capitanio 1996), though that may be related to higher levels of religiosity among African Americans (Egan and Sherrill 2009). Bernstein, Kostelac, and Gaarder (2003) find that African Americans are typically more supportive of civil liberties for lesbians and gay men than are white Americans. Explanations for these relationships stress that lesbians and gay men may threaten one's psychological sense of self in terms of sexuality, masculinity, and group identity. These approaches also stress the importance of contact with lesbians and gay men as a factor that minimizes prejudice and maximizes intergroup cooperation (Herek and Glunt 1993; Jordan 1997; Yang 1998).

Recent sociological approaches (Bernstein and Kostelac 2002; Bernstein, Kostelac, and Gaarder 2003; Bernstein 2004) pay closer attention to the interplay between the social construction of minorities and the role that organized groups play in fostering those constructions. Gay-rights opponents express status concerns when faced with lesbian and gay demands for equality. Dynamic interactions between diverse groups that have a stake in maintaining homophobia influence a group's sense of its proper position. From the group-position perspective, certain religions and social movements based on particular religious interpretations may indicate a commitment to group status based on self-interest as much as on psychological factors.

Sexuality scholars also examine the ways in which LGBT people of color may experience "secondary marginalization" (Cohen 1999) within the broader LGBT movement as well as within communities of color (Bennett and Battle 2001; Takagi 1994). This research is particularly important in examining the complex ways in which race, class, culture, and sexual identity influence the experience of sexuality, negotiations around sexuality, and family relations (Bernstein and Reimann 2001; Asencio 2009; Battle 2009).

Sexuality scholars also debate whether social movement strategies, identities, and goals challenge or support heteronormativity. For example, scholars question the value of the institution of marriage and debate the wisdom of pursuing same-sex marriage as a goal of the LGBT movement (Walters 2001; Warner 2000). For lesbian and gay rights activists, extending the right to marry to same-sex couples would simply give them the same rights and legitimacy as different-sex couples. In contrast, queer activists view extending the right to marry to same-sex couples as expanding current conceptions of what is normal to include same-sex married couples. Marriage equality would not ultimately challenge the very notions of normality that define LGBT people as other and would offer no support to people with nonnormative family structures.

Historical research on the emergence of the categories "lesbian," "gay," and "bisexual" finds that these categories, which are supposed to represent fixed sexual identities, are historically and culturally specific ways of organizing erotic desire and behavior. Even defining people in terms of sexual identity is a recent phenomenon (Katz 2007; Foucault 1978). Research on non-Western cultures finds that there are multiple ways of organizing same-sex desire and gender/transgender behavior. For example, sexual relations may be differentiated by biological sex, gender, and age (Herdt 1994, 1997; Drucker 2000). Western sexual and gender categories cannot be mapped onto non-Western configurations, such as the *aravani* or *hijras* of India (Herdt 1994; Waites 2009) or the *nahdle* of the Navajo/Dine culture, who are considered to belong to a third gender.

Studies of LGBT movements in the developing world show that homosexuality is often constructed as "Western," something that is not indigenous but is instead a colonial imposition (Adam, Duyvendak, and Krouwel 1999). These arguments are used as a way to deny basic human rights protection for intimate sexual behavior and other rights based on sexual orientation and point to the significance of discourse, culture, and colonialism for explaining inequality based on sexual orientation.

Sex Education and Sexual Health

In the United States, heteronormativity structures contemporary sex-education programs and research on sexual health. Rather than addressing how to empower women within sexual relations, research on sexual health and behavior focuses on sexuality as a social problem. As a result, such research centers on explaining what contributes to unwed motherhood, sexually transmitted infections (STIs), and adolescent sexuality with its presumed negative consequences, such as pregnancy, disease, and poor mental health. This is also reflected in battles over sex education (Irvine 2002; Luker 2006).

The United States has supported abstinence-only sex education since 1981. According to SIECUS (2010), "Moreover, many abstinence-only-until-marriage programs rely on fear, shame, and guilt to try to control young people's sexual behavior.

These programs include negative messages about sexuality, distort information about condoms and STDs, and promote biases based on gender, sexual orientation, marriage, family structure, and pregnancy options." Sexualities research has shown consistently that abstinence-only education is ineffective in changing rates of vaginal intercourse or number of sexual partners (Underhill, Montgomery, and Operario 2007). In contrast, comprehensive sex-education programs present information on methods of birth control and discuss STIs, but these programs nonetheless present sexuality in terms of fear of pregnancy and risk of diseases. Ignored are discussions of how to empower girls around sexuality to say both no and yes. In other words, even comprehensive sex education fails to acknowledge that sexuality can be pleasurable, operating instead from the perspective of risk and fear. More recent work has focused on understanding "sexual subjectivity" (Horne and Zimmer-Gembeck 2005)—that is, on girls and women as sexual agents who can experience entitlement to sexual desire and pleasure (Tolman 1994; Martin 1996). In 2010, the United States dedicated money for comprehensive sexuality education. States may also choose to apply for funding for abstinence-only-until-marriage programs (SIECUS 2010).

The Sex Industry

Debates over the sex industry generally rest on the view that sex workers are either victims of male domination or are romanticized as the "happy hooker" (Weitzer 2000). Sociologists contend that neither view is correct. Instead, scholars examine the extent to which sex workers have agency in constructing their lives and work choices. By viewing sex work as an occupation, one can examine differences in terms of social status (e.g., street versus indoor prostitution), control over working conditions (e.g., the ability to choose or refuse clients, access to resources for safety and protection, independence or dependence on managers or pimps, and the ability to leave sex work), and experiences at work (prevalence of rape and assault and the risk of STIs) (Weitzer 2000). While some women may have more control over their working conditions in the sex industry, others may have no control, as in women who are victims of "sex trafficking," "a modern-day form of slavery in which a commercial sex act is induced by force, fraud, or coercion, or in which the person induced to perform such an act is under the age of 18 years" (US Department of Health and Human Services 2010).

Race, Ethnicity, and Sexuality

Sociologists of sexualities argue that sexuality is intimately linked to racialized systems of domination. For example, cross dressing and homosexual relations were commonplace among many indigenous peoples in the Americas (Terl 2000). European colonizers exported their views on such practices to the Americas as they worked to eradicate sodomy among indigenous people through terror and exter-mination. Viewed as an offense to their Christian god, the colonizers embarked on a campaign of mass destruction and appropriation of Native land, carried out partially in the name of abolishing sin (Fone 2000).

Slavery in the United States depended on sexualized and racialized stereotypes that provided whites with a convenient means of justifying exploitation. For example, stereotypes that Africans were overly sexual provided white slaveholders with a way to justify the rape of black women. Not only did this constitute sexual exploitation, but the children born of these rapes were considered slaves, thus providing an economic benefit to the slaveholder. This became particularly important economically after the transatlantic slave trade was abolished and reproduction became the only way to produce new slaves. Other racialized sexual stereotypes served to keep African and African American men in line. Viewing African and African American men as overly sexual and predatory justified lynching black men who even looked at a white woman or were simply accused of doing so. These stereotypes also served to keep white women afraid and dependent on white men for protection (Dowd 1993). Collins describes a series of sexual stereotypes of black women rooted in slavery that have "been essential to the political economy of domination fostering Black women's oppression" (2000, 67). Other sexual stereotypes linked to ethnicity are an integral part of nationalist discourse, colonization, sex tourism, and globalization (Nagel 2003).

Scholars of sexuality find that sexuality is linked to immigration. For example, Cantú (2009) examines why Mexican men who have sex with men (MSM) immigrate to the United States. Most research on immigration assumes that people immigrate for financial reasons but ignores the ways in which socioeconomic structures are linked to inequalities like sexuality, race, and gender. Men who have sex with men are marginalized and suffer discrimination and prejudice, which constrains their socioeconomic opportunities. MSMs who do not create a heteronormative family unit as an adult are subject to more discrimination. And thus, for some MSMs, sexuality contributes to a lack of financial opportunities, which pushes them to immigrate.

STUDYING SEXUALITIES

The early study of sexualities was dominated by psychiatrists using the case-study approach, which was limited by not having control groups of people in nonclinical settings. Alfred Kinsey was the first researcher to conduct sexuality research on a large scale. However, his study did not employ random sampling techniques, likely skewing his findings (Kinsey, Pomeroy, and Martin 1948). In the mid-1950s, William Masters and Virginia Johnson conducted a major study of sexual physiology to measure exactly what human bodies do during sexual encounters. However, they limited their study to volunteers who were orgasmic and had experience masturbating and ignored the meaning of sexuality to the participants. The result is that sexual dysfunction, including diagnosis in the American Psychiatric Association's *Diagnostic and Statistical Manual of Mental Disorders*, is related to the failure of body parts to work appropriately. This has led to a view of sexuality that is not representative of female experience and ignores emotional attachment, which far more women than men define as key to their sexual satisfaction (Tiefer 2004).

Laumann et al. (2000) launched the National Health and Social Life (NHSL) Survey in the 1990s using a national random sample of adults and face-to-face interviews. Their study found Americans to be rather conservative in terms of sex. However, the accuracy of these findings has been questioned, based on the idea that respondents may "lie, or fudge, or misremember, or leave things out" and the fact that the study was done at a point in the AIDS scare where people were afraid that sex with the wrong partner could kill them (Adelson 2001, 63).

Large-scale, quantitative sociological research on adolescent sexuality emerged in a conservative context with public concern over teen pregnancy, the spread of STIs, and the reproduction of those deemed "undeserving," namely, the poor, immigrants, and racial minorities. For example, early incarnations of the National Longitudinal Study of Adolescent Health (Add Health) assumed that race and class differences, as well as biological factors such as hormones, accounted for differences in sexuality. Recent versions of Add Health focus on explaining teen sexual activity by looking at the impact of peers, family, religion, community, and schools (Cavanagh 2007; Wilkinson and Pearson 2009; Harding 2007; Bearman and Bruckner 2001). While important, these studies lack attention to the meaning of sexual activity and assume a framework of sexuality as harm. Some recent quantitative work, in contrast, has examined positive effects of sexuality as well as what contributes to female sexual empowerment (Horne and Zimmer-Gembeck 2005).

Sexuality research is difficult to fund, and it is always political (DiMauro 1995; Ericksen and Steffen 2001). The US government has canceled funding for many sexuality studies, including the NHSL survey, which was ultimately funded by private donors. There is a fear that simply asking people about sexual behavior or reporting on what others do will lead them to engage in those sexual acts and that findings will challenge some people's moral and religious views (Adelson 2001).

Qualitative research on sexuality typically focuses on the meaning of sexual activity, sexual development, and experience (Diamond 2006). Ethnography, in-depth interviews, discourse, and content analysis are also important staples of sexuality scholarship. These methods provide insight into the symbolic meaning that sexual activity may hold for respondents and may uncover new sexual scripts (Bogle 2008) that develop in response to broader demographic and cultural trends. Many of these works question the universality of the categories that are used in the contemporary West to define gender and sexual orientation (Valentine 2007; Katz 2007). One of the most important implications of this work is that care must be paid when utilizing the categories "sexual orientation" and "gender identity" in international human rights advocacy and law.

WHAT CAN THE HUMAN RIGHTS PARADIGM LEARN FROM THE STUDY OF SEXUALITIES?

Sexualities research illustrates that the categories used to describe sexual orientation (gay, lesbian, and bisexual) and gender (male, female, transgender, gender identity) in the West are socially constructed. Scholars also illustrate that sexuality can be understood as fluid rather than fixed. While same-sex erotic behavior and attraction exist in every culture across time, how they are organized and whether they are used to define categories of persons is historically contingent (Rupp 2009; Greenberg 1988). Similarly, many cultures have had ways of instituting transgender behavior that differs from Western models (Kulick 1998). Therefore, human rights scholars and activists can work to identify indigenous forms of same-sex erotic behavior in order to sever the link that conservatives often make between "being gay" and the imperialism and excesses of Western bourgeois culture. As Waites (2009) points out, we must have a language to use, but care must be taken to ensure that "sexual orientation" and "gender identity" are understood in diverse ways.

Human rights activists have created a list of principles designed to protect people on the basis of sexual orientation and gender identity. The Yogyakarta Principles also outline the deleterious consequences that people suffer because of their sexual orientation or gender identity: "They include extra-judicial killings, torture and ill-treatment, sexual assault and rape, invasions of privacy, arbitrary detention, denial of employment and education opportunities, and serious discrimination in relation to the enjoyment of other human rights" (Corrêa and Muntarbhorn 2007, 6).

The sociology of sexualities also shows how practices such as female genital mutilation and surgery on intersexed children are rooted in views about appropriate genitals, bodily integrity, and sexual fulfillment. Surgeries on intersexed children and female genital mutilation often impair later sexual functioning, can curtail the ability to experience sexual pleasure, and can result in other health complications. Human rights groups opposed to male circumcision, female genital mutilation, and surgery on intersexed infants argue for children's rights to bodily integrity and to be free from unnecessary medical procedures.

Studies of sexual negotiations and sex education point human rights scholars toward understanding that strategies for preventing unwanted pregnancy and reducing the spread of STIs and HIV are linked not only to providing access to condoms, birth control, and education about safer sex but to women's becoming empowered in sexual encounters. If girls and women continue to be charged with saying no in sexual encounters, then old sexual scripts that perpetuate male dominance will linger.

The push for same-sex marriage and parental rights shows the importance of equality for those who want to enter into the institution of marriage, but the debate has also shown that the traditional family structure is not the only one deserving of state support. Human rights scholars and activists must push for recognition of a variety of family forms and policies that support the economic, emotional, and caretaking needs of all people.

WHAT HAPPENS WHEN WE CENTER THE HUMAN RIGHTS PARADIGM ON SEXUALITIES RESEARCH?

Centering the human rights paradigm pushes the sexual health literature away from focusing on models of disease and pregnancy prevention to ask more questions about sexual empowerment and control and how that is linked to basic issues of human rights and dignity. A human rights perspective should help sexuality scholars focus on how eliminating economic disparities between men and women will facilitate greater equality of power in negotiating sexual encounters.

Sociologists of sexualities need to incorporate a more global perspective on sexualities and incorporate human rights perspectives into their research. While it is important to be aware of how the goals of the LGBT movement may reinforce heteronormativity, as in the case of same-sex marriage, or reinstantiate the closet, as in the case of decriminalizing homosexuality based on a right to privacy, scholars must be aware that, according to the International Lesbian and Gay Human Rights Commission, "over 80 countries currently have sodomy laws or other legal provisions criminalizing homosexuality" (IGLHRC 2011). In such contexts, challenging heteronormativity may be neither desirable nor realistic. Obtaining basic human rights protections may be paramount.

In other ways, many sexualities scholars have already begun to link issues of sexual rights to the broader project of seeking fundamental human dignity. All too often, those who advocate rights for sex workers and those who advocate the abolition of sex work are speaking past each other, not acknowledging the variation that exists in the experience of sex workers. Chapkis (2000) offers a middle position, arguing that the best way to help women in the sex industry is by giving all women greater economic opportunities to do other types of work and by working to ensure that those who choose to be in the sex industry have control over their working conditions. So rather than take an abolitionist approach, human rights activists should work to improve conditions for all sex workers, eliminate forced sexual slavery, and increase economic opportunities for women and those who are transgendered, many of whom only turn to sex work as a means of survival. Sexuality scholars can also do much to link broader patterns of militarization to the sexual exploitation of women and global economic inequality that fosters sex tourism.

CHAPTER TEN

ANIMALS AND SOCIETY

Victoria Johnson and John Sanbonmatsu

What is the relationship between human rights and animal rights? Is the notion of human rights, as a protected domain of universal moral and legal rights, premised on the exclusion of nonhuman animals from that domain? Does the systemic exploitation and killing of other conscious beings by human beings indicate instability or incoherence in the notion of universal rights? What are the social implications of the fact that our mass killing of other animals continues to be rationalized on the basis of discourses implicated in genocide—in presumptions of biological difference and worthlessness, lack of intelligence, or simply weakness?

Although some scholars and activists have sought to distance human rights from animal rights, the two are historically and conceptually intertwined. The question of animal rights intersects the question of human rights in at least four ways. First, historically, animal rights developed at the same time as human rights and on the basis of a similar set of moral and social concerns. Second, the social institutions, ideologies, and practices that lead to the oppression and dehumanization of human beings derive in part from the structures, beliefs, and practices used by human beings to control, dominate, and kill nonhuman animals. Third, and conversely, systems of human oppression that justify the conquest of nature confound attempts to protect members of both vulnerable human groups and other species from exploitation and violence. Fourth, the notion of human rights itself rests on unexamined anthropocentric assumptions about human superiority and nonhuman inferiority based on biological difference. This chapter explores these and related questions.

WHAT IS THE SCOPE OF ANIMAL RIGHTS?

Various philosophers and critics over the centuries, among them Pythagoras, Plutarch, Montaigne, David Hume, Jeremy Bentham, Arthur Schopenhauer, Leo Tolstoy, and Henry Salt, opposed human violence and cruelty against other animals and advocated for their protection (Walters and Portness 1999; Steiner 2010). While there are premodern antecedents for the protection of other animals from human cruelty, the concept of animal rights as such is a modern notion, one closely tied to the earliest development of modern human and civil rights (West 1841). By the late eighteenth century, ethical vegetarianism had become a serious intellectual current in the British isles (Stuart 2006), and by 1822, the British parliament had enacted the first of many subsequent animal-cruelty laws (Shevelow 2008).

Despite these and other developments, however, it was not until the early 1970s, especially with the publication of Peter Singer's book defending animal interests, *Animal Liberation* (2005), that the question of animal rights as such entered popular discourse. In the 1970s, the work of analytic moral philosophers such as Singer, Tom Regan, and Mary Midgley and a handful of sympathetic legal scholars firmly established animal rights theory as a recognized subfield of contemporary moral theory (Midgley 1995). Today, the animal rights movement is a significant international social movement, and animal studies is a growing field of interdisciplinary study involving thousands of academics working in dozens of different fields.

If there is consensus among animal studies scholars, it is that the long-neglected "animal question" is one of the most important questions of the twenty-first century. Because human exploitation of animals is so deeply woven into the fabric of human cultures—with billions being killed for their flesh and skin, used in scientific laboratories, and incorporated in myriad rituals, from Islamic animal sacrifice to Thanksgiving dinner to the lamb shank bone on Jewish seder plates—the range of possible scholarly concerns is overwhelming. Scholars are now asking questions about the relationship between human and nonhuman animals that simply have not been asked before.

One implication of the existing research is that human approaches to knowledge need to be rethought in a truly fundamental way. Over the past few decades, scientific research has demonstrated far more evolutionary and ontological similarities among humans and other animals—including nonmammalian species—than had been previously thought, at least in modern times. There is no longer any clear or distinct line separating humans from nonhuman animals vis-à-vis such traditional measures of human distinction as tool use, transmission of culture, intelligence, emotion, or even language (Armstrong and Botzler 2008; Stamp Dawkins 2006; Beckoff 2002; Rogers 1998). What we think we know about ourselves as a species turns out to be grounded in deeply embedded ideologies of supremacy that justify the exploitation and killing of those who are perceived to be lacking in reason. As a result, scholars are finding it necessary to revise traditional categories of human understanding, ontology, and science. If the animal rights critique turns out to be justified—that is, if we determine that there are good reasons to reject the exploitation, killing, and domination of other sentient beings and even to proscribe such behaviors by law—then the moral, legal, and economic organization of existing human societies must be found to be deeply flawed and in need of change.

How Do Animal Rights Intersect with Human Rights?

The current animal rights movement derives from the same historical and cultural context as the modern human rights movement—specifically, the bourgeois democratic revolutions of the late eighteenth century that legitimated and codified the belief in natural and inalienable rights. These rights, originally secured for propertied European males, have through popular struggles over time been expanded to include (at least formally) men of color and women. Now animal rights activists and scholars seek to extend legal protections to sentient nonhuman animals—beings capable of suffering and of experiencing the world.

The human rights template has been criticized for its origins in a European Enlightenment tradition that privileges reason (Kennedy 2002). Since the 1990s, a growing number of critical theorists have attacked the very notion of human rights, suggesting that the invocation of "rights" in fact serves to obscure the social inequalities and power differentials that produce international violence and inequality (Žižek 2005). In a similar vein, self-described posthumanist scholars in animal studies have drawn on poststructuralist thought to express skepticism toward animal rights too, effectively seeing rights as an epiphenomenon of state repression. However, other scholars have sought to expand the language of rights to include other sentient beings (Regan 2004; Wise 2005; Francione 2000; Jamieson 2003).

Animal rights scholars thus draw upon the human rights template to gain legal status for nonhuman animals as "moral subjects." But human rights scholars also stand to gain from animal rights scholarship, for example, in helping them gain a better understanding of the ways in which discourses operate to exclude entire categories of subjects. The scholarship in animal studies also reveals some of the underlying contradictions within human rights theory itself. For example, current definitions of human rights have been codified through the United Nations' 1945 Universal Declaration of Human Rights proposing that human beings be granted inalienable rights due to their "reason" and "conscience." Article 1 states, "All human beings are born free and equal in dignity and rights. They are endowed with reason and conscience and should act towards one another in a spirit of brotherhood" (UN 2010).

A variety of animal rights critics, however, have argued that neither moral concern nor legal equality should be contingent upon reason or reasonableness. Peter Singer, for example, pointedly observes that criteria such as the ability to reason or to use language would place not only (some) animals, but also human babies and severely mentally disabled human beings, outside the realm of moral consideration. (We could add the mentally ill and some categories of the human elderly to Singer's list as well.) The current codified justification for human rights in the Universal Declaration of Human Rights therefore excludes most animals from the domain of universal rights and some categories of human beings as well. This problematic logic poses a particular challenge to critics who express skepticism that animals can or should have "rights" at all on grounds that rights bearers must first be capable of knowledgeably entering into a social contract with others in a rights-granting community, which other animals cannot (Cohen 1986; Scruton 2000; Nobis 2004).

Animal rights studies contribute to the analysis of human rights in other ways as well. Historically, particularly in Kantian moral theory, philosophical concern about the human mistreatment of other species was seen as a problem only insofar as sadism and violence toward other animals could lead to abuse of humans

(Regan 2004). However, if it is true, as the psychological and sociological evidence suggests, that causing harm to nonhumans paves the way for the abuse of human beings (Bierne 2009; Linzey 2009; Fitzgerald, Kalof, and Dietz 2009), the reverse may hold true as well: that is, human social hierarchies and forms of power that are anathema to universal human rights, often involving ideologies that justify the conquest over "nature," are also related to enslaving and hurting other sentient beings closely identified with them.

Some animal studies critics maintain that we can better understand the processes of capitalist exploitation and environmental destruction through the lens of animal domination. In *Animal Rights/Human Rights*, for example, David Nibert (2002) shows how the exploitation of workers and animals is mutually reinforcing within capitalist relations. Subsequent scholars have further elaborated on the coconstitution of international capital and animal industries, both at the level of material production and semiosis (Shukin 2009; Torres 2007). Meanwhile, substantial scientific and sociological literatures now address the role of meat production in the global ecological crisis. Factory farming is one of the leading causes of anthropogenic climate change (global warming) and a major polluter of freshwater resources (UNFAO 2006). The international trade in animal flesh has meanwhile led to massive deforestation in the "third world" and to the impoverishment and political oppression of rural workers in Latin America (Nibert 2009). The oppression of other animals is thus intertwined with the oppression of vulnerable human populations.

One recent branch of research has taken up the controversial parallels between human mass extermination of other animals and genocide, including the Holocaust (Patterson 2002; Derrida 2004; Coetzee 1999). Critics ask whether there is a relationship between the beliefs and practices that justify the exploitation and murder of animals and the wholesale extermination of human groups. The common reply to the question of what gives humans the right to dominate and kill billions of other animals is that other species are our inferiors. Specifically, our superiority and right to domination are justified by reference to a precategorical and unchanging "nature." When applied to human beings, however, such beliefs are recognizably fascist and provide schemas for the "animalization" of different human groups (Johnson 2011).

As we see, then, in recent decades animal rights scholarship has begun to push questions about the treatment of nonhuman animals from the philosophical margins to the center of debates about social inequalities, human rights, the origins of violence, and environmental policy. An eclectic community of activists and scholars has posed challenging questions about the relationship of animal domination to racial, gender, disability, and other modes of domination. In *The Dreaded Comparison: Human and Animal Slavery*, Marjorie Spiegel (1988) delineates some of the many overlapping ideological and cultural practices that link human domination of animals with human social domination, that is, slavery. In 1990, Carol Adams focused feminist attention on the overlapping institutional and semiotic structure of patriarchy, the domination of nature, and speciesism in *The Sexual Politics of Meat*. She and other feminist scholars have since extended this critique (Donovan and Adams 1995, 2007). Diverse cultural understandings of human/animal relationships of love and hate and the processes through which we reify formerly conscious beings as "meat" are being analyzed by scholars through new theoretical lenses that illuminate cultural contradictions within human relationships with nonhuman animals (Oliver 2009; Vialles 1994). New questions and perspectives continue to emerge.

THE ANIMAL RIGHTS/HUMAN RIGHTS DIVIDE

The human rights paradigm seems ambiguous or unstable so long as it cannot find a way to incorporate the "other" upon which it has constituted its own identity as a discourse of liberation. By definition, the discourse of human rights evokes a universal claim concerning both the nature of human beings as possessing reason and conscience and the normative juridical and civil framework that such an ontological assertion entails. However, by defining the human against the nonhuman—that is, against beings presumed not to be reasonable or not to have a conscience (or to be self-conscious), hence not to have inherent rights to be free—the discourse re-creates the very conditions of violent exclusion it would undo. The solution to this problem is therefore perhaps to be sought in a "third term" between animal and human rights, or perhaps in a new conception in which the human/animal divide is dissolved altogether. The disambiguation of "human rights" thus stands as one of the greatest challenges facing contemporary theorists.

Despite the many similarities between the animal rights cause, social movements, and human rights campaigns—for example, struggles against the exploitation and oppression of devalued beings, unjust practices of torture and mass killing, and so on—activists in other movements have largely greeted the animal rights movement with skepticism, if not outright hostility. Most of the objections stem from the perception that taking animal interests seriously would "trivialize" human rights and social justice by implicitly drawing an analogy between humans and animals. However, as John Sorenson (2011) points out, such objections, voiced with equal fervor on the political left and right of the spectrum, rest firmly on an irrational speciesist ideology whose starting premise—that other animals simply do not matter— is rooted solely in prejudice against beings perceived to be so fundamentally and biologically different from ourselves that they fall completely outside the sphere of our moral concern.

Too often critics of animal rights scholarship and activism propose a false dichotomy between human or animals rights. It seems obvious that just as the interests of human individuals and groups clash with one another, we might expect human interests to clash with nonhuman ones, particularly in the context of increasing natural resource scarcity and widening habitat destruction due to unchecked human expansion. In fact, in a small number of cases animal rights seem to be in tension with some important human ones—consider, for example, past efforts by animal rights activists to end some seal hunts and whaling by Native peoples. However, few if any scholars today believe that the vast majority of existing human practices of domination and violence toward other animals can be justified on grounds of necessity. Gary Francione rightly observes that of the myriad practices we engage in at the expense of our fellow creatures, "most of the suffering that we impose on animals is completely unnecessary *however* we interpret" the notion of necessity itself (2000, xxiv).

Like the women's movement and the gay rights movement before it, the animal rights movement has been charged with being "bourgeois" or privileged—remaining a predominantly white, middle-class, Western phenomenon. Such characterizations obscure two important points, however. First, the identity of the individuals advancing a particular moral or political claim bears no necessary relation to the underlying validity of that claim. Thus, the fact that many of the leaders of the American abolition movement were white, propertied men was irrelevant to the essential justness of the antislavery cause. Second, it is well established within the social-movements literature that lacking resources, movements do not get very far (McCarthy and Zald 1977; McAdam 1999). Having social privilege can in fact free individuals in ways that enable them more readily to organize into social movements and dedicate their labor and resources to activism. The civil rights movement was organized by the African American middle class, the moderate and radical branches of the women's liberation movement came from middle-class backgrounds, and skilled, employed workers played a pivotal role in the making of the modern labor movement. Perhaps the more relevant point, taking into consideration the intersection of race, gender, and class, concerns the ways in which social location narrows or opens the scope of possibilities and commitments. It should come as no surprise that people of color and the poor (with the majority of the poor being women) may gravitate toward social issues of more immediate material and political concern to them than animal rights.

In fact, however, many animal rights activists and scholars are women, and a significant number of animal rights scholars and activists appear to come from working-class backgrounds. Furthermore, the animal rights issue has recently received more sympathetic attention from communities of color (Harper 2010). Vegans of Color, for example, a new movement organization located in Oakland, California, affirms its commitment to a variety of social causes—"Because we don't have the luxury of being single issue"—a nod to the ways in which identities of race and gender intersect with animal rights (Vegans of Color 2011). Many activists and scholars concerned with animal rights themselves come from diverse research and activist backgrounds that enable them to connect the oppression of other animals to other forms of inequality and injustice.

Finally, the charge that animal rights is solely a "first world" phenomenon ignores the fact that any number of religious and spiritual traditions in regions we now associate with the "third world" have highlighted our moral duties toward other animals for many centuries, including Mahayana Buddhism, Jainism, and Hinduism. While the multiple branches and sects of these religious traditions vary in their doctrinal beliefs toward nonhuman beings, with some advocating vegetarianism and some not, they all defend the principle of practicing nonharm toward other sentient beings, citing both the integrity of the animals themselves and the detrimental impact of killing and eating nonhuman animals on the spiritual development of human societies (Gandhi 2002; Shah 1998).

NEW QUESTIONS AND FUTURE DIRECTIONS

Three broad trends can be discerned in the field. First is the convergence between humanities scholarship and the biological sciences (particularly cognitive ethology, or the study of animal mind) concerning the complexity and phenomenology of nonhuman consciousness and experience, as well as the ethical implications of the new scientific research. Second, there has been increasing politicization of the field in the form of renewed interest in the intersection of speciesism with other forms of social inequality and violence, including capitalism, colonialism, gender oppression, and racism. In recent years, a determined group of activist intellectuals has endeavored to redefine the field as critical animal studies. The Institute of Critical Animal Studies, founded in 2001, now sponsors conferences, publishes an online journal, and has embarked on an international book series. Unifying this approach is the so-called critical theoretical tradition—broadly speaking, the radical, or "left," and feminist traditions in social and political thought. Drawing on, for example, Marx's critique of capital or on contemporary anticolonial theories of race, such critics emphasize the political, social, and historical dimensions of speciesism. They also affirm the traditional critical understanding of theory as a form of praxis for revealing truth and changing social reality (Sanbonmatsu 2011). By the same token, such critics (or a portion of them) emphasize that overcoming speciesism will in turn ultimately require the dissolution of inegalitarian social institutions and modes of development, including patriarchy and capitalism.

A third development is the marked professionalization of the field, which can be seen in the growing number of international conferences, peer-reviewed journals such as *Animal Law*, credentialed courses, and specialized degree-granting programs in the area (including some at the graduate level), as well as the formation of professional societies such as the American Sociological Association's Animals and Society Section (2011) and the online Society and Animals Forum. As in other instances where an advocacy movement has entered academia, however, tensions have emerged over the proper relationship between scholarly inquiry and activist praxis. As an increasingly legitimate and expansive field of scholarly research, animal studies may face the same dilemma or historical crisis confronting similar academic fields that owe their original impetus to social-movement activity: political irrelevance. The academic incorporation and professionalization of the women's movement, for example, came after that movement had crested and gone into decline. Animal studies faces a similar danger that it may refine the instruments of analysis and inquiry but play little role in the actual reform of society and social institutions. However, while some researchers have called for a more "disinterested" approach, the majority of scholars appear to identify their work as contributing to animal rights and social change, and those involved in critical animal studies continue to build bridges between activist and academic communities, with some success.

In any event, the greater challenge for animal rights is not academic irrelevance, per se, but speciesism itself as a mode of production, or way of producing and reproducing human societies. On the one hand, activists and scholars continue to make meaningful headway in extending the idea of rights, with its implicit notion of the dignity and inviolability of the person, to other sentient beings. On the other hand, the economic incentives for maintaining and indeed expanding the global system of species exploitation are stronger than they have ever been. Meanwhile, the cultural and ideological systems reinforcing speciesism show great resilience. Like other social movements for emancipation, then, the animal rights movement faces daunting obstacles in the years ahead, including an inhospitable organizing environment overdetermined by resource scarcity; the social, political, and economic pressures of neoliberalization; global warming; regional war; massive socioeconomic inequality; and the residue of thousands of years of cultural practices that treat the exploitation of nonhuman animals as natural and right.

Yet these social forces also have the potential to spark new scholarly research and ignite movements to explain and challenge the inequitable global distribution of resources, including unsustainable agricultural practices involving "meat" production. While the problem of world hunger is not yet a problem of scarcity but rather one of distribution and production, animal agriculture, as a grossly inefficient and ecologically damaging form of agriculture, has greatly amplified economic inequality and exacerbated the food crisis. Wealthy nations where "meat" consumption is the highest rely heavily on cattle-export economies in the "third world" that utilize agricultural practices that result in deforestation, displaced rural communities, and loss of land for local food production. Mitigating ecological crisis in the twenty-first century will require that "first world" nations phase out cattle-export practices, while also providing the resources for poorer nations to have options to change practices toward animals and the environment. In other words, solving the growing problems of global poverty and environmental destruction in the twenty-first century will require scholars, activists, and citizens to rethink philosophies, religions, and historical practices in very different ways, thereby creating a transformative potential to minimize the suffering and expand the rights of both human and nonhuman animals.

CHAPTER ELEVEN

DISABILITY AND SOCIETY

Jean M. Lynch

One thing is perfectly clear with respect to disability: for a long time there has been an empty seat at the human rights table. Compared to other minority groups, and with respect to related issues of inequality, disability has received very little attention from sociologists and human rights activists. What about disability—compared to other human rights issues, such as sex and gender, labor and labor movements, and the sociology of emotion—leads us so often to disregard it as an issue worthy of our attention? Disability as a human rights issue is simply ignored.

DISABILITY SCHOLARSHIP

Two competing models offer radically different conceptualizations of and perspectives on disability. Each model conceptualizes disability by outlining the causes of and appropriate responses to disability, shapes public perceptions, determines media images, and subsequently suggests the roles and scripts that the able-bodied and the disabled should assume in their interactions with each other. But they do so very differently.

THE MEDICAL MODEL OF DISABILITY

The traditional model, the medical/essentialist/individualist model, is the one primarily subscribed to by medical professionals. It emphasizes individualism. In the medical model, able-bodiedness is a normative ideal against which disability is compared (Switzer 2003). The goals of cure and rehabilitation are paramount (Silvers 1998b); it is assumed that the disabled want, and should want, to become as physically and mentally similar to able-bodied individuals as possible.

In the medical model, disability becomes the person's sole, salient identity; the focus is on the inability to function and individual reliance on others for care (Evans, Assadi, and Herriott 2005). It is assumed that there are no other relevant statuses (e.g., occupational, parental) occupied by those with disabilities, or if there are, they are not important. The person is infantilized and subject to others' perceptions and judgments (Longmore 2003). The true experts, the disabled themselves, remain almost totally excluded from the discourse! In this model, individuals should comply with medical prescriptions regarding treatment plans and goals whether or not they agree with these plans, consider them in their best interest, or perceive them as aligned with their life goals. The power of the professional is paramount, so much so that professionals can exercise social control, including denial of services, if the patient fails to comply with the professionals' directives (Adkins 2003; Barnes and Mercer 2010). Problematically, even decisions about types of medical equipment, definitions of the quality of life, and issues surrounding euthanasia—when based on empirical data—typically derive from data collected from able-bodied respondents (Silvers 1998a; Timmermans 2001). In a society where public perceptions rest on stereotypic assumptions about the disabled, the findings from such questionable data-collection procedures frequently yield policies and programs that further the exclusion and disadvantages already levied against this group (Silvers 1998a).

Indeed, the vast majority of media images are based on the medical model. These images present disability as an individual flaw and a personal tragedy due entirely to natural causes. Living with a disability is a "fate worse than death" (Fleischer and Zames 2001; Longmore 2003). Normalization depicts the disabled as "other," as the victims of an arbitrary fate who, if they attend to and comply with medical directives, can overcome their inferiority (Fleischer and Zames 2001). The disabled person is responsible for managing or controlling the consequences of the disability. The patient is exhorted to "psychologically manage" the disease, minimizing the effects of the disability as much as possible (Barnes and Mercer 2010).

Among many other things, the medical model fails to consider external sources that impact disability and does not attend to the conflicts embedded in the social relations between the disabled and the able-bodied; the focus is on changing the individual, not on modifying the environment—an environment that typically reflects only the dominant group's preferences (Silvers 1998a). The medical model fails to capture the experience of disability, including the goals of many with disability who focus on objectives other than cure. No attention is paid to the social, economic, and physical barriers that limit the opportunities of the disabled or to the conflicts embedded in the social relations between the disabled and the able-bodied (Silvers 1998a).

THE SOCIAL MODEL OF DISABILITY

The alternative model is the social model, which views disability as a creation of society. This model emphasizes inclusion and accessibility through modification of the environment (Switzer 2003). Social models of disability propose that disability is socially constructed and that the barriers to disability can be matters of physical accessibility or created by negative attitudes of the able-bodied toward those with disability. The impact of these barriers can only be reduced through social change

(Adkins 2003). Unlike the medical model, in which the individual is responsible for the disability and for failures that result from it, in the social model, society is at fault for the problems those with disability confront (Pfeiffer 2001).

In the social model, the professional is not the expert; nor are the able-bodied considered a normative ideal. The experts are those who are disabled, and their voices and experiences are central. The social model encourages arrangements that promote maximum mainstream social and economic participation. Rather than a focus on cure, maximizing the potential and life satisfaction of individuals in accordance with their own preferences is paramount (Asch 2001; Barnes 1996; Barnes and Mercer 2010; Silvers 1998b). The social model recognizes that people with disability are stigmatized and negatively labeled. Such recognition justifies the need for disability to be included in broader human rights conversations.

Recently, the limitations of the social model have been recognized within disability studies (Barnes and Mercer 2010; Shakespeare and Watson 2001). The social-constructionist model originally provided advantages over the medical model—primarily in making the voices of the disability community central to the conversation on disability. However, the model ultimately excludes much of what is essential to the lived experience of disability. For example, the model ignores impairment (physical or mental abnormalities or functional loss), recognizing only disability (the result of the former; a restriction or lack of an ability considered "normal" for a typical person [Barbotte, Guillemin, and Chau 2002]). There are other limitations in using the social model as the sole perspective on disability. The model does not lend itself to empirical observation as the concepts are not easily operationalized. It fails to recognize that those with disabilities are a heterogeneous group—for instance, in creating a solution to one person's issues we might create additional obstacles for another individual (Barnes and Mercer 2010; Shakespeare and Watson 2001). Perhaps most significantly, the model does not lend itself to the development of policy resolutions or strategies of resistance.

Despite these limitations, the social model shifts attention away from the individual and explicitly emphasizes social responsibility. It suggests an important alternative to the perception of disability as a tragic, individual phenomenon and instead emphasizes a recognition of social responsibility. Most importantly, it helps mobilize the disability community (Barnes and Mercer 2010), which hopefully will result in the community's ability to resist discrimination and to demand essential human rights.

RESEARCH ON DISABILITY

Disability studies differ across cultural contexts. For example, in Britain, disability studies were originally located within sociology, whereas in the United States disability scholarship originated in literature and rhetoric (Gordon and Rosenblum 2001). These beginnings have impacted future concerns with disability, including which models predominated then—and now. Since sociologists emphasize the social-constructionist model in considering minority groups (e.g., race, gender, sex, and age) and variations in privilege, it is surprising when people with disabilities are not included as a minority group. At least in the United States, disability is still frequently presented under the medical model and conceptualized as an individual rather than a social experience.

Space constraints prevent an exhaustive review of research findings; however, we can briefly present key findings from areas in which the most research has been completed. First, there has been a plethora of studies (e.g., Keller and Siegrist 2010; Leasher, Miller, and Gooden 2009; Ouellette-Kuntz et al. 2010; Scheid 2005) on attitudes toward persons with disabilities in a variety of settings (e.g., employment, educational institutions) and among different populations (e.g., college students). These studies provide specific understandings of how people perceive people with disability. For example, younger and more educated individuals hold more positive attitudes toward those with intellectual disabilities (Ouellette-Kuntz et al. 2010). People who like other people have more positive perceptions of people with physical disabilities; the reverse is true for those who believe in a just world (Keller and Siegrist 2010). We know that direct experiences, indirect experiences, and the attitudes of one's primary social group toward people with disabilities are central to an individual's attitude formation (Farnell and Smith 1999; Keller and Siegrist 2010). In addition, studies indicate that the amount of control we have over contact with people with disabilities and the amount of information we possess about disability both influence our attitudes (Krahe and Altwasser 2006; Pettigrew and Tropp 2006; Yuker 1994). For example, the less control we exert over an interaction, the more negative our attitudes, and the more intimate the contact situation, the less positively we feel about it. The more knowledge we have about disability, the more positive our attitudes (Berry and Jones 1991; Evans, Assadi, and Herriott 2005; Krahe and Altwasser 2006).

Second, there is a substantial amount of literature on specific types of disabilities (e.g., learning disabilities). These studies are of use to individuals diagnosed with those disabilities, their allies, and professionals who are invested in those particular disabilities (Dudley-Marling 2004; Phemister and Crewe 2004). Unfortunately, these findings offer little understanding in general about the lives of those with disability and how best to advance our knowledge of disability as a human rights issue.

Third, a moderate amount of literature describes the disability movement over time. Some of these findings provide an historical overview of the growth of the community and demonstrate the ways in which the disability community attempts to advance its cause (Dowse 2001; Foster-Fishman et al. 2007; Pfeiffer 1993). Fourth, the Americans with Disabilities Act has received a fair amount of attention, including evaluations of how it has influenced certain types of cases (e.g., employment cases) and how it has helped or hindered the disability community (e.g., Blau and Moncada 2006; Colker 2005; Fleischer and Zames 2001; Switzer 2003). Recent scholarship describes the changes made to the Americans with Disabilities Act to alleviate some of the initial drawbacks it posed for the disability community (Long 2008).

Two additional categories of literature have received significant attention and offer interesting insights for disability and the human rights agenda. First are content analyses of various genres. This work ranges from images of disability in children's books (Matthews 2009) to the presentations of disability in films (Black and Pretes 2007) and in the news (Haller, Dorries, and Rahn 2006). Second, euthanasia and eugenics have received a disproportionate share of attention, at least considering the scant amount of such scholarship that has been conducted within disability studies or by those with expertise in disability studies (Shakespeare 2006). Rather, these studies often rely on a medical perspective and are conducted by members of the able-bodied population (Grue 2010).

DISABILITY RESEARCH AND CONTENT ANALYSIS

One of the most popular kinds of sociological research on disability is content analyses of various media genres. These studies (e.g., Black and Pretes 2007; Safran 2001; Switzer 2003) are particularly instructive because they demonstrate how the social construction of disability occurs. Content analysis examines one or more media genres looking for recurring words or themes; after analyzing a sample of a particular genre, the researcher combines similar words or themes into categories that provide an overall picture of the images that depict a particular type of person, issue, event, and so on. Content analyses of media are instructive, as they can tell us about public perceptions and public attitudes. It is through the media and most often through films that the public is provided with what is often their only experience with disability. Safran, who analyzed six Academy Award–winning films that featured disability and war, argues that films "project representations of how individuals fit into a nation's social and political landscape" (2001, 223). These images are consistent with the medical model portrayal of disability; they depict disability as tragic (Switzer 2003) and the disabled as frequently incapable of adjusting to these tragedies and in need of help from the able-bodied to adapt, to provide care, or to access cures (Longmore 2003). The disabled are cast as unidimensional and rarely seen as anything but their disability; they rarely live successfully, whether success is measured occupationally, educationally, or through the ability to create or maintain intimate relationships (Black and Pretes 2007). Worse, the media provides many audiences with what may be their only socialization into relationships between the able-bodied and the disabled. Incapable of adjusting to their own life circumstances, the disabled must depend on the able-bodied, who are shown as emotionally, intellectually, and socially superior.

Some images that are perceived as positive by the able-bodied are considered by many members of the disability community as evidence of stereotypes and detrimental to the community and to persons with disabilities. One such image is the "supercrip." Often portrayed in fictional films and presented in news stories as well, supercrips are individuals who not only live very successfully with a disability (a fate worse than death) but also accomplish some spectacular feat (e.g., climb Mount Everest, play the violin with their tongue) (Black and Pretes 2007). This is comparable to Horatio Alger stories about people who pull themselves up by their bootstraps and attain enormous success and wealth despite being raised in an environment of extreme poverty. The ideology behind these messages is clear:

disabilities can be overcome if one simply works at it hard; those who fail to do so are just not trying enough.

Unfortunately, such imagery does disservice to the disabled. First, these presentations bear little connection to the experiences and the lives of the majority of those who live with disabilities. Second, these images provide the public with unrealistic standards that are then used to downplay the very real obstacles and barriers that do confront those with disabilities. Third, they also provide the able-bodied public with an "out," an image that they can assume would reflect their reality were they to become disabled.

With respect to the social construction of disability, the media is used to perpetuate ableist images of disability and send messages to the audience about what disability is like, what the lives of those with disability are about, how those with disability should behave and live, and how those who are able-bodied should perceive and treat the disabled. The function of these images is to absolve able-bodied individuals of any responsibility for the disabled and for the obstacles and barriers that confront individuals with disability.

Certain images of disability are particularly prevalent and becoming more frequent over time (Black and Pretes 2007). These images communicate the message that death through suicide or other means is an intelligent and responsible solution to the problem of living with a disability, one that a reasonable individual would choose. Increasingly films depict individuals with disabilities as wanting and fighting for the right to die. In a recent content analysis of films, almost half contained attempted, successful, or assisted suicide, and many included the "right to die" as a major theme (Black and Pretes 2007); media portrayal of disability as a fate worse than death is quite common (Black and Pretes 2007; Fleischer and Zames 2001; Longmore 2003). This evokes the fear in the disability community that the "right to decide to live and die may become a duty to die" (Mackelprang and Mackelprang 2005, 323). In reality, the disabled find themselves in situations where they need to fight for the "right to live." Although most people with disability may experience a brief period during which adjusting to the disability is difficult, research on the lives of the disabled and memoirs demonstrate the majority of those with disability lead happy and successful lives and would not choose suicide as an option.

EUTHANASIA AND EUGENICS

Recent questions posed by bioethicists include, What is a life of quality? Are there life situations not of value? Should this life be saved? These questions have intruded into the scholarship on disability, particularly that which considers eugenics and euthanasia (Asch 2001; Koch 2004). Exploring what is meant by human rights, Blau and Moncada (2005) speak as if euthanasia only exists in cultures removed from our own. Furthermore, they argue that in discussions of human rights, the focus is "everyday rights," not "human rights violations *in extremis*." Issues such as euthanasia and eugenics are not typically tied to human rights; yet for people with disability, they are very much aligned with their human rights. The suggestion that the lives of those with disabilities might be of lesser value than those of the able-bodied must be considered under the human rights umbrella. Many disability-studies scholars and some sociologists (e.g., Gordon and Rosenblum 2001; Grue 2010; Jotkowitz, Glick, and Gesundheit 2008; Koch 2004) claim that threats of euthanasia and eugenics are increasingly encroaching on the lives of those with disability.

Recent scholars suggest that contemporary thoughts about euthanasia and disability are not unlike the perspectives seen during the Nazi regime (Grue 2010; Jotkowitz, Glick, and Gesundheit 2008). Grue (2010) claims that we pacify ourselves by asserting that the German euthanasia programs and ideologies of eugenics disappeared after World War II, but she admonishes that there is little difference between our culture and Germany of the past, or between the physicians involved in genocide then and our own present-day physicians who support assisted suicide and link decisions about euthanasia to disability.

Research demonstrates that our evaluation of the value of a person's life is influenced by the fact of his or her disability (Fleischer and Zames 2001). For example, Mackelprang and Mackelprang (2005) indicate that favorable judgments are more likely to be handed down in right-to-die cases when the individual who requests the "right to die" is disabled. It is not that individuals should not be able to choose whether to live or to die; it is that our responses should not be tied to whether a person is disabled.

Many contemporary decisions about euthanasia rely on quality-of-life measures; yet these are not valid operationalizations of the will to live. Asch (2001) reports that persons with disabilities who seek to terminate their lives are typically recently disabled. Having lived in a world where media images portray disability as tragic and the lives of those with disability as miserable, is it any wonder that the onset of disability is accompanied by a wish to commit suicide? Given time, adjustments in accessibility, new learning, and attitude changes, most persons with disabilities quickly change their mind and choose to live. Most persons with disabilities describe their lives as happy and successful, a description most medical professionals and the public do not envision, given the lack of images that portray such a perspective (Asch 2001). Our reluctance to consider persons with disabilities as experts on living with a disability and our overreliance on physicians' views and on public perceptions of disability do not bode well for the future of euthanasia of the disabled.

Timmermans (2001) found that hospital medical staff typically consider certain patients as socially dead; although biologically alive, they are treated as if they were corpses. In resuscitation attempts, disabled patients are much more likely to be defined as socially dead than are able-bodied patients and more likely to be the recipients of passive euthanasia. In interviews with medical staff, attitudes toward the value of life for those with disability parallel public perceptions of disability (Timmermans 2001).

Although many persons with disability support issues of choice, there is a legitimate fear that the "right to die" will become a "duty to die" (Mackelprang and Mackelprang 2005). Already such pressure is placed on people with disabilities (Fleischer and Zames 2001). Under the capitalist system, the disabled are presumed to be living in nonexploitable and therefore valueless bodies. There is little hope that the public, holding the negative attitudes they do, will lend support if (or when) cost-benefit analyses are applied to life-and-death choices about the disabled. Hockenberry (1995) argues that much more effort is put into cure than into integrating persons with disabilities into society and suggests that the disabled are made to feel that if they cannot be cured, they have a civic responsibility to die.

The same issues exist in the area of eugenics. The fact that we have tests that allow people to ensure that they will not bear children with certain conditions can be perceived either as progress or as encouragement to eventually produce a purely able-bodied society. The assumption is that such a society would be a good one. There is no discussion about diversity; nor is there suggestion of the benefits that the disabled provide to society. The message to the public and to the disability community is clear: having individuals with disabilities is something to be avoided at all costs.

I believe we cannot discuss eugenics or euthanasia in any morally responsible way until we first disseminate accurate, realistic, and complete information about disability. Presently, decision-makers' views are informed by media images that fail to depict any objective view of what life with a disability is like and, instead, rely on public perceptions of disability and medical professionals' views. These perceptions generate unrealistic fears of disability. Severely lacking are the perceptions of those who live with a disability and accurate recognition of the social, economic, and environmental barriers they confront. It is one thing to decide not to have a child with a disability based on illusions and incomplete and misguided information. It is another decision entirely when one has been privy to complete objective, scientific, and experiential testimony and knowledge that includes both positive and negative information about the reality of that disability.

Singer's claim that "killing a disabled infant is not morally equivalent to killing a person; very often is not morally wrong at all" (1993, 191) is typical of the thinking that accompanies decisions about eugenics and euthanasia. If we replaced the phrase "disabled infant" with another identity or group, there would be moral outrage. Yet we live in a world where we allow decisions that reinforce the medical model and support the notion that it is disability, not discrimination against persons with disabilities, that we should eliminate. Whether eugenics or euthanasia is morally justifiable is beyond the confines of this chapter. It is essential, however, to consider whether we can tie eugenics and euthanasia to the fact of a person's disability or any other minority status. Making a decision about quality of life, especially when the majority of the information is based on possibly questionable operationalizations of such (if any at all), cannot be justified.

WHAT HUMAN RIGHTS OFFER DISABILITY STUDIES

As noted above, we lack a model that captures the experience of disability. The medical model is clearly deficient, but recently the disability community has recognized that the social-constructionist model has outlived its usefulness (Barnes and Mercer 2010). Originally the latter helped to mobilize the disability community; however, it is not a comprehensive model in that it fails to include significant aspects of being disabled, most notably impairment.

One way in which human rights scholarship benefits disability studies is the capabilities approach. This model suggests that human capabilities are universal and that people have the right, and therefore must be afforded opportunities, to develop their capabilities (Sen 1999b). Burchardt (2004) suggests that the capabilities model offers a useful complement to (not a replacement for) the social-constructionist approach. The strength of the capabilities approach is its focus on ends and opportunities rather than on means and the "typical" or actual. That is, the model suggests that mobility and accessibility are important; less important are the means through which those are achieved. It matters little whether mobility is achieved by walking or that accessibility is possible through sight; what is significant is that each equal human being, disabled or able-bodied, is afforded opportunities for accessibility and mobility (Blau and Moncada 2009).

It is difficult to discuss what else human rights offers disability since disability is so rarely considered under the human rights banner. One possibility is that human rights has much to offer people with disability—as for all minority groups—yet, because of its exclusion, it is difficult to identify specific aspects of the human rights agenda and its implications for studying persons with disabilities. One obvious priority is to include disability in the human rights conversation and for human rights advocates to place people with disabilities and the disability movement on an equal footing with other rights movements. People with disabilities must be seen as suffering not from an individual tragedy but from the ways in which disability has been socially constructed and people with disability have been denied opportunities to develop their capabilities and to participate equally in social, economic, and political life. We rely on human rights activists to promote human rights; yet they seem loath to include those with disability among the litany of groups for whom they advocate. Even though people with disability are clearly the "other," the activists who should know better ignore disability and avoid the "messiness" that accompanies it. We need to figure out why and what to do about this.

THE FUTURE OF DISABILITY AND HUMAN RIGHTS

The most pressing issue that faces disability as a human rights issue is to ensure that people who consider themselves human rights activists understand how and in what way disability is a human rights issue, along with gender, sex, poverty, race, age, and other identity characteristics that are routinely denied privilege. Currently, disability is an afterthought in human rights conversations and considerations. Some suspect this is because disability is one of the only statuses that can be entered at any moment without warning. Why it is avoided matters less than the fact of its avoidance and the necessity of rendering this avoidance obsolete.

We need to encourage human rights advocates to become allies to people with disabilities. Allies are "members of dominant social groups who are working to end the system of oppression that gives them greater privilege and power based on their social-group membership" (Broido 2000, 3). The ally identity is a unique status chosen by dominant group members who work for social justice, who believe in a society based on equity and justice. According to scholarship on the adoption of an ally identity, working as an ally, realizing and helping to break down the system that benefits dominant groups and disadvantages minority groups, liberates everyone (Bell 1997; Edwards 2006). As Freire (2000) and Brod (1987) argue, members of both minority groups and the dominant group suffer from participation in systems of oppression. History instructs us that most struggles for civil rights have been accomplished through the coordinated efforts of the "other" and their allies. Successful movements and achievements along the way owe much to the efforts and struggles of allies who had and offered the resources, power, and privilege to help groups denied privilege and human rights.

More research needs to be conducted on issues of disability. So much of the extant work was conducted from a medical-model perspective rather than from a social-constructionist or capabilities model. As a result, we have little substantive information regarding the social, environmental, and economic barriers that produce difficulties for people with disabilities. Nor do we know the ways in which interaction and systems of oppression are created and maintained between people with disabilities and people who are able-bodied. We need to know much more about how disability is socially constructed and why. We need to discover how to provide opportunities for people to realize their capabilities and opportunities. Disability deserves a seat at the human rights table as these discussions evolve.

Two

INSTITUTIONS IN SOCIETY

CHAPTER TWELVE

MEDICAL SOCIOLOGY

Susan W. Hinze and Heidi L. Taylor

Medical sociology emerged as a distinct subfield in the early to mid-twentieth century as sociologists brought their research skills to medical settings, studying doctor-patient relationships, the expansion of medicine as a profession, and the organization of medical systems, health care, and health policy (Bird, Conrad, and Fremont 2000; Bloom 2000). While the establishment of a formal American Sociological Association (ASA) section in 1959 is relatively recent, the intellectual roots of the specialty date back to the 1840s in classical works such as Friedrich Engels's writings on the health of factory workers and German pathologist Rudolph Virchow's work on the social origins of illness (Waitzkin 1981). Indeed, the struggle for economic and political rights for the working classes in the mid-nineteenth and early twentieth centuries was intertwined with concerns about the health status and rights of workers and citizens.

Fast-forward to the present, and medical sociology in the early twenty-first century is one of the largest subfields in the ASA, continuing to expand and diversify at a rapid speed as scholars explore societal consequences of the swift growth of the institution of medicine, the organizational fluidity of the health-care system, and the rapidly changing health conditions of global citizens. The internationalization of sociology is evident in publications by medical sociologists around the world in the past two decades, although the use of a human rights perspective within medical sociology is infrequent (see Dumas and Turner 2007 and Turner 2006 for exceptions).

While medical sociologists have rarely used the language of human rights in framing their scholarship, work within medical sociology contributes to a human rights framework in three important ways: (1) by providing evidence of and explanations for the unequal distribution of health within and between countries; (2) by presenting comparative research on access to health care and the evolution of health policies; and (3) by highlighting the dangers of the expansion of (Western) biomedicalization and the concomitant rise in corporate power—processes that may threaten the right to health, health care, and self-determination at local, national, and global levels.

BARRIERS TO THE RIGHT TO HEALTH

Article 25 of the Universal Declaration of Human Rights (UN General Assembly, 1948) specifies, "Everyone has the right to a standard of living adequate for the health and well-being of himself and his family, including ... medical care ... and the right to security in the event of ... sickness [and/or] disability." Implicit in the human rights framework is an understanding that the protection and promotion of human rights is essential to the protection and promotion of health (Mann 1996). Others have eloquently called for the protection and promotion of health as fundamental to protecting and promoting human rights (Farmer 2010). Clearly, human rights and the right to health are reciprocal and mutually constitutive. In short, the right to health is a basic human right, a sentiment captured by the language used in the Constitution of the World Health Organization (1948) specifying the enjoyment of the highest attainable standard of health as a fundamental right of every human being. Furthermore, the constitution champions equal development of the promotion of health and control of disease and the extension of the benefits of medical, psychological, and related knowledge to all.

How close are we—as a global community—to meeting the standards laid out by the Universal Declaration of Human Rights and the World Health Organization? Medical sociologists have helped to answer this question by documenting the disproportionate burden of illness, disability, and early mortality for certain individuals, groups, countries, and regions. Furthermore, medical sociologists explore the social conditions that produce health inequalities or violate the "right-to-health" principle. Virchow asked scholars to collect medical statistics in order to "weigh life for life, and see where the dead lie thicker, among the workers or among the privileged" (1848, 182). In general, decades of empirical research reveal the short answer to be "among the workers," or among individuals, groups, countries, and regions where social power is low (Marmot 2004; Robert and House 2000; Wilkinson 1992, 1996). The enduring survival gap between those in the upper versus the lower social echelons persists across times and place, even as causes of mortality shift from infectious disease to chronic illness due to rising standards of living, nutrition, and sanitation (Olshansky and Ault 1986; Omran 1971).

A major contribution by medical sociologists to our understanding of health inequalities is the focus on macro-level social structural conditions, rather than genetic, biological, and psychological conditions, that contribute to poor health. Social scientists employing a wide range of methodologies have used within-country, between-country, and individual-level data analysis to understand how macro-level forces (e.g., political economy, social-class relations, racism) and micro-level forces (e.g., individual risk factors, social support, patient-provider relationships) together contribute to health inequalities.

For the better part of two centuries, persistent health inequalities have closely mirrored social hierarchies, and sociologists (along with epidemiologists, health-service researchers, public health scholars, and others) have tracked how and why poor health accumulates in poor communities. One well-established empirical regularity in population health is the strong association between per capita income and life expectancy. Life expectancy rises rapidly with increasing GNP per capita, but the relationship holds only up to a certain level, after which there are diminishing returns (Wilkinson 1992, 1996). Income distribution within the country is also of critical importance; countries with the smallest income differentials have the highest average life expectancies.

From a human rights perspective, then, the right to health is more easily accomplished when citizens have a basic level of economic stability and live in countries or regions with less economic inequality. Farmer (2003) reminds us that macro-level forces, including global class relations, can do "violence" to individuals and communities by depriving them of the conditions necessary for good health. Analyses of health and medicine that incorporate critical views of class relations are important contributions by sociologists. For example, Navarro asks, how do "class structure, class exploitation, and class struggle appear, reproduce, and affect the health and quality of life of our populations?" (2004, 92–93).

Also important are studies using individual-level data, such as occupational indicators, income, and education, to reveal how poor social and economic circumstances affect health throughout the life course (House et al. 1994; Mirowsky, Ross, and Reynolds 2000; Robert and House 2000). In their watershed piece, Link and Phelan (1995) propose a theory of fundamental causes to explain persistent inequalities in overall health and mortality across time, despite the changing nature of diseases and risk factors.

Sociological research on individual-level health inequalities supports policies that address fundamental or root causes of poor health. Providing high-quality educational opportunities for all would go a long way toward improving health, as would protections against poverty and economic instability. Improving health also requires protecting workers and providing the right to autonomy on the job (Marmot 2004).

Other social factors that place people at risk for poor health outcomes include race/ethnicity, gender, and sexuality. Early sociologist W. E. B. DuBois (1899) implicated racial inequality as a social factor in the high levels of poor health for blacks. Unfortunately, DuBois's insights were overlooked because, for many decades, racial differences in health were generally viewed as biological (due to genetic differences) or as behavioral (due to lifestyle choices). However, we now have a wealth of evidence to show how one's life circumstances—especially in confronting classism, racism, and sexism—are increasingly viewed as leading sources of illness and death in the United States (Krieger et al. 1993; Krieger 2000). While recognizing race as a social construction and not a biological reality, most contemporary medical sociologists still use race and ethnicity as variables in research (for criticisms, see LaVeist 2002) primarily because, while imperfect, they highlight the disproportionate burden of disease, disability, and death borne by African Americans, Hispanic Americans, Native Americans, and some Asian Americans. In their overview of racial and ethnic inequalities in health, Williams and Sternthal (2010) illustrate how social exposures combine with biology to affect the social distribution of disease. They emphasize the disproportionate impact of socioeconomic status on certain racial/ethnic groups at the individual level (e.g., lower incomes, less education, less wealth, higher unemployment, increased occupational hazards) and community level (e.g., racial segregation, economic hardship, concentrated disadvantage, environmental toxins, poor-quality housing, criminal victimization). As well, they implicate racism—expressed through institutional and individual-level discrimination, stigma, racial prejudice, and stereotypes—as detrimental to the health of certain racial/ethnic minority groups.

Medical sociologists have been at the forefront in their examination of how gender "gets under the skin" with dramatic consequences for the health of women and men. In short, women get sicker, but men die quicker: in almost every nation, women live longer than men but have higher morbidity rates and a diminished quality of life in later years (Lorber and Moore 2002; Rieker, Bird, and Lang 2010). Much of this difference can be captured by social factors such as higher rates of alcoholism, substance abuse, and death by homicide and accident in part to due to expectations surrounding the male gender role or, as contemporary gender scholars phrase it, the risks of "doing gender" in line with hegemonic masculinity. In nations facing extreme poverty, both women and men die at relatively early ages, with women being particularly at risk because they often have fewer resources, such as education, food, and medical care (Rieker, Bird, and Lang 2010). Women in poor countries and poor women in better-off countries are at higher risk for complications from childbearing.

On a global level, members of the LGBT community experience higher rates of physical violence, suicide, depression, substance abuse, and other indicators of psychological distress than do heterosexuals (Herek and Berrill 1992; Krieger and Sidney 1997). Also, transwomen and transmen are especially at risk of homicide.

Since health disparities reflect social relations between people and not inherent qualities possessed by them, scholars caution against the use of certain variables, such as race/ethnicity or gender, as "explanatory." Smaje writes, "People do not experience the world through a set of partial coefficients, but as embodied social actors" (2000, 116). As sociologists have long asserted, these social factors are intertwined and intersect in important ways. For example, differences in health status by race/ethnicity often disappear when we adjust for social class; yet at each socioeconomic level, blacks have worse health status than whites (Williams and Sternthal 2010). Scholars employing a feminist, intersectionality perspective remind us to pay attention to how the mutually constitutive dimensions of race/ethnicity, gender, sexual orientation, and social class influence health (e.g., Hinze, Lin, and Andersson 2011; Richardson and Brown 2011).

Removing barriers to good health for members of marginalized groups necessitates bringing attention to racism and sexism as features of institutions. For example, policies and practices adopted by governments and corporations contribute to racial segregation and environmental racism (Bullard 1993; LaVeist 2002; Takechi, Walton, and Leung 2010), including toxic dumps and increased risk of pollution in certain areas (Brown 2000; Brown and Mikkelsen 1990). Medicine as an institution is not exempt. Historically, health-care providers in the Western world have held prejudices and biases that have resulted in poorer care for members of certain groups, including racial/ethnic minorities, women, members of the LGBT community, and people of lower socioeconomic status (Hinze et al. 2009; Sarver et al. 2003; McKinlay 1996).

In summary, health inequalities are not inevitable but are inherent in social systems where distributions of power are vastly unequal. As the next section makes clear, health services are not evenly distributed either among social groups within societies or between nations (Quadagno 2005; Wright and Perry 2010). After providing an overview of critical scholarship by medical sociologists on how nations finance and deliver health care, we consider how the spread of biomedical approaches to health is a risky proposition and a potential threat to human rights.

National Approaches to Health Care as a Human Right

The constitutions of 67 percent of UN member nations make provisions guaranteeing the right to universal health care, reflecting broad ideological support for the Universal Declaration of Human Rights. Unfortunately, no association has been found between a nation's constitutional pledge and its financial investment in health-care resources (Kinney and Clark 2004). Without concrete government action, affirming the right to health care is an empty promise if access is limited, quality is poor, and cost is prohibitive. The constitution of Haiti, for example, decrees, "The state has the absolute obligation to guarantee the right to life and health." This assurance is impossible in a country plagued by government corruption and economic and political instability (Farmer 2011).

In the struggle to ensure population health, nations must balance three inherently competing goals: equity, cost containment, and quality. Which of these goals becomes central to shaping a country's system, and how, is influenced by each nation's ideological, social, political, and economic realities (Gran 2008; Mechanic 1997; Wright and Perry 2010). Medical sociologists have developed useful comparative frameworks for examining national health-care systems and advancing research into the linkages between health outcomes and health-delivery systems of different countries (Kikuzawa, Olafsdottir, and Pescosolido 2008; Matcha 2003; Mechanic and McAlpin 2010; Stevens 2001). While not grounded in rights-based discourse, this comparative work is increasingly turning from examination of structural components to exploring principles and ideals underlying health-care systems. Challenging assumptions about the value neutrality of medical policy and practice lays bare culturally specific notions about distributive justice and human rights.

The growing comparative focus in medical sociology is also useful for understanding points of convergence and divergence between national approaches to health-care delivery and the multiplicity of factors shaping a country's system (Stevens 2001). In a landmark twenty-one-nation study, Kikuzawa, Olafsdottir, and Pescosolido (2008) found that residents of "Insurance Model" nations such as the United States, with a small state role in the provision of health care, are much less likely than people in National Health Service countries to agree that government should be responsible for health care. Yet a majority of people in countries such as the United States retain a belief in the fundamental right to health and health care (Jenkins and Hsu 2008). Medical sociologists can provide empirical data and theoretical underpinnings to illuminate the disjuncture between the moral convictions of individuals and health-care policies that do not uphold these values.

Along with international comparisons of health-care systems, it is essential to examine the rights of those individuals who remain on the sidelines of health-care policy. Though citizenship guarantees health-care services in most industrialized nations, indigenous and immigrant populations are often denied equal access to care (Turner 1993). Medical sociologists have chronicled health-policy barriers to access for indigenous populations, including the Roma in Europe (Sienkiewicz 2010), Aboriginals in Canada and Australia (Benoit, Carroll, and Chaudhry 2003), and Native Americans in the United States (Garroutte 2001, 2003), among others.

Of particular concern, from a health and human rights perspective, is the absence of provisions for illegal immigrant populations in almost all areas of policy. Even in the European Union, with a newly ratified health and human rights treaty, only Spain guarantees care for illegal immigrants (Romero-Ortuno 2004). Immigrants, both legal and illegal, face ineligibility and may forgo health services due to fears of arrest or deportation. Individual-level barriers include lack of knowledge of available services, language barriers, and cultural insensitivity of providers (Shuval 2001). Meeting the health needs of immigrant populations requires not only extending the right to health care to noncitizens and working to improve access for this population but providing a broader bundle of services, including translation, housing, education, and occupational opportunities. Immigrant health is particularly a problem for nations with large numbers of refugees (e.g., Kenya), rapidly growing immigrant populations (e.g., Spain), and nations such as the United States with millions of undocumented immigrants.

As the only industrialized nation that does not guarantee health-care access to all its citizens, the United States is uniquely situated in the debate over the right to health care. With health-care spending standing at nearly 18 percent of the GDP, the US system relies on a patchwork of public and private services that, despite being the most expensive system in the world, leaves 50 million people, or 17 percent of the US population, without health care. Fully one-third of young adults are uninsured, and at all ages insurance status is highly associated with race/ethnicity, with 14 percent of whites, 22 percent of blacks, and 34 percent of Latinos lacking health insurance (Streeter et al. 2011) The uninsured face higher levels of morbidity and mortality, delayed treatment, and inferior medical care; they have poorer medical outcomes and are more likely to be denied care (Chirayath 2007; Quesnel-Vallee 2004). While the 2010 Obama health-care legislation increases access to care, it does little to address health-care quality or cost, and many foresee a potential shift toward explicit rationing due to insufficient resources and health-care personnel to care for millions of newly insured.

Nations with universal health-care systems prioritize the goal of access, treating health care as a collective good and containing costs through implicit rationing based on medical need. However, the value placed on individual responsibility in the United States renders health care a commodity, not a right, and services are rationed on the basis of income instead of medical need (Jost 2003). Though the highest burden of disease lies with the poor, it is the wealthier and healthier Americans who "earn" the privilege of accessing the medical care required to maintain their physical and mental well-being. While policy-makers in the United States decry the rationing used in universal health-care systems, medical sociologists have been on the forefront of demonstrating ways in which explicit rationing occurs at multiple levels in the US system (Mechanic 1997; Stevens 2001). Medical sociologists (among others) point to the failure of competition in the medical marketplace to control costs and argue that health care cannot be considered a commodity because ill patients are not rational actors who can "shop around" for medical care as they can with other goods and services (Matcha 2003; Mechanic 1997). Navarro (2004) reminds us that wherever the corporate class is very strong and the working class is very weak, you find weak welfare states in which social services, including health care, are paltry. Without dismantling the market-driven commodification of health care, the US health-care system will stand at odds with the values of distributive justice and human rights.

The promotion of health care as a human right cannot be achieved through national health-care policy alone. Recent studies in Canada and the United Kingdom remind us that universal health-care systems do not ameliorate health disparities (Wright and Perry 2010). Access to health care must be coupled with political and financial investments in other "life-affirming opportunities" that protect disadvantaged populations from daily acts of structural violence (Matcha 2003, 184; Farmer 2003). Research in medical sociology confirms that the poor have difficulties seeking medical care if they do not have transportation, cannot leave work, or do not have child care. Physical and mental well-being suffer if housing is substandard, food is unsafe, crime goes unchecked, air quality is poor, working conditions are dangerous, and employment is scarce. Governing bodies at local, national, and global levels must recognize their role in the protection and promotion of health and take proactive steps to uphold the human rights of their peoples.

EXPANSION OF (WESTERN) BIOMEDICALIZATION

As the above sections make clear, medical sociologists have been at the forefront of research on inequalities in health and health care, providing contextual explanations that emphasize ideological barriers as well as social, political, and economic structures. In this section, we explore how a primary focus on biomedical solutions has potential to violate the "first, do no harm" axiom taught to health-care providers early in their medical educations. In short, medical sociologists have cautioned that the ascendancy, dominance, and expansion of biomedical approaches to health and illness, along with increasing commodification of medical care, carry significant risks to local, national, and global health, in part because they eclipse contextual explanations but also because they raise the specter of biomedical colonialism. Whether they frame it as medicalization (Conrad 2007), biomedicalization (Clark et al. 2003), geneticization (Lippman 1991; Shostak and Freese

2010), or pharmaceuticalization (Abraham 2010), medical sociologists and other scholars of trends in medicine warn of the dangers inherent in promoting Western biomedical models worldwide. A few examples bring to light the dilemmas and highlight potential threats to human rights.

First, sociologist Troy Duster's (2003, 2005) scholarship on the problematic social consequences of genetic research is a case in point. Genetic research is supported by extensive public-sector investment, yet reinforces the individualization of health and illness and reifies racial categories. The advent of "personalized medicine" (reserved primarily for the well-off) is based upon individual genetic profiles and locates health problems inside the body rather than with the social forces, social arrangements, and government policies that contribute to poor health. Additionally, racialized medicine promotes biomedical fixes for different races without attention to the role of structural forces that create racial and ethnic health disparities. (See also Conrad [2000] and Shostak and Freese [2010] for sociological critiques of the rise of the genetic paradigm, or genetic medicalization.)

Second, while sociologists are at the forefront (along with epidemiologists and public health scholars) of data collection on health disparities, it has become increasingly clear that data collection can impede the provision of health services. According to Adams (2010), global health efforts rooted in bench science can shift resources from the delivery of vaccines and treatment to laboratory research—often for pharmaceutical development—with clinical trial subjects and blood samples. Adams asserts that "turning the world of international health into a laboratory space for research" can interrupt the practices of physician activists and caregivers and divert scarce resources away from the provision of care to people and toward "good statistics" that accompany evidence-based medicine (2010, 54). If the only way for the poor to obtain health care is to enroll in clinical trials, then the objectives of public health are displaced.

Third, the promotion of Western biomedical models globally introduces a phenomenon Gaines (2011) terms "the biomedical entourage." In short, global health programs grounded in the Western biomedical model can impose costly and impersonal curative medicine resulting in a form of biocultural colonialism. A biomedical entourage comprised of pharmaceutical companies and medical technologies (both with enormous influence over medical research and practice), along with a universal bioethical approach that neglects local context (and is gender biased), accompanies many global health programs without attention to local biology, healing alternatives from the local culture, and even local medicines and medical practice.

Finally, while scholars and activists worldwide recognize the value of medical advances and technologies for improving health, Conrad (2007) reminds us of the "dark side" of medicalization. As more human conditions and problems come to be identified and treated as medical conditions, medicine and accompanying industries (e.g., insurance and pharmaceutical companies) become institutions of surveillance and control, laying claim to birth, death, and everything in between. At a general level, greater exposure to medical treatment opens the door to higher rates of medical abuses and iatrogenesis. For example, approximately two hundred thousand people die each year due to preventable medical errors (Harmon 2009). As well, history books are rife with examples of medical abuses, such as the infamous Tuskegee study, thalidomide deaths, and complications from the Dalkon Shield. In addition, and as touched upon above, certain health conditions, like depression or obesity, become decontexualized with a focus on diagnosis and biomedical treatment trumping collective social action necessary to change social conditions that contribute to increases in physical and mental illnesses. Karp's (1996) work on the experience of depression raises important questions about a postmodern world that may contribute to emotional exhaustion and alienation. As well, several scholars have exposed the role upstream social conditions (e.g., tobacco and fast-food industries) play in contributing to health problems downstream (McKinlay 1974). Yet, the biomedical model—and even public health and epidemiology—can very narrowly focus on individual risk behaviors and medical interventions. Medical sociologists keep health and human rights issues on the table by pushing questions of political economy and the market-based commodification of medicine to the forefront of academic attention.

Indeed, the spread of biomedicalization in its current form also invites exploitation by corporations, including pharmaceutical and technology companies, which may place medical treatments outside the realm of possibility for the poor, further exacerbating existing health inequalities. As Farmer and Smith note, "The better the therapy, the more injustice meted out to those not treated" (1999, 267). Market-based approaches to health care, combined with shrinking state investment in public solutions, will only deepen structural inequality, widening the health gaps between those with and those without resources. Roberts asserts, "The social immorality of biotechnological advances not only will ensure that their benefits are distributed unequally to the most privileged citizens, but will reinforce inequitable social structures and neoliberal political trends that impede social change" (2010, 69).

CONCLUSION

Anthropologist and physician Paul Farmer (2010) and the late public health scholar Jonathan Mann (1996) have argued that taking a "health angle" will help promote human rights globally. Medical sociologists contribute by providing vital theory and data on the causes and consequences of early mortality, excessive morbidity, and disability. In this chapter, we've argued that some bodies are more at risk than others and that structural forces and institutions have collective power to protect vulnerable bodies or do great damage to them. Turner argues for grounding sociological analyses of human rights in the concept of human frailty, generating "collective sympathy for the plight of others" and leading to the creation of moral communities in support of human rights (1993, 489). Since human frailty is a universal condition, bringing the plight of the vulnerable to light can increase collective support for a human rights paradigm.

Furthermore, a focus on health brings much to the struggle for human rights because public health, medicine, and social scientists occupy privileged spaces from which to promote a broader human rights agenda (Farmer 2010). One enduring conundrum is how scholars from Economic North countries often argue for "positive" civil rights (e.g., economic, social, and cultural) across the globe when their own countries fail to uphold the right to food, shelter, and medical care as human rights. Critical sociologists draw attention to the ideological and cultural resistance to the notion that the right to health care is a legitimate, basic human right (see, e.g., An-Na'im 2001). Findings from research in this tradition sharpen our understanding of the political processes at work in many Economic North countries and foster a greater understanding of cultural and geographic differences around the question of who deserves basic human rights. Sociologists can highlight the tensions between public support for civil and political rights worldwide on the one hand and public inability to support economic and social rights on the other. Bringing the tensions to light helps scholars, policy-makers, and activists craft agendas for the promotion of economic and social rights locally, nationally, and globally.

In the early years of the subdiscipline, medical sociologists embraced the academic tradition of moral neutrality in order to earn legitimacy within the scientific world of medicine. Currently, sociologists versed in the study of tangible social phenomena struggle with the conceptual vagueness of the language of human rights, which is "distinctly slippery, polysemic, and promiscuous" (Somers and Roberts 2008, 412). Yet, in the past fifty years, public sociology, feminist theory, and critical race theory have emancipated sociology from claims of moral neutrality, paving the way for a burgeoning sociology of human rights. According to Blau, while the role of sociologists has long been limited to observation and analysis of social inequalities, "human rights provide sociologists with the authority to assert that homelessness is *wrong*, racism is *wrong*, poverty is *wrong* (and, yes, even capitalism is wrong, if you are so inclined" (2006, 1). Increasingly, medical sociologists are adopting rights-based frameworks in their study of health inequalities and rejecting a rigid form of positivism (and even its later shift to cultural relativism), which led them to eschew normative judgments and universal values (Frezzo 2008; Turner 1993).

As social actors, medical sociologists inhabit multiple roles through which to make a case for health as a human right. We can advance awareness of human rights efforts through research drawing on local knowledge and "capturing realities on the ground" (Moncada and Blau 2006, 120). Medical sociologists need to guard against becoming handmaidens of the biomedical paradigm and must ensure that rights-based work remains guided by sociological perspectives. Blau and Smith argue that though they are rarely leaders in activism and policy, sociologists "become their advocates when they conceptualize the forms and the processes [and disseminate] their findings and interpretations in publications" (2006, xiv). For medical sociologists to embrace their role in advocating for health as a human right, a commitment must extend from their positions as authors, editors, and members of professional organizations and the broader academic community.

We also have the option of weaving advocacy for the basic right to health into our academic home: the classroom. Paolo Freire (2000) would remind us that our pedagogy cultivates humanitarian values and social action when we forge community with our students—future leaders who will harness new forms of social engagement to advocate for the protection and promotion of health as a fundamental human right.

Medical sociology is uniquely positioned to lay bare the ways in which myriad inequities around the world strip individuals, particularly the disenfranchised, of their basic right to health and well-being. By making the case for a right to health, to health care, and to autonomy from medical sovereignty, medical sociologists can help lay a solid foundation for the human rights paradigm.

≈

CHAPTER THIRTEEN

CRIME, LAW, AND DEVIANCE

Joachim J. Savelsberg

The relationship between the sociology of crime, law, and deviance and the study of human rights—those basic political, civil, and social rights that are granted to all human beings irrespective of their citizenship—is crucial but problematic. It is crucial because violations of human rights (and humanitarian law) constitute not just deviant but also law-breaking and at times criminal behaviors. They include war crimes, crimes against humanity, and genocide that have cost manifold more human lives and caused more suffering than all street crimes combined in the twentieth century alone. The relatively recent definition of these behaviors as crimes poses challenges to criminology and to the practice and sociology of law.

The relationship between crime, law, and deviance and human rights issues is also problematic. Scholars who address human rights and their criminal violations, especially political scientists, historians, lawyers, and philosophers, tend to know little about the wealth of sociological insights into issues of crime and law. Simultaneously, only a few sociologists of crime, law, and deviance have investigated human rights violations and legal responses to them (early: Turk 1982; Chambliss 1989; Barak 1991; more recently: e.g., Brannigan and Hardwick 2003; Ermann and Lundman 2002; Friedrichs 2009; Hagan 2003; Hagan and Greer 2002; Hagan and Levi 2005; Hagan, Rymond-Richmond, and Parker 2005; Hagan, Schoenfeld, and Palloni 2006; Hagan and Rymond-Richmond 2008, 2009; Maier-Katkin, Mears, and Bernard 2011; Mullins, Kauzlarich, and Rothe 2004; Savelsberg 2010; Savelsberg and King 2011; Woolford 2006). Yet, these themes should find a central place in the sociology of crime, law, and deviance, while these sociological specialties should simultaneously export their insights to other disciplines.

ATROCITIES: A MAINSTAY OF HUMAN HISTORY

Atrocities, today defined as humanitarian and human rights crimes, are a mainstay of human history. Myths and history tell us about mass killings during antiquity, hundreds of thousands slaughtered at the command of rulers and conquerors such as Genghis Khan and his successors, sultans of the Ottoman Empire, or rulers of the Aztecs (Rummel 1994). Europeans contributed to this history. In 1099, after the conquest of Jerusalem, Christian Crusaders butchered forty to seventy thousand of the city's Jewish and Muslim inhabitants. Eyewitnesses depict unimaginable cruelties and bloodshed (William, Archbishop of Tyre 1943). During the plagues of the fourteenth century, European Christians used their Jewish neighbors as scapegoats, and tens of thousands were killed. The Spanish Crown murdered some eighteen thousand Protestants in the Low Countries between 1567 and 1573, and the French royal court initiated the massacre of tens of thousands of Protestant Huguenots during the infamous St. Bartholomew night of 1572. The Revolutionary Councils of the French Revolution ordered the execution of some twenty thousand members of the nobility, political opponents, and alleged traitors. The Catholic Church had tens of thousands of heretics killed by fire, miserable prison conditions, and torture between 1480 and 1809, and Protestant witch hunts cost the lives of thousands of women (Jensen 2007).

Colonial rule also involved massive atrocities that victimized millions, including the early twentieth-century genocide against the Herero in today's Namibia by German colonial forces (Steinmetz 2007). Further, between the sixteenth and nineteenth centuries, up to 2 million African slaves were killed by the deplorable conditions of their voyage across the Atlantic Ocean. Millions more perished during transports to the Middle East and the Orient. The total death toll is estimated at somewhere between 17 and 65 million (Rummel 1994, 48).

Those responsible for atrocities throughout most of human history were not prosecuted and condemned but typically celebrated as heroes. "Victims," those on whom "heroes" imposed great sacrifices, were discounted, perceived as evil or "polluted" (*victima* in Latin means those set aside to be sacrificed) (Giesen 2004).

The long history of state-committed or -sponsored mass killings continued, as we know, into current times. The twentieth century outdid many of its predecessors in light of the technological advances and organizational potentials of modern states, especially totalitarian ones (Bauman 1989; Cooney 1997; Horowitz 2002). Rummel (1994) estimates the number of people killed by governments from the beginning of the twentieth century until 1987 at close to 170 million, not counting tens of millions who died as a consequence of regular warfare. Here, the percentage of civilian casualties of war increased from fourteen in World War I to sixty-seven in World War II and up to ninety in the century's final decades (Hagan and Rymond-Richmond 2009, 63f.). These horrifying numbers do not even account for the millions of women raped, houses and cities looted, and lands and livelihoods destroyed. The degree of victimization is of a magnitude that easily dwarfs that caused by regular street crime.

Reactions to atrocities have changed, however. While denial is still common (Cohen 2001), perpetrations often cause moral outrage, and the search for preventive measures and remedies and the punishment of offenders has begun. Several international conventions and UN initiatives speak to such innovation. Consider also diverse ad hoc courts and the new International Criminal Court (ICC), truth commissions (Hayner 2001), apologies (Bilder 2006), amnesties (Mallinder 2008), and other mechanisms of transitional justice (Teitel 2000).

EXPLANATIONS OF HUMANITARIAN AND HUMAN RIGHTS CRIMES

Crimes against humanitarian and human rights law always involve collective, often organizational action, but they can never be committed without individual action. In this respect they resemble white-collar crime, and terminology from that literature can be applied to human rights crimes too: *organizational crimes*, supported by often legitimate organizations whose goals they are meant to advance; *organized crimes*, committed by organizations set up for the purpose of engaging in law-breaking behavior; and *occupational crime*, "committed by individuals in the course of their occupation for their personal gain and without organizational support" (Coleman 2006, 11). Individual actors involved in such crime include frontline, low-level perpetrators who execute the dirty work (Hughes 1963), as well as leaders whose hands remain untainted by the blood they ultimately bear responsibility for shedding. These crimes demand complex explanatory approaches that go beyond much of what criminology has developed to address juvenile delinquency and street crimes (Chambliss 1989).

Innovative work on human rights crime thus seeks to link distinct levels of analysis and types of actors. Consider a simultaneous application of Randall Collins's micro-sociological, situation-focused approach to violence and Diane Vaughan's organizational model to the explanation of massacres (Savelsberg 2010, 75–85). Discussing the My Lai massacre against hundreds of civilians, committed by an American military company in the course of the Vietnam War, Collins focuses on situations that are "shaped by an emotional field of tension and fear" (2008, 18), turned into emotional energy that drives violent action. Resulting "forward panics" are particularly frequent in the context of guerrilla warfare, especially when troops are brought into a landing zone by helicopter in the middle of enemy territory (as in My Lai). Here "frenzied attacks of forward panic" become likely.

Importantly, military leadership frequently placed American soldiers in such situations during the Vietnam War (see also the 1972 documentary film *Winter Soldier*). Thus, actions by members of Company C cannot be understood without considering organizational context. Diane Vaughan (1999, 2002) stresses that members of organizations are likely to resort to the violation of laws, rules, and regulations in order to meet organizational goals, especially where divisions by hierarchy and specialization create "structural secrecy," where risk of detection is minimized. Organizational processes such as the "normalization of deviance" (i.e., acceptance of deviant behavior as normal) provide normative support for illegality, as has previously been documented in white-collar crime literature. Further organizational conditions (all identified for My Lai) include ambiguous orders and pleas for more aggressiveness perceived as authorization to engage in "sanctioned massacres" (Kelman and Hamilton 2002, 210); organized rituals that drive emotions to a high pitch (e.g., a funeral of a fallen comrade when orders for the attack were given); and organizational culture ("permissive attitude toward the treatment and safeguarding of non-combatants ... almost total disregard for the lives and property of the civilian population" [Goldstein, Marshall, and Schwartz 1976, 314]).

A sufficiently complex approach needs to incorporate, in addition to micro-dynamics and organizational conditions, the larger environment of organizations, where environmental uncertainty and "liability of newness" (Vaughn 2002, 275) further advance routine nonconformity (e.g., in My Lai, brief military training, neglected knowledge about local culture, and "the handling and treatment of civilians or refugees" [Goldstein, Marshall, and Schwartz 1976, 81]). The organizational environment also included definitions of the enemy as "commies," fighters for "ultimate evil" in the Cold War, and racist attitudes, reflected in the derogatory term "gooks" (Kelman and Hamilton 2002, 215).

In short, a complex approach that merges the study of situational, organizational, and environmental conditions is needed to explain grave human rights violations. Individual agency also matters. Some soldiers refused to participate in the My Lai case as elsewhere (for Police Battalion 101 during the Holocaust, see Browning 1998).

The sociology of crime has also finally begun to address genocide, the "crime of crimes," introducing innovative and complex methodological and theoretical tools (e.g., Hagan 2003; Hagan and Rymond-Richmond 2008, 2009; Savelsberg 2010). John Hagan and collaborators, after work on genocidal action in the Balkan wars and the building of the International Criminal Tribunal for the Former Yugoslavia (ICTY) (Hagan 2003), engaged the genocide in the Darfur region of Sudan (Hagan and Rymond-Richmond 2008, 2009). They utilized the Atrocities Documentation Survey, a rich victimization survey of some eleven hundred Darfurians in the refugee camps in neighboring Chad.

Horrifying narratives of victimization are backed up by statistical analysis: most victimization occurred where the land was most fertile, and total and sexual victimization were highest where attacks were most often accompanied by racial slurs. Expressions of racial hatred thus appear to ignite collective fury that encourages killing and raping. In a "joint criminal enterprise," individual liability exists in the context of collective action. Genocide is documented as the criteria of its legal definition are backed up with empirical evidence: members of a group are being killed, serious bodily and mental harm is being inflicted, conditions of life calculated to bring about their physical destruction are imposed, and empirical evidence of intent to destroy, in whole or in part, a racial or ethnic group is produced. The tools of crime, law, and deviance scholarship are thus used to document genocide.

Tools from crime, law, and deviance scholarship are also suited to explain genocide. Hagan and Rymond-Richmond (2009) put to productive use Ross Matsueda's (2006) complex criminological theory that links together Sutherland's expansion of social-psychological ideas about differential association toward differential organization, associated network ideas, and Goffmanian framing analysis. Collective-action frames (Benford and Snow 2000) are especially effective if they define the root of the problem and its solution collectively ("we are all in this together"), the antagonists as "us" versus "them" (e.g., "Jews versus Arians"; "blacks versus Arabs"), and a problem or injustice caused by "them" that can be challenged by "us." Closed and dense social networks with such collective-action frames are most likely to produce collective efficacy, "the willingness ... [of groups] to intervene for the common good [evil from the perspective of the other side]" (Sampson and Raudenbusch 1999, 919). "Social efficacy" of actors who are central to local networks, but who also are linked to the outside world, enables creation of "consensus over group ...

objectives and procedures, and translate[s] these procedures into action" (Matsueda 2006, 24). Capable of recognizing interests of their local group and of outside institutions and able to switch between local and universal codes, such actors play crucial roles in manipulating local groups on behalf of collective goals, including a state's genocidal project. Hagan and Rymond-Richmond link central elements of the Matsueda model with Coleman's (1990) famous micro/macro scheme and creatively apply this amalgam to explain the genocide in Darfur.

Linking theoretical arguments by Collins and Vaughan, applying them to massacres (Savelsberg 2010, 75–85), and merging models by Matsueda and Coleman to explain genocide (Hagan and Rymond-Richmond 2009, 117–121, 162–169) takes into account micro and macro factors and organizational and individual actors at different levels of hierarchy, thus engaging traditional tools from the sociology of crime in the explanation of the gravest of offenses. Other traditional criminological approaches await application to human rights crimes, including Messner and Rosenfeld's (2007) ideas about the imbalance of societal sectors, ideas on criminal learning and culture as enduring versus adaptive (Anderson 1994), especially if enriched by a wealth of differentiated ideas on the emergence of anti-Semitism (Friedländer 2007), and ideas about anomie and strain (Merton 1938) and their interaction with social instability (for suggestions, see Savelsberg 2010, 49–66; Maier-Katkin, Mears, and Bernard 2011, 239–247).

LEGAL REGULATION: NORMS AND COURT INTERVENTION

Responses to atrocities have changed dramatically in recent history. They limit the notion of national sovereignty, according to which domestic rulers can act toward their populations at will. Resulting from the 1648 Peace Treaty of Westphalia that ended the Thirty Years' War, sovereignty was meant to reduce foreign interventions and international warfare, but it opened up room for massive domestic abuses. The nineteenth century saw the establishment of humanitarian law (Geneva and Hague conventions), seeking to protect noncombatants against mistreatment in times of international warfare while still respecting national sovereignty. Yet, the Nazis' domestic terror and their later expansion into occupied and allied lands brought into plain sight the need for international regulation not only in the pursuit of war but also when states engage in outrageous victimization during times of peace. The foundation was laid, in immediate reaction to the Nazi terror, by the 1948 Universal Declaration of Human Rights (UDHR), guaranteeing civil, political, social, and economic rights. Also in 1948 the Convention on the Prevention and Punishment of the Crime of Genocide was approved by representatives of fifty nations. It finally entered into force on January 12, 1951. Genocide now constituted a crime, and perpetrators were to be punished, be they "constitutionally responsible rulers, public officials or private individuals" (Article 4). Other human rights conventions address the protection of women (1979), children (1990), and indigenous peoples (1991). The Convention against Torture and Other Cruel, Inhumane and Degrading Treatment or Punishment (1987), like the genocide convention, applies standards of criminal liability. Finally, the Rome Statute of the ICC established the first independent and permanent international criminal court to try "persons accused of the most serious crimes of international concern" (ICC 2011). It entered into force on July 1, 2002, and had been joined by 105 nations by October 2008, not including the United States. With jurisdiction over genocidal atrocities, crimes against humanity, and war crimes, it backs up a multitude of domestic and foreign courts (for critical debate on the criminalization of human rights offenses, see Blau and Moncada 2007a; Hagan and Levi 2007; Cerulo 2007).

Why did the twentieth century, despite its many competitors in the execution of excessive cruelties, become the first to get serious about developing control responses (Minow 1998, 2002)? Satisfactory explanations should simultaneously draw on human rights literature, the sociology of law, and other branches of sociology. They need to speak to the universalization of human rights (global norms trump state sovereignty), individualization of responses (individuals, not just nations, can be held liable), and criminalization of offenses.

Universalization was advanced by the globalization of economies and new technologies that enhanced the flow of ideas, capital, goods, and workers across national boundaries. New international governmental organizations, such as the United Nations, were supplemented by international nongovernmental organizations that now represent a form of civil society at the global level (Keck and Sikkink 1998). Comparable to national civil societies, they contribute to the creation of global cognitive and normative scripts, which, once produced, direct actions of national governments (Meyer et al. 1997). Policies passed in compliance with international human rights norms spread and become effective at the local level (e.g., Boyle 2002; Boyle and Corl 2010 on female genital cutting; for more cautionary conclusions, see Cole 2005).

Individual criminal accountability in international human rights law is advanced by structural and cultural forces: the changing balance of power (growing interdependence of nations), the emergence of global civil society, and the occasional backing of criminal justice intervention by powerful countries or international government organizations. The rapid establishment of criminal liability after the 1980s was advanced by the end of the Cold War, during which the two superpowers blocked any move toward international criminal justice (Turk 1982). The selection of leaders from relatively weak countries for criminal prosecution partially mirrors massive power differentials in the international community.

Cultural forces also promote criminalization of offenses. Émile Durkheim wrote—as Erving Goffman would later do—about the most sacred good in modern society, expressed in the "cult of the individual" (Smith 2008, 18). This new dignity of individuals combines with the sensitization of modern humans to physical violence resulting from the civilizing process with its massive decrease in interpersonal violence in everyday life (Elias 1978; Johnson and Monkkonen 1996). A cultural approach simultaneously recognizes punishment not as (just) a rational application of disciplinary knowledge but as a didactic exercise (Garland 1990; Smith 2008). Rituals of court trials signify, in line with Durkheimian ideas, the sacred—human dignity in modern society—versus the evil.

But what about the timing of the criminalization of human rights violations, specifically in the post–World War II era? In light of the new sensibilities to which Durkheim and Elias speak, the Holocaust evoked responses that created a universal cultural trauma: through symbolic extension of the Shoah and psychological identification with the victims, members of a world audience became traumatized by an experience that they themselves had not shared (Alexander et al. 2004, 251). The legal proceeding of the International Military Tribunal, subsequent Nuremberg trials (Heberer and Matthäus 2008), and punishment of leading Nazi perpetrators were performative or demonstrative in Durkheim's terms. They provided images, symbols, totems, myths, and stories and thus contributed to the formation of a collective memory of evil. Once established as universal evil, the Holocaust served as "analogical bridging" to reinterpret and dramatize later events in light of this earlier trauma (Alexander 2004, 245–249). Cultural trauma thus further advanced global consensus regarding the dignity of individuals.

In short, as a result of structural and cultural changes, human rights law became universalized, and individual criminal liability was introduced for perpetrators of state-organized crimes. The application of such law by courts poses the next challenge to which the sociology of law responds.

Recent work in the sociology of law has addressed the conditions of domestic, foreign, and international human rights courts (e.g., Hagan 2003 applying Bourdieu's field theory to the ICTY). Yet, central debates on consequences of human rights trials tend to bypass the sociology of law—much to their detriment. While conservative lawyers and political scientists (e.g., Goldsmith and Krasner 2003; Snyder and Vinjamuri 2003/2004) express skepticism about the application of international or domestic criminal law, liberals are optimistic regarding the effects of human rights trials (e.g., Sikkink 2011; Payne 2009). The former base their often effective arguments on case studies. The latter, however, have stronger ammunition in the form of systematic data sets with large numbers of transitional justice situations. Sikkink's analyses, for example, indicate that countries with truth commissions and trials substantially improved human rights records; countries with criminal trials alone still showed significant improvement. Yet, these analyses do not resolve the issue of causality. Could third factors, such as past states of democracy and liberal law, explain both the holding of trials in transitional situations and the later improvement of human rights?

Also, what might explain the effectiveness of trials, should the association indeed represent a causal relation? Classical and new arguments from the sociology of crime, law, and deviance provide a look into the black box between intervention and outcomes. A long line of research on deterrence, consistent with rational-choice ideas, suggests that the certainty of punishment deters more than its severity (Matsueda, Kreager, and Huizinga 2006). In the case of human rights crimes, the certainty of punishment moves away from zero, suggesting a deterrent effect (Sikkink and Kim 2009).

Newer cultural arguments focus on the memory-building functions of trials that may thoroughly delegitimize previous regimes and their atrocities (Osiel 1997; Savelsberg and King 2007, 2011). This new line of work on collective memory

(Halbwachs 1992) and cultural trauma (Alexander et al. 2004) is inspired by classic Durkheimian ideas. It is in line with arguments by historic actors such as President Franklin D. Roosevelt and Justice Robert H. Jackson, who assigned a history-writing function to the international military tribunal (Landsman 2005, 6). A cautionary note is warranted though. Trials follow a particular institutional logic, targeting individuals, not the social processes and cultural patterns sociologists might focus on; focusing on actions covered by legal classifications (producers of inflammatory rhetoric may not be criminally liable); focusing on defendants (voices of victims are heard only when they serve the court; on the ICTY, see Stover 2005); and considering defendants guilty or not guilty, a gross simplification by psychological standards.

Historical case studies indicate that trials do shape memory—albeit in line with the institutional logic of law (Bass 2000; Giesen 2004; Landsman 2005; Heberer and Matthäus 2008). Further, trials that unfold under conditions of regime continuity typically focus on low-level perpetrators and may be less successful. Most American history textbooks, for example, do not mention the My Lai massacre. Those that do tend to present the crime in line with the trial outcome, focusing on the deeds of 2nd Lt. William Calley, while silencing the role played by higher ranks and the attempted cover-up of the massacre (Savelsberg and King 2011). Such processing of past atrocities may have advanced uncritical attitudes toward the institution of the military (Smith 2009) and contributed to a willingness by American military in current conflicts to offend against norms of humanitarian law (Mental Health Advisory Team IV 2006).

In short, through deterrence and collective-memory functions, criminal trials may—under specific conditions—help transitions to democracy and peace and prevent the repetition of past evil. Optimism, however, must be tempered by insights into the selectivity and inaccuracy of trial-based memories, by the focus on "small fish" in the absence of regime transitions, and by transition problems that trials may cause in some contexts. Much more work on the conditions and effects of national, foreign, and international courts is needed.

MUTUAL GAINS IN METHODS AND THEORY: SOCIOLOGY OF CRIME, LAW, AND DEVIANCE AND HUMAN RIGHTS SCHOLARSHIP

This chapter indicates that the study of human rights and grave offenses such as genocide, mostly executed by historians, lawyers, and political scientists, can gain conceptually, theoretically, and methodologically from the sociology of crime, law, and deviance—and vice versa. Many human rights offenses constitute crimes, but the fields that most prominently study human rights have barely sought inspiration from the sociology of crime, law, and deviance, which has engaged issues of crime and its control for more than a century. This particularly striking example of the problems of disciplinary segmentation should be remedied. There are many potential gains. On the conceptual front, genocide scholars discuss totalitarianism, war and social instability, and racist and anti-Semitic ideologies. Crime, law, and deviance scholars tend to use broader concepts such as learning and culture, strain and anomie, social control and social disorganization. The application of each, historically specific and broader theoretical concepts, comes with costs and benefits, and drawing on both should yield substantial gain.

Genocide scholars' frequent concern with single cases yields profound insights. It contrasts with crime, law, and deviance scholars' typical interest in general patterns. Linking insights from both perspectives and advancing historical-comparative studies is highly promising (e.g., Weitz 2003 on genocide).

Historians are primarily concerned with past cases, while crime, law, and deviance scholars tend to focus on current-day phenomena. Yet, there is a history of the present (or very recent past), and historical criminology has become an important branch of this field.

While crime, law, and deviance scholars often proceed deductively, testing general theories with empirical data, genocide scholars commonly proceed inductively, weaving together a rich tapestry of empirical findings to arrive at explanations. In practice elements of induction and deduction enrich each other in the work of both historians and sociologist-criminologists. Mutual recognition is warranted.

Human rights scholars and sociologists of crime, law, and deviance tend to work with different types of data (e.g., archives versus surveys). Merging insights from different data sources can only enrich our understanding of social phenomena generally and of grave human rights violations specifically. One example for the use of crime, law, and deviance data that are new to human rights scholarship is large-scale victimization surveys and accompanying sophisticated statistical analysis, as in the work on Darfur by Hagan and Rymond-Richmond (2008, 2009). Also the use of nonparticipant observation and in-depth interviews can enrich human rights scholarship (e.g., Hagan 2003). Other methods include systematic content analysis to capture the memory and framing of grave human rights violations (e.g., Savelsberg and King 2011), historic comparative analysis, and—already common in human rights scholarship—archival research (e.g., Chambliss 1989).

Crime, law, and deviance scholars typically focus on individuals and their offenses (or aggregations to rates), much in line with criminal law's notion of individual criminal liability. Leviathan, the state as the creator and enforcer of law, is typically excluded as the potential culprit. In both respects, genocide scholars show much more independence from a state-centered perspective (e.g., on the role of physicians and lawyers in the service of the state, see Stolleis 2007; on collaborating governments, Fein 1979).

Human rights scholars speculate on the effect of criminal justice intervention on abuses. Crime, law, and deviance scholarship's deterrence research (Matsueda, Kreager, and Huizinga 2006) and new work on the collective-memory function of criminal trials (Osiel 1997; Savelsberg and King 2011) can provide guidance.

Sociologists of crime, law, and deviance have engaged in at-times-sterile debates on cultural versus structural conditions of crime. Historical genocide scholarship holds profound lessons on ways in which both are intertwined (e.g., Friedländer 2007).

Finally, and not covered in this chapter, responses to street crime, excessive incarceration, and the death penalty may at least potentially constitute human rights offenses. Much common crime, law, and deviance sociology should thus be examined through the human rights prism. Today, many Native Americans and African Americans live in miserable conditions, partly due to a legacy of discriminatory practices (Sampson and Wilson 1995). The federal and state governments have used massive force against members of these groups (Hagan and Peterson 1995; see also Hagan and Rymond-Richmond's 2009 link between Darfur and the position of minorities in the United States). The "war on drugs" has been a major contributor to the vast overrepresentation of blacks in America's prisons, and federal authorities anticipated this consequence from the outset (Tonry 1995). Felon disenfranchisement laws have been motivated by aggressive attitudes against African Americans and have further weakened their political representation (Manza and Uggen 2006). The practice of capital punishment has also been driven by resentments against minorities, and it continues to disproportionally affect blacks (Peffley and Hurwitz 2007; Jacobs et al. 2007).

CONCLUSION

To address major humanitarian law and human rights violations, crime, law, and deviance scholarship must develop more complex approaches. Previous work on white-collar and organizational crime particularly might lead the way. Crime, law, and deviance scholarship must also abandon its state centeredness, recognizing the state as a potential perpetrator, and adjust its conceptual and theoretical tools accordingly. Simultaneously, the response side of crime, law, and deviance scholarship must contribute to our understanding of the newly founded institutions of human rights law and international criminal justice. Debates in international relations reveal profound uncertainties about the likely outcomes of interventions. This is not surprising, as much human rights scholarship has only recently recognized criminal behavior and criminal-justice institutions as subjects of study and, indeed, as international institutions of criminal justice are historically new. Work on this front is only beginning, and cooperation between traditional human rights scholarship and the sociology of crime, law, and deviance is crucial.

CHAPTER FOURTEEN

EDUCATION

Nathalia E. Jaramillo, Peter McLaren, and Jean J. Ryoo

The importance of education as a human right has become widely accepted, in theory, with the 1948 publication of the Universal Declaration of Human Rights and the subsequent 1990 UNESCO World Declaration on Education for All. Both these documents, partial artifacts of a post–World War II climate, referenced existing educational disparities among states as well as an ideological shift toward addressing the "root" causes of social turmoil and strife. These documents also advanced a predominantly modernist paradigm for education in the wake of massive industrialization and uneven economic and social development/ exploitation between the world's periphery states and the capitalist core (Ishay 2008). The growing connections among education, state building, capitalist development, and liberal-progressive models of democratic governance gave credence to universal tropes associated with education as a human right within these global frameworks in terms of education providing means necessary for citizens' meaningful participation in society. This is not to suggest, however, that either of these treaties provided an elaborate or even sufficient definition of education per se. In fact, neither did. While Education for All identified literacy, numeracy, and basic problem-solving skills as fundamental to social progress and human welfare, many questions remained unanswered about how to justify education as a human right and how to define education altogether, given cultural, historical, and material differences (Spring 2000).

We could say, however, that a general consensus supports the notion that education is necessary and central to development of a state and its people. Education is considered, in the simplest sense, an institution and social practice that can aid in "self-reliance," as well as personal and social improvement, and contribute to a "safer, healthier and more prosperous sound world" (UNESCO 1990). Within the sociology of education, these preliminary understandings have resulted in various analyses and theoretical contributions to education as a human right. Interrogating relations between social and educational actors at both individual and societal levels, the sociology of education has, for the most part, focused on questions of access, inclusion, and exclusion and how they are addressed in both industrial and so-called developing nations. In more contemporary terms, the sociology of education has also examined roles of race/ethnicity, gender, sexuality, class, and disability in relation to differentiated distribution of educational services and practices (Sadovnik 2007; Weis 2008). It has given primary concern to the individual situated in a wider sphere of social relations and antagonisms that limit equal access to education. Further, questions about the relationship among schooling, states, and development of an active and participatory citizenry have been of concern from the sociology of education's inception.

Social inquiries into education as a human right have looked very different south of the equator, however, with questions of colonialism, coloniality and sanctity of culture, freedom of expression (religious, linguistic, or otherwise), and spatial sovereignty central to understanding and analyzing the relationship between education and society. Documented by friars and missionaries during brutal colonization efforts, indigenous testimonies and narratives have yielded profound historical archives from which to examine teaching's role and learning as a strategy for "conquering" mind, body, and spirit. We are confronted with the continuing legacy of what Nelson Maldonado-Torres (2007) refers to as "coloniality of being"—the idea that effects of colonialism do more than subjugate subaltern knowledges and practices through imposition of sovereign discourses; they also constitute a way of being that is embodied or enfleshed (McLaren 1999). Here the emphasis is on how lived oppression becomes naturalized as a way of life.

While we share the belief that education is a human right, our intent is not to reify the modernist tropes of progressive education as they have been articulated within the literature. Rather, we propose a decolonial and materialist shift in addressing social and pedagogical dimensions of knowledge production mutually evident in our conceptions of self, state, and rights/justice.

KEY FINDINGS IN THE SOCIOLOGY OF EDUCATION

Sociological research into education has traditionally been broken down into three general categories: functionalism, conflict theory, and symbolic interactionism. Following Durkheim (1956, 1962, 1977), functionalists focus on ways schools establish and maintain social order. Many believe that schools serve the interests of society's dominant groups/citizens by teaching children mainstream moral values, inculcating attributes of civic and national patriotism, manufacturing consent to that society's dominant political and social order, ensuring that students acquire academic skills necessary to understand majority-shared forms of knowledge, and facilitating a smooth ideological transition into the capitalist workplace. Modern functionalists often focus on the role of education in fostering a belief in meritocracy—an ideological disposition that assumes all people have more or less equal opportunities and that individual hard work and determination (not social or economic status) produce educational results—and thus suggest that students who fail to succeed in school or society are not meant to be its leaders (Davis and Moore 1945; Parsons

1959). Conflict theorists, on the other hand, illuminate how education imposes dominant groups' ideas on nondominant populations through subordination and manipulation in school spaces where administrators/teachers, teachers/students, teachers/parents, and so on engage in constant power struggles. Conflict theorists reveal how schools sort students based on social status instead of abilities, such that schools' organizations reflect organization of power relations in society at large (Bowles and Gintis 1976). Finally, sociologists in education who work from a symbolic interactionism perspective consider how peoples' engagement with education or learning is constantly in dialogue with socially constructed processes of making meaning of schooling experiences or practices (Rist 1970, 1973, 1977). Sociologists of education have offered analyses of schooling that complicate these three theoretical frameworks, pushing us to reconsider the relationship between society and educational institutions. For example, Basil Bernstein's (1970, 1977, 1990, 1996) "code theory" illuminates how differences in communication systems reflect differences in class, power relations, and social division of labor and how, due to ways schools value certain communication systems and language-use patterns over others, only specific groups are slated to succeed in such schools.

The conflict-theory school has strongly influenced work in social justice education and human rights, including early work within sociology of knowledge (Durkheim, Mannheim, Weber) and later work by Michel Foucault, the Frankfurt School, and Michael D. F. Young, as well as Joe Feagin and Hernan Vera's (2008) liberation sociology, Michael Burawoy's (2004, 2006) development of a public sociology, and phenomenological sociology. Sociologists of education working within this "critical school" recognize that larger society's asymmetrical relations of power and privilege are largely reproduced in school settings in which class exploitation and other social differences continue to obstruct access to equitable educational opportunities for student populations outside the dominant social order. However, such a view often fails to consider social and political agency of nondominant individuals and groups. Thus, several scholars have made an effort to highlight that schools can be sites of resistance that disrupt and challenge schools' dominant social arrangements (Freire 2000; Giroux 1983a, 1983b; Illich 1971; McLaren and Jaramillo 2007). For example, Freire (2000) notes how education is a potentially liberating space where oppressed and oppressor, student and teacher alike, can challenge educational and societal power hierarchies, examine personal roles in society, and create new visions of participation in our communities that are humanizing for all. In this sense, Freire recognized that education is a political act.

Antonio Gramsci's (1982) work—especially development of the theory of hegemony and function of organic intellectuals—has also been foundational to development of a critical sociology of education. For Gramsci, hegemony signified moral and intellectual leadership and management used to produce consent to specific interests of the ruling class or historic bloc. Here, Gramsci teaches that social integration at the level of culture and ideology required practice of moral and intellectual leadership in producing a unified will of the masses. Political power always involves coercion and consent, or a balance between political (coercive) forces and social (normative) functions. Gramsci distinguishes between a war of position (ideological battle for the "will" of the people) and a war of maneuver (a direct and violent frontal assault on the state) as two possible strategies for social transformation.

Freire's ideas, like those of Gramsci, have proved to be profoundly influential in the field of progressive education, providing the ideational spine for many of critical pedagogy's theoretical trajectories (Giroux 1983a, 1983b; McLaren 1989) and for those of revolutionary critical pedagogy (Allman 2001; McLaren 2005; McLaren and Jaramillo 2007) that recognize the potential for students and teachers to accomplish social-justice agendas.

As an emancipatory philosophy committed to empowering nondominant students, critical pedagogy urges educational researchers, theorists, and practitioners to (1) recognize traditional schooling's political nature (Giroux 1997; McLaren 1989; Shor 1992), (2) understand how educational reform must engage communities' experiences and belief systems (Duncan-Andrade and Morrell 2008; Valenzuela 1999), (3) replace banking education and rote memorization practices with classroom and teaching practices that support critical-thinking skills (Freire 2000), (4) challenge the teacher-student hierarchy by employing a dialogic approach to pedagogy (Freire 2000; McLaren 1989, 2005), (5) encourage student agency by providing students with support and knowledge necessary to understand and change the world in positive ways (Morrell 2008; Freire 2000; Freire and Macedo 1987), and (6) support a dialectical perspective that embraces critical praxis—uniting theory and practice—as a tool for envisioning and fomenting social change through engaged inquiry, reflection, dialogue, and collective action (Freire 2000; Giroux 1997; McLaren 1989).

Going further, revolutionary critical pedagogy proves useful for both sociology of education and human rights by reframing how we think about knowledge production and the purpose of learning through an anticapitalist framework and decolonialization of human subjectivity and struggle. Recognizing its own intellectual, historical roots in a white, male, Western, heterosexual, academic world, revolutionary critical pedagogy acknowledges the importance of self-critique and reflexivity in knowledge production and analysis of schooling.

This move to both historicize and draw attention to material social relations that yield knowledge production provides a fecund ground for extending more orthodox interpretations of Marxist theory in education. Sandy Grande (2004) has given due consideration to both omissions and affordances of revolutionary critical pedagogy from an indigenous standpoint. Grande's (2004) examination of teleological and linear tendencies of predominantly Western social theory occasions consideration of "deep structures of colonialist consciousness" that defines progress as change, separates faith and reason in overly positivistic, empirical ways of knowing, marks divine conceptualizations of reality as "primitive superstition," values individualism over community, and considers humans the only creatures capable of rational thought (69–70).

Catherine Walsh (2010) has extended such work in terms of "interculturality," a concept she characterizes as an analysis and reflection of the foundational principles of knowledge production that include both marginal and dominant ways of knowing. For Walsh, interculturality provokes "social, political, ethical, and epistemic considerations regarding society, State, life, and even ourselves" (2010, para. 16). An intercultural framework's intent is to avoid merely thinking about subaltern subjects and, rather, to enter into dialogue and thinking with such subjects and to learn from their "distinct knowledges, beings, logics, cosmovision, and forms of living" (Walsh 2010, para. 16). Such thinking and dialogue has as its aim transformation of social structures and institutions that continue to inflict colonialist ways of knowing and being upon aggrieved populations. Here, sociology of education becomes concerned with questions of identity, in the sense of the identity politics associated not with the postmodern turn in social theory but with what Walter Mignolo (2010) describes as "identity in politics," or historicity of identities. Questions raised by scholars and activists working within an intercultural framework concern the right of peoples to express their identities, knowledges, and ways of being in the context of existing social institutions and formations. Inquiries into "rights" and "access" to education have less to do with gaining entry into the assemblage of educational services and credentials offered by states/public agencies and more to do with transforming existing monolithic forms of thought into more inclusive and pluriversal understandings of the social organization of learning. The concept of social difference in this instance is seen as a way to open "new intercultural perspectives of living 'with,' of co-living or co-existence" (Walsh 2010, para. 16).

KEY METHODS IN THE SOCIOLOGY OF EDUCATION

Research methods used to explore how society affects schooling and how schooling, in turn, affects society include quantitative and qualitative approaches. While efforts have been made to be purely objective when conducting educational research in sociology, a critique of such scientific positivism has been embraced by many sociologists of education who recognize that complete objectivity—even in quantitative methods—is simply impossible. Drawing from Kant's (1993 [1788]) work that explored how pure objectivity and knowledge of "truth" are unattainable for humans submerged in a world where popular dogma masquerades as "truth," Marx and Engels (1976 [1846]) in *The German Ideology* develop a critical theory of consciousness that has proven useful for researchers in sociology of education. Contesting that human consciousness is separate from material world experiences, as well as that all consciousness is simply a sensory projection of that material world, Marx and Engels (1976 [1846]) describe a dialectical relationship between consciousness and material practice, human objectivity and subjectivity, such that only praxis between human thought and sensuous activity—attainable through researcher reflexivity—can reveal deeper understanding and consciousness. In response, critical researchers in sociology of education have sought to be more rigorous in their methods by using a "self-conscious criticism" that Kincheloe and McLaren describe as an awareness of "the ideological imperatives and epistemological presuppositions that inform their research as well as their own subjective, intersubjective, and normative reference claims" (1994, 140).

Recent work has explored more participatory, action-oriented research and decolonial research practices in an effort to describe educational experiences from the perspectives of actors involved rather than from the researcher's perspective. In such research methods, researchers, educators, and students collaborate to analyze classroom practice and social relations that inform their daily lives. The act of research becomes more pedagogical in the sense that guided inquiry is intended to provide students with tools necessary to generate their own conclusions about social reality and the potential transformative activity within their surroundings (see Duncan-Andrade and Morrell 2008). Questions about the subject-neutrality of research are considered, given the premises from which many educators-activists conduct their inquiries. Orlando Fals-Borda (1988), the founding "father" of participatory action research, clearly refuted the objective neutrality often associated with positivist research practice. Fals-Borda, a native Colombian, recognized early on the political and politicized elements of social research. For Fals-Borda (1988), participatory research methods needed to bring together action-reflection and theory-practice, in participation with others. Research needed to be "endogenous" so as to foster mutual confidence in shared goals of social transformation and people's power in the research process. Further, Fals-Borda encouraged educators-scholars-activists to connect the development of "local" knowledge and practices with the wider goals of democratic social change as part of the stated objectives or goals of a research project. The research process itself needed to be determined by the social-political-economic necessities of the very people who were both the subjects and objects of research.

Indigenous and decolonizing scholars have been at the forefront of articulating educational research practices that support community development. Importantly, research in this vein has sought not only to critique and dispel colonizing forces of imperialist research practices but to advance in its stead a humanizing and grounded research praxis that benefits communities. While recognizing the heterogeneous, multifaceted characteristic of native peoples, Linda Smith is among the most prominent researchers/educators to reshape qualitative methods by what she terms "Kaupapa Maori research" (2005, 125). The "genealogy of indigenous approaches to research" utilized by Smith takes into consideration relationships and connections between "indigenous aspirations, political activism, scholarship and other social justice movements and scholarly work" (2007, 87). Research is guided by the ethic of self-determination and development in an effort to undo the historical legacy of research practices that extract information/observations from the "native" rather than contributing to the community. As Smith reflects on the role of power in the research process, a particular Maori research methodology emerges that "sets out to make a positive difference for Maori that incorporates a model of social change or transformation, that privileges Maori knowledge and ways of being" (2007, 90). Though this is but one example, we can see how methodologically indigenous and decolonizing scholars within the sociology of education have extended the field to incorporate notions of power and self-determination as constitutive of the research process. Such efforts are different from those of the earliest progenitors of the field, who examined the school-society relationship from the macro structures of nation building, religious orthodoxy, and an evolving capitalist society. We could say that in the latter case, the subjective dimensions of social inquiry take precedence (at the level of "identity in politics"), given the immediacy of needs that present themselves in communities that have experienced grave degrees of isolation and exploitation.

THE SOCIOLOGY OF EDUCATION IN RELATION TO HUMAN RIGHTS

Research findings in sociology of education reveal that the current human rights paradigm regarding peoples' rights to education, as defined by Article 26 of the Universal Declaration of Human Rights, fails to acknowledge how schooling is affected by class exploitation, racism, sexism, colonization, and neoliberal globalization.

The human rights paradigm acknowledges that all parents have a right to choose what kind of education their children receive and that all people have a right to an education that is free, equally accessible, and merit based toward the development of a personality that respects human rights, freedom, tolerance, and peace.

Yet, applying the sociology of education to this human rights paradigm, one might begin to ask, While everyone has a right to education, to what kind of education do people have a right? Who determines the core subject matter that should make up that education and how such subjects are taught? Should literacy learning involve engaging critical-thinking skills necessary to read and write in multiple media forms so that one is able to read into deeper or hidden meanings found in advertising, film, television, radio, and so on? In many countries, education may be free, but are all schools equally accessible to all students? The sociology of education's exploration of US public education paints a picture of glaring inequality for nonwhite students (Velez et al. 2008; Yosso et al. 2009). How can we address differences in access to quality education based on overriding relations of class exploitation in capitalist society? How can we address differences in access to quality education based on other factors, such as race, gender, sexuality, or religion? How does such difference affect the ways that students learn about tolerance, human rights, and understanding across nations, races, or religions? Indeed, the human rights paradigm may uphold the importance of tolerance; yet education in all nations across the globe is fraught with intolerable inequalities based on race, gender, sexuality, religion, language, and more.

Needed is a globalized curriculum grounded in human rights education. No one has provoked more international debate on a globalized curriculum grounded in the human right to education than Joel Spring. The universal right to education should, in Spring's view, be underpinned by the struggle for happiness and longevity and accompanied by progressive human rights and environmental traditions. Spring has developed a prototype for a global school that combines eco-pedagogy to protect the biosphere and human rights to support the well-being of students, staff, teachers, and the immediate community. In Spring's own words, "The goal is to promote the longevity and happiness of school administrators, teachers, and students, while preparing students to assume the responsibility to ensure their own long life and happiness and that of others" (2007, 135).

In addition, Spring has been instrumental in drawing the link between colonialism/postcolonialism and the universal right to education. For Spring, it is necessary to justify the universal right to education according to people's culture and their location in an overriding global economy. The justification for the universal right to an education, according to Spring, includes the need for all people to know how the global culture and economy created by colonialism and postcolonialism affect their lives and what benefits or harm might result; the necessity of achieving other human rights that guarantee equal economic and social opportunities in the global economy; protection against economic and social exploitation; freedom of expression and thought; and the right to an education that does not serve nationalistic or particular political ends by indoctrination, and so on (2000, 75).

RESITUATING THE HUMAN RIGHTS PARADIGM
THROUGH THE SOCIOLOGY OF EDUCATION

To resituate the human rights paradigm using sociology of education as a crucial theoretical and methodological lens, we must acknowledge a deeper purpose in schooling beyond preparing students merely to be workers in our global, capitalist, military-industrial system. We must engage in sociology of education that is intercultural at the root—in both theory and practice—and that opens up new spaces for interrogating the relationship between education and various social formations. The focus here is on developing an approach that allows for individuals to express themselves freely, to exercise their rights to maintain and produce multiple knowledges, and to develop their capacities to participate fully in the social world. Of course, there is the danger of falling prey to a reductive solipsism that does not lend itself to building solidarity or community across groups or to developing a universal understanding of what it means to advance a human rights paradigm in education. We argue, however, that it is possible to generate a universal conception of human rights in sociology of education that attends to various geopolitical conditions of peoples across the globe and simultaneously addresses the overriding logic of capitalist exploitation that hinders overall human development. In this sense, our review of sociology of education has yielded two primary considerations for situating the field in a human rights paradigm: (1) an examination of the "objective" structures and internal relations of class exploitation characteristic of capitalist society, and (2) a due deliberation on "subjective" dimensions of what Mignolo (2010) terms "identity in politics" in relationship to the historical legacy of coloniality and imperialism through the apparatus of schooling. On these points we elaborate further.

Theoretically and methodologically, this paradigm must acknowledge the multiple ways in which people define "rights." Human rights must move beyond liberal-progressive notions of equity and access and into the deeper spheres of addressing human development. Taking into consideration macro-level structures and relations that shape our global social order, we find it necessary to reflect upon Marx's thinking on human development. Marx envisioned a society that emphasized full development of human beings as a result of protagonistic activity in revolutionary praxis—the simultaneous changing of circumstances and human activity, or self-change. This key link in Marx is the concept of human development and practice. In other words, as Marx makes clear, there are always two products resulting from our activity, change in circumstances and change in people themselves. Socialist human beings produce themselves only through their own activity (Lebowitz 2010). So the question becomes, How do we transcend the conflicts today that lead to overidentification and disidentification? According to Marx, transcendence means not only abolishing dehumanizing conditions under capitalism but going beyond the given to create conditions of possibility for individuals to shape their own destiny, read anew the past, and demythify and generate meaning from multiple contexts people inhabit. It is a process, one in which we have in mind the betterment of our social condition, of which education forms a central part.

Sociology of education within a human rights paradigm can and should address social structures and social relations that negate us as human beings. This includes aspects of classroom life: authoritarianism but not authority, apathy and a heightened sense of individualism, fear of speaking about difficult topics, resistance to moving outside disciplinary boundaries, and questioning the interrelationship of ideas and practices. If we could depict our own unity, what would we create? And furthermore, how would we define human development in the context of class antagonisms and social contradictions at the epistemological and ontological levels? The answer for us comes down to praxis. Sociology of education grounded in a critical praxis has potential to become both a reading practice, where we read the word in the context of the world, and a practical activity, where we write ourselves as subjective forces into the text of history. Praxis is directed at understanding the word and the world dialectically as an effect of contradictions. An engaged and grounded sociology of education is a way of challenging the popular imaginary (which has no "outside" to the text) that normalizes the core cultural foundations of capitalism and normative force of the state. A critical sociology of education is a reading of and acting upon the social totality by turning abstract "things" into a material force, by helping abstract thought lead to praxis, to revolutionary praxis, to bringing about a social universe concerned with human development as opposed to human exploitation.

This brings us to the distinction between abstract and concrete utopian praxis. A concrete utopianism is grounded in creative potential of human beings living in the messy web of capitalist social relations to overcome and transform conditions of unfreedom. Knowledge production as a liberatory act must include an *actio in proximis*, meaning that the epistemology in question must have a practical effect in the world. This echoes Walter Benjamin's argument that if we merely contemplate the world, we will only arrive at a knowledge of evil (see McNally 2001). Knowledge of the good is knowledge of a practice designed to change reality; it derives from action, from contemplation. We judge the truth of our actions in their effects on the lives of the oppressed. But an epistemology of everyday praxis is not enough, because such acts or forms of praxis need a larger rudder and heavier ballast, something to give the emancipatory act direction. That is, it must also be implicated in an *actio in distans*, or the utopian aspect of knowledge production, which, in our case, is part of our struggle to diminish exploitation and suffering and promote justice. An *actio in proximis* is very much like a form of emancipatory praxis, whereas the *actio in distans* is the larger movement within these forms of praxis toward a utopia built upon the principles of equality and participatory democracy. It is precisely the double valence, or mixture of the two acts, that prevents the utopia from becoming abstract and metaphysical and prevents everyday acts of emancipatory praxis from becoming free floating and directionless, detached from the larger project of global emancipation. It directs praxis toward a concrete utopia, grounded in everyday struggle.

Looking Forward

Sociology of education is ripe with possibilities for developing a transformative research praxis. The questions we have posed in this chapter are intended to incite debate and consideration of those issues that we deem relatively absent in a human rights paradigm in education. These have to do with attending to the complexity of defining "rights" within the multilayered and multidimensional social system in which we live that largely ascribes meaning to education as a mechanism for inculcating in generations of youth the norms of a preexisting social order. Our fundamental premise is simple. The global capitalist social order in which we live denies people the right to pursue a meaningful and humane life. To undo education's historical legacy as a means of social control and assimilation into a preexisting mode of work, citizenship, and general livelihood, sociology of education must address capitalist society's fundamental contradictions. This approach, which some may claim is universalizing in its approach and economically reductionist in its philosophy, needs to be considered in light of popular struggles currently waged on behalf of the disenfranchised. It is on this point that work on decoloniality and an engagement with the geopolitics of knowledge becomes fundamental to expanding the field into a pluriversal and intercultural undertaking.

CHAPTER FIFTEEN

FAMILY

Angela J. Hattery and Earl Smith

A s we enter the second decade of the twenty-first century, sociologists of the family consider changes in family form and ask, Is the family dying, or is it merely changing in response to social conditions? In a 2010 poll of American millennials—aged eighteen to twenty-nine—the PEW Research Center reports that marriage is no longer a top priority. In fact, though half of millennials indicate that they prioritize being a good parent, less than a third prioritize having a successful marriage (see Figure 15.1).

Simultaneously, but with very little awareness of the other, scholars of human rights—a relatively new paradigm—are raising questions about the fundamental rights of individuals and groups everywhere. In this chapter, we use the human rights paradigm to frame questions and a discussion about the contemporary American family. We argue that the family is not only an appropriate area for study but also in desperate need of attention by human rights scholars. Second, we argue that reframing many of the discussions around the central tenets of human rights would significantly advance family sociology. Third, the bulk of the chapter is devoted to a discussion of specific issues facing the contemporary family and the insights that a human rights approach brings to bear on the study of these issues.

KEY QUESTIONS FACING FAMILY SCHOLARS

In addition to the debate around the changing nature of the American family, a second key question seeks to investigate the health of the American family in the twenty-first century; the focus is on the degree to which families are able to provide for the basic needs of their members and how any shortfall is being filled. Third is the question of choice: Do all Americans have an equal right to found families, marrying and engaging in childbearing as they see fit? These questions bring us around to the role that the human rights paradigm can play in researching and interrogating US families in the twenty-first century. We begin by reviewing some of the major changes in the American family over the last hundred years.

Figure 15.1 Percentage of millennials saying that ___ is one of the most important things in their lives

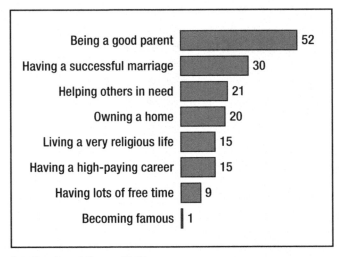

Note: Based on adults ages 18–29

AN OVERVIEW OF THE EVOLVING AMERICAN FAMILY

As a result of many social forces, including changes in the economy, urbanization, lower fertility rates, access to birth control, the civil rights movement, the "feminist revolution," and others, the shape of the American family is changing (Collins 1994; Coontz 1992, 1997). For example, the percentage of families that are "nuclear" dropped across the second half of the twentieth century from a high of 45 percent in 1960 to fewer than 25 percent in 2010 (Cherlin 2008). The most recent analysis by the Marriage Project (2010) reveals that these changes in marriage and the nuclear family form are largely shaped by race and social class. In short, the more highly educated and those with more financial stability are more likely to marry, less likely to divorce, and more likely to live in nuclear family households. A peculiar aspect of marriage decline and cohabitation increase in heterosexual relationships in the United States is that more Americans are turning to social media for relationships, love, and marriage.

Women's labor force participation changed dramatically across the twentieth century, such that the *Leave It to Beaver* family form, which hit its peak in the 1950s, is not only more or less a myth but certainly no longer exists today (Coontz 1992, 1997). According to a Bureau of Labor Statistics report in 2007, not only were 70 percent of married women employed, but 60 percent of mothers with preschoolers were as well (Cohany and Sok 2007).

Marriage also changed. Overall, marriage has declined. In 1960, 70 percent of Americans were married; today, that number has dropped to approximately 50 percent, with tremendous differences by race and social class (Marriage Project 2010). And those who do marry do so later—the average age of first marriage for women has risen to twenty-five (from twenty in 1960), and for men it has risen to twenty-seven (from twenty-two in 1960) (Marriage Project 2010).

Because there are structural advantages to marriage—for example, health benefits, inheritance-law preferences, and taxes—and because the middle and upper classes and whites have significantly higher rates of marriage, the advantages of being married and the disadvantages of not being married—in addition to those benefits and disadvantages already associated with differences related to class location—accrue disproportionately by social class and race.

Divorce remains common. The divorce rate more than doubled between 1970 and 1980, with financial stress being the greatest risk factor influencing one's chances of becoming divorced. The impact of social class on the likelihood of divorce stems from many factors, including arguments about money, differences regarding financial management, which can be more difficult to resolve in families with fewer resources, and the potential gains of staying married, which are highly tied to the perception that divorce results in a decline in social class for women (Stevenson and Wolfers 2007). Perhaps most importantly, unemployment and underemployment of men is a key risk factor for divorce, according to Stevenson and Wolfers (2007, 49), because of the perception that the male is not meeting expectations associated with masculinity and breadwinning (Kimmel 2005). Divorce rates peaked in 1980 and have since declined slightly and leveled off. In 1960 only 2 percent of the population was divorced, and in 2010 nearly 10 percent was; the overall divorce rate is 40 to 50 percent for new marriages, but because many divorced people get remarried, the percentage of Americans who are divorced at any given time remains approximately 10 percent. As Bumpass and Sweet (1989) predicted twenty years ago, by 2000 half of all children in the United States spent at least some of their childhood in single-parent households. As with most changes in the American family, divorce is also shaped significantly by social class in ways that compound class disadvantages, especially for children (Marriage Project 2010).

In contrast to declining rates of marriage, the rate of cohabitation has exploded. Today nearly 10 percent of all families involve a cohabiting couple, some of whom are raising their own children or are raising children as part of a blended family. One question that many scholars raise, including ourselves, is what role cohabitation does or does not play in supplanting marriage. The cohabitation rate increased fifteen times between 1960 and 2010. Today 25 percent of people between the ages of twenty-five and thirty-nine are cohabiting; an additional 25 percent reportedly cohabited in the past, and 60 percent of all marriages are preceded by cohabitation (Marriage Project 2010). In addition to the question of cohabitation supplanting marriage, it is also important to consider the question of resources, especially for children, and the degree to which children are shaped by the living arrangements of parents. For example, do children living in a household with cohabiting parents suffer in any measurable ways relative to those living in households in which parents are married? This is a complex question to answer and may be most easily understood by considering who chooses to marry and who does not. The Marriage Project (2010) data show that cohabitation rates are strongly shaped by race and social class. That is, cohabitation is on the rise, but not for every race/ethnic group. African Americans remain one ethnic group that generally chooses cohabitation over marriage. And, increasingly, middle-class Americans are cohabiting and never marrying.

The fertility behaviors of American families have changed over the last century. Fertility, by and large, has been steadily declining since 1900 (Coontz 1997; Hattery 2001). This may be one of the most significant trends in American families over the last hundred years. That said, fertility rates vary tremendously by race and social class; African American and Hispanic families have significantly higher fertility rates than whites (National Data Book). Because African Americans are disproportionately likely to be poor, and due to changes in the welfare laws that create significant burdens for women who continue to have children while receiving welfare, these differences in fertility likely contribute significantly to a racialized gap in standard of living for women and their children. We address this issue at length later in the chapter.

Perhaps one of the biggest changes in family life is the dramatic increase in nonmarital childbearing; in 2007, 40 percent of all babies were born to single mothers, more than double the rate in 1980. And, as is the case with most of the statistics associated with the family, this phenomenon is particularly racialized: 75 percent of African American babies are born to single mothers. Thus, the new norm of childbearing in the African American community is for marriage and childbearing to be decoupled (Burton 1990; Hattery and Smith 2007; Burton et al. 2010).

Finally, perhaps the key touch-button issue facing Americans in the early twenty-first century is the issue of gay marriage. As any casual news consumer is well aware, gay marriage is a highly contentious issue on which Americans have polarized views. Battles over gay marriage are currently fought in US voting booths, courts, and churches. That said, same-sex marriages are up. Period. Though gay marriage is still only legal in a handful of states and, at the time of this writing, is being fought over in the California court system, clearly the number of gay marriages has exponentially increased relative to just a decade ago. The issue of gay marriage is perhaps the one area of family scholarship in which a human rights paradigm has been applied; thus it is critical for us to review this argument. However, our focus in this chapter builds on the ways in which gay marriage as a human rights issue can shape our discussions of other issues facing the contemporary family.

In sum, the reader can see that the American family has been changing for at least the last hundred years, and there is no evidence to suggest that it will stop evolving. Though this perspective is highly contentious among sociologists who study the family, we stand firmly in our belief that when taking a longer, historical perspective, it is clear that there is no evidence to suggest that the family is disappearing in importance in American life; rather, it is evolving in response to a variety of institutional, legal, economic, and cultural pressures. Operating from this assumption, in this chapter we focus on the American family as a site for interrogation by the human rights paradigm. We focus our discussion on two key issues: (1) the right to create a family—to marry, have children, adopt, and so on—and (2) the right to have one's basic needs—for housing, food, access to education, and personal safety—met inside the family. We argue that on both accounts, the US government is not supporting the basic rights or meeting the basic needs of the family. We conclude by suggesting some changes to US policies regarding families that would result in both the basic rights and the basic needs of families being met (or restored) in ways that return the family, rather then the government, to the position of being the building block of society.

HOW ARE FAMILIES STUDIED BY SOCIOLOGISTS?

The primary methods that have been used to investigate families, attitudes toward families, and trends in everything from rates of interracial marriage to labor-force participation are surveys, specifically the national-level surveys conducted by the US Census Bureau and its related "arms," including the Bureau of Labor Statistics and the Current Population Survey; interviews (Garey 1999; Hattery 2001; Hays 2003); and ethnography (Burton 1990). In particular we highlight the use of government surveys, including data collected by the decennial census and Bureau of Labor Statistics, as these allow sociologists to examine trends among the entire US population. Because these data have been collected for decades, we can examine trends and changes across time.

As noted above, central to a human rights analysis of the American family are two basic rights: (1) the right to form one's own family—to marry and to control fertility—and (2) the right to have one's basic needs met inside the family. And though traditional sociological methods help to address these questions in terms of trends and predictions, as we will argue when data are collected primarily via large-scale surveys, there are limits to the analysis that can be performed through the lens provided by the human rights paradigm. Thus, in order to address human rights concerns as they apply to the evolving US family, additional methods will have to be employed. Specifically, human rights scholars who wish to study family life would rely on many qualitative methods, including interviews, ethnographic research, and policy analysis in order to generate the types of data appropriate for analysis and theory building. We point to the work of Linda Burton (1990) as an example of how ethnographic research can be used to disrupt underdeveloped and widely held beliefs and theories about teen childbearing.

THE SCOPE OF HUMAN RIGHTS CONCERNS REGARDING THE US FAMILY

We would argue that, largely, the core questions we are raising regarding the US family are national as well as global issues. The question of who controls the right to form a family—who can marry and who controls childbearing—is indeed global in scope. For example, the majority of other countries in the developed and developing world have either recently confronted or are currently grappling with the same issues, including gay marriage and abortion rights. Similarly, though the United States has long been characterized as one of the richest nations in the world, the recession that impacted us here is also global; the impact in Europe, for example, is particularly devastating. Outside the developed world, where the recession itself may have less impact, the conditions themselves threaten the very survival of most individuals and families living there. Thus, the questions we pose are indeed of both national and global importance.

INSTITUTIONS AND LEADERS SHAPE THE US FAMILY

Based on our definitions of the human rights issues facing American families, the key structures that impact or prohibit access to rights are (1) the legal structure, (2) the political structure, (3) the institution of religion, (4) the criminal justice system, (5) the economy, and (6) the system of social welfare.

First and foremost, the social structures that govern our lives are heavily shaped by our laws. Quite simply, for example, if gay marriage is not legal, then the right to form a family is threatened by the legal system. More complexly, the laws that shape eligibility for welfare indirectly threaten the fundamental right of the poor (and not those with financial resources) to control their childbearing. Other examples of this include issues such as retirement and financing a college education. For example, low-income individuals and families who live with employment instability or employment without benefits will rely entirely on the Social Security system to fund their retirement, whereas those with professional or unionized employment will likely have private, employer-contributed retirement plans. Similarly, though there are some programs for low-income students to attend college, these are competitive and often underfunded. For example, the most widely used government-funded program, the Pell Grant, recently limited awards to $2,500 per year. In contrast, middle- and upper-income families may be able to take advantage of 529 programs, which permit anyone to contribute to a student's college savings and benefit from tax deductions for the contribution, and the earnings are tax-free. Thus, the law is critical in shaping the basic human rights of families with regard to family formation. Similarly, with regard to the right to meet the basic needs of one's family, laws that shape the economy as well as the receipt of welfare are critical. For example, the minimum wage is set by law. The fact that the minimum wage does not provide a living wage is a major contributor to families' inabilities to meet their basic needs, as illustrated by the debate at the end of 2010 about the extension of unemployment benefits for the long-term unemployed.

We cannot undersell the importance of the development of hegemonic ideologies in shaping the options for families. At the most basic level, hegemonic ideologies impact and shape individuals' beliefs such that, for example, they may or may not support gay marriage rights. As important as this is, the real power of hegemonic ideology is how it is generated by the "state" (Therborn 1980), which in turn shapes state policies—for example, the law! Thus, hegemonic ideologies are a powerful force in shaping marriage rights and welfare. And, as Therborn (1980) notes, hegemonic ideologies are always constructed to uphold the interests of the state rather than individual citizens, and thus it is not uncommon for hegemonic ideologies and therefore policies to lag behind public opinion. Gay marriage rights and Don't Ask, Don't Tell are two contemporary examples of this.

The power elite—leaders of the government and corporate America (Zweigenhaft and Domhoff 2006)—influence all the major US institutions, including the military, the legal system, the criminal justice system, the economy and financial system, the system of education, the institution of religion, and the creation of ideology. Thus, the power elite either directly or indirectly influence the American family. Directly the elite influence the family by making laws that impact family rights—for example, the right to marry—and indirectly they influence the family, for example, through an economic system and set of laws and policies that prevent the minimum wage from being a living wage. The working poor barely live above the poverty line and find it difficult, if not impossible, to meet the basic needs—for shelter, food, and clothing—of the family.

RELEVANT EMPIRICAL FINDINGS

We focus our discussion around two key issues: the right to form a family and the right to meet the basic needs of the family.

THE RIGHT TO FORM A FAMILY

The right to form a family and to determine who will be a part of that family is not a guaranteed human right in the United States. Here we explore two different aspects of this issue: the right to marry and the right to bear children. Beginning with the right to marry, the United States—both the citizenry and the polity—is embroiled in a heated debate surrounding the rights of gays and lesbians to marry. This debate has been raging for the last decade and centers on several key issues. First and foremost are the beliefs of individuals regarding the fundamental right to marry. Currently, a third of Americans believe that gay marriage should be legal, and nearly half (41 percent) believe that civil unions—legal arrangements that provide the same legal benefits as marriage—should be legal (PEW Research Center for the People and the Press 2010). In contrast, the support for gay marriage among the power elite is far smaller, at least publicly. For example, more than a decade ago, in 1996, then–President Bill Clinton signed the Defense of Marriage Act (DOMA), which was intended to create a federal prohibition on gay marriage that would override the rights of individual states to grant marriages to gay and lesbian citizens. While the percentage of Americans favoring some sort of legal relationship for gays and lesbians continues to grow, both President George W. Bush and President Barack Obama affirmed the key tenets of DOMA.

At the heart, the fight for gay marriage rights is about the right of all Americans to form families. Additionally, of course, legal marriage carries many benefits, including the right to inherit property or visit one's partner in the emergency room or intensive care unit, as well as countless other rights and financial benefits that are part of various laws. Thus, the fight for gay marriage is about more than the right to form a family; it is also about the right to care for one's family and take advantage of the same benefits that married heterosexuals enjoy.

Rarely talked about is another aspect of family formation: the right to have and raise children. With regard to gay and lesbian couples and single parents, this issue centers primarily on adoption. A number of states currently allow gays and lesbians to adopt, but most have some policies that make it difficult, and several prohibit adoption by gays and lesbians, including Florida, Mississippi, Nebraska, Oklahoma, Utah, and Virginia. Additionally, we know anecdotally that in our home community of Winston-Salem, North Carolina, physicians at North Carolina Baptist Hospital refused to perform an in vitro fertilization procedure on a colleague of ours who happens to be a lesbian. Thus, the gap between policies and actual practices may be a gulf.

Even more invisible are the ways in which the welfare system seeks to control the family formation and reproductive rights of low-income Americans. At the height of the most recent welfare reform that culminated in the 1996 Personal Responsibility and Work Opportunity Act, various "experiments" were explored. "Bridefare" was a program that paid higher welfare benefits to single mothers who married the fathers of their children. On the surface this may sound like a palatable idea, but when one digs deeper, one realizes that it is no more than an attempt at social engineering for the poor.

Though "bridefare" did not last long, one element of social engineering of poor families has become a central piece of our current welfare system. Hays (2003) explicates a policy designed explicitly to limit the fertility of women on welfare; a stipulation in the eligibility rules for Temporary Aid to Needy Families states that any child born to a woman currently receiving welfare benefits—termed a "CAP baby"—is permanently ineligible for benefits. Though again, on the surface, this might seem like a prudent idea designed to reduce childbearing among women who are receiving welfare, we identify at least two key problems with this policy. First, though designed to penalize the mother, the impact of this rule effectually penalizes the child. The child will not be covered by Medicaid, and due to her mother's ineligibility, the child will not benefit from additional cash assistance, food stamps, housing allowances, or child-care subsidies. This penalty continues into adulthood; as an adult, the child is ineligible for welfare assistance. Second, like "bridefare," this policy uses financial incentives to place restrictions on poor women's family formation, thereby restricting, even outright denying, the basic human right to bear children.

THE RIGHT TO PROVIDE FOR THE FAMILY'S BASIC NEEDS

Many structures make it difficult for a family to meet the basic needs of its members—namely, the economy, the labor market, and the welfare system. As the reader and authors are well aware, the recession that began in 2007 has wreaked havoc on American families, though as scholars of poverty and social inequality have argued, this has been a slow process that has been happening for years. Kristoff summarizes the data on the trend of growing income and wealth inequality in the United States by noting, "C.E.O.'s of the largest American companies earned an average of 42 times as much as the average worker in 1980, but 531 times as much in 2001. Perhaps the most astounding statistic is this: From 1980 to 2005, more than four-fifths of the total increase in American incomes went to the richest 1 percent" (Kristoff 2010).

Another way of examining this trend is to note that if the minimum wage had kept pace with CEO pay, today the minimum wage would be about $15 per hour and provide an annual income for full-time workers of $30,000–$10,000 above the poverty line for a family of four. Thus, since 1980, the average worker has been falling behind. As a result, not only is the middle class being virtually eliminated, but the average worker has lost his or her ability to provide the basic necessities for a family. In the 1960s and 1970s, families with a full-time minimum-wage worker were able to afford to buy a home and, with scrimping and saving, even send a child to college. Today, a family relying on a single minimum-wage worker will fall below the poverty line—full-time minimum-wage employment yields about $16,500 per year, and the poverty line for a family of three is around $20,000—and will be eligible for welfare. Thus, a worker's right to earn a living that can provide for a family has been eroded, and that same worker must now rely on the government in order to meet the family's basic needs. And welfare dependency "costs" in terms of rights. A simple example will illustrate: Imagine two families in the local grocery store. One family is paying for its purchases with cash (or check or debit card), and the other is paying for its purchases with food stamps. Now imagine that a youngster in both families would like a candy bar in the checkout line. The family paying with cash has the right to decide whether to indulge the youngster or not. In contrast, the family paying with food stamps has to forfeit this right; candy is not an eligible purchase for food stamps. Though this is a simple example, the point remains that families of today who work in minimum-wage jobs—which, we note, are an increasingly large sector of the economy—often not only face difficulties in providing for basic necessities but must forfeit some of their rights because of their welfare reliance. The shedding of relatively high-paying, often unionized manufacturing jobs has been exacerbated by the recession. Thus, as Kristoff (2010) argues, income and wealth inequalities are likely to continue to grow in the United States. Accompanying this trend will be the forfeiture of more individuals' basic human right to earn a living wage.

APPLYING A HUMAN RIGHTS PERSPECTIVE TO THE STUDY OF THE FAMILY

Rarely do family sociologists frame anything with regard to rights—for example, the right to marriage, the rights of children, or the basic right of families to control their own destinies. In this chapter, we have provided two examples of critical issues facing contemporary US families and how these issues might be reframed as human rights issues. Here we conclude the chapter with specific examples of the ways in which a human rights approach would transform the study of the family.

Family sociology would be transformed if it were to consider the human rights paradigm. For example, if intimate-partner violence were recast as a denial of rights to personal safety and security, then questions and solutions proposed would be very different (Hattery 2009). A welfare system that focused on the child, rather than the parent, would prioritize a child's right to stable, secure housing and nutritious food, regardless of parents' decisions about marriage, employment, drug use, and so on. If the right to marry were considered a "human right," then the debate over gay marriage and its impact would change. If the right to work included the right to earn a living wage, then not only would minimum-wage and employment laws change, but US income inequality would decrease, as would related threats to human rights, such as dependence on welfare and other social-welfare programs.

Processes of research would change. Quite obviously, how researchers frame their questions determines the data that are generated. So, for example, if family scholars interested in marriage simply ask respondents for their marital status and do not ask if they would like the right to marry, then data on the right to family formation will not be generated. Thus, applying a human rights perspective to the study of the contemporary family will change, in many significant ways, the types of questions that scholars ask and the kinds of data collected for analysis.

APPLYING FAMILY SOCIOLOGY TO HUMAN RIGHTS RESEARCH

Just as family sociology is ripe for transformation through application of the human rights paradigm, the field of human rights can be transformed by family sociology. Quite simply, human rights research and theory rarely focus on the institution of the family; nor is the family generally conceptualized as a unit for analysis. In fact, as we have shown, the family is one of the most basic and fundamental institutions in which human rights play out. For example, human rights scholars study and pontificate about bride burning in India. Few rigorously examine intimate-partner violence in the United States, a phenomenon annually affecting millions of Americans and resulting in fifteen hundred murders. Similarly, human rights scholars conceptualize the US welfare system as a class (or race) issue but rarely examine the ways in which it restricts family life. Thus, we argue that scholars of the human rights paradigm are obligated to turn their attention to family sociology issues.

We agree with our colleagues Blau and Moncada that "every human being has moral rights to equality and has moral obligations not to violate or ignore the rights of others" (2005, 5). The right to equality and the protection of this right includes the family. Our chapter encourages family sociologists to see the ways in which the human rights paradigm would transform the field and, in turn, challenges human rights scholars to consider how their work could impact family sociology.

CHAPTER SIXTEEN

ORGANIZATIONS, OCCUPATIONS, AND WORK

J. Kenneth Benson

A commitment to the advancement of human rights for all people underlies this chapter. In the following pages, I analyze the implications of this commitment for the study of organizations, occupations, and work. I am indebted to the call of Gideon Sjoberg, Ted Vaughan, and their coauthors who have argued for the development of a sociology of human rights and for the grounding of the discipline in a concern with human rights. Burawoy (2005, 2006) recognizes different kinds of sociologies—professional, critical, policy, and public—and argues for reflexive interactions between them. Professional studies then would provide knowledge of existing realities, and critical and public sociologies would criticize those realities and design ways to alter them. In this view, human rights concerns would be a part of critical and public sociologies that take account of the theories and findings of professional sociology but subject those findings to critical, reflexive examination and advocate alternative realities. Organic public sociologists directly participate in publics—for example, social movements—carrying on an extended dialogue between the discipline and the publics (Burawoy 2005, 7). I distinguish between forms of sociological work along the lines suggested by Burawoy and deal with their interactions. I argue that existing studies of organizations, occupations, and work offer many conceptual and theoretical insights relevant to the analysis and realization of human rights. At the same time I contend that a practical and theoretical concern with the realization of human rights requires a thorough rethinking of these fields. The social organization of human societies has profound implications for the realization of human freedom and development of human potentialities. Systems of domination built into organizations, occupations, and work contribute to powerlessness, social isolation, and meaninglessness in human life. Social systems consisting in large part of interdependent patterns of work, occupations, and organizations can destroy the possibility of realizing the potentiality for people to democratically produce their social worlds. Guarantees and protections of human rights provide openings for the collective activity, the social movements, through which new, more humane social worlds might be created. Studies of organizations, occupations, and work have been dominated by deterministic theories and methodologies that make existing systems appear inevitable and necessary (Gouldner 1955).

In recent decades, however, critiques and alternative theories and methodologies have gained a foothold. The dominant perspectives are now contested by a number of alternatives. The critical alternatives have gained a hearing and some influence within the professional discourse of sociology and related fields such as management and political science.

Organizations, Occupations, and Work: The State of the Field

Foundational Puzzles

I focus here on a series of theoretical puzzles pursued in these fields that intersect in significant ways with human rights. I consider the implications of these puzzles for our understanding of human rights—that is, how these puzzles illuminate the tasks of developing and defending human rights. I also deal with the implications of a human rights–oriented praxis for the study of organizations, occupations, and work.

Although joined in the American Sociological Association's Section on Organizations, Occupations, and Work, these fields are somewhat distinct. It is common in the curricula of sociology departments to find separate courses for each field. However, here I identify some central theoretical puzzles that tie the fields together and argue that these central puzzles have profound implications for the realization of human rights.

A theoretical puzzle consists of a set of intersecting arguments about an aspect of social life. The arguments identify a centrally important complex of social phenomena and a set of possible, but potentially conflicting, explanations for those phenomena. Often the puzzles originate in the works of a classical theorist, such as Karl Marx, Émile Durkheim, or Max Weber (1968 [1920]), who defended opposing conceptions of the phenomena and conflicting explanations. These puzzles derive from the efforts of early theorists to understand the modernization of human societies, especially in the West.

The foundational puzzles include the following:

1. *The causes and consequences of bureaucracy:* Why do human societies undergoing modernization organize many spheres of activity into highly differentiated, hierarchical structures featuring elaborate systems of rules? What are the consequences of these organizational structures for the performance of the tasks of human societies and for the development of human societies? Are there any viable alternatives to bureaucracy for modernizing societies?

2. *The causes and consequences of technological change:* Why do human societies develop increasingly complex and sophisticated technologies, including especially increasingly complex machines and coordinated routines, that reorganize work and the administrative control structures governing work? How do these technological changes and diverse technological forms affect the development of human societies?

Are there alternative technologies and work organizations that are effective but less alienating for people?

3. *The causes and consequences of structural inequality:* Why do human societies develop organizational structures featuring varied forms of inequality between positions, organizations, and institutional sectors? How do these structured inequalities affect the development of human actors? Are alternative organizational forms featuring less inequality possible?

4. *The causes and consequences of such decentralized, participatory organizational systems:* "Professional control" (Freidson 2001), "responsible autonomy" (Friedman 1977), "workers' participation" (Poole 1975), and "self-management" (Markovic 1974) offer some measure of relief from bureaucracy.

5. *The causes and consequences of alienation:* Marx (1964 [1844]) argued that alienation in the sense of powerlessness, meaninglessness, and self-estrangement is driven by the normal operation of the capitalist mode of production. Bureaucracy, industrial technology, and power inequalities are endemic features of capitalist societies that break down the possibilities of people to control their own lives and their communities. Civil societies are destroyed by the advance of these forces. Durkheim's (1964 [1893]) analysis of the division of labor draws out similar themes. The human-relations approach to industrial management (Mayo 1933; Roethlisberger and Dickson 1947) developed techniques for engaging industrial workers in their tasks and integrating them into their work groups.

OPPOSING EXPLANATORY PARADIGMS IN THE STUDY OF ORGANIZATIONS, OCCUPATIONS, AND WORK

Theoretical work in this area has produced a lively debate about the causes of variation in social organization. Distinct paradigms and research programs developed out of the theoretical puzzles. These are a part of what Burawoy (2005) calls "professional sociology." A rational model growing out of the work of Weber (1968 [1920]) and the practical problems of industrial management (Taylor 1967 [1910]) has been challenged by a number of alternatives. The rational model remains especially powerful in organizational and industrial sociology and had considerable impact on studies of work and occupations. Alternatives drew to a considerable extent on the work of Durkheim as channeled through structural-functional theories of Parsons (1951), Merton (1968), and others. Influential occupation/work scholars (Hughes 1971; Strauss 1978) often formulated their ideas in conflict with the rational and functional approaches.

The Rational Model

Some influential organization theorists developed deterministic arguments linking causes and effects through the tendency of the organization to make rational choices. Thus, for example, in order to be effective, complex technologies require a decentralized and somewhat flexible organizational structure (Perrow 1967), or large organizations require a hierarchical and differentiated structure (Blau and Schoenherr 1971). These kinds of arguments assume, explicitly or implicitly, a rational decision process producing efficient or effective organizations (Benson 1983). Organizations choose structures and practices that produce efficiency or effectiveness. The perspective is based on two major elements.

> *Boundary assumption:* The organization is a self-controlling entity with boundaries allowing it to select its own internal structural arrangements. In much of the literature, the boundaries of organizations are taken to be real and effective limits, containing the causal forces that shape the organization.
>
> *Selection assumption:* The organization selects its tasks, strategies, and structures in ways intended to produce success in reaching goals. Thus, observed organizational patterns—hierarchies, divisions of labor, technologies, reward systems, and other features—are explained by the rational pursuit of goals.

The boundary and selection assumptions are obviously based on a simplification of reality. Selections of strategies and structures are often imposed from outside the organization—for example, in legislation, contracts, or incorporating documents. But the model permits the formulation of predictions and explanations.

Transaction-cost theory (Williamson 1985), a version of the rational model, was developed by economists extending rational-choice theory to explain the social organization of firms and industries. They offer explanations for the development of bureaucratic organizations (firms and other hierarchies) rather than markets to govern economic activities. They argue that the cost of transactions in markets sometimes makes it more efficient to merge firms or extend the boundaries of firms rather than to connect to other firms through markets and contracts. In this way the presence of nonmarket arrangements can be given a rational explanation, and predictions can be generated.

Challenges to the Rational Model

Challenges to rational explanations are numerous. Here I briefly review some of the prominent alternatives. Dobbin (2005) provides a similar review of theoretical approaches.

Open-systems theory challenges the boundary and selection assumptions. The boundaries are seen as porous and vulnerable to intrusions by social forces beyond the control of the organization. Political, economic, and cultural conditions shape the options of the organization and its decision-makers. Internally, too, there are opposing tendencies, recalcitrant units, interest conflicts, and competing loyalties. The organization must also meet its needs to maintain itself as a system, and the fulfillment of needs sometimes requires the sacrifice or compromise of goals. Decision-makers monitor the external environment and respond to its pressures, threats, and opportunities. They also try to manage the internal sources of resistance, irrationality, and apathy. Balancing these various pressures, they try to ensure the survival, health, and success of the organization. Scott (1998) covers this view extensively in his encyclopedic textbook, in which even Marxist ideas find a place within the open-system framework.

Symbolic interaction studies of organizations and work developed alternatives to bureaucracy. Strauss (1978, 1993), Hall (1972), Hall and McGinty (2001), and others developed a negotiated-order model. They have seen this as an alternative to the bureaucracy model derived from the work of Max Weber and developed in mainstream studies of organizations. Strauss and his associates in various studies showed that hospitals do not follow a bureaucratic model of hierarchical authority, strict role differentiation, and extensive rule-following behavior. They observed many situations in hospitals and elsewhere where professionals controlled their own work through "negotiations" carried out in everyday work situations. Hierarchies and strict divisions of labor broke down in the face of work to be accomplished and problems to be solved.

There are also power theories where Heydebrand (1977), Clegg (1989), Perrow (2002), Roy (1997), and others developed explanations focused on opposing interests and differential power to pursue interests. They contend that various interests have a stake in the shaping of organizations, and organizational practices are controlled by those with more power to defend their interests. There are factional divisions within organizations, and they are often linked to external interest formations. So, interest divisions and related power structures determine the strategies and structures of organizations. In work and occupation studies too, power approaches are prominent. Freidson (1970) analyzed the US medical-care system as a case of "medical dominance."

Constructionist theories, like that of Czarniawska (1997), argue that organizational practices are repeated and become accepted, normalized rituals. So, people repeat them many times over without engaging in a rational decision to select them.

Institutionalists—old (Selznick 1947, Stinchcombe 1997) and new (Scott 2001)— contend that organizations are shaped by previously established practices that have become normative and entrenched in relationships to other organizations (Nee 2005). In a classic formulation, Selznick (1947) argued that the Tennessee Valley Authority (TVA), in an effort to survive in an established organizational environment, compromised its goal of reducing the social inequalities of the American South and developed mutually supportive relations with the previously existing power holders and entrenched organizations of the region. The TVA had to adjust to an environment consisting of other organizations and established authorities with entrenched power bases. Goals were developed and modified through the struggle to survive as an organization in such an environment. Selznick drew ideas and inspiration from Michels's (1962 [1915]) study of a left-wing political party that became internally oligarchical in violation of its democratic ideology.

The "new institutionalists" propose normative and cultural explanations for organizational patterns. These arguments stress regulations, normative practices, and cognitive models as explanations for organizational structural formations (Scott 2001). Dobbin (1994), for example, has argued that during the nineteenth century, France, Britain, and the United States enacted different systems for organizing and regulating railroads, and the selected systems grew out of previously established organizing models in the societies. Here, too, there is an argument about repetition of previously established patterns of thinking. These repetitions come not only from practices required by law or rules but also from cognitive models, ideas carried in the minds of participants. The argument at this point is similar to theories of Bourdieu (1984) about cultural transmission and reproduction of established practices.

Institutionalism shows that there are variant forms of organizations, occupational systems, and work arrangements. Bureaucratization is affected by forces such as increasing scale (size) and technology, but these are not immutable forces beyond the control of human actors (agents) or independent of shaping by political, economic, and cultural contexts. These variant forms have differing implications for the realization of human rights. Different forms of capitalism have varying implications for the welfare of human beings and the realization of human rights (Sabel and Zeitlin 1997; Hall and Soskice 2001). The differences are not just a matter of culture but depend also on combinations of circumstances in the formative stages of institutions. Varying sets of interest combinations might have the upper hand in particular times and places, thus institutionalizing different forms of capitalism (Roy 1997, 263).

Marxist theories of industrial-capitalist societies (Burawoy 1983; Braverman 1974; Burawoy and Lukacs, 1992) identify the macro structures composed of multiple organizations, institutional sectors, and their organizing logics and contradictions. The recent literature on the labor process (Knights and Willmott 1990) was stimulated by the work of Braverman (1974). Working in the Marxist tradition, Braverman thought of the labor process as the seeking of capitalists to extract surplus value from the employment of labor power. He argued that capitalists seek more and more efficient ways to use labor and to link labor power efficiently to increasingly sophisticated machines. Increasing mechanization of production reduces the skills necessary in workers. Workers then are deskilled as the conception of work is separated from its execution. Braverman's argument predicts an inevitable deskilling of labor as capitalists seek profits through changes in technologies and divisions of labor. Some of the counterarguments (Clawson 1980) stress power, for example, contending that capitalists seek power and control over the labor process through rationalization of work and technologies. Bureaucratic organization and mechanization take skill and control away from workers and deliver control to managers and owners. Some (Burawoy 1979) see capitalists gaining greater control by creating ideologies, technologies, and incentive systems that harness workers to capitalist objectives. Power and ideology arguments were mounted to challenge deterministic rationalism in both cases. Some analysts, Murphy (1990) shows, extended the deskilling hypothesis to the professions and argued that they are undergoing proletarianization.

THE KEY CONCERNS OF THE FIELD

The concerns underlying and expressed in the fields of organizations, occupations, and work are varied and contested. Here I review the major alternatives.

RATIONAL STRUCTURING

Organizations, occupations, and work are studied in order to find and implement the most rational ways of organizing. The ideas of the field are still shaped to a considerable degree by the practical problems of making organizations, occupations, and work more efficient, productive, and profitable. These are legitimate and important questions but should not, and do not, define the boundaries of acceptable discourse. Rational structuring is not only a concern of business and industrial production but also an issue in government, professional, religious, and other organizations. In some settings questions about efficiency can challenge patterns of domination—for example, the excessive bureaucratic centralization of the Soviet bureaucracies. But values, beyond efficiency and effectiveness in reaching goals, should be part of the discourse about organizations. The human rights paradigm should be a part of the ongoing debates about organizational forms. The commitment to rational structuring may be lodged in decision-making bodies external to the organization—for example, ownership groups such as shareholders or governing authorities—that intervene periodically to keep the organization on track to achieve its goals.

INTERPRETIVE CONCERNS

Some scholars are concerned with providing interpretations of people and events in organizations and work situations. They typically utilize subjective research methods, including both observational studies and analysis of texts produced or utilized in a setting. The intent is to render a sensitive account of events and actions that permits others to better understand the situation. Abolafia (2001) analyzed the social construction of markets by traders on the New York Stock Exchange. He shows both how trading is shaped by its institutional context and how traders construct their work.

MORAL CONCERNS

The classic theorists—Marx, Durkheim, Weber, Simmel, Tönnies, and others—were morally concerned with the state of contemporary societies, and their theories were tied into their moral concerns (Wardell and Turner 1986). The human rights paradigm offers an opportunity to reflect upon the moral issues embedded in studies of social organization and to develop a set of explicit moral concerns about social organization. Reflecting on descriptive findings of social scientists opens alternative possibilities for organizing human societies and for moral engagement with the alternatives. The human rights paradigm provides an explicit formulation of a set of moral concerns that can challenge the dominance of the praxis of rational structuring.

EXPLANATORY CONCERNS

Much of the work in these fields is driven by a search for causal explanations, with practical concerns with efficiency or effectiveness in the background. Which organizational structures are associated with particular functions or tasks? For example, are research-and-development units structured in a less hierarchical way than production units? Are decentralized firms quicker to make technological innovations or to enter new markets? Are professionals less alienated in less centralized, participatory organizations? In many of these inquiries, the researchers may say little or nothing about the search for the most rational or efficient ways of organizing. However, the rationality concern is so deeply institutionalized that such inquiries are implicitly tied into the praxis of rational structuring. Czarniawska (1997) uses a narrative method to give the reader an understanding of how people working in organizations follow routines that have grown up around the established tasks or functions. With repetition these become rituals that are disconnected from the goals and formal procedures of the bureaucracies. These accounts provide a unique understanding of the settings. Her accounts are similar to those from interactionist studies in the research tradition of Strauss (1993).

EMANCIPATORY CONCERNS

These fields include some scholars who focus explicitly on liberation or emancipation of people and institutions from centers of power and domination. They invoke values beyond the pursuit of "formal rationality" through making organizations effective and efficient in reaching goals. There are a number of important directions of emancipatory work (for example, Alvesson 2009; Alvesson and Willmott 1992, 2003; Adams and Balfour 1998). Some of these are emancipatory by undercutting the claims of rationality within the rational model. Dorothy Smith (1990, 1987, 1999) accomplishes this by revealing another social world hidden but coexisting within the bureaucracies.

FINDINGS

The study of organizations, occupations, and work has produced a large number of findings over the years. The findings are embedded in and grow out of research programs. The "findings" are contentions supported by empirical evidence to some degree but also by the orienting arguments of research groups. The research programs represent a "contested terrain" (Edwards 1979).

Rationalization accompanies and grows with the modernization of societies. Thus, organizations, occupations, and work in modernizing societies are increasingly governed by norms of rationality extending across an array of institutions—industry, government, science, education. For example, see Thomas et al. (1987).

Bureaucracy increases in extent and complexity with the size of organizations (Blau and Schoenherr 1970). Specifically, organizations become more hierarchical and differentiated as they grow in size. This relationship is said to be a result of organizations seeking to reach goals efficiently as organizations grow. It is assumed that hierarchy and differentiation are effective means for coordinating work in large organizations. For critiques of this line of research, see Gouldner (1965) and Turner (1977). For an influential defense, see Donaldson (1987).

Administrative structures—hierarchy, differentiation, and rule systems—vary with the technologies, goals, and/or functions of organizations. It is assumed that the structures are selected for their fit. Etzioni (1961), Perrow (1967), and others developed this argument in the 1960s. The perspective remains as an important set of explanatory ideas that are invoked, sometimes in conjunction with other arguments.

Administrative structures vary with the strategic decisions of managers, owners, and administrators. These strategic decisions represent rational judgments made in specific circumstances such as market conditions or opportunities. This is a finding from managerialist studies, which generally see managers making rational decisions in the context of the circumstances and opportunities confronting their firms at particular times. These findings by scholars such as Chandler (1962, 1977) in his series of business histories open the way to another kind of argument and supporting set of findings. These involve the analysis of changing management ideologies and reasoning frameworks or logics, a direction that Child (1972) used to open managerial logics to analysis. Managers' strategic decisions are an independent source of variation, not just rational responses to circumstances and opportunities presented by the market or new technologies. If the managerial logics are not simply based on objectively rational responses to the challenges and opportunities faced by an organization, then many alternative outcomes are possible. Child's work connects to an older stream of thought associated with March and Simon (1958), which suggests careful studies of management decision-making, including the internal political processes in organizations through which powerful departments select managers with strategic views supportive of their interests (Cyert and March 1963).

Organizations with their associated work and occupational practices are shaped by their institutional, organizational, and political environments (Fligstein 2001). Organizations, occupations, and work are arranged in different ways, find different solutions to similar problems, and develop in accord with different institutional models and political systems. Politically negotiated regimes enforce models and control systems.

These effects blunt or redirect the effects of rational choice, technology, and size. Organizational arrangements are swept along by forces beyond their boundaries and their control (March and Olson 1984).

Technologies are shaped by social and political processes in organizations and the larger social world. Thomas (1994) has shown how high-technology manufacturing companies develop and adopt new technologies through a complex political negotiation among interest groups based in the different departments of the organizations.

Organizational, occupational, and work structures and practices are shaped by the modes of production—for example, different forms of capitalist, social democratic, and socialist systems. The contradictions of the larger mode of production and its class conflicts shape the organization of work and power structures in organizations. Burawoy (1983) and others have developed this line of thought. Burawoy and Lukács (1992) in particular analyzed the similarities and differences in work organizations between capitalist and socialist industrial work. They found that factories in the United States and in socialist Hungary were incorporated into larger corporate or state administrative structures, but the Hungarian factories were subjected to scarcities that caused workers to be innovative and resourceful in order to do their work and earn their pay. In earlier comparative work, Burawoy (1983) argued that "factory regimes," the systems of discipline and control of factory workers, varied among capitalist countries. Thus, there is not just one capitalist mode of production but multiple forms of capitalism featuring divergent ways of organizing production and distribution (Hall and Soskice 2001; Sabel and Zeitlin 1997).

Multiorganizational systems are beset by contradictions and tensions that generate opposing interests and social movements within and beyond the systems (Offe 1984, 1985). These interests and movements produce instability and social change in the operation of the organizations and systems. Studies of the policy process by Hall and McGinty (1997) show that public policies, once made by legislation, are transformed through the pulling and hauling of the implementers; so they conclude that policy-making is the "transformation of intentions." Social movements form around the contradictions and tensions and reshape the directions of the organizations and systems (Davis et al. 2005).

Networks are increasingly powerful compared to hierarchical bureaucracies in contemporary societies (Castells 2000). Clegg (1990) argues that recent decades have seen a reversal of the long-term trend toward centralization of administrative structures and consolidation of power in bureaucratic organizations. Guillén (2001) finds that international business networks provide opportunities for innovation leading to diverse national models rather than convergence.

Many organizations persist despite failures to develop internally rational practices and meet objectives (Brunsson 1985; Meyer and Zucker 1989). This finding challenges the rational model.

Levels of alienation from work are affected by types of technologies of industries and varied ways of organizing workplaces. Assembly lines, bureaucratic hierarchies, responsible autonomy, and so on (Blauner 1964; Friedman 1977).

RESEARCH METHODOLOGIES

The methodologies of these fields are varied and, to a considerable extent, contested by the advocates and critics of particular approaches. Here I describe the contested methodological claims.

Fact/value separation versus fact/value contestation. The dominant methodological stance in these fields separates facts and values. Separation is defended by advocates of an exclusively scientific, empirically based discipline. Empirical observations are sought as a basis for building and testing theories. Statements of value or morality are separated from descriptive and predictive/explanatory theories, and this stance discounts the study of emergent possibilities and alternate models based on ideals. The scholar pursues empirical regularities and generalizations about causes and consequences based on rigorous empirical observations. If he or she has moral concerns about the phenomena observed, these might be set off in a footnote or an appendix or perhaps another kind of document altogether. In this methodology one must be careful not to allow values or moral concerns to contaminate the scientific observations and analyses. By contrast, Sjoberg and others argue that theories and methods (paradigms) in professional sociology have moral values and commitments inextricably built into them. The idea of a completely value-free sociology is illusory; thus it is necessary to illuminate those underlying moral values and commitments (Sjoberg, Gill, and Williams 2001).

Theorizing only the empirically observable versus challenging existing "realities" through "countersystem models." The positivist view is to deal only with concepts that can be observed and verified through empirical methods. This methodological stance makes it more difficult to see alternatives to the present realities and to analyze the possibilities for realization of human rights. Sjoberg, Gill, and Cain (2003) call these alternatives "countersystem models." The analyst might construct a model of how an organization based on human rights would be structured and compare that model to empirically observed organizations. Countersystem models then can be partly normative, based on human rights principles, and partly empirical, resting upon alternative realities held by participants. In an earlier formulation Gouldner (1965) suggested an "iron law of democracy" to counter the deterministic pessimism of Michels's "iron law of oligarchy" and Weber's "iron cage" of inevitable bureaucratization. Blau and Moncada (2005), in an argument compatible with countersystem analysis, develop an ideal type of a society built on human rights for all people.

Value neutrality versus reflexive engagement with social movements. The positivist methodology requires that research be carried out from a detached, distinterested stance. Touraine (1981, 1983), by contrast, advocates reflexive engagement with social movements. He argues that sociologists can assist activist groups in analyzing their objectives and strategies, interpreting their movements, and locating them within historical trajectories. The observer assists the group in self-study to reach a reflexive understanding of its position and objectives. In doing so, the sociologist must be immersed in the work of the group but still maintain distance to permit objective analysis. The sociologist must be reflexive about his or her engagement with the movement and with the analytical tools and theories of the discipline. This engagement by the sociologist can help to keep the group engaged with the larger society and developing its discourse (Touraine 1981, 167–222). Touraine (1983) engaged in such reflexive intervention with the Solidarity social movement in Poland. In this way the sociologist can look for emerging possibilities, alternative conceptions of reality, repressed ideas, and social movements within organizations and their extensions beyond their conventional boundaries. A human rights concern leads to a sensitivity to oppressed and hidden movements and fractures of the organizational order of things. Giving voice to these movements may open routes to transformations of the organizations. Davis et al. (2005) call attention to the intersections of organization studies and the study of social movements.

Separating versus contextualizing organizations, occupations, and work in larger social formations and analyzing how the transformations of the social formations move back and forth through the micro, meso, and macro levels of analysis. Burawoy (2006) argues that a professional sociology connected to public sociology must address the embedding of observed phenomena in larger institutional contexts. It must analyze the connections between local and international events. In recent decades the neoliberal political agenda has overwhelmed the protective barriers that restrained market forces in the past. The defenses afforded by labor unions, professional associations, tenure systems, retirement systems, and health-care systems have been gradually compromised and threatened. Market forces have been allowed freer movement of workplaces and reorganizations of firms to pursue market advantages (Streeck 1992). Shareholder value as a logic of action has been allowed to destroy firms and disrupt communities (Fligstein 2001). States have retreated from their powers to shape and defend the systems of economic organizations, networks, and industries. It is important to sustain forms of sociological analysis that examine and critique the larger forces shaping the fields of economic action (Bourdieu 1998). It also important to develop the methodological resources for understanding forces emanating from the micro and meso levels of social formations. Hall and his associates have developed ways of conceptualizing and examining the back-and-forth, up-and-down movements of public policies. Policies emanating from one level are transformed during implementation at other levels (Hall and McGinty 1997).

Determinism versus possibilism. Studies of organizations, occupations, and work have been guided to a considerable extent by a search for deterministic variables that provide causal explanations and predictions. The proposed determinants include economic rationality in the prediction that the most efficient or effective social arrangements will prevail. Mancur Olson (1982) argued that nation-states and other political-economic units that had discarded their entrenched bargains, regulations, and restrictions on capital were most likely to experience rapid economic growth. Olson's view was characterized by Esping-Anderson as a thesis of "institutional sclerosis" (1994, 723). Douglas North argued that stability and order in regulatory regimes are essential to the growth and prosperity of business organizations. Weberian scholars have argued that rationalization of organizations and work is an inevitable tendency in modernizing societies, driven by the persistent search for more and more rational social arrangements. Some Marxists have predicted the inevitability of class conflict and reorganization of capitalist institutions toward production efficiency (Bottomore 1985). However, many scholars in these fields have argued for a kind of "possibilism" stressing multiple causes and contingent combinations of causes and uncertainty of outcomes. Weber himself took such a position (Kalberg 1994) as did Henri Lefebvre (1968), a French Marxist. Touraine (1981, 1983) develops a similar stance in his social-movement approach to social organization, as does Prechel (2000) in his work on corporate organizational structures, specifically, the development of firms with many subsidiaries. In the study of professions, historical comparative studies have challenged the adequacy of deterministic arguments such as Braverman's deskilling thesis (Murphy 1990).

LEARNING FROM STUDIES OF ORGANIZATIONS, OCCUPATIONS, AND WORK

The sociology of organizations, occupations, and work offers some lessons for the development of a human rights paradigm. Social organization has significant implications for the realization of human rights. Often human rights are denied or diminished by the social organization in these areas. The problems include the following: First, excessive domination denying actors the opportunity to control or participate meaningfully in the construction of their work settings, political systems, and communities. The result can be a pervasive alienation both in the structural sense and the social-psychological sense. In some cases it produces the complete collapse of the civil society through which people form communities and identities.

Second, the excessive and debilitating differentiation of work and other organizational settings denies people the opportunity to develop their capacities as human beings, narrowing the freedoms of people to pursue their own intellectual, cultural, and social development.

Third, inequalities and uneven development of social organization can narrow the range of opportunities available to minorities and to regional and sectoral divisions. Often the divisions of organizations, occupational categories, and work assignments correspond to spatial and ethnic differentiations of a society or international formation. The differentiations of the population are built into the structure of the organizations and occupational categories. Durkheim (1964 [1893]) referred to this pattern as the "forced division of labor," one of his "abnormal forms." Weber referred to "closure," and Marx wrote about "uneven development." Contemporary writers (Baron 1984) have analyzed the contribution of organizations to the construction and reproduction of social inequalities.

Fourth, multiorganizational networks, differentiated but coordinated systems, and competing fields (linked industries and governmental departments) exert control over huge sectors of social life. Policy-making and implementing organizations bring together the interests and powers of these multiorganizational systems. These multiorganizational systems are highly stratified with well-understood positions of dominance and subordination among the units. Policy-makers who would change or reform these systems struggle to find traction for movement and power resources to influence directions. Korpi (1983) analyzed such political processes in Sweden. Benson (1975, 1982) provided some early theoretical ideas on the topic. Many others have contributed to the development of the problem. Scott et al. (2000) drew upon several strands of theory to analyze the US health-care system. Bourdieu (1984, 1998), DiMaggio and Powell (1983), Fligstein (2001), and others have utilized the "field" as a meso-level concept for dealing with these issues.

The forces and powers outlined above show the need for the declaration, implementation, and protection of human rights. These forces and powers greatly restrict the capacity of human beings to collectively, democratically, and cooperatively construct their social worlds and build alternative futures that realize more nearly the dignity and potentiality of the human condition. Yet dismantling the complex networks, organizations, and fields in favor of free and open markets is not a viable option. Bourdieu (1998), among many others, has stated effectively the dangers of that option. Instead we have to reconstruct the organizations, occupations, networks, and fields.

I suggest six steps in the reconstruction:

1. *Working reflexively as organic intellectuals in the social-movement organizations supporting human rights.* Touraine's (1981, 1983) model of engagement with social movements provides some guidelines. Sociologists and others studying human rights organizations may choose to be critical partisans rather than objective, detached observers. In this way theory and praxis may be more perfectly and fruitfully connected.
2. *Broadening decision-making in organizations to include participants and recipients in more significant ways.* Critical organization theory challenges the powers of central authorities and centers of power. We must develop stakeholder theory to guide this effort.
3. *Challenging the rights of business corporations.* Corporations are treated in American law and practice as actors with legal rights and powers. Vaughan, Sjoberg, and Reynolds (1993) and Sjoberg, Gill, and Williams (2001) have made this point very strongly in several publications. The powers vested in corporations must be challenged, debated, limited, and revised through democratic processes. In social democratic societies such debates and limitations have been accomplished to some extent, for example, in codetermination laws.

4. *Designing multiorganizational systems extending and defending human rights regimes.* The system of property rights must be challenged and redesigned. Limits must be placed on the property rights of capitalist corporations, in effect reducing the power of corporations, for example, by limiting the right to reorganize the labor process in pursuit of profit.

5. *Designing new institutional arrangements to make possible a viable civil society, following up Burawoy's argument that both the market and the state must be countered by civil society.* What kinds of organizational structures would be supportive of civil society? Network and field studies can be utilized in the development of these objectives. Can you build a set of interdependent relationships between organizations that support a robust discourse in civil society?

6. *Recognizing the variety of organizational arrangements and taking a constructionist view of possibilities.* This would entail rejecting the assumption that "there is no alternative" (Clegg 1990). But possibilism does not mean that anything is possible. Markovic (1974) argued there were only three possible futures for Yugoslavia: bureaucracy, capitalism, or self-management. Rather, possibilism entails analyzing the possibilities for effective action for human rights at a particular time and place. Some possibilities are open and others are closed at a given time. The set of boundaries and limits to negotiation at a given time is an aspect of social structure (Abbott 1988). Activists for human rights must analyze the situation, mobilize resources, and institutionalize their gains. Consider Korpi's (1983) argument about mobilizing power resources, husbanding them wisely, utilizing them effectively, building investments of resources into the system, and preparing for the next opening. Also, consider building movement organizations that are dialectical in the sense that diverse perspectives are included rather than excluded and the processes for democratically confronting differences is built. White (1974) calls this kind of system a "dialectical organization."

A RESITUATION OF THE AREA/FIELD

Here we consider how the study of organizations, occupations, and work might be reshaped by its connection to the human rights paradigm. Previously I argued that the field should be guided by a praxis of liberating people from systems of domination (Benson 1977). A "public sociology for human rights" (Burawoy 2006) gives more specificity to that proposal. The discipline would be concerned with building organizations and reorganizing work and occupational structures to realize human rights, specifically the right to participate meaningfully in the design and control of work and the right to democratically, collectively, and cooperatively guide the development of societies.

A praxis of human rights would also shape the research agendas of these fields. Social-movement organizations and NGOs concerned with human rights can be studied and made more effective. Conventional organization theory and social-movement theory may be useful in this connection. It may be possible to study human rights organizations in ways that connect their goals and strategies more effectively—that is, to make strategic choices and develop administrative means that move the organizations more efficiently toward the realization of their goals. However, the range of studies must include critical, reflexive perspectives. The organizational means that are used to address human rights must themselves be operated in a way that upholds human rights. The internal methods of governing the social-movement organizations and relationships with constituents must be consistent with human rights principles. Exploitation, domination, subordination, and other methods resulting in alienation of participants must be resisted. Also the role of the scholar must be addressed. One way is to follow Touraine's (1981, 1983) model of reflexive engagement with the movement. Extending organizational liberation beyond the borders of any one nation and studying how to build global networks of democratic organizations would be important too.

Concentrations of power must be continuously challenged. Burawoy (2006) and others argue that this ongoing challenge requires a strong "civil society" consisting of social movements and movement organizations that can mobilize the population and develop power resources for limiting and revising the powers of centralized corporate and governmental bureaucracies. Scholars who criticized Soviet bureaucracies noted the destruction of mediating organizations and institutions. The Soviet bureaucracy drew all powers into itself and crushed organizations outside its control. Two Polish scholars (Kostecki and Mrela 1984) writing in the period of the Solidarity movement referred to these as "powdered" societies in the sense that all sources of possible challenge to bureaucratic power had been pulverized, leaving people as isolated particles subject to absolute control from above. They argued that these bureaucracies had produced a vacuum in the space that had been civil society. Solidarity was able to move into this space and create an effective challenge to the bureaucracy.

Developing stakeholder theory (Freeman 1984) is an approach to business management that runs counter to shareholder value as the dominant criterion for decisions. The general idea is that many different kinds of interests are affected by corporate actions. These include employees, the community, consumers, and so on. In this view, actions such as building a plant, closing a factory, or investing in a new technology would be made through consideration of and consultation with the various stakeholders. We might argue that human rights would call for the expansion and implementation of something similar to stakeholder rights. Also, it would be important that the rights of people not be infringed by corporate decisions in which these individuals have no voice or mechanism for being heard.

A robust civil society would include an extensive array of interorganizational networks. While some have championed networks as a more democratic step forward, networks do not necessarily end systems of domination (Sjoberg, Gill, and Williams 2001). We already have numerous studies that reveal power inequalities in networks (Laumann and Knoke 1987). Peter Bogason (2006), a social scientist in Denmark, is associated with a Centre on Democratic Network Governance and has written about such networks.

Developing nongovernmental network organizations can resolve many conflicts. Elinor Ostrom (1990) has studied and advocated the formation of networks that various interests form to settle differences and arrive at solutions to common problems. For example, farmers and other interests sometimes form associations to govern water rights. For her efforts in this direction she was awarded a Nobel Prize in economics a few years ago.

A LOOK FORWARD: NEW QUESTIONS AND NEW POSSIBILITIES FOR BOTH THE AREA/FIELD AND HUMAN RIGHTS REALIZATIONS

Alvin Gouldner (1965) confronted the pessimistic determinism of the classical theorists. We now face new sources of metaphysical pathos in current assessments of the future of democracy. The nation-state as a protector of human rights has diminished power vis-à-vis international corporations. In any case its policies are dominated by the unregulated powers of those corporations. The labor movement has lost much of its power to protect even workers' rights. International organizations facilitate the movements of capital and industrial jobs to low-wage countries where rights are not protected. The rational model, in new forms such as transaction-cost economics, still legitimates these developments. Studies of organizations, occupations, and work have never been more important.

The history of research and theory in these fields includes many challenges to the dominance of the rational model. But rationalization goes on and reaches new heights of achievement and degradation. It is to be hoped that the human rights movement will successfully challenge these trends. The events themselves generate increasingly glaring contradictions. By addressing those in the interest of human rights, we can contribute to the emancipatory possibilities of human action. Theories of the past and present provide openings for thought and action.

CHAPTER SEVENTEEN

POLITICAL SOCIOLOGY

Thomas Janoski

Influenced by nineteenth-century Enlightenment universalism, the concept of human rights has deep roots in the politics of Europe and America (Delanty 2009). After World War II, human rights became pervasive as states derived much of their legitimacy from being embedded in the larger world of the United Nations, with its legitimating values in human rights declarations. As notions of citizenship, human rights, and individuality spread across state boundaries as well, more organizations, institutions, and social movements created a common human rights culture in the world, especially after the fall of communism. Yet, human rights still has many tensions, contradictions, and violations.

Political sociology has thoroughly addressed citizenship rights within countries, but it has been in slow opening up to global human rights. This survey of political sociology and human rights examines four areas concerning this relationship. First, it looks at key questions of morality and philosophies of law, then major theories of political sociology. Second, the most important findings in the field are examined in the area of revolutions, internal rights processes, world governments, and the most current human rights scenario. Third, the different methods in the field are reviewed. Fourth, the reorientation of political sociology toward human rights and future research is addressed.

KEY QUESTIONS AND THEORIES

HUMAN RIGHTS AS A SOCIOLOGICAL TOPIC

Theories of human rights often invoke morality and are at odds with value-free social science. Human rights theories tend to come out of a particular philosophy of law called natural law. Yet, at the same time, two other philosophies of law—legal positivism and legal realism—would not cede human rights to natural law alone. However, developing empirical proof of human rights as residing in religion is generally not possible, nor is finding the sociological evidence for some natural condition of humanity embedded in all of us. Political sociology frequently has a stronger basis in legal positivism, which is typically tied to ideas of rationality and/or legal realism, which are approached in terms of interests, emotions, and traditions. Even though sociologists commonly assume that these rights are innate, sociology has difficulty with human rights as natural rights because human rights' truth claims are difficult to pin down. However, sociology need not verify the truth claims of natural human rights because, according to the W. I. Thomas theorem, a sociologist views a situation as real if people define it as such and consequences follow. Thus, political sociologists can make claims for the consequences of people following ethics or natural law.

One weakness of the human rights tradition is that it tends to avoid duties and obligations. Rights and obligations exist in a system; speaking about one without the other is problematic (Janoski 1998). Because of the human rights focus on massive deprivations of rights, obligations may not stand out as important, but they are needed to enforce rights. Thus, the political sociologist must have a clear-minded view of both rights and duties.

POLITICAL THEORIES OF HUMAN RIGHTS

Five theories of political sociology deal with human rights. First, convergence theories claim that states respond to common social forces, social movements, and international organizations to adopt similar cultural norms that reinforce human rights. This may often occur through a diffusion process, but with theories of globalization, this process itself becomes an isomorphic force that pressures states to adopt human rights conventions. An initial component of this pressure is identifying inconsistencies in application of internal state constitutions and laws that obligate a state to treat everyone as equally endowed with various rights. Although China has been a significant exception, a second component, international human rights requirements, is powerful. Unless those requirements are satisfied, access to markets is not assured, and states will face boycotts or other sanctions.

This type of convergence theory can have an implicit structural-functionalist undercurrent. For instance, some claim that states must have a strong bourgeoisie and a capitalist system to gain democratic rights (Lipset 1981; Huntington 1991) because democracies and rights only emerge from the capitalist system with economic growth. Thus, as resources catch up to needs, societies will increasingly fulfill those needs. Convergence theories can be subject to the weaknesses of functionalism in that the mechanisms for the global convergence of ideas and human rights sometimes remain vague. Given emphases on convergence, retrenchment of rights is often ignored.

Second, power-constellations theory takes an interest-driven approach to human rights (Huber and Stephens 2001). People whose rights are not protected eventually realize their interests and mobilize resources to influence the state to enact those rights. Whether citizenship or human rights are enacted within states depends upon power resources of various social movements and political parties. Originally focused on class, this theory requires vigilance concerning the power bases of various human rights groups in their abilities to create membership, organization, finances, and even military capacities to press their claims. A wealth of information exists on how social movements and political parties gain these power resources within states to pass new legislation, change constitutions, or press legal claims in courts. The power-constellations approach has generalized power-resources approaches to consider gender, racial and ethnic, and other groups that mobilize resources to press human rights claims. Often these groups must operate within an institutionally structured environment that constrains state formation, but these constraints are usually what they are trying to change. The social movements it examines may often invoke human rights, but the theory itself sees interests rather than natural rights as motivating political processes.

Third, world polity is a global system of creating value through authority with rules, frames, or models (Meyer 2010; Boli and Thomas 1997, 172). States and organizations in civil society enact global models that create "more structuration" than internal societal processes of states would produce (Meyer et al. 1997, 173). These global movements have widely shared principles of human rights. The United Nations and voluntary civil society associations have played salient roles in implementing this order and spreading its moral culture. Once enacted, world culture consists of states as rational actors that operate according to formal and often universalistic rules. World culture exerts isomorphic pressure on human rights with causal factors based on seeking good will or assuaging guilt. The institutionalization of these world-cultural models leads to structural similarity as states adopt similar constitutional, public-educational, and welfare systems. International voluntary associations promote, extend, and sometimes actually implement global cultural principles (Boli and Thomas 1997). Inside states, this global culture pressures organized interests to enact new policies. This results in a social "dynamism that is generated by the rampant inconsistencies and conflicts within world culture itself" (Meyer et al. 1997, 172). Different ways to resolve those tensions lead to a variety of world-cultural models. World polity-theory then leads to empirical analysis of various human rights policies using new institutional theories (Schofer and Meyer 2005).

Fourth, Marxist theory and human rights constitute a paradox in political sociology. Marx was dismissive of individual rights in general as a "bourgeois ruse" that would prevent the eventual liberation of workers. Marxist discussion has derided rights as individualistic solutions to social problems and maintained that group rights—specifically workers' or working-class rights—are solutions. On the other hand, Marxist activists and scholars have always been very concerned about human rights abuses and open to ethnic and women's rights. But to a large degree, human rights became a major weakness in communist societies once the capitalist system was eliminated.

As a version of Marxist theory, world-systems theory, with its focus on core and peripheral nation-states, has a twist on human rights. Starting with the Dutch in the United Provinces, the core power has an interest in toleration and human rights within the core. World-systems theory sees this relationship as being in the core's interests to develop new ideas and attract talent from the periphery in order to pursue political-economic dominance and empire (Wallerstein 1974; Hall 2002).

However, human rights in the periphery continue to be trampled upon. World-systems theory does not propose a unique solution to promoting human rights, but it does lay open the contradiction that often exists between rights in the core and the periphery (Hardt and Negri 2009).

Fifth, cosmopolitanism theory has developed along with globalization in the 1990s and promotion of universalistic human rights (Delanty 2009; Beck 2007a). This theory focuses on supranational organizations as guarantors of justice (e.g., world courts, government, and media) and transnational or international nongovernmental organizations (INGOs) and social movements as dynamic factors that create and motivate these institutions (Held 2010; Archibugi 2008). Cosmopolitan theory is highly normative, claiming that the state no longer has sovereignty as INGOs assume power. While state decline is exaggerated, cosmopolitan theory makes recommendations about how to change global institutions and enhance human rights.

KEY FINDINGS IN POLITICAL SOCIOLOGY

The findings of political sociology on human rights consist of four historical contexts of revolutions, states, world governments, and the current and complex global human rights situation.

HUMAN RIGHTS REVOLUTIONS

The age of revolutions directly brought down repressive regimes and indirectly affected many other states, including encouraging steps toward democracy. Explanations of these political changes are theories of state centrism and rising expectations that lead to mobilization (Goodwin 2001). Two outcomes emerged from the ensuing revolutions. First, the American and eventually the French revolutions brought democracy directly to those countries and established foundational documents concerning human rights, the Declaration of Independence in 1776 and the Declaration of the Rights of Man in 1789 (Hunt 2007). Second, communist movements emerged out of the Industrial Revolution to create a second burst of revolutions that resulted in an emphasis on social rights. But these Soviet-led communist revolutions exhibited difficulty in adopting political rights after the first group of democratic countries attained their social and participation rights (Janoski 1998). As a result, communist revolutions led to (1) state-led deprivations of political and human rights that were not overcome, and (2) an East-West stalemate on rights enforcement in the United Nations during the Cold War. The difficulties of communist states adopting human/citizenship rights remains important since mainland China, Cuba, and North Korea are still caught in this conundrum.

While the prevalence of revolutions and human rights was marked during this period, two nonrevolutionary movements should not be ignored. First, internal abolitionist movements from 1820 to 1870 led to states rejecting the slave trade and then banning slavery inside their borders (Hunt 2007). Second, the Crimean

War led to a long-term international social movement to prevent inhumane treatment during wars. From 1859 to 2008, two major transnational institutions were created: the International Red Cross and the Geneva Conventions for the treatment of prisoners (Forsythe 2007; Bennett 2006). The women's rights movement started during this period but did not peak until the end of the twentieth century.

CREATING RIGHTS INSIDE STATES

Although constitutional conventions sometimes create human rights, they are generally enacted out of the proposals made by legislative political parties. These proposals are often propelled by developments in civil society, the media, and social movements. For the Organization for Economic Cooperation and Development (OECD) countries, modern-welfare-state research has shown how citizenship rights were developed through the efforts of left parties with the support of labor and civil rights movements (Huber and Stephens 2001). Cultural values shape developments in different countries. More liberal and left parties, along with some religious groups, promoted human rights in earlier periods. In the courts, judges have influenced internal human rights. Where democracy is weak, social movements may prove especially important, as with Solidarity in Poland or the Mothers of the Plaza de Mayo demonstrations in Argentina. In sum, every country has an internal explanation.

WORLD GOVERNMENTS

After the armistice of 1918, sentiment arose to end arms races, secret diplomacy, and nation-state ambitions. The Paris Peace Conference created the League of Nations in the final Treaty of Versailles. But from a political standpoint, the treaty was flawed by failure to pass the Japanese proposal on the equality of races and then doomed by the American refusal to ratify it.

World War II proved to be even more horrible, with mass genocide, prompting strong international pressure from the Allies to act decisively on guaranteeing peace. The leaders of the most powerful states worked with internal elites to establish the United Nations. The human rights movement with independent elites and INGOs stressed universal and global rights and a responsibility to support these rights in the world, independent of state boundaries. After the Security Council was established, representing the dominant states, and the General Assembly was created, representing all member states, the United Nations passed a series of human rights declarations that large numbers of states ratified (Cole 2005; Donnelly 2006; Wejnert 2005; Morsink 1999).

Research studies have tracked the rapid expansion of human rights treaties, intergovernmental organizations, INGOs, and popular and professional discourses advocating human rights (Pubantz 2005). Since 1970, the world human rights movement has expanded its earlier focus on individual legal protections to a more empowering focus on human rights education. INGOs and social movements have taken the place of states as primary forces. The United Nations expanded refugee

protection through an international asylum regime led by the UN High Commission on Refugees (Morris 2010). By the 1980s, refugees and asylum seekers became
an official category with their own statistics collected by the OECD and others.
While there are still problems and sometimes backlashes, the focus on human
rights with institutions helping refugees and other victims has risen to a new and
encouraging level.

Part of the reason for creating the United Nations was to prevent genocide. This
was capped in the post–World War II era with events such as the Nuremberg trials,
which prosecuted and punished war criminals. Perhaps the greatest achievement
in terms of human rights was the relatively peaceful end of the apartheid regime
in South Africa, which was followed by the Truth and Reconciliation Commission
hearings that created a mass mea culpa with no intention of prosecution. While
some were dissatisfied with the lack of convictions, the subsequent calm and democracy that characterized the country compares favorably to the condemnation of all
Bath Party leaders in Iraq, which led to their recruitment as terrorists.

The United Nations created the International Court of Justice in 1945 to resolve
disputes between nation-states, but this has proven to be ineffective concerning
human rights claims. The court requires that both states acquiesce to its decisions,
and one country usually does not do so. However, the United Nations created
the International Criminal Court in the 1990s, which has convicted individuals
representing states or rogue groups. Nonetheless, preventing genocide remains a
difficult issue.

THE CURRENT GLOBAL HUMAN RIGHTS SCENARIO

The usefulness of the United Nations in promoting human rights was limited by
the deadlock of the Cold War. But the fall of communism led to a new approach to
human rights throughout the world. Four processes and institutions are important
in these developments: INGOs, the United Nations, new courts, and global agencies.

First and perhaps foremost in these developments have been the INGOs, such
as Amnesty International and Human Rights Watch, that pressure and expose
governments on human rights violations (Hafner-Burton and Montgomery 2008;
Hopgood 2006; Shanks, Jacobson, and Kaplan 1996; Smith and Wiest 2005).
Many of these organizations annually provide detailed information on how well
governments are fulfilling human rights expectations. WikiLeaks falls into this
category, but its impact is in revealing information and indirectly in judging human
rights. Another type of INGO (e.g., the Red Cross or Green Crescent, Oxfam,
and Doctors Without Borders) has provided direct relief aid and services while
proliferating and gaining direct access to various arms of the United Nations,
including the Security Council. Many of these INGOs are religious organizations
that raise considerable money but may conflict with other cultures. The impact
of these efforts on human rights abuses is somewhat mixed (Lebovic and Voeten
2006). Hafner-Burton (2008, 713) shows that from 1975 to 2000 in 145 countries,
"naming and shaming" by INGOs, the UN Commission on Human Rights, and
the media had some positive impact on political rights but also increased political

terror. Definitive solutions can be elusive. A critical indirect issue is how much these same policies influence the world polity to bring pressure on governments to improve human rights policies.

Second, the United Nations has continued to be active throughout this period, with increasing influence in creating international criminal courts and additional human rights declarations. However, the enforcement of these declared rights is a weakness of the UN rights regime, and this has not been aided by a number of corruption scandals at the United Nations.

Many international bureaucracies have filled this enforcement gap, and two cosmopolitan thinkers, Held (2010) and Archibugi (2008), make strong arguments that new types of political institutions need to be developed to improve UN action on human rights. Archibugi recommends the expansion of the UN Security Council to include a few more members on a rotating basis and limit the use of the veto power of permanent members. More powerful states would oppose adding to the Security Council, so Singer (2009) recommends proportional representation. Both authors recommend strengthening the General Assembly on human rights by (1) having the people of each country elect an additional representative to the assembly (the other would continue to be appointed by state leaders), and (2) creating an independent UN law-enforcement organization to keep the peace and enforce directives. Archibugi recommends expanding to all countries the International Court of Justice and International Criminal Court and establishing a World Parliamentary Assembly that would perform national citizenship audits, steer political action toward democracy, and evaluate the human rights regimes using smart sanctions (i.e., targeted toward specific and workable areas) for violators. And Held would create a world referendum process across country boundaries at regional and global levels to implement human rights policies. These recommendations are unlikely to pass anytime soon, but this plan for reform delineates clear reforms that would make the United Nations more responsive to human rights crises. A promising development since 2006 is the UN Human Rights Council, which conducts four-year periodic reviews of violations and makes its findings known to member states (OHCHR 2010).

Third, the United Nations established the International Criminal Tribunal for the Former Yugoslavia (ICTY). It has grown from an unfunded UN resolution to an institution with more than a $100 million budget and one thousand employees. Its success opens up international justice to serious consideration by offending states as it is the first effective international court since Nuremberg. The ICTY has crossed borders, overcoming political and organizational difficulties to create a new and effective tribunal. Chief prosecutors Louise Arbour and Carla del Ponte worked with others to reverse its initial failures to arrest and convict significant figures and advance the tribunal's agenda. In particular, they used secret indictments and unexpected arrests to bring prominent war criminals, from soldiers to Slobodan Milošević, to justice. Using the investigations and criminal proceedings of the tribunal, Hagan and Levi (2005) show how the ICTY as an institution was founded and transformed by determined prosecutors into a new transnational legal field (Ginsburg 2009).

The establishment of the world criminal courts brought some triumphant cases and convictions, but subsequent events have been less successful (Hagan and Levi 2005; Hagan and Kutnjak 2006). The UN peacekeeping effort in Rwanda had too few troops and came too late, and the International Criminal Tribunal for Rwanda faced major obstacles. Many efforts in Somalia were fraught with the contradiction of peacekeeping creating more violence (Hagan and Kutnjak 2006; Power 2002). Later difficulties emerged with the prosecution of Sudanese leaders responsible for the tragedy in Darfur. While problems with these courts and peacekeeping efforts to prevent genocide have not been solved, these courts are an important new development.

In a "multicultural critique of international human rights," Stacy (2009) asks whether universal standards of human behavior can gain any real traction in a world of diverse religious, cultural, and national beliefs. Regional courts can help solve this problem. The European Court of Justice and, more recently (1998), the European Court of Human Rights provide an increasingly popular way to address human rights violations. In the Americas, the Organization of American States has the Inter-American Court of Human Rights, which plays an important but not decisive role in protecting those rights. The African Union has an African Court on Human and Peoples' Rights, which is a promising start. The countries of the Association of Southeast Asian Nations have a fledgling human rights system. But the Muslim countries in the Middle East and Africa lack a larger regional framework, which is important since their laws are generally decentralized but powerful within states. Currently, the European regional courts are the strongest institutions in this category, but many liken the Europeanization process to state building, and others contend that the various European courts concentrate too much on interstate jurisdictional disputes (rather than within-state problems). Nonetheless, these European courts are an example to be followed by other regions. Finally, two powerful states have been reluctant participants in these and wider types of courts—the United States and China—except when referring to other countries' violations (Blau et al. 2008; Quigley 2009; Amnesty International 2010).

Fourth, human rights can also be enforced or abridged in organizations such as the World Trade Organization (WTO), World Bank, and International Monetary Fund (Hafner-Burton 2009). These organizations have formulated rules and forums that displace parts of many state legal systems. Held (2010) wants these organizations to be more open, perhaps with the public election of representatives who would be more likely to uncover hidden practices. Archibugi (2008) indicates that these organizations should endorse human rights, democracy, and nonviolence and exert pressure for these values inside authoritarian and transitional states.

This legal implementation can be achieved in at least four ways (Kingsbury, Krisch, and Stewart 2005). First, transnational networks may coordinate with various states under the umbrella of a global decision-making structure that has little or no coercive power (e.g., the Basel Committee on Banking Supervision that coordinates central bank policy). Second, distributed administration exists where the regulatory agencies of states act in concert with INGOs to create policies that are then returned to the regulatory agencies of all states (e.g., the WTO appellate body) (Alvarez-Jimenez

2009). Third, hybrid (intergovernmental-private) administration exists with INGOs that give feedback to a federation that produces policy that it transfers to a larger global government. In turn, this governmental agency directs standards for the INGO members. This reflects the most common interaction of INGOs and global governments through humanitarian services (e.g., the WTO, International Labour Organization, and UN institutions described in Reimann 2006). Fourth, private governments consisting of INGOs regulate limited areas (e.g., the Codex Alimentarius Commission that develops food-safety regulations or the Internet Corporation for Assigned Names and Numbers that manages part of the Internet).

There are two larger problems in enforcing global rights. First, NGOs are given a very strong role to play but may not be strong enough to enforce global citizenship rights and obligations. If organizational learning improves, these INGOs may enforce multidimensional citizenship. Second, states may withdraw from international organizations when they do not like decisions or possible prosecutions, and many states are still not willing to delegate these functions within their borders (Quigley 2009).

KEY METHODOLOGICAL ISSUES

There are many methodological approaches to the political sociology of human rights. Some of the most compelling are qualitative case studies of personal and group struggles. Other studies have been historical and legal and examine evidence and court documents. Welfare-state studies that involve citizenship rights, which strongly overlap with human rights, have used many different types of quantitative regression methods, often with pooled time and space techniques. The world-polity literature has examined large numbers of countries with event history methods, and the world-systems approach has used network analysis to look at economic organization and sometimes human rights (Meyer et al. 1997; Meyer 2010).

Recent cosmopolitan theorists have been extremely critical of using the state for human rights analysis because focusing on the state draws attention away from central actors in global human rights struggles (Beck and Sznaider 2006; Levy and Sznaider 2006). World-systems theorists frequently tout an "n of one" as their unit of analysis (Hall 2002; Wallerstein 1974). They call for the use of social-network analysis of the world-system. However, the nodes of these networks (i.e., their units of analysis) are still states. Beck and Sznaider advocate "alternative units of research" and mention "transnational regimes of politics" and "transnational spaces and cultures of memory" (2006, 14–15). This suggests an institutional approach that might be a form of "policy domain" where a variety of state, corporate, and nonstate actors may reach various decisions.

One possible solution to this issue is to seek the smallest political unit possible and then to use various forms of hierarchical linear modeling or multilevel statistical analysis. For instance, one might take the county, parish, or census tract as a unit of analysis and then see how various influential regional, national, and supranational entities (including corporations) influence human rights. Or one could use states, provinces, or departments as the unit of analysis. This might be a way of operationalizing Beck and Sznaider's (2006) politics of "perspectives" or "scale" where they describe the integration of local, national, transnational, and global foci. This challenge is far from settled.

CRITIQUE OF POLITICAL SOCIOLOGY AND HUMAN RIGHTS

Sociology in general and political sociology in particular have been criticized for not taking on the moral cause of human rights more actively, whether in an explanatory or normative context (Sjoberg, Gill, and Williams 2001; Blau and Moncada 2005; Turner 1993). It is clear that cosmopolitan theory embracing human rights has been much more active in the United Kingdom and Germany than in the United States (e.g., two special issues of the *British Journal of Sociology* were voted to the topic in 2006 and 2010). Political sociology has touched but not embraced human rights, yet it can have a much stronger impact in this area. Action research combined with service learning within universities may present opportunities (Touraine 1981). Finally, Sociologists Without Borders is one of a number of possible extensions of the political-sociological charge, as are many other political party and social-movement activities (Moncado and Blau 2006).

REPOSITIONING POLITICAL SOCIOLOGY VIS-À-VIS HUMAN RIGHTS

Given the critique of political sociology, how can this field better position itself toward human rights without abandoning any claim to being a social science? Political sociology would appear to be caught between opposing theories. On the one hand, there is an optimistic cosmopolitan naïveté of a withered state being tamed by INGOs. On the other hand, the pessimistic view of world-systems theory sees multinational corporations and capitalism pushing societies and states into their global shadow. Neither is convincing. A more useful theory might recognize the importance of states, while making morally driven policy recommendations about improving international institutions and rights protections. Further, a more general theory of globalization might well recognize the usefulness of reforming international institutions with INGOs and social movements.

Political sociology could benefit from a more global and process-oriented view of policy. One indicator of this change is that political sociologists (as opposed to political scientists) have not published much in international relations or organizations journals. The age of globalization would call for a redirection into international political sociology. Cosmopolitan solutions point to these innovative solutions, and political sociological research could be designed to improve the implementation of cosmopolitan recommendations and reforms of the exploitative aspects of the global economy.

Looking Forward to the Political Sociology of Human Rights

Political sociology will continue to examine power conflicts over inequality and human rights violations in both rich and poor countries. These studies will require new methods to fulfill the nonstate approach, but case-study comparisons and participant-observation studies will continue to be undertaken. This process will not be unilinear, but what is different at this point in history is the existence of transnational movements, global institutions, and bureaucracies that will continue to focus attention on human rights abuses. As such, the politics of fighting human rights abuses will no longer be built from within countries alone.

Chapter Eighteen

Culture

Mark D. Jacobs and Lester R. Kurtz

A major legacy of the Enlightenment, first formalized as a result of the American and French revolutions, wrought upon the experience of twentieth-century Holocaust and given worldwide legitimacy and force by the declarations, treaties, and institutions of the United Nations, the concept of human rights would seem to be one of the signature triumphs of the modern age. Yet systematic abuses of human rights persist. Indeed the very concept of human rights remains ambiguous. The sociology of culture—whose force derives more from the series of exegetical questions it asks than a body knowledge it has accumulated—can turn that ambiguity to productive use by posing a series of questions salient to human rights.

Are human rights defined *globally* or *locally*? Are they *universal*, a foundation of natural law, or *particularistic*, dependent on uniquely individual contexts? Are they *essential*, one of the very defining characteristics of what it means to be human, or *constructed*, negotiated through emergent processes of social interaction? Is their purpose *instrumental*, to increase societal effectiveness or efficiency, or *expressive*, to endow human experience with deeper meaning? How can social actors exercise *agency* to resist or transform a *structure* that appears to them all-powerful and impervious to change? And perhaps of greatest practical consequence, is the social order they help constitute *beneficial* or *exploitative* for the mass of the population?

Cultural analysis cuts through to the root issues of freedom and necessity, existence and identity. The sociology of culture is of special relevance to human rights because it has the capacity to denaturalize and reenvision categories of understanding them. If, as Gideon Sjoberg, Elizabeth Gill, and Norma Williams (2001) insist, human rights are best defined as "claims against organized power," the sociology of culture is especially useful in revealing and demystifying the ordinary workings of power embedded in habit or "common sense." As both neoliberal theorists of "soft power" and neo-Marxist proponents of the "dominant ideology thesis" argue, power functions most effectively when it does so seamlessly—without recourse to coercion—because subjects unreflectively regard as natural ways of acting that serve its ends. A cultural lens helps foreground the social dynamics that marginalize and victimize groups according to class, race, gender, sexuality, or nationality to penetrate more fully the underlying complexity of social process. Analysis that focuses exclusively on the ways that culture aligns with power or material interests, however, falls into a trap of reductionism by ignoring the autonomy of culture as a quest for meaning.

QUESTIONS POSED BY CLASSICAL THEORISTS

The twentieth-century marked the creation of mass society, the nature of which remains a subject of underlying debate. For such sociologists as Edward Shils (1975), mass society represents the broader and closer integration of "peripheral" populations into "the center," that zone of values and institutions with the most concentrated sacral powers. Shils and others endorse the claim of T. H. Marshall (1964) that modern history describes a path of progress in extending to the masses an expanding set of rights—from political to social and then economic ones. For the neo-Marxist "critical theorists" of the Frankfurt School, such as Max Horkheimer and Theodor Adorno (1993 [1944]), and other proponents of the "hermeneutics of suspicion," on the other hand, mass society operates as a form of exploitative manipulation of the masses, resting on a popular-culture industry that neutralizes possibilities for meaningful resistance by transforming subjects into passive consumers of regressive cultural products.

The most influential founding sociologists of the nineteenth-century laid the groundwork for this debate by interpreting the dizzying effects of societal transformation—of simultaneous global political, economic, industrial, scientific, religious, intellectual, and urban revolutions—in ways that emphasized both their promise and their dangers. Max Weber (1946, 1968 [1920]) discerned in these multiple transformations a process of "rationalization"—the achievement of technical mastery of the universe so that in principle all things were calculable, but at the tragic cost of "disenchantment," the loss of meaning. In a contrarian reading of the Weberian corpus, Donald Levine (1985) argues that in ways partly obscured by the stunted translation of Weber's texts into English, Weber conceived so many different types of "rationality" and "freedom" that he was able to entertain the possibility that rationality could actually expand the realm of freedom.

Émile Durkheim (1933, 1995) explored the promise and danger of industrial capitalism by focusing on the transformation of the *conscience collective* expressive of social organization based on "mechanical" solidarity into that expressive of social organization based on "organic" solidarity. Ideally, the specialized division of labor that characterizes modern industrial society should increase the level of social solidarity, despite the increasing individualism it creates. But instead, Durkheim (1951a) observed the alarming acceleration, in his time, of increase in the incidence of egoism and anomie—social-psychological pathologies indicated by rates of suicide under different conditions of modernity. These pathological weakenings of solidarity Durkheim attributed, in a succession of different works (1933, 1951b, 1995), to such causes as obsolete institutions of socialization, a forced and unjust division of labor, and a lack of civic rituals.

Today's sociology of culture continues to draw on the traditions of Weber and Durkheim. Wendy Griswold explicates those two traditions: the Weberian approach, on the one hand, emphasizes how culture in the form of ideas and world images "shapes action by defining what people want and how they imagine they can get it. Cultural analysis focuses on the complex systems of ideas that shape individuals' motives for action" (1995, 25). The Durkheimian approach, on the other hand, explores how representations, rituals, and symbols concretize "collective consciousness." Relevant to the underlying research problem of measuring the relative benefits and harms of late modernity, Weber bequeaths to the sociology of culture one major subproblem: How, amid a general decline in meaning and cultural authority, is it possible to exercise critical-normative judgment about issues of public and civic consequence? Durkheim bequeaths another: how do we increase social solidarity amid the growing recognition of individual and group difference?

SEMANTIC TENSIONS IN THE SOCIOLOGY OF CULTURE

Culture may be provisionally defined as the constant making and remaking of meaning, the medium of lived experience expressive of practical dilemmas. The very concept of human rights is a cultural construct, as is the concept of culture itself.

Since the "cultural turn" in the late 1980s, culture has been the subject of the most intense sociological study. The Section on the Sociology of Culture of the American Sociological Association is the largest and fastest-growing section, whose continued vitality is presaged by its claiming the largest contingent of graduate student members. The subfield is still generating enough intellectual ferment to defy codification; the elements of culture are variously denoted as symbols, rituals, metaphors, schemas, templates, frames, classification systems, boundaries, practices, discourses, cognitions, narratives, performances, and semiotic codes, among others, not to mention values and norms. Rather than being a linearly accumulating corpus of knowledge, the subfield is unified by a set of semantic tensions. Since this same set of tensions is common to the sociology of human rights, it is instructive to review how the concept of culture mediates them. Without presuming to engage in systematic codification, these semantic tensions can be illustrated with reference to selected exemplary cultural analyses.

If, taking advantage of modern technology, immigrant families steadily maintain real-time communication with relatives left behind, visit them periodically, and keep alive the dream of returning "home," where is the geographical locus of the family? Given the prevalence of international monetary and population flows, even the "local community" has gone global. Social organization is no longer local or global but a dynamic interplay of both. As Peggy Levitt (2005) demonstrates in her study of Pakistani Americans in New England, urban ethnography must now be multisited and transnational. Analogously, Diana Crane (2005) operationalizes "globalization" in a range of action spheres from governance to art markets as a multidirectional set of cultural flows involving a complex array of actors—individual and corporate; public, private, and civic; international, transnational, and regional; grouped and networked.

Is "the law" a body of doctrine, imbued with sacral force—the perfect example of a social fact—as Durkheim believed, or is it a negotiable set of behaviors and practices? Susan Silbey (2005) notes that the attitudes of ordinary citizens exhibit the same chasm that exists in legal scholarship between these two views. In interviews that she and Patricia Ewick conducted, people told stories about the different ways they oriented themselves to the law as it entered their everyday lives. Some orientations were essentialistic, respecting the law's transcendent impartiality and authority; others were constructed, regarding the law as a resource to be employed in interactions with others or something itself manipulable. Silbey insightfully observes that the very plurality of these orientations strengthens the stability of the law as an institution. What she calls "the cultural construction of legality" must embrace this plurality, since no one orientation can reflect all the varied ways that people actually experience the law, and the law would lose credibility if it had to exclusively match a single orientation.

In what ways does Jürgen Habermas's original ideal of a universal public sphere— a forum for critical-rational discussion of civic matters of greatest concern, free from the "steering mechanisms" of power and money—violate the very possibilities for communicative action Habermas intended to promote? Nancy Fraser (1992) argues that since, in practice, members of marginalized groups cannot participate equally in such a forum, the universal public sphere can only exist as a remotely conceivable utopian outcome of dialogue among particularistic public spheres, each consisting of peers whose voice more nearly commands equal respect. Michele Dillon (2005) demonstrates that, conversely, universal identifications can strengthen particularistic bonds, as in the case of gay Catholics whose devotion to the more general tenets of Catholicism, despite the church's intolerance of homosexuality, strengthens their allegiance to each other.

Why would Howard Becker, in his seminal study *Art Worlds* (1982), insist on viewing art from the perspective of the sociology of work? Don't artists primarily seek to create beauty, and isn't their activity different from any other kind of work, somehow transcendent? And isn't mundane work primarily motivated by the search to achieve maximum productive efficiency? Yet, as Becker documents, any form of artistic production involves the coordination of a varied and far-reaching division of labor, so the effectiveness of that coordination is a necessary condition for the production of the artwork. And as John Dewey (1980 [1934])—a major influence on Becker—explains, even the most mundane activity attains esthetic quality if it represents a "consummation" of experience through the resolution of tension. Instrumental activity, action governed primarily by a logic of utility, has the potential to be fully meaningful, while expressive activity, action governed primarily by a logic of meaning, can be nothing but humdrum. Either form of activity, to be fulfilling, must transform "experience" into "an experience." Rather than denoting different types of action, "expressive" and "instrumental" denote necessarily complementary qualities of any single activity.

How can individuals or groups challenge the powerful structures that appear to them as essentially unchangeable? How, for example, could members of art and poetry circles transform Japan from an authoritarian feudal society into a modern nation-state so suddenly under the Meiji Restoration in the second half of the nineteenth century? Eiko Ikegami (2005) offers a "public-centered" explanation. Drawing on the work of Harrison White, William Sewell, and others, she recognizes that structure exists as a multiplicity of networks, each carrying distinctive cultural schemas. "Publics" are sites (such as arts circles) where individuals from different networks physically interact, affording them the emergent opportunity to switch network identifications along with the associated schemas. Japanese artists could evade official prohibitions against political party formation by switching the nature of their associations, instantly creating a culture of national identification and a structure of political participation. Agency and structure are not antithetical but rather mutually constitutive, each enabling as well as constraining the other. Publics are central sites of cultural production and transformation. They offer a compelling example of how culture links micro-level subjectivities with macro-level structures and indeed of how culture is the very switch point of agency and structure (Jacobs and Spillman 2005).

Global and local, universalistic and particularistic, essential and constructed, instrumental and expressive, structure and agency—these semantic tensions describe the deep structure of the sociology of culture. They prove to be false dualisms, better treated as paradoxes, that require the contrasting terms to be held in suspension with each other. Cultural analysis aims to mediate semantic tensions—including in human rights conflicts.

SEMANTIC TENSIONS IN HUMAN RIGHTS DISCOURSE

How do these semantic tensions find expression in the discourse of human rights—in such arenas as the media, UN agencies, and national and international courts and tribunals? How do these tensions shape human rights dilemmas, and what paradoxical strategies do they suggest for reenvisioning them? These tensions both reflect and act back upon the everyday lived experience of real human beings, including victims of human rights abuses and those who serve as their advocates. Although human rights struggles are often represented in the dominant media as a simple dialogue between a unified global center—the "international community"—and a nation on the periphery, a cultural lens helps bring out the multiplicity of human voices involved, as well as the power interests at play. The cultural flows of information and opinion are both bottom up and top down, as what Robert Benford and David Snow (2000) call a "framing contest" emerges in the public sphere.

What is to be done, for instance, if practices of a particular local culture are considered cruel, inhuman, or degrading according to principles propagated by the so-called international community, enforced by international agreements? Or if local governments must comply with transnational ultimatums about rights as conditions of participation in the global economy? The universal principles of human rights paradoxically include the right of indigenous cultures to protect their traditions, so a local government can defend its challenged practices by an appeal to its own traditions.

This paradox of universalism and particularism is inflected by tensions of essentialism and constructivism, as well as globalism and localism. Are standards of human rights essential to the nature of all humans or constructed by a political process dominated by the United States and Europe in violation of other cultural traditions? The dominant definition of human rights proffered by international institutions is often criticized as an imposition, which itself violates the rights of non-Western peoples to maintain their own values and practices. Shu-Ju Ada Cheng and Lester Kurtz argue that "Western-based rights discourse, rooted in the liberal individualist tradition, focuses mainly on civil and political rights. The principle of natural rights, the root of the human rights discourse, emphasizes individual dignity, well-being, and freedom" (1998, 1).

A partial way to resolve this dilemma is to reframe the universalizing process as also addressing particular interests, by representing a common set of agreed-upon rights and enforcement institutions in such a way that the various particular societies see them as legitimate from their own cultural perspectives (see Snow et al. 1986; Benford and Snow 2000). Abdullahi Ahmed An-Na'im too suggests that "people are more likely to observe normative propositions if they believe them to be sanctioned by their own cultural traditions" (1992, 20). If the right to free elections, for example, is advocated in a Muslim culture as a natural right within the tradition of the Qur'an and the teachings of the Prophet Muhammad, rather than in some Western parliamentary sense, it is more likely to resonate within the culture, as we saw happening in the Arab uprisings in Tunisia, Egypt, and elsewhere in 2011 (see Esposito and Voll 2001).

Claims about global, universalistic, essentialistic rights are not always expressions of Western cultural hegemony. Particularistic variations create divides not only among nations but also within them. It is important to note, as An-Na'im does, that even within a single society, "there are either actual or potential differences in perceptions and interpretations of cultural values and norms" (1992, 20). Dominant groups attempt to foster the impression of consensus about "cultural values and norms that are supportive of their own interests, proclaiming them to be the only valid view of that culture" (An-Na'im 1992, 69). Female genital mutilation, soundly criticized by international human rights activists, is more a matter of patriarchal interests in maintaining control over women in a particular population than a widely shared value within that population.

HUMAN RIGHTS IN CHINA

In the Chinese case, although government officials may reject Western allegations of human rights abuse with countercharges of cultural interference, millions of Chinese themselves have challenged the system through dissident movements demanding their rights that wax and wane over the decades.

Yet the People's Republic of China, while failing to protect individual liberties, has raised 1 billion people out of poverty in the past half century. While Chinese citizens may lack freedom of speech, their basic human needs are being met by the political system. This case provides an instructive example of the different cultural definitions of basic human rights, a major issue during the Cold War and now resurfacing in conflicts over human rights between China and the United States. Western rights activists, on the one hand, attack China for its refusal to protect political dissent, freedom of speech, and the ability to organize opposition political parties—basic rights as defined by the Western paradigm. On the other hand, the Chinese development project, often deliberately designed to prioritize economic development over individual freedoms, has profoundly changed the social and economic conditions of its citizens, with dramatic improvements in the standard of living, health, education, and general well-being of the nation's population.

When we look at cultural mediations of this dilemma, a number of possibilities emerge. First, a new global culture is under construction, with its increasing unity and diversity; we are conscious of both the global village in which we live and our own cultures, which sometimes butt up against the globalizing process—hence the emergence of fundamentalist movements that resist globalization by asserting their own countertruth, sometimes violently. The human rights movement itself is part of a dynamic process that involves confrontations and consultations between particular cultures and interests on many levels.

China's ambivalent embrace of the Internet illustrates how the process of globalization creates cultural flows in more than one direction. The Chinese government had to accept Google's search engine as a communication tool necessary for economic development. But Google threatened governmental control of the population by allowing its users to circumvent official censorship and to interact with each other as a virtual public. The government effectively forced Google to revise its global commitment to the free flow of information as a condition of doing business in China. Despite its technical ability to establish servers in Hong Kong and elsewhere around the entire globe, Google was confronted with a choice of accommodating China's censorship policy or losing that crucial market. The universal communication technology of globalization bent to the force of Chinese particularism.

Yet the virtual public created by the Internet has also frustrated the efforts of the Chinese government to resist the celebration of human rights as a globally shared value. The government was unable to repress either the local hero of discontent Liu Xiaobo or the news of his award of the 2010 Nobel Peace Prize. Instead, its attempt to do so backfired, causing negative fallout for China worldwide and an avalanche of critical Internet communication within the country. Ying Chan, dean of Cheung Kong School of Journalism and Communication at Shantou University, followed the overwhelming unofficial response in China on her BlackBerry and laptop. "I was following the actions of these free-thinking strangers in real time without ever setting foot outside," she declared, in an act of resistance that made her local site global (Kurtz 2010).

The Occupy Movement

The Occupy Movement that first emerged (as Occupy Wall Street) in New York in the fall of 2011 offers another example of all the semantic tensions that animate human rights. It resulted from, and in turn produced, cultural flows moving in all directions around the world. Inspired by the "occupation" of Tahrir Square, half a world away, a few months earlier, encampments of protesters sprung up, first in New York and then in thousands of other sites around the world. These sites can easily be seen as examples of the "publics" described by Eiko Ikegami (2005), offering opportunities for the dramatic exercise of agency in transforming economic and political structures through the switching of network identifications and cultural schemas. Each encampment modeled the tension of universalism and particularism: there were no identified leaders, and all decisions were made in assemblies of the whole, with the expectation that the diverse participants would meld their particularistic interests into a collective stance. The slogan "We are the 99%"—signifying concern for widespread suffering and economic injustice in the midst of especially hard times—instantly evoked deep resonance in the encampments and beyond, even in the mainstream press.

It is too early to assess the impact of the movement. But the gatherings were not solely (or even primarily) instrumental in nature. As many observers found puzzling, the "occupiers" did not even issue lists of concrete, specific demands. The expressive objectives of the occupations were manifest: a mood of communion developed in and among the encampments. "Occupy" helped answer a major research problem about the quiescent public reaction to the axial financial crisis that has so exacerbated economic distress and inequality: where was the "piacular" ritual (or ritual of atonement) that Durkheim claimed was necessary to preserve collective solidarity in the face of a calamity of such magnitude (Jacobs 2012)? The protests—and the spirit of communion among the protesters—served the expressive function of providing just such a ritual. In Sjoberg, Gill, and Williams's (2001) definition of human rights as claims against organized power, "Occupy" is both an expressive and an instrumental example of the struggle for human rights.

Mahatma Gandhi and the Indian Independence Movement

Making explicit the play of semantic tensions also helps better explain the remarkable achievement of Mahatma Gandhi, often cited as the modern source of inspiration for human rights movements. Indeed, this form of cultural analysis suggests answers to research problems that have frustrated traditional political analysis. How could a frail, nonviolent man exercise such agency against the might of the British Empire? How could he so thoroughly reverse the flow of global/local influence? Was his world-changing activity politically instrumental or spiritually expressive?

Gandhi brought together a series of particularisms into a universal approach to the problem of rights, starting with the warrior and pacifist motifs that run through the world's religious and ethical traditions regarding the use of violence and force to address issues of injustice. The warrior believes it a sacred duty to fight, and the pacifist believes it just as important not to harm. Gandhi's nonviolent civil resister fights like the warrior but also like the pacifist, without doing harm (see Kurtz 2008). Similarly, he drew on multiple religious traditions—starting with the Hindu and Islamic—bringing these multiple traditional worlds together in a recipe for revolution. Gandhi had not read his own Bhagavad Gita, recited with his mother in the temple when he was growing up in India, until he went to study law in England. He combined Jesus's Sermon on the Mount with Hindu and Buddhist concepts of *ahimsa*, nonharmfulness, and the idea of nonattached action: do what is right without focusing on the act's consequences. He brought together East and West, North and South, as well as the spiritual and the political, and redefined power as something that grows not out of the barrel of a gun but from the collaborative noncooperation of a mobilized people.

The dramas of resistance and liberation that he presented on the world stage were also politically strategic. The cloth and boycott struck at the heart of a colonial structure based on the industrial revolution in textiles, the exploitation of raw materials, and global trade. His Salt March in 1930 was at once a religious procession and an act of political resistance that gathered increasing crowds and attention as he marched to the Indian Ocean to make salt, in defiance of a British monopoly over the necessities of daily life. Applying the terms of Ikegami's (2005) analysis to these mass gatherings, these events can be seen as "publics" and these dramatisms as the newly popular cultural schemas that emerge from them, constituting counterstructures to the structure of British colonialism.

WHY A CULTURAL ANALYSIS OF HUMAN RIGHTS IS ESSENTIAL

These cases of China, Occupy, and Gandhi suggest the value of the sociology of culture for understanding human rights. Since the concept of human rights is a cultural construct, human rights issues are inflected by the same set of semantic tensions as the culture concept itself. The sociology of culture thus recommends a method for studying human rights: to explicate—indeed, to weave into an exegetical deep structure—those various tensions. This helps us to see beneath the distortions that power and other forms of domination introduce into the discourse of human rights and to recognize the full multiplicity of interests and voices.

Therefore, cultural analysis also recommends practical strategies for addressing human rights issues. A semantic tension poses a paradox. The resolution of paradox always involves enlarging the problem frame to uncover the larger unity between the terms. Analytically and practically, it is a mistake to seek a one-dimensional solution rather than holding the contrasting terms in suspense. Thus, for example, an enlarged problem frame reveals the strategic advantage of stating universalistic claims in particularistic terms and particularistic claims in universalistic ones.

These reflections on cultural analysis of human rights issues also suggest ways to broaden the sociology of culture. Indeed, they suggest the need for an "esthetic conception of culture" (Jacobs and Hanrahan 2005). Like art itself, in such a conception culture has the capacity to hold difference in suspension and express a higher unity. Like art itself, it suggests grounds of normative evaluation even in the absence of measurable or objective standards. As Jaeger and Selznick (1964) explain in "A Normative Theory of Culture," a translation into sociological terms of Dewey's *Art as Experience,* culture can and should be evaluated according to its "human-centeredness." Like art itself, in this conception culture reenvisions the actually existing world. Great "masters" earn that status, as Dewey (1980 [1934], 301) observes, "precisely because they do not follow either models or rules but subdue both of these things to serve enlargement of personal experience."

This conception broadens the sociology of culture by adding a tradition emanating from Georg Simmel to the ones emanating from his contemporary peers Max Weber and Émile Durkheim. Simmel, trained as an esthetician, developed an approach to sociology focused on the interrelated forms of social interaction and objective culture. His approach anticipated the understanding of art as "feeling embodied in form" famously proposed by modern esthetician Suzanne Langer (1953). An esthetic conception of culture suggests ways of addressing the major problems bequeathed by Weber and Durkheim—to exercise evaluative judgment amid cultural disenchantment and to increase social solidarity amid the growing recognition of individual and group difference. In the balance of these problems hangs the future of human rights.

CHAPTER NINETEEN

SCIENCE, KNOWLEDGE, AND TECHNOLOGY

Jennifer L. Croissant

The sociology of science, knowledge, and technology and its affiliated field of science and technology studies (STS) comprise a heterogeneous discipline (Hess 1997; Hackett et al. 2007) that embodies contradictory approaches to considerations of human rights. These contradictions emerge from the specific intellectual trajectories that shape the major approaches in the field and the legacy of theory and methodology that shapes inquiry in these areas.

WHAT'S GOING ON

There are two general intellectual orientations within the social studies of science and technology: institutional studies and knowledge studies. These are, of course, approximations that elide the cross-fertilizations and trafficking across the subfields. The study of technology, as technology, is situated uneasily within each of these research trajectories. The distinction between these orientations, which I problematize below, is based on what might be termed the "Mertonian exemption," where Merton's (1973) institutional sociology of knowledge largely exempted the content of scientific knowledge claims from sociological examination. Unlike Mannheim (1936), who did not exempt scientific knowledge from the problems of ideology, Merton also avoided the utopian ambivalence of Marx, for whom a true "science" would emerge in a noncapitalist society (Perelman 1978). Merton's legacy in institutional studies of science generally posits that in a democratic social order, scientific institutions informed by functioning social norms of communalism, disinterestedness, organized skepticism, and universalism would work for the betterment of humankind and be freed from ideologies that might derive from or justify forms of oppression. Science, in this perspective, both needs and is good for democracy, although capitalism can produce distorting "interests" that lead to limited research or outright fraud. The institutional approach has informed science policy, such as the formulation of responsible-conduct-of-research (RCR) guidelines or pedagogical resources (COSEPUP 1995), even if as an unacknowledged narrative or set of assumptions.

Within institutional studies, there are thriving subspecialties that examine science as an occupation and organization, studies of scientific disciplines, and surveys of the public understanding of science. Each of these intersects with questions of human rights on several levels in contemporary research agendas. In terms of studying science as an occupation, the determinants of successful scientific careers, issues of equity, and access to scientific networks are long-standing yet continuously productive research areas (DiPrete and Eirich 2006; Fox 2010). The methods here include quantitative survey work, analyses of curriculum vitae, and interviews and qualitative observational work on the socialization of scientists. Recent findings of particular interest to those interested in human rights include considerations of family and gender equity, mentoring, and related issues in access to scientific careers, which indicate that there are no unambiguous effects of issues such as childrearing on scientific productivity and that there are mixed results regarding organizational structure and institutional equity (see Roth and Sonnert 2011; Fox 2008; Smith-Doerr 2004).

The study of science at a global, institutional level indicates that the late-twentieth-century emergence of a common template of a functioning state, both on practical and symbolic levels, is connected to the adoption of a relatively standardized educational system and to the use of Western science as the global common denominator of policy (Drori et al. 2003). This is an expression of and facilitates science's global cultural authority. Despite differences (such as gender patterns by field of specialization or areas of emphasis between "hard" and "soft" sciences based on specific historical trajectories of nations), there are complex trends, highly dependent on the indicator selected, suggesting the continued spread of global institutional forms of science along with global models of human rights. For example, formerly communist states and states with lower current metrics of democratic participation have greater emphasis on the natural rather than social sciences, while more internationalist states with high levels of democratic participation both demonstrate expertise about and produce policy in support of social-science research (Drori et al. 2003, 202). These trends are not without contradictory impulses. There are also questions about the loose coupling between matters of national policy and the specific organization of science, and again between the organizations and the actual practices of scientists. This is a finer-grained set of distinctions than Merton's overall claims about the productive relationship between science and democracy.

At a less global or macroscopic scale, the study of the organization of scientific disciplines has been transformed by the availability of low-cost and simplified scientometric and bibliometric tools and data sets, which put quantitative assessment of scientific networks within reach of a broad range of scholars. Focusing on the information gleaned from formal scientific publications, such as citation patterns, coauthorship, institutional alliances, and funding sources, current research questions include the spatialization or development of geographic referents for scientific networks, ranging from field level (such as genomics or nanotechnology) to regional innovation system analysis (Leydesdorff and Schank 2008). The new bibliometrics analyze the structure of scientific networks as represented in the published scientific literature. For example, the structure of scientific consensus in controversies such as vaccination's noncorrelation with autism or the noncarcinogeneity of coffee is very dense and stable, unlike the continued public debate on these issues (Shwed and Bearman 2010). Work such as this, however, must remain agnostic as to the veracity of the consensus (because today's consensus can be upended by tomorrow's discoveries) and provides few mechanisms that explain the persistence of the controversy in the public sector. The relative closure of many kinds of controversies in the scientific literature may also show the constraints of the current regimes of proof, where the establishment of causality is strictly linked to statistical significance measures that make disproof easier than proof. To the extent that the invocation of "science" can be used to quell public debate (Ehrenfeld 2002), there is some concern that this kind of work can add to the appeal of technocracy as a political theory that substitutes administration for politics, as if the science itself were neutral. Such goals illustrate the power that the scientific register has in public discourse. The achievement of this power has yet to be sufficiently explained.

The gap between professional scientific discourse and public understanding of science has vexed scholars and policy-makers for a long time. Until innovations by scholars such as Irwin and Wynne (1996), which interrogate local knowledge in relation to formal scientific knowledge, and the uptake and coproduction of science by "lay experts" (Epstein 1998), the primary model of public understanding was a deficit model of inadequate literacy, primarily examined through surveys of "known" scientific knowledge and belief. The deficit model is, at least in scholarship, superseded by analyses that take local knowledges seriously and also recognize hybrid social roles.

The organization of knowledge at the interface of scientific communities and the public is also engaged in what might be called critical institutional studies, which examine the emergence and circulation of new knowledges, also attuned to questions of power, ideology, and social justice. While human rights, per se, are not a frequent key phrase, this kind of work, ranging from the historical to the contemporary ethnographic, engages the coproduction of knowledge, expertise, identity, and policy (Frickel and Moore 2006). For example, how do people engaged in local environmental-quality controversies seek out and produce scientific knowledge, and what are the responses by policy-makers to multiple knowledge claims? An important dimension to this is the increasing attention to gaps in knowledge, whether due to intentionally withheld information or "undone science." As scientific priorities are set through complex processes that often reflect entrenched interests, it is often difficult to get science done by or on behalf of a broad public interest not defined by a potential market share. And there are also problems of "willful ignorance," such as in the case of homeowners in post-Katrina Louisiana not wanting to assess the toxicology of their property as that knowledge would make it unsalable (Frickel and Vincent 2007). It is in these kinds of studies that the field moves from studies of the organization of science as an institution to an engagement with studies of the organization of science as a fluid body of knowledge.

Not to be excluded from the question of science and human rights are questions about the science of human rights and about access to science as a human right.

As an example of the latter, questions about scientists' access to international data resources are framed as a human right with regard to their ability to participate in the international scientific community (Arzberger et al. 2004). Similarly, the United Nations presents an unstated definition of science in its articulation of property rights from scientific discovery and privileges "the freedom indispensable for scientific research" (UNHCR 1966). In the case of the former, establishing human rights violations can be an issue of establishing matters of fact (Orentlicher 1990), engaging epistemological questions about what counts as evidence, and exploring methodological questions about indices and measures. Finally, of course, the incorporation of human rights into human-subjects-protection protocols based on a model of autonomous human agents working under conditions of informed consent both protects human subjects and the legitimacy of scientific research and reinscribes that particular model of an individuated subject.

The role of science and scientists in human rights discourse has a long and complicated trajectory. For example, Barnett (1948) argued for the separation of science and human rights based on a traditional (modernist) separation of matters of fact from matters of value, rights being a matter of value. Moore (2008), however, outlines the ways in which scientists themselves have challenged that separation on personal and institutional levels, particularly around issues of militarization but more generally opening up discussion around the social responsibilities of science. While the contemporary RCR enterprise is currently focused on internal dynamics of scientific conduct, such as fraud, falsification, and plagiarism, it remains to be seen if this rapidly emerging field will move from procedural ethics and issues of research compliance and policy to engaging substantive, or "macro," ethics and issues of distributive justice, human rights, and social responsibility on a different scale and moral register (Herkert 2004). At worst, the RCR approach contributes to a laissez-faire approach to science policy and ethics. The policy-making process for science, particularly in setting research priorities, may lead to neglect of matters of broad human rights concern if they do not fit into market-driven solutions.

The laissez-faire approach is clearly central to a great deal of scholarship on technology (see Baumol 2002). This approach generally conflates economic "democracy" of free markets with ideas about social democracy and rights. These sorts of innovation studies (see Comin and Hobijn 2004) are focused on a specific model of economic development and growth. More nuanced studies (Weeramantry 1993) that problematize the social changes surrounding importing Western technology into new contexts (such as women losing land rights when industrial farm implements are imported) circulate as case studies and moral warnings but often do not impinge on the quantitative development models (and despite the emergence of alternative accounting systems, such as Waring 2003). As Adas (2006) argues, US development efforts are justified by assumptions about technological superiority and technological necessity. As technology is a presumed good, its negative impacts in new contexts are attributed to insufficient preparation on the part of recipients or cultural backwardness rather than to the inappropriateness of the new technologies and the required infrastructure and cultural changes needed to support their implementation.

Current research in technology and human rights has become infatuated with information and communication technology (ICT) and its role as a tool for economic development and the expansion of human rights. This orientation is embodied in "one-laptop-per-child" programs, which have been criticized as imperialist, irrelevant, and a distraction from pressing basic issues (Smith 2005). And while it is clear that ICTs have had a role in global social movement organization and mobilization, be it flash mobs organized by cell-phone users or the transmission of information to global news sources (Van Aelst and Walgrave 2002), it is not clear that they are the panacea for global development in that government tracking and content restrictions impinge on these network solutions (see Shirazi, Ngwenyama, and Morawczynski 2010).

CHALLENGES

Significant challenges to the human rights paradigm emerge from methodological and epistemological consequences of studies in the sociology of science, knowledge, and technology and STS. The challenges emerge from three primary orientations: The first is in the empirical standpoint of postcolonial scholars such as Vandana Shiva (1997), who maintain that the spread of Western knowledge regimes and their intertwined property regimes has intensified inequalities, led to ecological disasters, and decreased human rights. The second challenge emerges from traditional Marxist orientations that identify science and technology as the product of capitalism and thus unable to contribute to humane modes of existence (Aronowitz 1988).

The third, final challenge to the human rights paradigm emerges from nuanced poststructuralist scholarship, particularly actor-network theory (ANT) (Law and Hassard 1999; Latour 2007) and posthumanist and anti-Enlightenment paradigms, often informed by Haraway's "A Cyborg Manifesto" (1991) and feminist critiques of rights discourses (Brown 1995). In that it applies itself to both knowledge and technologies, the term "technoscience" emerges from studies in the social construction of technology and ANT and becomes an important signifier of the organized networks of innovation. ANT may be, arguably, mislabeled as a theory and more effectively understood as a methodology in which the relations among things are traced out and their properties become attributes related to their perception and use in networks. That is, as with other networks studies, it remains to be seen whether the network is explanatory or needs itself to be explained.

ANT and its convergence with ethnomethodological and poststructuralist methodologies together produce an agnosticism about the key terms "human" and "rights," which inform human rights discourse, as well as "science" and "technology." As an antiessentialist move, ANT eschews the attribution of properties to technologies and other nonhuman entities except as they are instantiated through the relations of the networks of humans and nonhuman actants. ANT has proven a valuable framework for posthuman scholarship in the way it shifts focus from considering innate properties of things to problematizing the attribution of properties of actants such as rights or agency as emergent properties semiotically and materially produced in relation to an overall network. Callon's (1986) study of scallops and their goals in a controversy over scallop fishing or Latour's "Sociology of a Door Closer" (Johnson 1988), which explores the delegation of human agency to objects such as speed bumps and automatic door closers, are examples of this approach.

In this light, human rights are problematic in that that the boundary between human and nonhuman is permeable and seen as culturally specific, as a product of networks of attribution and action. As Butler (1993) argues, the point of a critical poststructuralist approach is not to determine what, in her case, the body "really is" as either a discursive or material thing, whether it is cultural or natural, but to examine what is at stake in dragging it to one side or the other of the discursively produced nature-culture divide. Similarly, the dualisms of "technical" and "social" or "technical" and "political" are rendered problematic, examined as the outcome of network processes. ANT as a form of poststructuralist inquiry eschewing essential distinctions such as "social," "technological," "political," "scientific," and "human" or "nonhuman" has thus been convergent with innovative extensions of rights to nonhumans, such as animals. The second term in the phrase "human rights" is similarly challenged by scholars, particularly in that rights discourses generally represent a propertarian orientation that reinstantiates individualism and the role of the state as the guarantor of rights (Brown 1995). What becomes apparent in this loose configuration of approaches is a destabilization of both terms of the phrase "human rights," as well as ideas about science as a value-free or objective enterprise. Thus the question for the expansion of human rights becomes a question about what counts as human, whether or not rights are guarantors of (human) well-being, and what power structures and ideologies are reproduced with the expansion of discourses of (human) rights.

Conversely, a focus on human rights, broadly defined, may challenge the approaches to science, knowledge, and technology that do not problematize the current institutional configuration of science and its relation to capital and the state. For example, the "triple-helix" model (Etzkowitz 2003) of government-university-industry relations in innovation is instantiated in policy across international boundaries (e.g., Rivera Vargas 2010), takes for granted that this configuration is both necessary and sufficient for progress, and unproblematically assumes a specific model of intellectual property, economic growth, and neoliberal subjectivity.

Additionally, technoscience is expensive. The consequences of this range from disparities in health research favoring the wealthy (e.g., prioritizing heart disease research over research on infectious diseases) to the problems of the appropriation of intellectual property from so-called third-world countries. Much is assumed in the vision of Western technoscience as the epitome of human achievement and as the end point of international development (Adas 2006). Clearly Western technoscience is seen as problematic for postcolonial scholars such as Shiva (1997). And yet, evidence, measurement, and proof are important to numerous social movements, whether related to environmental justice, antiglobalization, or human rights organizations (see Orentlicher 1990).

There is thus probably no single "future" to which the intellectual orientations of the sociology of science, knowledge, and technology and STS point, except perhaps a hopeful heterogeneity. Science as a social institution holds great sway as an arbiter of public life, and science operates as a powerful register of discourse. Similarly, there is a great deal of ambivalence about access to technology as both a marker and a guarantor of rights. For those interested in promoting human welfare, science has always produced a great deal of ambivalence: its tools can be used either to sustain or resist forms of oppression or to argue for the expansion or contraction of rights (Croissant and Restivo 1995).

≈≋

CHAPTER TWENTY

SOCIOLOGY OF LAW

Christopher N. J. Roberts

The biggest challenge for the sociological study of human rights can be posed in five words: What is a human right? Traditional intellectual divisions of labor typically have left this question for lawyers, philosophers, political scientists, and advocates—not sociologists. Evidence of custom, however, is not a sufficient reason for its preservation. As human rights have become an undeniable social force in contemporary life, increasing numbers of sociologists have undertaken their study. This is fitting. The sociological canon is in many respects tailor-made for examining the most complex and pressing contemporary human rights problems. After all, human rights at their most basic level are about people as they exist in society. Yet the standard approaches to human rights—most often rooted in law, politics, and philosophy—often conceive of human rights in a way that dislocates them from these social moorings. Such conceptions of human rights, therefore, are not well suited for sociological inquiry.

As the "pioneers" in the sociological field of human rights well know, offering a sociological definition of the human rights concept is a deceptively challenging task (e.g., Turner 1993, 1995; Rowland 1995; Connell 1995; Waters 1995; Barbalet 1995). This, however, is not a task to begin anew. Examining new categories of transnationalism, globalization, or international treaty making—the very places one would first think to look for an answer—provides much less guidance than one might assume. Instead, this chapter looks to several foundational debates within the subfield of the sociology of law. In fact, all the necessary pieces of a robust sociological framework for studying human rights already exist, and most of the groundwork has already been laid.

In selecting a sociological answer to the question posed at the outset of this chapter, there are three important preliminary considerations. First, there is the multiplicity issue. The multitude of distinct forms that human rights manifest can make it an extremely complicated topic of inquiry—particularly in the context of a social-scientific analysis where specificity and precision are essential. The great difficulty is that the same term invokes a multiplicity of "registers"—an incredible array of disparate definitions and an intractable range of conflicting foundational sources (Somers and Roberts 2008). The term "human rights" can be thought of as a "free-floating" or "empty" signifier—a concept that is constantly deployed, yet vague, highly variable, and stripped of context and specified meaning (Derrida 1978). For example, when the phrase "human rights" is invoked, it is entirely unclear whether it refers to the eighteenth-century French "rights of man and citizen," the fundamental right of citizenship Hannah Arendt discusses in the context of European statelessness, or the rights associated within the modern post–World War II international human rights regime. As a broad starting point for the study of human rights, a sociological definition or framework for studying rights should narrow the field of study to identify the object of study at a level that provides sufficient sociological meaning, yet still captures the breadth of the subject in all its guises and myriad forms.

Second, the definition must conceive of human rights in a way that is amenable to sociological inquiry. Common notions of human rights will often require some degree of empirical translation. Human rights, for example, share much with natural rights arguments based on supposed inherent human traits, fundamental laws of nature, religious principles, historical experience, morality, and so forth. The problem for sociology is that such natural rights concepts exist within a universe that is unassailable and unknowable. An individual's inherent dignity, for example, can never be drafted away by treaty, plundered by tyrants, or proven spurious by social scientists (no matter their methodological rigor). But it can be studied as a sociological entity, within a categorically precise sociological framework that will permit access to human rights in all of their guises on a sociological plane.

Finally, as a broad orientation the sociological study of human rights is much more than sociologists who just happen to be studying human rights. Indeed, there should be something unique and different about a sociological approach to the study of human rights that distinguishes it from other approaches rooted in law, philosophy, and political science, for example. But just being different from other disciplines does not justify the effort. It should shed new light on a particular aspect of the world or present new understandings that are not available through existing approaches. There must be a sociological advantage.

Although the topic of human rights is broader than what typically counts as "the law," the debates and central questions that have emerged within the sociology of law subfield help in constructing a sociological framework for the study of human rights by identifying the central concerns, critical divisions, fault lines, and disciplinary boundaries. A comprehensive overview of the entire subfield of the sociology of law is of course not possible here (for overviews, see Cotterrell 2007, 1418; Deflem 2008; Freeman 2006; Trevino 1996). This chapter focuses narrowly on the problems and implications raised by four key sociology-of-law debates surrounding (1) normativity versus objectivity, (2) sociological empiricism, (3) levels of analysis, and (4) order versus conflict.

The subfield of the sociology of law has provided a space for these disciplinary discussions to define the subfield while shaping the contours of the broader discipline. Looking to these debates provides guidance not only in addressing the essential "What is a human right?" question, but also in establishing a conceptual space for disciplinary dialogue and debate within the emergent human rights subfield.

These debates show that, at its essence, human rights is a sociological concept, for any statement of rights is a statement of social relationships. This understanding of human rights is broad and best operates as a starting point for sociological analysis. Because an understanding of human rights as social relationships applies equally well to the rights concept, throughout this chapter the terms "rights" and "human rights" are used interchangeably.

THE DEBATES, PROBLEMS, AND IMPLICATIONS

PROBLEM #1 FOR THE SOCIOLOGICAL STUDY OF HUMAN RIGHTS

Human rights are inherently value-laden entities. Is there a place for the normative component within an epistemological context that favors scientific objectivity and value freedom?

The tensions surrounding this fact/value question are foundational in the sociology of the law and in the broader discipline as well. In their respective studies of the law, both Max Weber and Émile Durkheim sought to distinguish juris-prudential or normative studies of the law from its sociological or social-scientific study (Durkheim 1982). Other early sociologists presumed that a "sociology of law" was "logically" and "theoretically impossible" given the incompatible nature of sociological inquiry (a study of what is) and the study of the law (what ought to be) (Timasheff 1941, 233). More recently within the subfield of the sociology of law, scholars have engaged in intense debates over whether and how to keep normative inquiry separate from scientific objectivity in the study of the law. Scholars such as Donald Black have argued that a sociological approach must only focus on what is scientifically knowable, thus leaving the more normative concerns to philosophers and jurists. For Black, the "study of fact" as a scientific venture must, in sociology, "be distinguished from the study of value" (1972, 1093). Others, most notably Philip Selznick, have called for an approach in which underlying philosophical, jurisprudential, or policy aspirations are incorporated within the framework of the sociological study. In a series of spirited exchanges with Black, Selznick urged sociologists not to shrink away from the normative and more philosophical elements of the law, for distanced neutrality was not the most appropriate role (or goal) for sociologists of the law. Instead, they "should be ready to explore the meaning of legality itself, to assess its moral authority, and to clarify the role of social science in creating a society based on justice" (Selznick 1959, 124).

Though international human rights were not on the agenda for Black or Selznick, the fault lines between fact and value exhibited in these debates cannot be ignored. Interestingly, each side sacrifices in proportion to what it seeks to maintain. An objective scientific approach, for example, may attempt to maintain a value-free perspective by reducing rights to strictly empirical phenomena. But to completely divorce rights from their normativity threatens to alter an essential feature of the object under investigation. For it is precisely the normative element within rights that makes them distinct entities that possess social importance and causal power in the first place. Doing so dramatically alters an entire field of inquiry before it can be analyzed. It can be argued, in fact, that separating a right from its normativity alters the object of study so completely that it quite possibly is no longer a "right."

On the other hand, an approach that seeks to integrate the underlying normativity rests on a very shaky scientific foundation. An overly normative study might not even be "sociology," but might bleed into other categories, such as jurisprudence, philosophy, social activism, or some other endeavor altogether. So one way (among others) the tensions between fact and value play out is this: study rights as empirical facts and sacrifice an essential piece of their nature, or integrate the normative elements within the study and risk sacrificing the epistemological orientation that makes sociology, sociology. As discussed below, these two paths are not necessarily mutually exclusive—the best framework for the sociological study of rights is one that is faithful to the nature of the object of study but still amenable to social-scientific methods.

PROBLEM #2 FOR THE SOCIOLOGICAL STUDY OF HUMAN RIGHTS

Human rights are not empirical entities.

Even if one were to adopt Black's supposedly scientific and objective empirical approach—his "pure sociology of law" (1972, 1087)—there remains a major problem: the law (and certainly human rights) cannot be found in the empirical world. While at the conceptual level they are each very real, powerful, and thus a worthy (if not a necessary) aspect of sociological inquiry, no one has ever seen a human right or touched the law. They are nonempirical entities. For Black, "Every scientific idea requires a concrete empirical referent of some kind. A science can only order experience, and has no way of gaining access to non-empirical domains of knowledge" (1972, 1086).

The key question, then, for gaining access is how to identify the tangible, empirical indicators that represent these concepts. In this sense, the empirical difficulties that emerge for the sociological study of rights are no different from those for other sociological areas of study, such as race, gender, inequality, culture, the family, emotions, and the law. Defining the concept under investigation is the necessary first step of an empirical study, which in turn points to where such visible, empirical indicators reside. Black (1972, 1976), for instance, views the law in terms of behavior. This moves him out of the normative (and epistemologically alien) realms of jurisprudence and moral philosophy, for example, and into a venue in which the tangible indicators of the law—human action and interaction—can be studied sociologically. While human rights are much more than "behavior," it is similarly necessary to narrow the concept down to a meaningful range of phenomena that can then be examined empirically.

There is significant breadth in the approaches used in the sociology of law to locate, measure, assess, and understand such empirical indicators. Quantitative and qualitative research techniques, as well as positivist, interpretive, ethnographic, and historical approaches, are equally at home within the sociology of law. Whether a particular approach is more or less appropriate than another depends upon the research question(s) posed at the outset, the available data, and the nature of the object of study. But regardless of the particular methodological approach employed, it must place the object under investigation within a contextual frame of reference in which distinctions can be drawn among categorically like objects.

A sociological framework must therefore define human rights and identify the relevant empirical indicators. The definition must at once incorporate a broad spectrum of competing definitions, while being narrow enough to possess sociological meaning.

PROBLEM #3 FOR THE SOCIOLOGICAL STUDY OF HUMAN RIGHTS

It remains unclear what the appropriate analytic level for studying human rights is.

A key difficulty for defining human rights is that so much remains unknown about what they in fact are, how they operate, and where they do their work. This question concerning location of the concept and its empirical referents is a particularly knotty one that reveals another dimension of the multiplicity issue. Common understandings of human rights seem to imply that they reside simultaneously at a variety of conflicting levels. Human rights can be thought of as individual-level, state-level, global, or universal phenomena. So how does one define human rights so that the research framework does not assume away the very questions that researchers need to ask?

Human rights are often assumed to be a category of individual right. The individual notion of rights is captured well in the many colloquial expressions—for example, "right holder," "right bearer," or one's "bundle of rights"—that tend to imply that rights are exclusive to the individual and are possessed or owned, independently of other aspects of the social world. Rooting the concept within the individual, however, places the concept in a realm that is less amenable to sociological methods and social-scientific epistemologies. Sociological studies of the law have approached this problem by viewing individual actors not exclusively on their own terms but as they are constituted within a broader matrix of social relationships, interactions, and structures (Deflem 2008; Durkheim 1982; Edelman 2004; Sanders 1990). As Edelman writes, "Ideas, norms, and rituals evolve at the group or societal level and help to constitute individual identities, needs, preferences, and behaviors. Individual action cannot be understood apart from the social environment that gives meaning to that action" (2004, 186).

But at what level does "society" exist in the contemporary world? While the boundaries of law are often presumed to begin and end at the level of the state, new patterns of transnational activity—migration, NGO activity, and international legal and economic processes, to name a few examples—reflect new spheres of social action and identity formation that do not necessarily coincide with the political and geographic boundaries of the state.

Sociologists of the law such as Boyle (2007) suggest that researchers must now grapple with "multiple levels of analysis." Halliday and Osinsky, however, advise empirical researchers to "maintain a studied skepticism about excessive claims made of globalization and its impact" (2006, 466). These warnings are particularly relevant for the study of human rights. Common understandings of human rights are freighted with notions of internationalism, global norms, and universal truths (or, conversely, of individual nature, human dignity). From a sociological perspective, these vague though normatively and heuristically compelling statements about the nature of reality are just that—statements. In sociological terms, they are "social facts." To assume within the empirical research framework that human rights are indeed "universal" or "individual" is to accept an ontology that assumes away the importance of the very sociological indicators—that is, social relationships—that reveal the essence of the concept. A sociological framework should therefore receive human rights on this sociological plane—one, for example, that conceives of human rights as basic statements of social relationships.

PROBLEM #4 FOR THE SOCIOLOGICAL STUDY OF HUMAN RIGHTS

Should sociologists view human rights in terms of stability and shared norms or conflict and change?

A major sociological debate in the post–World War II period concerns competing ideas about how society operates. Structural-functionalist approaches view society as an integrated system comprising a series of subsystems. Although these ideas can be traced to nineteenth-century thinkers such as Auguste Comte and Durkheim, the rise of structural functionalism in the post–World War II sociological canon is perhaps most associated with Talcott Parsons. As a broad orientation, structural-functionalist ideas typically view the law in its capacity for social integration, focusing, for instance, on its ability to inform social values and consensual norms and to achieve social equilibrium (Trevino 1996, 333). Interestingly, a significant portion of the impact of structural-functionalist thought on the sociology of law can be attributed to the work of its critics. Conflict theorists such as Ralf Dahrendorf (1958) believe that the structural-functionalist approach, slanted in its focus on harmony, stability, and consensus, overlooks a key part of social reality—authority within a system not only is integrative but can also be divisive and coercive. Thus, conflict-model theorists argue that coercion and conflict should be studied as an important element of society in its capacity to both preserve the social order and facilitate social change (for examples of conflict-theoretical work in the sociology of law, see Quinney 1970; Chambliss 1964).

In the sociology of the law, each of these starting assumptions about how society operates has a marked effect on how the law is conceived. Austin Turk explains it this way: "If one assumes that social order is an expression of general agreement among the members of a population on how they should go about business of social life ... then legality will probably be defined as a characteristic of norms which the people consider important enough to protect against the few who do not go along with the majority" (1969, 30). On the other hand, Turk writes, "if order is seen as largely a pattern of conflict among parties seeking to protect and improve their life chances ... then legality becomes an attribute of whatever words and deeds are defined as legal by those able to use to their advantage the machinery for making and enforcing rules" (1969, 31–32). These starting assumptions about social order or social conflict therefore have a profound effect on the entire research program, influencing the questions posed, the data sought, the inferences made, and the theories developed. But despite their incredible influence, Turk argues, such assumptions in the sociological study of the law are often left implicit and unstated.

The existence of unspoken apriorities is particularly relevant in the study of human rights. It is a common assumption that human rights represent basic, shared values or that they embody statements of fundamental principles that will (when adhered to) provide stability and social harmony. These assumptions might lead to questions about how to honor, enforce, and protect individuals' human rights. This, in turn, might lead to an empirical focus on processes of integration, the spreading of shared norms around core human rights, and how to use the law to promote and enforce human rights laws and norms. These assumptions—quite prevalent in human rights research—are not in and of themselves incorrect. They do, however, present a very particularized view of the world.

Human rights ideas are never free from conflict and struggle. The very fact that human rights might be needed in the first place underscores the lack of shared norms. In fact, during the 1940s and 1950s, when the foundations of the modern international human rights regime was being created, the human rights concept spurred incredible opposition and resistance as imperial powers such as Great Britain and influential political factions in the United States feared that human rights would alter existing social relationships and hierarchies. Interestingly, during the same period, prominent professional organizations such as the American Bar Association, the American Anthropological Association, and the American Medical Association, as well as progressive thinkers like Hannah Arendt and Mohandas Gandhi—all for their own reasons—also rejected key ideas within the emerging human rights concept. This opposition has had lasting effects on the modern international human rights concept. But because of how the human rights concept is usually defined (and the a priori assumptions that lie within), these influential social struggles and conflicts over human rights have, to date, received very little notice (see Roberts, forthcoming).

This, however, is not at all to argue that a conflict perspective is the only appropriate approach to human rights. As Dahrendorf says, "We need for the explanation of sociological problems both the equilibrium and the conflict models of society; and it may well be that, in a philosophical sense, society has two faces of equal reality: one of stability, harmony, and consensus and one of change, conflict, and constraint" (1958, 127). Although conflict, opposition, and resistance should always be expected in the empirical field of human rights, over time, the outcomes of such struggles can become integrated into the social structures, institutions, practices, laws, and ideas that define a social order and hold it together. The very relationships that were once contested and opposed, over time may become accepted and naturalized (or, in rights parlance, self-evident, inherent, fundamental, and natural).

A sociological lens used to study the process in which social struggles transcend their existence as social action and become a structural entity known as "human rights" must be able to account for what keeps a society together and what moves it forward. It must therefore be able to account for cyclical processes of conflict and order, stasis and transformation, social struggles, and the naturalization of social relationships.

A SOCIOLOGICAL FRAMEWORK

The nebulous and indistinct nature of human rights presents a number of difficulties for their sociological study. But a number of the core issues that have emerged in the subfield of the sociology of law help to illuminate the disciplinary tensions, fault lines, and boundaries within which a sociological framework for the study of human rights must operate. The issues discussed in this chapter certainly are not the only relevant ones. They are, however, central concerns that sociologists interested in studying human rights cannot ignore. As mentioned above, the sociological idea that human rights are statements of social relationships represents a broad analytic orientation. It is a conceptual starting point, an analytic framework for their study that is grounded in sociological ideas as old as the discipline.

A sociological conception of human rights is a "thin" conception purposely devoid of the typical substantive and normative claims associated with human rights (e.g., which categories of rights are "core," whether positive rights are more "real" than natural rights, and so forth). It does not claim to know whether human rights exist and operate at a global, local, or national level, and it leaves open the possibility that human rights operate through processes of both conflict and consensus. It therefore allows researchers to answer such questions through empirical study rather than to assume them away in the definition.

The one issue not yet settled is how to deal with the inherent normativity of human rights. As soon as a definition is offered for what a human right is, the normativity problem discussed in problem #1 presents itself in full force. This is true when defining any social concept. Selecting any single definition over others is always a normative move that has political implications and social consequences. In this sociological framework, though, it is important to note that the normativity does not reside within the human rights concept (where it generally resides in scholarship). Implicit within such an approach is the acknowledgment that human rights, if implemented, have the potential to reshape (or solidify) existing social configurations. As such, human rights can be agents of sweeping change by extending recognition to new categories of social actors. Conversely, they can also be the servants of the status quo by transferring older social hierarchies into the language and structures of human rights. Indeed, within this framework human rights are not inherently good or bad. As representations of social relationships, they have been used to justify bringing an end to Jim Crow and colonialism. Ironically, they have also been used to support the continuance of Jim Crow and colonialism (Roberts, forthcoming). This is already a dramatic departure from the typical normative-heavy understanding of human rights. Human rights are certainly important causal forces. But how, where, and the extent to which they do their work are all empirical, not normative, questions.

The normative component that exists within this sociological framework resides within the idea of social relationships. The importance of social relationships, social embeddedness, and the individual's existence as a social being is taken as a given in sociology. This is what makes the discipline unique and its conception of human rights sociological and not something else. Within this normative, sociological framework that views human rights as statements of social relationships, unbiased, objective, empirical research can take place.

The sociological canon and the past debates within the sociology of law provide much guidance for those who wish to study the underlying sociality that inheres within rights. As a subfield, however, the sociology of human rights is not simply a lesser subunit of the sociology of law. For one, what counts as human rights is broader than even the broadest articulations of what "the law" is. But neither is it merely a diffuse or indistinct topic of study within the broader discipline. So if the sociology of human rights is worthy of being its own subfield, those who occupy this space must embrace the shared questions and burdens of the greater discipline while simultaneously contributing distinct modes of inquiry and categories of knowledge that are not otherwise possible.

This process is not free from conflict. As the debates that helped to define the sociology of the law illustrate, the development of new knowledge will at times challenge prevailing orthodoxies, stir new debates, and redefine the contours of accepted thought and practice. And this process will move the entire discipline along.

Already, the nascent subfield promises to resituate some of the assumed antinomic relationships between fact and value and order and conflict, for example. Each of these two dichotomies exists and operates not to the exclusion of the other but as a necessary and essential component of what makes human rights what they are. Within the present framework these quarrelling categories are now housed within the same analytic quarters to do their work together. So rather than replicating the intellectual divisions that are perhaps no longer as deep or as impassable as they once were, this framework for studying human rights aims to be an analytic counterpart to the reality it attempts to understand.

The new research techniques, innovative modes of thought, and intellectual relationships that will continue to emerge within this new area of study, however, are not exclusive to the field of human rights. The law and its sociological study exist within a very similar contextual space as human rights. By "sociologizing" human rights, the concept and its study become a new conceptual space for intra-disciplinary dialogue and debate.

As with all research programs, this framework is not in any way a final statement. Nor is it the only possible sociological approach. It is one among many possible others. This approach represents a particularized orientation for studying rights that other scholars can hopefully use for their own research while contributing their own insights, helping to refine it along the way. Human rights formation is an ongoing process—as new issues emerge and the parameters of existing social relationships inevitably shift, so too must the various social meanings of the human rights concept, as well as the various ways of studying it.

≈≋

CHAPTER TWENTY-ONE

RELIGION

David V. Brewington

The sociology of religion poses a wide variety of questions about human rights. Here I focus on four families of questions:

1. What are the sociological foundations of human rights?
2. What is religion's status regarding violations of human rights?
3. How do religious and political institutions interact with respect to rights?
4. What is religious freedom's status as a human right?

These basic questions serve as an entry point into understanding how the sociology of religion addresses issues surrounding human rights. I elaborate on each question by discussing first the substantive question and then the level of reality or realities to which the question pertains and the social structures, actors, institutions, and processes relevant to it.

The most fundamental question the sociology of religion asks regarding human rights concerns its foundations. How, why, and where do human rights develop in history as idea and practice? What sociological factors play roles in this development? These questions recognize that human rights, like any other idea and practice, are not innate to the human condition. Human rights have a history situated in time, place, social structure, process, actor, and institution. Does religion play a role in this history?

A second important question the sociology of religion poses concerning human rights is how religion is involved in human rights violations. This question has two poles: Does religion as an institution have a role in advocating for human rights, and does it have a role in violations of human rights? Why, how, and when do religious actors, be they nation-states, organizations, or individuals, play a role in actions for human rights or violations of rights of humans?

Religion as an institution interacts with political institutions. At times this interaction directly concerns human rights practices and ideas. What shape does this interaction take? Do political institutions violate religious practices? Do religious institutions and organizations interact with political institutions to bolster or minimize human rights practice?

Finally, the practice of religion and conscience is recognized as a fundamental human right in both international law and many national constitutions. What is religious liberty's status, then? What can we say about kinds and levels of religious-liberty violations? Where and when do they take place? What do religious organizations do in response to violations? What do they do to prevent violations? These questions will form this chapter's basis.

ORIGINS, ADVOCATES, VIOLATIONS, AND FRAMES

How has the sociology of religion accounted for origins of human rights? There are two senses in which religion as an institution is implicated in human rights foundations. The first sense is how, historically, human rights come to be in the first place, while the second sense is how human rights practices and ideals are disseminated.

SECULARIZATION AND HUMAN RIGHTS: A FOUNDATIONAL ACCOUNT

Sociologist of religion William Garrett (2001) provides an account of the origins of religious liberty and human rights and identifies secularization as the process responsible. Secularization, in simplest terms, is a decline of religious authority (Chaves 1994) through time. Garrett locates the beginning of secularization in institutional differentiation during the Papal Revolution of the eleventh to thirteenth centuries. Prior to this period, religious and political bodies were one and the same. This was the case in Europe with the Holy Roman emperor and also under William the Conqueror in Normandy and the English Isles.

In the mid eleventh century, Pope Gregory VII began to assert the power of God over the emperor's secular power in selecting churchmen for church offices. Known as the lay investiture, the pope felt that secular powers were exerting too much authority over the church, raising questions of religious integrity. Only God and his agents on earth should have the power to appoint men to church offices.

For Garrett this created an interesting problem for the papacy. How did a pope establish a novel claim to authority "when he lacked both an army and customary practice to lend credibility to his innovations" (2001, 295)? The answer is that the pope turned to legal authority, and this unleashed 150 years of research, development, and codification of canon law through a revival of Roman law and Stoic natural law. This extended act of legal codification for Garrett is the big bang of Western secularization because it "transformed the church into a corporation" (2001, 295), a body unto itself, and in turn created the need for the political body to do the same. Thus, in a dialectic of legal corporatizing, religious and political institutions of the West devolve out of each other as separate bodies.

Though much legal innovation occurred in the intervening centuries, what is important for Garrett as the second great movement of secularization is that the lawyers and scholars working out secular rules and laws endeavored to develop secularized legal foundations without resorting to religious grounds for political institutions. Substantively they were not successful, but they did succeed in convincing later scholars that nonreligious institutions needed to be grounded in secular rather than religious foundational theories. This secular foundational thrust culminated in the US colonies' specific solutions to issues of church and state: human rights law emerged as a wall forbidding the state to intervene in religious issues.

Garrett (2001, 322–327) finds the first appeals to unlimited guarantee of freedom of religion and conscience with Roger Williams and the settlement he founded in Rhode Island and with the Levellers serving in Oliver Cromwell's New Model Army, both in the 1640s, as well as with Isaac Backus, a Baptist minister who emerged out of the first Great Awakening in the colonies in the 1770s. Each of these developed understandings of religious rights in the face of "a similar set of religiously repressive social conditions" through distinctively religious understandings of an individual's capacities and duties to conscience. For Williams, it was only through a deeply free conscience that individuals could come to a right understanding of the Christian god. The Levellers came to their understanding of human rights through a belief that the Christian god granted each person an ownership of his or her own person. From this ownership all other rights were derived. Backus derived his rights framework from the idea that "all persons are born equally free and independent" (Garrett 2001, 327).

The religious origins of each of these early enunciations of comprehensive human rights derived from the sacred origins of individuals and were born in religious repression. Whereas the Levellers' ideas in the United Kingdom did not survive the demise of the movement, by Garrett's account the religious environment in the United States afforded the ideas of Williams and Backus a means of fermentation and dissemination to the masses. Baptist and Separatist sects were bursting at the seams with new converts after the Great Awakening of the 1730s and 1740s, and their clergy preached religious and other freedoms borne of their own religious persecution. This created a mass appeal for rights discourse that resonated later with Thomas Jefferson's more Lockean natural rights theories of equality and inalienable rights (Garrett 2001, 329).

The religious reasoning behind the American human rights tradition and political reasoning behind the natural law tradition found sufficient expression in the American context to effect resolution of what Garrett (2001, 330) regards as a significant sociological problem: how to build a secular state and keep it out of the business of religion while simultaneously keeping religion out of the business of the state. Religious reasoning behind freedom of conscience defined sacredness as a property of the human individual deriving directly from Christian divinity, while political reasoning defined the state as a secular entity divorced of religious foundations and connections. These lines of reasoning converged in the US Bill of Rights, legally institutionalizing human rights and serving as an institutional model for human rights and religious liberty in subsequent constitutions and international instruments (see Gill 2008).

RELIGIONS AS CARRIERS OF HUMAN RIGHTS

Garrett's account provides a view of human rights foundations from a sociology-of-religion perspective. In addition to its importance in the foundation of human rights, religion has also been a prominent carrier of human rights ideas and practices. The origins of numerous transnational human rights advocacy campaigns can be traced to religious voices, and religiously minded individuals and religious organizations have often sustained these movements. An incomplete list of religious bodies and their campaigns includes, in the nineteenth century, the Quakers, Methodists, Unitarians, and Presbyterians' work in the antislavery movement in America and the United Kingdom (Keck and Sikkink 1998, 41–51; Chabbott 1999, 228; Rabben 2002, 8–12); the Woman's Christian Temperance Movement's involvement in the women's suffrage movement (Keck and Sikkink 1998, 54; Berkovitch 1999); the Calvinist Henry Dunant's campaign leading to the Geneva Conventions and the International Society of the Red Cross/Crescent (ICRC 1998; Finnemore 1999); and Christian missionaries' anti-foot-binding movement in China (Keck and Sikkink 1998, 59–66). In the twentieth century we see Protestant organizations and the Catholic Church pushing for the inclusion of human rights in the UN Charter and in the drafting of the Universal Declaration of Human Rights (UDHR) (Traer 1991, 173–185); the Catholic Church's efforts to highlight human rights atrocities in Chile under Augusto Pinochet and in East Timor under Suharto (Risse 2000, 193–195); the Catholic group Pax Romana and the Quaker UN Office advocating at the United Nations for the inclusion of conscientious objection as a human right (Hovey 1997); and Catholics and Protestants as one segment of the Jubilee 2000 movement to eliminate third-world debt (Lechner 2005).

It is evident from this list that religious organizations and individuals are tied to the human rights paradigm's development. But religion has not always been on the side of human rights.

RELIGIOUS VIOLATIONS OF HUMAN RIGHTS?

While religious actors and social processes involving religion are foundational to human rights, examples exist of religion not acting as a human rights advocate. The actions of nineteen al-Qaeda hijackers on September 11, 2001, constitute the most sensational example of religious actors violating human rights in recent memory. Other less astounding examples abound. Members of the People's Temple, a new religious movement (NRM), murdered children as part of a mass suicide (Hall 1987). Government authorities intervene when NRM leaders are accused of child molestation, which occurred with the Peoples Temple in the 1970s and the Branch Davidians in the 1990s (Hall 1987; Hall, Schuyler, and Trinh 2000).

Lest we think that human rights violations are the product of peripheral organizations, we should consider more mainstream religions and their roles in human rights abuses. The ongoing child-molestation claims made by Catholic parishioners against the Catholic Church (Berry 1992; Burkett and Bruni 1993; Hidalgo 2007;

Shupe 1998; Shupe 2007) point to clear violations of children's rights. The advocacy activities of conservative evangelical Protestant organizations in pursuing antiabortion and "natural" marriage legislation are framed by some as violations of reproductive rights and civil liberties. It is possible that Hindus of the untouchable caste would regard their status by birth as a violation of their rights.

These examples illustrate that religion and its actors can be violators as much as they can be advocates of human rights. The same religious organization can utilize organizational capacities, theological precepts, and moral teachings to promote human rights and at the same time violate human rights. Sociologists of religion can greatly expand their research programs by examining human rights as a frame of reference.

How Do Religious and Political Institutions Interact?

The interaction of political and religious institutions is fundamental to considerations of human rights. A frequent subject for the sociology of religion is interaction of religion and state, which often concerns freedom of religious believers to practice their faith, especially where minority religions are concerned. It is instructive to reflect on how the secularization process can be utilized to understand how a state might be expected to treat religion within its territories. Martin (1978) begins with the historical frame in which a society enters secularization. This frame structures society's subsequent history such that a society's path from secularization and subsequent treatment of religion within its borders are dependent on the frame through which it enters secularization.

Martin strongly associates religious pluralism with democratic pluralism and religious monopoly with strong secularism, while considering the impact of the size of religious minorities. The nature of specific religions also plays a role. Catholicism is associated with strong political power in the monopoly situation, and in the minority situation Catholics stress their beliefs' universal aspects. Protestants are inclined toward individual achievement, inhibiting organic formations in both majority and minority situations. Martin associates Protestantism with intrinsic pluralism and democracy—salvation for all tends to produce tolerance, if unintentionally.

The path through which a state enters secularization frames the relationship between religion and state. We can see examples of this path dependence in how national legal systems address religious issues. In France in 2010, the full-face veil was banned in public places (Ajrouch 2007; Haddad 2007; Read 2007; Wallerstein 2005b). Religious and immigration histories of the United States and France shape their responses to the veil (Ajrouch 2007; Read 2007).

NRMs are also the subject of much legal scrutiny. Scientology has encountered hostile legal systems in much of the West, including the United States, Germany, France, Spain, Canada, Belgium, Denmark, Greece, Ireland, Italy, and others. Typically the legal cases involving Scientology concern whether it should be designated as a religious organization and accrue benefits from that status, including tax exemptions. The German state went so far as to put Scientology on its list of extremist groups, which also includes neo-Nazi factions (Seiwert 1999; Seiwert 2003; Simon 2010; Taylor 2003).

Religion-state interactions do not always surround human rights conflicts. In the United States, a consortium of religious organizations joined together with allies in Congress to send the International Religious Freedom Act to President Bill Clinton in 1998. The bill was signed into law and mandated that religious freedom become one of the criteria through which the US State Department evaluates other states (Farr et al. 2009; Fore 2002; Gunn 2000; Mousin 2003; Pastor 2005; Wales 2002).

While the sociology of religion provides a contextual frame for understanding these controversies (i.e., that of Martin 1978), very seldom does sociology of religion address these issues through human rights frames. As before, opportunities for sociology of religion to consider these issues in human rights contexts are considerable.

Religious Freedom as a Human Right

Religious freedom is codified in the UDHR as follows: "Everyone has the right to freedom of thought, conscience and religion; this right includes freedom to change his religion or belief, and freedom, either alone or in community with others and in public or private, to manifest his religion or belief in teaching, practice, worship and observance" (UN 1948). Based on recent research by the PEW Forum on Religion and Public Life (2009), only 7 countries out of the 198 they examined, or 4 percent, had no constitutional protection for religious freedom. At the same time, the PEW report finds that for the 191 national constitutions that provide some level of protection of freedom of religion, 146 (74 percent) also include language that appears "to qualify or substantially contradict the concept of 'religious freedom'" (2009, 54). Only forty-four nations (22 percent) do not have contradictory or qualifying language circumscribing religious freedom. According to PEW's Government Restrictions Index, nearly 22 percent of all countries have high levels of restrictions, including China, Iran, and Saudi Arabia. Moderate levels of restriction are found in 18.2 percent of countries, including Ethiopia, France, Mexico, and Venezuela. More than 60 percent of states impose low levels of restrictions, such as Costa Rica, Poland, and Senegal.

The national government of 141 countries (71 percent) either fully respects religious freedom in practice or generally respects religious freedom in practice with exceptions in some locations. National governments in fifty-nine countries (29 percent) do not respect religious freedom in practice generally or at all. Countries in this latter category tend to be in the Middle East and North Africa or Asia-Pacific. However, European nations are not exemplars in religious freedom. Former communist countries tend to favor one state-recognized religion, and western European countries "have laws aimed at protecting citizens from what the government considers dangerous cults or sects" (PEW 2009, 15).

While these national participation measures are important, they omit a piece of the religious-freedom story. This is the realm of not-for-profit advocacy organizations that work within national and international jurisdictions to call attention to religious-freedom issues. The PEW Research Center is a recent organization in a long tradition. Two early formal human rights international nongovernmental organizations (INGOs) dedicated to religious liberty are the International Religious Liberty Association, founded in 1893, and the International Association for Religious Freedom, founded in 1900.

Scholarly research on religious-liberty INGOs is unfortunately scant, but some of it provides an interesting comparison with other types of human rights advocacy. Religious-liberty INGOs are far more likely to be religious than all other human rights INGOs (Brewington 2005). They are less likely to have consultative status with the United Nations than INGOs for children's, women's, or people's rights. In absolute numbers, there were far fewer religious-liberty INGOs than children's, women's, or people's rights INGOs as of 1994 (Brewington 2005). Despite being one of the first formally organized human rights areas, religious liberty is less institutionalized in the UN system, the size of the population is relatively smaller than "younger" rights, and these organizations are much more likely to have religious origins than all other human rights INGOs. Religious-rights advocates are of predominantly three types: secular with a universalistic approach (freedom of religion is advocated for all humans), religious with a universalistic approach, and religious with a particularistic approach (freedom of religion is advanced for a particular faith) (Brewington 2011). The latter type of human rights organization is fairly rare in human rights advocacy. These early findings suggest some puzzles to which scholars of the sociology of religion and globalization need to pay more attention (see Brewington 2011).

LEVELS OF REALITY, SOCIAL STRUCTURES, ACTORS, INSTITUTIONS, AND PROCESSES

Multiple levels of reality are implicated in questions that sociology of religion asks of human rights. Much of the focus is on national levels, however, and historically these questions have been asked of specific national contexts—the United States and western European states. There are two main reasons for this. First, sociology as a discipline and sociology of religion as a subdiscipline are historically embedded in the West. The mythic founders in sociology—Weber, Marx, Durkheim, and Simmel—were all interested in religious questions as they observed the social, structural, and cultural changes around them in the context of the emergence of the modern era in Europe and the United States. When these and later authors referred to society, they were typically conflating US and European national societies, which became the default subject of study. Second, national governments are the actors held "responsible" for the rights of the people living within their territorial boundaries. Constitutional protections of rights are extended by states to the inhabitants of their national territories.

There are many relevant social structures at play in approaches that sociology of religion takes toward human rights. In most studies, the individual and the state are the most relevant actors. The individual, who possesses rights, and the state, as the entity that both protects and violates rights of its residents, are taken for granted by most sociologists and sociologists of religion as involved actors. Group or collective rights are also implicated in how sociologists of religion address human rights. By virtue of its being religious community, a group sometimes asserts rights as necessary for it to practice its faith. Proselytism, or an active effort to change a person's faith, is one practice that is often viewed as a violation of a religious group's collective rights. At the same time, most international human rights instruments provide for the right to conversion—to change one's belief. Assertions of collective rights and individual rights, especially regarding religious rights, can be quite controversial (Thomas 2004; Thomas 2001).

Religion as an institution is also implicated in the answers put forth by sociologists of religion to questions outlined above. A corollary is that religion as an institution is one among many institutions at play in national society. With respect to human rights, religion as an institution especially interacts with the national polity—the system of government, laws, and norms enacted within a specified territory.

Religious organizations, comprised of practitioners or political advocates, constitute actors of interest in the sociologist of religion's research. These actors are worshipers' organizations, secular or religious NGOs advocating for religious liberty, or religious NGOs advocating for human rights in general. International governmental organizations, especially the United Nations, are the target of much human rights advocacy.

The global level of reality is increasingly of interest to sociologists of religion studying human rights. Global processes, including the accelerating flows of information, ideas, norms, models, people, and materials, structure the phenomena of human rights of interest to sociologists of religion.

What Can the Human Rights Paradigm Learn from Work in Sociology of Religion?

The sociological study of religion in general and its specific analysis of human rights in particular do offer some important lessons for studying human rights. The first lesson concerns the ambivalent disposition of religion toward human rights. Religious actors and processes can be a catalyst simultaneously for the expansion of the human rights paradigm and for the promotion of human rights violators. This is not to say that these occur concurrently, but through history one religious actor may be a human rights advocate in one context and complicit in violations in another.

The philosopher Jacque Maritain (1952, 110–111), one of the principle architects of the UDHR, said that human rights ideology was indeed like a civic or secular religion. Others, in the tradition of Émile Durkheim, have examined human rights as a "cult of the individual" (Elliott 2007, 2008). We do not have to go as far as these scholars and claim that human rights ideology has religious properties, but the religious dimensions of human rights in its foundations and implementations suggest that the sociologist of religion should have several points of advice for scholars of human rights. Religion, as a realm of texts and discourse, is subject to the contexts in which it is interpreted, and interpretation is mutable. Human rights scholars should be sensitive to and understand how human rights ideology changes over time and is interpreted contextually.

A second offering from scholars of the sociology of religion would be that human rights scholars should be sensitive to the fact that human rights ideology is contested, as is religion, precisely because it is mutable in its interpretations, especially in an era of globalization (Beyer 2001; Beyer 2006; Robertson 1992). One example concerns Islamic members of the UN Human Rights Commission who have put forward resolutions seeking to define criticism of religion as a violation of practitioners' rights. Critics immediately point out that this is itself a violation of the right to free speech. Neoinstitutional sociological approaches to human rights point out that conflicting claims are expected with the global expansion of human rights (Elliott 2008; Elliott 2007; W. H. Thomas 2004; J. Thomas 2001): rights claims can overlap in ways that produce controversy and contestation.

A final offering that sociologists of religion would make to scholars of human rights is to remind them that however universal human rights might seem, they are in fact products of particular histories. While it would be simplistic to label the current conception of human rights as "Western," there is still truth to the claim, and interpreters of human rights do indeed criticize them as being of Western origin (Ishay 2004a).

Sociologist of religion and globalization Roland Robertson (1992) has captured much of these cautions in his work on globalization as a process whereby the particular becomes universal and the universal becomes particular. Simply put, human rights ideology is a particularistic product of a particular culture promulgated as a universal (i.e., as applying to all humans globally). This universal ideology is then received in particularistic ways—it is interpreted vis-à-vis the local context it is being situated within. While freedom of religion is conceived of as a universal human right, its local application is context specific. Thus, even while the US and French constitutions espouse freedom of religion as a citizen's right, the historical relationship between religion and state conditions the practice and regulation of religious liberty. As we saw earlier in the French context, the full-face veil that some Muslim women wear has been banned in public spaces. This coheres with the French context in which religious symbols are not as welcomed in public life as in US contexts.

WHAT CAN THE SOCIOLOGY OF RELIGION LEARN FROM HUMAN RIGHTS SCHOLARSHIP?

The sociology of religion has much to learn from human rights scholarship. One branch of human rights scholarship approaches its subject matter from a neoinstitutional or world-polity approach (Boli and Thomas 1999; Lechner and Boli 2005; Powell and DiMaggio 1991; Thomas 1987). Simply put, neoinstitutional scholars take culture very seriously and promote a definition that goes deeper than conventional notions of culture. The environment in which social entities find themselves is filled with rules, norms, and models. Entities in this environment do not act; they enact. These rules, norms, and models are the culture to which neoinstitutionalists pay attention because they structure what and how entities enact within a given environment. Human rights scholars in this tradition would interpret the fact that 96 percent of all national constitutions have some stated protection for religious liberty as suggesting that they are enacting globally accessible norms that imply there better be at least some lip-service to religious freedom.

A popular approach in sociology of religion in the last twenty to twenty-five years is that of the rational-choice tradition, which is sensitive to the manner in which actors behave in their own self-interest. While interest maximization is undoubtedly a factor, it leaves out a great deal of sociologically interesting material to which neo-institutional approaches are sensitive. From where did the idea of religious liberty come? From where do the individual's preferences for one religion over another come? In short, if sociologists of religion pay attention chiefly to interest maximization, they miss capturing key factors in their explanations of religious phenomena.

Sociology of religion can also learn from human rights scholars to pay more attention to issues of globalization. While a number of sociologists of religion, such as Robertson, Peter Beyer, and Jose Casanova, certainly take the global level seriously, it seems that human rights scholars are ahead in studying how globalization as a process is important to human rights study. Neoinstitutional scholars are among those who study human rights as a global process, but international relations scholars such as Keck and Sikkink (1998), Hafner-Burton and Tsutsui (2005), and Florini et al. (2000) were also at the forefront in studying human rights advocates in global contexts.

What Is the Future?

Where should the sociology of religion go in researching human rights? My hope, as a scholar of religion, human rights, and globalization, is that the sociology of religion will expand its understanding of human rights by taking the global level of reality more seriously and that it will feed other subdisciplines (e.g., social movements, organizations) by fleshing out the special nature of religion with respect to human rights: it is a progenitor of human rights but can be both advocate and violator of them. In light of what sociologists of religion might advise human rights scholars, it is my hope that the human rights paradigm will explore itself reflexively and understand that it is itself a source of ongoing controversy.

CHAPTER TWENTY-TWO

ECONOMIC SOCIOLOGY

Clarence Y. H. Lo

The field of economic sociology examines how economic institutions and elites operate in the global context and what social inequalities are produced thereby. Economic sociology (otherwise known as the field of economy and society) focuses on a critique of models of rational self-interest, commonly used to explain economic phenomena. To many in the discipline of economics, rational self-interest models of microeconomic behavior provide a workable blueprint of an economy that can produce growth and efficiency without coercion, thereby justifying free markets and private, for-profit ownership of businesses (Friedman 1962). The field of economic sociology advocates an alternate vision, which has insisted that rational self-interest models ignore cultural and social factors that can be powerful explanations of economic life. With its view of economic, cultural, and social factors, economic sociology is well positioned to inform knowledge of human rights

THEORETICAL CRITIQUES OF MARKETS IN ECONOMIC SOCIOLOGY

In its critique of market individualism, economic sociology draws insights from organizational theory, which says that businesses in reality do not rationally choose the best policy from the available options. Rather, firms "satisfice" (Simon 1947), picking the first satisfactory solution. Searching for more information to find a better solution is avoided, since it entails significant costs for the firm. What is defined as "satisfactory" is socially and culturally determined, highly variable and context dependent, and thus a fitting subject for sociologists.

The New Institutionalism (Powell and DiMaggio 1991), which analyzes economies as social institutions, also goes beyond rational optimization as an explanation and argues that cultural processes lead organizations and their policies to resemble each other. Instead of pursuing optimally effective policies, organizations develop policies as rituals or because of their symbolic dimensions and in relation to professional groups or more powerful or esteemed organizations.

Economic sociologists have pointed to other limitations of conceptualizing the economy as propertied individual actors maximizing self-interest. Even when individual decision-making is the unit to be analyzed, many economic sociologists argue that trust, sympathy, and morality are the lynchpins of economic life, a prerequisite before rational self-interest can begin to function—a perspective shared by no one other than Adam Smith ([2002] 1759). Although individual ownership of physical and money capital was fundamental to industrial society, Bourdieu (1984) argues that different forms of capital, social capital and cultural capital, are now important in the perpetuation of class position. Economic sociologists have examined the varied forms of cultural capital for social classes in different contexts (Lamont 2000).

Network analysts have contributed to economic sociology by adopting as their unit of analysis not individual maximizers but rather social relations, such as patterns of networks, to explain phenomena, for instance, successful job searches (Granovetter 1973). In technical and bureaucratic settings, the right to participate in decisions is contested by networks of actors that form to gain participation on a particular issue. In government, consultations with technical officials through such networks develop as an alternative to the intervention of elected representatives (Callon, Lascoumes, and Barthe 2009). Putnam (2000) argues, following Tocqueville's (1960 [1835]) analysis of nineteenth-century America, that the social relations of civic life are the foundation of American prosperity. In short, economic activity is best studied not as a rational choice abstracted from society but rather as action embedded in social relations, institutions, and culture (Polanyi 1944).

Thus, economic sociologists have pointed out that market models have been conceptually limited and have constructed inadequate explanations ignoring sociocultural factors. These same weaknesses, as will be evident below, have led economic sociologists to raise significant questions about the ability of markets to produce efficiently, yield economic growth, and provide for the well-being of workers, consumers, and society. Economic sociology has provided the values, standards, evaluative processes, and underlying causal factors by which market behavior and its outcomes have been judged and can be further criticized.

ECONOMIC SOCIOLOGY'S FINDINGS

Much of economic sociology casts doubt on the notion that market forces alone are capable of guiding the economy, let alone ordering society. Leading scholars in the field of economy and society have demonstrated that active governance and policy-making, by political leaders and economic elites, have been crucial factors of economic life since the beginning of the Industrial Revolution (Hobsbawm 1962; Krugman 2007).

Scholarship in the field of economy and society has demonstrated that the unparalleled prosperity after World War II in the United States and the rest of the capitalist world has been the result not of free markets but rather of government intervention. In the United States, the continuation of the New Deal from the 1930s brought about an acceptance of Keynesian fiscal policy (Lekachman 1966). In Europe, government takeovers of some industries led to a mixed economy, social democracy, and an elaborated welfare state. Labor unions were an integral part of the postwar boom, giving their blessing to technical advances in productivity in the United States and holding formal power on industry councils ("codetermination") in Germany, Sweden, and other western European nations (Hollingsworth et al 1994).

However, after 1973, higher oil prices destabilized global financial flows, as inflation disrupted Keynesian fiscal policy. Stagnant standards of living and youth unemployment upset political establishments, as did the earlier rise of the civil rights, antiwar, students', and women's movements around the world, complicating the task of legitimizing governments and their economic policies (Mishra 1984).

The field of economic sociology has analyzed the origins and implementation of, and the opposition to, the governmental market-privatization policies, which were the reaction to the economic turmoil after 1973. Deregulating airlines and banking, reducing nondefense spending, turning over government functions of prisons and education to private corporations, weakening environmental and consumer regulations, and other free market policies were promulgated by business interest groups and right-wing political parties around 1980. Among the most prominent implementers of such policies were US President Ronald Reagan and Prime Minister Margaret Thatcher in England (Harvey 2005).

The implementation of market privatization (also known as neoliberalism, or the Washington Consensus) necessitated government budget and service cutbacks, which in turn required changes in political organizations, processes, and rules, such as executive centralization (Steinmo, Thelen, and Longstreth 1992). Similar policies establishing markets and private business ownership were adopted by the Augusto Pinochet regime in Chile and elsewhere in Latin America (Centeno and Cohen 2010), as well as in the former Soviet Union and in Eastern Europe (Lo 2008). Such regimes increased economic inequalities between workers and those who managed large businesses and owned significant blocks of stock. For workers and retirees, neoliberal policies disrupted the security and subsidies that had offered some protection against economic adversities (Esping-Andersen 1999), thereby negatively affecting human rights.

Although market privatization has led to some signs of prosperity, such as increases in stock prices, asset values, and high-end consumption, critics have pointed out that such signs are indicative of speculative bubbles, which in the past have invariably burst (Kindleberger and Alibler 2005), with disastrous results for the human rights of populations. A prime example was the Tulip mania, in which bourgeois families spent huge sums for imported tulip bulbs that later collapsed in value in 1637. Later bubbles included the Roaring Twenties, leading to the Great Depression. In the 1970s and 1980s, the widespread marketing of high-yield ("junk") bonds, pioneered by Michael Milkin and the firm Drexel Burnham Lambert, financed a wave of corporate mergers and takeovers. The junk-bond boom and bust resulted in high fees and profits for Wall Street firms but layoffs and plant closings as well. In Harrison and Bluestone's (1988) words, the "casino society" had produced a lack of productive investments that had deindustrialized the United States (Perrucci and Perrucci 2009), putting at risk the basic rights of populations.

Comparative historical analysis has been the methodology of choice for economic sociologists. The work of Esping-Andersen (1999) on different types of welfare states is cross-national quantitative research. The work of Skocpol (1992) is based on carefully documented studies comparing leading cases across time and key nations. The latest work by economic sociologists on the 2008 financial meltdown, collected in *Markets on Trial: The Economic Sociology of the U.S. Financial Crisis* (Lounsbury and Hirsch 2010), effectively uses a case-study methodology to argue that the 2008 crisis can be understood only if the economy is seen not as an effectively functioning free market but rather as a social institution that became a risky gamble because of inadequate government regulation.

This latest work in economic sociology thus continues the theoretical and practical critique of free markets. Theoretically, the market is not seen as intrinsically rational but rather as premised on social characteristics such as confidence (Swedberg 2010). The mortgage-securities markets that collapsed in 2008 were not free of government but rather were creatures of government entities like Fannie Mae that had greatly expanded housing-mortgage lending (Fligstein and Goldstein 2010). Government policy such as the Graham Leach Bliley Act of 1999 created a plethora of nonbank institutions that were minimally regulated and hence could rapidly increase subprime loans and repackage them as sound investments (Campbell 2010). Social institutions, financial and regulatory, sustained a perception that the mortgage markets could be trusted to rationally handle any risk that arose.

CONTRIBUTIONS OF ECONOMIC SOCIOLOGY TO HISTORICAL ANALYSIS OF HUMAN RIGHTS

The field of economic sociology, aided by its use of historical comparative methodology, seeks to comprehend how various types of human rights have been advanced in different economic formations in historical periods throughout world history.

Philosophers and theorists of human rights, such as the French Enlightenment thinkers and Immanuel Kant, have emphasized the universal nature of rights across all humanity, regardless of national borders or the stage of societal development. Economic sociology has added the specificity of a historical and practical dimension to our understanding of human rights. The context of economic life at a particular place in time affects which rights are salient and how those rights are conceptualized. Sociologists have generated knowledge about the economic contexts from which specific rights are articulated, thereby contributing to grounded theorizing about human rights.

Economic sociology directly relates key historical developments of commerce, industry, and modernization to transformations in the thinking about human rights, as well as the actualization of specific rights in constitutions and laws and in everyday economic practice and norms. Many scholars have contributed to the analysis of the historical construction of rights from the beginning of early modern Europe.

Karl Polanyi (1944) argued that with the first stirrings of the commercial transformation of the English countryside, populations struggled to have their traditional statuses and rights preserved and recognized. T. H. Marshall (1964) argued that the Industrial Revolution in the nineteenth century had gradually but inextricably led to the progressive winning of different types of rights. Civil rights, such as free speech and the right to security of person and property against despotic governments, were won by democratic revolutions, such as in the United States in 1776 and France in 1789. Political rights (expanding voting to include middle-class men and then most other male citizens) occurred in the late nineteenth century. By the first half of the twentieth century, political rights were being used in elections to win economic and social rights, including accident, unemployment, and old-age insurance. These gains led to campaigns for extension of the right to vote to women and broadening the conceptualization of social and economic rights to include better housing, free public education, and health care.

In the context of American prosperity between the end of World War II through 1973, the increasing importance of Marshall's socioeconomic rights figures prominently in a key philosophical text of the time on equality and rights, John Rawls's *A Theory of Justice* (1971). Rawls emphasized the importance of individual liberty, the civil rights about which Marshall wrote. Rawls also argued that social arrangements are just only insofar as the condition of the worst off is improved; Rawls thereby included Marshall's economic rights in his thinking about justice. When Rawls sketched a possible economic system that would be consistent with his principles of justice, the system was a social democracy, a society that was politically democratic with regulated, privately owned businesses and a public sector for investment in social programs, the type of society in Europe that economic sociologists were studying to counterpose against the free market-model.

The first oil-price spike of 1973, in the name of the rights of oil-producing nations, put the world, economic sociologists included, on notice that the global character of the economy shapes human rights, for better or worse. A robust literature on transnational corporations emerged. Wallerstein (1976) argued that the structure of the contemporary world-system could be traced back to the "modern" world-system of 1450. William Appleman Williams (1962) and his students critiqued US market policies such as free trade, the open door, and the consequent imposing of regimes by the United States on former Spanish colonies by demonstrating that such policies in the US sphere of influence violated the American principles of democracy and human rights, even though US presidents justified those policies with the rhetoric of American freedoms. Williams's analysis of US "imperial anticolonialism" foreshadowed the work of later scholars of the postcolonial condition (Hardt and Negri 2000). By the end of the twentieth century, there was an outpouring of academic writing on the issue of "globalism" and its relation to democratic and human rights (Held 2004).

As a result of the growing academic interest in global inequalities, scholars interested in economy and society have explored new definitions of human rights, apart from American conceptions of electoral democracy and business freedom, which would be more relevant to those in the impoverished Global South. Sen (1992) revisits Rawls's (1971) discussion of which rights in the constellation should be primary to focus on defining what kind of equality would be most important to address in the developing world. Sen argues that more fundamental than equalities of wealth and income are equalities in the capabilities of individuals to accomplish a variety of ends. Health-care rights and public-health measures are necessary to enable the population to work and go on to raise further issues of rights of livelihood. Sen enables us to better comprehend how campaigns for public health in developing areas are crucial for the realization of a range of human rights.

The globalization of the economy has led to human rights issues that have transcended not only geographic borders but the narrow borders of conceptualization of rights as economic rights for labor. Narrow issues of distribution of material goods have spilled over into new definitions of political and social rights demanded by the feminist, antiwar, environmental, and black-consciousness movements (Laclau and Mouffe 1985), which have raised economic issues of equality and sustainability in ways different from earlier trade unions and old left political parties.

Fraser and Honneth (2003) argue that a basic right is for groups to be positively recognized so that group members can participate in a full range of interactions, without barriers or stigmatization. To be accomplished, recognition must include participation in democratic institutions. The democratic elitism of the periodic election of leaders must be replaced with a deeper and more inclusive participatory democracy (Fung and Wright 2003).

Racial-justice, feminist, environmental, and other social movements have increased recognition and participation of subordinate groups around the world. Global social movements, exemplified by world social forums (Chase-Dunn and Reese 2010), global feminisms (Naples and Desai 2002), environmental justice movements, and the movement for climate justice, put new definitions of human rights squarely on the bargaining table. At the same time the advance of economic globalism challenges the centrality of the state, national politics, and the entire system of sovereignty that arose with the Treaty of Westphalia (1648), which ended the Thirty Years' War in Europe.

Fraser (2009) argues that with a globalized economy, issues of justice and human rights cannot be effectively handled by nation-states, which can only alter policies within their borders. The key questions include who the global actors are and what standards of justice should be applied. Global social movements have been, and will continue to be, active players in the ongoing process of defining human rights.

Thus, human rights are not solely and narrowly an issue of economic rights; human rights require participatory politics to form a collective will whereby communities of citizens engage in the processes of learning to implement human rights by changing the rules in institutions (Bowles and Gintis 1986). Human rights cannot only be gauged by the metrics of individual equality, for a fundamental human right is to determine public policies collectively. Levine (1999) argues for going beyond individual egalitarianism to advocate the value of democratic political rights used to cooperatively guide the sources of economic productivity in a society.

The recent work of Margaret Somers (2008) in *Genealogies of Citizenship* reprises previous historical investigations of economic sociologists and goes on to show how the themes that form the basis for research in the field of economic sociology— namely, the critique of markets and the establishment of the theoretical primacy of grounded societal institutions—can sharpen the conceptualization of human rights and citizenship rights. The development of market liberalism into a dominant ideology over the past 170 years has reduced the concept of rights to mere freedom from state intervention, making remaining rights contractual, activated only if individuals are successful in market exchanges in obtaining the resources needed to activate their rights.

For Somers, contemporary events provide searing episodes of how the practical and ideological primacy of the market can lead to the abridgements of citizenship and hence human rights. American conservatives have argued that rights to the good life should only be extended to those individuals who prove themselves worthy through participation in work and the labor market (the "responsibility crusade"); conversely, those individuals who are morally failures through their own free decision are undeserving (the "perversity thesis"). The poor and black residents of New Orleans, whose marginal participation in the economy afforded them neither means of transportation nor social respect, remained in the city as a shocking example of how basic human rights have been contractualized, afforded only to those who succeed in markets.

Somers argues for a fuller definition of citizenship as a basic human right that would be grounded not in market relations, as in neoliberalism, but rather in the social relations that economic sociologists see as more important than market relationships. For Somers, citizenship rights require social inclusion, the recognition of groups in society as worthy members of a community who, as Somers puts it, have the "right to have rights." Human rights, then, are fundamentally constituted by society and crucially depend on the strength of institutions in civil society as opposed to the state or the market.

REDEFINITION OF ECONOMIC SOCIOLOGY WITHIN A HUMAN RIGHTS PARADIGM

Economic sociology thus contributes to the human rights perspective by historicizing and specifying the particular human rights that have shaped economic life in the progression from an agrarian society, through mercantilism and the stages of the Industrial Revolution, to advanced capitalism and a global economy. Conversely, a human rights perspective can contribute to economic sociology by prompting research into how different ideals of human rights come to influence specific debates in economic policy, as well as the actual policies themselves.

Rearticulated concepts of human rights and standards of justice challenge some of the ideologies that justify inequalities, such as racial hierarchy, market exchange, and the sanctity of property rights enshrined in the modern corporation. Ideologies of racial domination, as Omi and Winant (1994) point out, are continually reformulated due to the stirrings of social movements. The collision of human rights principles and racial and ethnic hierarchy produces new hybrid forms of discourse characteristic of governance institutions in the age that Hardt and Negri (2000) characterize as postcolonial empire. Similarly, a human rights perspective can contribute to economic sociology by exploring the conflicts between human rights and the fundamentals of the capitalist economy, such as private property and markets. These conflicts result in changing temporary compromises or "fixes" that can be studied as Omi and Winant studied racial formations.

Equality and other human rights contend with property rights to form a series of compromises, among them the notion of "fairness." Fairness leads to reforms that are considerably less sweeping than a drive for full equality. Notions of fairness or "equity," rather than equality, exemplify the development of hybrid concepts of rights that may be found, for example, in global discussions where advocates of women's equality collided with those who sought to rearticulate inequalities.

Equality of rights and the economic condition for women has been advanced through the UN Convention on the Elimination of All Forms of Discrimination against Women (1979) and at UN-sponsored forums such as the Fourth World Conference on Women held in Beijing in 1995. There, representatives from areas with traditional religious views argued that universalistic definitions of equality need to be tempered with national customs as to what is proper. Full equality of educational and economic opportunity, so the argument went, was not realistic and should be replaced with equity as a more modest goal (Facio and Morgan 2009).

Human rights discourses, in addition to operating at the global level, also permeate local contexts. Human rights discourses constitute knowledge used in institutions such as the media, popular culture, law, and professional and academic disciplines (Powell and DiMaggio 1991). Elster (1992) establishes a theoretical framework that can be used to analyze how different concepts of equality and justice are applied in the knowledge, culture, and routines of specific institutions. As Glenn (2002) points out, the civil, political, and economic rights theorized by Marshall (1964) are contested and altered in their application to educational institutions and other forms of civic life in local communities.

The conflicts between human rights such as universal equality and contrary principles that support property rights and markets have produced hybrid concepts about equity and fairness in many institutions. In US federal courts, the hybridities between the class-based discourse of property rights and the popular discourse of economic rights were articulated in a series of legal compromises in the early twentieth century. The doctrines of court majorities responded to political debates couched in terms of long-standing American rights and new definitions of those rights stemming from the claims of social movements. Court decisions led to further commentary by politicians and social movements (Friedman 2002). The notion that the rights of small producers were violated by monopolistic agreements among large companies spawned political rhetoric, even more litigation, and eventually the legal doctrine of ruinous competition—that price cutting among producers could become cutthroat and hence destructive for the common person as well. Another legal doctrine of the time was the "rule of reason," articulated by justices such as Edward Douglass White, Oliver Wendell Holmes, and Louis Brandeis, who argued that the rights of small producers should not sweep away all trusts and all their restraints of trade; some restraints were reasonable and therefore permissible under the Sherman Antitrust Act (Hovenkamp 1991; Peritz 1996).

Legal discourses affect political speech in Congress and in presidential campaigns, such as the election of 1912 (Sklar 1988), and vice versa. New temporary resolutions of the tensions between two contrary grand principles, human rights and property rights, originate in one area of the public sphere and reverberate through others. Hybridities can begin in the discourse in one discipline, such as the law, and travel to spawn other hybridities in another discipline, such as political theory. The human rights perspective has given rise to major works in economic and political sociology that detail the legal, political, and regulatory consequences of conflicts between human versus business rights. The resulting regulations that were passed and administered were crucial for the rise of the large industrial corporation (Peritz 1996) and the development of a global economic system of advanced capitalism (Sassen 2006b).

As I argue in my new book (Lo, forthcoming), through a discourse interwoven with conflicting rights, Americans developed a sense of what was fair, or "equitable," on the market. Some argued that markets were fair; they just had to be left alone. Some argued that injustices of the market were so glaring that they could only be made fair through reform pushed through by government power. Such was the debate following the Great Recession of 2008.

NEW POSSIBILITIES FOR ECONOMIC SOCIOLOGY AND HUMAN RIGHTS REALIZATION

The ebb and flow of hybrid rights and justice discourses has animated debates over economic reforms. Economic sociology that is focused on human rights can identify, analyze, legitimize, and promulgate new concepts of rights, thereby contributing to the success of reform. For example, many of the leading empirical works in the field of economic sociology have already sought, quite explicitly, to advance different types of human rights—democratic political and participatory rights (Etzioni 1988, 2009), economic security (Esping-Andersen 1999), women's rights (Walby 2009), individual opportunity (Giddens 1998), and social democracy.

Many arguments for policies to advance human rights are grounded in an economic-sociology critique of markets, such as the failure of markets to deal adequately with externalities or provide economic security (Esping-Andersen 1999). Langewoort (1996) argues that the widespread failure of individuals to behave rationally during investment booms necessitates the US federal government's taking on additional responsibilities to see to it that small investors are protected. During periods of speculative fervor, individuals are prone to judge the present situation in light of recent gains, attributing upside profit to skill rather than luck. Regulation is needed, Langewoort argues, to save us from our own behavior in markets, which is irrational despite what the models claim.

In the area of labor rights, Margaret Weir (1992) argues that political rhetoric and processes in Congress led to the concretization of specific employment rights. Following the 2008 recession, the AFL-CIO used a new language of rights when it argued for employees' right to sick leave as an extension of the right to free association. In addition, labor used rights-based arguments to advocate for the Employee Free Choice Act, which would give unions additional opportunities to organize workplaces through gathering signatures rather than gaining votes in an election (Clawson 2003).

The emergent ways in which rights are defined have greatly impacted the success of movements to gain credit rights. Credit rights can be defined as the right of an individual woman to be fairly considered for loans or, alternatively, as the right of a depositor to benefit from a proper fiduciary relationship with the local bank to whom she has entrusted her money. It was the latter definition of rights that led to the successful passage of the Community Reinvestment Act of 1977 (Krippner 2010). Economic sociology, using conceptions of human rights as an analytic tool, can discover which definitions of rights have actually led to reforms that have most advanced the cause of human rights.

THREE

LIVING TOGETHER LOCALLY AND GLOBALLY

CHAPTER TWENTY-THREE

COMMUNITY AND URBAN SOCIOLOGY

Kenneth Neubeck

The contemporary human rights paradigm is quite a recent development, sparked by the signing of the UN Charter and the founding of the United Nations in 1945. UN members quickly reached consensus on a common standard of human rights achievement in the Universal Declaration of Human Rights (UDHR), adopted by the UN General Assembly in 1948. The UDHR, while not a treaty and thus not carrying the force of international law, prompted drafting and adoption of key international human rights treaties and other important human rights instruments (Forsythe 2000; Donnelly 2003). The UDHR's provisions are today reflected in constitutions, laws, and judicial decisions of many nations (Blau and Moncada 2005; Blau and Frezzo 2011). The declaration has also played a role in inspiring social-justice movements around the world.

The contemporary human rights paradigm, crafted largely in response to the horrors and human suffering resulting from World War II, calls for governments at all levels to take forward-looking actions based on a vision of a better world (Lauren 1998). This vision is founded on the belief that there are rights that all people have simply by virtue of being human and that respecting, protecting, and fulfilling these rights is a precondition for individuals to live their lives in freedom and with dignity. The rights involved are political, civil, social, economic, and cultural. They are not only deemed to be inalienable but also, equally importantly, interconnected with and interdependent on one another (Howard 1995).

While sociology, with its nineteenth-century western European origins, is obviously much older than the human rights paradigm, the discipline's adherents and proponents have long maintained that sociologists should study human society and its features to provide knowledge helpful to guiding social change that will improve people's lives. Some European founders of sociological thinking concluded that positive social change would naturally come about and counseled people to accommodate themselves to the prevailing order so as not to disrupt it and thus inhibit social progress. Others, in contrast, argued that social progress would not occur without people actively struggling against injustice and deprivation, and they counseled people to take collective action to bring about change (Zeitlin 2000).

Regardless of differences in how they have thought society could best get there, influential sociological thinkers have shared a belief that sociological knowledge could be used for human betterment.

Unfortunately, human rights advocacy and sociological scholarship have typically been carried out in separate silos. At worst, this has meant that one really has had little to do with the other; at best, there has been a tension between the two that relates to sociologists' tendency to self-identify professionally as scholars as opposed to rights advocates (Frezzo 2011). However, growing interest around the world and within the United States in implementing human rights at the local level, to be discussed later in this chapter, offers possibilities and opportunities for these two silos to merge. As is shown below, both community and urban sociology (CUS) and the human rights paradigm are concerned with serious problems in living that are adversely affecting people's life experiences and life chances. In addition, many of those who are engaged in CUS share human rights advocates' belief that knowledge gained from listening to the voices of those experiencing these problems provides an important basis for crafting solutions. The mutual benefits that can come from collaboration between CUS scholars and human rights advocates is addressed at the end of this chapter.

COMMUNITY AND URBAN SOCIOLOGY AS HUMAN RIGHTS WORK

Community and urban sociology in the United States has often reflected a reformist orientation. While CUS covers an enormous range of topics, since the early-twentieth-century city-centered scholarship of the Chicago School (Bulmer 1984; Fine 1995), there has been a tradition of sociologists studying "urban problems." In doing so, many CUS scholars have documented instances or effects of what human rights advocates call human rights violations. The rights being violated are fundamental to the framework of human rights set forth in the 1948 UDHR and incorporated into international law through subsequent UN human rights treaties.

The human right to freedom from discrimination is a key component of the human rights framework, as is the right to an adequate living standard. CUS scholarship has documented ways in which racism and poverty impact and severely limit the life chances of many who inhabit cities (Wilson 2009) and has shown ways in which these phenomena contribute to residential segregation and social isolation, and vice versa (Saito 2009). Segregation is both economic (Dreier, Mollenkopf, and Swanstrom 2005) and racial (Hartman and Squires 2009). CUS scholars have shown the negative outcomes of segregation and social exclusion for city dwellers (Peterson and Krivo 2010; Zukin 2011). Among these outcomes are ways in which segregation places structural limitations on people's opportunities to rise out of poverty and overcome social marginalization (Squires and Kubrin 2006).

The human rights framework also embraces the right to education, which is seen as necessary for the full development of the human personality. Access to equal educational opportunities and to quality education are directly affected by economic and racial segregation. Such segregation adds to disadvantages many children already face due to low family incomes and institutional racism embedded in schooling (Neckerman 2010). CUS researchers have found that not only disparities in income but also unacknowledged disparities in wealth distribution directly shape urban children's educational choices, opportunities, and ultimate achievements (Johnson 2006). Income and wealth also impact such basic matters as an urban family's choice of day-care facilities for its preschooler, which in turn has important impacts on the child's development of opportunity networks and social capital (Small 2009).

The rights to work and to just and favorable remuneration are likewise central to the human rights framework. Urban poverty largely reflects high rates of unemployment and underemployment, and many city dwellers are permanently trapped in the low-wage job market (O'Connor, Tilly, and Bobo 2001; Newman 2008). Lack of jobs and low wages have been found to exacerbate struggles of low-income female-headed families (Edin 2005) and contribute to failure of federal and state welfare reforms to remedy the extreme poverty in which many such families exist (Edin, Lein, and Jencks 1997). Many city residents have no choice but to derive income from within their city's underground economy (Venkatesh 2009). Without an adequate living standard, families are incapable of achieving the human right to housing and increasingly are found by CUS scholars to be among the nation's homeless (Wright 2009). Nonetheless, many poverty-stricken people do manage to survive with surprising resilience (Sanchez-Jankowski 2008). This includes immigrants, who in the United States have increasingly been people of color (Kasinitz et al. 2009), subject to their own forms of racialization and mistreatment (Merenstein 2008).

The human rights framework also includes rights to security of person and to equal treatment and protection under the law. While crime has been declining in US cities over the last decade, CUS scholars have found that street crime and threats to personal security remain highly problematic in many urban areas (Parker 2008). Involvement in criminal activity has become equivalent to a lifestyle and a form of fictive employment for some urban residents (Anderson 2000; St. Jean 2007). Policing in US cities of people who are poor and of color is often harsh, harassing, and sometimes accompanied by police brutality (Holmes 2008). CUS scholars have found that new forms of social control are increasingly being added to traditional policing powers, such as the creation of "exclusion zones" that enable police and courts to banish class and color "undesirables" from certain parts of cities (Beckett and Herbert 2009). Despite ongoing economic and racial dynamics that function to keep different population segments apart in urban settings, CUS scholars have also investigated the ubiquity and importance of common spaces where people can and do safely interact with civility across class and race lines (Anderson 2011).

The human rights to health and to medical care are important parts of the human rights framework. While the health of people who lack adequate incomes (and health insurance) is a chronic concern across the United States, cities are often the object of special environmental health concerns. CUS scholars have addressed environmental racism in urban settings and environmental justice movements that have arisen in response to urban environmental hazards to which people who are poor or of color are disproportionately exposed (Bullard 2000). In the wake of natural and environmental disasters in the United States that have destroyed or disrupted the lives of tens of thousands, such as low-income people of color disproportionately killed or displaced in New Orleans by Hurricane Katrina, CUS has examined the importance of place and racial and class politics of disaster response in urban settings (Bullard and Wright 2009).

The human rights framework also includes the right to political participation in order that government will reflect the will of the people rather than privileged special interests. CUS scholars have studied cities' power structures, which provide the local governing context within which all harmful conditions mentioned above occur (Strom and Mollenkopf 2006). Urban power structures have been analyzed by CUS scholars with attention to the role that race often plays in the conduct and outcome of city politics (Pattillo 2007; Saito 2009). Much research has also been directed at the dominant role that the local "growth machine" of bankers, real estate developers, and other private stakeholders often plays in influencing decision-making by city officials (Domhoff 2005; Logan and Molotch 2007). CUS has examined the impact of local grassroots movements by urban residents opposing private-sector dominance on affecting decision-making by local governments (Gendron and Domhoff 2008).

Finally, there has been progressive realization within CUS that many conditions existing within US cities are greatly affected by uneven forces of globalization, forces that affect people's abilities to realize their human rights "at home." Scholars have been examining exemplars of "the global city" to understand their dynamics and trajectories and the implications of these processes for the quality of life of urban inhabitants (Sassen 2001, 2006a). Urban dwellers may feel fallout from globalization but not really understand why or what can be done about it. There has been, however, growing popular protest in various urban locales against growth machine politics-as-usual and local neoliberal taxation and spending policies that are resulting in disinvestment in city services (e.g., public education, public safety, public parks and recreation, income assistance, job training) on which many city dwellers, especially low-income people, heavily rely (Hackworth 2007). CUS scholars are now drawing attention to local-level movements that call for a "right to the city" and demanding popular democratic control over city space and its uses (Brenner, Marcuse, and Mayer 2011).

THE POWER OF METHODS EMPLOYED BY COMMUNITY AND URBAN SOCIOLOGISTS

The cumulative power of the body of CUS scholarship on urban problems reviewed above rests in large part on researchers' use of a wide range of sociological research methods. A diverse tool kit of both qualitative and quantitative methods has been used to (1) clarify origins and overall magnitude of selected urban problems, and (2) assess their everyday, on-the-ground, human consequences. Selection of different methods for these two purposes has been the hallmark of CUS for years and is reflected in what are considered some of CUS's most classic works. The widely acclaimed *American Apartheid* (Massey and Denton 1993) demonstrated how discriminatory US housing policies produced urban racial ghettos, providing a model of the use of structural, sociodemographic, and policy analysis for assessing directions in which cities and their populations were heading. In contrast, the classic ethnography *Tally's Corner* (Liebow 2003) illustrated the power of studying the voices of the oppressed to understand devastating sociopsychological effects of poverty affecting people residing in urban racial ghettos, in this case impoverishment driven by male breadwinners' under- and unemployment. Human rights advocates need data that can be derived from such a wide range of methods, insofar as these data provide documentation of injuries stemming from human rights violations; reveal how these injuries are socially, politically, and economically constructed; and suggest what must change to eliminate violations.

In short, just as human rights advocates are concerned with conditions that undermine an individual's dignity and freedom—for example, discrimination, poverty, and powerlessness—so are many scholars engaged in CUS. Indeed, much CUS scholarship can be viewed as a form of human rights work, even if scholars do not realize this or have not framed their work with human rights in mind. I return to this point toward the end of this chapter after providing an overview of emergent worldwide interest in the implementation of international human rights at the local level. The latter is a topic on which CUS scholars and human rights advocates can have a lot to say to one another and on which they can find grounds for fruitful collaboration.

THE "HUMAN RIGHTS CITY" CONCEPT AND LOCAL IMPLEMENTATION OF HUMAN RIGHTS

CREATING HUMAN RIGHTS CITIES

The concept of Human Rights Cities was initiated and pioneered by the People's Decade for Human Rights Education (PDHRE), also called the People's Movement for Human Rights Learning, a nonprofit, international organization founded in New York City in 1989 (PDHRE 2011). The following definition captures the essence of the concept (Marks and Modrowski 2008, 39–40):

> Human Rights Cities are community-based initiatives, locally conceived and directed by local groups around the world, which combine participation, empowerment and social change with international solidarity based on agreed principles of human rights education and sustainable development.

PDHRE (2011) has consulted with human rights advocates around the world on ways that human rights learning can best be carried out locally; how advocates can turn city inhabitants' learning about human rights into action; and how mechanisms can be created across the city to embed human rights norms into every aspect of people's daily lives.

The most important initial step that PDHRE advises cities to take is establish-ment of a democratically functioning Human Rights City steering committee that represents all sectors of the city, not simply municipal government. Voices of all groups in the city are to be at the table, particularly those that historically have been marginalized or excluded from participating in decision-making.

PDHRE (2011) has helped facilitate the creation worldwide of more than seven-teen Human Rights Cities that are now either firmly established or in the process of formation. Examples include Rosario, Argentina; Graz, Austria; Nagpur, India; Korogocho, Kenya; Bucuy Municipality, Philippines; Edmonton, Winnipeg, Canada; and Kaohsiung, Taiwan, China.

But not all efforts at local human rights implementation adhere to the Human Rights Cities concept. Cities around the world and in the United States are taking a variety of approaches to local human rights implementation.

COUNCIL OF EUROPE CONGRESS OF LOCAL AND REGIONAL AUTHORITIES

Europe has a strong human rights regime and an advanced legal system for address-ing the full range of universal human rights. The pan-European Council of Europe (2011), composed of forty-seven member countries, works to implement European Convention principles and other European and international human rights instru-ments across Europe.

In 2010, the Council of Europe's Congress of Local and Regional Authorities adopted a resolution calling for local and regional European authorities to imple-ment measures to further promotion and protection of human rights in day-to-day operations of local and regional governments. These measures include establishing indicators or indices of human rights fulfillment, action plans for human rights imple-mentation, city budgeting that is guided by human rights standards, independent complaint mechanisms, human rights training for elected officials and staff, nondis-crimination in accessibility of public services, and accountability and quality control in cases where services are being privatized (Council of Europe Congress 2010a).

In their deliberations, participants in the congress drew lessons from the examples of a number of European cities that have taken steps in this direction. These include Graz and Salzburg, Austria; Paris, France; Nuremberg, Germany; Utrecht, Netherlands; and Malopolska, Poland.

2011 WORLD HUMAN RIGHTS CITIES FORUM, GWANGJU, SOUTH KOREA

The movement to implement human rights locally in Asian nations has lagged behind Europe. In 2011, more than one hundred mayors, city representatives, UN experts, scholars, and members of civic and human rights NGOs gathered in South Korea for the first World Human Rights Cities Forum, hosted by Gwangju Metropolitan City.

Gwangju, the site of nationally influential protests against Japanese occupa-tion and a leader in local pro-democracy uprisings against a succession of Korean dictators, is now drawing upon this historical legacy of human rights advocacy in framing its rationale for becoming a Human Rights City. City authorities have now created a Human Rights Office, begun to draft a charter that will guide local human rights implementation, initiated ways to promote human rights learning throughout the city, and started crafting an initial action plan linked to a human rights index that will help city officials monitor progress and change (Gwangju Metropolitan City 2011).

The 2011 World Human Rights Cities Forum showcased the Human Rights City work occurring in Gwangju and also provided an opportunity for participants to hear about other cities' experiences. Forum participants also collectively adopted the Gwangju Declaration on Human Rights City. In this declaration, participants committed to "making the vision of a human rights city a reality on the ground by implementing international human rights norms and standards" (Gwangju World Human Rights Cities Forum 2011).

US EXCEPTIONALISM AND "BRINGING HUMAN RIGHTS HOME" TO THE LOCAL LEVEL

A BRIEF COMMENT ON US EXCEPTIONALISM

The United States is often characterized as an "outlier" regarding its failure to apply the human rights framework to its own legal system and to problems within its own borders (Schulz 2009). In the face of the general US failure to "bring human rights home" and to respect, protect, and fulfill them domestically, a US human rights movement has arisen and gathered strength over the last decade or so (see, e.g., US Human Rights Network 2011). This movement, eclectic and growing in membership, is aimed at pressuring government at all levels to address major domestic issues through a human rights lens (Hertel and Libal 2011).

The drive in the United States to implement human rights principles and standards locally has become a part of the larger domestic movement to bring the US government into conformity with international human rights norms (Soohoo, Albisa, and Davis 2008). Human rights advocates are coming to see local implementation not only as valuable for its own sake but as a means of influencing the US government to meet its human rights obligations (Finnegan, Saltsman, and White 2010). In the United States, city-level efforts at local implementation have taken a number of forms (US Human Rights Fund 2010; Columbia Law School Human Rights Institute and IAOHRA 2010; Sok and Neubeck, forthcoming). Some examples follow.

HUMAN RIGHTS CITY EFFORTS IN THE UNITED STATES

In 2008, the Washington, DC, City Council (2008) passed a resolution declaring its intention to be the first Human Rights City in the United States. Since then, human rights advocates in Chapel Hill and Carrboro, North Carolina; Richmond, California; and a few other US municipalities have taken initial steps toward or expressed interest in becoming Human Rights Cities (see, e.g., Chapel Hill and

Carrboro Human Rights Center 2011). All have been influenced by the PDHRE model discussed above.

Human rights resolutions are not ordinances and do not carry the force of law. However, they may serve to legitimize local human rights advocates' work as they carry out human rights education and help to mobilize city inhabitants to press for the creation of legal frameworks and structural mechanisms to institutionalize local human rights implementation.

SAN FRANCISCO: PROVIDING HUMAN RIGHTS PROTECTIONS FOR WOMEN

San Francisco was the first US city to implement human rights by passing a local version of an international human rights treaty (Menon 2010). In 1998, the San Francisco Board of Supervisors approved an ordinance modeled on the Convention on the Elimination of All Forms of Discrimination against Women (CEDAW), a key international human rights treaty that the US government has not ratified (WILD for Human Rights 2006).

The 1998 ordinance supports women's rights as human rights. Implementation of the San Francisco CEDAW ordinance has included conduct of gender audits in city departments, development of departmental action plans to remedy unintentional discrimination, and a system for overseeing and monitoring action-plan outcomes. An evaluation report issued on the tenth anniversary of the San Francisco ordinance found that its implementation had prompted many policy changes, from ending unintentional discrimination against women and girls in delivery of city services to providing family-friendly employment practices that have improved women's city government employment opportunities and supported employees' work-life balance (Liebowitz 2008).

THE NEW YORK CITY HUMAN RIGHTS INITIATIVE: STILL AN ASPIRATION

Human rights advocates in New York City were inspired by implementation of San Francisco's CEDAW ordinance, launching in 2002 a campaign to adopt a similar law (New York City Human Rights Initiative 2011). This proposed Human Rights in Government Operations Audit Law (GOAL) calls for human rights audits, action plans, and systematic monitoring of all city departments. It is aimed at remedying and preventing discrimination in delivery of city services, budgeting decisions, and staffing. GOAL was introduced as a bill for consideration by sympathetic city council members in 2004 and 2008 and again in 2010. New York City mayor Michael Bloomberg and his council allies have thus far successfully blocked the bill from a council vote, using arguments that GOAL is unnecessary and would be an added expense.

THE EUGENE (OREGON) HUMAN RIGHTS CITY PROJECT: A WORK IN PROGRESS

Local human rights implementation in Eugene, Oregon, has been driven by its city council–appointed Human Rights Commission. Since 2007 the commission has explored ways that Eugene city government can implement UDHR standards and principles across all its departments and operations (US Human Rights Fund 2010, 95–96). It has conducted citywide human rights awareness events, organized local social-justice groups and their allies into an informal human rights coalition, used mass media to address the need for local implementation, and held a major human rights community summit to identify Eugene's pressing human rights issues (Eugene Human Rights City Project 2011).

City staff have initiated a five-year Diversity and Equity Strategic Plan (2009–2014) that calls for Eugene to "integrate Human Rights City concepts into City policies and procedures" (City of Eugene 2011a). City staff are also developing a Triple Bottom Line Tool that can be used to assess impacts of program, policy, and budget decisions. The social-equity component of the tool "places priority upon protecting, respecting, and fulfilling the full range of human rights, including civil, political, economic, social, and cultural rights" (City of Eugene 2011b).

OTHER LOCAL IMPLEMENTATION ACTIVITIES

As interest in local implementation of human rights has grown, US efforts have taken different forms (US Human Rights Fund 2010; Columbia Law School Human Rights Institute and IAOHRA 2010):

1. The Chicago City Council passed a resolution in 2009 supporting alignment of the city's children- and family-support policies with the UN Convention on the Rights of the Child.
2. In 2009, the Berkeley, California, City Council passed an ordinance requiring the city to report on its compliance with international human rights treaties directly to the US State Department.
3. The Los Angeles County Human Relations Commission is using international human rights in advocating for death-penalty abolition in California and in its campaign to address violence against people who are homeless.
4. Approximately fifty cities and twenty counties have passed resolutions in support of the Convention on the Elimination of All Forms of Discrimination against Women.
5. Human rights and human relations commissions in Milwaukee, Wisconsin; Portland, Oregon; and several other US cities have adopted the UDHR as a guiding standard for their human rights activities.

THE BENEFITS OF COLLABORATION BETWEEN COMMUNITY AND URBAN SOCIOLOGISTS AND HUMAN RIGHTS ADVOCATES

COMMUNITY AND URBAN SOCIOLOGISTS CAN CONTRIBUTE TO LOCAL HUMAN RIGHTS IMPLEMENTATION

Much CUS research, if we use research on cities in the United States as a case in point, is actually human rights work. Emerging research findings can easily be translated into or reframed in human right terms and provide a scholarly window to assess the breadth and extent of US human rights violations affecting urban inhabitants. The knowledge and skills of those working in CUS can be mobilized and tailored to assist local human rights advocates in their data gathering, organizing, and local implementation efforts. CUS sociologists can contribute directly to a city's human rights implementation efforts by employing demographic skills to document and analyze the city's history and extent of economic and racial segregation, as well as relevant population characteristics (e.g., disaggregated poverty rates, school attendance and dropout rates, unemployment rates, crime rates, and arrest patterns). CUS sociologists can use ethnographic research skills, interviewing, facilitation of focus groups, listening sessions, and online and questionnaire surveys to help determine city inhabitants' level of human rights education, their human rights concerns, and what they experience to be the institutional and interpersonal sources of their concerns. They can use existing research to inform local institutional analyses and data gathering based on testing by volunteers in order to uncover sources and patterns of discrimination (in municipal services, employment agencies, real estate, and banking) that rise above and beyond the interpersonal level. CUS sociologists can employ knowledge of social-movement research to help human rights advocates develop messaging and organizing strategies that are effective in mobilizing civil society around the goal of local implementation of human rights. CUS sociologists can assist in the development of human rights indicators or other metrics that will help identify and measure progress following local human rights implementation efforts. Finally, CUS sociologists can invite human rights advocates and victims of human rights violations to be speakers in classrooms and at other campus venues in order to extend institutional recognition to local human rights efforts, encourage human rights learning on campus, and inform students about volunteer opportunities in local human rights implementation activities.

ADDRESSING LOCAL IMPLEMENTATION WILL ENRICH COMMUNITY AND URBAN SOCIOLOGY

The movement to implement international human rights locally offers opportunities for CUS to become not only a contributor but also a beneficiary of collaborating with human rights advocates at initial stages of what is promising to become a worldwide movement. Such collaborations will prove beneficial by providing CUS theorists with local laboratories for exploring conflicts arising between the goals of human rights implementation and the interests of major private-sector stakeholders. These collaborations will give CUS theorists of local power structure opportunities to analyze and assess struggles between proponents of neoliberal urban social policies and human rights advocates. These collaborative opportunities will provide unique data-gathering opportunities for CUS scholars who use their ethnographic skills to gain entrée and establish rapport with and to solicit data from disempowered and marginalized population segments whose voices must be heard and brought to the table throughout the local human rights implementation process. These collaborations will open up opportunities for CUS researchers to test theoretical propositions regarding on-the-ground, urban, grassroots human rights movements as participant observers while playing legitimate roles as interested researchers. They will add to theoretical knowledge of CUS regarding how, why, and under what conditions the human rights framework functions to bring groups together across racial and class lines that have not normally collaborated or that political actors have successfully kept at odds. The collaborations will encourage networking and collaborative sharing of professional research interests among CUS scholars in different cities and countries who are functioning as scholarly allies in support of the international human rights movement. These opportunities will offer new opportunities for community service contributions by CUS scholars, whether they choose to use their methodological and analytical skills as behind-the-scenes consultants or as public sociologists assuming active human rights advocacy roles. Collaborations will show students a new and exciting way to think about the relevance of CUS, the contributions it can make to society, and how the knowledge and skills they are acquiring in their CUS studies can be used to help protect, promote, and fulfill human rights.

CHAPTER TWENTY-FOUR

PEACE, WAR, AND SOCIAL CONFLICT

Nader Saiedi

A human rights–centered sociology must directly address the questions of war and peace. Indeed, it can be argued that security is a human right and that no lasting peace is conceivable without the realization of justice and human rights. In an age of nuclear weapons and the globalization of violence, no social problem is more pressing than war and no need more urgent than peace. Yet, surprisingly, mainstream sociology has largely overlooked both issues. In a study of American and European main sociological journals, Garnett (1988) found that war is not perceived as an important research topic in sociology. Fortunately, there has been a recent resurgence of interest among a specialized circle of sociologists in the study of violence and war (Collins 2008; Giddens 1985; Joas 2003; Kestnbaum 2009; Malesevic 2010; Mann 1988; Shaw 2000; Skocpol 1979; Tilly 1992).

Many sociologists, including Giddens (1985), Mann (1988), and Joas (2003), have commented on the neglect of the issues of war and peace in classical sociological literature. Three main reasons for this neglect have been proposed: the appearance of a relatively long period of peace in nineteenth-century Europe between 1815 and 1914, the reduction of the concept of society to the category of nation-state, and the optimistic faith in modernity as the age of rationality, progress, and development.

Yet Malesevic (2010, 17-49) proposes that classical sociological theory was dominated by the bellicose tradition. However, after World War II, the revulsion against war brought about a reinvention of the classical tradition and turned it into a peaceful tradition. Malesevic reminds us of authors like Gumplowicz, Ratzenhofer, Ward, Simmel, Oppenheimer, Rostow, Pareto, and Mosca, who presented a sociological theory centered in war and national conflict.

WAR AND OTHER FORMS OF VIOLENCE

There is a dialectical relationship between war and other forms of violence. On the one hand, war is a special case of violence whose proper analysis requires understanding the mutual relationships among alternate types of violence. On the other hand, war is a unique form of violence. The emphasis on the mutual interaction of war and other forms of violent conflict is one of the central contributions of socio-logical literature. Consequently a sociological analysis of war or peace will address questions of justice and structural violence. Thus, for example, religious fanaticism, patriarchy, racism, ideologies of national superiority, poverty, social inequality, and class oppression are linked to militarism, war, and the dehumanization of the enemy.

Such sociological insight is compatible with a positive definition of peace. Nega-tive peace is the absence of war. For Galtung (1996), however, war is the absence of peace. Positive peace refers to an objective form of social relations that foster harmony, mutual growth, communication, and unity among the interacting part-ners. In such a definition, the absence of coercive conflicts is a necessary, but not a sufficient, condition of peace. Positive peace therefore depends on the existence of social justice and a culture of communication, peace, and human rights. Violence is conceptualized as systematic denial of human needs and human rights. It can be direct or structural, physical or ideal. The idea of positive peace assigns conceptual primacy to peace rather than war. It is in this spirit that Collins (1974) distinguishes between three types of violence as ferociousness or direct coercion against others, callousness or impersonal structural violence, and asceticism or violence directed against one's own self.

At the same time, wars are highly organized forms of social conflict that are qualitatively different from ordinary forms of violence. In his book *Violence*, Col-lins (2008) discusses ordinary forms of violence to highlight the fact that contrary to the prevalent ideas, human beings abhor violence, try to avoid it, and seek alternative ways to save face without engaging in physical fights. The principal error of various macro theories of violence is that they all assume that violence comes easily to individuals. Collins argues that contrary to a common Hollywood portrayal of violence, ordinary violence rarely occurs, is very short in duration, is not infectious, and is accompanied by intense anxiety rather than a joking attitude. Even literature on war shows that soldiers frequently prefer to escape rather than fight and are intensely afraid and anxious, a fact that explains the prevalence of friendly fire (Picq 2006; Marshall 1947). Such a perspective is completely at odds with a neo–social Darwinist ideology that sees aggression as a biologically induced tendency among young males in order to further the reproduction of their genes (Wilson 1978, 125–130).

Extensive social organization is necessary in order to compel individuals to engage in military conflict and kill other human beings. As Malesevic argues, human beings, left to their own devices, "are generally incapable of violence and unwilling to kill and die." Therefore, it is the "institutional trappings of the net-works of organizations and ideological doctrines that make us act more violently" (Maelsevic 2010, 117).

PEACE AND WAR IN CLASSICAL SOCIOLOGICAL THEORY

War and peace were central questions in the social theories of both Auguste Comte (1970) and Herbert Spencer (1967). Both theorists conceived of social change as evolutionary movements toward progress and characterized the emerging modern society as industrial rather than military. Industrial society is a peaceful society in which military conquest aimed at acquisition of land is replaced with economic and industrial competition. For Comte this is part of his "law of three stages." Spencer defined a military society as a form of society in which the social function of regulation is dominant. Conversely, in an industrial society it is the economic function that becomes predominant.

With the onset of World War I, most of the social theorists sided with their own country. A unique case is Georg Simmel (1990), who identified war as an "absolute situation" in which ordinary and selfish preoccupations of the individuals with an impersonal money economy are replaced with an ultimate life-and-death situation. Thus war liberates moral impulse from the boredom of routine life and makes individuals willing to sacrifice their lives for the good of society. Simmel's (1968) idea is partly rooted in his theory of conflict in which conflict becomes a force of group integration and solidarity.

On the other side, we see Durkheim and Mead, who both take strong positions against Germany. Discussing Heinrich von Treitschke's worship of war and German superiority, Durkheim (1915) writes of a "German mentality" that led to the militaristic politics of that country. Such militarism is an outdated morality that is opposed to an existing "universal conscience and a universal opinion, and it is no more possible to escape the empire of these than to escape that of physical laws, for they are forces which, when they are violated, react against those who offend them" (Durkheim 1915, 44). A similar analysis is found in the writings of Mead, who contrasts German militaristic politics with Allied liberal constitutions. Immanuel Kant's distinction between the realm of appearances and the things in themselves has led to a theory in which reason is capable of legislating only the form, not the content, of the moral act. The determination of practical life is then left in the hands of military elites. Romantic and idealist schools, represented by Fichte, Schelling, and Hegel, connect this abstract individual to the absolute self, demanding obedience to the dictates of the Prussian state. Such a state "could by definition only rest upon force. Militarism became the necessary form of its life" (Mead 2008 [1918], 167). While liberal democratic countries conceptualize the state as a technical means for realizing individual rights, their full realization of democracy requires institutionalization of substantive social rights for the people. Only in a democratic society with a democratic nationalism will the rule of force and militarism be abandoned both within and between national borders (Mead 2008 [1918], 159–174).

Another classic thinker who wrote on war and peace during World War I is Veblen, who applies his theory of pecuniary emulation to the question of international relations. In his analysis of the leisure class, Veblen (1991) argues that consumption has become the main indicator of social honor. Ownership is mainly sought for its role in claiming prestige. It is the emulation of the wealthy and competition for honor that are the main motivators of human behavior. Thus, both wasteful conspicuous consumption and leisure become the mark of success in pecuniary emulation. However, this same process of emulation is the basis of the claims for national honor and patriotism. According to Veblen, patriotism is "a sense of partisan solidarity in respect of prestige," for "the patriotic spirit is a spirit of emulation" (1998, 31–33). No permanent peace is possible without a fundamental transformation of these patriotic habits of thought. Veblen regards the dynastic militarism of imperial Germany and Japan as a feudal vestige based on the subservience of people to ruling individuals. Such a system necessarily seeks imperial expansion and initiates war. Liberal states are based on impersonal loyalty to things rather than individuals, and they avoid initiating wars. However, the other cause of war is the economic interests of the captains of business and finance. The persistent inequality of possession and control in liberal societies may lead to revolution by the poor. In this situation the liberal states may be tempted to initiate war in order to diffuse the revolutionary sentiments of the workers and farmers. The only thing that is common between the rich and the poor is the sense of patriotism.

Another significant classical theorist who made contributions to the study of war is Werner Sombart. Like Weber, Sombart was interested in understanding the causes of modern capitalism and emphasized the centrality of both religious and political/military factors in its development. Sombart (1913) argued that war between the European states was a major factor in the development of capitalism. The development of a standing army and the state's demand for military uniforms, weapons, and naval ships created the first mass demand for economic production, leading to the development of large-scale capitalistic enterprise. Modernity, in other words, is unthinkable without its genesis in war.

No discussion of classical social theorists is complete without referring to the ideas of Marx and Weber. Both are indispensable for any analysis of war or peace. Marxist tradition has always been a main theoretical model for such analysis. On the other hand, most of the recent sociological contributions to the issue of war and violence are inspired by a Weberian model emphasizing the significance of the modern state and the rationalization of coercion and discipline.

PRINCIPAL THEORIES OF WAR AND PEACE

Social-scientific literature seeks social reasons for war and investigates the social conditions that are conducive to peace. Five such theories are discussed below.

REALISM

Realism is the dominant theory in the field of international relations, and it is rooted in a Machiavellian and Hobbesian conception of human beings. Waltz (1979) introduced the theory of structural realism, according to which states are the main actors in international relations. However, the main determinant of a state's decision to engage in war or peace is the international political and military structure. This international structure, however, is none other than international anarchy. In other words, the Hobbesian state of nature is the dominant reality at the level of international relations since there is no binding global law or authority in the world. States are left in a situation of self-help. Consequently, each state regards all other states as a potential or actual threat to its security. Thus arms races and militarism are rational strategies for safeguarding national security. States must act in rational and pragmatic ways and must not be bound by either internal politics or moral principles in determining their policies. In this situation there is no chance for permanent peace. War is a normal result of the structure of international relations. For Waltz, however, the primary interest of states is security. Therefore, states seek a balance of power. Discussing the so-called long peace during the Cold War, he argues that this peace was the product of the two structural conditions of bipolarity and nuclear armament. Another realist, Mearsheimer (2001), introduced offensive structural realism. In this model, states are primarily interested in attaining or securing a hegemonic position.

The closest allies of the realist model in sociological literature are the classical bellicose authors, who conceived of social change in terms of a state-centered theory of war and military conflict. Weber partly defends a state-centered concept of realpolitik. His emphasis on the relativity of all values, his rejection of the ethics of ultimate ends, and his support for the ethics of responsibility in the context of political decision-making are various expressions of this position (Weber 1948b). Yet, for Weber and the neo-Weberians, realism is an inadequate theory because the state represents the intersection of the internal and the external (Skocpol 1979). Furthermore, sociological literature conceives of international structure in terms of both political/military and economic characteristics. Realist theory is criticized from many directions. In a sense, all other theories of war and peace are various forms of rejection of realism.

Joseph (1993) calls for a change of paradigm in understanding the idea of security, replacing a war politics of national security with a peace politics of global security. According to Joseph, realism sees the other states as the main threat to security, whereas peace politics emphasizes the common threats to humanity, namely, environmental pollution, global inequality, poverty, violation of human rights, and nuclear disaster. War politics considers the appropriate response as militarism, whereas peace politics finds demilitarization and global cooperation to be the rational strategy. War politics defines peace in negative terms, while peace politics regards it in positive terms.

DEMOCRATIC PEACE THEORY

One of the best-known theories in relation to war and peace is a liberal theory according to which democracies rarely, if ever, engage in war with each other. Kant first advanced this doctrine in 1875 in his historic work *Perpetual Peace*. Contrary to realism, democratic peace theory seeks the root cause of war or peace in the internal political structure of societies. Varieties of empirical tests have confirmed the existence of a significant positive correlation between democracy and peace (Oneal and Russet 2001). Two sets of explanations have been offered for this relationship. Institutional explanations emphasize the existence of systematic restraining forces in democracies. The vote of the people matters in democracies, and therefore war is less likely to occur because the people, rather than the rulers, will pay the ultimate price of war. Cultural explanations argue that democracies respect other democracies and therefore are more willing to engage in peaceful resolution of conflicts. The internal habit of democratic resolution of conflicts is said to be extended to the realm of foreign relations. Among classical social theorists, there is considerable sympathy for this idea. Durkheim, Mead, and Veblen all identify the undemocratic culture and politics of Germany and Japan as the cause of World War I. Similarly, Spencer (1967) finds political democracy compatible with peace.

However, a sociological discussion of democratic peace theory may point to a number of modifications. First, it reexamines the concept of democracy and defines it in both formal and substantive ways. Marxists and critical theorists, as well as Durkheim, Mead, and Veblen, emphasize the necessity of social democracy in addition to formal political democracy for the existence of a genuine participatory democracy. Second, as Held (1995) argues, in a globalized world, where the most important decisions are blind outcomes of the anarchy of particularistic decisions made by states and transnational corporations, democratization of nation-states does not furnish a real democracy. Consequently, an adequate theory of democratization must address the issue of arbitrary and particularistic decision-making in the context of international anarchy. Such a perspective emphasizes the need for a further extension of democratic decision-making to the global level. Strengthening institutions such as the United Nations, the World Court, and global civil societies becomes a vital step in attaining peace.

MARXIST THEORY

The Marxist theory of violence can be discussed in terms of three issues: the relation of capitalism to war or peace, the role of violence in transition from capitalism to communism, and the impact of colonialism on the development of colonized societies. The dominant Marxist views on these issues are usually at odds with Marx's own positions.

Marx did not address the issue of war and peace extensively. He shared the nineteenth century's optimism about the outdated character of interstate wars. In fact, he mostly believed that capitalism benefits from peace. Marx (1956, ch. 6) considered Napoleon's war a product of Napoleon's obsession with fame and glory. As Mann (1987) argues, Marx saw capitalism as a transnational system and therefore regarded it as a cause of peace rather than war. He believed that violence is mostly necessary for revolution but affirmed the possibility of peaceful transition to socialism in the most developed capitalist societies. Furthermore, Marx saw colonization of the non-European societies as mostly beneficial for the development of those stagnant societies, a development that would in turn lead to socialist revolutions (Kara 1968).

In the midst of World War I, Lenin (1939) radically changed Marxist theory of war and peace. He argued that imperialism, or the competition for colonial conquest, necessarily brings Western capitalist states into war with each other. This war would destroy capitalism and lead to the triumph of socialism. Furthermore, violence was the only possible way of attaining socialism (Kara 1968). The main opposition to Lenin's ideas was Kautsky's (1931) defense of a democratic and parliamentary way of achieving socialism. Lenin's predictions proved to be wrong. In the early twenty-first century, we witness peace among Western capitalist states. More recent Marxist theories are divided in two camps: some find capitalism engendering war between the imperialist (North) and dependent (South) countries, while others see it triggering war within and among poor countries (Frank 1991; Bauman 2001).

Marxist theory has inspired many sociological theories of war and peace. A prominent case is C. Wright Mills's (1956) famous thesis of the military-industrial complex, in which the complex unity of military and industrial enterprises creates conditions conducive to war. Another influence can be found in Wallerstein's (1984) theory of the world capitalist system. Through networks of exchange and trade, the world is divided into center, periphery, and semiperiphery. The structure of this system is the main explanation for wars, including hegemonic ones.

SYMBOLIC INTERACTIONISM AND SOCIAL CONSTRUCTIVISM

A sociological perspective that has influenced the field of international relations is the theory of social constructivism. The main advocate of this theory in discussions of war and peace is Alexander Wendt, who systematically criticizes the realist perspective. Emphasizing the symbolic and interpretive character of social relations and practices, Wendt (1999) argues that the objective anarchy of international relations by itself does not lead to a system of mutual threat, antagonism, and self-help. Rather, it is the interpretation of the behavior that determines whether anarchy leads to a system of cooperation and trust among nations or a system of antagonism and distrust. For example, Canada and the United States are two sovereign states neighboring each other. Yet the relationship is mutually interpreted as one of trust and cooperation. Similarly, the development of a single nuclear missile in North Korea creates security panic in the United States, whereas the existence of a massive nuclear arsenal in England creates no such concern. Consequently, it is how states perceive and interpret identities and interests that determines the prospects of peace and war.

Wendt's theory is influenced by symbolic interactionism. Mead's (1967) emphasis on the social and interactive construction of self, whereby it comes into existence through language and internalization of the generalized other, is compatible with a host of philosophical and sociological theories that have emphasized the significance of language in defining human reality. Unlike utilitarian and rationalist theories that perceive humans as selfish and competitive, the linguistic turn has emphasized the social and cooperative nature of human beings. Being with others is not an external addition to human consciousness. Rather, it is the very constitutive element of human consciousness and self. For Habermas (1979), for example, the very structure of language presupposes acknowledgment of the presence and legitimate claim of the other. Thus, in the very structure of language, the normative legitimacy of arguments and communication is implicit as the regulating principle of social life.

CULTURE-OF-VIOLENCE/-PEACE THEORY

Cultural theories emphasize the causal significance of the culture of violence or peace as the main determinant of war or peace. Mueller (1989) argues that prior to the twentieth century, war was perceived as a natural, moral, and rational phenomenon. However, through World Wars I and II, this culture changed. According to Mueller, the Western world is moving increasingly in the direction of a culture of peace, with the non-Western world lagging behind. But the future is bright since we are moving in this direction.

Such a perspective may be compatible with Durkheim's (1964) view of organic solidarity. For Durkheim, the appropriate culture corresponding to the modern division of labor is a culture of solidarity that recognizes differences in the context of the equal right of all individuals to self-determination. Therefore, Durkheim believes, the individual's right to autonomy and individuality becomes the new sacred of the modern society. However, for Durkheim, organic solidarity is associated with the rise of a global human consciousness, where such right is extended to all human beings (Lukes 1972, 550).

Lasting peace, therefore, requires a critique of various forms of the culture of violence. These include, among others, cultures of patriarchy, racism, social Darwinism, religious fanaticism, and aggressive nationalism. For example, a culture of violence defines identities through the opposition of the self to the other, whereas a culture of peace defines identities through their mutual interdependence. Patriarchy becomes particularly important because a patriarchal system is likely to produce a negative type of male identity, one that is defined in terms of the negation of the female (Reardon 1985). This is due to the absence of fathers from home and the consequent negative definition of the father image as nonmother.

There is an extensive debate on the reciprocal effects of patriarchy and militarism. Authors like Caprioli (2000) have found a positive correlation between patriarchy and war, where the low social, political, and economic status of women leads to a higher likelihood of interstate wars. On the other hand, many anthropologists (Ember and Ember 1994; Goldstein 2001) have argued that it is war and militarism that lead to violent socialization of males.

A culture of violence is accompanied by a culture of othering and estrangement characterized by the dehumanization of others, reducing them to the level of biology, and violence of singular identity (Sen 2006). Concepts of both social justice and human rights are inseparable principles of a culture of peace.

MODERNITY, WAR, AND THE NEW WARS

As Malesevic (2010, 118–145) notes, a most perplexing characteristic of the twentieth century is the fact that while it was a century of almost universal acceptance of the principles of human rights and peace, it was the bloodiest century in the history of humankind. Modernity represents the increasing integration of the state, the military, technology, and the economy. War requires extensive and massive social organization. Consequently, the history of modernity is a history of such militaristic, technological, and nationalistic integration and mobilization. Sociologists such as Mann (1988), Giddens (1985), and Tilly (1992) have studied the rise of the modern state and nationalist ideologies. Their main inspiration is Weber's concept of the modern state and bureaucratization. War and coercion played a crucial role in the creation of the present system of nationalism. Military competition among the European states led to the military revolution, the rise of the standing army, the emergence of the conscript army, military discipline, and national integration of the populace in war industry. It was partly this bureaucratization of the army that led to the bureaucratization of other aspects of society, shaping the factory in the image of the army.

Weber defined the modern state as having monopolistic control of the means of coercion. In the modern state, industry, technology, and war become increasingly integrated. The machine gun, the train, the telegraph, airplanes, and high-tech/nuclear war have transformed the nature of modern warfare. Equally important has been the rise of nationalistic ideologies, which opened the masses to militarism. Napoleon introduced national mobilization of people, propaganda, and revolutionary zeal to the art of death and militarism, replacing the old army with a conscript citizen army. Nationalism increasingly became the most powerful determinant of identity in the modern world, replacing religion as the center of the mobilization of emotions.

The paradox of the twentieth century can therefore be explained by the interaction of various causes. First, the destructive character of recent military technology has increased the deadly nature of war. Second, the rise of popular nationalism has led to mass participation of citizens with patriotic and ideological zeal in war. Third, the justification of violence by an instrumental ethics has legitimized all kinds of wars in the name of peace and justice. Fourth, the integration of industry and the military has eroded the distinction between civilian and military institutions. In spite of modern agreements to confine war to the military sector and protect civilians from military violence, the twentieth century became the century of total war. Both popular support for war and the integration of industry and the military encouraged the destruction of the industrial and civilian infrastructure of the enemy. World War II was a major expression of this type of war. It eroded the distinction between the soldier and the civilian. The enemy's civilian industry and infrastructure became the legitimate target of military attack.

Yet three developments—the end of modernism, the end of the Cold War, and globalization—have led to some weakening of national sovereignty and nationalistic identification. They have turned some social movements, such as human rights, environment, and peace movements, into global civil societies. As Kaldor (2003) notes, this development represents a hopeful path of peace for the future.

But they also have triggered the rise of new wars and global uncivil societies. According to Kaldor (1999), new wars are qualitatively different from the old wars. The aim of new war is usually extermination or mass expulsion of the other, whereas in the old war the aim was securing geopolitical control. New war is frequently based on identity politics, and therefore the other must be eliminated. The means utilized by old war were a centralized professional military. New war uses gangs of decentralized warlords and criminal groups, even child soldiers, for murder. The basis of finance of old war was the state treasury and taxation, whereas its base in new war is criminal enterprise as well as the financial support of sympathetic people in other parts of the world. New wars are usually associated with failed states unable to have any meaningful control of the means of coercion in their territory. Both the end of the Cold War and globalization of economic competition contribute to state failure.

What emerges from the story of new wars is the insightful removal of the distinction between the war hero and the criminal, corresponding to the elimination of the distinction between military and civilian targets. However, new war is partly a further extension of the modern concept of total war. Critique of nationalism is indeed a critique of this distinction.

A NEW SOCIOLOGY

A human rights–centered sociology will define peace in positive ways, emphasize the connection between violence and injustice, assign theoretical primacy to the study of peace rather than war, and question the pervasive and alienating cultural and institutional habits of thought related to identity politics, nationalism, and national security, while promoting a holistic orientation to the study of war and peace. In addition, such a paradigm will question the traditional distinction between facts and values and approach peace studies in the same way that positive science approaches medical studies. In both cases the study of facts is accompanied by a normative commitment to universalism and health. Methodologically, this perspective will embrace not only positivistic but also hermeneutical and critical methods of studying war and peace. The human rights perspective will encourage the discourse of war and peace to overcome disciplinary reifications and to include questions regarding nationalism, national security, and the connection of war to patriarchy, racism, and social inequality—issues that are normally excluded in the dominant literature on international relations. Finally, a human rights paradigm will transcend the nationalistic heritage of nineteenth-century sociology, appropriate the discourse of globalization in all sociological studies, and, consequently, address issues of war and peace as central questions of sociological theory.

Chapter Twenty-Five

Environment and Technology

Francis O. Adeola and J. Steven Picou

The relationships between technology, environment, and human rights have not been thoroughly addressed by social-science research. Study of the nexus between human rights, environment, and technology is a recent development and does not enjoy the methodological rigor or sophistication and richness of theories and empirical data that characterize more established fields (see Coosmans, Grunfeld, and Kamminga 2010). An important question yet to be resolved is whether technology represents a cure for environmental and human rights ills or, rather, is the major culprit behind or catalyst for these problems. In other words, does technology represent a blessing or a curse for both environmental and human rights protection? A second question facing human rights scholars and activists addresses the extent to which the environment is universally recognized as a component of human rights. Issues of environmental justice are seminal, as the human rights of minority, indigenous, and low-income people are compromised by negative externalities of industrial production and other environmental risks (Bullard 2000, 2005; Bevc et al. 2007; Washington 2010; Wakefield and Baxter 2010; Lerner 2010). These communities are often regarded as "sacrifice zones" for economic and national-security imperatives. Also posing a challenge to human rights scholars is the question of whether access to technologies and protection from adverse effects of technologies is part and parcel of basic human rights demands. These questions remain unsettled and will be addressed in this chapter through an analysis of the relationships between the concepts of technology, environment, and human rights and their historical development.

Are technological impacts universally regarded as positive or negative? While there are quantitative or objective impacts that tend to draw a universal consensus, the qualitative impacts that are socially constructed at the local or regional level may not be universally agreed upon, especially due to cultural differences in risk perception (see Douglas and Wildavsky 1982; Lupton 1999; Slovic 2000; Adeola 2004). We contend that technologies are used to subdue nature as well as to control and dominate other humans. As stated more than thirty-nine years ago by Leon Kass, "What we really mean by 'Man's Power over Nature' is a power exercised by some men over other men, with a knowledge of nature as their instrument" (1971, 782).

Cases involving the use of technology to oppress, subdue, and annihilate technologically challenged people and to commit other types of human rights violations have been documented around the globe, both before and after the original Universal Declaration of Human Rights (UDHR) (Wronka 1998; Ackerly 2008). Using sociological theory regarding technology, the environment, and human rights, it is possible to respond to human rights abuses.

DEFINING THE ENVIRONMENT AND SOME REASONS FOR CONCERN

The concept of the natural environment encompasses conditions and factors in the surroundings of an organism or group of organisms, including living and nonliving components, as well as the complex of sociocultural conditions associated with individuals, groups, communities, and populations of various species (Cunningham and Cunningham 2008). A distinction is often made between the natural and built environments within which various populations, communities, and organisms live and interact. The built environment consists of physical structures within communities, in cities and towns where people live, work, go to school, play, and conduct daily activities. From architectural designs to city- and town-planning features, industrial structures, extensive street and road networks, and technical infrastructure, the role of technology in the design and maintenance of the built environment is undeniable in modern societies. The natural environment has relatively less human modification, as found in rural areas, the undisturbed wilderness, and ecosystems. However, with technological encroachment, the undisturbed ecosystems around the globe are vanishing at an alarming rate (Brown 2009; Chew 2001). In fact, as pointed out by a number of scholars, human civilization seems to face imminent risk as a result of our application of technology to resource exploitation and subsequent degradation of the environment (Beck 1996, 1999, 2007b). Our growing population and voracious appetite for resources are both directly linked to global environmental problems and resource depletion (see DeSouza, Williams, and Meyerson 2003; Brown 2009).

The decline of the natural environment and the proliferation of emerging risks to the human community are occurring at an alarming rate (Beck 2007b; Barry and Woods 2009). A single generation is witnessing the rapid disappearance of thousands of animal and plant species, the destruction of habitats, and declining air and water quality (De Souza, Williams, and Meyerson 2003; Brown 2009; Gardner and Prugh 2008). Erratic and unusual weather patterns with catastrophic outcomes are becoming common (Adikari and Yoshitani 2009; International Federation of Red Cross and Red Crescent Societies 2004). Resource-induced conflicts and human rights violations are occurring in many regions of the world (World Resources Institute's Earth Trends 2008). Fossil-fuel reserves have been depleted, which is one reason for venturing into fragile ecosystems to extract fossil fuels through the application of remote sensing devices and other sophisticated technologies to find oil deposits in delicate geological zones (World Resources Institute's Earth Trends 2008). The Gulf Coast is just one among many cases where multinational oil corporations have destroyed the environment and violated human rights—including causing deaths, health diminution, violence, deprivation of livelihoods, and insecurity—in order to extract oil and gas (see Adeola 2000a, 2001, 2009; Barry and Woods 2009; Freudenburg and Gramling 2010; Maas 2009; Okonta and Douglas 2001; Sachs 1996). The aggressive use of modern technological systems has resulted in serious human rights violations and the wanton destruction of sensitive environmental resources.

TECHNOLOGY: THE BRIGHT AND DARK SIDES

Technology has been defined in numerous ways by different authors (Volti 1995; Weinstein 2010; Gould 2009; Headrick 2010). The term "technology" was originally coined by Harvard professor Jacob Bigelow (1831) in his book *Elements of Technology*, first published in 1829, in which he describes technology as systematic knowledge, tools, implements, techniques, and machines employed in the production and distribution of goods and services in society. According to Volti (1995, 6), technology is a system based on the application of knowledge, manifested in physical objects and organizational forms, for the attainment of specific objectives. Technologies are created and used to accomplish otherwise impossible tasks or to perform tasks more efficiently—that is, more cheaply, quickly, and easily, with less drudgery. For Gould (2009, 97), technology is simply a series of entanglements with social systems and ecosystems, close and far, obvious and hidden. In other words, there is a social dimension to technology that shapes the division of labor, how tasks are structured, how technologies are used, and how goals are attained. The concept of technology refers to those aspects of material culture used in the manipulation and exploitation of the biophysical environment for the purpose of meeting the material needs of people in society. As such, technology is a critical part of modern society and has helped to advance improved quality of life for untold millions around the globe.

Technology is involved in the process of social interaction, as well as in the process of human interaction with the biophysical environment. Headrick (2010, 3) defines technology as all the ways in which humans harness the materials and energy in the environment for their own ends, beyond what they can do with their own bodies. Weinstein (2010) refers to technology as a stock of know-how developed or borrowed by a population to extend its members' abilities to transcend natural and biological limits. He describes technology as a uniquely human possession that has provided Homo sapiens with a powerful advantage over all other species on the planet, resulting in some species being driven to extinction, as well as threatening human survival (Weinstein 2010, 194). Humans are different from all other species given their intelligence and ability to acquire and transmit knowledge and to apply this knowledge to create tools and techniques.

Along these lines, Volti (1995, 4) has noted that without the human capacity to invent and use a great variety of technologies, humankind would never have been able to establish itself in virtually every part of the globe and exploit every ecosystem on the planet. Volti (1995, 4) further contends that our dependence on technology is as old as the species, and any evils that have accompanied the application of a particular technology are not enough to indict technology as being unnatural. He states that our past, present, and future are inextricably linked to our capacity to shape our existence through the invention and application of implements and techniques that enable us to transcend our own limited physical endowment. The history of technology has been described as the history of human society's increasing adaptability. This pattern of adaptation identifies human prowess and the increasing ability of the species to manipulate nature—from Stone Age primitive axes to nuclear bombs, from small dugout canoes to supertankers, from simple horticulture and gardening to genetic engineering and the creation of genetically modified crops (Headrick 2010). Yet, following patterns of social stratification, modern technologies are not evenly distributed throughout society; it is always advantageous to own technology, especially in nonegalitarian societies. Technological systems are often concentrated in the hands of those who can afford them.

Technology has both positive and negative exponential impacts on the biophysical environment and across different dimensions of society (see Mesthene 2000). On the positive side, technological advances have led to increased life expectancy, less infant mortality, increased food production, economic growth, better standards of living, improved communication and transportation systems, and accelerated rates of diffusion of sociocultural elements, including technological innovations (Mesthene 2000; Khalili-Borna 2007; Haugen 2008). Globalization, the rapid or accelerated flow of capital, information, and cultural elements around the world, is driven by technological innovation (Haynes 2008). Technology represents the engine of sociocultural transformation (Nolan and Lenski 2011; Takacs-Santa 2004) and is a key element for enhancing progress and prosperity. Technology holds the solutions to most, if not all, of our social problems, including the liberation of individuals from tyranny (Mesthene 2000). Essentially, technology has shaped civilizations and defined societal progress, from major medical breakthroughs to space missions, the production of arrays of materials goods and services, and the innovation and diffusion of ideas across the globe.

The globalization of technology is a transformative force with the potential to improve human rights monitoring and protection around the globe. For example, Lauren (2008) indicates that revolutionary changes in transportation and communication systems played a pivotal role in bringing human rights abuses in one region of the world to the attention of people and governments in other areas. Human rights abusers are increasingly finding it difficult to hide or deny information about their oppressive and inhumane actions. Global awareness of human suffering rose sharply during the nineteenth century with advances in transportation and communication systems, the mass media, transistor radios, telegraphy, photography, and the invention of relatively inexpensive postage stamps. These initial advances have continued at an accelerated pace.

Now, as a product of the electronic and Internet revolution of the twentieth and twenty-first centuries and the powerful forces of globalization, there are abundant technological devices readily available to monitor the breach of international human rights norms even in the most remote regions of the world. Both Apocada (2007) and Lauren (2008, 97) have compiled lists of technological accoutrements available for use to safeguard human rights, including handheld portable electronic devices such as cellular phones, iPods, and MP3 players equipped with digital cameras and text-messaging options, as well as video cameras, fax machines, laptop computers, the Internet, scanners, YouTube, and television cable networks. The most repressive regimes around the world are increasingly finding it difficult to stop the diffusion of information through the use of these tools. Nonetheless, public protests in Egypt in 2011 resulted in the government's obliteration of Facebook, Twitter, BlackBerry Messenger, and the Internet as operative resources; it appears that astute hackers and sympathizers within Egypt's borders thwarted the government's action. Although communications technologies are liberating in one sense, they can be controlled by repressive governments (Hendawi 2011). How much control a government can exert is open to debate, especially in the wake of WikiLeaks and unsuccessful attempts by many Arab countries facing revolutionary changes. It is also important to understand that a large proportion of the world population is still excluded from the benefits of science and technology. According to Human Rights Watch (2010, 7–8), many societies remain closed to international human rights scrutiny. Some governments are so repressive that no domestic human rights organization or movement can exist openly. Visits or penetrations by international human rights monitors are typically discouraged by these governments, such as in Burma (Myanmar), Eritrea, Iran, North Korea, Somalia, and Turkmenistan.

Technologies can be used to commit human rights atrocities. As noted by Volti (1995, 16), it has become a cliché that a particular technology can be used for either good or evil purposes: while a construction team employs dynamite to build a road, a terrorist uses it to blow up an airplane, automobile, or people. Transportation and communication technologies propelling globalization are the same tools of choice for trafficking women and children across international borders for prostitution and child slavery, as well as for drug trafficking. Computer and communication technologies are also resources for spreading political misinformation and propaganda or jamming information-transmission channels (Apocada 2007; Lauren 2008; Hendawi 2011). Many terrorist groups use computers, the Internet, and handheld portable electronic devices to plan and achieve their violent objectives. The basic rights to life and a safe and healthy environment are imperiled by the invention and production of weapons of mass destruction, such as nuclear, chemical, and biological weapons, that can be misused by terrorist groups or irrational leaders of rogue states.

About thirty-two years ago, David Orr indicated that a society becomes vulnerable to catastrophe the moment it becomes dependent upon complex, energy- and capital-intensive "high" technologies that radically extend control over nature and at the same time increase the potential for catastrophic side effects and social dysfunction. For instance, the development of automobiles, chemical pesticides, nuclear energy, supersonic transports, supertankers, recombinant DNA, and so on suggests a large number of potential disasters due to latent effects that often manifest as surprises when accidents occur. The earthquake-tsunami-triggered nuclear-meltdown potential at the Fukushima Daiichi nuclear power plant in

Japan is a recent example of complex technological surprise (Clayton 2011). Risk in contemporary modern societies is viewed as a function of high technology, which is primarily a product of the growth and diffusion of technologies that took place after 1945 (Orr 1979, 43).

Among other negative impacts of technologies on society are the rising numbers of casualties associated with a variety of catastrophic events triggered or exacerbated by technology. For example, technological disasters, wars, crimes, terrorism, health problems, global pollution, environmental injustice, and threats of global climate change all reflect human rights abuse (Adeola 2001). Historically, science and technology have been implicated in several atrocities involving the blatant violation of human rights—including their application as instruments of mass repression, torture, genocide, ethnic cleansing, and slavery both before and after the UDHR (Toney et al. 2010; Evans 2007). Technology has been employed in cases of infanticide in many parts of Asia, including India, Pakistan, and China. There are also cases of eugenics, the Tuskegee experiment, the poisoning of Vietnam residents with Agent Orange, and the strategic deployment of weapons of mass destruction (Khalili-Borna 2008; Toney et al. 2010). The detonation of atomic bombs over Hiroshima and Nagasaki in Japan provides further examples of massive loss of life and environmental destruction spanning several generations (Erikson 1994). Unfortunately, the jury is still out in terms of whether the benefits of technology outweigh the costs. It is important to note that humanity is a part of nature and is systematically involved with nature's continuity and evolution. Nonetheless, science and technology have the untoward potential to cause the elimination of humankind through misapplication (Szell 1994).

HUMAN RIGHTS: THE IMPORTANCE OF ENVIRONMENT AND TECHNOLOGY

In both first- and second-generation rights, environmental rights and rights to technology were not clearly addressed. This is not surprising given the anthropocentric nature of the human rights movement and UDHR. Also, it is important to note that even though a number of scholars raised alarms about environmental pollution and the problems associated with pesticide use as far back as the 1960s, especially with the 1962 publication of *Silent Spring* by Rachel Carson, environmental rights did not emerge as a primary concern both in the United States and within the United Nations until the late 1960s and the 1970s (Carson 1962; Johansen 2003). A number of memorable events, such as the passage of the National Environmental Policy Act, the establishment of the Environmental Protection Agency, the celebration of the first Earth Day, the Santa Barbara oil spill, the energy crisis, the Three Mile Island disaster, and other disturbing environmental-contamination episodes in the 1970s, sparked vigorous modern environmental movements within the United States and global outrage about environmental problems (Carson 1962; Giddens 1999; Hernan 2010; Johansen 2003; Perrow 1999). The issue of illegal waste movements from the Global North to the Global South has also gained international attention (Clapp 2001; Pellow 2007). These modern environmental risks are often invisible, transgenerational, transnational, and uninsurable and pose the ultimate threat to human rights and human security (Beck 1996, 1999; Giddens 1999).

The Declaration of the United Nations Conference on the Human Environment held in Stockholm is often regarded as the first international attempt to address pressing environmental problems. Representatives of 113 countries attended the conference, and as contentious as environmental issues were at the time, they all agreed to twenty-six principles that direct governments to cooperate in protecting and improving the natural environment. Shortly after the Stockholm conference, several environmental catastrophes occurred both in the United States and other parts of the world, raising social consciousness about threats to environmental sustainability and the latent dysfunctions of modern complex technologies. Among these, the dioxin contamination of Seveso in Italy in 1976; the toxic waste contamination at Love Canal, New York; the Three Mile Island nuclear reactor accident; the deadly contamination of a neighborhood in Woburn, Massachusetts; the mass killings of thousands of people by poisonous gas released at the Union Carbide Corporation factory in Bhopal, India; the mega nuclear reactor meltdown at Chernobyl, Ukraine, in 1986; and the massive *Exxon Valdez* oil spill in Prince William Sound, Alaska, provided growing evidence of the problem of technological failure and environmental destruction (Erikson 1994; Picou, Gill, and Cohen 1997). In addition, a plethora of alarming cases of toxic contamination across the United States, especially in lower-income, minority communities, provide evidence of the risks that threaten human rights to life, a safe and healthy environment, and psychosocial well-being (see Adeola 2011; Hernan 2010; Marshall and Picou 2008; Gill and Picou 1998). Clearly, most of these cases depict the dark side of technology for humans and all other organisms in the environment. Citizens, sociologists, and environmental activists have increasingly addressed patterns of environmental injustice and how these events expose issues related to human rights, technology, and the environment (Bullard 2000, 2005). Sociologists have also played a key role in the environmental health movement, addressing the manifest and latent outcomes of technologies and their psychosocial impacts (see Perrow 1999, 2008; Erikson 1994; Gill and Picou 1998). They are increasingly involved in applied research offering policy guidelines and choices to public administrators.

Social vulnerability to changes in the environment and environmental hazards is a direct function of technology and social relations. The history of global inequality makes some groups more vulnerable to environmental hazards than others. Despite the existence of the UN instruments, as well as other local, national, and regional structures establishing human rights, some groups experience a disproportionate share of negative environmental externalities imposed by technology and industrial activities. As emphasized in the environmental-justice literature, disadvantaged groups—including racial and ethnic minorities, indigenous peoples, people of color, and the poor all over the world—are more vulnerable to environmental hazards than other groups (Bullard 2000, 2005). For people who live with disadvantages, the rights to healthy habitats, clean natural resources, including air and water, and occupational safety are considered expendable for the sake of economic gain, national security, and national energy imperatives (Johnston 1995). Many communities of color are regarded and treated as "paths of least resistance" for absorbing the deleterious consequences of industrial pollution. These communities exist within and contiguous to sources of toxic emissions that threaten health and social well-being (Adeola 1994; Johnston 1995; Bullard 2000, 2005; Agyeman 2005). These increased risks also characterize third-world countries where hazardous wastes from affluent societies of the Global North are overtly or covertly dumped, showing a global pattern of environmental injustice (Adeola 2000a; Pellow 2007; Clapp 2001). To mitigate this pattern of environmental injustice against the people as well as against the biophysical environment, the World People's Conference on Climate Change and the Rights of Mother Earth convened in April 2010 in Bolivia and developed a draft Universal Declaration of the Rights of Mother Earth.

Does every human being have a right to the positive benefits of environment and technology? A consideration of global and local structured social inequality suggests that unequal command of technology results in exposure to deadly environmental hazards regardless of existing human rights. The rights to a clean environment and positive applications of technology are often considered as part of the third-generation rights recently recognized within the United Nations (Johnston 1995; Glazebrook 2009; Ruppel 2009). This category of human rights has become controversial because addressing this issue is contingent upon both the positive and negative duties of the state, individuals, and organizations (Wronka 1998; Ishay 2004a; Boersema 2011). As mentioned, among these third-generation rights are the rights to development, to peace, to a healthy environment, to the benefits of science and technology, and to intergenerational equity. As mentioned by Ruppel (2009), the right to a clean environment requires healthy human habitats that are free of pollutants, toxins, or hazards that pose threats to human health. The right to a healthy environment therefore requires the commitment of states (1) to refrain from directly or indirectly interfering with the enjoyment of the right to a healthy environment; (2) to guard against third parties, such as corporations, interfering with the right to a healthy and productive environment; and (3) to adopt all necessary measures to achieve the full realization of the right to a safe and healthy environment (Ruppel 2009).

The principal instruments asserting the third- and fourth-generation category of rights are the African Charter on Human and People's Rights of 1981 and the Declaration of the Rights of Indigenous Peoples of 2007 (Battersby and Siracusa 2009). Indigenous rights are considered under the purview of conventions addressing biodiversity and intellectual property. Even though genetic research delivers medical benefits, it is also argued that biotechnologies have allowed food and drug companies to distill and manipulate the genetic structure of plants known to indigenous communities for their medicinal qualities. Such genetically modified crops pose threats to indigenous cultures and traditional biophysical environments.

While most of the first- and second-generation rights have been ratified by many states and codified within international laws, the third- and emerging fourth-generation rights remain controversial. This was apparent at the 1992 Earth

Summit convened in Rio de Janeiro, Brazil, where concerns for economic development among the less developed countries were pitted against the protection of the biophysical environment advocated by most affluent nations of the Global North. Instead of focusing on an ecocentric approach to addressing environmental rights for people, emphasis was shifted to the goal of sustainable development. Nevertheless, the Earth Summit gave impetus to a Framework Convention on Climate Change, which addresses the problem of global warming. The World Summit on Sustainable Development held in Johannesburg, South Africa, in 2002 focused on sustainable development as reflected in the Johannesburg Declaration (UN 2002). These developing trends in human rights advances clearly reveal the emerging role of environmental concern for protecting the health and well-being of citizens throughout the world.

CONCLUSION

The future of human rights in the twenty-first century poses many challenges and opportunities for humankind. In particular, issues directly related to the biophysical environment and technological advances will increasingly become a permanent source of controversy and a potential platform for advances in the human rights arena. Human rights scholars need to address the fact that technological systems are far from perfect, and the lesson from Hurricane Katrina's destruction of New Orleans is that even natural catastrophes can be technologically engineered (Freudenburg, Gramling, and Laska 2009). The failure of technology is a "normal" event, and as technological systems become increasingly complex, humankind faces "surprises" and "worst-case scenarios" that have the potential to obliterate the scientific advances of the last century (see Perrow 1999, 2008; Clarke 2006). This increasing inventory of risk permeates the social fabric and is embedded throughout the global biophysical environment (Beck 2007b). As such, technological advances and failures, coupled with environmental degradation, become inextricably linked to our consciousness of issues for advancing human rights. These advances can be fostered by declarations of global organizations, such as the United Nations, by international agreements, and also by raising individual consciousness through educational empowerment, or individualization (Beck 1996).

From a social-policy standpoint, Hayward (2005) suggests the usefulness of embedding environmental rights within national constitutions, which would serve a broader purpose than simply providing for the protection of the environment by legal actions. A potential effect of environmental human rights would be mandating several procedural rights, including the right to know, to be informed of any proposed developments in one's locality, to information about environmental-impact and technological-impact assessments, to information about toxic releases into the environment, and to freedom of assembly to facilitate protests against locally undesirable land uses, such as creation of brown fields and erection of noxious facilities, as well as extensive rights to self-determination, encompassing the right to participate in decision-making forums. As noted by Barry and Woods (2009, 324), the legal recognition of these rights would enhance the democratic efficacy of environmental decision-making processes, thereby facilitating environmental justice while at the same time promoting an ethic of custodianship of the biophysical environment. The mandatory precautionary principle (the notion that we should strive to prevent harm to human health and the environment even in the face of scientific uncertainty about risks) has also been advanced in the literature and within the United Nations as an important mechanism for ensuring environmental justice, human rights, and protection of the integrity of nature. In fact, the precautionary principle has become a key component of EU environmental policy and is included in Principle 15 of the Rio Declaration. The extent to which all the declarations have been implemented remains subject to debate. Several NGOs, such as Human Rights Watch, Amnesty International, and Earth Justice, among others, are monitoring and reporting human-environmental rights situations across nations.

The relationship between the biophysical environment, technology, and human rights is complex and critical for understanding the human condition in the twenty-first century. While human rights encompass the right to life, a clean environment, liberty, and security, guaranteed access to environmental amenities and protection against environmental harms for present and future generations remain elusive. Although the application of technology as a liberating force for enhancing quality of life and economic development is a laudable and important goal, alternative outcomes that ensure the protection of ecological integrity, human rights, and sustainable development need to be addressed. The irresponsible application of modern technologies has resulted in massive contamination of the natural environment, loss of life, and the destruction of human communities. Coinciding with this "dark side" of technology are numerous examples of the worldwide violation of human rights emphasized in this chapter. Sociological research should become more actively engaged in understanding the dynamic linkage between technology, environment, populations, level of affluence, political regime characteristics, and human rights around the globe in an attempt to positively influence social change in the twenty-first century. Hopefully this chapter will be a source of encouragement for future inquiry.

CHAPTER TWENTY-SIX

POPULATION

Jenniffer M. Santos-Hernández

In 1993 Bryan Turner explored and proposed the creation of a theory of human rights within the discipline of sociology. Over the last two decades, several sociologists have focused on understanding the value of moving beyond the limited engagement of our discipline in normative debates (Waters 1996; Hafner-Burton and Tsutsui 2005; Blau and Frezzo 2011). In the summer of 2005, Michael Burawoy, in his presidential address to the American Sociological Association, called for a public sociology and stressed our responsibility to focus on understanding and preventing the devastation of society. He highlighted the widespread appeal of human rights as a framework to ensure human dignity and stand against human atrocities.

This chapter discusses some opportunities for the human rights paradigm for cross-disciplinary collaborations between demographers and sociologists interested in population studies and human rights. It is important to highlight that studies in population have greatly contributed to securing and extending human rights. Research in demography is at the heart of human rights discussions. For example, the Population Division of the United Nations Department of Economic and Social Affairs is one of the main international organizations collecting, monitoring, analyzing, and distributing global population data. The data collected by the Population Division is used by all dependencies in the UN system to create policies and to monitor their implementation. Externally, the data offered by the UN Population Division presents information that governments can use to explore demographic trends in other countries.

THE GROWTH OF WORLD POPULATION AND POPULATION STUDIES

Sometime during the last quarter of 2011, the world's population reached 7 billion. The growth is not because people are having more children. In contrast with common belief, people are in fact having fewer children. Fertility, or the average number of children per woman, has steadily declined in the last fifty years. What has happened is that after the second half of the nineteenth century, the world was transformed dramatically through several processes of change, including secularization, industrialization, increased access to education, and improvements in sanitation and health services, among others. People are now living longer, and their children are less likely to die of communicable or preventable diseases. As a result of all these changes, the world's population has grown faster than ever before. What is interesting about these changes is the fact that they occurred as part of a larger and longer process of social change that demographers have named the "demographic transition" (Caldwell 2006).

Improvements in transportation and communication systems have also transformed societies. The world is now connected in ways that seemed unimaginable a century ago, facilitating the flows of people and objects and leading to the emergence of not only a network society (Castells 2000), but also a world economy (Goldfrank 2000). The challenge is that the relationship among countries is not equal; rather, it has led to the emergence of a global division of labor or social structure that renders some countries and their citizens as subordinates to the market demands of others (Wallerstein 1974). With all the changes mentioned, human rights emerged as a universal set of rules for interactions among all humans (Donnelly 2003).

Sociology as a discipline emerged to study the social changes that in many ways have facilitated the demographic-transition process and the development of states that are now increasingly part of this global society. Current debates in our discipline discuss the need to extend beyond the boundaries of states and allow for the development of a "connected sociology" that emerges from the bottom up and integrates challenging perspectives in order to reconstruct our understanding of society and the sociological endeavor.

While not all demographers are sociologists and not all sociologists are demographers, the two fields have long been related. Demography has truly evolved as a multidisciplinary area of inquiry, attracting researchers who study how changes in a wide variety of phenomena affect people and how they react to those effects. For instance, demographers are interested in questions such as, How many children are born? To what families are children being born? In what types of housing arrangements do those families live? What are the characteristics of their neighborhoods? What resources are accessible to them? How do people move? How many people die? What is their cause of death? Where are all these events and processes happening? To answer such questions, the field of demography has increasingly relied on statistical methods that allow us to standardize and systematize data-collection procedures (Hinde 1998). In addition, the development of information-system technologies has also improved the study of population by reducing the uncertainty of the data collected and increasingly making the data available in formats that are easier to use and understand.

Demographers have also focused on refining demographic theories. The field of demography has long been criticized for the lack of depth of its associated theories (Crimmins 1993). Micklin and Poston (2005) argue that despite their disagreement with such a view, evaluating and clarifying demographic theories remains a challenge. They argue that the challenge is not necessarily due to the complexity of those theories but stems from the diversity of demographic theories used in population studies. The collaboration of sociologists and demographers is promising because it affords an opportunity to extend critical approaches within demography and reflect on the characteristics and patterns observed in a group (Horton 1999). For example, instead of assuming progress by relying on proxy variables that seek to measure progress toward the attainment of specific human rights, a contextualized approach that captures how the global order affects the rights of citizens in different societies would be more effective in advancing the promise of human rights. The importance of such cross-disciplinary collaboration lies in the opportunity to really understand the situation of people in a particular social context instead of simply assuming that progress is being made because of a reduction in the prevalence of a characteristic or indicator.

POPULATION STUDIES AND HUMAN RIGHTS

The collection of information about the population in a political jurisdiction dates back to the beginning of civilization. Population data are used by governments for a wide variety of reasons, including taxation, military recruitment, development of military strategies, provision of public services, allocation of government funds, and assessment of the effects of policies implemented. Population data collected by states around the world has functioned as a mechanism to facilitate governance.

In an ideal situation, population data would always be used to ensure the welfare of individuals. However, the social categories used to group individuals are not socially neutral. On several occasions, information about a population has also been used to target vulnerable groups (Seltzer and Anderson 2002). In other cases, marginalized groups have been systematically excluded from data-collection efforts (Anderson and Fienberg 2001). Table 26.1 provides an overview of crimes against humanity and the populations affected.

At the same time, realization of the human rights of some and enhancements in their standard of living have sometimes come at the cost of the human freedoms of marginalized groups. These changes are, to a great extent, a result of population policies. Some population policies have transformed societies through programs that facilitate institutional arrangements that treat everyone equally and with dignity. Those population policies allow men and women to plan their futures and their families and to make decisions with a clear understanding of their consequences. Other population policies have failed to respect the rights of men and women. Some of them have focused on neo-Malthusian or eugenics beliefs and have targeted specific groups, resulting in some of the most atrocious crimes against humanity (Levine and Bashford 2010), as Table 26.1 shows. Some of those appalling policies have led to social movements or to civil and/or military conflicts.

For example, modern family-planning methods have facilitated a reduction in fertility, the emergence of smaller families, the integration of women into the labor market, and the alleviation of poverty. Nevertheless, for many women in

Table 26.1 Selected crimes against humanity

Country	System
South Africa: apartheid	Apartheid was a racial-segregation system in place in South Africa until the mid-1990s. The system maintained four categories—black, colored, Indian, and white—and prevented them from interacting with each other through physical separation and prohibition of intermarriage. Institutional power was held by whites, and other groups were denied the right to participate in politics (Ozler 2007).
Germany: Holocaust	During World War II, approximately 6 million Jews were killed by the Nazi government (Longerich 2010; Bauman 1988).
Guatemala: genocide	During the 1980s, more than two hundred thousand people were killed by the military in more than six hundred Mayan villages (Higonnet 2009).
Rwanda: genocide	More than five hundred thousand were killed in a conflict against the Tutsi ethnic minority in the 1990s. About a third of the Tutsi population was killed (Barnett 2003).
Bosnia: genocide	More than one hundred thousand Bosnians and Croatians were killed in the 1990s by military forces (Ching 2009).
Darfur, Sudan: genocide	Ongoing state-led genocide in Darfur has resulted in more than 400,000 people killed and 2.5 million displaced (Suleiman 2011).

Puerto Rico, Haiti, and other countries, the potential side effects of the use of contraceptives, such as permanent sterilization, were not well understood when these methods were adopted (Salvo, Powers, and Cooney 1992; López 1993; Briggs 1998). In fact, birth-control programs implemented in many countries throughout the world were built around neo-Malthusian and eugenic-supremacy beliefs (López 2008). Researchers have long documented that women often accepted undergoing sterilization procedures offered by government social workers at no cost because they believed the procedures were reversible. The main idea behind such policies was that poverty was caused by overpopulation. As such, in order to reduce poverty and promote economic development, population-control policies were perceived as necessary to reduce reproduction among those on the lower rungs of society. Similarly, in the United States many people of color and those considered inferior because of physical or mental limitations were sterilized in the first half of the twentieth century. While these family-planning initiatives can allow people to make their own childbearing choices, when family-planning methods are mandatory or target specific groups, or when all potential consequences are not understood, they fail to recognize the rights of those who adopt them.

POPULATION GROWTH, ADAPTATION TO CLIMATE CHANGE, AND HUMAN RIGHTS

Research in population will continue to be vital for the advancement of human rights. Moreover, assisting in the realization of human rights will depend on the methods we use and how well they capture the experiences of those we group into larger categories. Society now confronts the most crucial challenge of all times: climate change (Giddens 2009). Modernization has brought great advances but also has accelerated the degradation of our environment. Climate change is already affecting the lives of people around the world (Stringer et al. 2009).

Moreover, although fertility continues to decline, the world's population will continue expanding for the upcoming decades, with the fastest growth taking place in the poorest nations (Campbell-Lendrum and Lusti-Narasimhan 2009). Why? Because more people live in less advanced societies that are at an earlier stage of the demographic-transition process. The challenge is to develop a way of living that can sustain the current population, adapt to an increasingly changing climate, and account for the needs of the population that is being added to our planet.

While we often take for granted the food we eat and the water we drink, in some areas of the world drought-driven famines have profound social and political impacts. In other areas of the world (e.g., the Horn of Africa), famines have been caused or triggered not by droughts but by faulty governments, civil conflicts, and war (Wisner et al. 2004; Sen 1981). In many areas of countries such as China, Pakistan, Somalia, Sudan, and Iraq, people are increasingly affected by food and water scarcity, living in poverty, and oppression by authoritarian political regimes. Therefore, the challenge of climate change calls upon sociologists to examine the dialectical relationship between society and environment (Grundmann and Stehr 2010).

SOCIOLOGY AND POPULATION STUDIES FOR THE FUTURE OF HUMAN RIGHTS

The transformation of social life and the enhancement of infrastructure to facilitate the exchange of goods and resources have created a new global community that extends beyond the boundaries of states. With the transformation of societies, human rights emerged to provide guidance regarding social interactions. Population research has been crucial in the advancement of human rights by providing much-needed information to support the development of policy that addresses the needs of those whose rights are being denied or postponed. Drawing on the strengths of population and sociological research affords an opportunity to critically examine the past, understand the challenges of the present, and in doing so prevent the future devastation of society.

The development of effective population policy in the twenty-first century is essential to confront the challenges of a changing climate. Sociology can greatly contribute to addressing the fissures of current social arrangements and can help reduce the pressures that human activities place on the environment. Climate change challenges not only our current social arrangements but our capacity to ensure the realization of human rights for others. Population studies and sociology can greatly contribute to understanding how the current world order affects the capacity of different groups and societies to secure the human rights of their members. Moreover, population studies and sociology can greatly contribute to the process of identifying challenges and opportunities for securing the human rights of citizens as we also adapt to the challenges posed by a changing climate.

Chapter Twenty-Seven

COLLECTIVE BEHAVIOR AND SOCIAL MOVEMENTS
Lyndi Hewitt

R ichard Flacks has characterized the study of social movements as an examination of "the conditions under which human beings become capable of
wanting freedom and acting freely" (2005, 4). Thought about in this way, social
movement research goes to the very heart of human rights, linking intellectual
and political endeavors for actors in the academy and in the field. In collaboration with interlocutors from political science, sociologists of collective behavior
and social movements (CBSM) have long striven to illuminate the multilayered
action of social movement participants in their efforts to achieve social change.
Taking up questions around the emergence, trajectories, and outcomes of collective
action, movement scholars offer theoretical and empirical insights of considerable
relevance to human rights.

Scholars of social movements have addressed human rights to the extent that
the political actors they study are (1) engaging human rights frameworks in their
struggles, (2) documenting human rights abuses as a form of advocacy, (3) contesting
and reshaping political and public understandings of human rights, and (4) fighting to secure the rights of oppressed groups. Not surprisingly, then, the literatures
examining transnational resistance to neoliberalism and struggles for the rights of
women are particularly active sites for such work; I focus on these literatures here.
Surveys, case studies, qualitative interviewing, document analysis, comparative
historical approaches, field research, and more have been used to address questions
where human rights and movements intersect. And while it is not uncommon
for scholars to be deeply engaged with the movements they study, there is ample
room for more explicit adoption of participatory and human rights approaches to
movement research.

This chapter briefly reviews key threads, questions, and recent developments in
the social movements literature and, further, argues that conceptual and empirical
work on social movements offers important insights into understanding human
rights. Social movement scholars are well positioned to facilitate the advancement of
human rights activism but must work diligently to develop praxis-oriented research
agendas in order to maximize their impact.

HISTORY AND KEY QUESTIONS OF CBSM SCHOLARSHIP

Scholars generally agree that social movements are defined by (relatively) sustained and organized efforts on the part of collectivities engaging in at least some noninstitutionalized tactics and seeking to achieve or resist social change. Prior to the 1960s and 1970s, dominant understandings of collective action focused heavily on the role of grievances and depicted movement participants as largely irrational actors. The field then shifted and expanded substantially as the US civil rights, women's, student, and antiwar movements illustrated the shortcomings of existing explanations of collective action. Researchers, many of whom were activists themselves, studied these agitations and ultimately rejected psychologically driven approaches to explaining mobilization in favor of more structural perspectives that took into account factors such as resources, organizations, networks, and political context. Leading scholars, including Charles Tilly, William Gamson, Doug McAdam, and Sidney Tarrow, demonstrated the influence of these structural factors across a range of mobilization efforts and carved out ambitious research agendas for the field of movement studies.

Researchers have consistently investigated influences on the emergence, trajectories, and outcomes of collective action at local, national, and increasingly transnational levels. Key questions have included, Why do people protest? How do contextual conditions support or hinder collective action? How do movements influence cultural attitudes and policy change? What differentiates a successful from an unsuccessful movement? In their efforts to describe and analyze these multiple sites of collective action, movement scholars have highlighted the importance of resources, political and cultural contexts, and also the agency of movement actors. The resource mobilization perspective (Jenkins 1983; McCarthy and Zald 1977) emphasized the importance of organizational resources in catalyzing movement action. Early conversations about resources yielded useful concepts, such as social movement organization, social movement industry, and social movement sector, that facilitated systematic empirical study. Generally speaking, research in this tradition demonstrates that higher levels of resources are beneficial for mobilization efforts (Cress and Snow 1996; Zald 1992), with the importance of different types of resources (e.g., material, human, social) varying according to the nature and phase of the movement. Scholars have also explored the consequences of resource accumulation and professionalization, concluding that the effects on movement trajectories are mixed (Piven and Cloward 1977; Staggenborg 1988).

The notion of political opportunities (Kitschelt 1986; Meyer 2004) further transformed the field of social movement study, illuminating the role of factors such as elite allies and the openness of political systems in facilitating or preventing protest. Political opportunity is the crucial ingredient in what became known as the political process model of collective action (Kriesi 2004; McAdam 1982), which remains a dominant perspective. The political process model synthesized existing insights in the field and prioritized the influence of political opportunities and threats, or lack thereof, in understanding movement development. Shifting opportunities over time and across locales have helped explain why collective action emerges and/or succeeds in some situations but not in others. Even while the political process perspective was arguably at its height, though, scholars worried about the overextension of key concepts (Gamson and Meyer 1996). While numerous studies attempted to measure and assess the impact of contextual conditions, they often utilized different indicators. At the same time, studies exploring the cultural and emotional aspects of movements were on the rise.

Although resource mobilization and political process models contributed a great deal to understandings of collective action, scant attention was paid to the ways that culture, ideology, and meaning construction came to bear on the emergence and development of social movements. The "cultural turn" in social movement theory brought with it more careful attention to the role of framing, emotions, and collective identity in building and sustaining movements. This gradual shift in the study of social movements over the past twenty-five years has been well documented by social science researchers (Benford and Snow 2000; Gamson 1992; Goodwin and Jasper 2004; Johnston and Klandermans 1995; McAdam 1994), and the explosion of research on collective action frames and framing processes is the most prominent example of this phenomenon (Johnston and Noakes 2005). The considerable influence of collective action frames in movement emergence, development, and outcomes is now widely recognized (Cress and Snow 2000; Gamson 1992; McCammon et al. 2007; Zuo and Benford 1995). Scholars of social movements have come to understand framing processes as the means by which movement actors translate grievances into action, as a major impetus for participation in protest, and as a vehicle for creating and sustaining collective identity (McAdam, McCarthy, and Zald 1996; Benford and Snow 2000; Snow 2004). This symbolic, or "signifying," work is an important tool not only for recruiting participants during the early life of a movement but also for maintaining membership and morale and communicating with other targets, such as the media, the state, and movement opponents, in order to achieve both political and cultural outcomes (Cress and Snow 2000; McAdam, McCarthy, and Zald 1996; McCammon 2001).

Some of the research in this cultural vein fundamentally challenged structural approaches (e.g., Jasper 1997), but other culturally focused research developed in tandem with structurally centered explanations of collective action rather than seeking to overhaul them. However, the dominance of political process approaches to the study of social movements has been increasingly criticized in recent years by scholars calling for more nuanced, dynamic approaches that make central the agency and strategic choices of movement actors (Goodwin and Jasper 2004; Jasper 2004). While scholars continue to debate the relative importance of contextual conditions and agency in determining movement trajectories and outcomes, other criticisms have also been raised about the relationships between researchers and activists. Cox and Fominaya argue that

> Contemporary social movement studies as it now exists, institutionalized as an increasingly canonized body of knowledge within North American and West European academia, has become increasingly distant from any relationship to movements other than the descriptive and analytic—despite the fact that a

number of its most significant authors started from positions sympathetic to social movements, if not actually within them. (2009, 6)

A lack of strong, equitable connections between researchers and the movements they study poses a particular obstacle to the political usefulness of social movement theory as a whole. I explore this issue in greater detail in a later section but turn first to a brief review of CBSM scholarship examining human rights activism.

HUMAN RIGHTS MOVEMENTS: FINDINGS FROM THE CBSM FIELD

Although rights claims are invoked in local, national, and transnational struggles, a substantial portion of social movement theory has been generated through examinations of US-based movements, which tend to use human rights frameworks less frequently than others. But explosive growth in human rights activism, much of it outside the United States, over the past two decades has encouraged movement scholars to turn their attention to various dynamics of transnational human rights organizing (Bandy and Smith 2005; Bob 2005, 2009; Della Porta et al. 2006; Ferree and Tripp 2006; Keck and Sikkink 1998; Risse, Ropp, and Sikkink 1999; Smith, Pagnucco, and López 1998; Tarrow 2005). The rise of transnational advocacy networks (TANs) has been an especially influential topic of study in the field. Keck and Sikkink write, "What is novel in these networks is the ability of nontraditional international actors to mobilize information strategically to help create new issues and categories and to persuade, pressure, and gain leverage over much more powerful organizations and governments" (1998, 2). On human rights issues, in particular, TANs have been successful in transforming global norms through the use of information politics, symbolic politics, leverage politics, and accountability politics.

While some refer to a "human rights movement," one is hard-pressed to discern where the human rights movement ends and the global justice movement begins. In a political era characterized by global network relationships, overlapping issues, and a commonly shared diagnosis of neoliberalism, many movements consider themselves part of a broader human rights movement. Many transnational organizations have also moved away from single-issue foci toward multi-issue agendas that encompass and even emphasize economic rights (Smith 2004). This is made possible in part by the inclusive, indivisible notion of human rights that has gained steam since the early 1990s. Feminist activists in particular have pushed for inclusive and interdependent notions of human rights that go beyond civil and political rights to account for economic, social, and cultural rights violations, as well as those that occur in the private sphere (Ackerly 2008; Ackerly and D'Costa 2005; Bunch 1990).

The language of human rights has long been embraced by the United Nations, as evidenced by numerous key documents, such as the Universal Declaration of Human Rights, the Convention on the Rights of the Child, the Vienna Declaration, the Beijing Platform for Action, and the Millennium Development Goals. Thanks in large part to the efforts of activists, many governments have joined the United

Nations in its promotion of a human rights framework, helping these discourses gain greater traction transnationally. Human rights ideas have thus become part of the "dominant symbolic repertoire" (Woehrle, Coy, and Maney 2008), which has enabled not only transnational but also local movements working on a range of issues (e.g., violence, environment, labor, peace, sexuality) to harness and adapt the human rights discourse to further their goals (Ackerly and D'Costa 2005; Levitt and Merry 2009).

The global justice movement represents one of the most active and fruitful areas of scholarship addressing human rights and social movements (Blau and Karides 2008; Cox and Nilsen 2007; Della Porta et al. 2006; Juris 2008; Smith 2008; Smith et al. 2008). Local, regional, national, and transnational movement organizations have articulated a shared set of grievances identifying ubiquitous neoliberal values and policies as the common target (Blau and Karides 2008; Naples and Desai 2002; Tazreiter 2010). Many of these organizations have also adopted master frames of human rights and democracy as alternatives to the existing neoliberal order. In 2001, the World Social Forum (WSF) emerged under the banner "Another World Is Possible" as a site for shared resistance to neoliberalism. The WSF and the ongoing social forum process more generally have spawned a proliferation of new research among scholars in many disciplines and parts of the world.

Jackie Smith, along with multiple colleagues, has been at the forefront of documenting the emergence and trajectories of transnational organizations and of the global justice movement (Bandy and Smith 2005; Smith 2008; Smith and Johnston 2002). Smith (2008) provides one of the most comprehensive examinations to date of the global justice movement. Her analysis illuminates the complex relationships between rival networks of neoliberal actors (e.g., corporations, the commercial media, the International Monetary Fund) and the activist globalizers from below who seek to prioritize democracy and human rights over profit.

The global women's movement may be the single best contemporary illustration of activists working for the advancement of human rights while simultaneously transforming understandings of them (Antrobus 2004; Ferree and Tripp 2006; Friedman 2003; Keck and Sikkink 1998; Naples and Desai 2002; Moghadam 2005; Peters and Wolper 1995). Feminists and women's rights activists have continuously pushed for a human rights perspective that transcends multiple issues and identities. Utilizing opportunities such as the UN conferences of the early 1990s and the social forums since 2001, women's and feminist activists built alliances with other movements and insisted that no rights are secure unless all rights are secure. They rejected a silo model of human rights and encouraged other movements to do the same, with considerable success.

While the scholarship mentioned above represents a growing and dynamic body of work, the intersection of social movements and human rights is, on the whole, surprisingly understudied. In a somewhat rare endeavor that explicitly examines the relationship between social movements and human rights, political scientist Neil Stammers (1999, 2009) makes a compelling, historically informed case that social movements have always been key players in shaping social values. Drawing on the work of Melucci (1989), Stammers (1999, 987–988) emphasizes the dual instrumental and expressive dimensions of social movements, arguing that the role movement actors play in constructing and reconstructing human rights is no less important than their role in actually securing those rights. Moreover, Stammers reminds us that expansive human rights claims that move beyond civil and political rights to encompass economic and social rights are not new but rather emerged in the context of eighteenth-century workers' struggles. Finally, he considers the relatively recent movements against corporate-led globalization to hold tremendous potential for advancing human rights.

METHODS IN CBSM SCHOLARSHIP

Methods of data collection and analysis in social movement scholarship run the gamut. CBSM researchers have used participant observation and in-depth interviews with activists, protest-event analysis, case studies, discourse and frame analysis, comparative historical designs, statistical analysis of survey data, and mathematical simulations to investigate the dynamics of collective action (Klandermans and Staggenborg 2002). The Yearbook of International Organizations has been a popular source of data for scholars using quantitative methods to study human rights and other transnational movement organizations (Smith, Pagnucco, and López 1998). Recently, Internet technology has enabled scholars to examine movement identity and framing more systematically through information available on organizational websites (Ferree and Pudrovska 2006; Hewitt 2009). Network analysis has also been used to map connections among different organizations and sectors affiliated with the broader global justice movement (Chase-Dunn et al. 2007).

The methodological diversity in the study of social movements is widely viewed as a great strength. In their edited volume *Methods of Social Movement Research*, Klandermans and Staggenborg (2002) note that movement scholars have always been quick to assess and revise theoretical developments through rigorous empirical study, and the use of and respect for multiple methodological approaches has been a driving force behind the tremendous growth and advancement in the field.

THE UTILITY OF SOCIAL MOVEMENT THINKING FOR THE HUMAN RIGHTS PARADIGM

Because social movements play such a critical role in constructing human rights and achieving them, researchers in the CBSM field have much to offer. Flacks argues that social movement research is "essential for those engaged in social struggle, helping to provide them with the theoretical and practical knowledge needed for effective action" (2005, 4). Perhaps most importantly, movement researchers can help document the theoretical insights of activists and bring them to bear on public thinking and conversations about human rights. That movements generate theory is widely recognized but not sufficiently discussed in academic circles. CBSM scholars can and should capture this theorizing, with proper attribution and respect. Baxi

(2002) has argued that social movements of oppressed peoples have long been the unrecognized intellectual engines of human rights thinking. Feminist political theorist Brooke Ackerly (2008) highlights the important contributions of women's human rights activists in developing a theory of human rights that is universal without being universalizing.

The idea of universal human rights is often pitted against cultural relativism, but feminist activists have repeatedly insisted that cultural sensitivity and respect for human rights can coexist. Transnational women's movements have been especially successful at building human rights coalitions and infusing human rights language into international institutions (Desai 2002; Friedman 2003; Moghadam 2005; Ferree and Tripp 2006; Joachim 2003). Perhaps more than any other movement, they have been forced to confront tensions between universalist and relativist approaches to human rights and have modeled ways of building solidarities across differences of class, race, culture, religion, and sexuality (Desai 2005). The theoretical lessons emerging from women's human rights struggles and documented by movement scholars continue to be influential in critiquing and shaping the human rights paradigm.

In addition to illuminating the theoretical insights of activists, movement scholars can also document the challenges and successes of activists, making visible patterns of strategic efficacy for human rights movements. Organizations working for human rights face a multitude of obstacles and threats. Most are eager to learn from the strategies and experiences of other organizations, but some have limited opportunity to interact. This is particularly true for under-resourced groups that do not have regular access to Internet communication. CBSM scholars may be able to increase the strategic capacity of social movement organizations by synthesizing and sharing insights based on their research.

The social movements literature helps us remain attentive to the multiple stakeholders constituting the landscape of rights struggles and to the varying organizational, political, and cultural contexts in which they do their work. Researchers are thus well situated to integrate the theoretical and strategic lessons of multiple movements. From a more aerial view, they can identify potential allies and facilitate connections. Furthermore, they may be able to assist movement actors in making their cases to donors and grant makers, a vitally important task in this era of shrinking funding for many social-change efforts.

In short, social movement theory and research can be useful to human rights activism. While the potential exists, utility has been limited thus far and will continue to be limited without heightened attention to relevance. The onus is on scholars to demonstrate the added value of academic research to movement actors working for human rights advancement.

CBSM SCHOLARSHIP INFORMED BY A HUMAN RIGHTS PARADIGM

A human rights lens would surely compel us to ask different research questions, but more importantly it would lead us to develop our questions and methods differently, often in collaboration with movement actors. If we believe in human dignity for all, and if we attend to activists' theorizing around the indivisibility of human rights, what are our responsibilities as scholars? Considering this question and its implications may require both an epistemological and a methodological shift. Where do our questions come from? How do we study them? How do we develop and use concepts? Where and how do we disseminate our work?

I want to suggest that CBSM scholarship is a natural site in the academy for supporting human rights struggles; however, taking seriously a human rights approach to CBSM scholarship makes the calls for movement-relevant scholarship all the more urgent (Flacks 2004, 2005; Bevington and Dixon 2005). While CBSM scholars engaging in praxis-oriented research have been grappling with these issues for some time (e.g., Croteau, Hoynes, and Ryan 2005), they have not been at the forefront of the field. Recent developments are promising, though, and indicate that movement scholars may be returning in earnest to their more grounded beginnings. At the recent CBSM workshop held just before the 2011 American Sociological Association meetings in Las Vegas, producing useable knowledge was a key organizing theme. In the opening plenary of that workshop, Maney (2011) argued for movement-based research that entails collective critical inquiry, sustained relationships with activists, and respect for multiple forms of knowledge. He asserted that movement-based research is equally rigorous as, if not more so than, traditional approaches and presented clear examples from collaborative projects, several of which dealt directly with protecting human rights. While Maney's model implies study of and with contemporary movements, much as Bevington and Dixon's (2005) framework calls for "direct engagement," scholars investigating historical movements can also elucidate movement-relevant knowledge. McCammon et al.'s (2008, 2012) work on strategic adaptation among advocates for US women's jury rights in the twentieth century reveals how specific strategic practices on the part of movement organizations influence the pace of outcome achievement. Given that a key goal of any movement is to achieve one or more favorable outcomes, and in the case of human rights movements to ensure that all people can exercise the full range of human rights, strategic insights may be particularly important.

Doing movement research from a human rights perspective also requires us to think more carefully about dissemination. In order for knowledge to be accessible to all stakeholders for consumption and critique, movement scholars need to think outside the boundaries of traditional academic publishing. As I have argued elsewhere (Hewitt 2008), we should share our work at earlier stages, solicit feedback from activists, and create more spaces for open dialogue. Human rights activists have demonstrated effective, democratic models of sharing knowledge for years, and scholars could learn from their examples. *Interface: A Journal for and about Social Movements*, a peer-reviewed periodical that published its first issue in 2009, is devoted explicitly to promoting dialogue between movement researchers and practitioners.

THE ROAD AHEAD

Cassie Schwerner writes, "If movement scholars wish to continue theorizing about social movements in the manner in which we have done for the past forty years, that is clearly a personal choice. These scholars, however, must recognize that their work is not being used by activists who need their insights the most" (2005, 171). Most CBSM scholars have an interest in producing useable knowledge, which means that some reflection is in order. As CBSM scholars set future agendas, they would do well to attend carefully to the intellectual, political, and moral dimensions of movement studies and to make the methodological adjustments required to do so. Specifically, CBSM scholars should deepen their commitment to ethical relationships with movement actors and make a more concerted effort to include actors not only in data collection but also in other research stages such as question formation and data analysis.

The most critical questions in the years to come will likely focus on movement strategy and outcomes. And if recent events are any indication, CBSM researchers will have no shortage of new research questions and empirical material to engage. In the wake of the Arab Spring and Occupy movements, questions about repressive states, police aggression, and Internet communication have moved front and center. Protesters have forcefully articulated the inextricability of political, civil, economic, and social rights and demanded the public's and the media's attention. Furthermore, scholars have only just begun to examine the newly significant role of e-mail campaigns and social media in facilitating information exchange and propelling protest (Earl and Kimport 2011). In this era of rapid technological and political change, movement scholars have their work cut out for them.

CHAPTER TWENTY-EIGHT

ALCOHOL, DRUGS, AND TOBACCO

Jennifer Bronson

Through time and space, alcohol, drugs, and tobacco have been, and continue to be, a feature of social and cultural life. Today, substance use is less likely to have ceremonial or ritual purposes and more likely to manifest through a complex intersection of social fragmentation, poverty, alienation, anomie, and urbanization inherent in modern life (UNODC 1997). Historical shifts have also occurred in the realms of drug control and regulation, with the dominant players in this changing construction of drugs coming from a place of privilege. Global economic, political, and social forces create and perpetuate human rights violations at the individual and community levels around the world. The United States is a key player in the current state of alcohol-, drug-, and tobacco-related issues, both as the highest consumer of illicit drugs in the world and as a leader in shaping international drug policy regarding legal sanctions (Oppenheimer 1991).

Whether legal or illegal, drugs are inherently shaped by social context. By locating alcohol, drugs, and tobacco within their sociocultural context, sociology provides an important foundation for understanding patterns of use, media and advertising influences, and social-control mechanisms. Despite invaluable contributions made by sociologists to drug-related research, it is not a principal topic within the discipline (Blum 1984). In addition, a definition of sociological alcohol, drug, and tobacco research does not exist (Bucholz and Robins 1989), which results in the absence of a coherent position within the discipline (Zajdow 2005). The complex, multifaceted nature of drugs, alcohol, and tobacco necessitates transversal research; therefore, fields such as public health, medicine, psychology, economics, criminology and criminal justice, anthropology, international studies, and policy studies crosscut research and analysis of drugs, alcohol, and tobacco (Bucholz and Robins 1989; Husak 2003; Peretti-Watel 2003).

In order to unite the different disciplines and address drug-related problems worldwide, we should place human rights at the center of a discussion on alcohol, drugs, and tobacco. A human rights perspective provides an organizing set of principles to guide, direct, and maintain the universal freedoms of individuals that instill equality, as well as accomplishes public health and public security aims. Human rights documents, such as the Universal Declaration of Human

Rights, outline the broad responsibilities of the state to respect, protect, and fulfill the complete range of interdependent, inalienable, and indivisible rights belonging to all persons (UNODC 2010). Yet many states fail to extend these concepts to drug-related matters. A human rights lens enables us to examine macro-level violations created through the transnational production and consumption of drugs, as well as to preserve not only the rights of substance users and those convicted of criminal offenses, but also individuals' abilities to seek appropriate treatment with dignity.

HISTORICAL SHIFTS: DEFINING AND REGULATING DRUGS

Variations exist between sociocultural groups and nations with regard to their attitudes toward and the acceptability of drug use and production. Neilson and Bamyeh note that, historically, most drugs were governed by some sort of social-control mechanisms geared "towards aims that served, protected or enhanced the customary order" (2009, 4). For example, tobacco was most often used by Native American cultures for religious purposes (Courtwright 2001), and in Morocco only elderly members of society could smoke hashish (Neilson and Bamyeh 2009). These mechanisms serve to proscribe social norms surrounding drug substances, which separates them from today's rigid sanctions and arbitrary prohibition policies.

The rise of capitalism contributed to the development of the plantation-based slave economy in the Americas (Moulier Boutang 1998) and helped define the acceptability of some "drugs" over others. Plantations based on production of sugar cane for rum, tobacco, and coffee beans dominated the economies of the Caribbean and the American South for centuries and shaped other economies as well, while perpetrating one of the largest cases of human rights violations in world history. In addition, capitalism was a central factor in the determination of the legality and acceptability of particular drugs. Those labeled licit were substances "more compatible with the emergent capitalist order" (Courtwright 2001, 59). Stimulants such as tobacco and coffee became subsumed by capitalism because they were easy to grow, transport, and distribute (Courtwright 2001). The production and sale of tobacco, alcohol, and coffee generated vast profits for capitalists while offering escapism and relief for the laboring masses.

During the early twentieth century, a coalition of political, religious, moral, and medical forces united to ban alcohol in the United States. This was accompanied by an overall reframing of "illicit drugs" that was codified into law (Husak 2003). Political power and money were the largest influences in dichotomizing drugs into legal or illicit designations, and Courtwright (2001) posits that the use of tobacco and alcohol by elites is likely the reason for selective prohibition. This selective regulation does not correspond to the degree to which actual harm is inflicted by a particular substance (Husak 2003; Courtwright 2001). For example, tobacco and alcohol are the first and third most common causes, respectively, of preventable death in the United States (CDC 2011). This contrasts starkly with the zero deaths attributed to marijuana use, which is illegal.

QUESTIONS SOCIOLOGISTS ASK AND WHAT THEY FIND

WHO USES ILLEGAL DRUGS? PATTERNS OF USE

Research on patterns of tobacco, alcohol, and illicit drug use based on any number of organizing variables dominates sociological literature. While by no means constituting a comprehensive list of the breadth and scope of the research, past and present studies examine alcohol, drug, and tobacco use and the following: age (Peretti-Watel 2003; Filmore 1987a), sex (Peretti-Watel 2003; Wilsnack and Cheloha 1987; Filmore 1987b; Sobell et al. 1986; Hoffmann 2006), type of school (Peretti-Watel 2003; Hoffmann 2006), religiosity (Wallace et al. 2007; Shields et al. 2007; Gillum 2005), race and ethnicity (Kitano 1988; Caetano 1984b; Weibgel-Orlando 1989; Herd 1988), degree of assimilation (Caetano 1987), and self-esteem (Peretti-Watel 2003). The role of the media and advertising (Kohn and Smart 1984; Sobell et al. 1986; Atkin et al. 1983; Strickland 1983; Lindsay 2009), as well as the social construction of space for purposes of engaging in drug-related activities, is also discussed in the literature.

Of particular interest to a human rights perspective on alcohol, drugs, and tobacco are discriminations related to one's race or ethnicity. According to some sociologists, the significance of race in the United States influences cultural and political processes, resulting in the definition of certain drugs and behaviors in racialized terms (Brubaker, Lovemen, and Stamatov 2004; Hall et al. 1978). Although blacks have lower rates of alcohol and drug consumption, they suffer from stiffer social consequences than their white counterparts due to the erroneous belief that blacks are the primary users and sellers of illicit drugs. This belief is evident in a 1986 federal law that created sentencing disparities for possession of crack cocaine and powdered cocaine, with the former used more by blacks. Under this law possession of five grams of crack cocaine warranted a five-year sentence, whereas an offender would have to be holding five hundred grams of powdered cocaine to receive the same punishment (Duster 1997; Tonry 1995). This law was overturned in 2010, but a sentencing disparity of eighteen to one still remains (ACLU 2010).

A discussion of racial injustice in the United States is incomplete without a class analysis. Research shows that harmful drug use is disproportionately concentrated in poor communities of color (Beckett et al. 2005), stemming from systemic social and economic inequality (Baumer 1994; Currie 1994; Duster 1997; Hagan 1994). High rates of addiction are often correlated with a lack of opportunities, high unemployment or underemployment, low-paying jobs, overwork, stress, and poor health (Beckett et al. 2005).

DEFINING ABUSE AND ADDICTION: IS A MEDICAL MODEL CORRECT?

An area of debate in sociological research on alcohol, drugs, and tobacco concerns whether substance addiction is a medical disorder or a behavioral or moral problem. This is an important question, and one unresolved by the field, because whether addiction is viewed as a disease or a failure of personal character is reflected in society's responses to alcoholism. Sociologists Conrad and Schneider theorize that deviance, such as drug and alcohol addiction, has become medicalized and argue that "medicalization of deviance changes the social response to such behavior to one of treatment rather than punishment" (1992, 28). Thus, a medical model of deviance demands a corresponding medical intervention by trained professionals to treat or cure the illness (Conrad and Schneider 1992). Others are weary of applying a medical model to addiction. These critics believe that although a moral-defect approach is significantly flawed, a medical approach is too limiting to represent the full spectrum of addiction experiences and consequences (Valliant 1983; Leigh and Gerrish 1986). As patterns of experimentation, use, and addiction vary across social and economic classes, with the greatest consequences disproportionally experienced by the poor and people of color, a disease model cannot explain these variations or rationalize the prohibition of some drugs over others (Husak 2003).

COMMON TOOLS AND METHODS

Sociology has a rich history of qualitative studies of drug and alcohol users. Examples include studies of cannabis users (Becker 1963), Alcoholics Anonymous (Denzin 1997), homeless heroin and crack addicts (Bourgois and Schonberg 2009), and teenage drug users (Dixon and Maher 2002). These participant observation and ethnographic studies connect seemingly insignificant elements of life to larger social processes (Zajdow and Lindsay 2010), provide insight into people's motives for substance use, and uncover the learned behaviors related to drug use (Hughes 2003).

There is a preference toward quantitative data in sociology. In quantitative studies on alcohol, drugs, and tobacco topics, sociologists often utilize cross-disciplinary instruments and surveys (Bucholz and Robins 1989). For example, the Federal Bureau of Investigation's Uniform Crime Reports compile police-department incident reports with data on race, crime of arrest, and drug involved in drug arrests (Beckett et al. 2005). Quantitative research on alcohol, drugs, and tobacco is not without its problems, regardless of an abundance of available statistical instruments and survey data (Peretti-Watel 2003). Statistical data simply do not provide a full picture of a person's experiences, motives, and feelings surrounding drug use. It also removes the individual from the larger sociocultural context of drugs and the transnational drug circuit. Additionally, this type of data may be flawed, as social desirability can bias the accuracy of self-reported usage (Gillum 2005), or indicators may not be correctly operationalized.

A mixed-method approach may be best suited to understanding the individual, local, national, and international dimensions of drug-related social problems and human rights violations.

FILLING IN THE GAPS WITH A HUMAN RIGHTS PARADIGM

Although sociology has contributed to research on drugs, it offers few answers (Bucholz and Robins 1989) and remains underdeveloped (Bucholz and Robins 1989; Zajdow 2005). Sociology could better address macro-level dynamics such as the role of economic forces in shaping transnational alcohol, drug, and tobacco demand and production patterns, the effects of drug trafficking on citizens and communities, and the influence of the capitalist political-economic system on drug-related policies. Despite applicable globalization and commodities theories, such as Wallerstein's (1983) world-systems theory, sociologists seem hesitant to analyze alcohol, drugs, and tobacco and the individual user in the context of an interconnected global market. A discussion of drugs should not omit "the larger and connected realms of cross-border politics, economics, and culture" (Neilson and Bamyeh 2009, 5).

A human rights perspective can enhance the sociological literature by connecting patterns of individual-level actions to global forces and help to evaluate the impact of alcohol, drugs, and tobacco on human dignity, freedoms, and equality. This framework highlights the flaws in the dominant legal-sanctions model that perpetuates human rights abuses and excludes those persons most in need of treatment and rehabilitation (UNODC 2010). Additionally, given the well-documented connection between poverty and increased participation in all levels of drug-related activities, it is likely that rising economic inequality will increase the current global drug cycle (Neilson and Bamyeh 2009). The United Nations General Assembly states that the world drug problem is best addressed in principles of universal human rights and fundamental freedoms (UNODC 2010).

HUMAN RIGHTS VIOLATIONS: UNJUST DUE PROCESS, SENTENCING, AND LEGAL ENFORCEMENT

According to the United Nations Office on Drugs and Crime (UNODC), effective drug control cannot exist without fair criminal justice and successful crime prevention. While formal sanctions and policies concerning drug-related activities can easily be instituted in a manner that is not damaging to human rights, often they are not. Nations vary in the severity of punishments for drug-related activity as well as in the number and types of crimes deemed illegal. From a human rights perspective, the most extreme and unacceptable is the utilization of the death penalty for drug-related offenses, as practiced by China (UNODC 2010). In other countries, such as the United States, human rights violations can manifest through the creation, implementation, and enforcement of racially biased or classist laws (HRW 2000).

The United States has been a leader in advocating and promulgating rigid legal sanctions for a host of minor and substantial drug-related offenses. Since President Richard Nixon first declared the "war on drugs" in the 1970s, drug-related human rights violations have increased domestically and internationally. The strict legislation and enhanced law enforcement that followed led to an astronomical number of people arrested and convicted for drug-related offenses. This spike in incarceration is widely documented as affecting African Americans disproportionately (McWhorter 2011; HRW 2000; SAMHSA 2010). A 2000 report by Human Rights Watch estimated that blacks comprised 62.7 percent and whites 36.7 percent of all drug offenders in prison, despite the fact that five times more whites use drugs than blacks (HRW 2000). According to a recent Bureau of Justice Statistics report, the arrest rate in 2009 for African Americans was three times that of whites for drug possession and four times that of whites for drug sale or manufacture (Snyder 2011). Human dignity cannot be delinked from the principle of nondiscrimination, and current US efforts are clearly biased against nonwhites. To be effective, criminal-justice processes must ensure that law-enforcement activities are evidence based and not carried out solely on the grounds of racial or class bias (UNODC 2010).

Less widely known is that the "war on drugs" produced a "war" on the rights to education, social security, and housing. Policies enacted in the 1990s resulted in the denial of high school education or college opportunities to tens of thousands of American students (Blumenson and Nilsen 2002). Due to federal zero-tolerance policies for drugs, 80 percent of students charged with drug or alcohol infractions were suspended or expelled from school in 2001 (CASA 2001), with African Americans being the most likely to be expelled or suspended. In 1998, black students comprised 17 percent of the American public-school student body but accounted for 33 percent of zero-tolerance suspensions or expulsions (CASA 2001). Poor or low-income students are doubly penalized in that they cannot afford private school.

Further representing an attack on the right to education is the US Drug-Free Student Loan Act of 1998, which can deny federal college loans and grants to students convicted of a misdemeanor or felony controlled-substances offense (Blumenson and Nilsen 2002; GAO 2005). It is estimated that during the 2003–2004 academic year alone, this act resulted in the disqualification of about forty-one thousand applicants for postsecondary education loans and grants (GAO 2005).

As regards rights to social security and an adequate standard of living, dignity, and affordable housing, under the Personal Responsibility and Work Opportunity Reconciliation Act of 1996, offenders convicted of a felony drug offense can be denied receipt of Temporary Assistance to Needy Families (TANF) and food stamps. Federal law mandates a lifetime ban on receiving these benefits, unless the stricture is modified by state law. In 2005, eighteen states had fully implemented the TANF ban (GAO 2005). It has been estimated that approximately 5 percent of public-housing applicants are disqualified because of a drug-related offense (GAO 2005).

The US Government Accountability Office report titled *Denial of Federal Benefits* explicitly states that these policies only affect those drug offenders who would otherwise meet the eligibility requirements for federal benefits, representing clear discrimination against poor and low-income individuals. In some cases, drug offenders can be exempt from these bans in federal service if they undergo rehabilitation or treatment services. However, this provision is biased against low-income persons—the very group most in need of student loans and college opportunities—who may not be able to afford the cost of treatment, transportation costs, or the lost wages from attending classes (Blumenson and Nilsen 2002).

HUMAN RIGHTS VIOLATIONS: INTERNATIONAL IMPLICATIONS OF US POLICY

While the United States is the largest consumer of illicit drugs, the vast majority of drug production occurs in other countries. Therefore, US drug policy extends around the world to reduce and contain the supply of drugs entering the country.

Targeted governments, particularly those in the Andean region of South America, argue that military-like policies are misdirected, and efforts should focus on the social and economic structural roots of the problem. Furthermore, while widespread impoverishment and the need to make an income spur many to become involved in drug production and trafficking, these activities exist largely to satisfy the large American market (Youngers and Rosin 2005).

An example of human rights violations produced through US drug-control strategies can be observed in Colombia. Because 90 percent of the cocaine in the United States originates in that country, aerial fumigation of coca fields emerged as a central strategy in the early 1980s and intensified under Plan Colombia. It is estimated that between 2000 and 2003, fumigation efforts destroyed coca on 380,000 hectares, or approximately 8 percent of Colombia's arable land (Lemus, Stanton, and Walsh 2005). Fumigation not only destroyed the environment but ruined the only economic option for peasants who grew coca. Between 2001 and 2003, more than seventy-five thousand Columbians were displaced due to crop fumigation, food scarcity, and, according to reports, painful skin, respiratory, and other ailments (Lemus, Stanton, and Walsh 2005).

A latent effect of efforts to reduce cocaine production and trafficking in Colombia has been the rise of Mexican drug cartels to take their place. The Department of Justice (2010) estimates that Mexican drug cartels directly control illegal drug markets in at least 230 American cities. Violence in Mexico has sharply escalated, largely due to the increase in drug-production and -trafficking activities. Since 2006, more than thirty-five thousand people have been killed in drug-related violence in Mexico (*Los Angeles Times* 2011). This does not include the countless others who have been kidnapped or tortured. Much of this violence initially took place between rival drug cartels, but now it is not unusual for civilians, police officials, activists, and family members of cartel members also to fall victim.

As a last example, the United States' labeling of drug traffickers as terrorists and cartels as terrorist organizations violates rules of war and human rights. This policy effectively renders nonmilitary persons objects for "justified" military intervention, despite international rhetoric condemning this position (Gallahue 2010). Although monies from drug production and distribution can and do benefit insurgent movements, this is not an activity that costs civilians their protected status and invalidates their placement on a "kill list." Drug trafficking is not synonymous with combat, and therefore such acts cannot be equated with direct military or combat participation (US 111th Cong. 2009). Yet, in 2009, the US Pentagon announced that fifty Afghan drug traffickers were now listed as people "to be killed or captured" (US 111th Cong. 2009).

HUMAN RIGHTS VIOLATIONS RELATED TO DEVELOPING NATIONS AND MARKET EXPLOITATION

The exploitation of land, labor, and people inherent in capitalism continues to shape alcohol, drug, and tobacco markets. The United States is a driving force behind consumer culture, including sale of alcohol and tobacco. These industries increasingly target developing nations as new markets. As such, we are seeing a global rise in alcohol and tobacco use, along with its individual and social consequences (Sengupta 2003). However, we fail to see a corresponding increase in the export of either accessible, affordable, and dignified treatment options for individuals who become addicted or just legislation related to illicit drugs. Perhaps this is because treatment is underemphasized in America, with approximately 10 percent of those who need treatment actually receiving it (SAMHSA 2010).

As the antismoking campaign gained momentum in the United States, multinational tobacco companies turned to undeveloped markets in impoverished countries. Although persons of consenting age are permitted to smoke cigarettes, the issue here is whether individuals in these nations are sufficiently aware of smoking's health consequences. Not only did marketing efforts entice people to smoke, but pro-tobacco policies extended to agriculture as well. To encourage peasant farmers in these nations to grow tobacco, tobacco corporations, the World Bank, and the UN Food and Agriculture Organization offered loans, extension advice, pesticides, and tobacco seeds (Motley 1987; Muller 1983). One estimate places the value of World Bank loans for tobacco production at $1 billion and rising (Nichter and Cartwright 1991). In most cases, this assistance has eroded traditional economies and endangered the production of food crops in lieu of tobacco's higher profits (Nichter and Cartwright 1991).

The word "drug" signifies both a substance that is illegal and prohibited by formal regulations and a substance to cure illness (Neilson and Bamyeh 2009). Economic forces shape pharmaceutical distribution as well. Pharmaceutical companies generate profit by controlling drug patents and monopolizing knowledge. Research, development, and marketing efforts are not solely driven by illness and disease patterns; rather, they are influenced by the profit motive and who can pay for treatment. Today, pharmaceutical research and development is skewed toward drugs for diseases most prevalent in developed countries, such as cancer, or "lifestyle" drugs, such as Viagra. Research estimates that only 4 percent of pharmaceutical research money goes toward developing new drugs for diseases, such as cholera, prevalent in developing countries. This means that only 10 percent of the $56 billion spent annually on medical research is for ailments that affect 90 percent of the world's population (Sengupta 2003).

THE RIGHT TO USE ALCOHOL, DRUGS, AND TOBACCO AND TO SEEK TREATMENT

The rights of the individual to use alcohol, drugs, or tobacco and to seek accessible, appropriate, and dignified treatment are also important. A caveat is that these rights are compromised when personal agency and informed choice are removed or when crimes are committed due to drug use (UNODC 2010). This is not to say that human rights principles support a general "right to abuse drugs" (UNODC 2010); rather, this position reminds us that personal responsibilities are interrelated with freedoms and rights. For example, the rights of smokers and nonsmokers are debated as smoking in public spaces is banned through national or local legislation around the world. At the center of this issue is informed consent as to the well-documented health risks associated with smoking. One on side, antismoking advocates point to the dangers of secondhand smoke and the inability of nonsmokers, children, and fetuses to give informed consent to smoking (Bailey 2004). However, smokers, tobacco corporations, and pro-tobacco lobbyists insist that adult smokers have the right to smoke and to incur associated risks so long as an "informed consumer risk" policy is in place (Viscusi 1998).

Drug dependency is recognized by virtually all international bodies and national organizations as a medical condition or disorder. From a human rights perspective, the right to health applies equally to drug dependency as it does to any other health condition. Through criminalization efforts to curb drug use, dependent drug users, particularly injecting drug users, suffer not only from the condition itself but also from a lack of effective programs, such as clean-needle and -syringe exchanges, and dignified psychosocial and pharmacological treatment (UNODC 2010; Elliott et al. 2005). These and similar socially responsible programs are fully compatible with international drug-control conventions (UNODC 2010), yet we continue to see a scarcity of such services nationally and globally. Intravenous drug users with HIV/AIDS are particularly vulnerable to human rights infringements (Wodak 1998; Elliot et al. 2005; Oppenheimer 1991), as criminal sanctions against drug use contribute to a lack of services and treatment options for this population. At the other end of the spectrum is the issue of forced or coerced substance-abuse treatment or drug testing. Nonconsensual treatment or testing endangers the right to health, to freedom from inhuman or degrading treatment, and to liberty and security of person, as well as the right not to be subjected to arbitrary or unlawful interference with privacy (UNODC 2010).

EMPLOYING A HUMAN RIGHTS APPROACH TO ALCOHOL, DRUGS, AND TOBACCO

As noted by the UN High Commissioner for Human Rights, drug laws frequently overemphasize criminalization and punishment while underemphasizing treatment and respect for human rights (UNODC 2010). Law-enforcement approaches toward drug policy are costly, ineffective, and often counterproductive to policy aims, yet law enforcement remains the major response toward illicit drugs in the United States and the international community. This trend is especially evident in the United States, where 82 percent of the 1.6 million arrests in 2009 were for drug possession alone (DOJ 2010). Despite high incarceration rates for drug possession, the threat of prison has not deterred Americans from using illicit drugs, which more than 47 percent of persons over the age of twelve admit to having done (SAMHSA 2010). The default position of the criminal-justice system is to punish substance users simply for using or being addicted to an illegal substance (Husak 2003).

As stricter drug possessions laws have not deterred drug use in America and are enacted across color lines, sociologists should reframe their research, applying a harm-reduction approach rather than a criminal-justice approach. In recent years, international and intergovernmental drug-policy reforms have attempted to incorporate protections of human rights for drug users through harm-reduction programs (Elliot et al. 2005). These programs differ from criminal-justice approaches because they work to decrease substance use and abuse in a dignified and just manner, rather than penalizing users and addicts. Informed consent, legalization, and decreased regulation of marijuana and other illicit drugs also fall under harm reduction. Many harm-reduction programs in the United Kingdom, Switzerland, and the Netherlands show evidence of positive outcomes and the protection of human rights.

We must revise legislation on substance addiction and abuse treatment based on current knowledge and human rights awareness. By curbing the demand for illegal drugs, we curb production, trafficking, and deadly violence. This entails the understanding that problems related to drugs and alcohol go beyond dependent individuals. Substance abuse cannot be examined or treated in a vacuum; therefore, prevention efforts should aim to improve human lives and communities, including by providing access to health care, education, and gainful employment (WHO 2001). As views toward addiction and substance abuse vary cross-culturally, the World Health Organization advises treatment programs to consider political feasibility, the capacity of a country or community to treat individuals, public acceptability, and the likelihood of impact (2001).

Lastly, we should invest in people and communities to eliminate poverty, provide fiscal opportunities within the mainstream of socioculturally acceptable limits, promote education, and give people the resources they need to make informed and rational choices to engage in drug-related activities of any sort. The United States can play a role by ending its "war on drugs" and fostering more equitable partnerships with drug-producing and -trafficking nations. To do this effectively, it should shape drug-control policy based on the sociocultural context within which drug production and circulation occur, and local needs and views. If this shift were to occur, poverty elimination and democratic development would become the centerpiece of the US drug policy in Latin America and the Caribbean (Youngers 2005).

Human rights violations related to alcohol, drugs, and tobacco occur on a continuum, but they all prevent individuals from realizing a dignified life in some manner. Drug-related problems are best analyzed within appropriate sociocultural frameworks. Sociology provides direction and methods to examine many of these problems, and its emphasis on the individual can clarify the different variations in drug-related activities across social groups. Further, sociology has shed light on the social inequalities created by unjust drug policies and the effects these laws have on individuals and their communities. This information on patterns of drug use and abuse complements human rights principles. A synthesis of sociology and human rights theory can locate these patterns in a globally situated analysis of the international drug circuit to better pinpoint areas for social change.

CHAPTER TWENTY-NINE

RATIONALITY AND SOCIETY

Valeska P. Korff, Mimi Zou, Tom Zwart, and Rafael Wittek

One of the key objectives of the international human rights movement is to institutionalize adherence to human rights principles in societies around the world. Institutionalization refers to a situation in which a set of rules is considered as legitimate, widely accepted, and "infused with value" (Selznick 1957, 17). The key argument we seek to elaborate in this chapter is that rational-choice theory and its core methodological principle, structural individualism, offers a valuable contribution to the human rights paradigm in general and to explaining variations in the institutionalization of human rights in particular. Structural individualism posits that all social phenomena on the macro and meso levels—like the institutionalization of human rights—need to be explained by referring, or descending, to the micro level of individual decisions and behavior. Hence, when explaining the structural conditions under which human rights become institutionalized in a society, we need to understand the decision-making and behavior of the involved actors.

While challenging the macro-level focus of human rights discourse, this proposition in fact is linked to a seminal development in legal conception: the emergence of the field of international criminal law. International criminal law and international human rights law are interlinked in many ways (De Than and Shorts 2003), whereby the former can basically be regarded as an individual-centered subcategory of the latter. Presupposing the responsibility of individual offenders for human rights violations, international criminal law departs from the main focus of international law on obligations of states. With the implementation of the Rome Statute and the establishment of the International Criminal Court (ICC), the individual has taken center stage in the area of international human rights. As we will elaborate, rational-choice theory provides a framework to accommodate the role of actors relevant in this context: offenders, prosecutors, and judges. By specifying the factors that shape these actors' decisions and behaviors, it allows us to systematize the inquiry into the conditions influencing the protection and promotion of human rights on the state or macro level.

KEY ASSUMPTIONS AND CONCEPTS OF RATIONAL-CHOICE THEORY

The theoretical tradition generally referred to as rational-choice theory incorporates a multiplicity of theoretical and methodological approaches (for accessible introductions, see, e.g., Elster [1989, 2007] and Little [1991, ch. 3]; for a more comprehensive treatment in sociology and philosophy, see, respectively, Coleman [1990] and Mele and Rawling [2004]). These share the key conviction that all social phenomena need to be explained as the outcomes of individual actions that can in some way be construed as rational (Goldthorpe 2007). Rationality refers to goal-directed behavior: individuals try to realize their preferences by selecting the best action alternative, taking into consideration the opportunities and constraints of the situation in which the decision takes place. This set of core assumptions underlies all rational-choice approaches and allows for theory building and formal modeling. While the respective interpretations of these core assumptions vary substantially between rational-choice approaches, all of them share the conviction that rationality, preferences, and individualism are crucial categories needed to explain human behavior and societal development.

Rationality assumptions refer to the extent to which an individual's decisions meet a set of internal consistency conditions (Bhattacharyya, Pattanaik, and Xu 2011). Individual rationality is shaped by an actor's perception of existing decision alternatives. This perception is in turn influenced by an actor's beliefs and the available information allowing for the evaluation of decision alternatives and their probable outcomes. Rational action is always based on the available information and beliefs, which together generate means-end frames (Simon 1957).

Preference assumptions refer to the extent to which individual decision-makers are selfish egoists striving to maximize material gain. Preference assumptions within the rational-choice paradigm range from "self-seeking with guile" to "linked-utility" assumptions in which individuals derive utility from solidarity acts toward others, without direct personal and material benefit for themselves.

Individualism is a methodological principle holding that any societal phenomena at the macro level can only be explained in a satisfactory way if the preferences, constraints, and behaviors of the involved individuals have been explicated. Thus, while the theoretical primacy (that is, the phenomenon to be explained) is situated at the macro level, the analytical primacy (that is, the social mechanisms leading to the behavior of individual actors) is located at the micro level of individual choices. While all rational-choice theory approaches uphold some individualism assumption, these can differ in the degree to which macro- and meso-level conditions, such as institutions or social structures, are incorporated into the explanation. Most sociological perspectives consider individual decision-makers as embedded in social contexts and influenced by institutions in their preferences and rationality (Udehn 2001). Consequently, a sociological rational-choice explanation needs to specify three steps: first, a macro-micro step, or *situational mechanism*, explicating how the social situation at the macro level affects the preferences and constraints of individual actors; second, a micro-micro step, or *action-generating mechanism*, specifying intra-individual decision-making processes and the resulting action; and third, a micro-macro step, or *transformation mechanism*, to explain the aggregation of individual action on the macro level (Hedström and Swedberg 1998). The relation between macro-level factors, individual perception and behavior, and macro-level outcomes is illustrated in Figure 29.1.

Figure 29.1 Mechanisms linking macro-level phenomena and micro-level behavior

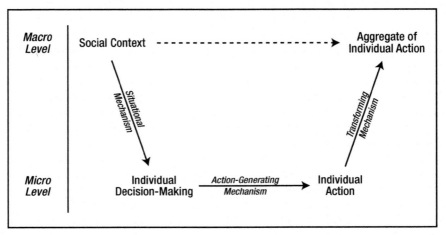

Flexibility in the interpretation of core assumptions makes rational-choice theory a broad and highly diverse theoretical paradigm integrating such distinct approaches as neoclassical economics and social-rationality conceptualizations (Lindenberg 2006a, 2006b; Macy and Flache 1995). Variation, however, is not limited to theoretical reasoning. In terms of empirical application, rational-choice models have been used to examine systematically a broad variety of social phenomena pertaining to basically all areas of human behavior and interaction. These studies make use of all methods commonly applied in the social sciences, including quantitative survey studies, psychological experiments, qualitative interviews, text analyses, ethnographic observations, and computer-assisted simulations. Irrespective of the chosen method, the focus of all rational-choice research is on individual behavior as the primary explanans of macro-level phenomena. Applying a rational-choice perspective to the study of the institutionalization of human rights accordingly implies a departure from the macro-level perspective common in this field and a new focus on the role of the diverse actors involved in the process.

INTERNATIONAL CRIMINAL LAW

International criminal law is a distinct body of law that comprises both principles of public international law—which human rights law has become part of (Brownlie

2008)—and criminal law. Its relatively recent development over the past fifty years reflects a departure from the "traditional" focus of international law, which only recognized rights and obligations of states and tended to ignore the individual as a subject of law. As an extension of criminal law at the national level, international criminal law regulates and punishes the conduct of individuals rather than states. Many of the crimes now defined by international law are also considered violations of the human rights of individuals (Ratner, Abrams, and Bischoff 2009).

International criminal law encompasses substantive aspects of international law that deal with defining and punishing international crimes and mechanisms and procedures used by states to facilitate international cooperation in investigating and enforcing national criminal law (Brown 2011). The sources of international criminal law are those of international law, which are usually considered to be treaty law, customary international law (a body of peremptory rules of international law, known as *jus cogens,* "the compelling law," from which states may not derogate), and general principles of law recognized by the world's major national legal systems (see Statute of the International Court of Justice, Article 38). It is not always straightforward to determine what constitutes a crime under international law. International treaties rarely explicitly declare something to be an international crime. Broadly speaking, crimes that have risen to the level of international *jus cogens* include aggression, genocide, crimes against humanity, and war crimes (Cassese et al. 2011).

The first international criminal tribunals were set up after World War II, when the Nuremberg and Tokyo International Military Tribunals tried key "war criminals" of the Axis powers for crimes against peace, crimes against humanity, and traditional war crimes. These trials marked the beginning of jurisprudence regarding individual criminal responsibility under international law. The next important step in the process was taken with the setting up of two ad hoc tribunals for the prosecution of crimes committed, respectively, in the former Yugoslavia (ICTY) in 1993 and in Rwanda (ICTR) in 1994. These tribunals represent major progress toward the institution of a kind of permanent jurisdiction (hybrid domestic-international tribunals have been established in Sierra Leone [2000], East Timor [2000], Kosovo [2000], Cambodia [2003], Bosnia [2005], and Lebanon [2007]). A permanent international criminal tribunal was finally established in 2002, when the Rome Statute of the ICC entered into force.

There is growing attention to the relationship between international criminal law and human rights law (Ratner, Abrams, and Bischoff 2009; De Than and Shorts 2003). Some recently adopted provisions of international criminal law appear to be influenced by human rights rules and standards of protection. For example, the Rome Statute refers to concepts such as "personal dignity," prohibition of "humiliating and degrading treatment," "judicial guarantees," and prohibition of group-/collective-based "persecution," discrimination, and apartheid. These concepts have all been established in the main UN instruments for the protection of the rights of the individual.

As a result of the establishment of numerous ad hoc and hybrid tribunals, as well as the permanent ICC, the individual has taken center stage in the area of international human rights.

A Rational-Choice Perspective on the Commitment, Prosecution, and Judgment of International Crimes

The recognition of individual responsibility in the prosecution of human rights violations under international criminal law calls for a better understanding of the motives and behavioral alternatives of the involved actors—offenders as well as prosecutors and judges. Rational-choice theory provides a heuristic suitable for such venture.

As previously described, the basic assumption underlying all rational-choice approaches is the notion that individuals act rationally in pursuit of their goals. Following the fundamental convictions of rational-choice theory, this rationality (that is, the actual decision-making process) is influenced by three factors: the actor's perception of decision alternatives, the preferences of the actor in the sense of the goals strategically pursued, and the constraints and opportunities faced by the actor, which determine behavioral alternatives. Examining the realization of these three dimensions forms the basis for understanding individual rational action. It allows tracing the reasoning that underlies observed behavior. Accordingly, these three dimensions form the core of the rational-choice research framework, which we propose in this chapter. The three dimensions not only directly shape the decision-making process but are also interrelated. Constraints and opportunities in the institutional and social environments influence the perceptions as well as the preferences of an actor. The available information and beliefs about opportunities and constraints shape an actor's evaluation of decision alternatives, which in turn influences preferences. Thus, an analysis of individual rationality implies the consideration of the available information and beliefs, of goals and preferences, and of opportunity/constraint structures simultaneously and in relation to each other.

Explaining Violations of International Criminal Law

Understanding the prevalence of structural human rights violations requires examining the conditions under which individuals violate international criminal law. Accordingly, as a first step we turn our attention to the offenders to inquire about the factors influencing their decisions to act in violation of international criminal law. Applying the above-outlined research framework, we assume that international crimes are a product of rational decision-making, influenced by the perpetrator's goals, perception of decision alternatives, and constraints and opportunities faced.

The case of the strategic use of violence against civilians by the Ugandan Allied Democratic Forces, including killing, looting, and forcible recruitment, constitutes a suitable example to explore this relation. Fundamentally, violence against civilians in civil wars appears irrational as it jeopardizes the loyalty of the very citizens for which both insurgents and incumbents compete. In the case of the Allied Democratic Forces, repeated attacks on villages and refugee camps indeed showed no substantial benefits in a military sense. Hovil and Werker (2005) argue that the violence was a rational tactic that served to maintain the support of external financiers, which included state sponsors such as Zaire and Sudan, as well as radical Islamist groups like al-Qaeda, which had a shared interest in destabilizing the Ugandan government. In a situation of asymmetric information between the insurgents and their financiers, where the latter were, due to being distanced from the actual events, not in a position to judge the reality of the battle, the highly visible atrocities and excessive violence were a credible signal through which the rebels could demonstrate their true commitment to the rebellion. Looking at the three analytical dimensions outlined above, the underlying reasoning becomes comprehensible. A main goal of the Allied Democratic Forces was to secure its survival as an organization. Strong dependence on the resources provided by external financiers posed a major constraint. At the same time, the threat of sanctions for violence against civilians was very limited. Finally, in terms of perception, the asymmetric information structure between Allied Democratic Forces and financiers led the Allied Democratic Forces to consider excessive campaigns against civilians as a necessary signal of commitment to the financier. Under these conditions, the apparently irrational and ineffective strategy of violence against civilians appears in a different light and can be understood as a result of a rational effort to maintain financier support.

EXPLAINING PROSECUTION DECISIONS

The second aspect to consider is the prosecution of international crimes. The powers of the prosecutor who acts before the ICC are mainly discretionary. Although the Rome Statute offers some criteria, they are vague enough not to fetter the prosecutor. Accordingly, critical inquiries are needed to understand how the prosecutor's beliefs and goals and the constraint/opportunity structure influence the decision to bring a case before an international tribunal.

The Republic of Uganda submitted the first case to the ICC, which related to the atrocities committed by the Lord's Resistance Army (LRA), a violent rebel group, in the northern part of the country. There are strong indications that President Yoweri Museveni made the referral for strategic reasons (Nouwen and Werner 2010; Branch 2007): unable to beat the LRA, he saw "outsourcing" the fight to the ICC as a viable option. Involvement in an ICC case would delegitimize the LRA, which would diminish its support by external suppliers. Interestingly, the prosecutor accepted the referral in the proposed form. In a statement he declared that even though both sides may have engaged in crimes, those committed by the regular army were not of "sufficient gravity"—which is one of the admissibility criteria in the Rome Statute—while those committed by the LRA were. This meant that only atrocities by the LRA were actually brought before the ICC.

Taking into account the constraint and opportunity structure faced by the prosecutor, this startling decision becomes comprehensible. As a fully equipped court without any live cases, the ICC had increasingly come under criticism. The fundamental goal of the prosecutor under these conditions was the legitimization of the ICC. Prosecuting the LRA, while granting immunity to the regular army, generated a case urgently needed to establish the legitimacy and relevance of the ICC. The prosecutor went to even further lengths to secure this case, thereby effectively limiting his power to discontinue a case and substantially fettering his discretion. While apparently irrational, this approach likely constitutes a structural strategy of depoliticizing through legalizing (Ferguson 1994). Portraying the Office of the Prosecutor as a neutral, expert body that is unwilling to engage in political negotiations, the prosecutor justifies his actions by presenting them as dictated by law and by downplaying the political dimension.

EXPLAINING TRIBUNAL DECISIONS

The final rationality to examine is that of the court, or, more specifically, the decision-making that informs the ruling of judges. In order to examine the factors influencing such decisions, we draw on Epstein and Knight's (1998) work on the strategic behavior of judges.

This perspective considers judges and courts as strategic actors who make rational decisions in pursuit of a variety of goals. The implementation of his or her own policy preferences may be the goal of the judge, but there are other potential aims as well, such as the desire to reach "principled" decisions based on impartial doctrines, the strengthening of the institutional legitimacy of the court, and using a career on the court as a stepping stone for political office. In addition, the strategic model assumes that judges carefully calculate the consequences of their choices. It postulates that judges are strategic actors who realize that their ability to achieve their goals depends on a consideration not only of the preferences of others, such as their colleagues on the bench, the political branches, and the public at large, but of the choices they expect others to make. Judges will also take into consideration the institutional context within which they act, for instance, the concept of stare decisis, which can constrain them from acting on their individual policy preferences. Epstein and Knight's (1998) assumptions concerning the factors influencing judges' rulings correspond closely to our previously outlined research framework. A judge's ruling is shaped by his or her goals as well as by his or her general perception of decision alternatives and potential outcomes, given existing constraints and opportunities.

While the ICC has yet to hand down a judgment, in its dealings with prospective cases, strategic behavior can be observed. The above-mentioned example of the LRA case again illustrates this. The ICC's Pre-Trial Chamber, much like the prosecutor and likely for similar reasons, did its best to secure the first case. When it became known that national proceedings were being initiated that might trump the ICC's jurisdiction under the concept of complementarity, it made clear, on its own initiative, that the ICC and not Uganda determines whether a case is admissible (Nouwen and Werner 2010, 17).

Previously, however, the Trial Chamber has twice decided to discontinue proceedings against a defendant because the prosecutor, in its view, did not play by the rules. On the first occasion, Trial Chamber judges suspended the trial against Lubanga, a Congolese militia leader accused of recruiting and deploying child soldiers, because the prosecutor was unwilling to disclose information that might exonerate the defendant. On the second occasion, Trial Chamber judges found that the prosecutor had ignored their order to reveal the identity of an intermediary who had been assisting witnesses. Several possible explanations for the judges' position have been put forward. It has been argued that the Trial Chamber judges showed their commitment to a fair trial to enhance the ICC's legitimacy (Anoushirvani 2010). An alternative view is that the judges were eager to slap the prosecutor on the wrist for ignoring due-process requirements to achieve results (Verrijn 2008). In each instance there was a risk that Lubanga would walk free as a result of these actions, which would have been a very serious consequence. However, in both cases the prosecutor was saved by the Appeals Chamber. In the second case, while agreeing with the Trial Chamber judges that the prosecutor had violated the rules, judges of the Appeals Chamber emphasized that there were less drastic means to correct that behavior, compared to letting Lubanga walk away, such as imposing sanctions on the prosecutor. The Appeals Chamber judges felt that the Trial Chamber judges should have considered imposing disciplinary sanctions on the prosecutor as an alternative in this case. It looks as though the Appeals Chamber was eager to caution and reprimand the prosecutor—perhaps to display the fair-trial image—while being unwilling to let the trial collapse.

In their acceptance or rejection of cases, the different chambers of the ICC obviously pursue a variety of goals: sanctioning perceived misbehavior of the prosecutor, establishing legitimacy, and demonstrating authority. Their actions thereby are influenced by each other, as well as by the general political environment. Thus, the judges certainly do not decide in an apolitical and mechanical way; on the contrary, they appear to navigate complex constraint and opportunity structures in their pursuit of diverse and partly even contradictory goals.

THE (DE)INSTITUTIONALIZATION OF HUMAN RIGHTS

Rational-choice theory contends that macro-level phenomena are aggregate outcomes of micro-level action. Thus, the institutionalization of a human rights regime depends on the behavior of individual actors, which in turn is guided by their rational pursuit of goals. Individual actors' rationality, hence their behavior, is influenced by three factors: their perception of decision alternatives based on the available information and their general beliefs, their distinct preferences and goals, and the constraints and opportunities they face.

These fundamental assumptions are of crucial relevance to understanding the institutionalization of human rights on the macro level. Following them we can deduce that the institutionalization of human rights in a society requires that individual actors act in accordance with the related legal and normative principles. As actors are rational and goal-oriented, acting in accordance with human rights has to be the most advantageous and beneficial action alternative for the individual. Finally, as the evaluation of decision alternatives fundamentally depends on an actor's beliefs, the information available to him or her, and the constraints and opportunities faced, these factors can be considered determinants for the successful institutionalization of a human rights regime.

More specifically, in order to make it rational for individual actors to act in accordance with and in support of human rights, several conditions need to be fulfilled: First, individuals need to be well educated about human rights and the consequences of violating them. Second, these consequences or sanctions—both formal and informal—need to be substantial and to outweigh the potential benefits of defection. Third, opportunities need to favor behavior that respects human rights. Fourth, resources need to be available to allow for the provision of information about human rights and for the implementation of sanctions—positive and negative. Under such conditions, human rights adherence is the most sensible option, which in the aggregate enables the institutionalization of human rights. Responsibility for establishing and implementing the necessary conditions lies with the state and its agencies. The ideologies represented and the sanctions enforced by a government have fundamental effects on the behavior of its subjects.

Genocides, as the structural and systematic destruction of a people by a state bureaucracy, constitute the most horrifying expressions of just how intensive such influence can be (Horowitz 1980). Cases such as Nazi Germany, the former Yugoslavia, and Rwanda exemplify the potentially devastating capacity of states to reframe their subjects' perceptions (e.g., Sekulic, Massey, and Hodson 2006; Prunier 1997; Brubaker 1996). The systematic dehumanization of certain social groups, together with the creation of opportunities for members of the majority to benefit from the exertion of violence, creates a frame in which systematic violations of human rights become a rational means of goal pursuit. This certainly paints a bleak picture, yet at the same time creates a ray of hope. If governments can succeed in making rational individuals commit heinous acts that require the repression of fundamental feelings of empathy and pity, they are also able to make it reasonable for individuals to respect each other's dignity and act in accordance with the principles of human rights.

Human rights are not just an abstract ideal transcending social reality, but also can become integrated as guiding principles of rational human action. The "receptor approach" developed at the Netherlands Institute of Human Rights constitutes an original and auspicious perspective on how such integration could be implemented (Zou and Zwart 2011). Following Moore (1978) in conceptualizing behavior as influenced by a diversity of institutions—informal norms and values as well as the formal legal framework—this approach contends that human rights need to be aligned to the local context in order to be successfully implemented. Such alignment is facilitated by identifying local institutions that match certain human rights and can serve as "receptors" through which the respective principles can be introduced (Zou and Zwart 2011). Preventing dissonance between the formal legal structure and local institutions, the receptor approach provides a strategy to make human rights an influential factor in individual decision-making.

LEARNING FROM A HUMAN RIGHTS PARADIGM

Rational-choice theory is a general theory of action. As any such theory, its core assumptions (e.g., concerning human nature) are subject to constant refinement, and it has to face empirical findings that do not match its theoretical predictions.

Human rights issues are one of the many substantive domains in which the theory can be applied. Their empirical investigation may shed light on a classical puzzle of rational-choice theory: the explanation for cooperation and collective action where actors incur considerable costs without expecting immediate benefits (Scott 2000). The historical and social process of the development and dissemination of the human rights paradigm constitutes a powerful example. Looking at the implementation of human rights in a nation's legislation requires understanding why a government is willing to invest in an effort that effectively restricts its power without necessarily involving immediate benefits. Which considerations and motivations, or, more specifically, which rationalities, underlie such behavior? Or, as human rights scholar David Moore summarizes it, "Rational choice theory has not provided a comprehensive explanation of why a nation would find it in its self-interest to conform to human rights norms when it is not compelled to do so by domestic influences and is not coerced" (2003, 880). Inspired by this problem, Moore develops a signaling model of states' human rights compliance, building on assumptions of strategic rationality as formulated in game theory. More generally, empirical research on the institutionalization of human rights regimes and on the conditions of compliance with or violation of human rights principles may provide invaluable case material to inform recent rational-choice scholarship on altruistic or costly punishment in particular (Fehr and Gächter 2002) and the link between decision theory and morality in general (Dreier 2004).

The establishment of a human rights regime requires the realization of actors' perceptions of decision alternatives, goals and preferences, and opportunities and constraints in a way that makes acting in accordance with human rights principles the most advantageous, hence rational, action alternative. It is the responsibility of governments to implement such conditions. A culturally sensitive approach that aligns general human rights principles and local institutions presumably constitutes the most viable strategy to achieve this objective, thus making human rights the rational choice.

CHAPTER THIRTY

INTERNATIONAL MIGRATION

Tanya Golash-Boza

A human rights perspective presumes the fundamental dignity of all people, regardless of national origin, and recognizes that people are members of families and communities (Blau and Moncada 2005, 29). A consideration of the human rights impact of international migration requires the recognition that people have rights not just as citizens of a particular nation-state but as human beings. A human rights analysis necessitates a consideration of how immigration policies affect all people—not solely or primarily citizens of particular countries.

Taking a human rights perspective, we are compelled to see migrants not simply as workers but as husbands, fathers, brothers, wives, mothers, sisters, and community members. As human beings, migrants have the right to be with their families and to be full members of the communities in which they live. These family and community rights are enshrined in the Universal Declaration of Human Rights (UDHR), as well as other declarations. Not only is the importance of these rights internationally recognized, but their realization is fundamental to creating a better society for all. Although the UDHR is not a legally binding doctrine in the United States, it can serve as a moral compass for those of us who believe that all human beings deserve rights and dignity, regardless of national origin.

When we center the human rights paradigm in international-migration scholarship, we change our focus from the costs and benefits of international migration for sending and receiving countries and begin to consider the global, human impact of international migration and immigration control. Centering the human rights paradigm in the field of international migration would fundamentally change how sociologists approach the study of international migration.

THE SOCIOLOGY OF INTERNATIONAL MIGRATION

International-migration scholars are concerned with the movement of people across borders. Sociologists who study international migration ask how many people migrate, who migrates, why people migrate, what happens to them once they arrive in the host country, and how migration affects sending communities.

HOW MANY INTERNATIONAL MIGRANTS ARE THERE?

To understand how many international migrants there are in the world and in a given country, international-migration scholars develop models. These models measure migration flows, estimate how many immigrants are legally and illegally present in a given country, and consider the extent to which migration is temporary or permanent. Quantifying international migration allows for an analysis of how migration flows change over time and in response to structural forces and changes. Gaining an understanding of the scope of international migration lays the groundwork for other sociological explorations of this phenomenon.

HOW MANY MIGRANTS ARE THERE AROUND THE WORLD?

According to the United Nations, there were 214 million international migrants worldwide—3 percent of the world's population—in 2010. International migration has been on the rise over the past few decades: there were 155 million international migrants in 1990 and 178 million at the turn of the twenty-first century. About half of all migrants are women. The gender balance has been constant since at least 1990 (UN 2008).

HOW MANY MIGRANTS ARE THERE IN THE UNITED STATES?

About a fifth of all international migrants—43 million people—can be found in the United States. International migrants account for 13 percent of the US population (UN 2008). About 10 million of these migrants are undocumented; 85 percent of undocumented migrants in the United States come from just ten countries: Mexico (6.65 million), El Salvador (530,000), Guatemala (480,000), Honduras (320,000), Philippines (270,000), India (200,000), Korea (200,000), Ecuador (170,000), Brazil (150,000), and China (120,000) (Rytina, Hoefer, and Baker 2010). Although many undocumented migrants come from Asia, Asian migrants are rarely deported from the United States: 95 percent of the 393,289 people deported from the United States in 2009 were from just ten countries, all in Latin America (Department of Homeland Security 2010, "Immigration Enforcement Actions: 2009").

WHY DO PEOPLE EMIGRATE?

Most people in the world never leave their home country. Why, then, do some decide to venture out across international borders? International-migration scholars answer these questions by considering how the agency of individual migrants intersects with the structural constraints and possibilities of migration.

A major area of scholarship is the development of theories to explain international migration. Some contend that migration is linked to relations between countries. These scholars argue that foreign direct investment, trade, labor recruitment, and military interventions influence migration flows (Sassen 1989; Golash-Boza 2011). These analyses explain why most migrants to the United States come from just a few countries. Others point to the importance of migrant networks to explain why migration is highly localized—people leave one village in Mexico or Thailand and move to the same neighborhood in San Francisco, California, or Winston-Salem, North Carolina (Rumbaut 1994; Massey, Durand, and Malone 2002). Although one set of factors may lead to migration, once migration flows have begun, new circumstances develop that lead to the perpetuation of these flows (Massey, Durand, and Malone 2002).

International-migration scholars explain that people migrate due to a combination of individual and structural factors. They point out that Emma Lazarus's poem engraved on the Statue of Liberty, which describes immigrants as poor, huddled masses, is inaccurate: the people who migrate to the United States are not the most destitute in the world. In 2009, more than 1 million people became legal permanent residents of the United States. Only 6,718 of them came from the five poorest countries in the world. Nearly half (3,165) of the migrants from the five poorest countries hailed from Afghanistan, a country in the midst of a US military occupation. Niger, the poorest country in the world, only sent 183 legal permanent residents to the United States in 2009 (UN Human Development Reports 2010; Department of Homeland Security 2009).

Documented and undocumented migrants do not come to the United States simply because they are poor, according to international-migration scholars. They come because of strong ties to the United States. Labor recruitment, military interventions, and foreign direct investment create and sustain migration flows (Sassen 1989; Golash-Boza 2011). Countries with long histories of labor migration, such as Mexico and the Philippines, continue to send migrants to the United States because these histories have created strong ties between the countries. In addition, family-reunification policies in the United States encourage further migration by giving preference to those with family members living in the country. This process is known as cumulative causation: migration begets more migration (Massey, Durand, and Malone 2002; Massey 1988).

Military intervention can lead to migration due to the ties it creates as well as the turmoil that ensues. Migration flows develop due to amorous relationships between US soldiers and locals and the emergence of close ties between people in the United States and the country at hand, such as, for example, when Filipinos were recruited to join the US Navy (Rumbaut 1994). The United States has been involved militarily with nearly all the countries that send migrants to the United States (Golash-Boza 2011). In some cases, military interventions create outflows of refugees because of the violence of military operations.

Scholars who look specifically at refugee flows analyze the reasons people find themselves forced to leave their countries of birth. The concept of the refugee was developed in the aftermath of World War I to describe the situation of Armenians fleeing Turkey and Russians fleeing the revolution there (Petersen 1978). Over the past century, the numbers of refugees have increased, and refugees come from dozens of countries. The United Nations High Commissioner for Refugees (2010) estimated that there were more than 15 million refugees in need of resettlement in 2010.

Foreign direct investment creates migration flows through its inevitable effects on the local economy and the integration of the country into the global economy. In an analysis of twenty-five developing countries, Sanderson and Kentor found that "the stock of foreign direct investment has a long-term positive effect on emigration" (2008, 529). These factors have led to both legal and illegal migration to the United States.

WHAT HAPPENS TO MIGRANTS?

Another major area of study for international-migration scholars involves an analysis of what happens to voluntary labor migrants and refugees upon reaching their destinations. These scholars consider both how immigrants incorporate into the host society and the extent to which they maintain ties to the home country. Scholars whose primary framework involves an analysis of assimilation measure the extent to which migrants maintain their culture and language, their incorporation into the labor market, and residential patterns (see Alba and Nee 1997; Gans 1997; Gordon 1964; Portes and Rumbaut 2001). Those whose primary mode of analysis revolves around transnational ties consider the extent to which migrants maintain ties to their home country through travel, international communications, and links to conationals in the host country (see Goldring 1998; Guarnizo, Portes, and Haller 2003; Guarnizo and Smith 1998; Mahler 1998; Popkin 1999).

Migrants Assimilate

There are two kinds of international migrants: sojourners and settlers. Sojourners are those who travel to a new country for a fixed period to work, visit, or study and plan to return to their country of origin. Settlers are those who intend to stay. Sociologists often explore the incorporation processes for settlers. The dominant paradigm in sociology is assimilation: the process by which an immigrant settler and future generations of immigrants become part of the host country. The concept of assimilation has been criticized insofar as it seems to imply that immigrants have no option but to become part of a monolithic culture; in reality, the host culture often changes with the arrival of immigrants, and immigrants vary greatly in the ways that they become part of the host society. Scholars such as Richard Alba and Victor Nee (1997) defend the concept of assimilation by pointing out that immigrants can assimilate in many ways: the descendants of the Irish may become part of the Euro-American mainstream, whereas the descendants of Caribbean black immigrants may become part of the African American community.

Migrants Maintain Transnational Ties

Although many international migrants seek to remain in their host countries, they are often inclined to maintain ties with their home countries. Sociologists refer to the cross-border interactions of international migrants as transnational ties. The concept of transnationalism derives from the works of anthropologists

Linda Basch, Nina Glick Schiller, and Cristina Szanton Blanc (1994), who argue that contemporary cross-border connections are qualitatively and quantitatively different from those in previous eras in that the relations are more intimate and persistent than ever before.

Recent work in sociology questions both how assimilation works and the extent to which migrants maintain transnational ties. Luis Guarnizo, Alejandro Portes, and William Haller (2003) point out that the maintenance of contacts across borders is perhaps as old as international migration itself, and they contend that only a small subset of international migrants actually engages in cross-border activities on a consistent basis. Remarkably, they also find that transnationalism and assimilation are not at odds: migrants' lengths of stay in the United States do not reduce the likelihood of their maintaining contact with their home countries.

WHAT ARE THE CONSEQUENCES OF INTERNATIONAL MIGRATION?

Sociologists join economists and other scholars in exploring the cultural, social, and economic impact of international migration on sending and receiving locales (Borjas 2004). Understanding the economic impact allows social scientists to inform policy-makers. Discussions of the cultural and social impact of international migration permit scholars to help communities plan for the future of their changing locales. In terms of sending communities, two primary areas of concern revolve around the "brain drain" and the extent to which migration helps or hinders economic and social development in poor countries (Meyer 2001). Concerns over the exodus of highly trained professionals have been present for migrant-sending nations at least since the 1960s (Petersen 1978). The debate over whether migration helps or hinders development is far from settled. Hein De Hass (2010) posits that the contention over the benefits of emigration and remittances arises from the fact that each community and country presents a unique situation. In some cases, remittances help local development; in other cases, emigration upsets local economies and unsettles whole communities.

Sociologists also explore the extent to which migrants help or hinder the economy, the effects of immigration on crime, and how immigrants transform the cities and towns in which they live (Ghosh 1992; Lipton 1980; Lisborg 1993; Rumbaut and Ewing 2007; Taylor 1999). Although many people in the United States associate undocumented migration with crime, Rubén Rumbaut and Walter Ewing (2007) demonstrate with convincing data that immigrants in the United States have lower crime and incarceration rates than their native-born counterparts. They further contend that the flow of immigrants into the United States in recent years is one reason that crime rates in the United States have declined. Their study provides one example of how immigration can change receiving communities in profound ways.

WHAT TOOLS DO SOCIOLOGISTS USE TO STUDY MIGRATION?

Sociologists use a variety of methodological tools to study migration. Those who wish to gain an in-depth understanding of the local-level effects of international migration and to comprehend the decision-making processes of migrants use ethnography and in-depth interviews (Levitt 2001). Scholars who are interested in large-scale trends of international migration draw from census data and surveys (Guarnizo, Portes, and Haller 2003; Rumbaut and Portes 2001). Demographers paint broad pictures of flows around the world (Durand et al. 1996). Those scholars interested in media and popular-cultural representations draw from textual and content analyses (Diaz-McConnell 2011), and comparative historical sociologists often use archival data in addition to other sources (Brubaker 1990). Sociologists also use mixed methods: one of the most innovative techniques developed by Douglas Massey and his colleagues specifically for the study of international migration is the ethnosurvey, which combines qualitative and quantitative data in a single data-gathering and -analysis strategy (Massey and Zenteno 2000).

WHAT CAN THE HUMAN RIGHTS PARADIGM LEARN FROM THE STUDY OF INTERNATIONAL MIGRATION?

Work in the field of international migration renders it evident that migrants do not live in a vacuum and that connections between countries are intimate and persistent. Human rights scholars who ponder the ethical and philosophical bases of immigration controls can learn from migration scholars that (1) people emigrate from one community to another because of specific ties between their communities, (2) emigration affects sending communities because of the transnational ties it creates and the social and economic remittances migrants send, (3) sojourners often become settlers because of restrictive immigration controls, and (4) the impacts of immigrants on communities in the receiving countries are often profound and frequently positive. The findings from the work of international-migration scholars have important implications for any consideration of the right to mobility.

The work of international migration scholars on the incorporation patterns of migrants also has important bearings for consideration of the cultural rights of migrants. Human rights researchers who ask what protections should hold for migrants' rights to their cultural beliefs and customs can learn from international-migration researchers about the ways in which holding on to cultural beliefs can inhibit as well as enhance migrants' success. Human rights scholars can learn from this field that states' efforts at inclusion can have wide-ranging effects on migrants as well as the communities in which they live.

WHAT HAPPENS WHEN WE CENTER THE HUMAN RIGHTS PARADIGM IN INTERNATIONAL-MIGRATION RESEARCH?

International-migration scholars most often ask why people migrate and what happens to them once they do. This work often takes national borders as givens—people cross or do not cross these borders for a variety of reasons.

A human rights paradigm pushes us to ask a whole new set of questions. What fundamental human dignities are people deprived of in their choice to migrate? What human rights violations do they experience upon arriving in their host countries? What special arrangements need to be made for refugees and asylees? How does the international community deal with migrants deprived of a nationality and who have no country to which they can return? To what extent does international migration allow people to realize their full potential? How are transnational ties necessary to ensure the human rights of migrants and their families? How would ideas of assimilation change were human rights to be considered? And how could we create a world in which people's right not to migrate would be realized?

Whereas international-migration scholars tend to focus on the citizenship rights of individuals, the human rights paradigm allows us to focus on the fundamental rights all people share—not as members of particular nation-states but by virtue of their status as human beings.

Debates in the field of international migration frequently revolve around the economic and cultural costs and benefits of immigration. A human rights analysis compels us to calculate the human costs and benefits. Putting human rights first means asking a different set of questions. For example, some critics who argue that undocumented migration has a negative economic impact include the costs of education for US-citizen children of undocumented migrants in their analyses. A human rights analysis would see education as a fundamental human right and children as deserving of special protections. Others argue that undocumented migrants bring down wages. For example, George Borjas (2004) contends that low-skilled immigrants are only beneficial to their employers, whereas they lower the wages of their native low-skilled counterparts. A human rights analysis would insist that all workers deserve a living wage. Economist Barry Chiswick (1988) points out that low-skilled foreign workers can be economically beneficial, so long as they do not bring their nonworking family members with them to the United States. A human rights analysis considers family unity to be an inalienable right.

WHERE DO WE GO FROM HERE?

Human beings—no matter their national origin—possess fundamental human dignity. The task for researchers is to figure out ways to make it clear that people's rights should depend not on their national origin but on their status as human beings. How can we convince the public and governing bodies that recognizing human rights should take precedence in all decisions? How can we develop scholarship that demonstrates that the rights to mobility, to be with one's family, to shelter, and to a clean environment are all fundamental human rights that should be recognized? How can we render it clear that rather than, Why are they here? the question is, How can we create a world in which the decision to migrate (or not) is a choice and not a survival tactic?

As sociologists, we have a wealth of information and data that can demonstrate the importance of the right to mobility in a globalizing world. We would do well to use that data to bolster human rights claims. A prime example is that sociologists have extensive evidence of how emigration changes sending communities. Human rights scholars who debate the moral bases of the right to mobility benefit when they are able to take into account not only the ways that emigration can be economically beneficial to an individual, but also the extent to which it can change the nature of the community he or she leaves behind.

In human rights scholarship, debate continues around what a right to mobility would look like. For instance, does the right to mobility require open borders and the free movement of people? Does it imply that all people deserve the economic capital requisite for international travel? Or does it shift the burden of proof to states, saying that they must admit noncitizens unless they can provide a valid reason to deny them entry? The right to mobility is undertheorized and underdeveloped both in sociology and in human rights scholarship more generally.

The right to mobility does not form part of current human rights documents. In the human rights tradition, the right to leave one's country is recognized. However, the right to enter another country does not form part of existing human rights conventions and treaties. This leads many critics to argue that the right to mobility is a serious omission in human rights treaties. The right to emigrate is effectively useless if there is no country to which one can migrate (Pécoud and de Guchteneire 2006). Joseph Nevins (2003) adds to this discussion the fact that, in a globalizing world rampant with economic inequality, the human rights to free choice of employment and to an adequate standard of living enshrined in the UDHR are difficult to achieve without the ability to leave one's country of origin.

If human beings had the right to mobility, then states would have to provide compelling reasons to deny individuals the right to enter their territories. One possibility would be to shift the burden of proof, such that states would be required to provide reasons a person should not enter as opposed to the current situation, where it is up to individuals to prove that they deserve to enter another country. This would be one way of incorporating the right to mobility into human rights doctrine. Can we imagine human rights doctrines holding that states shall, except when compelling reasons of national security otherwise require, allow noncitizens to enter their territories? What does the right to mobility mean? What would it actually look like? Crucially, does the right to mobility require open borders?

These questions remain unanswered for human rights scholars (Pécoud and de Guchteneire 2006; Bauböck 2009). There certainly are many immigration scholars who argue for open borders, including, for example, Nandita Sharma, Kevin Johnson, Jonathan Moses, Jane Guskin, and David Wilson. As Guskin and Wilson (2007) point out, open borders would save us billions of dollars in immigration law enforcement, increase tax revenues since all workers would pay payroll taxes, raise wages and improve working conditions since we would no longer have a disenfranchised workforce, and eliminate criminal activity associated with undocumented migration, such as identity theft and human trafficking.

It is now time for human rights scholars to take on these questions and to begin a conversation within the United Nations that explores the extent to which a right to mobility could be incorporated into human rights doctrine.

CHAPTER THIRTY-ONE

LABOR AND LABOR MOVEMENTS

Héctor L. Delgado

The human rights and labor rights movements share the fundamental goal of improving human beings' quality of life. While the labor movement is more focused on ensuring that workers can feed themselves and their families, work in a safe environment, and have a voice in the workplace, the ability of workers to secure these rights has consequences far beyond the workplace and typically requires the right to associate freely, a fundamental human right found in several human rights instruments. It is difficult to imagine an aspect of workers' lives with farther-reaching consequences than their ability to secure food and lodging for themselves and their families. In fact, fulfillment of many human rights depends, in some measure at least, on individuals' ability to do just that. Yet, as Leary observes in her seminal article on labor rights as human rights, "the human rights movement and the labor movement run on tracks that are sometimes parallel and rarely meet" (1996, 22). Since Leary's observation in 1996, however, the tracks have started to converge and on occasion cross.

A good bellwether of human rights status, Leary (1996, 22) observes, is workers' rights. But human rights activists have not paid nearly the same attention to economic and social rights as they have to civil and political rights abuses, such as genocide, torture, murder by death squads, and arbitrary arrests and imprisonment (Gross and Compa 2009; Leary 1996; Craven 1995). The tendency has been to view workers' rights, principally if not purely, as economic disputes between workers and their bosses. The following statement by the United Nations Committee on Economic, Social, and Cultural Rights in 1993, however, suggests that some human rights activists recognize the need to pay more attention to labor rights: "Despite the rhetoric, violations of civil and political rights continue to be treated as though they were far more serious, and more patently intolerable, than massive and direct denials of economic, social, and cultural rights" (quoted in Steiner, Alston, and Goodman 2008, 264).

Labor activists and scholars, in turn, have rarely employed a human rights perspective or analysis. But this appears to be changing. In 2005, the AFL-CIO issued a brief stating that freedom of association is a human right that employers too often deny workers, created a "Voice at Work" campaign that referred to the right to organize for a better life as a "basic human right," and held more than one hundred demonstrations and took out full-page ads in newspapers throughout the country in support of workers' human rights, enlisting the signatures of eleven Nobel Prize winners, including the Dalai Lama and Archbishop Desmond Tutu.

The National Employment Law Project (NELP) was created to protect immigrant workers' rights. NELP has filed numerous complaints with international agencies on behalf of immigrant workers in the United States. In concert with Mexican colleagues, NELP sought and received a favorable opinion from the Inter-American Court regarding mistreatment of undocumented workers in the United States. The AFL-CIO filed a complaint with the International Labour Organization's (ILO) Committee on Freedom of Association in response to the US Supreme Court's *Hoffman Plastic Compounds, Inc. v. NLRB* (2002) decision denying undocumented workers back-pay remedies in the event of an unfair labor practice by the employer (Gross 2009).

Observing that sociology should contribute more to scholarly discussions of human rights, the University of Warwick's Sociology of Human Rights website posted a list of question areas sociologists can help find answers to: "historical questions about the emergence of human rights; conceptual questions concerning the relation of human rights to other forms of rights, including civil, political and social rights; normative questions concerning the right of all human beings to have rights; and critical questions concerning the legitimacy of human rights." The first two areas are especially relevant to sociologists of labor and labor movements. Why did it take so long for the labor and human rights movements to collaborate, if not merge, and how can the human rights movement's emphasis on civil, political, and individual rights be reconciled with the labor movement's emphasis on economic, social, and collective rights? Despite labor activists' and scholars' significant movement toward a human rights paradigm, there is still a long road ahead, and it is not one without hazards.

RESEARCH ON LABOR AND THE LABOR MOVEMENT

Sociologists are indeed assigning greater importance to human rights, as evidenced by new human rights sections of the American Sociological Association and the International Sociological Association and new publications such as this edited volume and Blau and Frezzo's *Sociology and Human Rights: A Bill of Rights for the Twentieth-First Century.* For the first half of the twentieth century, the study of labor and the labor movement was dominated by the Wisconsin School and economists and labor historians Richard Ely (1886), Selig Perlman (1922, 1928), and John Commons (Commons et al. 1910–1911, 1918–1935). The Wisconsin School played an important role in the creation of industrial relations as a field of serious scholarship and helped to pave the road for US business unionism, but it began to diminish in importance in academic circles after World War II as new scholars introduced new perspectives and approaches (Devinatz 2003). Among these new scholars were David Brody (1960, 1965, 1979), Irving Bernstein

(1960b, 1970), and Herbert Gutman (1961, 1962, 1976). They and a new crop of labor historians were inspired by work of British historians E. P. Thompson (1963) and Eric Hobsbawm (1964) to write a "new labor history" from workers' perspectives.

Scholarly interest in labor has not waned since the 1970s; rather, it has flourished, as Kimeldorf and Stepan-Norris (1992) note in a review of historical and sociological studies of the US labor movement. This research has been driven by several key questions, beginning with the notion of exceptionalism in terms of why the US labor movement has failed to develop a socialist philosophy or program (see Laslett 1970; Laslett and Lipset 1974; Mink 1986; Zolberg 1986; Wilentz 1984; Foner 1984) and issues such as employers' sustained assault on unionization and workers' rights (see Klare 1978; Casebeer 1989; Cornfield 1989; Quadagno 1988; Goldfield 1989; McCammon 1990; Wallace, Rubin, and Smith 1988). A second set of questions, Kimeldorf and Stepan-Norris (1992) observe, focuses on workplace dynamics in the industrial sector, which includes research on one of the most important questions for labor scholars: What explains the rapid decline in union membership over the past fifty years? Some scholars have identified as culprits the migration of production from high-union-density regions to regions less friendly to unions and the decline in blue-collar jobs. Other scholars attribute blame to organized labor's failure to invest more resources into organizing and employers' resistance to unionization (see Bluestone and Harrison 1982; Bernstein 1960a; Goldfield 1987; Freeman and Medoff 1984; Lipset 1960; Fantasia 1988; Griffin, Wallace, and Rubin 1986). Measures employers adopt to resist unionization, both legal and illegal, deserve sociological analyses that focus on what a human rights regime deems to be the universal human right to form organizations.

Other studies have focused on the labor movement's organizational history, especially major events in that history that helped to shape the movement. Here, as Kimeldorf and Stepan-Norris (1992) observe, recent sociological work makes an important contribution by linking unionization efforts to larger processes, essential in any discussion of labor rights as human rights (for a review of this literature, see Brody 1979; Kimeldorf 1991). Another important body of research has drawn on concepts of social-movement research. This social-movements approach is especially relevant to a discussion of labor rights as human rights as well. "Thinking of organized labor as a social movement ... has been a needed corrective—emphasizing contingency and contestation—to earlier sociological analysis, which focused on trade unions as organizations and workers as individuals with varying political attitudes (or on the individual correlates of their political behavior)" (Kimeldorf and Stepan-Norris 1992, 509; see also Griffin, Wallace, and Rubin 1986; Voss 1992; Moody 1997).

Rights Discourse

If the labor movement succeeds in casting labor issues as human rights, it may benefit from a rights language, or discourse, that has existed in the United States from its inception and especially since the civil rights movement. Sociology is unrivaled in its scholarship on the black civil, women's, gay/lesbian, and other rights movements. "In no other large country is rights consciousness of greater potency, in the law, in culture, in foreign policy, in the subtleties of daily life and language" (Lichtenstein 2003, 64). But some of these studies reveal that the labor movement was slow to support the civil rights struggles of the 1950s. The mainstream labor movement, which had fought doggedly for higher wages and better working conditions for white workers for more than a century, was much less dogged about the rights of black workers. In fact, for much of its history, organized labor closed its doors to native workers of color and immigrants. Slowly, however, the mainstream labor movement began supporting important civil rights legislation, such as the Civil Rights Act of 1964 and the Voting Rights Act of 1965.

Reluctant to organize immigrant workers initially, unions began to organize them principally out of necessity. Eventually the AFL-CIO leadership officially endorsed the organization of immigrant workers, including the undocumented, when in 2000 its executive council adopted a pro-immigrant resolution in favor of a new amnesty program for undocumented immigrants and repeal of the employer-sanctions provision of the Immigration Reform and Control Act of 1986. By defending the rights of black and immigrant workers, the AFL-CIO put itself in a better position to invoke a rights discourse and to regain trust lost abroad due to the activities of several foreign arms, including the federation's principal Latin American arm, the government-funded and CIA-connected American Institute for Free Labor Development (Sims 1992; Cantor and Schor 1987).

WHY UNIONS MATTER

In many respects, the demands of the black civil rights movement were fundamentally the same as labor's, as the Reverend Martin Luther King Jr. proclaimed at the AFL-CIO's Fourth Constitutional Convention in December 1961: "Our needs are identical with labor's needs: Decent wages, fair working conditions, livable housing, old-age security, health and welfare measures, conditions in which families can grow, have education for their children, and respect in the community" (1986). Unions have played an indispensable role in securing these things for workers. In an Economic Policy Institute (EPI) briefing paper, Mishel and Walters (2003) noted that unionized workers' wages were 20 percent higher than those of their nonunion counterparts, and unionized workers were more likely to have paid leave, health insurance provided by their employer, and a pension plan. It is worth noting as well that the labor movement played an integral role in the enactment of laws and regulations protecting all workers, including the Social Security, Occupational Safety and Health, and Family Medical Leave acts, measures addressing fundamental human rights. Furthermore, unions have secured for workers, especially for their members, recognition that workers are not simply commodities but human beings with rights, including the right to be treated with dignity and respect (see Freeman and Medoff 1984; Yates 2009). The erosion of union membership and power over the past fifty years, then, should alarm human rights activists as much as it does their organized labor counterparts.

Since Dr. King's proclamation in 1961, union membership has declined precipitously. In 2010, 6.9 percent of nonagricultural, private-sector workers enjoyed union representation, down from 37 percent in 1960. Unionization among public-sector workers is much higher at 36.2 percent but is in danger of falling if Republican governors and legislators are successful in their bids to weaken public-sector unions (Bureau of Labor Statistics 2011). At the same time, the income and wealth gaps in the United States have widened appreciably. For example, in 2009 the top 1 percent of the US population averaged nearly $14 million in wealth, while the lowest quintile, on average, owed more than their assets' value. The top 1 percent of the population owned 35.6 percent of all net worth, while the bottom 90 percent owned only 25 percent of all net worth (Allegretto 2011). Between 1949 and 1979, the richest 10 percent of the country received 33 percent of the growth in income, but between 2000 and 2007, it received all the growth (EPI 2011). While organized labor's interest in a human rights regime is opening up new research avenues and is likely to lead to more international and interdisciplinary labor scholarship, sociologists can argue for expansion of human rights or, at minimum, prevail on the human rights community to assign far greater importance to economic, social, and cultural rights.

To claim the human and labor rights movements historically have run on parallel tracks is not to say that human rights bodies have not promoted rights of relevance to workers. Founded in 1919 following the end of World War I, the International Labour Organization (ILO) focuses on social justice as a means of promoting peace. Its Convention 98, adopted in 1949, recognizes workers' right to organize and bargain collectively, free from employer interference. Other conventions supporting workers' rights can be found in the Universal Declaration of Human Rights (UDHR), the International Covenant on Civil and Political Rights, and the International Covenant on Economic, Social, and Cultural Rights (ICESCR). The rights in these declarations or covenants include freedom of association, such as the right to join trade unions and bargain collectively; the rights to be paid equally for comparable work, to protection from discrimination in employment, and to be safe in the workplace; and child labor prohibitions. UDHR Article 23 includes rights "to just and favourable conditions of work," to "remuneration ensuring for [oneself] and [one's] family an existence worthy of human dignity," and "to join trade unions for the protection of [one's] interests." Existence of these rights creates space for the labor movement to promote workers' rights.

HUMAN RIGHTS AND LABOR RIGHTS DISCOURSES

Organized labor may gain by adopting discourse and strategies that have proved effective for the human rights movement, especially given labor's waning membership, power, and popularity. In fact, according to a 2010 PEW Research survey, only 41 percent of people polled had a favorable opinion of unions, down 19 percent from 2007. While 61 percent agreed that unions were necessary to protect working people, an equal percentage agreed that unions had too much power—up from 52 percent in 1999 (PEW 2010). Clearly, unions have a lot of heavy lifting to do on the public-relations front, but labor might lighten its load if it adopts a human rights approach and if the human rights movement serves increasingly as an advocate for labor rights (Kolben 2010, 461). But this approach is likely to have an empowering psychological impact on union members as well (Gross and Compa 2009, 8).

While the marriage of human and labor rights seems obvious, not everyone agrees; at the very least, there are those who believe labor should proceed with caution. As Kolben observes,

> While strategic deployment of human rights discourse might appear to be advantageous in the short run, the fundamental differences between this discourse and that of labor rights may inhibit the long-term effectiveness of this approach.... The strategies, politics, culture, and ideologies that inform much of the U.S. human rights establishment are quite at odds with those of the labor rights movement, and a serious human rights turn risks weakening commitment to the economic justice and workplace democracy principles that have long underpinned labor rights thought and practice. (2010, 452)

Kolben is not alone. In the *Harvard Law School Human Rights Journal*, Kennedy (2002) recommends a more pragmatic attitude toward human rights due to the fact that they do not address a central issue for labor: redistribution. Another area of concern for Kennedy (2002) is whether human rights might minimize the focus on collective responsibility, a salient difference between labor and human rights, also noted by Kolben. "While human rights concern individuals and, arguably, achieve outcomes such as better working conditions, labor rights are more collectively oriented, and worker mobilization and negotiations processes take precedence" (Kolben 2010, 452). In a similar vein, labor historian David Brody (2001) expressed his own misgivings in a critique of Human Rights Watch's (HRW) 2000 report on labor rights in the United States.

Brody observed that in promoting stronger free speech for workers and not less for employers, the report failed to apprehend what the 1934 Wagner Act's authors understood: that employer speech is more powerful and "inherently" coercive. Employers did understand and worked successfully to restore such speech. In 1947, the Taft-Hartley Act gave employers relatively free rein to use measures to prevent unionization, including mandatory captive-audience meetings with workers and plant-closure threats if workers voted for union representation. Taft-Hartley weakened workers' position dramatically. Recent attempts to enact the Employee Free Choice Act, an antidote to Taft-Hartley, have not gained much traction. US workers are on their own in a legal system that favors their employers. Brody's concern is that "human rights analysis" might deflect workers from this reality and the "hard thinking" required "to negotiate a way through, or around" it (2001, 604). In addition, proponents of a labor rights as human rights perspective face some human rights advocates who treat workers' claims as goals, not rights.

RIGHTS VERSUS GOALS

"Human rights" typically refers to civil and political rights, with an individual rights emphasis. Economic and social rights take a back seat to these rights and are seen by some, if not many, human rights activists principally as desirable goals rather than as rights in the same sense as, for example, the right not to be tortured. Do individuals, for example, have a right to a subsistence wage and basic health care? Do collectivities have rights comparable to individual rights? International human rights documents, despite their emphasis on civil, political, and individual rights, do contain provisions that reflect a concern for rights deemed economic or social, and even collective, with the freedom of association being the most notable. Instead of adding economic and social rights to their list of human rights, the United Nations drafted the International Covenant on Economic, Social, and Cultural Rights, adopted by the General Assembly in 1966, to address them.

The covenant recognizes, in accordance with the UDHR, people's right to self-determination and to pursue "economic, social and cultural development" (Article 1, 1). In Article 7, parties to the covenant agree to recognize everyone's right to enjoy fair and favorable work conditions. Article 8 (a) recognizes the right of "everyone" to form and join trade unions. The United Nations is more equivocal about these rights than it is about civic and political rights. The same article states that no restrictions can be placed on these rights, "other than those prescribed by law and which are necessary in a democratic society in the interests of national security or public order or for the protection of the rights and freedoms of others." The right to strike must conform to national laws in which a union operates. The most ominous provision in the article for organized labor, at least in the United States, says, "This article shall not prevent the imposition of lawful restrictions on the exercise of these rights by members of the armed forces or of the police or of the administration of the State."

The covenant does refer to the 1948 ILO convention, especially its granting of freedom of association and the right to organize, stating that nothing in the covenant authorizes legislative bodies to pass laws that would "prejudice" guarantees that the ILO convention provides. But while the ILO convention provides important guarantees for workers, an Article 2 provision makes very clear that economic, social, and cultural rights enumerated in the ICESCR convention lack the urgency of civic and political rights. In effect, economic and social "rights" are characterized more as goals than as rights. The fact that limitations to these rights can only be exercised to promote "the general welfare in a democratic society" is of little consolation in a country in which a growing majority believes that unions benefit their members but harm society.

Historically, for a claim to constitute a right, it had to satisfy several conditions. According to Beetham, "It must be fundamental and universal; it must in principle be definable in justiciable form; it should be clear who has the duty to uphold or implement the right; and the responsible agency should possess the capacity to fulfill its obligation" (1995, 41–42). Arguably, the rights specified in the ICESCR covenant do not satisfy these conditions. This is not only an intellectual but a political explanation for why economic and social claims do not (and should not) rise to the level of rights, since these types of claims, as Kennedy notes (2002), typically require a redistribution of power and wealth down, which economic and political elites are reluctant to embrace. But another factor works against a program to guarantee basic economic and social rights: market forces have eroded governments' capacities to determine their economic destinies. "The structures of power and interest and the forces at work in the international economy and within developing countries themselves," Beetham observes, "pull remorselessly in the opposite direction to a basic rights agenda" (1995, 56–57).

Freedom of association and collective bargaining, abolition of forced labor, elimination of child labor, and freedom from discrimination, according to Kolben, differ from other labor rights because they "do not necessarily require a given level of economic advancement and arguably do not impact comparative advantage" (2010, 454). Organized labor's focus is on the first freedom, but Kolben notes a more expansive view among some scholars. These include a number of "social" rights, such as the right to "full and productive employment," as found in the ICESCR and labor-related social rights contained in the UDHR. Other scholars disagree. Social rights, they argue, depend on economic context, in effect converting a right into a goal and thereby diluting its moral authority. Goals, however, Nickel (2010) avers, can approximate rights if formulated correctly.

Goals gain currency when you are able to assign responsibility, identify beneficiaries, provide reasons for their importance, and assign a level of urgency. International agencies must monitor goals. One advantage of treating rights as goals is that they do not then appear ridiculous in those instances in which a country simply does not have the resources to realize them. "Goals are inherently ability-calibrated" (Nickel 2010). While it is easy to see why someone would characterize a goal as a poor substitute for a right, the goal would still have more power and a greater sense of urgency if it were endorsed internationally and by human rights organizations. The countries that ratified the ICESCR, Nickel points out, agreed to "take steps, individually and through international assistance and co-operation to the maximum of [their] available resources, with a view to achieving progressively the full realization of the rights recognized in the present Covenant" (2010). In a move reminiscent of US affirmative action, and drawing on sociological literature on institutional discrimination, international bodies could conceivably require a plan and timetable and apply sanctions to governments not making good-faith efforts to realize goals.

INTERNATIONALIZING LABOR RIGHTS

While the US decline in union membership and power in the past forty years has been especially pronounced, it is a worldwide phenomenon. Globalization has blurred the employer-employee relationship. "Whereas employees used to work for an identifiable common employer, today they occupy an uncertain location on a global production and distribution chain" (Lichtenstein 2003, 61). In this environment unions are challenged to organize workers and protect their rights. To the degree that unions are principally focused on workers' rights in their own countries, and to the degree that union federations are simply another arm of the government, as they are in some countries, the task is a daunting one. It is difficult to imagine, however, completing the task without a universal standard of labor rights or goals and a labor movement that is not boxed in by national borders. Capital certainly is not.

The human rights movement, international in makeup and scope, can serve both as a model for an international labor movement and as a vehicle for workers' rights advocates. The human rights movement has not experienced the same decline as the labor movement and, in fact, can claim to be stronger today than it was forty years ago. HRW, for example, saw its budget increase from $200,000 in 1979 to $20 million by 2001 (Lichtenstein 2003, 63). Consequently, in its attempts to survive, let alone retrieve lost members and power, US organized labor may not have a choice but to cast labor issues as human rights issues and to align itself when and where it can with the human rights movement, labor movements in other countries, and other progressive US movements and organizations. The task is facilitated by the fact that many human rights documents contain provisions that speak to workers' rights. In the process, organized labor will position itself to persuade international human rights groups to broaden their human rights definitions and to rethink the mutually exclusive distinction made between civil and political rights on the one hand and economic and social rights on the other.

While establishing a set of workers' rights recognized by the international community is essential, enforcement is problematic. Government inspectors, Lichtenstein (2003) notes, are incapable, adding that only an organization representing workers has the resources and expertise to ensure protection of workers' rights, just as the NAACP and other organizations have worked to protect the rights of and advocate for African Americans. A second problem noted by Lichtenstein is that settlement of disputes is taken out of the hands of those most directly affected and placed instead in the hands of government bureaucrats if workers do not have their own representative organizations. Third, workers end up having less control over the work environment because they cannot confront capital directly. Finally, the rights revolution has done little to create a climate conducive to a strong labor movement or to scale back capital's power in determining economic conditions under which workers labor.

Lichtenstein and others are not saying that a vigorous human rights movement is not important to labor. He applauds the ILO's and other international bodies' conventions and the work of organizations such as Amnesty International and Human Rights Watch. The enforcement of civil and human rights in the workplace and of any right that impacts an individual's ability to make a living and to provide for a family is essential. But "without a bold and society-shaping political and social program, human rights can devolve into something approximating libertarian individualism" (Lichtenstein 2003, 71). Trade unions, especially an international trade union movement, can be the vehicles for this "society-shaping political and social program." Whether they can be that and still pitch economic concerns in human rights terms is less certain and certainly a question that sociologists should attempt to answer. It seems clear that doing so will require an expansive view of human rights, expressed succinctly by Beetham: "The idea of economic and social rights as human rights expresses the moral intuition that, in a world rich in resources and the accumulation of human knowledge, everyone ought to be guaranteed the basic means for sustaining life, and that those denied these are victims of a fundamental injustice" (1995, 44).

The culprits, as the human rights movement suggests, are individual states, but the lion's share of the blame is perhaps best placed on corporations—extraordinarily powerful entities that not only are not reined in easily by states but can in fact dictate to states. The United Nations is not a formidable adversary either for these behemoths. At the national level, a resurgent labor movement is one of the few counterweights to this kind of power. Ultimately, a unified and powerful international trade union movement is needed to check the power of these multinational corporations. Without it and a strong international human rights movement, human and labor rights are not likely to flourish. The human rights and labor movements may not need to run on the same track. Parallel tracks that at various junctions converge may not only be sufficient but in fact may be preferable to allow each movement the freedom it needs to secure fundamental rights for everyone, including workers. Their respective goals, however, must at least be compatible, if not the same.

≋

CHAPTER THIRTY-TWO

EVOLUTION, BIOLOGY, AND SOCIETY

Rosemary L. Hopcroft

The Evolution, Biology and Society Section of the American Sociological Association was established in 2004 to facilitate the integration of biology into what was at the time, and still is, a highly biophobic discipline. Much of this biophobia stems from early work attempting to incorporate biology into sociology in such a way as to reinforce the prejudices of the researcher and justify existing social inequalities between classes, races, and sexes (see Gould 1981 for a review of this work). Yet current biosocial sociologists distance themselves from the faulty methods and reasoning of this early work. Rather than exacerbating existing social inequalities and reinforcing prejudices, I argue in this chapter that integration of biology into sociology can help to further the most humane goals of sociologists, in particular a concern for human rights. The biological unity of humankind and the universality of human nature underline the notion "that all men are created equal," an assumption that is the basis of most declarations of human rights. The biosocial view argues strongly against biologically based divisions between groups, but it does not deny that socially created divisions between groups exist. I argue that dissemination of information about the biological unity of the human group, coupled with understandings of the biological underpinnings of many social phenomena, can contribute to the breaking down of social divisions.

Scholars from a variety of areas were involved in the creation of the Evolution, Biology and Society Section, which is reflected in the wide range of topics it currently encompasses. Topics range from micro- to macrosociological, with the unifying feature being an acknowledgment of the role of biology in human social life. Researchers in the area use a variety of sociological methodologies as well as research results from a wide array of disciplines, including anthropology, history, primatology, paleoanthropology, biology, psychology, and neurology. The questions asked pertain to actors from individuals to whole societies and are relevant to all social institutions and structures.

The field focuses on how the universal, evolved human biology interacts with particular social environments to produce and respond simultaneously to social institutions and structures. In what follows I review the major strands of research within the evolution, biology, and society field (emotions and social behavior, neurosociology, evolution and social behavior, genes and social behavior, hormones and social behavior, and evolutionary macrosociology) and describe some of the major methods and findings within each. I also discuss what the human rights paradigm can learn from the work in this area and, conversely, what the field can learn from the human rights paradigm.

EMOTIONS AND SOCIAL BEHAVIOR

The first major strand of research within the area is microsociological in orientation in that it begins with individual emotions. The primary question for these researchers is, How are our social, symbolic, and emotional selves grounded in our shared, evolved human biology? Turner (2007) and others (Turner and Maryanski 2008; Turner and Stets 2006; Massey 2004) have focused on the implications of evolution for human emotions and the role of emotions in both social solidarity and social change. Their work is based on information from primatology, behavioral ecology, and paleoanthropology.

Turner and Maryanski (2008) trace the evolution of the human species from the early primates, through the last common ancestor of all apes, to the emergence of modern humans. They suggest that for hominoid societies to exist on the open savannah after leaving the relative shelter and safety of the forest, there was likely selection for stronger ties between individuals. They suggest that selection pressures leading to heightened individual emotions, first selected as a means to control noise levels in new, more dangerous environments, were the basis on which social solidarity could build. They show how the areas of the human brain (particularly the amygdala) that control emotions are much larger in humans than in other, less social apes. They draw on contemporary research showing the importance of emotions for human bonding, social interaction, and human reasoning. They further suggest that selection pressures for stronger ties produced the nuclear family and the hunting-and-gathering band. In another work, Turner and Maryanski (2005) argue that the development of incest taboos helped to consolidate human solidarity. Turner and Maryanski (2005, 2008) thus draw a picture of the evolved human that emerged some 150,000 years ago and has changed little since: an individualistic hominid, linked by emotional ties to group members but resistant to domination by other hominids. They note that this is the human nature that cultures have built on but not eradicated.

Other scholars within this group examine how social relations and situations in turn influence human emotions (Stets and Asencio 2008; TenHouten 2005). For example, TenHouten (2005) shows how experiences with four elementary social relations, described as market pricing, authority ranking, communal sharing, and equality matching, are linked to eight basic emotions (acceptance, disgust, happiness, sadness, anger, fear, anticipation, and surprise). Robinson, Rogalin, and Smith-Lovin (2004) discuss how the experience of in-group interactions (e.g., having high or low status) influences emotional and physiological states. Much of the research shows that occupying a low-status position is more stressful than occupying a high-status position. Massey (2004) argues that long-term exposure to stress and violence produces a high allostatic load in African Americans, and this has a variety of deleterious health and cognitive outcomes (see also Davis and Were 2008).

This research reveals the nature of humans as emotional beings with a fundamental social focus, and the human rights paradigm can benefit from a consideration of the social and emotional, as well as the economic, needs of individuals. Researchers in the area can contribute to human rights goals by examining how human emotions and social solidarity can be used both to support and to violate human rights goals.

NEUROSOCIOLOGY

The second primary area of research in the section may be referred to as neurosociology. Franks (2010) and others (Franks and Smith 2009; Smith 2004; Hammond 2004) have been interested in work in neuroscience as it relates to emotions and other aspects of cognition. They examine the neurological basis of emotions, unconscious behavior, the role of mirror neurons in imitation and empathy, and how the social self is based on brain processes. This draws on findings in neurological research using fMRI and PET scans to examine how different parts of the brain are involved in social behaviors and emotions.

Findings include the importance of normal social interactions for the development of the individual brain and the development of the self. Another finding is the fact that the individual is not conscious of the large majority of what the brain does, perhaps as much as 80 percent. Last, contrary to many beliefs, emotion is the basis of rational decision-making. For people to make sensible decisions, the available choices must have an emotional valence. When that emotional valence is missing, for whatever reason, the person cannot make rational decisions.

Franks (2010) notes that research on mirror neurons supports the work of the Chicago pragmatists. Mirror neurons are neurons in the brain that mimic the neurons of others. So when a person falls and feels pain neurons in his or her brain fire, the same neurons in the brain of a person witnessing the event also fire. This means that, to a certain extent, the witness actually feels the faller's pain. As a result, mirror neurons are importantly involved in empathy. They are also involved in helping individuals to see how others see them, and this is an important component of the development of self-identity and self-esteem. This is the mechanism for what Charles Horton Cooley referred to as the "looking-glass self," although Cooley, of course, was not aware of the neural basis of the phenomenon he described (Franks 2010). Other neurosociologists show how additional social processes are based on the existing neurology of the human brain. For example, Hammond (2004) shows how social experiences such as religious experience piggyback on neurological circuits evolved for different purposes.

The area of neurosociology once again shows the importance of a normal social life for individual well-being. The human rights paradigm can shape work in this area through a renewed focus on the implications of our neurology for the functioning of small groups—for example, group solidarity, status processes, and conflict—and their consequences for human rights. Methodologically, more work with groups from outside Western cultures would be helpful.

EVOLUTION AND SOCIAL BEHAVIOR

This next area of research takes the opposite stance to the microsociological research discussed above—that is, evolved human universals are assumed to shape culture and aggregate social behavior in all societies, and the question is how they do so. The focus is thus on aggregate trends across human societies. Research has been done primarily in six areas: family processes and fertility, sex differences, religion, crime, ethnic behavior, and sociological theory. Each of these areas is discussed below. Methods used include standard statistical methods such as survey methods and analysis of existing data, experimental methods, as well as more qualitative methods such as field research and comparative historical sociology.

Pioneering work in the area of the family using the evolutionary perspective was done by van den Berghe (1979). He notes the centrality of kin processes in all societies, as well as commonalities in mate choice and parenting across societies. For example, in all human societies women marry men who are older than they are, on average, although the age gap varies across cultures. In all human societies women perform the majority of childcare, whether for their own children or the children of others (Brewster and Rindfuss 2000, 272). In the United States, Biblarz and Raftery (1999) found the counterintuitive finding that single mothers are better at sponsoring the educational and occupational attainment of their children than reconstituted families, and they note this is consistent with evolutionary theory that posits greater investment by women than men in their children, on average. In terms of measured investment, adopted children receive more investment than biological children, but this is because adoptive parents have higher socioeconomic status than other parents (Hamilton, Cheng, and Powell 2007). Adjusting for parental income, adoptive parents invest at the same rate as biological parents. There have been tests of the Trivers-Willard hypothesis of biased investment in sons and daughters by family income in the United States, with mixed results both supportive of Trivers-Willard (Hopcroft 2005) and not supportive (Freese and Powell 1999). Work focusing on male fertility finds that for men, and not women, personal earnings are positively associated with number of biological children in the United States, Sweden, and the United Kingdom (Hopcroft 2005; Fieder and Huber 2007; Nettle and Pollet 2008)

Researchers also note a variety of sex differences they suggest have an evolved basis. A comprehensive survey of sex differences was published by Ellis et al. (2008). Rossi (1984) noted sex differences in parenting behavior in the United States. Other researchers have examined the sex difference in depression (Hopcroft and Bradley 2007); some have examined the implications of sex differences for gender inequality (Huber 2007; Ellis 2001; Hopcroft 2009).

Sanderson (2008) has argued for an evolutionary perspective on religion. He argues that during the human evolutionary period religiosity was an adaptive trait—that is, it helped individuals survive and reproduce—and this has ensured a universal predisposition toward religious sentiments. Miller and Stark (2002) have suggested that the sex difference in religiosity may be innate and hence evolved, although others prefer socialization arguments (e.g., Collett and Lizardo 2009).

Regarding crime, Ellis (2004; see also Savage and Vila 2003) notes that universally young men are more involved in crime than any other group. Ellis argues that there are evolutionary reasons to explain this. Crime may be seen as a risky way of attaining status and resources. In the evolutionary environment, there was likely selection for traits promoting status-striving behavior in males. This encourages males to use a variety of methods to attain status—even risky methods if others are not available. Ethnic behavior such as altruism to fellow ethnic group members is another universal human phenomenon, examined by van den Berghe (1981), who argues that ethnic behavior may be seen as an extension of kin selection to the wider ethnic group (see also Whitmeyer 1997).

The implications of evolutionary theory for sociological theory have been evaluated by a number of authors. Blute (2006, 2010) examines the possibility of using models from evolutionary biology to model cultural evolution. Kiser and Welser (2010) have made a similar argument for comparative historical sociology. Sanderson (2001, 2007; see also Horne 2004) has argued that materialist theories need help from evolutionary theories particularly to explain many nonrational behaviors. Hopcroft (2008) has suggested that evolutionary theory can help create a unifying paradigm for sociology, as many of the pro-social behaviors of interest to sociologists (within the family, for example) are likely based on evolved predispositions.

Much work remains to be done on the entire range of human social behaviors—family, race and ethnicity, stratification, fertility, and gender. Family is of particular interest to the human rights paradigm, as the Universal Declaration of Human Rights singles out special protection for the family as follows: "The family is the natural and fundamental group unit of society and is entitled to protection by society." Understanding human universals in the family and how they contribute to individual well-being will further both this subfield and the human rights paradigm.

GENES AND SOCIAL BEHAVIOR

The next area is primarily focused on individual variation and is the focus of significant current research. The central question in this area is, How do human genetic potentials interact with specific social contexts to produce social behavior? This is macrosociology because the researchers generally use statistical methods to find patterns in large data sets. Much of this research relies on DNA data collection along with typical survey data on attitudes and behaviors. One of the major data sets is the National Longitudinal Study of Adolescent Health (Add Health), collected by researchers at the University of North Carolina, Chapel Hill. Using these data, criminologist Kevin Beaver (2008; Vaughn et al. 2009) and Guang Guo,

Michael Roettger, and Tianji Cai have examined the interaction between genes and environment in criminal and delinquent behavior. Using a variety of data sets, researchers have examined the interaction of genes and environment in substance dependence (Button et al. 2009), smoking (Boardman, Blalock, and Pampel 2010), and drinking (Pescosolido et al. 2008; Guo et al. 2009). A variety of studies also examine the interaction of genes and social contexts in physical and mental health (Adkins, Wang, and Elder 2008; Kendler, Jaffee, and Romer 2010). Other researchers have examined the relative effects of genes on educational attainment (Shanahan, Bauldry, and Freeman 2008), happiness (Schnittker 2008), age at first intercourse (Guo and Tong 2006), number of sexual partners (Guo, Tong, and Cai 2008), and fertility behavior (Kohler, Rodgers, and Christensen 1999, 2002).

One general finding that emerges from a number of these studies is that genetic influence on behavior is stronger during affluent periods when individuals (presumably) have more choice. This has been capitalized on by Nielsen (2006), who suggests that the degree to which individuals achieve genetic potential can reflect the opportunities present in their societies (see also Adkins and Vaisey 2009). Although this generally rises with affluence, there is variation in such opportunities across developed societies.

One limitation of this area, as Perrin and Hedwig (2007) have argued, is that it focuses too much on individuals and too little on social contexts. This is in part because most of the early research in the area was produced by nonsociologists, who are less aware of social contexts and their roles in shaping behavior. Sociologists engaging in this work are less likely to make this mistake (Shanahan et al. 2010). A human rights approach should maintain the focus on the importance of context and keep in mind that individual variability exists within overarching universals. After all, human beings share the vast majority of their genes, and genetic variants are only a tiny fraction of the entire human genome.

HORMONES AND SOCIAL BEHAVIOR

Other researchers examine the effects of various hormones on individual behavior. The central question in this area is, What is the role of hormones in human social behavior? Some of this research shows the direct relationship between hormones and social behavior. For example, Mazur (2004; Mazur and Booth 1998) has shown that the hormone testosterone fluctuates with social position: winning competitions causes a rise in testosterone; conversely losing in competitions causes a fall in testosterone. These effects of winning and losing even extend to people who watch sports. During the 1994 World Cup in which Brazil beat Italy, the Brazilian fans who watched the match on TV saw a rise in testosterone after the game, whereas the Italian fans who watched the match saw a decline (Dabbs and Dabbs 2000). Udry (2000) examined how different in utero exposure to testosterone was associated with women's gendered behavior thirty years later.

Other researchers note there is a complex interaction between hormones and social context. Updegraff, Booth, and Thayer (2006) show that testosterone's effects are dependent on social context: when boys had close relationships with their moth-ers and sisters, testosterone was positively associated with peer involvement and competence; the reverse held when they did not have close relationships with their mothers and sisters. Booth, Johnson, and Granger (2005) likewise found that the effects of husbands' testosterone levels on marital quality depended on whether the husbands perceived high levels of role overload.

Much of this research has focused on easily measured biochemicals such as testosterone and cortisol (e.g., Booth, Granger, and Shirtcliff 2008), and much of it has focused on the effects in males. Much less research has focused on females. A human rights perspective necessitates that more attention be given to women. Future work should examine the range of socially related biochemicals and their interactions with social contexts, as well as examine both women and men. Another area of study promoted by human rights approaches is the effect of human-made biochemicals (such as antibiotics and steroids routinely given to farm animals, biochemical residuals in the water supply, etc.) in the environment and their effects on human health.

EVOLUTIONARY MACROSOCIOLOGY

The last area is a macrosociological one that examines large-scale societal change and the evolution of human societies. The primary question for these researchers is, What are the constraints placed by human nature on social arrangements and social change at the macro-level? The primary method is comparative-historical.

Gerhard Lenski (1966, 2005), the pioneering scholar in this area, was the first to note the importance of subsistence technology in shaping social arrange-ments and the degree of social stratification. Lenski's conclusion that a society's subsistence technology (hunting and gathering, horticulture, plow agriculture, or industrialization) predicts its population (size), social organization, and ideology is well known and much used. The association of complexity of subsistence technol-ogy with complexity in occupational and political structures is also well known. Lenski's (1966) finding that social inequality increases with increased complexity of subsistence technology until we reach industrial societies has also been widely recognized (Nielsen 2004). Others note the implications of subsistence technology for gender stratification. While the amount of gender stratification in society most often tracks the degree of stratification in general, Blumberg (2004) suggests that the most important factor influencing gender stratification in a society is women's relative control of key economic resources. Women are more likely to have a higher status in societies where they contribute to the society's main productive activities, but women's work does not enhance gender equality unless it also results in control of significant economic resources.

Lenski and Nolan (2005) hypothesized that societies that were previously agrarian do better in terms of various measures of development than societies that were previously horticultural. The hypothesis is strongly supported empirically. Lenski's theory also has implications for the failures of Marxist societies, which in

Lenski's view stemmed from the failure of Marxism to fully understand human nature. Marxist societies ended with a concentration of power at the top, resulting in communist societies more closely resembling monarchies and oligarchies in agrarian societies. This form of government is also associated with many human rights abuses, both in the Soviet case and the current Chinese market-oriented communist regime.

Unlike Lenski, who focuses on internal characteristics of societies for explaining societal evolution, other authors link the process of societal evolution to the society's place in the modern world-system and adopt a world-systems theoretical perspective (e.g., Chase-Dunn 2005). Hall and Fenelon (2009) have looked at the distinctiveness of indigenous movements and how they have responded to recent policy reforms and globalization. Findings from this research highlight the importance of the influence of global and historical forces on indigenous movements.

One of the primary limitations of this research is that most studies are qualitative—few scholars employ quantitative methodologies. This is partly because good-quality, comparable quantitative data are not available for many historical societies. A human rights focus also necessitates more quantitative comparative research, as abuses of human rights are often most effectively documented with quantitative evidence.

IMPLICATIONS OF THE EVOLUTION, BIOLOGY, AND SOCIETY AREA FOR THE HUMAN RIGHTS PARADIGM

All these subtopics within the evolution, biology, and society area stress the interaction of human biology with social contexts in explaining social phenomena. Unlike earlier attempts to incorporate biology into sociology, however, this research mitigates against biological divisions between human groups, as it stresses the fundamental biological unity of humankind. Most of the great variation in social behavior exists because of differing social, cultural, and economic contexts of peoples around the world. Only a small amount of this variation in social behavior exists because of individual differences in biological makeup, although genetically based individual variation does exist and can be consequential for individual behavior. Whether it is or not, once again, depends on the social, cultural, and economic context.

This research demonstrates the importance for all humans of experiencing a socially rich life, as well as the deleterious effects of social and economic deprivation and stress. Research in this area also shows how some social, cultural, and economic contexts are better at enabling individuals to live normal lives, achieve their potential as individuals, and avoid violence, hunger, and stress. Generally, more affluent societies are better at this, although there is variation among developed societies.

These findings have a variety of implications for the human rights paradigm. First, it is important that the paradigm acknowledge the role that this research suggests economic development and the acquisition of affluence play in promoting individual well-being and the achievement of individual potential. At the same time, development that forces people to sever social ties or that does not promote meritocracy is unlikely to further human well-being. One-size-fits-all development policies should be avoided in favor of policies that offer maximum flexibility to all individuals.

The evolution, biology, and society area can also benefit from a consideration of the human rights paradigm. For example, researchers in the area should give more explicit attention to the implications for human rights and well-being and to policy recommendations. Furthermore, researchers should be careful to state that findings apply to the average person and not each individual, and policy-makers should ensure that policies based on findings of this research allow for individual variation.

Four

Methodology, Practice, and Theory

CHAPTER THIRTY-THREE

METHODOLOGY

Amir B. Marvasti and Karyn D. McKinney

A s sociologists, we are new to the study of human rights. Frankly, it used to be that when we heard the phrase "human rights," we immediately associated it with the fields of international law and politics. However, it seems that sociologists are increasingly taking an interest in human rights. For example, the American Sociological Association recently established a section on human rights, and esteemed sociologists like Judith Blau and Alberto Moncada (2009; see also Blau and Moncada 2007a, 2007b) and Norman Denzin (2010) have published books explicitly on this topic. Contrary to common perception, human rights is not the specific provenance of law or politics. Indeed, to the degree that the study of human rights concerns how people are, or should be, treated by others, American sociology has long been interested in the topic, but without explicitly referring to it as such. For example, C. Wright Mills (1956, 1959; see also Hayden 2006), whose research focused on oppression and the necessity of social change, could be viewed as an early champion of human rights. So we begin this chapter with the assumption that, in some ways, sociology has always been about rights, though that inclination has become more explicit in recent years.

Before we discuss a qualitative approach to the study of human rights, the focus of this chapter, we should note that the choice of research methods does not help advocate or hinder human rights. More specifically, quantitative data and methods are not inherently anti–human rights. In fact, numerical data can be very useful for producing evidence of inequality (e.g., the difference between the rich and the poor in terms of education, access to health care, quality of life, or treatment in the criminal justice system). On the other hand, certain features of quantitative methods make them less appealing to human rights researchers. In particular, the dominant paradigm of objective truth and positivism sometimes discounts the experiential reports of human rights violations on the grounds that they are based only on anecdotal evidence.

Returning to the task at hand, what can we say about the relationship between qualitative research methods and the study of human rights? Here we highlight the unique strengths of qualitative methods and analysis for the study of human rights.

CONCEPTUALIZING AND MEASURING RIGHTS QUALITATIVELY

From a methodological perspective, conceptualization and measurement are foundational and interrelated concerns: one must have a working definition of the thing to be studied before proceeding to observe or measure it. In particular, a qualitative approach to human rights must begin with the question, What are rights? We suggest that the answer to this question is neither self-evident nor universal. To illustrate this point, let us begin with the UN Universal Declaration of Human Rights (UDHR). Among other things, this document calls for a "spirit of brotherhood." One might ask, Why not "a spirit of sisterhood"? Why is one half of humanity implicitly excluded from a statement about human rights? Similarly, Article 5 of the declaration states, "No one shall be subjected to torture or to cruel, inhuman or degrading treatment or punishment." One need only look at recent debates over what constitutes torture in the context of the so-called War on Terror to realize that even the seemingly self-evident is not exempt from definitional quandaries.

Thus the first challenge for scholarly research is pinning down the very definition of rights. The many questions (adapted from Fields 2010 and Brinkmann 2010) that complicate this task are, What is the level of analysis (group or individual rights)? What is the topical focus of analysis (social, political, civil, or economic rights)? What is the theoretical/epistemological foundation of rights (international/universal law versus traditional, local, or tribal law)? Who is the affected population for the purpose of analysis (human, animal, or plant rights)? A qualitatively oriented study of human rights favors a pragmatic approach that is focused on the empirical dispute at hand as it is lived or experienced in everyday settings as opposed to a priori normative assumptions about what human rights are or should be.

OBSERVING WRONGS

Human rights tend to become conspicuous through their absence; for the purposes of empirical social science, human rights often become socially or politically relevant because they have been violated. Arguably, human rights are rarely debated outside perceived or actual violations of those rights. Returning to the UDHR, it is important to note that the rationale for the document was the deplorable violations of human rights in the course of World War II. Indeed, this is noted in the preamble: "Whereas disregard and contempt for human rights have resulted in barbarous acts which have outraged the conscience of mankind.... Now, therefore, the General Assembly proclaims this Universal Declaration of Human Rights as a common standard of achievement for all peoples and all nations" (OHCHR 1998, 3–4). Thus, rights become realized in reaction to imagined or actual violations or wrongs.

This intricate rights-violation relationship is made clear by Svend Brinkmann's (2010) discussion of "human vulnerabilities" as being inseparable from human rights. In particular, Brinkmann argues,

If we educate students in qualitative inquiry so that they see it as their duty to understand rights as a central part of social life in-the-making—both for ethical and epistemic reasons—then we could possibly assist in generating a public where the sufferings and rights violations of each and every human being ultimately come to matter. (2010, 97)

Similarly, Norman Denzin and Michael Giardina state,

Hope alone will not produce change. First there must be pain, and despair. Persons must make pain the object of conscious reflection, the desire to resist, to change. This desire must be wedded to a conscious struggle to change the conditions that create pain in the first place. (2010, 29)

For the purpose of this chapter, defining rights in terms of possible and actual wrongs allows us (1) to focus on the observable disputes or claims about rights, and (2) to circumvent a priori definitions of rights and instead rely, phenomenologically, on members' own definitions. This in turn helps us feature the strengths of qualitative research, especially in terms of its capacity for analyzing rhetoric, claims, justifications, and narratives of wrongs as ongoing and always in the making. In short, with this phenomenological emphasis, we can use qualitative methods as a way of understanding the language, culture, and practices within which rights and wrongs are contested.

In the following section, we illustrate the qualitative research paradigm using examples, first in terms of data-collection strategies (i.e., methods of soliciting data) and then in terms of analytical themes (i.e., ways of making sense of data). Readers should note that the methods described here are not mutually exclusive, nor are they inherently pro–human rights. The goal here is to offer examples of how qualitative methods could be used to study and advocate human rights and not to argue that they indeed are or should be supportive of human rights.

Data-Solicitation Strategies

Whether it is study of human rights, wrongs, or any other subject matter, as an empirical enterprise, social-science research begins with the collection of some form of data that is later analyzed and represented to a given audience. Three of the most common qualitative data-collection strategies are discussed below.

In-Depth Interviews

The interview in all its variations (e.g., open-ended, closed-ended, focus group, etc.) is a procedure used by social scientists to gather information from their research respondents. Among qualitative researchers, the in-depth interview is particularly common (Johnson 2001). The in-depth interview basically involves a face-to-face encounter during which a researcher poses a series of questions to respondents. The goal is to use fairly flexible lines of inquiry (open-ended or unstructured questions) that will allow respondents to tell their stories with minimal interference from the researcher. The stories are expected to be in-depth in the sense that they are usually longer and more detailed than responses to a survey, for example.

Applied to the study of human rights, the in-depth interview itself becomes a way of exercising the right to tell one's story. Thus the act of telling itself is potentially liberating and therapeutic for the respondent. Furthermore, the stories help document (1) the suffering of those whose rights have been violated, and (2) their needs or demands for rights. Seen in this way, in-depth interviews have long been used by qualitative researchers to convey the experiences of the victims of human rights violations (see, e.g., Cohen 2007; Matthus 2009) and the less privileged or marginal members of society in general. Of course, interviews can also be used to investigate (or reveal) the attitudes or accounts of the violators of human rights (see, e.g., Straus and Lyons 2006).

ETHNOGRAPHY

With its long history of affiliation with the field of anthropology, ethnography (loosely defined as writing about culture) is a mainstay of qualitative research and uniquely suited for the cross-cultural comparisons involved in human rights research. Additionally, the wide range of representational practices that exist under the broad umbrella of ethnography makes this research methodology particularly appealing for those interested in documenting and telling stories of rights and wrongs in innovative ways (see Goodale 2009). For example, consider Ruth Behar's (1997) approach to writing ethnography described in her book *The Vulnerable Observer: Anthropology That Breaks Your Heart*. As the book's title indicates, the goal here is to tell stories with an emotional impact. Far from adhering to the positivistic mandate to stay value-free or neutral, Behar and other feminist and critical ethnographers try to engage readers using first-person accounts (autoethnography) and other innovative writing practices (e.g., poetic prose). To the extent that the study of human rights involves subjectivity, voice, and advocacy on behalf of those whose rights have been violated, the writing practices and strategies developed by critical and feminist ethnographers could be immensely relevant and useful to the practitioners in this field.

Another strength of ethnography, as applied to human rights research, is the ability to show how universal norms or ideals are actually practiced in a specific local context. For example, in her book *Human Rights and Gender Violence: Translating International Law into Local Justice*, Sally E. Merry uses ethnography to explore the tension between what she calls "transnational elites and local actors" (2006, 3). As she puts it, "The challenge is to study placeless phenomena in a place ... to locate sites where the global, national, and local practices are revealed in the social life of small groups" (Merry 2006, 29). Ethnography is well suited to close analysis of both unique contexts and universality.

CONTENT ANALYSIS OF EXISTING DOCUMENTS

Broadly defined, content analysis refers to the systematic analysis of texts (e.g., written documents, pictures, movies). Typically, the analysis begins with a sampling of a body of text (i.e., all articles related to topic *x* published in a daily paper) and then proceeds with categorizing these data into themes. In the context of human rights research, researchers are often interested in learning about the cultural climate that makes the systematic violation of human rights possible. In this regard, content analysis of newspapers, for example, could help expose the cultural sentiments, or the propaganda, that eventually lead to mass murders of the innocent (see, e.g., Stephens 1979). Explorations of sexism in popular culture have often relied on content analyses to show how, for example, women are treated as objects in advertising (see, e.g., Goffman 1979; Kilbourne 1999). This area of research has more recently expanded to include analyses of sexism in other forms of media, such as music videos (see, e.g., *Dreamworlds 4*, a documentary by the Media Education Foundation). Finally, content analysis has been used to expose racist ideologies promoted on the Internet (see, e.g., Gerstenfeld, Grant, and Chiang's 2003 analysis of online hate groups).

ANALYTICAL THEMES

A large portion of research on human rights is devoted to international legal studies that focus on variations in human rights around the world and their enforcement, or lack thereof. With few exceptions (see, e.g., Merry 2006; Hinton and O'Neill 2009), it seems that in this context, legal documents, treaties, or conventions are the primary sources of data and are taken at face value, detached from the micro, everyday-life situations in which they are interpreted and practiced. As an alternative, a qualitative orientation to human rights is more concerned with lived experience as something fluid and culturally embedded.

More specifically, qualitative researchers' ontological commitment to lived experience and the right to be heard leads to a focus on three analytical themes. Studies of power and discourse in practice examine the understanding that human rights is about not just documents, as in the US Constitution, but their interpretation and application in practice (the rhetoric of right and wrong in practice). This requires attention to how conflicting parties use words rhetorically to advance and legitimize their interests at the expense of their opponents. In narratives, researchers explore the recognition that the conflict over human rights involves battles over narratives of who deserves what and under what conditions and, more fundamentally, which side has the right to tell its story. For example, researchers might examine how narratives of national identity help demonize certain groups, which are subsequently stripped of their human rights. Finally, studies of voice and subjectivity embrace the value of subjectivity and voice as a way of telling what it feels like to be wronged. In this context, generalities are set aside in favor of the nuances of how oppressed individuals express themselves from their unique perspectives. The particulars are featured in the analysis to bring to life the experience of being wronged.

ADVANTAGES OF QUALITATIVE METHODS FOR THE STUDY OF HUMAN RIGHTS

Qualitative methods are uniquely suited for the study of human rights, especially to the extent that these methods can be used to document violations of human rights (wrongs) from the perspectives of the people involved in such disputes. Broadly speaking, qualitative methods are especially useful in this regard for three reasons.

LOGISTICAL ADVANTAGES

Qualitative research has the advantages of being user-friendly and cheap. It is often less expensive than surveys because a small research team can conduct qualitative research with less standardized training. All of these features make qualitative research more accessible for advocacy groups, which often have few resources. In addition, at the level of audience reception and dissemination of findings, qualitative research manuscripts do not require prior knowledge of statistics and thus tend to be easier to comprehend for average readers. Because of this accessibility, qualitative studies tend to resonate with broad, mainstream audiences.

SUBSTANTIVE COMMITMENT

There is a long history of qualitative studies with a focus on the less privileged. Whether one considers William F. Whyte's *Street Corner Society* (1943), Erving Goffman's *Asylums* (1961), Howard Becker's *Outsiders* (1963), or Elliot Liebow's *Tell Them Who I Am: The Lives of Homeless Women* (1993), qualitative research is a field rich with accounts of marginalized people whose rights have been violated in one way or another by mainstream society and its institutions. In part, it is this substantive interest in "social outcasts" that informs the methodological choices of qualitative researchers. Specifically, it is often difficult to collect large random samples of deviant populations, especially if their actions are deemed to violate the laws of the state. Thus a rigid quantitative analysis of their lives is not practical. By comparison, any deviant group can be studied using a small sample and ethnographic techniques, for example. This orientation easily transfers to research on the human rights of marginalized people who are in hiding, for example, because they fear persecution from state authorities.

THEORETICAL COMMITMENT

Qualitative research is generally better suited to measuring or studying abstract concepts (how a person would like to be treated as a human being) as opposed to more concrete variables or immediate outcomes (e.g., the respondents' earnings in US dollars or how they might vote in an upcoming election). Additionally, a different conception of validity and "truthfulness" in qualitative research aids the study of human rights as abstract ideals. Rather than judging research participants' statements and actions against predetermined or taken-for-granted norms, qualitative researchers tend to be more interested in how they make sense of their own world. Indeed, qualitative researchers are cautioned not to "argue with members" (Gubrium and Holstein 2012) and to be faithful to the members' own accounts. In addition to the attentive and accurate description of participants' perspectives, qualitative research is theoretically committed to the agency and autonomy of the research subjects. This is often reflected in both (1) the way data are solicited from respondents (e.g., using open-ended questions that allow for a fluid and unrestricted account), and (2) the way respondents are encouraged to aid the researchers and in some cases become part of the research (e.g., autoethnography and collaborative ethnography). In the words of Antjie Krog, as qualitative researchers interested in human rights,

> we have to find new ways in which the marginalized can enter our discourses in their own genres and their own terms so that we can learn to hear them. They have a universal right to impart information and ideas through any media regardless of frontiers, and we have a duty to listen and understand them through engaging in new acts of becoming. (2010, 134)

Collectively, these strategies allow qualitative researchers to treat their respondents as equals (if not as experts in their own right). To understand them, we must listen to respondents' words and their versions of events; the researcher is not the sole arbiter of truth.

Additionally, at least some qualitative researchers are committed to telling the stories of those who are less fortunate with the goal of creating positive social change. This direction is best described by Norman Denzin in his book *The Qualitative Manifesto: A Call to Arms*, which calls on qualitative researchers to "change the world, and to change it in ways that resist injustice while celebrating freedom, and full, inclusive, participatory democracy" (2010, 32).

POTENTIAL PITFALLS

Because of their face-to-face and experiential nature, qualitative studies of human rights pose unique challenges for researchers. Qualitative methods and related analytical strategies are not without their pitfalls. Specifically, the observational techniques used by qualitative researchers could in fact be more exploitive and destructive to native populations than the more quantitative counterparts. The very personal and interactional nature of qualitative research often fosters relationships between participants and researchers. In this context, there is a real possibility that the researcher and participants will have differing views of the nature of the relationship and its objectives. What the researcher believes to be an "interesting case" or an opportunity to illustrate a violation of human rights might be viewed by the respondent as an ongoing personal relationship.

Additionally, there is a danger of researchers implying that they have more power and authority to change people's lives than they actually do (i.e., making promises they cannot keep). In the context of human rights research, this problem can, quite literally, have deadly consequences for the participants. Consider, for example, a researcher who encourages former political prisoners to speak about how they were tortured during their incarceration. In this case, it is very likely that the political prisoners are still under government surveillance, and while the researcher is in a position to collect the stories and walk away to his or her next publication, the former inmates could fall victim to retaliation from the authorities, who are not pleased with the bad press. At a minimum, it is crucial for qualitative researchers in such scenarios to warn participants of potential risks and not to imply that they are in a position to provide legal immunity.

THE FUTURE OF QUALITATIVE METHODS AND HUMAN RIGHTS

Research methods, whether quantitative or qualitative, continue to expand and change. Technological innovations and new theoretical paradigms constantly challenge researchers to rethink and adapt the ways they collect, analyze, and write their observations. For example, mixed methods offer exciting possibilities for combining different types of data to tell a story (Morse and Niehaus 2009). In this context, researchers are encouraged to set aside methodological fixations in favor of what works for the task at hand. Additionally, the digital revolution will profoundly change the definition and practice of social research. For example, new technologies make it possible for native populations and the oppressed to tell their own stories and communicate them with an international audience through the Internet. Indigenous people no longer need Western, university-trained academics to publish their stories in some obscure book or journal; they can tell their stories in real time to the rest of the world. Bloggers, for example, have been instrumental in bringing attention to human rights abuses in the Middle East.

We imagine certain things will remain constant, however, as we peer into the future. Namely, we believe it is necessary for researchers to continue to adhere to the idealistic, perhaps naïve, interpretation of science as a quest for knowledge, irrespective of its methodology. In order to retain any degree of legitimacy, to have a reason to speak and be heard in a sea of voices, our research enterprise has to remain focused on liberation from ignorance as an end in itself. Science is about questioning the fundamental nature of reality in all its forms (social and physical). It is ultimately "the relentless critique of the status quo" that is the goal, regardless of the particular method of study. This means thinking of human rights and wrongs as emergent and ongoing ideas and practices. Guided by something along the lines of a rights-centered scientific pragmatism, researchers will have to constantly judge the moral positions they are advocating in the context of the empirical evidence at hand and the realities of the situation under analysis.

CHAPTER THIRTY-FOUR

MATHEMATICAL SOCIOLOGY

Guillermina Jasso

Thou hast ordered all things in measure, and number, and weight.
—Wisdom 11:21

The Book of Nature is ... written in mathematical characters.
—Galileo

Mathematical sociology has assembled a marvelous set of tools for addressing the questions of interest in all the subfields of sociology. The tools include mathematical functions, probability distributions, matrices, and inequality measures. The ideas of a population of persons (or a network of persons), relations between characteristics of persons, and relations between persons enable clear description of individuals and societies and of the links between them. The tools of mathematical sociology can be used to build rich theories with abundant testable predictions. Importantly, they enable clarity and transparency in statements about human nature and human behavior, spanning the gamut from the most abstract to the most concrete concerns of sociology.

I begin this exploration of mathematical sociology and human rights with three remarks.

Remark 1. Mathematics is our human heritage. Humans are born with a foundation for mathematics. This foundation is evident in many ways, perhaps most vividly in the spontaneous and unconscious way that we solve difficult differential equations every time we approach an intersection and, in the face of traffic, decide whether to stop or cross. Mathematics brings clarity to the mind and joy to the soul. It is thus a fundamental failure of human rights that mathematics is sometimes thought the province of a subset of humans—whether the subset is defined by gender or race or class or discipline. And it is a dual tragedy when the excluded applaud and defend their exclusion.

Remark 2. Unease about mathematics may be lower in regions where the language has grammatical gender (as do the Romance languages) and some mathematical terms are feminine. For example, the basic mathematical terms to be discussed in a later section of this chapter, "function," "equation," "distribution," and "matrix," are all feminine in Spanish, as are the words for "mathematics" and for the basic terms of empirical sociology, "variable" and "regression." Perhaps the sting of mathematics is native only to regions whose languages have no gender. And perhaps the relative exclusion of mathematics from sociology has been spread, along with neglect of fundamental tu-vous processes (Brown and Gilman 1960), by a sociology expressed in English, a language that has begun to shed its stratifying elements and thus, paradoxically, is oblivious of both the humanizing and dehumanizing effects of languages with gender and tu-vous distinctions.

Remark 3. The clarity and transparency of mathematical sociology makes it an ideal way to describe and assess basic issues of human rights.

KEY BUILDING BLOCKS OF MATHEMATICAL SOCIOLOGY

This section examines the key elements in mathematical sociology. Any mathematical model or theory will contain one or more of these elements. They play prominent parts in the history of mathematical sociology, including the foundational monographs—Coleman (1964), Fararo (1973), and Leik and Meeker (1975)—and the *Journal of Mathematical Sociology*, founded in 1971.

THEORETICAL MEASUREMENT OF PERSONAL CHARACTERISTICS

Humans notice their own and others' characteristics—their attractiveness, income, skill, and so on. These characteristics can be classified according to whether they are quantitative or qualitative. The idea that there are two kinds of personal characteristics, quantitative and qualitative, and that they differ in their social operation was pioneered by Blau (1974).

PERSONAL QUANTITATIVE CHARACTERISTICS

Quantitative characteristics are characteristics of which individuals can have more or fewer. They may be cardinal (like wealth) or ordinal (like beauty). Cardinal characteristics are measured in their own units (such as dollars or acres). Ordinal characteristics are measured as relative ranks within a group or population.

Quantitative characteristics of which more is preferred to less are called goods; if less is preferred to more, they are called bads. To illustrate, for most people, wealth is a good, and taxes are a bad. We will denote the quantitative characteristics by X.

Sometimes cardinal things are called possessions and ordinal things are called attributes.

PERSONAL QUALITATIVE CHARACTERISTICS

Qualitative characteristics, in contrast to quantitative characteristics, describe features of individuals that have no inherent ordering but can be used to classify them into groups or categories. Qualitative characteristics may be binary (such as gender) or polytomous (such as race and ethnicity).

SPECIFICATION OF MATHEMATICAL FUNCTIONS FOR LINKING PERSONAL QUANTITATIVE CHARACTERISTICS WITHIN POPULATIONS FORMED BY CATEGORIES OF PERSONAL QUALITATIVE CHARACTERISTICS

Humans not only notice their own and others' characteristics but also link two or more characteristics. The most basic kind of link is between two quantitative characteristics. For example, students (or their parents) may talk about the link between years of schooling and earnings. They may say things like, as years of schooling increase, earnings increase. Formally, we say that a dependent variable y is a function of an independent variable x or, more generally, of a set of independent variables, writing,

$$(1) \qquad\qquad y = f(x_1, x_2, x_3, ..., x_k)$$

Choosing—or discovering—the independent variables that affect a dependent variable is the first step in specifying a function.

The second step is to specify, based either on theory or previous empirical research, the direction of the effects of each of the independent variables. For example, the researcher may believe that y is an increasing function of one independent variable, a decreasing function of another, and a nonmonotonic function of still another. This "signing" of the effects is often represented by the first partial derivatives; for example, a positive first partial derivative indicates that, holding constant the other independent variables, as an independent variable increases, so does the dependent variable.

The stage is now set for the third step, which introduces a specific function and/or a set of second derivatives. The second derivative indicates whether the rate of change is increasing, decreasing, or constant. For example, the combination of a positive first derivative and a positive second derivative indicates that as the independent variable increases, the dependent variable increases at an increasing rate.

The second derivative is of the greatest importance in sociology because many outcomes vary with the same independent variables, and thus the challenge is to specify what is distinctive about each relation. To illustrate, power, status, and self-esteem all vary with wealth, and the task is to discover what is distinctive about each of these relations. Or are power, status, and self-esteem merely synonyms?

The second derivative can unlock many mysteries—for example, gravity in the physical world and the difference between status and power in the social world.

Figure 34.1 depicts the basic set of monotonic functions—increasing functions in the first row, decreasing functions in the second row, and the single constant function in the third row. The first and second row each include three graphs, one each to depict the rate of change—increasing, decreasing, and constant.

Nonmonotonic functions are also important in sociology. For example, in the study of immigrant selection, two of the major types of selectivity are a U-shaped pattern (Lee 1966), such that the probability of migrating is highest at the lower and upper extremes of the distribution of schooling or income, and an inverse U-shaped pattern (Chiquiar and Hanson 2005), such that the probability of migrating is highest at an intermediate level of schooling or income.

Classic books on mathematical functions and calculus include the little Thompson (1946 [1910]), the two-volume Courant (1937 [1934]), and the great Bronshtein and Semendyayev (1985).[1]

Figure 34.1 Monotonic functions

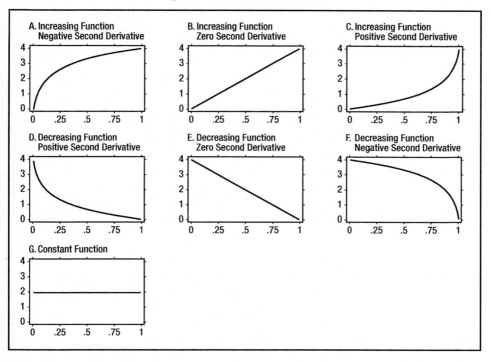

1. Samuel Kotz (Nadarajah 2002:222) recalls studying the Russian 1945 edition of Bronshtein and Semendyayev "from cover to cover" in his youth and still using it decades later.

SPECIFICATION OF PROBABILITY DISTRIBUTIONS REPRESENTING PERSONAL QUANTITATIVE CHARACTERISTICS

Probability distributions represent a variable's array. Some variables are so important—for example, wealth, power, and status—that we might say their distribution provides a picture of society. Moreover, they work together with mathematical functions to provide seamless passage from the distribution of an independent variable to the distribution of a dependent variable. For example, if we know the distribution of the independent variable x, and we also know the function that converts x into y, we can obtain the distribution of y.

It is a good idea to have handy an introduction to probability distributions and a dictionary of distributions. A prominent introduction is *Distribution Theory*, the first volume in the two-volume edition of *The Advanced Theory of Statistics* first published by Kendall in 1943 and the three-volume edition first published by Kendall and Stuart in 1958, and continued in Stuart and Ord (1987). As for dictionaries of distributions, there are three kinds of sources. The first consists of the large books that assemble all the principal information about each of the major known distributions. The most prominent exemplar is the compendia originated by Johnson and Kotz (1969–1972) and continued by Johnson, Kotz, and Balakrishnan (1994, 1995). The second source consists of a little handbook first published by Hastings and Peacock (1974) and now in its fourth edition as Forbes et al. (2011). For many scientists, this little handbook is like Mary's little lamb. The third source is the Internet, where the US National Institute of Standards and Technology (NIST) posts an *Engineering Statistics Handbook*, with the remarkable Section 1.3.6 on probability distributions.

SPECIFICATION OF MATRICES REPRESENTING SELF-OTHER RELATIONS

In many areas of social life, the important x and y variables can be arrayed in a matrix. Three examples include the following: (1) a group of wage-setters recommends the earnings for each worker in a group, (2) every member of a group accords status to every other member, and (3) observers form ideas about the just reward (which can be a good, like earnings, or a bad, like time in prison) for a set of rewardees.

SPECIFICATION OF INEQUALITY DYNAMICS

At least four major types of inequality dynamics arise in sociology. The first is a link between overall inequality and subgroup inequality. The second is a link between the coefficients of a reward function and inequality in the reward's distribution. The third is a link between inequality in an input and inequality in an outcome. The fourth is a link between the configuration of inputs (viz., their number and intercorrelation) and inequality in the sociobehavioral outcome they generate.

USING THE KEY BUILDING BLOCKS

MATHEMATICAL FUNCTIONS

The Status Function

The status function specifies the magnitude of status as a function of relative rank for valued personal quantitative characteristics:

$$(2) \qquad S = \ln\left(\frac{1}{1 - r_x}\right)$$

where S denotes status, and r denotes the relative rank on the valued good X within a group or population. The status function, which was proposed by Sørensen (1979), embeds the convexity property described by Goode (1978), whereby status rises steeply with rank.

The Comparison Function

Comparison processes are outcomes that are generated by comparison of an actual amount or level of a characteristic to an amount or level desired, envisioned, or thought just or appropriate. Some examples are self-esteem, relative deprivation, and the justice evaluation. The comparison function specifies the outcome as a function of the logarithm of the ratio of the actual amount to the comparison amount:

$$(3) \qquad Z = \theta \ln\left(\frac{X}{X^*}\right)$$

where Z denotes any of the comparison outcomes, X is as above the valued good, X^* denotes the comparison standard, and θ is the signature constant whose sign indicates whether the reward is viewed as a good or a bad and whose absolute value denotes expressiveness. The comparison function, which was proposed by Jasso (1978, 1990), embeds the property that deficiency is more keenly felt than comparable excess, a property considered fundamental in justice research (Wagner and Berger 1985, 719). The log-ratio function is also the only function that satisfies scale invariance and additivity.

   In the special case of the justice-evaluation function, the general comparison outcome variable Z is replaced by the justice evaluation J, and the variables in the ratio are usually called the actual reward and just reward.

PROBABILITY DISTRIBUTIONS

For Ordinal Characteristics—the Rectangular

Ordinal characteristics are naturally represented by relative ranks, and the set of relative ranks is in turn naturally represented by the rectangular distribution (also known as the uniform) specified on the unit interval and thus called the unit rectangular (or unit uniform). The rectangular distribution is a special case of the beta distribution. For further properties, see Johnson, Kotz, and Balakrishnan (1995, 210, 276–321).

For Cardinal Characteristics—the Lognormal, Pareto, and Power-Function

The distribution of a cardinal X may assume any of a wide variety of shapes. Theoretical analysis, although always seeking distribution-independent results, can yield useful results and insights by exploring the properties and behavior of outcome distributions generated by selected modeling distributions that vary in their support, tail behavior, and other features.

For this purpose, we begin with three widely used continuous univariate distributions whose properties are well known: the lognormal, Pareto, and power-function (Johnson, Kotz, and Balakrishnan 1994, 1995; Kleiber and Kotz 2003); see Figure 34.2.

Figure 34.2 Basic associated functions (PDF, CDF, and QF) in three continuous univariate distributions: lognormal, Pareto, and power-function. Arithmetic mean fixed at unity and displayed as either a vertical line (PDF and CDF) or a horizontal line (QF).

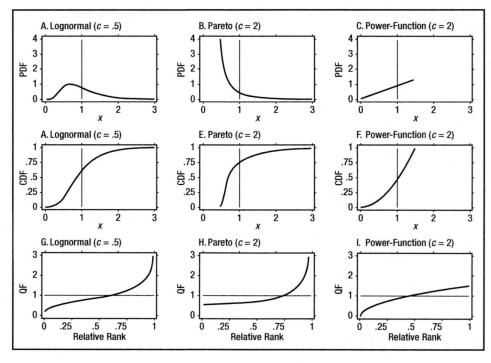

MATRICES

The Wage Matrix

Consider a group or population in which wage-setters—whose number may range from a small committee to the entire population—recommend the wage amounts for every person in the population. Thus, the final wage distribution is a weighted sum of all the recommended wage distributions. Analysis of this model yields interesting results about the effects of the number of wage-setters and their independence of mind on the ensuing wage inequality (Jasso 2009), as will be seen below. Table 34.1 shows the matrix formed by the recommended wage amounts.

The Self-Other Status Matrix

In the study of status, there are two fundamental actors, each conferring status on and receiving it from the other (Friedkin 1998; Goode 1978; Shils 1968). The self-other status matrix collects the magnitudes of status accorded by each actor to each other actor (Jasso 2001, 101), as shown in Table 34.2.

The Observer-Specific/Rewardee-Specific Justice Matrices

In the study of distributive/retributive justice, there are three matrices, corresponding to the three quantities in the justice-evaluation function: the actual reward, the just reward, and the justice evaluation. As shown in Table 34.3, each of these matrices has the same form.

Table 34.1 The wage matrix: N wage-setters and J workers

A. The Wage-Setter-Specific/Worker-Specific Wage

$$x_{ij}$$

where x denotes the recommended wage, and the wage-setters are indexed by i ($i =$ 1, ..., N) and the workers by j ($j = 1, ..., J$)

B. Wage Matrix

$$X = \begin{bmatrix} x_{11} & x_{12} & x_{13} & \cdots & x_{1J} \\ x_{21} & x_{22} & x_{23} & \cdots & x_{2J} \\ x_{31} & x_{32} & x_{33} & \cdots & x_{3J} \\ \vdots & \vdots & \vdots & \ddots & \vdots \\ x_{N1} & x_{N2} & x_{N3} & \cdots & x_{NJ} \end{bmatrix}$$

C. The Case of a Single Wage-Setter

If there is only one wage-setter, the wage matrix collapses to a vector:

$$x_{.j} = \begin{bmatrix} x_{.1} & x_{.2} & x_{.3} & \cdots & x_{.J} \end{bmatrix}$$

Table 34.2 The self-other status matrix

$$S = \begin{bmatrix} S_{11} & S_{12} & S_{13} & \cdots & S_{1J} \\ S_{21} & S_{22} & S_{23} & \cdots & S_{2J} \\ S_{31} & S_{32} & S_{33} & \cdots & S_{3J} \\ \vdots & \vdots & \vdots & \ddots & \vdots \\ S_{N1} & S_{N2} & S_{N3} & \cdots & S_{NJ} \end{bmatrix}$$

Notes: Each individual ($i = 1$ to N) accords status to each individual ($j = 1$ to J). Each row represents the status accorded by one individual (to self and to others), and each column represents the status received by one individual. Thus, each row represents the status structure in the mind of one person. In the special case of consensus, the matrix collapses to a vector.

Table 34.3 Observer-by-rewardee matrices of the just reward, the actual reward, and the justice evaluation

1. Just Reward Matrix

$$C = \begin{bmatrix} C_{11} & C_{12} & C_{13} & \cdots & C_{1R} \\ C_{21} & C_{22} & C_{23} & \cdots & C_{2R} \\ C_{31} & C_{32} & C_{33} & \cdots & C_{3R} \\ \vdots & \vdots & \vdots & \ddots & \vdots \\ C_{N1} & C_{N2} & C_{N3} & \cdots & C_{NR} \end{bmatrix}$$

2. Actual Reward Matrix

$$A_{.} = \begin{bmatrix} a_{11} & a_{12} & a_{13} & \cdots & a_{1R} \\ a_{21} & a_{22} & a_{23} & \cdots & a_{2R} \\ a_{31} & a_{32} & a_{33} & \cdots & a_{3R} \\ \vdots & \vdots & \vdots & \ddots & \vdots \\ a_{N1} & a_{N2} & a_{N3} & \cdots & a_{NR} \end{bmatrix}$$

If there are no perception errors, the actual reward matrix collapses to a vector:

$$a_{.} - [a_1 \, a_2 \, a_3 \ldots a_R]$$

3. Justice Evaluation Matrix

$$J = \begin{bmatrix} j_{11} & j_{12} & j_{13} & \cdots & j_{1R} \\ j_{21} & j_{22} & j_{23} & \cdots & j_{2R} \\ j_{31} & j_{32} & j_{33} & \cdots & j_{3R} \\ \vdots & \vdots & \vdots & \ddots & \vdots \\ j_{N1} & j_{N2} & j_{N3} & \cdots & j_{NR} \end{bmatrix}$$

Notes: Observers are indexed by $o = 1, \ldots, N$; rewardees are indexed by $r = 1, \ldots, R$. Thus, c_{or}, a_{or}, j_{or} represent the observer-specific/rewardee-specific just reward, actual reward, and justice evaluation, respectively.

The qualitative characteristics introduced above provide a natural way to form subgroups. For example, the group or population under study may be divided by gender or by race or by citizenship, nativity, mother tongue, or any of a host of qualitative characteristics. The subgroups obtained from such classifications are called preexisting subgroups because they preexist the operation of sociobehavioral phenomena such as status or comparison.

Sociobehavioral processes generate new subgroups, and these are called emergent subgroups. For example, justice processes generate three emergent subgroups, namely, the underrewarded, the justly rewarded, and the overrewarded.

Further, all the sociobehavioral outcomes—including status, comparison, and power—generate still another set of emergent subgroups based on the contrast between own outcome, average outcome in the preexisting subgroup, and average outcome in the whole group. Sociobehavioral theory proposes that individuals orient to or identify with self rather than with their preexisting subgroup if own outcome is greater than the subgroup average, and vice versa. For example, a person whose subgroup has a higher average status than his or her own status score will gain status from identifying with the subgroup. There can be contests between self and subgroup, between self and group, and between subgroup and group, as well as a three-way contest. Persons who orient to self, subgroup, or group are called *selfistas*, subgroupistas, and *groupistas*, respectively.

Figure 34.3 provides illustration of the status function in the case of a group with two subgroups of equal size (as might be the case when the subgroups are based on gender). The graph shows the graph of status as a function of relative rank—as in equation (2). The vertical line at $r = .5$ indicates the boundary between the two subgroups.

As shown in Figure 34.3, and as has been demonstrated algebraically, in a contest between self and preexisting subgroup, the lower-ranking persons are *subgroupistas* and the higher-ranking persons are *selfistas*. Thus, it is easy to see that important matters should not be entrusted to "the best and the brightest," because in a time of crisis, they will act in their own interests rather than in the interests of the preexisting subgroup.

In an application to residential segregation (Jasso 2010), the *selfistas* are integrationists and the *subgroupistas* are segregationists. In this case, the sociobehavioral dynamics generate a mixed group of integrationists, plus two groups of segregationists (one drawn from each race), which may form a coalition to preserve the segregated way of life. Figure 34.4 provides visual illustration of the proportions in the mixed group and the two segregated groups, by percentage black in the overall group.

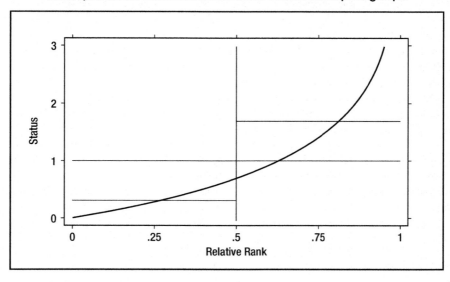

Figure 34.3 Status function, with subgroup and group averages. The long horizontal line represents the arithmetic mean of status in the population. The two short lines represent the arithmetic means in the bottom and top subgroups.

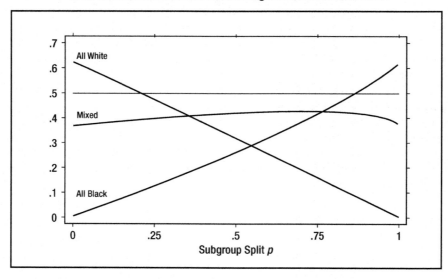

Figure 34.4 Segregation model: all-black, all-white, and mixed neighborhoods in a status society, by subgroup split p. For each magnitude of the subgroup split (or proportion black), the proportions in all-black, all-white, and mixed neighborhoods sum to one.

MEASURES OF OVERALL AND SUBGROUP INEQUALITY

The set of measures of overall inequality include the Gini coefficient, the coefficient of variation, one or more of the measures proposed by Atkinson (1970, 1975), and one or both of the measures proposed by Theil (1967).

Concomitantly, the measures of subgroup inequality contrast a variable, such as income, across the categories of a preexisting subgroup. Examples include the gender wage gap and the race wage gap.

Formulas for these measures are provided in Jasso and Kotz (2008). Fuller detail and insight are provided in Dagum (1983), Firebaugh (1999), Kleiber and Kotz (2003), and Liao (2006).

LITTLE MODELS AND BIG THEORIES

"Model" is a wonderful, all-purpose word. It is happily at home in many settings. There are theoretical models and empirical models, substantive models and methodological models, mathematical models and statistical models, applied theoretical models and ad hoc conceptual models. And as if that were not enough, "model" is also a verb. I will not attempt to constrain the word's all-terrain-vehicle nature. I will, however, introduce the better-behaved "theory" and discuss the difference between the two.

Though "theory" also has many meanings, in the world of scientific theory, there is one basic form of theory. A scientific theory has a two-part structure. It begins with an assumption or a small set of assumptions, and it ends with predictions or propositions.

Within this one form of theory, there are two main types: deductive and nondeductive. Within the deductive type of theory, there are two main subtypes: the gold-standard hypothetico-deductive form invented by Newton (and discussed by Toulmin 1978, 378–379) and a second form.

In the gold-standard hypothetico-deductive form of theory, the assumption(s) yield(s) a large and growing set of testable predictions, including novel predictions (Jasso 1988b). Because "assumption" is also at home in many settings (for example, not only as the starting point for a theory but also as the understandings about the unobservables in a statistical model), the word "postulate" is often used to refer to the assumptions of a hypothetico-deductive theory (the alliteration with "prediction" also helps). Tests of the predictions are used to assess the postulates' relative fidelity to the real world. The goal is a theory with a minimum of postulates and a maximum of predictions, where the postulates are "genuine guesses about the structure of the world," and the predictions display the "marvelous deductive unfolding" of the theory (Popper 1963, 245, 221). The postulates' fruitfulness is evident in the "derivations far afield from its original domain," which "permit an increasingly broad and diversified basis for testing the theory" (Danto 1967, 299–300).

In the other deductive subtype, the assumptions are known to be true—they may even be self-evident—or the assumptions may describe a set of arrangements under human control. Thus, the implications must be true. There are no guesses about the nature of the world.

In the nondeductive type of theory, owed to Toulmin (1953)—see also Fararo (1989)—the assumptions do not yield predictions. Instead the theorist links them to observable terms, producing testable propositions.

A theory can have several links with a model. Here I illustrate two. In both cases, a model is related to a deductive theory.

Consider the comparison function in equation (3). Its roots lie in a model of the justice-evaluation process, the process by which an observer judges the justice or injustice of the actual reward received by a rewardee (Jasso 1978). When the justice-evaluation function was first introduced in 1978, it was a model. It was not a theory, nor was it embedded in a theory as either postulate or prediction.

Of course, it had attractive features. In particular, it faithfully embodied the long-standing view that deficiency is felt more keenly than comparable excess (Wagner and Berger 1985, 719); it unified the two rival conceptions of justice contrasts as a difference and a ratio (because the logarithm of a ratio equals the difference between two logarithms); and it could immediately be applied to all cardinal goods, giving it an air of universality. In fact, it was so attractive that Jasso (1978) immediately proposed it as a candidate for a Law of Justice Evaluation.

But it was only a model. It was not a theory and not embedded in a theory.

Two years later it became part of a theory. Soon after its introduction, it became apparent that the justice-evaluation function could serve as a fruitful postulate. Thus, Jasso (1980) proposed a new theory whose first postulate was the justice-evaluation function. The initial statement of the theory did several things. First, it extended the class of rewards to which it was applicable from the cardinal goods of Jasso (1978) to ordinal goods (thus making the justice-evaluation function even more universal than it had at first appeared). Second, it showed that if the just reward is held constant at the arithmetic mean (which has the interpretation that the just reward is the equal reward), then information about the distribution of the actual reward (known automatically for ordinal goods) is sufficient to generate information about the distribution of justice evaluations—thus providing pictures of a society's justice life. Third, the postulates yielded both a set of initial predictions and a set of initial propositions, making it a hybrid form. Initial predictions included the prediction that if a society values an ordinal good—such as beauty or skill—the most overrewarded person is only modestly overrewarded compared to the most overrewarded person in a society that values a cardinal good (Jasso 1980, 12–13). Initial propositions included the proposition that the propensity to violent revolutionary conflict varies with the absolute magnitude of the lower extreme value of the distribution of justice evaluations (Jasso 1980, 8).

Thus, in this case, a model became the postulate of a theory. The very same occurred with the status function proposed by Sørensen (1979). At first it was a model. Later it became the postulate of a theory, generating a wealth of new predictions (Jasso 2001).

In both of these examples, the justice-evaluation function and the status function operate as Popperian guesses about the world. Tests of the derived predictions provide evidence to support or refute the initial guesses.

Of course, it is also possible for a model to become part of a theory by becoming a prediction of a theory. The textbook case involves Kepler's laws of planetary motion, which, fifty years later, Newton derived from his laws of motion and of universal gravitation. As schoolchildren learn, Kepler did not know why his laws worked; Newton provided the deeper explanatory framework.

Because the goal of scientific work is to understand more and more by less and less, we can expect that someday there will be deeper, more fundamental social-science theories capable of predicting the justice-evaluation function and the status function (and the power-function, too).

SOME KEY RESULTS, SUBSTANTIVE AND METHODOLOGICAL

SEAMLESS AND TRANSPARENT PASSAGE BETWEEN MICRO AND MACRO LEVELS OF ANALYSIS

Mathematics provides many bridges between micro and macro levels of analysis (Jasso 2010). For example, an analysis of marriage, based on justice theory, made transparent the links between (1) the individual-level justice evaluation, (2) the couple-level marital cohesiveness, and (3) the societal-level divorce rate (Jasso 1988a), as well as links connecting the mean and inequality in the husbands' and wives' income distributions to the societal divorce rate.

A DIAGNOSTIC FOR PROBABILITY DISTRIBUTIONS

Whenever any characteristic or outcome can be expressed as a function of relative rank, that function is itself the extremely useful quantile function. The quantile function signals the characteristic's probability distribution.

To see this remarkable fact in action, consider the status function in (2). Notice that it is a function solely of relative rank. If we go to a dictionary of distributions, we will quickly find a distribution whose quantile function is indeed the same as the status function. It is the exponential distribution (see, e.g., Forbes et al. 2011, 88).

Of course, not every function of relative rank we encounter has a counterpart among the quantile functions of the major known probability distributions. If the function has a special sociological meaning, and if substantial further searches fail to find a probability distribution with a quantile function the same as our function, then it means we have found a new probability distribution. This was the case recently when Jasso (2001) derived a new distribution representing the case in which status is generated by two characteristics that are perfectly negatively correlated. Initially called "Unnamed" (Jasso 2001, 122), it was introduced more formally several years later and given a proper name: the "mirror-exponential" (Jasso and Kotz 2007).[2]

Thus, functions of relative rank provide an extraordinary win-win situation. Either they lead us straight to the distribution of the characteristic, as in Sørensen's status function (1979), or they lead us to a new distribution (Jasso 2001; Jasso and Kotz 2007).

WAGE DISTRIBUTION AND WAGE INEQUALITY

The wage-setter model introduced above yields many results highlighting the connections between political arrangements and economic outcomes, including these two: First, inequality is reduced when the wage-setters have independence of mind and reduced further still when their views are diametrically opposed. Second, as the number of independent wage-setters increases, wage inequality decreases.

PROBABILITY DISTRIBUTIONS IN THE WORLD OF STATUS

As seen above, and known already to Sørensen, the basic status distribution, arising from consideration of one good, has the exponential form. Subsequent work has established that if people value more than one good—say, both beauty and wealth or both diplomatic skill and military skill—status assumes the form of two further families of distributions. In the case where the valued goods are independent, status is distributed as a general Erlang, and in the case where the valued goods are negatively associated, status is distributed as the new mirror-exponential (Jasso and Kotz 2007).

PROBABILITY DISTRIBUTIONS IN THE WORLD OF COMPARISON PROCESSES

Comparison processes, like justice and self-esteem, require more distributions for their full representation than does status. This greater complexity is due to two reasons: First, comparison processes notice the cardinal aspect of cardinal goods. Second, comparison outcomes are produced by two independent variables rather than one, not only the actual reward but also the just reward, so that the initial modeling requires not only a distribution for the actual reward but also something further, such as a distribution for the just reward or a condition on the set of others with whom self compares.

It thus turns out that the distributions of comparison outcomes obtained thus far include the following forms: negative and positive exponential, normal, symmetric and asymmetric Laplace, logistic and quasi-logistic, and two new families that arise when self compares to everyone below or to everyone above.

INEQUALITY DYNAMICS

A Link between Overall Inequality and Subgroup Inequality

It was recently shown that in a specified class of probability distributions—namely, continuous two-parameter distributions—and in the case in which the subgroups occupy distinct regions of the distribution (for example, the wealthiest person in one subgroup is less wealthy than the poorest person in the other subgroup), measures of overall inequality and of subgroup inequality are both monotonic functions of a general inequality parameter. Thus, as overall inequality increases, so does subgroup inequality. Jasso and Kotz (2008) report derivation of this result, together with discussion of the settings around the world that satisfy the condition of disjuncture between the subgroups.

A Link between Inequality in an Input and Inequality in an Outcome

Many results fall under this rubric, including these two: First, when the outcome is a linear function of the input (as believed for the power sociobehavioral outcome), the variance in the power outcome is quickly obtained from information about the variance of the input and the two parameters (intercept and slope). Second, when the sociobehavioral outcome is status, inequality in X is irrelevant to status inequality because the status function notices only ranks.

A Link between the Number and Intercorrelation of Valued
Goods and Inequality in the Sociobehavioral Outcome

Almost fifty years ago, Berger, Cohen, and Zelditch (1966, 44) showed that status inequality declines when individuals value negatively associated characteristics. Building on that pioneering result, Jasso and Kotz (2007, 316–318) showed that status inequality also declines when the multiple valued characteristics are statistically independent, with status inequality decreasing as the number of independent goods increases. These mechanisms apply not only to status but also to the other sociobehavioral outcomes.

A NEW UNIFIED THEORY OF SOCIOBEHAVIORAL FORCES

Building on the classic sociological idea that there are three basic sociobehavioral outcomes (Homans 1974, 231)—status, power, and justice (including the other comparison processes)—Jasso (2008) proposes a unification in which all three outcomes depend on the same inputs, but each has a distinctive rate of change.

The theory yields a broad array of testable predictions, including the following: (1) a thief's gain from theft is greater when stealing from a fellow group member than from an outsider, and this premium is greater in poor groups than in rich groups; (2) parents of two or more non-twin children will spend more of their toy budget on an annual gift-giving occasion than on the children's birthday; (3) blind persons are less at risk of eating disorders than are sighted persons; (4) veterans of wars fought on home soil have lower risk of posttraumatic stress syndrome than veterans of wars fought away from home; (5) vocations to the religious life are an increasing function of economic inequality; (6) a deposed leader is more likely to be executed if the people care about justice; and (7) in a status regime, people are closer to their neighbors below than to their neighbors above, but the opposite occurs in a comparison regime.

HUMAN RIGHTS AND MATHEMATICAL SOCIOLOGY

The study and practice of human rights demands great accuracy and precision. It is vital to know who did what to whom and when and who knew what and when. This is the kind of accuracy, precision, and transparency that mathematics enables.

TRANSPARENCY WITH RESPECT TO THE WEIGHT OF EACH ACTOR

When a salary committee makes recommendations for compensation, when panels of judges or juries make decisions on punishments, when a firm or organization makes hiring decisions, the weight of each decision-making actor is crucial. The weights may range from complete equality, to weighting schemes in which some actors have a larger say than others, to stark situations in which only one actor's voice counts. Verbal descriptions of the procedures can be vague or confusing. Explicit expression of a weight matrix enables full transparency. As a simple example, Table 34.4 provides the weight matrix associated with the wage matrix in Table 34.1.

Table 34.4 The weight matrix: N wage-setters and J workers

A. The Wage-Setter-Specific/Worker-Specific Weight

$$w_{ij}$$

where w denotes the weight, the wage-setters are indexed by i ($i = 1, ..., N$) and the workers by j ($j = 1, ..., J$), and the weights are nonnegative and for each worker sum to one. That is, $w_i \geq o$ and $\sum w_i = 1$.

B. Weight Matrix

$$W = \begin{bmatrix} w_{11} & w_{12} & w_{13} & \cdots & w_{1J} \\ w_{21} & w_{22} & w_{23} & \cdots & w_{2J} \\ w_{31} & w_{32} & w_{33} & \cdots & w_{3J} \\ \vdots & \vdots & \vdots & \ddots & \vdots \\ w_{N1} & w_{N2} & w_{N3} & \cdots & w_{NJ} \end{bmatrix}$$

C. The Case of a Wage-Setter with Absolute Power

If one wage-setter has absolute power, the weight matrix collapses to a vector:

$$w_{.j} = \begin{bmatrix} w_{.1} & w_{.2} & w_{.3} & \cdots & w_{.J} \end{bmatrix} = \begin{bmatrix} 1 & 1 & 1 & \cdots & 1 \end{bmatrix}$$

D. The Case of a Single Weighting Scheme for All Workers

If weights do not differ by worker, the weight matrix collapses to a vector:

$$w_{i.} = \begin{bmatrix} w_{1.} \\ w_{2.} \\ w_{3.} \\ \vdots \\ w_{N.} \end{bmatrix}$$

Weights also play an important part in the study of justice. Justice and injustice are subjective constructs and have no life independent of an observer; hence, the first task is to identify the observer(s) whose justice assessments are to be counted in discussions of justice. Three traditions provide answers to the problem of identifying the relevant observer whose justice judgments are to be counted. At one extreme is theology, in which the relevant observer is God. The theologian attempts to discover the sense of justice that is in the mind of God; notwithstanding the theologian's feats of reasoning, there is never any question that the only important judgment is God's and that the theologian's view is at best a faint approximation. At the other extreme is social science, in which the relevant observers are unambiguously everyone. Every person's justice assessments are of interest. Between theology and social science lies philosophy, in which the archetypal relevant observers are the Platonic societal guardians, but which extends from quasi-theological analyses in which the relevant observer is a being possessing certain God-like properties—such as Firth's (1952) "ideal observer" or Hare's (1981) "archangel"—to quasi-scientific analyses, such as that of Rawls (1971), who seeks to discover principles of justice with which all humans would agree. As in the wage example, a weight matrix may be used to assemble the weights of the observers.

TRANSPARENCY WITH RESPECT TO INCLUSION/EXCLUSION OF ACTORS IN A POPULATION

Mathematical representation of a population forces us to make explicit who is included or excluded from the population. For example, suppose that a firm or organization receives a windfall, and part of it will be distributed as supplementary funds to subunits or as bonuses for staffers. The group among whom the windfall will be distributed cannot be hidden in a mathematical representation. In the case of bonuses to individuals, mathematical representations will make clear that some receive nothing, as does the fraction of the population they represent. Thus, mathematics reveals the distribution of the bonuses and inequality across the recipients.

TRANSPARENCY WITH RESPECT TO ASSUMPTIONS AND MATHEMATICAL SPECIFICATIONS BY AND ABOUT INDIVIDUALS WITH DIFFERENT QUALITATIVE CHARACTERISTICS (GENDER, RACE, ETHNICITY, RELIGION, ETC.)

More broadly, decisions about who counts among decision-makers and who counts among rewardees may notice qualitative characteristics of the wage-setters, observers, and rewardees. Mathematical sociology forces such decisions to become explicit. For example, if the population allowed to vote or to own property or to work for pay includes only persons of a given gender or religion or citizenship or language, these features must be made explicit; they cannot be hidden behind a veil of words.

NEW QUESTIONS AT THE INTERSECTION OF MATHEMATICAL SOCIOLOGY AND HUMAN RIGHTS

JUSTICE, INCLUSION, AND EXCLUSION

Theories of distributive justice typically begin with a population and then proceed to discuss the principles of justice governing relations between members of the population. A more fundamental question concerns the definition of the population and the rules for inclusion. For example, some rules may apply only to natives. Foreigners may be the functional equivalents of slaves, women, or those without property in other eras.

JUSTICE, SPECIALISTS, AND ORDINARY PEOPLE

Procedures for combining individuals' ideas of justice—just pay, just punishments, just procedures, just war—sometimes give more weight to specialists. But a basic tenet of human rights is that all persons count equally. Thus, an important new question is to assess the determinants of granting unequal weights to the ideas of justice espoused by different persons.

A LOOK FORWARD

I believe that in the coming years there will be two kinds of progress at the intersection of mathematical sociology and human rights. First, there will be a new transparency in sociological models and new attentiveness to matters of inclusion and of the worth of persons. Second, the set of sociologists producing the new results will grow as more and more sociologists claim their mathematical heritage.

CHAPTER THIRTY-FIVE

ETHNOMETHODOLOGY AND CONVERSATION ANALYSIS

Peter Eglin

The demand that US President Barack Hussein Obama produce his birth certificate to show the bona fides of his occupancy of the White House had, of course, its precedents.

P: What's your name, boy?
D: Dr. Poussaint. I'm a physician.
P: What's your first name, boy?
D: Alvin.

On a street in Jackson, Mississippi, in 1966, a black doctor (D) is asked for his name by a white policeman (P), who addresses him with the derogatory term "boy." D answers with his title, last name, and occupation, to which P responds by asking for his first name and repeating the slur. D answers by providing his first name (Watson 1984, 63; Speier 1973, 188; Ervin-Tripp 1972, 218; Poussaint 1967). This brief episode is recognizable to any competent observer as a case of racial subordination of D by P, though no racial descriptors are used. It is clearly an abuse of D's human rights, being at least an "attack upon his honour" (Article 12 of the Universal Declaration of Human Rights [UDHR]).

To see what ethnomethodology (EM) might make of such an interactional episode, it is helpful to employ Francis and Hester's (2004, 25–26) three-step model of ethnomethodological methodology:

1. Notice something that is observably the case about some talk, activity, or setting.
2. Pose the question, How is it that this observable feature has been produced such that it is recognizable for what it is?
3. Consider, analyze, and describe the methods used in the production and recognition of the observable feature.

Step One

It is observably the case about this talk in interaction that it consists of a sequence of observable actions in the form of two question-answer exchanges. In the first exchange, P "asks" D for his name while insulting him by addressing him as "boy," which D observably attempts to counter by prefacing his last name with the honorific "Dr." and explicating it with the hearably high-status occupational title of "physician." In the third turn, P may be heard as doubling the insult by "asking" for D's first name and repeating "boy" (Speier 1973, 189). In the fourth turn it may be said that D hearably succumbs to P's demands by providing his first name.

Although it is not incorrect to say that the four turns consist of two (information-seeking) questions and two answers, it is more to the point to say that the question-format here conveys a demand or command rather than simply a request for information, so that in answering P's question, D may be heard to be complying or obeying rather than simply providing the information.

We may further notice that P is here acting as at least a police officer, that D is responding as at least a citizen or member of the public, and that P is engaged in what is at least a routine activity of police officers, namely, asking or demanding that a citizen identify him- or herself. But this episode is also hearably an instance of a white person humiliating and subordinating a black person in spite of, and perhaps because of, the latter's modest resistance.

Step Two

How is it that these actions and identities are recognizable for what they are? How is it that the four utterances represented in the four lines of the transcript are observably or hearably (or visibly, for the reader) a "sequence of turns of talk" in which the two parties are observably "talking to each other" by tying each subsequent turn to the one that preceded it (rather than the episode merely being a temporally contiguous but otherwise adventitious collection of speech-bits uttered to no one in particular)? How is it that P's utterances are observably performing the actions of "demanding identification," "insulting" the person being addressed, and doing so in a "racially motivated" way designed to put that person (back) in his place? How are D's utterances hearable as "resisting the put-down" and "complying with the demand"? How is it that P is here visibly acting "as a police officer" and D as a "citizen"? And how is it observable that this episode is relevantly one between a "white" and a "black" (rather than, say, between two guys out and about in the town)?

Step Three

Ethnomethodology is so named because it treats such questions as asking for an account that explicates the "methodology" societal members (or "ethnos") use to determine just such social facts as those listed above. Note that by using this method, parties to the interaction themselves "see" what action an utterance is performing. This method also allows participants to understand who is performing the actions, along with their own identity for the occasion in question.

Thus, D may find who he is for P on this occasion when P both asks him for his name and addresses him as "boy." "Police officer" is one of those occupational categories whose incumbents may "request the papers" of citizens or members of the public without introduction or explanation (the request being, in effect, a demand). This action is an entitlement of the category "police." The citizen has a corresponding obligation to comply, with attendant consequences for not doing so. The culturally available, and here-and-now occasioned, tie between the action of asking for one's name and the identity category "police" provides a method of practical reasoning by means of which one so addressed may see that "What's your name?" is such a request or demand (and not, say, a pickup line) and that the one making it is, for this occasion, a police officer, as his uniform signifies (and not a fellow player in the local bowling league, in or out of uniform). With such a method D can see that he is being asked for at least his last name, if not his full legal name. But P follows the name request with the word "boy," a customary address term by whites for blacks in the South. By invoking the visibly available color difference between them, D can now find that "boy" is on this occasion that racially evoca-tive epithet (and not a jovial greeting between friends), that he is relevantly for this occasion a black (and not just a citizen), and, moreover, that he is being subjected to customary white racism.

D's analysis of P's first turn is conveyed in D's first turn, in which he does more than give his name in response. Notice first, though, that "Dr. Poussaint. I'm a physi-cian" stands to be heard as an "answer" by virtue of its positioning immediately after what is hearably a question (by virtue of its interrogative format). (Otherwise it might be any number of things, including a person rehearsing introducing himself to an academic in need of medical assistance, where "Dr. Poussaint" is a term of address rather than a reference to the speaker.) Its observability as the motivated action of replying to a request or demand is dependent on its speaker having located it next to—that is, immediately following—a preceding question. That it is also hearable as doing the further interactional work of countering P's racial putdown is evident in D's adding to his last name "Dr." and "I'm a physician." D's going beyond the mere provision of his name is parallel to P's having gone beyond its mere solicitation. Of all the versions of one's name one might employ in fulfilling such a request (Sacks 1992, 1: 282–291, 2: 56–66, 68–69, 376–383; Watson 1981), D provides his professional name and occupation. D, that is, attempts to counter the putdown of "boy" by upping his status with "physician" (a status that also outranks that of police officer). For P, no doubt, D is being an "uppity n____r."

The foregoing analysis of an accessible case of social interaction embodying a transparent instance of a human rights violation based on race is intended to serve as a nontechnical entry to ethnomethodology for the purpose of considering its relation to human rights and as a preface to the more formal, abstracted account of the field that now follows. A more technical conversation-analytic account of the case returns below.

ETHNOMETHODOLOGY

Ethnomethodology is the discovery and invention of Harold Garfinkel (1917–2011), one of the greatest of twentieth-century sociologists (Lynch and Sharrock 2003; Rawls 2000), who died as I was revising this chapter (Weber 2011). Stephen Hester notes that the ethnomethodology program's "central recommendation" is stated on the first page of Garfinkel's first book, *Studies in Ethnomethodology* (1967):

> The following studies seek to treat practical activities, practical circumstances and practical sociological reasoning as topics of empirical study, and by paying to the most commonplace activities of daily life the attention usually afforded extraordinary events, seek to learn about them in their own right. Their central recommendation is that the activities whereby members produce and manage settings of organized everyday affairs are identical with members' procedures for making those settings "account-able." (2009, 240)

"Account-able" here means "observable-reportable." That is, ethnomethodology is (the study of) societal members' methods or procedures for making their and others' actions observable and reportable as those actions. It is (the study of) members' methods of making sense, where "making sense" refers to both the work through which members produce their actions as recognizable to others and the work by which members do the recognizing.

From his studies as a graduate student of Talcott Parsons in the 1940s (see Garfinkel 2006, 2008) to his death in 2011, Garfinkel sought to "respecify" the problem of social order as formulated by Parsons (Rawls 2006) to focus on social order's production from within the conduct of everyday affairs. "It is Garfinkel's central contention that order is already complete in the concrete" (Frank 1988; cited in Garfinkel and Wieder 1992, 176). In Garfinkel's words, "The objective reality of social facts [as] sociology's fundamental phenomenon ... is an astronomically massive domain of phenomena of social order" that are irremediably missed by social science's constructive-analytic methods (2002, 119). The ensuing and considerable body of studies by ethnomethodologists of that missing domain of phenomena is diverse in content and method (Maynard and Clayman 1991), but practitioners share a focus on seeking to elucidate members' local achievement of social order "at all points" (Sacks 1984, 22). They investigate members' practical sociological reasoning across all forms of social action and social practice, lay and professional, from air traffic control to basketball to surgery, from talk on the telephone to office-hour consultations, from congressional inquiries to forensic pathology and mathematics, from such sciences as astronomy and zoology to such arts as anthropology and Zen Buddhism, from cognitive psychology and linguistics to computer-supported cooperative work, including all substantive and methodological areas of sociology from education to gender, from medicine to race, from media to work, from asking questions to zeta coding and more.

A mass of studies resists easy summary, though Hester (2009, 240–243) has ably sketched the broad outlines as follows: studies of accountability, rule use, and mundane reasoning (e.g., Zimmerman 1970; Wieder 1974; Pollner 1987); conversation analysis (CA) comprising sequential analysis (SA) and membership categorization analysis (MCA) (Sacks 1992); the studies of work program (e.g., Garfinkel 1986; Button 1993); and what might be called the "Wittgensteinian ethnomethodology of mind" (e.g., Coulter 1979, 1989; Coulter and Sharrock 2007). See Paul ten Have's Ethno/CA News website (http://www.paultenhave.nl/EMCA.htm) for current activities, bibliographies, and the ongoing train of published studies in the field.

ETHNOMETHODOLOGY'S KEY FINDINGS—NOT!

Because EM, not to say sociology itself, properly understood (Winch 2008), is more akin to philosophy than to empirical science, there is a sense in which it is true to say that its "state" does not change (Hutchinson, Read, and Sharrock 2008, 91–112). EM does not have a collection of key findings since it is not a "discovering science" in the first place. As Sharrock puts it, "It is not motivated by the aspiration to make *discoveries* about the nature of social phenomena, but to undertake the *recovery* of what is already known—but is 'known' in the form of competent mastery of practical affairs—to the members of society" (2001, 258). Thus "findings" are its subject matter, not the outcome of its researches. How members of society going about the work of living find the objects, facts, and conclusions they do is its question and topic. This includes how members make these findings observable and reportable to others. You can say that what EM finds about the methods members use to make their findings is, in a sense, always the same. Such methods are taken for granted, locally occasioned, reflexively organized, interactional accomplishments. But what this amounts to in any instance is incarnate in the instances themselves.

ETHNOMETHODOLOGY'S METHODS—NOT!

Accordingly, just as EM "does not aspire to the formation of *theory*" (Sharrock 2001, 251; Rawls 2006; Hester 2009, 237–239), so it does not have "a set of distinctively *methodological*" concerns (Sharrock 2001, 252). It most certainly does not have specialized "methods of data collection" that are "distinct from everyday 'methodical' practices" (Hester 2009, 243), since "data is stuff that society itself makes available—what is found in an evening class in Kung Fu, what can be taped off TV, what can be witnessed or overheard in a courtroom, and so on and so on" (Hughes and Sharrock 2007, 264). Instead EM adopts a particular policy toward inquiry, an "analytic mentality" (Schenkein 1978) that attends exclusively to "instantiations of the array of practices comprising *practices of practical sociological* reasoning," lay and professional, without privileging the latter (Sharrock 2001, 252). How it does that is not (and could not be, given EM's take on social order) independent of the very ways in which the phenomena comprising the subject matter of EM's inquiries make themselves available for observation and report (Hester and Eglin 1997b, 1)—that is, are "account-able" in Garfinkel's terms. "There is ... no prohibition against using any research procedure whatsoever, if it is *adequate* to the particular phenomenon under study" (Lynch 1996, 267; see part

2 of Hughes and Sharrock [2007] for extended discussion of method's adequacy or faithfulness to phenomena).

What EM does require is immersion in the phenomena under study, whether the unreflective immersion attending participation in the ordinary interactional business of everyday life (like talking), self-reflection on one's own actions (like reading the newspaper), or acquired immersion in some specialized activity (like courtroom litigation or long-haul truck driving) (Francis and Hester 2004, 26; Hester 2009, 243–244). Garfinkel refers to immersion as the "unique adequacy requirement of methods" (Garfinkel and Wieder 1992, 182–184). This is not to say, however, that conversation analysis, as a partially independent offshoot of EM, has not developed "particular research techniques" (Lynch 1996, 267), as will become evident below.

CONVERSATION ANALYSIS AND THE CASE IN POINT RESUMED

Conversation analysis was developed by Harvey Sacks (1992) in relation to ethnomethodology (Garfinkel and Sacks 1970) and in collaboration with Emanuel Schegloff and Gail Jefferson. It has long since become its own substantial field (Drew and Heritage 2006). From the start it has had two emphases, namely, sequential analysis of the turn-taking system for conversation and derivative speech-exchange systems (Sacks, Schegloff, and Jefferson 1974; Schegloff, Jefferson, and Sacks 1977) and membership categorization analysis of the terminology of person-description (Sacks 1972a, 1972b). While there have always been studies that have not only combined the two emphases but seen them as interdependent (Watson 1997; Hester and Eglin 1997b: 2–3, 165n2), the two have become identifiable subfields in their own right (Jayyusi 1984; Hester and Eglin 1997a; Schegloff 2007a, 2007b, 2007c). Space availability does not permit giving an adequate account of either branch of CA, but some idea of their analytic practices (or research techniques) can be gleaned from taking up our case in point in their technical terms.

Thus, in terms of SA of turn taking, we may refer to the four utterances as four turns at talk that consist of two adjacency-paired exchanges.

In its minimal, basic, unexpanded form, an adjacency pair is characterized by certain features. It is

(a) composed of two turns
(b) by different speakers
(c) adjacently placed; that is, one after the other
(d) these two turns are relatively ordered; that is, they are differentiated into "first pair parts" (Fs for short) and "second pair parts" (Ss for short). First pair parts are utterance types such as question, request, offer, invitation, announcement, etc.—types that *initiate* some exchange. Second pair parts are utterance types such as answer, grant, reject, accept, decline, agree/disagree, acknowledge, etc.—types that are *responsive* to the action of a prior turn.... Besides being differentiated into Fs and Ss, the components of an adjacency pair are

(e) pair-type related; that is, not every second pair part can properly follow any first pair part. Adjacency pairs compose pair types; types are exchanges such as greeting-greeting, question-answer, offer/accept/decline, and the like. . . .
 The basic practice or rule of operation, then, by which the minimal form of the adjacency pair is produced is: given the recognizable production of a first pair part, on its first possible completion its speaker should stop, a next speaker should start . . . and should produce a second pair part of the same pair type. (Schegloff 2007c: 13–14)

It is evident that P and D produce their four turns as two consecutive adjacency-paired exchanges of questions and answers. But notice that this is their interactional achievement, a product of their sequential analysis of each other's talk. The turn-taking system is not formalizable since it is "participant-managed" (Button et al. 1995, 194, 197).

By means of this sequence type they perform certain actions—demanding and providing identification, addressing and responding to being so addressed, insulting and countering the insult, and so on. The recognizability of these actions for the parties themselves (and thereby for the overhearing professional sociological analyst) depends, however, upon the speakers' use of interactional resources other than the sequentially organized properties of the turn-taking system for conversation (or interrogation). That "What's your name?" as the first pair part of a question-answer adjacency pair stands to be heard as a demand for identification rather than a disinterested request for information or a preface to a solicitation for money derives from the speaker and hearer appreciating who is making it and how such a question relates to the categorial identity of the speaker. The parties may be said, that is, to be engaged in carrying out their own MCA of their situation. D may find that "What's your name?" is a demand that he identify himself by seeing the speaker as an incumbent of the category "police officer," where that category has been selected from a collection of occupational categories that, together with its rules of application, constitutes the membership categorization device (MCD) "occupation." In this way he may find that the inquirer is asking the question in his occupational capacity as such an officer, that indeed such an officer is entitled (if not required, depending on the circumstances) to make such an inquiry, and that he (D) is obliged to answer. In terms of professional MCA, that entitlement may be construed as a category-bound or category-tied predicate of the category "police officer." This tie between category and predicate then provides, when locally occasioned, a practical reasoning resource through the use of which the hearer may find both who is speaking to him (a police officer) and how he is being spoken to (he is being "questioned"). MCA refers to the locally occasioned use of such ties for such purposes as being in conformity with certain rules of application, such as the following "viewer's maxim":

If a member sees a category-bound activity being done, then, if one can see it being done by a member of a category to which the activity is bound, then: See it that way. (Sacks 1972b: 338)

But what gets to be interesting here are the categorial identities made pro-grammatically relevant for the one being addressed (D) when the speaker (P) speaks as a police officer. If "police officer" implicates the "occupation" MCD, then by virtue of what MCA calls the "consistency rule" and the "consistency rule corollary" (Hester and Eglin 1997b, 5), D can find it relevant to describe himself, and to be heard to be describing himself, with a category from the same device. Thus, "I'm a physician." Yet, when police officers question others, it is not as incumbents of specific occupations that they address them, but in terms of one or another of a closely related assortment of categories that may include "citizen," "member of the public," "person of interest," "suspect," "accused," "offender," "convict," "prisoner," and "ex-con." Here it appears to be (at least) "citizen." Such categories fall into pairs with police officer as the first pair part, and in each case the pairs imply a relationship between the parts, characterized by the normative entitlements and obligations already referred to. MCA calls such pairs asymmetric standardized relational pairs (SRPs) (Jayyusi 1984, 125). Moreover, although there is not space to pursue it, a third MCD may be relevant here, what Sacks (1972a: 37–40, 61–63) calls "K" (for "knowledge"), consisting of the two categories "professionals" and "laypeople." That is, with respect to matters of law enforcement and keeping the peace, the police may be said to be professionals, the rest of us, laypeople. Readers may wish to consult Jayyusi's chapter on "category-generated problems and some solutions" for a penetrating discussion of the interactional considerations attending members' invoking of this categorization device (1984, 123–150).

What, however, undoubtedly brings this episode to attention is its paradig-matic instantiation of a classic method of racial subordination, and thereby violation of D's human rights, without explicit reference to racial categories or descriptors. For EM/CA the question is how this is achieved, for it apparently consists of nothing more than the employment of a single word ("boy," twice) and the seemingly most innocent of inquiries ("What's your first name?"). The achievement in each case relies on what MCA calls the stage-of-life MCD, which consists of a positioned set of categories for referring to persons according to their stage of life—baby, toddler, infant, child, adolescent, teenager, adult, girl/woman, boy/man, and so on. One standard use of this categorization device is to praise or belittle persons by referring to or addressing them with a higher or lower positioned category, respectively, than they would otherwise be incum-bents of (Sacks 1972b: 336). To refer to a man as a boy is, without qualification, to demean him. To address him as such is perhaps even worse since it is done to his face. To do the second when one is in a position of authority not easily challenged by the recipient is especially humiliating. And to do it by invoking the SRP of white-black (Watson 1983) and thereby a whole history of racial oppression founded in at least the standardized, normative treatment of African American adults as children is to be cruel beyond words. D responds with the one interactional resource available to him for peaceful resistance in defense of his dignity, namely, the occupational status hierarchy invoked by P acting as a police officer. "Dr. Poussaint. I'm a physician," D says. But to no avail.

Whereas it is essential, if man is not to be compelled to have recourse, as a last resort, to rebellion against tyranny and oppression, that human rights should be protected by the rule of law. (Preamble, UDHR)

ETHNOMETHODOLOGY AND ITS RELATION TO HUMAN RIGHTS SOCIOLOGY

I hope to have conveyed, through a perspicuous demonstration of EM's analytic mentality in practice, its distinctiveness in relation to conventional sociology in general and human rights sociology in particular (Sharrock and Button 1991, 167). It is a category mistake to suppose that by explicating the interactional accomplishment of an answer to a question by sequential analysis of the adjacency-paired organization of turn taking, or of an attempt to counter a racial slur by membership categorization analysis of an occupational status contest, one is advancing the cause of universal human rights! Yet this is the stated purpose of the current project, which aims "to offer new insights into the social structures, relations and practices that will most fully support the *realization of human rights in the world*" and asks, "How can ethnomethodological sociology *further* human rights—as they are both conceptualized *and lived?*" (my emphasis). My point here is that EM and human rights sociology are simply two fundamentally different enterprises. And that's because EM and professional sociology, construed as "constructive analysis" (Garfinkel and Sacks 1970, 345–346, 358–362), are "two incommensurable, asymmetrically alternate technologies of social analysis" (Garfinkel and Wieder 1992; Garfinkel 2002, 117).

The relevant part of what this means for this discussion is that EM is "ethnomethodologically indifferent" (Garfinkel and Sacks 1970, 345–346) to any practical, normative, moral, or political import members of society may attribute to the phenomena under investigation. This position stands in clear and stark contrast to the attitude that informs human rights sociology, the practitioners of which are hardly indifferent to the question of moral responsibility for intolerable states of human affairs represented by egregious violations of human rights. For, like not only Marxist and feminist sociology but what Garfinkel calls the whole "world-wide social science movement," human rights sociology is itself heir to and part of a movement, in this case the human rights movement. However much practitioners may "academicize" (Fish 2008, 27–30) their research and teaching in human rights, the concept itself is thoroughly value laden and inseparable from the movement bearing its name. Indeed, the problems that sociologists in general take up are routinely driven by practical, rather than theoretical, considerations, such that the concepts they employ are not simply descriptive of some state of affairs in the world but embody some evaluation of it (Sharrock 1980, 121–122; for Weber, see Hughes, Martin, and Sharrock 1995, 128–129). This is surely true of human rights sociology.

Clearly, EM's position stands in radical contrast to the main thrust of the social sciences, whose practitioners (including me as a teacher of human rights) not only want their (my) science to be useful, whether for reform or revolution, but build that desire into their (my) conceptualizing. They (we) stand in the great Comtean tradition in which sociology is the queen of John Stuart Mill's moral sciences, of the worldwide social science movement. As Émile Durkheim put it in 1893, "If we separate carefully the theoretical from the practical problems, it is not to the neglect of the latter; but, on the contrary, to be in a better position to solve them" (1964 [1893], 33). But that cunning phrase, "moral science," embodies a self-contradiction and, with it, the endless confounding of fact and value that dogs mainstream sociology. EM's strength is precisely its insistence on being ethnomethodologically indifferent to all such practical concerns. Moreover, in this way it stands in parallel with Wittgenstein's own fundamental declaration that "philosophy leaves everything as it is" (Sharrock and Anderson 1991, 62). Ethnomethodological indifference is EM's formal equivalent to Wittgenstein's stance and must necessarily be so if EM is to make practical action its subject. It should be supererogatory to state that, in being strictly methodological, this indifference has nothing to do with whether or not practitioners care about human rights or any other normative matter outside their ethnomethodological inquiries.

Thus EM is, in the strictest sense, ethnomethodologically indifferent to the fact that members of society may be described as "human beings" with, say, "inalienable rights." That members may "find" it relevant to describe themselves as "human beings" who bear "inalienable human rights" is itself, for EM, a social production, an interactional accomplishment. Alternatively, the human rights paradigm may be said to be founded in the distinction between citizen and state or, more broadly, between individual and society (see Coulter 1982; Jayyusi 1984; Sharrock and Watson 1988). From EM's point of view these categories and distinctions may be thought of as membership categorization devices (Hester and Eglin 1997c), methods for producing social order just like those of "occupation," "stage of life," and "police-citizen" in the analysis above.

Whether this chapter's demonstration of the practical sociological reasoning used to accomplish an instance of racial subordination is, as a contingent matter, of use or relevance for the theory and/or practice of human rights sociology is a matter to which EM, qua EM, cannot be anything but indifferent. Put even more bluntly, since "ethnomethodology is NOT a corrective enterprise ... NOT a rival science in the worldwide social science movement" (Garfinkel 2002, 121), it has nothing critical to teach human rights sociology. It can only study it (Jayyusi 1991, 235).

By the same token, and as should be abundantly evident by this point, human rights sociology has nothing to say to EM. EM cannot but appear as entirely and irrevocably irrelevant to its interests.

CHAPTER THIRTY-SIX

COMPARATIVE AND HISTORICAL SOCIOLOGY

Jean H. Quataert and Benita Roth

A historical and sociological approach to human rights activism raises new and challenging questions of interest to both historians and sociologists working in the field. Despite expectations of a growing convergence between the two disciplines, seen partly in the rise to prominence of historical sociology as a separate subfield of inquiry by the late 1970s, scholars in each discipline continue to approach research with distinct methods, questions, concepts, and purposes (Bonnell 1980; Skocpol 1984). And yet, human rights research offers a fruitful basis for renewed interdisciplinary dialogue and exchange, particularly with regard to transnationality in social movements. The historian's approach, with its attention to the specificity of time and place, as well as its roots in primary archival and published sources, offers precisely the rich empirical data with which sociologists can formulate, test, and refine theories and concepts. Historians also contribute a set of distinct questions reflecting the contingent nature of historical change. While a unique byproduct of the historical perspective, they are of potential interest to sociologists. In turn, sociologists reconstruct patterns of national and transnational claims making for rights, and historical sociologists also bring a discussion of historical details and contingency into the assessment of these patterns. Skocpol notes that historical sociological studies examine "concretely situated" dynamics and "address processes over time," with serious methodological focus on the way that actions take place in time and within structural constraints (1984, 4). As a historian and a historical sociologist, we demonstrate in this chapter a beneficial convergence of interests around the international and transnational nexus of organizing, transnational social-movement theories, gender, and global interactions among feminist activists.

A COMPARATIVE HISTORICAL EXAMINATION OF HUMAN RIGHTS

Historians are latecomers to studying the field of human rights, a topic still dominated by a focus on recent developments and time frames. A historical perspective thus has much to add to the discussions. Historians began to enter this research arena only several decades ago and, at the outset, concentrated on the origins (or genealogies) of human rights as ideals and norms. To date, however, much of this literature reproduces one or the other of two easily conflated fallacies. The first regards all historical expressions of rights and moral principles as forerunners of human rights and elides them (Ishay 1997). It is, to be sure, important to acknowledge the multiple moral traditions that have helped establish widely shared principles of justice and dignity. To claim these precepts are equivalent expressions of human rights in any operative or legal sense, however, is not historically accurate. Such a claim fails to differentiate the subtle complexities as well as the specific historical and cultural meanings around the notions of freedom, rights, liberties, privileges, and power over time and in different cultures. It is also historically inaccurate to think about human rights movements as such prior to the past two hundred years. As Tarrow (1998), Tilly (1978), and others have argued, modern social movements require at least the technological necessities of communication to transmit ideas and action repertoires that allow claims making to take place.

The second approach understands human rights to be a "revival" or "rebirth" of natural rights philosophy and law characteristic of European Enlightenment universalism. Drawing on the philosophical works of John Locke and Hugo Grotius, this liberal formulation imagined men with an equality of rights in the state of nature and limited state power to the protection of men's inalienable rights (Burgers 1992; Hunt 2007). But the revivalist view works to flatten historical time and also conflates natural rights and human rights, leading to less precision about the demands of activists. In addition, natural rights, historically, constructed sovereignty; human rights principles have the potential to subvert state sovereign prerogatives. Besides, the revivalist view also leaves out the whole post-Enlightenment history of political thought and actions taking place around the globe, not the least of which were the international organizing from the early 1800s to abolish slavery, the mid-nineteenth-century movement for women's rights, and the international movements on behalf of rights for workers. As in the transnational networks coordinating socialist, feminist, or anticolonial movements, many of these mobilizations reflected alternatives to liberal rights traditions. However, both major interpretations are framed in terms of "progress" and inevitable "human betterment."

The state of the field is much more complex now. Many historians and social scientists have come to acknowledge the Janus-faced nature of rights visions and interventions and their multiple, often contradictory uses in specific contexts, particularly, but not limited to, questions of gender. These new understandings work to displace the linear, progressive narratives of early rights history. For example, in a 2008 article, Eric Weitz coins the term "entangled history" to assess a major shift in the international order between the Vienna Peace Treaty (ending the Napoleonic Wars) and the Paris Peace Accords after World War I. From an international and European Great Power perspective, he shows how nineteenth-century diplomacy became increasingly focused on population policies and, specifically, on colonized and minority peoples in eastern Europe, Africa, and the Ottoman Empire. These new concerns led, on the one hand, to formulations of minority protections and a "civilizing" mission promising statehood at some distant future and, on the other, to strategies of forced population exchanges, expulsions, and efforts at annihilation.

Weitz (2008) posits that emerging rights protections and state-sanctioned violence were two sides of the same new diplomatic coin.

Also employing the interpretive perspective of Great Power politics, Mark Mazower (2004) sees the "strange" shift from minority protections under the League of Nations to individual human rights under the United Nations as a product of calculated state interests rather than solely a triumph of morality over "realpolitik" and "barbarism." Bringing gender analysis to this international perspective, Barbara Metzger looks at the larger historical context leading to passage of a Convention on the Suppression of Traffic in Women and Children (1921) under League auspices. She shows how European feminist concerns with appreciable "white slave traffic" networks expanded in the new arena of global interactions in interwar Geneva to address problems of trafficking worldwide. In response, some governments adopted progressive legislation, which "legalized prostitution, penalized procurement and provided for widespread health services to those in need." Illustrating unintended consequences, Metzger (2007, 62) also shows how governments used the new international agreements to restrict many women's efforts to move across borders for work.

Building on these detailed studies, human rights historians are recognizing the necessity of grounded empirical research to sustain new understandings of the complexity of human rights histories. These histories have been challenged recently by groundbreaking collections about feminist organizing in international and transnational scales by Sinha, Guy, and Woollacott (1999), Marx Ferree and Tripp (2006), and Basu (2010), all of which insist on reimagining historical understandings of human rights activism as centrally constructed by feminists and women's rights advocates. These edited collections, as well as monographs like those of Mohanty (2006) or Moghadam (2005), constitute a project at once political and scholarly aimed at creating at the same time a broader understanding of the perimeters of gender rights and human rights struggles. In a word, these efforts by feminist scholars are ambitious; as Sinha, Guy, and Woollacott state, "At its broadest, the history of feminisms and internationalism is a lens through which we can view modern world history" (1999, 3).

ASKING QUESTIONS ABOUT HUMAN RIGHTS

Of specific concern to historians' work are questions of time and chronology and, thus, the question of whether to write human rights narratives diachronically (as unfolding over time) or as a discontinuous process, with starts, stops, and gaps as well as high and low points of societal interest in all manner of rights issues. The other question of course is what counts as a human rights narrative, a question compelling in gender analysis, as noted above. Here the feminist political project corresponds to an empirical and historical one aimed at folding gender activism back into the picture of human rights activism, even though historically women's rights have been treated as requiring "special" attention—that is, through the 1979 Convention on the Elimination of All Forms of Discrimination against Women

(CEDAW), the most important international law proclaiming women's rights in the second half of the twentieth century. Historians and social scientists need to overcome this administrative fiat in writing their scholarly analyses. These matters of time and inclusion have been debated most intensely for the post–World War II period. For example, one body of recent historical scholarship sees the 1970s as the major turning point in human rights history. Although contested, its authors point to a confluence of global forces during the decade that vastly expanded human rights agendas into diplomatic discourses and transnational activism (Moyn 2010; Eckel 2009). Here, it is the historians' interest in timing that brings known evidence into new patterns. However, if feminist internationalist and transnationalist organizing is reintegrated into discussions of rights organizing, the picture looks much more continuous and less punctuated by spasms; several essays in the Sinha, Guy, and Woollacott (1999) collection see feminist efforts continuing beyond the interwar period in a number of places around the world, ironically spurred by the world war that was choking the life out of international feminist organizing in Europe (see, e.g., Miller 1999).

Complementing these questions, a wealth of newly gathered historical details helps provide some insights into the complex and varied meanings attached to human rights by people's struggles and mobilizations over time. After all, human rights crises are never generic; they may be about grave breaches of community norms of life, liberty, personal security, or social justice, but they take place at precise movements in time and in distinct communities. Human rights tragedies are tangible events about people with faces, names, families, and histories. They must be placed within their specific historical and social contexts. Historians and sociologists alike share these assumptions, sustaining fruitful exchanges of research findings. Historically, these questions have revolved around how and why human rights visions came to resonate among people at risk. More precisely put, when did human rights notions become believable, to whom, and in which specific contexts? A corollary question asks whether human rights movements are a new form of politics in the public arena. Do advocates at times deploy neutral or "humanitarian" languages for eminently political purposes? In addition, what ties connect human rights mobilizations; leftist, radical feminist, and solidarity movements; and movements for racial/ethnic liberation?

Finally, the historian's sensitivity to change raises questions about transitions and shifts in the meaning of terms and themes. Thus, for example, Quataert's empirical work explores the "knowledge revolution" that is at the basis of the shift from sex equality enshrined in the UN Charter to gender as a new category of human rights protections that underpinned the emergence of the global women's human rights movements during the UN Decade for Women (1975–1985). Others have catalogued changes in the meaning of key concepts such as self-determination, which emerged as colonial people's increasingly insistent calls for national liberation and independence. Linked to universal human rights principles by prominent leaders of new nations in the 1950s, self-determination served, by the late 1960s, to defend territorial sovereignty against any outside interference. Still later, some of the same postcolonial leaders used self-determination to push international law to protect states' vital economic resources against exploitative policies of powerful nations and multinational corporations. Others note the centrality of self-determination to women's struggles for sexual autonomy and state support of reproductive rights and health measures that emerged globally in the 1990s (Quataert 2010; Burke 2010; Anghie 2005; Reilly 2009, 83–88).

WHAT DO COMPARATIVE HISTORICAL RESEARCHERS' FINDINGS TELL US?

Despite the many contributions of historians to human rights research, it is difficult to summarize the key findings because there is no firm interpretive consensus. For the social sciences, it is a little easier to find a consensus, although here findings have generally focused on the generalizability of forms (rather than discrete issues) taken by transnational human rights organizing. For example, the hugely influential work of Keck and Sikkink (1998) on transnational advocacy networks has transformed understandings of the global and local. Keck and Sikkink theorize how advocacy for rights at the transnational level has a boomerang effect of strengthening the positions of local activists. Clearly influenced by Keck and Sikkink's analysis, for example, Moghadam posits transnational feminist networks, which she defines as "structures organized … above the national level that unite women from three or more countries around a common agenda, such as women's human rights, reproductive health and rights, violence against women, peace and antimilitarism, or feminist economics" (2005, 4). Similar efforts to identify wider patterns are also found among historians working in the period after 1945, who have identified a mainstream understanding (as opposed to form) in rights activism and lawmaking.

In *Advocating Dignity: Human Rights Mobilizations in Global Politics*, for example, Quataert (2009) introduces the term "orthodoxy" to describe a limitation in human rights thinking and implementation. Until the mid- to later 1970s, the heart of international debate and action on human rights violations focused on opposing the state's arbitrary use of power in repressing individual liberties, whether by legal racial segregation; denial of political rights, mobility, and freedoms; or infringement of the right to bodily integrity and liberty (Quataert 2009, 61–68). The emerging framework even generated its own influential symbolic politics—the so-called prisoner of conscience unjustly incarcerated for speaking out freely—deployed by Amnesty International when it was founded in 1961. International responses to these types of violations by UN organs and commissions as well as other regional security arrangements began to challenge the once sacrosanct norm of domestic jurisdiction, slowly eroding its authority at least in cases of the systematic abuse of political authority by state actors in the public arena. These violations were grave abuses of human rights, to be sure, but they were only part of the interdependency of rights understood as necessary for human well-being by the original architects of the Universal Declaration of Human Rights in 1948 (Morsink 1999).

Importantly, the notion of orthodoxy opens up new lines of interpretation. It means, historically, that feminist and women's activists (in women's rights movements and UN development agendas participating in UN women's world conferences during the Decade for Women) emerged as critics of mainstream human rights thinking while they expanded notions of human rights as gender rights beyond the orthodoxy of gender neutrality in considering the individual rights-bearing person. Coalescing around new understandings of gender-specific violations virtually unacknowledged in rights work to date, the global women's human rights movement challenged the language of the university as well as dominant definitions of rights, equality, and development (see, e.g., Ackerly 2008; Jain 2005). It also critiqued the public/private divide of original human rights legal thought that left the private realm of family and status law off limits to human rights discussions and mobilizations, opening new contestations among diverse feminist groups globally about common grounds for broad coalition building.

Comparative Historical Methodology

Historians are by training geared to historical precision, or what the guild calls "historicization." This method helps sustain human rights interdisciplinary dialogues because it puts themes, actions, and concrete actors in their precise historical and social contexts. Furthermore, it works to uncover historical conjunctures, those contingent but unmistakably powerful interplays of forces driving change, as in the end of formal empire and the internationalization of individual rights discourses or in the imposition of neoliberal thinking through dominant global financial structures and the proliferation of private NGO activities (Burke 2010; Mojab 2009). However, a sociological and global perspective on these same questions opens scholars up to thinking about modularity in activism, the way that repertoires travel across space given the inter- and transnationalization of communications, capital, and transportation, leading to additional pressures, constraints, and opportunities for actors. For example, Jackie Smith and Dawn Wiest (2005) have documented the exponential growth in transnationally oriented nongovernmental organizations as links among activists in various regions become easier to facilitate. Documenting this growth is one project; understanding it historically and contextually is a different one.

Human rights history also fits growing interest in global interconnections and the methodologies, specifically transnational and gender analysis, sustaining such research. From a historical vantage point, "transnational" is more than just a descriptive term capturing the ways human rights ideals in various modes of translation have spread across territorial borders and into many different communities and cultures over time. It also is a dynamic analytical tool that simultaneously keeps in focus local contexts and international settings. Historians and sociologists agree that using transnationality analytically (and distinguishing it from its earlier but still-kicking cousin, internationality) is a perspective that moves seamlessly from local through national and regional and international arenas and back again, all the while addressing the potential and actual transnational responses to local situations, on the one hand, and crediting the grassroots pressures on regional and international decision-making in law and policy, on the other. "Transnationalism" as a term is older than we usually imagine, coming into general use in the United States and Europe in the 1920s, according to Miller (1999). She and other feminist scholars use transnationalism to signal a form of engagement by groups or individuals that stands apart from "formal intergovernmental activities" in favor of direct connections among activists situated in different nation-states and territories (Miller 1999, 225). Transnational research also shows the limits of its approach. The method helps uncover the dense networks, agents, and NGOs that take rights into different settings, including negotiating norms at the international level (in UN commissions and human rights law oversight committees, for example). However, "transnational" alone cannot capture the precise meaning for activists engaged in day-to-day rights struggles, identify the key activists (including the role of exiles), or specify the cognitive and emotional appeal of rights talk. These details require empirical research at the micro level (Merry 2006).

Drawing on the global strands of feminist theory and the records of the transnational practices of feminist activism historically, women's and gender historians employ the analytical unit of gender to reassess human rights developments since 1945. Under this lens, the formal creation of the human rights system between 1945 and 1949 already bore the impact of nearly a century of women's international activism in many arenas around the globe, whether in the imperialist metropoles, the colonies, or urban centers in semicolonized lands such as the Ottoman and Chinese empires. Connected transnationally, as noted above, these early activists also established formal international organizations, with headquarters, membership rolls, and circulating media (Rupp 1997). It is not surprising, then, that prominent transnational women's activists shaped the new human rights system in three major ways. First, they helped insert the "sex-equality" clause into the Charter of the United Nations in San Francisco in 1945 as part of human rights promises of nondiscrimination; second, as members of the Human Rights Commission, they inserted essentially gender-neutral language into the Universal Declaration of Human Rights (in contrast to the "rights-of-man" traditions); and third, they ensured the establishment in 1946 of the Commission on the Status of Women as its own independent body, the only all-women organ in the United Nations at the time. Subsequently, women's disparate mobilizations around the globe, in emerging rights movements, national liberation struggles, and UN and national development agendas, have reflected the predominant end goal of equality between women and men. Recent research, as noted earlier, has analyzed the timing and impact of the new shift to gender in human rights discourses, with its emphasis on difference.

Recognizing people as gendered beings has meant a profound paradigm shift in human rights advocacy and law. It has called attention to forms of abuse and violation previously unrecognized by human rights monitoring bodies; broadened definitions of international crimes (for example, defining rape as violence against women and criminalizing sexual slavery and forced pregnancy in wartime); and written new sections of human rights instruments, such as section 1, paragraph 18 of the Vienna Declaration of Human Rights (1993), which for the first time in a rights document used gender as a distinct category of protection and prohibition

(Bunch and Reilly 1994, 150). Importantly, CEDAW was a bridge instrument, as law no longer committed to "equality" based on men's standards (advocating special affirmative measures) but did not fully embrace gender-specific legal safeguards. Reflecting the evolving quality of rights thinking, however, this privileging of gender as a new human rights category has come under scrutiny by some postcolonial feminists (Kapur 2005; Kempadoo 2005). Recognizing the major advances of the category in law making and advocacy but noting its potential to favor already advantaged groups, these scholars stress the ways gender intersects with other structures of oppression, such as class, race, and ethnicity. Paradoxically, this insight pushes toward the universal by acknowledging differences. Introduced historically into human rights debates through women's transnational networks, including emerging groups of lesbian activists, gender sustains attention to gay and transgender issues and also boy trafficking. Furthermore, by enriching social analysis, it also reframes many of the transnational crises addressed by human rights advocates, revealing the gendered dimensions, for example, of transnational labor migrations, refugee experiences, the global food crises, or environmental degradation.

How Can the Field of Human Rights Change Comparative Historical Research?

As the foregoing discussion has shown, the study of the field of human rights generally profits from historical and sociological perspectives. Historians and historical sociologists help unravel the complexities of human rights thinking over time, assess varying responses, and provide detailed empirical studies of their meanings in concrete situations. Historical perspectives add depth to the analysis as they show the changing face of human rights advocacy agendas over time. Historical contexts are essential to interdisciplinary work at the core of human rights scholarship, with its unique ties to academics and activists. Similarly, feminist insights and gender analysis in human rights, by taking seriously diverse women's agency within structural and discursive constraints, offer a continuous corrective to a simple narrative. They serve as a constant reminder that the presumed language of universality underpinning the effort to establish shared rights agendas at any one moment contains glaring biases—whether of assumed gender neutrality reinforcing, in effect, hierarchy or the failure to interconnect gender vulnerabilities with other broad social markers of disadvantage. Similarly, the dialogues they promote reveal divisions within global feminist communities precisely over the efficacy of bringing human rights methodologies and law to ongoing feminist and women's movements' causes and struggles.

The so-called master narratives of history rooted in the dominant national or territorial framework (which themselves are challenged by many subfields of the discipline, to be sure) have not accommodated transnational perspectives, let alone those dealing with human rights values and networks crossing boundaries in many directions and dimensions. Much of historical scholarship centers on nations, empires, and territories as discrete and privileged historical units of analysis, homogenizing the diverse components of intrastate and national developments. Early research in women's history also remained confined to national borders examining, for example, aspects of the German socialist or bourgeois women's movements or the development of women's movements in Uruguay. Human rights history and historical sociology focusing on rights movements in the modern era, therefore, are part of a broad scholarly effort to rethink and transform many of the major conceptual and organizing principles behind the writing of history. Such perspectives can also challenge hegemonic interpretations, which historically reflected predominantly Eurocentric and Western patterns of developments. In this sense, human rights perspectives and those of transnational feminism have major transformative potentials for the disciplines, a point acknowledged by their practitioners. The new history and social science involve a self-conscious critique of many of the assumptions in the older practices of history writing.

And yet, the climate for human rights activism has deteriorated today, necessarily affecting the nature of scholarly inquiry. The optimism and near-global extension of human rights and humanitarian activism in the 1990s (and their corollary texts rooted in notions of progress) have given way to a more difficult and troubled climate for human rights and humanitarian work in the real world of action. The US-led War on Terror after 2001, the invasion of Iraq in 2003 (or the morphing of "humanitarian intervention" into preemptive war), and continuing warfare in Afghanistan, to mention only the most visible Western state-led global military agendas, showed unmistakably the malleability of human rights notions and the ease with which they are used to justify invasion and accompany imperialist and elite projects.

Nowhere is this more clearly seen than in the matter of women's human rights, which have been instrumentalized by military invasion and occupation and by the political Right, as well as by fundamentalist thinkers in many domestic controversies and burgeoning anti-immigrant movements. No wonder that in this political climate there is no agreement among gender scholars in many different regions of the globe about the efficacy of human rights politics for feminist agendas. Serious theoretical and practical points of controversy must be addressed. And yet, the explosion of grassroots, democratic mobilizations in North Africa and the Middle East in early 2011 shows (whatever the outcome) that democracy (also appropriated by the Great Powers for so-called regime change) is a tangible and viable people's principle. In these protest movements, human rights principles of dignity and individual and self-determination, arguably, are a shared diagnostic, capturing the palpable anger at injustice, corruption, and sexual and political abuses. The prominent role of women in these movements reinforces the need for dialogues about the transformative potential of human rights politics as a common basis for action across women's differences. Critical human rights histories are a vital component of these pressing global debates.

CHAPTER THIRTY-SEVEN

POLITICAL ECONOMY OF THE WORLD-SYSTEM

Tarique Niazi and Jeremy Hein

Political economy of the world-system is a sociological perspective that developed in the 1970s. Based on the foundational work of sociologist Immanuel Wallerstein (1974, 1980), political economy of the world-system argues that the major political and economic events in individual countries result from the historical growth and change of the global capitalist system. Wallerstein's argument was considered radical when it first originated but in some respects is now conventional wisdom. Popular books, such as *The World Is Flat* (Friedmen 2005), routinely point out that economic events in one place quickly influence governments, companies, and communities in other parts of the world.

Political economy of the world-system, however, is not a synonym for globalization (Wallerstein 2005a). It is an explanation for economic inequality and numerous forms of social inequality, including health disparities, environmental problems, and threats to indigenous peoples (see Dunaway 2003). Precisely because political economy of the world-system examines cross-national trends in social inequality, some sociologists find it puzzling that the theory is rarely used to explain human rights violations (Blau 2005). A broader criticism is that political economy of the world-system focuses too much attention on the state and the market, thus neglecting the many other social institutions that are collectively referred to as civil society (Smith 2005). Political economy of the world-system has also been criticized for paying insufficient attention to local campaigns to limit the negative effects of systemic inequality (Wieviorka 2005).

In this chapter we extend political economy of the world-system further into the sociology of human rights using the literature on the world-system's environmental impact (Adeola 2000a; Chew 1997; Hornburg 1998; Prew 2003). The core of the world-system overconsumes natural resources from the periphery and externalizes environmental costs (such as pollution) to the periphery (Jorgenson 2003; Rice 2009). This appropriation causes numerous environmental problems in developing countries (see Kick and Jorgenson 2003). Many antisystem social movements are produced by local resistance to "the dominant models of development" and their "environmentally destructive practices that leave landscapes of ecological destruction" (Escobar 2006, 6).

Building on these insights from the political economy of the world-system literature, we propose a social-ecological theory of human rights. We argue that the most severe human rights violations in the twenty-first century are due to market-driven contradictions between ecosystems and social systems. Globalization has vastly increased the value of land, fresh water, wood, metals, gems, energy sources, and the transportation routes to move these commodities. Competition over access, appropriation, development, and shipping of natural resources leads to conflicts among resource-dependent local communities, resource-extractive states, and resource-commodifying elites. Often the result is human rights violations due to what we call violent development: state and elite coercion of subnational communities in resource-rich areas in order to rapidly produce wealth for the global market.

STRUCTURAL, EMBEDDED, AND EMERGENT VIEWS OF HUMAN RIGHTS

Wallerstein developed world-system theory in the 1970s, but the addition of the political-economy perspective that forms political economy of the world-system actually occurred during the 1990s. It is therefore important to keep in mind that what we now call political economy of the world-system combines two distinct sets of concepts: political economy, which focuses on the relationship between government (state) and the market in one or more countries, and world-system, which focuses on transnational trends in financial profit-making.

World-system refers to the modern capitalist economy in the core and its expansion into the periphery in search of profit (Wallerstein 2005b). This profit (surplus value) is created by minimizing the costs of labor, natural resources, and taxation. Profit accumulation declines over time as corporations lose their monopolies over production and face greater demands from labor to pay more to workers in the form of wages as well as the taxes that fund the social welfare system. As profit declines in one area, corporations expand further into the periphery, creating a "constant geographical shift of the zones of production" (Wallerstein 2005a, 1270).

Political economy examines the two most central institutions in a modern, developed society: the state and the market. "The state" refers to the people and organizations that control political authority and power through government. "The market" refers the people and organizations that control the valuation and exchange of natural resources, goods, services, and labor. States depend on markets for taxes and the wealth that provides the basis for power over other states. Markets depend on states to contain labor movements that threaten profits and to rescue corporations with public funds when shortsighted greed threatens the long-run stability of the market.

Since human rights tend to take the form of laws and other social policy, the main question for political economy of the world-system is how independent (autonomous) the state is from the market (Fortman 2011). This question is important because political economy of the world-system argues that the more the state is independent from the economic interests of dominant groups, the more it can provide human rights protections. The political economy of the world-system literature offers three different answers to that question. The structural view sees little or no state autonomy, the embedded view sees moderate autonomy, and the emergent view sees extensive autonomy.

From a structural perspective, human rights violations are permanent and cannot be ameliorated under the present world-system because it is based on exploitation (Bonilla-Silva and Mayorga 2009; Jalata 2008). Human rights violations are pervasive and simply take different forms in different parts of the world-system. Strong states in the core appear to respect constitutional guarantees of human rights, although ethnic minorities experience severe inequality. Weak states in the periphery routinely violate the human rights of individual citizens in shocking ways. But many of these human rights problems in the periphery result from core states fomenting armed conflict and labor exploitation.

The embedded perspective sees the state as having partial autonomy and thus a greater ability to guarantee human rights through citizenship (Somers 2008). The rights of citizens derive from the sovereignty of the territorial state, which offers citizens protections and liberties. The territorial state is itself embedded in the modern nation-state system, which was first formulated in Europe by the Treaty of Westphalia (1648) to end the Thirty Years' War.

The watershed year of 1648 culminated in many trends favoring human rights (Israel 2011). Central according to the embedded perspective was the Enlightenment's notions of individual freedoms from oppressive feudal authority. The Enlightenment produced a political model holding that human rights are inalienable rather than based on wealth and power, such as in a plutocracy or oligarchy and under feudal lords or emperors. To tell the story of how rights moved from kings to citizens, the embedded explanation of human rights begins with the Magna Carta (1215) and largely ends with the French Revolution (1789).

The emergent perspective views the state as very autonomous from dominant groups. This view posits that the greatest expansion in real, as opposed to ideal, human rights results from the post–World War II international system (Clapham 2007). According to the emergent perspective, while the Magna Carta may be the seed, the 1948 Universal Declaration of Human Rights is the flower of human rights. From this perspective, the United Nations and regional political entities, such as the European Union and African Union, are the main promoters of transnational human rights policies through treaties, protocols, and other agreements.

The main emergent theory, called world-polity institutionalism, argues that there is a global trend toward increasing respect for human rights (Boli and Thomas 1997; Meyer et al. 1997). Koo and Ramirez (2009) document what they term the "human rights revolution" during the 1990s and early 2000s. During this period, numerous countries established ombudsmen for justice and for human rights, as well as human rights offices, centers, and commissions. By 2004, about 70 percent of all nation-states had developed some form of national human rights institution. The main determinants of this trend, Koo and Ramirez argue, is the national incorporation of the international human rights regime: "Nation-states are embedded in a wider world and influenced by world models of proper nation-state identity" (2009, 1329). This emerging world model of human rights manifests as world conferences, international organizations, treaties, and cumulative adoption by more and more countries (Hafner-Burton and Tsutsui 2005).

INTRA- AND INTERSTATE EXPLANATIONS OF HUMAN RIGHTS

The embedded and emergent views of human rights are broad perspectives on whether respect for human rights is old (since the 1600s) or new (since the 1990s). But both raise the question of why there is cross-national variation in human rights violations. The embedded view focuses on citizenship guarantees by a sovereign territorial state and therefore suggests an intrastate answer. The emergent view focuses on global trends that may influence countries and thus suggests an interstate answer.

Intrastate explanations focus on the structural precondition for human rights in a society. Three hypotheses have been widely tested. The economic hypothesis considers the effects of economic development on human rights practices (Hafner-Burton and Tsutsui 2005). Mitchell and McCormick (1988) offer the simple poverty thesis, which sees fertile ground for political conflict in economic resource scarcity, which in many cases prompts governments to resort to political repression. On the other hand, in an advanced economy where people are likely to have fewer grievances, political stability is often achieved more easily, reducing the likelihood of human rights violations (Henderson 1991).

The second hypothesis is a political one. Democracies are less likely to commit human rights violations than autocracies (Hafner-Burton and Tsutsui 2005). Howard and Donnelly (1986) contend that the protection of human rights requires a liberal state regime that respects the substantive conception of human dignity. Henderson (1991) also claims that democratic governments are more responsive to their citizens than autocratic governments and, hence, more likely to accommodate the demands of their citizens without violent conflict. Poe, Tate, and Keith (1999) and Mitchell and McCormick (1988) also indicate the positive effects of democracy on human rights.

The third argument is a demographic hypothesis. Population pressure can lead to resource stress, increasing the likelihood of governments' use of repression (Henderson 1993). When a state experiences rapid population growth, lack of resources quickly becomes a serious problem, pressuring the government to head in an authoritarian direction. Hafner-Burton and Tsutsui (2005) noted that population size also affects political repression; states with a larger population are more likely to violate human rights (Poe, Tate, and Keith 1999).

In contrast to these three intrastate hypotheses derived from political-economy theory, an alternative explanation is the interstate hypothesis derived from the transnational component of political economy of world society. The interstate hypothesis focuses on the relationships among countries as they experience global processes (Hafner-Burton and Tsutsui 2005).

Mitchell and McCormick (1988) introduce a Marxist argument drawing on Chomsky and Herman's (1979) contention that capitalist states, driven by economic interests, favor political stability in developing nations and thus fortify existing regimes even when government repression is endemic. As developing third-world governments receive economic support from capitalist nations whose primary goal is to maintain favorable conditions for investment, the likelihood of human rights violations increases.

Drawing on this analysis, Mitchell and McCormick (1988) hypothesize that economic ties with the United States and other advanced capitalist states encourage human rights violations in the periphery. Meyer (1996), on the other hand, examines the impact of multinational corporations on human rights practices, contending that they promote both socioeconomic rights and civil and political rights. The effects of multinational corporations on economic and social rights are direct, promoting development and hence improving quality of life. Multinational corporations also indirectly improve political rights insofar as they promote the expansion of a politically stable urban middle class, thus enhancing stability and political tolerance in the larger society. Smith et al. (1999), however, report contradictory findings, cautioning that the optimistic outlook on the roles of multinational corporations may not be warranted. Our cases of natural resource development in Xinjiang, China, the northeastern region of India, and Balochistan, Pakistan, corroborate the findings by Smith et al. (1999).

On a broader level, there are major debates about whether the spread of capitalism reduces or increases human rights. The expansion of markets and private ownership of property has arguably both positive and negative implications for human rights. World-system and political-economy approaches predict increased levels of human rights violations in the periphery following capital penetration (Mitchell and McCormick 1988; Chomsky and Herman 1979). Although in the minority, Myer (1996) finds a positive impact of multinational corporations on human rights practices. On the other hand, Smith et al. (1999) are cautious about the role of multinational corporations in human rights protection.

SUMMARY OF KEY METHODS

Research in the political economy of the world-system utilizes a wide range of methodologies, including historical narratives, case studies, comparative analyses, and cross-national and quantitative approaches. In another respect, however, political economy of the world-system methodology tends to be quite restricted. These four methods focus on individuals and overemphasize typologies at the expense of theory.

The historical narrative cites key events in order to demonstrate a recurring pattern over time. An example is *The Arab Mind* (Patai 2002). The primary weakness of this type of research is a tendency to invoke psychological traits.

The case study examines a single place or event in order to illustrate an important development. Examples include the Darfur region of Sudan and the Xinjiang region of China (Bhattacharji 2009; Prunier 2005). Case-study methodologies tend to rely on categorizing regime types, such as democratic, authoritarian, totalitarian, and failed state. Major human rights organizations such as Amnesty International, Human Rights Watch, as well as the US Department of State largely use case-study methods.

Comparative methods focus on the differences between societies that in other respects have much in common. Examples include research on the greater protection of human rights in Jordan compared to Iran. This methodology tends to emphasize typologies (Hafner-Burton and Tsutsui 2005; Rawls 2003).

Cross-national quantitative methods typically use coded categories of countries to produce an index of freedom and repression (Poe, Tate, and Keith 1999). Many are based on self-reports by national governments to UN agencies and thus lack reliability. Quantitative studies claim highly detailed measurements of certain variables. Yet many facets of human rights are not measurable. Since human rights involve humans, some facets are symbolic or evocative for what they reveal about the depths of human suffering.

The main limitation of all four methodologies is that they too often focus on the individual and thus miss the forest for the trees. Below we argue that human rights violations also have a collective dimension, especially in Asia, where these violations result from the state's coercive measures against minority groups that have been denied their economic, environmental, and social rights. This can be seen in the Uighur Muslim rights movement in Xinjiang, China, the Naxalite movement in northeastern India, and the Baloch rights movement in Pakistan.

RESITUATION OF THE FIELD: THE SOCIAL-ECOLOGICAL THEORY OF HUMAN RIGHTS

Political economy of the world-system has developed a considerable literature on the environmental problems caused by the world-system since analysis began in the late 1990s (Chew 1997; Goldfrank, Goodman, and Szasz 1999; Hornburg 1998). Environmental degradation in the periphery is now recognized as a form of human rights violation (Adeola 2000b, 2001). The broader problem of climate change has also been conceptualized as a human rights issue (UN Human Rights Council 2008). The notion of climate justice has even been advanced to increase recognition of this problem: "The adverse effects of climate change can already be felt in many areas with direct negative impact on the enjoyment of human rights, such as in agriculture and food security, biodiversity and ecosystems" (OHCHR 2011, 1).

While valuable, the political economy of the world-system literature tends to conceptualize the environment as merely an outcome of social systems (particularly the economy). For political economy of the world-system, nature is seen as merely two of three ways in which capitalism avoids (externalizes) the real costs of production in order to produce profit (Wallerstein 2005b). The nonenvironmental (i.e., social) externalization is that capitalism tries not to pay for the public infrastructure, such as schools, roads, and bridges, that supports the market. The other two forms of externalization are environmental: natural renewal of primary resources (letting nature produce more at no cost) and detoxification (cleaning up pollution).

Drawing on Bookchin's (1982) concept of social ecology, we argue that nature has a much more significant causal influence on social systems than political economy of the world-system has thus far recognized. According to Bookchin (1982), contemporary ecological problems arise from deep-seated social problems such as hierarchical societies. In his words, "The domination of nature by man stems from the very real domination of human by human" (Bookchin 1982, 1).

Social-ecological theory thus explains social conflicts by analyzing how power and resource allocation mediate humans' abilities to sustain themselves from nature (Vaillancourt 2010). This contradiction between ecosystems and social systems produces what appear to be "environmental problems." Social ecology therefore focuses on the underlying relationship between social systems and ecosystems. Combined with Wallerstein's (1976) analysis of world-system dynamics resulting from globalization, not nation-states or "countries," we can present a social-ecological theory of human rights.

Social-ecological theory argues that globalization prioritizes the rapid production of wealth from natural resources. Much prior research has documented the resulting economic, political, and demographic harms—for example, Worldwatch Institute's *State of the World Reports*, the World Bank's *World Development Reports*, and the UN Development Program's *Brundtland Report* (1987, subsequently republished as *Our Common Future*). Social-ecological theory identifies the common link among them: disruption of the social-natural nexus. Violent development around the world threatens resource-dependent communities, as will be evident from our cases of Xinjiang, northeastern India, and Balochistan.

We define violent development as state and elite coercion of subnational communities in resource-rich areas in order to rapidly produce wealth for the global market. Natural-resource extraction by state actors and resistance by nonstate actors lead to conflicts and human rights violations.

We argue that social-ecological theory can explain a wide range of human rights violations. As the following illustrations show, social-ecological theory is a complement, not a rival, to prevailing political economy of the world-system explanations. The common trends in these illustrations include state repression of local communities that resist the state's attempts at resource extraction without the communities' consent; state tendencies to define local communities' resistance as a law-and-order problem; and globalization's hunger for cheap raw materials and energy resources, which states advance as "national development."

CHINA

Xinjiang is China's autonomous Muslim-majority region, which forms China's westernmost boundary. Stretched over 635,833 square miles, Xinjiang comprises one-sixth of China's landmass, with a population of 23 million people. It is endowed with immense untapped energy resources of oil and natural gas that are measured in billions of barrels and trillions of cubic feet (Niazi 2005). China is investing $88 billion to develop its western territories, including Xinjiang, apparently to bring them to a par with coastal areas such as Shanghai. This development push has caused displace-ment of the Uighur Muslim majority in the area, especially from Xinjiang's capital city of Urumqi, where the native Uighur population has declined from 90 percent in 1949 to 49 percent in 2004 (Niazi 2005). The incoming non-native Han Chinese population in Urumqi has grown from 10 percent in 1949 to 49 percent in 2004.

The multi-billion-dollar development push, accompanied by demographic engi-neering of the region, has injected tensions between incoming Han Chinese and native Uighurs. In July 2009, riots erupted that claimed two hundred lives, leaving seventeen hundred wounded (Guardian 2010). In July 2011, Xinjiang's historic city of Kashgar became the scene of deadly violence between Han Chinese and Uighur Muslims, leaving eighteen people dead (Wines 2011).

State security forces and the East Turkistan Islamic Movement, which the United States designates as a terrorist organization, are the principal agents of violence in the region. At the core, however, is the singular agenda for developing the region's natural resources due to the astronomical growth of manufacturing since the 1980s, when China converted to a market economy. As a result, China's thirst for natural resources, particularly materials and energy, both at home and abroad, has become unquenchable. Violence in Xinjiang and oppression of its Uighur inhabitants are manifestations of this globally fueled development agenda.

INDIA

Naxalites in northeastern and southern India have been campaigning for land rights, control over mineral resources in their communities, and autonomy for forest-dwelling tribal populations since 1967. Their genesis is traced to a peasant uprising in India's Naxalbari district in 1967, which led to the founding of the Naxali movement (Dixit 2010). It has since organized itself around Maoism for "agrarian revolution" (Millet 2008).

Naxalites now have a presence in fourteen of India's states (The Economist 2006), control 20 percent of the territory, and enjoy the support of 50 percent of India's tribal population (Millet 2008). The Indian prime minister has graded "Naxalism" as "the greatest threat to our internal security" (Dixit 2010). Many analysts, even those sympathetic to the Indian government, blame the state for failing to address the "causes and conditions" that "sustain the movement" (Dixit 2010).

Fatalities from violence by state security forces and Naxalites, whom Millet (2008) calls "terrorists," are in the thousands. In 2007, as many as 2,765 people were killed. As Naxalites mobilize peasants for a "people's war" against the state and the state organizes militant groups such as Salwa Judum "to destroy" them, human rights violations register a dramatic uptick. Many Western companies are eager to see the Naxalite movement pacified in order to have access to the region's mineral riches. Under such pressure and in the name of "development," the state frames the Naxali resistance as a "law and order problem" (Dixit 2010) and reinforces security deployments to quell it, only to further exacerbate the human rights situation.

PAKISTAN

Balochistan, comprising one-half of Pakistan's landmass, is home to the country's Baloch ethnic minority. Members of this minority have long been engaged in an armed struggle to achieve autonomy and control of their natural resources, strategic waterways in the Indian Ocean, and hundreds of miles of their coastline.

Pakistan first set out to develop natural resources in Balochistan in the 1950s, which led to disputes between the local Baloch ethnic community and the state. The resource-dependent Baloch community wanted its say in the development of resources and apportionment of royalties. Instead, the state invoked "eminent domain" to push through its development agenda. These disagreements led to repeated eruptions of violence that have continued to occur every ten years since the 1950s. In August 2006, a legendry Baloch leader, Nawab Akber Bugti, was assassinated by state security forces while fighting for Baloch rights. There has since been a bloody conflict between Baloch armed fighters and state security forces, with hundreds of casualties each year. In 2011, dozens were killed.

Balochistan, which has been Pakistan's energy capital since the 1950s, is believed to be sitting on additional untapped natural wealth. The value of its natural resources and the state's attempts to access and appropriate them have increased since the collapse of the Soviet Union in the 1990s and a simultaneous onset of a wave of globalization. The United States and many other Western nations want to use Balochistan as a key link in their revived effort to relaunch the historical Silk Road.

Because of its proximity to Iran, Balochistan also will host a $10 billion oil pipeline from Iran to India and China. Another multi-billion-dollar oil pipeline is being planned from Turkmenistan-Afghanistan to Pakistan and India, which also will go through Balochistan. Balochs again want their say in these mega-development projects and view them as tempting targets of violence, which is met with counterviolence by state security forces.

A LOOK FORWARD

Our analysis of China, India, and Pakistan reveals that the political economy of the world-system provides a powerful explanation for global inequality, and the theory's insights can be easily extended to the sociology of human rights. Core and semiperipheral economies produce wealth at the expense of peripheral societies. As sites of production move further into the periphery, societies in Asia experience greater labor exploitation and environmental degradation. They also experience extreme human rights violations. This connection between human rights violation and profit maximization is the main contribution of political economy of the world-system scholarship.

To understand this connection, it is necessary to distinguish the two components of the political economy of the world-system: the capitalist world-system and the political economy of specific societies. The world-system expands by incorporating external areas into a periphery where profits can be maximized free from the constraints imposed by states and organized labor in the core. Local profit extraction in the periphery and semiperiphery itself has costs, including the use of force to appropriate natural resources and quell resistance. Peripheral and semiperipheral states and markets (political economy) carry out these human rights violations and, through trade and other global mechanisms, transfer the profit to the core.

This link between political economic exploitation and capitalist world-system profits first emerged in the 1500s with sugar production (Moore 2000). It led to human rights violations on a massive scale, including African slavery and the genocide of indigenous populations in the Caribbean and in North, Central, and South America. As our discussion of China, India, and Pakistan illustrates, a similar profit-exploitation process is occurring in the twenty-first century as a result of unprecedented globalization. Political economy of the world-system analysis takes us this far in understanding contemporary human rights violations. Our social-ecology theory completes the explanation.

According to social-ecological theory, distinguishing twenty-first-century profit extraction from that at the beginning of the world-system is the far more massive exploitation of surface (wood, water, and land) and especially subsurface (oil, gas, metals, minerals, and gems) natural resources. The search for wealth in more remote areas also raises the value of transportation systems to move commodities and the need for military installations to protect the routes. States and markets seek control of these natural resources at the expense of local communities, which have historically lived in balance with their environment. But the violent development of their natural resources creates a contradiction between ecosystem and social system. The result is human rights violations in the form of forced migration of locals who flee or counterinsurgency campaigns against locals who stay and resist.

Social-ecological theory's insights contribute both to the political economy of the world-system and the sociology of human rights. For the political economy of the world-system, it highlights the fact that globalization polarizes peripheral and semiperipheral areas by creating core regions within them. Thus, in Pakistan the comparatively developed Punjab seeks to profit from the natural resources of the less developed Balochistan. In China and India, similar regional polarities exist between internal core (Shanghai, Mumbai) and peripheral areas (Xinjiang, Andhra Pradesh).

For the sociology of human rights, social-ecological theory offers the following look forward. Economic development can promote human rights, but it can also be regressive and promote violence. At the root of this violence is conflict over local, national, or transnational control of natural resources. Human rights regimes that focus on the liberties and protection of individuals will not resolve these conflicts. Resource-rooted communities like those in Xinjiang, northeastern India, and Balochistan use collective identities and institutions to create a balance between ecosystems and social systems. It is states and markets that use individualism in the form of national citizenship and private property to appropriate natural resources.

CHAPTER THIRTY-EIGHT

SOCIAL PSYCHOLOGY

Steven Hitlin and Matthew Andersson

> *Dignity is a real, objective feature of human personhood. The question is not whether dignity exists, any more than whether the Grand Canyon exists. The question is whether human minds understand, acknowledge, and respond to the fact that human persons possess dignity.*
> —Christian Smith (2010, 434)

The Universal Declaration of Human Rights, which recently celebrated its sixtieth anniversary, vouches for the "dignity and rights" of all humankind. Social-psychological insights allow us to conceptualize and understand notions of human dignity that underlie cross-cultural notions of rights. In essence, social psychology as applied to the study of human rights pertains to the subjective experience of social inequalities and adversities; it offers a focus on how such experience is potentially buffered by individual self-conceptions and belief systems, as structured by cultural value systems and as enacted in particular local contexts. This chapter suggests avenues for undergirding the sociological study of human rights with established social-psychological mechanisms, principles, and theories.

We orient this review around the terminological pivot of dignity and, in particular, around relevant notions of human and social functioning that contribute to the sense of dignity at the very root of the Universal Declaration of Human Rights. We suggest that dignity rests on an individual's personal ability to satisfy culturally defined needs that may or may not involve consistency of the self (Turner and Gordon 1981), authenticity (Gecas 1991; Turner 1976), and autonomy (Deci and Ryan 2000). Dignity might be thought of, then, as ultimately reflecting a desire for personhood (see Smith 2010, 434–490).

Allport (1954) offers perhaps the quintessential statement of social psychology, paraphrased as the study of the actual, implied, and imagined presence of others in social action. As we will demonstrate, all three facets of Allport's vision are at play in the realization of human dignity. In actuality, others are continually involved in interpreting, sanctioning, and socializing our lines of action, whether through their physical presence or through social structures. By implication, these others are continually invoked as guideposts for our implicit and explicit beliefs and choices; by imagination, others provide us with meanings, audiences, and ideals.

In fact, general identification with the world, justice, and the global environment (termed "universalism" or "globalism") and identification with humanity proper are both necessary for an appreciation and proactive stance toward human rights (Crompton and Kasser 2009; McFarland 2010). Likewise, Max Weber originally envisioned a consideration of others and of collective resources as fundamental to social action. "Concretely it is social, for instance," Weber remarked, "if in relation to the actor's own consumption the future wants of others are taken into account and this becomes one consideration affecting the actor's own striving" (2007 [1914], 225).

With respect to social-psychological inquiry, House (1977) identifies the three faces: psychological social psychology, social structure and personality (SSP), and symbolic interactionism. In this chapter, we focus on the latter two, which are distinctively sociological. Before sampling relevant contributions from each of these faces, we offer a snapshot of these perspectives in terms of the questions they pose about human rights, the findings they offer, the research methods they typically utilize, and the limitations and future directions that characterize their frontiers of research.

Social Structure and Personality

Questions. How do macrostructures provide for as well as impede dignified functioning?

Findings. Researchers in this tradition find that individual values are shaped in patterned ways based on social-structural location and that national characteristics are important predictors of the types of values associated with a stronger concern for human rights.

Methods. Most research on social structure and personality uses survey-based techniques.

Limitations. Findings in this tradition are bound by the difficulty in establishing causality and are subject to the limitations of studying people in the aggregate.

Symbolic Interactionism

Questions. How are individuals socialized into various views of themselves and of social categories? How do they create meaning in extreme or adverse situations, such as homelessness and captivity?

Findings. Individuals utilize skillful mixes of closeness and distance in maintaining dignity. Also, group work can be a productive and effective way of achieving dignity.

Methods. Symbolic interactionists often employ qualitative methods, which allow for a rich and particularized conceptualization of mechanisms and processes.

Limitations. While comparatively good in identifying the various mechanisms and submechanisms by which individuals achieve dignity across time, this perspective often does not control for larger social forces that may be orchestrating or at least shaping what is being observed.

While these two sociological approaches differ largely in their methodological stances, they need not be viewed as oppositional. In fact, notable attempts (e.g., Stryker 1980) have attempted to merge their strengths to better understand the relationship between macro structures and micro-level beliefs and actions. In typical practice, however, one finds more statistically oriented researchers focused on the SSP approach, while symbolic interactionism is based on a century of observational research and theorizing.

SOCIAL STRUCTURE AND PERSONALITY

For social structure and personality, we draw on work by McLeod and Lively, focusing on their definition of the SSP perspective as "principles [that] direct our attention to the hierarchically organized processes through which macrostructures come to have relevance for the inner lives of individual persons and, in theory, the processes through which individual persons come to alter social systems" (2003, 77). According to House (1981), a full analysis of social structure and personality should touch upon the components, proximity, and psychological principles. The components principle states that sociologists should delineate the system of interest in terms of its theoretically relevant components. The proximity principle states that the macro dimensions of a social system should be understood in terms of "*proximate* social experiences and stimuli in a person's life" (House 1981, 540; emphasis in original). And finally, the psychological principle requires that researchers invoke substantive theories about attitudes, personality, and behavior in order to have a sense of when and how larger mechanisms are effective. In this section, we conceptualize societal values as a key component of interest, and we contend that various interpersonal experiences serve as the basis for the enactment and transmission of values. At the same time, we recognize that a consideration of humans as operative according to their values may rely too heavily on rational conceptions of the actor, and thus the researcher may need to appeal to more practical and habitual forms of social learning, an avenue that we explore later this chapter in conjunction with symbolic interactionism.

The social structure and personality framework has a long tradition in social psychology, and its influence has extended to the point that it is largely the basis for other sociological subfields (e.g., mental health), with principles that were once seen as novel now widely taken for granted. We illustrate one way that the SSP tradition might inform the sociological study of human rights by focusing on social elements underlying the individual development of values. Values are famously defined as "conceptions of the desirable" (see Rokeach 1973) and reflect possible end states from necessary elements of evolved group life (e.g., Schwartz 1992; Joas 2000). People develop values in patterned ways (see Hitlin and Piliavin 2004 for an overview), with commonalities being found by race, gender, and especially social class (see the long tradition of work by Kohn, Schooler, and colleagues). For instance, macro shifts in social structure and especially class-based labor opportunities can affect individual experiences and valuations of self-directedness (Kohn et al. 1997).

Values that contribute to a belief in human rights are anchored largely in a belief in the importance of universalism, a sense of concern for the well-being of the wider community. A series of studies by Inglehart (e.g., 1977, 1997) focuses on what he terms "postmaterialistic" values (a focus on the community and wider environment) that suggest concern for the well-being of others. In his body of work, he finds evidence that such values become more prevalent in societies that undergo economic growth. These universalistic values are fostered by living in highly economically developed societies, though cultural traditions moderate this general pattern (Inglehart and Baker 2000; see also Schwartz and Sagie 2000).

Yet, at the same time, cross-cultural research reveals that the pursuit of capitalist goals and values, such as being financially successful and having a favorable self-image, is diametrically opposed to the pursuit of spirituality and community (Grouzet et al. 2005; Schwartz 2006). More recently, Kasser (2011) found that a nation's pursuit of egalitarianism and harmony-based values was associated with children's well-being in the nation, generosity of legislation regarding maternal leave, a lower volume of advertising directed at children, and, finally, lower overall levels of carbon-dioxide emissions.

In total, it is likely that the highly complex moral climates of contemporary societies are resolved person by person, through choices made and habits developed at the individual level as a function of disposition and personal background. McFarland (2010) found across two studies that personal dispositions such as globalism, identification with humanity, and dispositional empathy are associated with support for human rights. Also, McFarland found that authoritarianism is negatively linked to human rights concerns; this effect is mediated through an ethnocentric in-group bias as well as reduced identification with humanity. In turn, the roots of authoritarian personality, ethnocentrism, and identification with others need to be explored in order to arrive at a micro-level conceptualization of human rights.

SYMBOLIC INTERACTIONISM

Transitioning our discussion to the micro level, we consider a symbolic-interactionist perspective so as to conceptualize how individual dispositions, attitudes, and perspectives are developed and maintained. Eleanor Roosevelt, one of the authors of the Universal Declaration of Human Rights, famously remarked that "nobody can make you feel inferior without your consent." As social psychologists, we can lend complexity to Roosevelt's notion of consent by suggesting how consent is shaped by individual and structural forces affecting one's ability to resist or negotiate interactional affronts, prejudices, and stigmatization. Actors are resourceful in their self-definitions insofar as their interpersonal, mental, and physical resources allow. From a purely materialistic standpoint, one might well claim that one's mix of resources enables one's sense of dignity. Indeed, we agree with Snow and Anderson's statement that "not all individuals have equal access to a measure of self-worth" (1987, 1339). However, at the same time, we emphasize agency and the negotiating abilities of the actor when it comes to situating him- or herself within a meaningful social order.

Thus, for symbolic interactionism, we take a micro approach by focusing on how individuals negotiate their own self-concepts amid extreme adversity and various kinds of interactional affronts. Long a tradition in social psychology (e.g., Fine 1993; Stryker and Vryan 2003), symbolic interaction largely focuses on the ways individuals create, understand, and collectively enact meaning and social reality.

Following Anderson and Snow, a symbolic-interactionist approach to human dignity "illuminates the various manifestations and contexts of inequality at the micro, everyday lot of social life" (2001, 395). Indebted to Goffman's (1963) pioneering study of stigma and "spoiled" identities, a symbolic-interactionist focus on dignity and human rights takes as its subject matter interactional affronts and stigmatization as they are either deflected or absorbed by the self-concept, which itself exists within a hierarchical social order. Rather than advocating a static, structuralist stance on the self-concept, which would view one's dignity and cognitive-emotional makeup as largely fixed, a symbolic-interactionist perspective focuses on the agentic ways that actors manage challenges to that sense of self. While we do not flesh this out in this space, we suggest that dignity is a variety of agency with particular relevance to the management of interactional affronts to the self.

One of social psychology's core areas of inquiry is the self-concept, where personal and social identities are reconciled. The self-concept is not fixed; it is sensitive to situational pressures. Indeed, Gecas and Burke maintain that "the reflected appraisals process does not operate all the time or under all conditions" (1995, 91). When it does operate, and to what extent, are key theoretical questions. The preservation of one's dignity is likely to involve ongoing negotiation and to be a deliberate affair that draws on limited mental resources. That is, the energy required to present and inhabit a dignified self should operate in line with depletion-based models of self-regulation (e.g., Muraven, Tice, and Baumeister 1998). It is likely that groups of inferior social standing exhibit high chronic levels of stress and also suffer disproportionately from mental and physical illness, which should make the ongoing regulation of self and therefore the achievement of dignity more difficult.

It is clear that a sense of dignity and a sense of self are fundamentally related. In fact, Christian Smith (2010) links the experience of dignity to the experience of personhood and suggests that to be a person is to be entitled to dignity. We would add that one's self-conceptions and beliefs about who one ought to be also shape the ongoing experience of dignity. According to a symbolic-interactionist formulation, the self-concept is established and then continually maintained through interactions with significant or close others (Berger and Luckmann 1966; Mead 1967). Indeed, Smith maintains that one hones a sense of dignity by practicing it toward others; thus, the social practice of dignity and dignified self-regard are mutually dependent.

In what follows, we first provide a brief overview of how socialization occurs and how it provides individuals with baselines for thinking about who they are, which social categories and groups they belong to, and how they (and others) deserve to be treated. We call these implicit and explicit beliefs about how dignity works "dignity perspectives." In particular, one's practical knowledge of human dignity is apt to be a function of past and ongoing social relationships, which shape our implicit and explicit understandings of what human dignity encompasses, how it is justified, what it looks like, and how it is enacted.

SOCIALIZATION

Berger and Luckmann maintain that "society, identity *and* reality are subjectively crystallized in the same process of internalization" (1966, 133). While many people are involved in socializing an individual, a handful of significant others (e.g., parents) exert a disproportionate influence in shaping a variety of one's generalized notions about human rights and dignity. Among these socially influenced beliefs are the ways oneself and others from different social backgrounds and groups ought to be treated and how well-being ought to be achieved and sustained on an ongoing basis. Through socialization experiences, we learn how to speak about our human condition as well as the conditions of others. Moreover, we learn ways of reasoning and dealing with authority figures, thus partly determining how we will handle ourselves in hierarchical situations as adults.

A rich example of socialization in action is Annette Lareau's (2003) work on unequal childhoods. She considers how one's class background shapes one's exposure to various kinds of conflict resolution. She finds that in a lower-class situation, one is more likely to learn to defer to authority and to follow directives, whereas middle- and upper-class childhoods are associated more with the development of reasoning and self-assertion skills. In any case, one's upbringing is a source of embodied resources or tools that are used to define the self across a variety of social contexts as one grows older. Thus, the practice of dignity and self-justification is apt to begin at a very young age with the assembly of a repertoire of self-maintenance skills (e.g., Swidler 1986). And, as Corsaro and Fingerson (2003) demonstrate, the process of socialization is not just passively inflicted on children; rather, children are active agents in shaping their own socialization. The interplay between individual volition and cultural value systems that shape this socialization is quite complex (see Heinz 2003).

SELF AND IDENTITY

The social-psychological study of selfhood is quite relevant to an emerging sociology of human rights (for overviews, see Gecas and Burke 1995; Stryker and Vryan 2003). Study of the self often focuses on explicit self-understandings, but an overlooked area of research—besides learning how to reason and assert oneself in different social situations (much of which is class based)—involves the development of implicit and explicit attitudes toward various social groups (e.g., Devine 1989), as shaped in part by the formation of friendships across different social categories. Pettigrew and Tropp (2006) conducted a meta-analysis of 375 studies involving intergroup contact and prejudice. They found that contact indeed leads to reduced prejudice and to improved relations with the out-group as a whole across contact settings. Also, they showed that while Allport's four optimal conditions of intergroup contact—equal status, common goals, cooperation, and institutional support—do lead to larger effect sizes, these factors tend to occur as an "interrelated bundle" and are not essential for significant improvements in attitudes (1954, 751). In general, contact may derive its efficacy by lessening the uncertainty associated with interracial encounters (Lee 2001); a reduction in intergroup anxiety is thought to mediate the inverse link between contact and prejudice (Stephan, Stephan, and Gudykunst 1999; Verkuyten, Thijs, and Bekhuis 2010). Dealing with people from different groups appears to break down stress and stereotypes and to increase the possibility of attributing human rights to members of those groups.

Across decades of social-psychological research, the in-group/out-group distinction has been shown to carry real and substantial implications for trust, cooperation, and the allocation of rewards (e.g., Brewer 1997), as well as for dignified functioning. For members of a racial or ethnic majority group, racial and ethnic minorities tend to be perceived as constituting an out-group. Weber long ago likened the concepts of honor and dignity, observing that positively and negatively privileged status groups derive their dignity from entirely different sources. For the positively privileged group, he argues, dignity derives from a form of nontranscendence, a kingdom of this world. On the other hand, a negatively privileged group must look elsewhere for dignity: toward the future, toward a potentially better state of affairs, toward some ultimate form of justice or retribution. In short, hope and faith sustain the negatively privileged group, whereas being in itself is sufficient, enjoyable, and perhaps sensed as righteous for members of a positively privileged group. Within majority and minority groups alike, complex psychological lines may be drawn such that generated factions exhibit prejudicial and disparaging attitudes toward each other.

As Tajfel's (1970) classic research on minimal intergroup distinctions makes abundantly clear, categorical forms of social cognition take hold with little effort and have profound consequences. Intergroup contact often does not occur or is stymied by intergroup forecasting errors (IFEs) (Mallett, Wilson, and Gilbert 2008). IFEs are expectation states that involve overestimating the number and extent of differences between oneself and an out-group member and underestimating the number and extent of similarities. Just as group lines can be cast with minimal information, IFEs can be reduced substantially by reflecting on even trivial similarities across groups, such as shared tastes in food (Mallett, Wilson, and Gilbert 2008). In turn, positive expectations for interactions can lead to better interactions and to enhanced friendship formation. Thus, persons or groups seen situationally to be a part of one's in-group will be subject to human rights concerns more than if they are seen as an out-group. The key insight of this research tradition is, however, that these group distinctions are fluid and respond to situational pressures.

INTERACTIONAL NEGOTIATIONS OF DIGNITY

Little sociological research has richly engaged the psychological substrates for a sense of dignity, which is perhaps the fundamental aspect of human rights. A well-known exception, however, is the work of Snow and Anderson (1987), which details how homeless persons participate in identity talk, which allows them to manage the stigma of their lowly social position. For instance, homeless individuals engage in distancing, embracement, and fictive storytelling. Together, these strategies represent mixed formulations of immersion and denial. As they acclimate themselves to the streets, homeless persons increasingly express themselves through various forms of embracement. This ethnographic account of identity negotiation is consistent with experimental research in psychology indicating that cognitive-emotional narratives of distressing life events take increasingly integrated forms with time (Pennebaker 1997). In turn, these integrated forms are associated with favorable mental- and physical-health outcomes. It seems that with the proper meaning-making tools, derived from one's cultural and social embeddedness, one can make sense of even severely distressing situations. The reestablishment of a sense of mastery of one's fate may be a key ingredient of the narrative-making process, and different degrees of distancing are likely to be necessary for optimal recovery, depending upon one's initial level of distress (Andersson and Conley 2008).

Viktor Frankl's (1984 [1959]) firsthand account of Holocaust captivity attests in poignant detail to the sustaining power of meaning making and hope; in doing so, it exemplifies Nietzsche's assertion that a "why" can weather any "how." According to Frankl, humans can habituate themselves to almost anything, including deprivation of sleep and food. Rather than the rejection of life, such near-total deprivation may instead lead to the "intensification of inner life" through interest in politics, religion, and culturally meaningful phenomena such as stories and the beauty of nature (Frankl 1984 [1959], 50). In fact, some prisoners attended cabaret-type shows hosted by camp officials, even though this necessarily involved missing their daily rations of bread and watery soup. Frankl himself struck up a comradeship with a fellow prisoner; the two men vowed to share one amusing story with each other daily. More than anything, though, Frankl's imagination of his wife, who was imprisoned in another corner of Auschwitz, became particularly keen: he imagined being close to her and having discussions with her.

Overall, Frankl's thesis is that one's dignity is maintained in extreme conditions through the decision of how to define one's situation. Even in the absence of opportunities to create and to enjoy, one can preserve oneself through responding to one's situation in meaningful ways that focus on one's close relationships, one's future, or one's responsibility to support fellow prisoners. And, as Frankl intimates, strategies of hope and survival are often developed in concert with one's fellow prisoners. This suggests that negotiations of dignity are often both individual and collective affairs. A social psychology of human rights would explore the factors that promote such a sense of personal self-worth (but see Crocker 2002 for one approach) and how they are anchored in community. Is there a relationship between attachment to one's society and the availability of tools for constructing a dignified sense of self?

Human actors understand themselves and sort out difficult events according to internalized voices provided by those individuals who are personally important (Higgins 1987; Morin and Everett 1990). For instance, Mason-Schrock (1996, 186–189) found that postoperative transsexuals sorted out their new gender identities by way of four principle strategies: modeling, guiding, affirming, and tactful blindness. First, as group members told their stories to each other, they arrived at intuitive senses of which elements were canonical (i.e., widely understood) and which were not. That is, they modeled basic story elements off each other's nascent narratives. Second, guiding, a more interactive strategy, involved normatively shaping group members' narratives by asking each other tailored questions about story elements relevant to the group culture. Third, group members affirmed each other's stories by reacting to them positively. And fourth, group members overlooked holes in each other's narratives so as to permit an air of definitiveness and reality. To have pointed out holes would have been to strip the narratives of their legitimacy and thus to undermine the dignity provided by the postoperatives' verbal constructions. Indeed, believing in the integrity of one's narrative seems integral to the experience of dignity.

SUMMARY

This chapter offers a social-psychological window through which to focus on studying the development of both an individual sense of dignity and wider social concern with dignity at the root of the current notion of human rights. We offer an admittedly brief introduction to literatures that ideally motivate and inform human rights research on some of the micro-level sociological processes that we believe are implicated. Beliefs about human rights, priorities about what elements of personhood are seen as universally valid, and individuals' ongoing notions of their own worthiness are all shaped socially and deserve further study.

Scholars interested in human rights can draw on a variety of established research traditions, discussed above, to inform their projects. We suggest research ranging from the sociocultural determinants of the scope of human rights down to microanalyses of the ways that individuals demonstrate and enact these beliefs within concrete situations. We suggest "dignity" as the terminological pivot that links societal beliefs to individual belief and action and that future research may look at dignity as both an independent and a dependent variable (to put it crudely).

Social psychology is often concerned with social mechanisms and their links to societal forces and is much less concerned with the political mission underlying the human rights paradigm. As such, the field is much better suited for offering mechanisms—theoretically specified and empirically tested—than for reshaping itself in line with a focus on human rights. We study all sorts of beliefs and actions, and that study is ideally helpful to those focused on human rights; the field itself is quite large and sprawling and thus difficult to redefine in light of any external paradigm.

Human rights scholars certainly can and should partner with sociological social psychologists to begin to address these macro-to-micro and vice versa issues of how societal forces lead individuals to understand and enact human rights. Future work can begin to specify what human rights beliefs fully entail, where they come from, and what influences they have on individual and societal behavior.

~

CHAPTER THIRTY-NINE

SOCIOLOGICAL PRACTICE AND PUBLIC SOCIOLOGY

Jan Marie Fritz

This chapter discusses clinical sociology, a type of sociological practice, and its relation to the human rights paradigm. Clinical sociology is a creative, rights-based, multidisciplinary specialization that seeks to improve life situations for individuals and collectivities (Fritz 2008, 1, 7–8). Clinical sociology needs to be creative in order to be innovative as well as useful. Creativity, a process as well as an outcome, refers to "ideas of duality and paradox, the combination of ideas into new and unexpected patterns, combinations of innovation and value, of different thinking styles, rationality and irrationality" (Bilton 2007, xiv). While individuals can hold on to paradoxical ideas that lead to unique outcomes, creativity is perhaps more likely to be found in the interplay that comes through networks or groups, particularly ones that include contributors with different disciplinary and practical backgrounds. A rights-based approach means that clinical analysis and intervention is expected to "promote and maintain a minimum standard of well-being to which all people ... would ideally possess a right" (Johnson and Forsyth 2002).

Clinical sociologists work with systems to assess situations and avoid, reduce, or eliminate problems through a combination of analysis and intervention (Fritz 2008, 1, 7–18). Clinical analysis is the critical assessment of beliefs, policies, or practices, with an interest in improving the situation. Intervention is based on continuing analysis; it is the creation of new systems as well as the change of existing systems and can include a focus on prevention or promotion (e.g., preventing illness or promoting healthy communities).

Clinical sociologists have different areas of expertise, such as counseling, small-group dynamics, organizational development, health promotion, conflict intervention, and policy development. They are concerned with the different levels—micro, meso, and macro—of intervention. Some are university professors (full- or part-time) who use their clinical expertise (e.g., in organizational development, participatory research, or mediation) on campus and/or in the community. Others can hold positions such as full- or part-time consultant or adviser, community organizer, sociotherapist, focus-group facilitator, social-policy implementer, action researcher, or manager. Clinical sociologists assist individuals, communities, public-sector organizations (government and nonprofit organizations), and for-profit enterprises that are publicly or privately owned.

Clinical sociologists often have education and training in more than one discipline and a great deal of experience in working with intervention teams whose members have a variety of backgrounds. In part because of their multidisciplinary training and practice, clinical sociologists use a range of theoretical approaches (e.g., grounded, standpoint, multicultural-liberationist, psychoanalytic, systems, land ethic, conflict, social-constructionist, symbolic-interactionist, critical, or social-exchange) and frequently integrate them in their work.

Clinical sociology is as old as the field of sociology, and its roots are found in many parts of the world (Fritz 2008, 2). The clinical sociology specialization is often traced to the fourteenth-century work of Arab scholar and statesperson Abd-al-Rahman Ibn Khaldun (1332–1406). Ibn Khaldun provided numerous clinical observations based on his work as secretary of state to the ruler of Morocco and chief judge of Egypt.

Auguste Comte (1798–1857), Émile Durkheim (1858–1917), Karl Marx (1818–1883), and Marcel Mauss (1872–1950) are among those who have been mentioned as contributing to the development of the specialization (Fritz 2008; Gaulejac 2008). Comte, the French scholar who coined the term "sociology," believed that the scientific study of societies would provide the basis for social action. Durkheim's work on the relation between levels of influence (e.g., social in relation to individual factors) led Alvin Gouldner (1965) to write, "More than any other classical sociologist [Durkheim] used a clinical model." Marx, as Alfred McClung Lee noted, brought to his written work "the grasp of human affairs only possible through extensive involvement in praxis" (1979, 488). Mauss gave us "some of the strongest ideas at the base of clinical sociology," including the importance of "lived experience" and "the need for sociology to take into account the meaning people give to their lives" (Gaulejac 2008, 59).

It is not surprising that many of the early sociologists in the United States were scholar-practitioners interested in reducing or solving the pressing social problems that confronted their communities (Fritz 2005). Sociology, in the late 1800s and early 1900s, emerged as a discipline when the nation was struggling with issues of democracy, capitalism, and social justice. There was rural and urban poverty and a growing need for economic security, women were still without the vote, and there were lynchings. At the turn of the twentieth century, frustration led to public protests and the development of public-interest groups and reform organizations.

In the United States, the earliest known written proposal using the words "clinical sociology" was put forward by Milton C. Winternitz, a physician who was dean of the Yale School of Medicine from 1920 through 1935 (Fritz 1989). At least as early as 1929, Winternitz planned to establish a department of clinical sociology within Yale's medical school. Winternitz wanted each medical student to have a chance to analyze cases based on a medical specialty as well as a specialty in clinical sociology.

The first published discussion of clinical sociology by a sociologist was Louis Wirth's (1931a) article "Clinical Sociology" in *American Journal of Sociology*. Wirth wrote at length about the possibility of sociologists working in child-development clinics and noted that this work may create a new form of clinical sociology. That same year, Wirth also wrote a career-development pamphlet in which he "urged [sociology students] to become specialists in one of the major divisions of sociology, such as social psychology, urban sociology … or clinical sociology" (1931b).

The first clinical sociology course in the United States was taught by Ernest W. Burgess at the University of Chicago (Fritz 2008, 28–29). In 1928 and 1929, the course was a "special" course, but it was a regular course from 1931 through 1933. Clinical sociology courses also were offered in the 1930s at Tulane University and New York University (Fritz 1991, 17–19). The Tulane University course was designed to give students the opportunity to learn about behavioral problems and social therapy. The New York University seminar in clinical practice, taught by Harvey Warren Zorbaugh and Agnes Conklin, provided undergraduate and graduate preparation for dealing with behavioral problems in schools to visiting teachers, educational counselors, clinicians, social workers, and school guidance administrators.

If one focuses on the use of the words "clinical sociology," the specialization has its longest history in the United States, where a good number of English-language publications are directly linked to the specialization. The American clinical sociologists focused on publication, emphasized intervention, designed a certification process, and helped establish a commission that accredits clinical as well as applied and engaged public sociology programs. Clinical sociology appeared in Canada (Quebec) in the 1950s (Rheaume 2008, 37), in France in the 1960s (van Bockstaele et al. 2008; Gaulejac 2008, 34), and in Japan in 1993 (Noguchi 2008, 72).

While the United States has the longest history under the name of clinical sociology and the only credentialing processes, most activity in this area (e.g., conferences, publications) are now in the French- and Spanish-speaking parts of the world. For example, a special conference was held (June 2010) in Paris to celebrate the fortieth anniversary of the Social Change Laboratory. The Grupo de Sociologia Clinica Uruguay held the Eighth International Congress of Psycho-sociology and Clinical Sociology in Montevideo (April 2011). In all areas of the world, however, the specialization has always had a central concern with justice, humanism, and/or rights in terms of definitions, research agendas, publications, and interventions.

Clinical sociology has developed in a number of countries around the world. The clinical sociology division (Research Committee 46) of the International Sociological Association, for instance, has members in at least twenty-two countries: Argentina, Australia, Belgium, Canada, Chile, France, Greece, India, Israel, Italy, Malaysia, Mexico, Nigeria, Norway, the Philippines, Romania, Russia, South Africa, Spain, Ukraine, the United States, and Venezuela. French is the language of many of the current international clinical sociology conferences, and many publications clearly linked to clinical sociology have appeared in Québec, Canada, and France. The French-speaking clinical sociologists emphasize clinical analysis and frequently focus on the relationship between psychology and sociology. They have a solid international and interdisciplinary network that is part of the clinical sociology division of the Association Internationale des Sociologues de la Langue Française

(International Association of French-Language Sociologists) and the Association Française de Sociologie (French Sociological Association).

KEY RESEARCH METHODS AND INTERVENTION TECHNIQUES

A clinical sociologist in the United States who is involved in analytic and intervention work may have an undergraduate or a graduate degree. Some, particularly at the bachelor's level, may not undertake much research or may form part of a team that is doing the research. Some practitioners (with any level of degree) may undertake a lot of research but not publish information about their work in the public domain because they are not interested in publication or because of their clients' preferences (Fritz 2008, 13). Practitioners also may not identify themselves as clinical sociologists or not belong to professional sociology organizations. They may work in areas of practice not necessarily identified with sociology (e.g., union organization, grief counseling, sports consulting) and may only be active in professional organizations in their areas of specialization. Thus, it is difficult to identify the key research methods and main intervention techniques. However, some points can be made about research and intervention based on what has been published as well as discussions with colleagues over the last thirty-five years.

RESEARCH

Clinical sociologists who conduct research may do so before beginning an intervention project (to assess the existing situation), during an intervention (to follow the process or possibly change directions), or after the completion of the intervention (in order to evaluate the outcomes) (Fritz 2008, 13). For some clinical sociologists, the research activity is an important part of their own clinical work, and they look for opportunities to conduct research. For instance, an organizational development specialist may study changes in organizations to improve the quality of her or his consulting work. Other clinical sociologists may be interested in research only in a very limited way and only as it is useful (e.g., for assessment) for a specific project. They may prefer to concentrate on the interventions and leave any research to others.

Clinical sociologists use a range of approaches in their research, but there is an emphasis on qualitative approaches—such as participatory/collaborative or life history—and qualitative case-study methods. French Canadian Robert Sevigny (2010), for instance, has been a consultant for a range of organizations and notes that his own work "has always been on the qualitative side" with an emphasis on "participation and communication." He says he has used "a participatory or action research approach whenever possible." Scholar-practitioner Emma Porio (2010), from the Philippines, says she "favors" participatory research as her "approach to housing, social justice and other urban issues" and has used "family/individual life history methods and focus groups" in her research about street children. French Canadian Jacques Rhéaume (2010) says that "in the community development field we use collective life stories or narratives as a global approach based on a clinical sociology perspective." Many US-based clinical sociologists use participatory (community-driven) or collaborative (e.g., researcher-driven but with strong community involvement) approaches and case studies (Fritz 2008) when studying areas such as employment conditions or environmental-justice concerns.

INTERVENTION TECHNIQUES

The role of the clinical sociologist can involve one or more levels of focus, from the individual to the global (Fritz 2008, 9–12). Even though the clinical sociologist specializes in one or two levels of intervention (e.g., individual counseling, neighborhood improvement), the practitioner will move among a number of levels (e.g., individual, organization, community, global) in order to analyze or intervene. Clinical sociologists focus on one level but also have an additional focus, or at least a background, in one or more other levels and integrate that knowledge in their work.

A basic intervention process with a client system (the individual or group using the assistance of a clinical sociologist or intervention team), as outlined by Ronald Lippett and his colleagues in 1958, is divided into seven stages:

(1) The client system discovers the need for help, sometimes with assistance from the change agent.
(2) The helping relationship is established and defined.
(3) The change problem is identified and clarified.
(4) Alternative possibilities for change are examined and the goals of the change are established.
(5) Change efforts are attempted.
(6) Change is generalized and stabilized.
(7) The helping relationship ends or a different type of continuing relationship is defined. (Fritz 2008, 9–10)

Two general points should be made about these stages. First, it is possible not only to progress through the stages but also to cycle back through them as necessary. Second, the length of time required for each stage will depend on a number of factors, including the kind of change under consideration.

Clinical sociologists differ in their consultation models (e.g., control or influence, extent of citizen participation) (Fritz 2008, 11–12). A consultant's approach might be, at one extreme, directive (telling clients what they might do), or it could be quite the opposite. The approach could be collaborative, with the consultant acting as part of a client group and, like other members of the group, offering his or her skills to help the group make a decision. Most clinical sociologists seem to operate in a facilitative (assisting rather than directing) or collaborative way.

The characteristics of the client system are particularly important during a period of change. The largest share of work in any change initiative generally must be undertaken by the client system. Therefore, the extent and quality of the change will depend, in large part, on the energy, capability (including available resources), and motivation of the client system.

It is useful to outline the principles, attitudes, and tools needed by clinical sociologists to conduct interventions (Fritz 2008, 12). While these can differ depending on the level of intervention (e.g., individual, community, nation), they generally include having a rights-based ethical framework, practicing inclusiveness, working with the people's interests and opportunities, encouraging recognition of other viewpoints, demonstrating interdependence as a factor in the change process, encouraging capacity building, having relevant knowledge and knowing how to access additional information, encouraging empowerment, and having a long-term perspective. Change agents need to work well with others and be open-minded as well as courageous.

The context in which change takes place is very important (Fritz 2008, 12). The clinical sociologist and the client system need to identify and review the internal and external forces that foster or resist change at the onset as well as throughout the process. This is a particularly creative part of the change agent's work. If one does this well, appropriate intervention tools and techniques will be selected that can lead to effective, sustainable change.

Clinical sociologists use many different intervention tools but also have similar approaches to their work. For instance, clinical sociologist Jean-Philippe Bouilloud (2010), who is with ESCP Europe (an international business school) in France, says that when he does intervention work with companies, he uses the "clinical tradition of co-construction of solutions" as well as role playing. Jan Marie Fritz (2004) uses a humanistic-integrated process approach in her work as a mediator and organizational consultant. Brazilian Norma Takeuti (2010), using an "interactive or dialogic model," works with young people "to make possible the inventive capacity of subjects" so they can reflect and examine "other futures." Her techniques include a biographical approach, a "workshop in the history of life in communities," and individual drawings (e.g., clay pictures) or some kind of collective work (e.g., writing). French sociologist Vincent de Gaulejac (2010) uses two main approaches in his research and intervention—organizing groups of involvement and retrieval (GIR) in which participants work on their life history and "organidrames" in which participants analyze the causes "of conflict structures at work or in social life."

KEY ISSUES IN THE FIELD AND SELECTED FINDINGS

Clinical sociologists are contributing to the discussion about and resolution of the most pressing issues of the day—such as violence reduction, community development, climate change, inclusion, and health promotion. Clinical sociologists also help individuals and groups analyze their own situations and assess their options. This work with clients may—or may not—focus on pressing issues of public concern.

Clinical sociologists address many different topics. Bouilloud (2010), for instance, notes that a number of clinical sociologists in France, like those in many countries, are concerned with work (e.g., pressures on workers, the impact of modernization, intellectual workers, unemployment). US scholar-practitioner Judith Blau (2010, 2011) founded the Human Rights Center in the town of Carrboro, North Carolina, and has been centrally involved in getting a city and town to become Human Rights Cities. Italy's Association of Clinical Sociology "runs a house for people with social problems and two multifunctional centers for children" (Gargano 2008, 155), and Fritz (2010, 2011) writes about improving the national actions plans for women that have been developed in a number of countries and are based on the UN Security Council resolutions concerned with women, peace, and security.

As there are many different areas of application (e.g., management, family counseling, community development) in clinical sociology and not all work is discussed publicly, it is a difficult task to discuss main findings. However, some points can be made. First, one area of shared general knowledge is the history of clinical sociology in various regions or countries. A 2008 publication (Fritz), for instance, highlights the histories of the field in French Canada, the United States, France, and Japan. The next steps will be when a number of people are writing about the history of clinical sociology in one country and when detailed comparisons are made between and among countries and regions.

Second, many clinical sociologists are using participatory and collaborative approaches in their work. These approaches are time-consuming, but broad-based involvement and rights-based analysis can support effective, sustainable change.

Third, research findings differ for the many areas within clinical sociology. Brabant, for instance, shows how "the shift from a psychological to a sociological perspective eliminates problems that have long perplexed bereavement theorists and clinicians" (2008, 112). Sevigny concludes that clinical sociology can be an effective approach "to the experience of severe mental illness with all its complexity" (2008). Billson showcases the creative ways focus groups can be used "to harness our collective understanding of the complexities of human interaction and help uncover layers of and types of information" (2008, 204). It is interesting to note that clinical sociology publications and presentations often provide findings as well as advice about options. For instance, Fritz (2010) has done this in analyzing special-education mediation and, with colleagues (Fritz, Bistak, and Auffrey 2000; Fritz, Doering, and Gumru 2011), in discussing public policy issues such as tobacco control and national action plans to improve the situation of women and girls.

THE CURRENT AND FUTURE RELATIONSHIP OF CLINICAL SOCIOLOGY AND HUMAN RIGHTS

At least three points should be made. First, the definitions of clinical sociology (as they have developed in various countries) have reflected a central concern with justice, humanism, and rights. There are varying degrees, however, to which individual practitioners see justice, humanism, and rights as central to their own work. As the world (and sociology) pay more attention to human rights, one can expect to see increasingly explicit references to human rights and human rights documents in the publications, presentations, and interventions of clinical sociologists.

Second, sociology students and sociologists who want to take part in intervention activities should be encouraged to receive appropriate education and training, including training in human rights, as well as to participate in supervised practice before engaging in independent interventions. The training and supervised practice will provide the appropriate skills and necessary experience as well as underline the importance of rights-based analysis and intervention.

Third, the participation of clinical sociologists in human rights groups within the International Sociological Association and national and specialty groups such as the American Sociological Association and the Association for Applied and Clinical Sociology will give increasing opportunities for human rights specialists and clinical sociologists to engage in joint analyses of situations. It will also, hopefully, encourage those who are specialists in human rights—but not clinical sociologists—to consider obtaining training and experience in intervention efforts and for those clinical sociologists who are not specialists in human rights to deepen their understanding of human rights documents.

꽃

Chapter Forty

Teaching and Learning

Corey Dolgon

Born as an effort to use science as a foundation for studying social problems, sociology is often caricatured as a dour discipline, well equipped to deconstruct what's wrong with the world but poorly positioned to teach students how they might change it for the better. While dismantling students' cherished ideologies and mythologies, sociology professors rarely demonstrate how the discipline can inform alternative systems of values and practices based on more peaceful, just, and humane premises. The social problems course, in particular, remains a general litany of the world's miseries instead of an inspiring peek at how a sociological imagination might empower students to use their individual and collective agency to make a better world.

Recently, however, movements toward service learning and public sociology, as well as the scholarship of teaching and learning, have advocated a more progressive pedagogical project linking research and teaching to community service, activism, and human rights. But the goal of infusing sociological teaching and learning with an engaged commitment to social justice and human rights is not entirely new, even if it has been mostly marginalized.

The Origins of Social-Justice Teaching in Sociology

Although sociology's earliest scholars and practitioners paid some attention to teaching and learning, they focused primarily on the standardization of course content and the formalization of departmental offerings. In 1909, only four years after the American Sociological Society's first meeting, the group created a committee to study and report on a core course and curriculum for the discipline. This course would establish the scope and field of sociology (Rhoades 1981). But the committee failed to accomplish this task due to its members' differing perspectives on what it meant to unify the literature. Instead, they suggested that coherence would come from a collation of thought and experience led by "competent teachers and institutions of rank" (Rhoades 1981). But who would be those competent teachers, and how would they be taught?

About that same time, Jane Addams and Florence Kelley were shaping the experience and pedagogy of many sociology students and faculty at the University of Chicago. Their book, *Hull House Maps and Papers*, compiled massive statistical data and drew sophisticated maps of Chicago's industrial development and working-class neighborhoods. They analyzed how economic and political institutions and social agencies structured the daily lives of working-class immigrants and others, while at the same time the culture of immigrant communities, labor struggles, and other formal and informal patterns of social life "restructured" those same daily lives. All of this work was done as part of a settlement house movement engrained in the life blood of urban, immigrant, and working-class communities, creating a direct link between the work of Hull House residents and sociologists at the University of Chicago (Deegan 1988; Reisch 2009).

Addams and Kelley advocated the importance of a deep relationship between research and one's social engagements; they carried out their work as part of an effort to educate and organize for social change (E. A. 1950a, 1950b; Deegan 2002). Thus, their pedagogical mission was not to impact sociology, per se, but to infuse struggling communities with the work of young people who wanted to make a difference. Addams, in particular, advocated an engaged pedagogy that taught young people about the potential of building communities for social change. Addams articulates her students' sentiments, describing a desire to fully understand and live democratically. Their feelings resonate strongly with what has become a human rights paradigm for education in sociology, especially in its approach to ideas of universal democracy and education, cultural integrity and dignity, and the rights of workers and other marginalized peoples. As many of the original Chicago School sociologists were shaped by their experiences at Hull House, Addams and Kelley's radical praxis and commitment to human rights education would characterize at least some of American sociology's earliest teaching (Lengerman and Niebrugge-Brantley 1998; Calhoun 2007; Jorgensen and Smith 2009).

But as Mary Jo Deegan and others have written, a serious tension existed between the sociological work at Hull House and the increasing "professionalization and elitism" of a formal academic discipline. Robert Park and other professional gatekeepers demonstrated contempt for Addams and her cohort. While Hull House scholar-activists did teach at the University of Chicago, their courses were usually restricted to campus extension programs or the School of Social Service Administration. According to a former graduate student, "There were occasional rumblings about the old maids downtown who were wet-nursing social reformers" (Queen 1981). Park himself distrusted progressive politics, suggesting that "the greatest damage done to the City of Chicago was not the product of corrupt politicians or criminals but the women reformers" (Sibley 1995).

An increasing separation between sociology and social work/social service emerged as disciplines evolved along gender, class, and political lines. Despite the high quality and groundbreaking nature of race and housing-market work by women such as Edith Abbott and Sophonisba Breckinridge, they remained marginalized from "professional" sociology. The resulting segregation of politically active and socially engaged scholarship and teaching in sociology not only isolated women and progressives in departments of social work but also left the teaching of sociology isolated from engaged human rights and social-justice paradigms (Lengerman and Niebrugge-Brantley 2002; MacLean and Williams 2009).

Instead college faculty shaped a discipline that became increasingly scientific, prioritizing theory and empirical research over reform (Bulmer 1984; DeVault 2007). Classroom pedagogy remained centered on lectures and discussions, with the occasional visit to correctional facilities, poorhouses, and other social institutions where the "underclass" could be further observed and stigmatized (Ellwood 1907). Even field-based study within sociology became formalized and professionalized; the work of developing questions, collecting data, and analyzing results remained exclusively the purview of expert scientists and their apprentices—not embedded in the communities being studied.

In one of the few published discussions on sociological pedagogy during this period, important figures in the discipline focused on lectures and theoretical discussions that integrated classical knowledge with a burgeoning social science. Two dissenting voices emerged, however, and it is interesting to note they came from Jeffrey Brackett, director of the School for Social Work in Boston, and J. Elbert Cutler, who spent most of his professional training at a women's college. Unlike others, Brackett (1907) suggested the need for more than simple visits to underclass institutions. Instead, he proposed an applied social ethics course requiring students to have consistent and systematic contact with poor and disadvantaged families. Cutler (1907), echoing Addams, suggested the necessity of fieldwork if the goal of education concerned citizenship. Unfortunately, such propositions became increasingly rare in sociology departments as many departments focused on basic science and elite theory. Human rights and social justice, if they were discussed at all, were assumed to be the products of a growing professionalized middle class whose scholarship contributed to elite notions of American democracy (Geiger 1986; O'Connor 2002). But even in the post–World War I era, persistent poverty, labor unrest, and other social conflicts proved that knowledge production generated from all classes, not just from "intellect workers." An engaged pedagogy linked to human rights and social justice would have to come from others elsewhere.

MOVING OFF CAMPUS: FINDING SOCIAL JUSTICE ON THE SHOP FLOOR AND CITY STREETS

Some of the most inspired human rights education during the post–World War I period emanated from American labor colleges. Places like the Works Peoples College, the Commonwealth College, and Brookwood Labor College all premised their pedagogy on the need to train organizers and activists in the labor movement (Cummins 1936; Altenbaugh 1990). Local efforts arose in New York City, Boston, Washington, DC, Chicago, Philadelphia, Denver, Seattle, San Francisco, and Portland, demonstrating a workers' education movement across the country (Lembcke 1984; Edwards and McCarthy 1992; Thayer-Bacon 2004).

Student movements also gained strength in the 1930s, empowered by a radical Left response to the Great Depression. Stronger labor unions, active and effective Socialist and Communist parties, and other political forces encouraged student movements for economic and racial justice. Groups such as the American Student Union, the Student League for Industrial Democracy, the Young People's Communist League, and the Young People's Socialist League, as well as youth-focused movements within the NAACP, all introduced students to intellectual and political activities on racial and class equality and peace and disarmament movements (Lewack 1953; Altbach and Peterson 1971; Bynum 2009). Inevitably, these student activities found their way back to campus through sponsored lectures, organizing events, and even demands for integration of local, national, and international politics into the curriculum.

The rapid growth of professional sociology between 1913 and the early 1930s was mostly an isolated, ivory-tower enterprise. While battles raged within the discipline, especially over notions of science, objectivity, and social reform, the teaching of sociology got little attention, and the issue of student learning engaged with movements for social justice and human rights received outright hostility (Turner 2007). Eventually, a more engaged sense of progressive purpose for sociology did emerge, primarily in the work of teachers and scholars like Robert and Helen Lynd. Their groundbreaking community studies of Muncie, Indiana, published as *Middletown* (1929), shifted some of the scientism and alienation of sociology. The Lynds' multi-methodological studies assumed that integrated and comprehensive institutional studies could help communities avoid provincial and reactionary approaches to social problems, instead "suggesting the possible utility of a deeper-cutting procedure that would involve a reexamination of the institutions themselves" (1929, 502).

Robert Lynd's later work, *Knowledge for What? The Place of the Social Sciences in American Culture* (1939), made clear his belief that social scientists needed to do more than simply analyze and draw inferences; they needed to strategize about the implementation of their findings. Known as a tireless and committed teacher whose meticulous readings of student works often resulted in commentary longer than the original papers, Lynd (1939, 1982) also inspired his students to consider the real human impact of their work—both the questions they pursued and the knowledge they produced.

Political tensions within sociology continued to manifest along gender and political lines, and hybrid sociologists–social workers like Mary van Kleeck (who maintained a focus on social justice and human rights) remained marginalized. As part of Social Work's Rank and File Movement in the 1930s and 1940s, Van Kleeck's research on the industrial conditions of women workers in New York City "convinced her that social justice for the lower classes in general and women in particular was possible only if the objectives of business were 'social' and not 'individualistic'" (Selmi and Hunter 2001, 790). Van Kleeck emphasized linking both the research and teaching of sociology (in general) and social work (in particular) to labor organizing for the benefit of both (Nyland and Rix 2000). Yet Van Kleeck, Lillian Gilbreth, and others faced alienation within the academy based on male domination, political intimidation, and the ensuing backlash against radical scholars (Abramovitz 1998; Karger 1989). Thus, at the same time that sociology (departments, courses, faculty positions, majors, etc.) grew in American higher education, there was a relative decline in social-justice courses (Bernard 1945).

Still, a strong relationship to labor organizing and early civil rights activity brought sociologists and other social scientists back into the heart of political struggles and, in particular, labor organizing. Despite the demise of the workers' education movement in the early 1930s, a new labor college movement rose again in the early 1940s and stood as a prime example of a growing practical relationship between academics and workers. Labor education projects sprouted across the country in New York City (Jefferson School), Detroit (Workers' Service Program), Chicago (Abraham Lincoln School), and especially in California, where schools in San Francisco (California Labor School) and Los Angeles (People's Education Center) counted numerous teachers from the University of California system on their faculty (California Legislature 1943; Kornbluh 1987; Denning 1998). Once again, social science was engaging students in the community and teaching outside the institution to implement a social-justice and human rights pedagogy.

After World War II, radical education projects outside the ivory tower continued, but more progressive faculty within the academy also took up a focus on human rights and social justice—especially those critiquing the role of an intellectual elite attendant to mainstream economic, political, and military power structures. C. Wright Mills and Alfred McClung Lee were two of the most eloquent voices examining the intricacies of institutional power and an intellectual culture bound up in serving the "ruling class." In books and lectures, Mills (1948) encouraged his students to use their "sociological imagination" to observe and challenge the growing centralization of power in the United States.

Meanwhile, sociologists such as Alfred McClung Lee asked their own versions of Lynd's "knowledge for what?" by wondering, Sociology for whom? Lee developed an interdisciplinary and humanist approach to sociology that drew power from the growing social movements of the 1950s and 1960s. Discussing the possibility of sociologists "serving man," Lee wrote,

> All social scientists need to keep their eyes trained and to encourage their students to keep their eyes trained ... upon the great and pressing problems and challenges of man's life in contemporary society. Thus they can help create social sciences to serve the needs of man rather than to aid the manipulations of present and future elites and tyrants. (1973, 201)

Lee and his wife, Betty, helped found the Society for the Study of Social Problems (1951) and the Association for Humanist Sociology (1976), professional organizations more openly political than the American Sociological Association (ASA).

This history of McCarthyism's impact on the academic Left is well documented, and it clearly challenged the ability for faculty to openly espouse and teach from a progressive human rights and social-justice framework (Schrecker 1986; Chomsky et al. 1998). Ironically, though, despite the infringement on free speech and the relatively conservative political landscape that McCarthyism inspired, student activism returned with a vengeance in the 1950s. Mills and Lee and a host of other radical and often politically engaged faculty called forth a new generation of progressive young activists, and soon their analytical perspectives and classroom teachings raised the critical consciousness of students (Scimecca 1976; Trevino 1998). From Berkeley's Free Speech Movement to the rise of the Student Nonviolent Coordinating Committee (SNCC) in southern black colleges, the teachings of radical faculty like C. Wright Mills and Howard Zinn inspired students such as Tom Hayden, Marian Wright Edelman, and Alice Walker.

And sometimes it was students who led such engagements. Bob Zellner, SNCC's first white field secretary, did graduate work in sociology at Brandeis. While the department was well known for its radical faculty, it was Zellner who often asked the secretary to interrupt classes because students were needed at sit-ins (Zellner et al. 2008). Professors usually consented.

But most of the engaged teaching about social justice and human rights came, once again, not in the classroom but from work in the streets. SNCC's Freedom Schools and the Students for a Democratic Society's Education Research Action Project brought hundreds of college students into poor urban ghettos and rural hamlets and challenged them to learn American history, sociology, and politics at the same time that they learned about oppression, struggle, democracy, love, and freedom (McDew 1966; Frost 2001). While these social movements would have transformative impacts on American society in general, nowhere was their impact felt more completely and fundamentally than on college and university campuses. And nowhere would the rise of racial and ethnic studies, feminism, women's and gender studies, and an overall sense of the need for civic engagement and social consciousness be felt more notably than in the teaching of undergraduate students.

BACK TO SCHOOL, BACK TO STRUGGLE: PRODIGAL STUDENTS DEMAND AND DESIGN NEW PEDAGOGY

Throughout the late 1960s and 1970s, many sociology students would take journeys back and forth between the classroom and the political work of social movements. The anthology *Radical Sociologists and the Movement: Experiences, Lessons, and Legacies* (Oppenheimer, Murray, and Levine 1991) shows that these experiences made political engagement a crucial element of how students learned and how, eventually, faculty would teach sociology. But as social movements waned in the mid- and late 1970s, and as some radical sociologists became entrenched in departments, the focus on engagement and social justice also shifted and diminished. And as the late twentieth century witnessed higher education becoming a primary economic engine, colleges and universities themselves adopted the techniques and practices of major corporations. Eventually, these changes would be encapsulated in what critics have called the "corporatization of the academy" (Soley 1999; White 2000; Tuchman 2011). For faculty, an increasing pressure to publish and a stratified star system of research and scholarship resulted in a hyper, yet disengaged, professionalism. Meanwhile, a growing bureaucratic hegemony created an obsession with measurement and assessment primarily focused on efficiency and ill-defined notions of "excellence" (Readings 1996; Scott 2004).

Internal and institutional reflexivity did result in some positive effects, however, such as the focus on teaching quality that eventually resulted in a movement toward scholarship of teaching and learning and the role of civic engagement and service learning in higher education. Discussions of pedagogy and engagement in teaching sociology had not been completely silenced by the initial split with social work or the discipline's patriarchal and political conservatism as symbolized by the marginalization of Addams, Kelley, and Hull House. In the late 1940s, David Fulcomer (1947) critiqued the "lecture-quiz section" method of teaching, suggesting it only elicited a "copy, memorize, and cram" style of learning. Instead, he lauded innovations in "project-based" pedagogy as well as using popular culture. But his primary proposal promoted using communities as laboratories where students participated in and learned from community life (Fulcomer 1947). Mirra Komarovsky (1951) and others echoed the need to examine pedagogy more systematically and substantially, but their voices in the early post–World War II period were few and far between.

According to Jay Howard, a kind of social movement occurred in the late 1960s and the 1970s, as those interested in examining pedagogy began collecting and mobilizing resources and support inside and outside the sociological profession. From the founding of the Committee on Teaching of Undergraduate Sociology (1966) to the establishment of the Section on Undergraduate Education (1972) and the initiation of its scholarly journal, *Teaching Sociology* (1973), the American Sociological Association began institutionalizing a commitment to the study of teaching sociology (Howard 2010). By the mid- to late 1970s, this movement's leader, Hans Mauksch, had further expanded the legitimacy and development of pedagogical inquiry in professional sociology. The growing attention to pedagogy did not, however, result in a focus on social justice or human rights. In fact, articles relating to pedagogy and social justice during this period were mostly linked to either social work or teaching outside higher education in prisons and other community settings. Such experience in and integrations with institutions and movements outside the academy remained crucial for infusing new pedagogical movements with a commitment to social justice.

For many, Ernst Boyer's (1997) call for an "engaged scholarship" initiated a "civic engagement" movement within higher education. Boyer argued that faculty needed to go beyond the three traditional categories of professional work (scholarship, teaching, and departmental or professional service) to include a fourth category of engagement. Citing a long line of historical, public engagements from American higher education's founding, Boyer (1997) contended that the public mission to create and produce "relevant" knowledge required an "engagement" with the public. This work and its followers had a major impact on both the scholarship of teaching and learning in general and engaged pedagogy and scholarship in particular (McKinney and Howery 2006).

Ironically, almost a decade before Boyer, Bob Sigmon (1990) published "three principles of service learning" in 1979, and by 1989 more than seventy organizations had consulted with the National Society for Experiential Education to produce "Principles of Good Practice for Combining Service and Learning" at the Johnson Foundation's Wingspread Conference Center in Wisconsin. By the mid-1990s, national networks for service learning had appeared, the *Michigan Journal for Community Service Learning* had been founded, and dozens of states had formed Campus Compact organizations with more than five hundred college and university members all committing to the goal of civic engagement in higher education.

Most "pioneers" in service learning and civic engagement acknowledge that their experiences with the social movements of the 1950s and 1960s significantly influenced their project of creating a more practical and politically engaged scholarship and pedagogy. They trace their inspiration for community-engaged teaching to high school and college experiences with civil rights work: the Freedom Rides and Freedom Schools, sit-ins, and local campaigns around free speech and equal employment opportunities (Stanton, Giles, and Cruz 1999; Ewen 1991; Ross 1991). As these activists became teachers and professors, they developed pedagogies that encouraged students to incorporate course readings and classroom reflection with experiences in community organizations and local institutions. Thus, Boyer's work, as influential as it was in articulating and inspiring both scholarship of teaching and learning and civic engagement, emanated amid an already burgeoning movement inspired by civil rights and other activists returning to college campuses in search of politically engaged teaching and scholarship.

As a pedagogy, service learning now pervades most college campuses and is supported by a myriad of national organizations, including the National Service-Learning Clearinghouse (Corporations for National and Community Service), the Campus Compact (thirty-five states and more than eleven hundred colleges and universities), and the American Democracy Project. Hundreds of articles and a number of books about sociology and community-based pedagogies (service learning, community-based research, etc.) have appeared since 1990, often under the leadership of activist scholars such as Sam Marullo, Kerry Strand, Randy Stoecker, and Phil Nyden. The service learning and civic engagement movement has come to symbolize one of the strongest pedagogical frameworks focused on human rights and social justice in the contemporary higher-education landscape (Annette 2005).

A PROFESSIONAL CRITIQUE AND THE FUTURE OF TEACHING SOCIOLOGY

This movement has many conservative critics who complain about watered-down courses, a lack of academic rigor, and the political indoctrination of students (Butin 2010; Arum 2011). The Left, too, has critiqued service learning's all-too-common link to charity and social-service work without a focus on the root causes and power structures that cause social problems to begin with (Roschelle, Turpin, and Elias 2000; Arena 2010; Dolgon et al. 2012). But advocates continue to see service learning as a powerful pedagogical tool and a foundation for what has become a trend toward combining civically engaged pedagogy with a focus on social justice and human rights (Lewis 2004; Hattery and Smith 2006; Dolgon and Baker 2010).

One of the most exciting possibilities on the contemporary pedagogical landscape has been the dovetailing of civic engagement with the growing movement toward public sociology. Corey Dolgon and Chris Baker (2010) go so far as to say that service learning is the pedagogy of public sociology. But others, such as Kathleen Korgen and Jonathan White (2010) and Melanie Bush and Deborah Little (2009), are not just writing extensively about the need to engage students actively in struggles for human rights and social justice; they are attempting to offer the requisite resources, tools, and pedagogical analyses needed to provide guidance for faculty who share the perspective that

> perhaps the greatest service sociology can offer to its students is to teach them to understand the ways in which what they perceive to be their "personal troubles" may in fact be "public issues" [and] how their own biographies—their loves, their demons—are oftentimes those of many others. Even more important, once the student understands his or her connection to "others" [and] to social structure, s/he [will] understand the ways in which that structure both creates those demons and how that structure might be changed to alleviate them. (Goodwin 1987, 19)

Despite the growth in scholarship of teaching and learning and community-based pedagogies, work on teaching and learning still remains marginal in professional sociology, even if the margins themselves have expanded as membership in ASA's Section on Teaching and Learning places this area among the top concentrations in the field. Meanwhile, general surveys of sociology as a professional discipline pay scant, if any, attention to teaching. The recent centennial epic edited by Craig Calhoun (2007), *Sociology in America: A History*, is a case in point: twenty-one chapters and more than nine hundred pages of incredibly eloquent writing on the history and trajectory of sociology in the United States include not one piece (or even index reference) relating to teaching or pedagogy.

The trend in higher education to take scholarship of teaching and learning more seriously has generated greater interest in the theory and practice of teaching. This developing awareness holds some potential for a more passionate and rigorous push toward teaching sociology that educates and inspires a new generation of students interested in social movements and social justice. Still, much of the focus on scholarship of teaching and learning continues to be driven by a bureaucratic and conservative assessment phenomenon. While the implementation of methodological and analytical rigor in the work of research on teaching is long overdue, within the current context of institutional rationalization and conservative ideological attacks, a pedagogical focus on the social justice and human rights impact of our teaching may remain marginalized by our professional discourse.

Still, the popularity of public sociology and civic engagement remains vibrant and vital. The growing number of majors and concentrations in public sociology and increases in campus offices and centers for civic engagement create the kind of institutional space for the active teaching of social action and social change. Within these contexts, Bush and Little's advocacy seems far from marginalized:

Academic sociologists can and should make social justice and political engagement a central part of sociological pedagogy, not only within the classroom but in the larger university environment. In particular, we suggest that connecting our students to the lived experiences of those involved in contemporary social justice activism and social movements is a core task of public sociology. (2009, 13)

More importantly, our students increasingly demand the kind of relevancy and critical knowledge that spirited a once apathetic 1950s college generation to take' to the streets. As I write this, the Occupy Wall Street protests are spreading like wildfire. My own students at a small, Catholic, liberal arts college (which research indicates is one of the least politically active but the seventh-happiest campus in the country and where students self-identify as living "in a bubble") have already organized two teach-ins, a march, and a demonstration, and they grow hungrier every day for a critical, politically engaged education. As has happened time and time again, sociology will be called on to provide the analytical and political tools for a new generation of activists hoping to establish a world based on human rights and dignity. Whether inside or outside the institution (or both), teaching sociology that aims for a more just and human world will be what captures the imaginations of our most engaged students—it will be why they want to "do" sociology and why we want to teach it.

Chapter Forty-One

History of Sociology

J. I. (Hans) Bakker

In order to discuss the relationship between human rights and sociology, we need to consider the discipline of sociology itself. There is no disciplinary unity within sociology; instead, sociology is a complex amalgam of many different perspectives. One author has argued that sociology is a multiparadigm "science." But even the term "science" is something that many sociologists would reject if science is viewed from a primarily positivistic, metaparadigmatic orientation. Interpretive, critical, feminist, and postmodernist sociological theorists reject all forms of "scientism." Indeed, almost all sociologists would reject the notion that we can best pursue socio- logical questions through strictly reductionistic, empiricist natural- and life-science approaches. While some life scientists, such as E. O. Wilson, argue for "consilience" among all the sciences, including the social sciences, that sociobiological and evolu- tionist position is widely rejected even by positivist sociologists. Due to the diversity of approaches that all fall under the umbrella word "sociology," it is no wonder there are approximately forty-five different sections of the American Sociological Associa- tion (ASA). No sociologist can possibly be well-read on all of American sociology, much less sociology worldwide. German, French, British, Indian, Argentinean, and many other sociological traditions vary greatly. Linguistic barriers prevent sociolo- gists from communicating effectively. While English is often used for publications, many important publications in other languages, especially German and French, are ignored by English-speaking sociologists. Hence, when an author is translated into English, his or her chance of receiving some recognition is greatly improved, as has been the case with a number of prominent theorists, including Jürgen Habermas and Michel Foucault. Since the early 1990s, sociological ideas from the West have circulated more freely in Russia and are beginning to be appreciated more widely in the People's Republic of China. It is safe to say that in those nation-states where human rights violations tend to be most severe, the impact of sociology has often been minimal. In Cambodia, Democratic Republic of the Congo, Republic of the Congo, Uganda, Sudan, Chile, and many other countries, the discipline of sociol- ogy is not widely viewed as having any real bearing on political and ethnic or racial realities. The network of Sociologists without Borders, which Judith Blau initiated, has made a small mark on a global picture that is not particularly encouraging. But even all the social sciences and humanities together have not prevented major human rights abuses during the last century. It is paradoxical that the rise of fascism in Italy and Germany was not significantly hampered by prominent Italian and German sociological thinkers. Moreover, many of the human rights abuses in the Soviet Union were exacerbated by a simplistic interpretation of the ideas of Karl Marx and various Marxists. Today, sociology is not much of a safeguard against the violation of human rights in the advanced industrialized nations, despite the huge outpouring of empirically based research studies. The Enlightenment ideal of a secular approach to sociopolitical problems has not been fully realized. Sociological theory remains a battlefield (Bakker 2010a). In order to grasp why that is the case, we have to return to the earliest roots of the very idea of individual rights.

WHAT IMPACT DID RELIGIOUS BELIEFS HAVE ON THE GENERAL CONCEPTUALIZATION OF HUMAN RIGHTS?

It is not possible to articulate a theory of the human rights of individuals until we have a clear idea of what a human being is as a legal person. The seedbed of the theory of human rights, sociologically speaking, is the earliest religious beliefs of ancient peoples, including Mediterranean, Middle Eastern, and Indic peoples. In the very long run, religious beliefs have contributed to a notion of individual humans having value. In the Roman Empire, a Roman citizen had a right to a fair trial, although that right was not always honored in practice. Slaves did not have any rights in the Roman Empire or the Holy Roman Empire.

The development of the notion of a dialectic between the concept of a lasting human soul (Sanskrit: *atman*) and the theological notion that the soul is not lasting (Sanskrit: *anatman*, Pali *anatta*) is one reasonable starting point. One of the first theorists of a sophisticated Buddhist-Hindu theory of the self is the Indic philosopher Nagarjuna (2007), a Brahmin who became very influential in Buddhist theology. A recent exchange between a Buddhist leader and a secular thinker (Dalai Lama and Eckman 2008) emphasizes the way in which human compassion is central to any notion of respect for the rights of others. In the strident political debate concerning Tibet, there may be a certain degree of romanticization of the freedoms of Tibetans in earlier eras, but it is difficult to conceive of the treatment accorded Tibetans by the government of the People's Republic of China as true liberation from feudal oppression.

We also need to mention Christian "catholic" (i.e., universal) beliefs in the individual human soul. In Christianity, as in Islam, all human beings potentially have everlasting life, starting at the moment of conception. However, the religious belief in the sacredness of human beings as mature and solitary political individuals did not emerge until the Protestant Reformation. During the Holy Roman Empire (c. AD 800–1812), members of groups (e.g., guilds), but not individuals, per se, had rights. The Holy Roman Empire and Roman Catholic Church did not emphasize human rights as a matter of universal citizenship. Later, Roman Catholic Church dogma involved a belief in the individual soul, which became a seed of the eventual right of certain persons, especially royalty and aristocrats, to be given a certain degree of deference (Bakker 2010a). The English Magna Carta of the thirteenth century (with its various formulations) first enunciated the notion of a right to trial by a jury of one's peers, but we have to remember that peer meant "peer of the realm" and certainly did not mean ordinary merchants or peasant cultivators. The peerage only won rights very gradually and certainly did not suddenly become empowered in 1225. As circumstances changed, retrospective legal thought may have exaggerated the idea of rights. We must not fall into the trap of thinking of human rights as only a western European phenomenon.

Many Islamic scholars have also stressed the sacred aspects of human life. Abdal-Rahman Ibn Khaldun, who is mentioned in many sociology theory textbooks as an important forerunner to sociology, can be cited as one example. That is because he had a theory about the oscillation of power between power holders in urban centers and those who were outside the gates of the cities, mainly the Bedouins. But Ibn Khaldun can also serve as an example of a thinker whose grasp of the notion of collectivities goes to the heart of the problem when it comes to thinking about the human rights of individuals. If the nation is all-important, then the rights of individual human beings have to suffer in times of war. Nevertheless, Islamic caliphates and both Sunni and Shiite Islamic theologians did not emphasize human rights.

Theology and social theory go hand in hand, often without explicit recognition of the mutual interdependence of the two. In this secular age, critics of religious beliefs often neglect the deep religious roots of fundamental human rights as nonscientific superstitions. But natural sciences do not directly involve any kind of belief in the worth and dignity of individual members of a species. The neo-Darwinian modern evolutionary synthesis contributes a view of the world that has great heuristic power for the life sciences, but the empirical research findings do not clearly indicate anything about the human rights of individuals or even groups. In fact, the misuse of Darwin's ideas by social Darwinists often involved some version of eugenics or ethnic cleansing, which was diametrically opposed to contemporary standards of universal human rights.

MODERN CAPITALISM AND THE EMERGENCE OF BOURGEOIS FREEDOMS

We need to be clear that religious beliefs concerning the sacredness of the individual human being are central to any first-stage notion of human rights. Much of what we now consider common sense comes to us through the fiercely fought Protestant Reformation in Europe. Moreover, the modern notion of human rights cannot be disassociated from modern capitalism. Whereas earlier religious insights about generic notions of human worth are important, the way in which we think about human rights today is part and parcel of the development of modern capitalism since the sixteenth century. The Renaissance, Reformation, and Enlightenment were key phases in the development of human rights and also in the course of the transformation from medieval feudalism to modern capitalism in western Europe.

No sociological theorist has provided a more adequate explanation of the transformation that took place than Max Weber (2011). Weber's famous Protestant Ethic thesis holds that there was a degree of association (or "elective affinity") between the post-Calvinist Protestant sects (e.g., the Quakers, Methodists, Baptists, Anabaptists such as Mennonites, and others) and the idea of a this-worldly calling that involved assiduous work. The asceticism that had been characteristic of monks and nuns in the Middle Ages (i.e., an otherworldly asceticism) could now be central to the lifestyles of ordinary, working people in this world, here and now.

Jeffrey Alexander (2010) has argued that the civil sphere can be considered vital as an umbrella for modern politics, outside the formal political arena. He emphasizes Weber's views on the ways in which power can be considered and adds a notion of social power that departs from the rigid view of power as coercion or the activities of a power elite. While elites and state bureaucracies have an important impact, moral ideas about citizenship rights and human rights in general are also very important. It may be true that the civil sphere sometimes gets idealized, but nevertheless, to the degree to which there is an effective representative democracy, the civil sphere will have some degree of autonomy and power. Recent scandals have rocked modern capitalist institutions such as the stock market, but without a notion of fundamental rights, instances of gross exploitation (e.g., Bernie Madoff's Ponzi scheme) would not be as clear. In most parts of the world, there is still a struggle for full citizenship. We now take it for granted, for example, that all citizens should have the right to vote, but we forget how recently that right became formalized in law. Informal political rights and privileges are part of a civil sphere that is not directly part of political and legal-juridical institutions (Alexander 2006).

Classical Sociological Theory and Human Rights

While Weber is often credited with explaining the key to the rise of modern capitalism in the sixteenth century, it was Karl Marx (1967) who critiqued the way in which work as a laborer in a modern capitalist firm involves the alienation of not only one's labor time but also one's self. A worker sells labor time, which becomes one of the forces of production. The way in which the forces of production are organized determines the relations of production in society. In other words, the social structure of modern capitalism is rooted in a system of buying and selling of labor time. Marx argues that such a system ultimately creates the seeds of its own destruction due to increased general alienation and misery of the proletarian workers. Some apologists of capitalism argue that the average worker in an industrialized country is not miserable but enjoys certain basic privileges and a very high standard of living. One could argue that high levels of unemployment and the vagaries of the labor market make such a rosy picture difficult to defend for all but a few members of the labor elite (i.e., young, well-educated, technically skilled workers and those in professions such as law, medicine, and teaching).

In the Global South, on the other hand, billions of people still do not lead comfortable lives. The citizens of the advanced industrialized nations are spared the worst features of modern capitalism through globalization, the newest stage of what formerly could have been called imperialism and finance capitalism. This Marxist argument is not accepted by everyone, but many thinkers have utilized the grain of truth in the Marxist notion of species being to argue in favor of a view of human beings that stresses realistic goals. A life well lived is a life that begins to approximate the ideal of species being, with the paradox that species being is our true nature, what we were intended to be from the beginning.

While he was very critical of Marx's theory of capital, Georg Simmel (1990) argued that a closer examination of superordination and subordination, as well as modern life in a metropolis, does tend to illustrate that there is a cost involved.

Later, the philosopher George Herbert Mead (1967) developed a theory of the importance of symbolic interaction for the development of the social self. Mead's ideas, when combined with those of the American pragmatist Charles Sanders Peirce, provide a very cogent, heuristic view of what it means to be an individual human being (Wiley 1994). The fact that the Mead-Peirce theory of the self is rarely brought up in discussions of human rights and freedoms indicates the low level of theorizing about legal persons and unalienated human beings.

CONTEMPORARY COMPARATIVE SOCIOLOGICAL THEORY AND HUMAN RIGHTS: THREE THINKERS

It is not just classical contributors to the discipline of sociology who have touched on the notion of human rights in various ways. Of all contemporary theorists, we can briefly mention three who stand out as especially important: Jürgen Habermas, Immanuel Wallerstein, and Dorothy Smith. Of course, it would be easy to add dozens of other names since hundreds of sociological thinkers have contributed to a better understanding of the individual and society.

Jürgen Habermas (1989 [1981]) is an expert on comparative law, and his sociology of law is of great importance for any full understanding of the rise of the notion of the legal person. His neo-Marxist critical-theory approach has been very influential. His views are comparative and historical. We often forget that peerage is not the same as citizenship. It was only in recent history that some of the highest offices in the governmental structure of the United Kingdom could be held by ordinary citizens. Habermas's notion of communicative action in the lifeworld (*Lebenswelt*) stresses the importance of social interaction outside the political, economic, and civil spheres. The lifeworld of ordinary persons was of very little importance in legal theory before the nineteenth century. It has been argued (Gutman and Thompson 2004) that in the light of contemporary mass media and the systematic distortion of information in postmodern societies, Habermas's views concerning consensus formation do not adequately support the kind of national value systems required for human rights to flourish. Rawls's theory of justice is important, and readers should carefully study the Habermas-Rawls arguments on both sides.

Immanuel Wallerstein (1979, 2002) is the founder of a neo-Marxist perspective that insists on the importance of measuring Marxist ideas concerning exploitation and alienation on a world scale. Hence, his writing is deeply historical and compara-tive. Rather than thinking primarily in terms of individual nation-states, as Marx tended to do, Wallerstein places globalization in the forefront. Even before the term "globalization" became popular in its contemporary meaning, the theory of a world capitalist system was an important modification of Marx's insights concerning the working of capital. The economic exploitation of the periphery and semiperiphery by hegemonic core states is central to a neo-Marxist view of the world that stresses the global impact of finance capital. Today, every business page of every newspaper illustrates the volatility of money markets and the interrelatedness of all parts of the capitalist system. But that interconnectedness was true, according to Wallerstein and other world-system theorists, from the very beginning of modern capitalism in the sixteenth century.

We need to also pay attention to feminist theorists when we discuss human rights, since the human rights of women have traditionally been undervalued in many ways. Despite the romanticization of motherhood in Victorian times, even upper-class elite and bourgeois women had few legal rights. Dorothy Smith (1990, 1999) in particular and standpoint theory and methodology in general (Harding 2003) correct some of the problems that characterized sociological thinking up until very recently. It is not difficult to see how Smith's methodology of institutional ethnography could be very helpful in comprehending the relationship between feminine gender identity and human rights.

CONCLUSION

From all of the above it is clear that the discipline of sociology, with its many branches and sections, has a great deal to say about human rights. Many social (and specifically sociological) theorists have dealt with a host of issues that have relevance to the study of human rights, especially when we consider human rights comparatively and historically. In a sense, the history of sociology as a discipline and the history of the development of contemporary conceptualizations of human rights go hand in hand.

Sociological theory helps us to comprehend human rights for several reasons. First, sociological theory helps us to understand the relationship between the individual and society (Holstein and Gubrium 2003). Societal structures make it possible for citizens of a nation-state to have certain guarantees of life and liberty, at least in theory. Citizens also benefit from cutting-edge legislation concerning harassment in the workplace. Second, the cultural traditions of specific societies keep the civil sphere and communicative action alive, in part through freedom of religion and freedom of the press.

Political scientists and political sociologists have analyzed the way in which totalitarian regimes, particularly the Hitlerian Nazi fascists in Germany and the Stalinist Marxist-Leninists in the Soviet Union, have completely abrogated human rights, even for natural-born citizens. In a nation-state where the individual has no legal rights, it is very easy for the state apparatus to develop a life of its own.

Such a state system is cumbersome and may only last for a few decades, but in the meantime, many people suffer in countless ways. Ironically, more than 26 million Soviet citizens (soldiers and civilians) died fighting the Nazi war machine, thereby saving the modern capitalist system from itself. The socialism that National Socialists espoused in Germany, Italy, Spain, and many other countries deviated completely from any notions of liberty and freedom. Ultimately, the Soviet ideal of communism, rather than the actual workings of the dictatorship of the proletariat, led to the defeat of the modern capitalist mutation we call fascism.

Many citizens in industrialized societies take certain rights for granted and tend to believe that the rights they are guaranteed in their own countries should also be available to all others, regardless of where they were born or now live. Unfortunately, the United Nations does not have the military power or even general persuasive ability to guarantee human rights in many parts of the world where human rights are threatened. In Myanmar (Burma), for example, a military dictatorship makes it impossible for ordinary citizens to feel free.

Moreover, if we move away from the discipline and simply think of pre-Enlightenment social theory, it is obvious that all theories of human rights are ultimately deeply embedded in theological principles and early social theorists writing from within a more religious worldview (Tarnas 1991). Mohandas Karamchand Gandhi was known to many as the Mahatma (Great Soul; Sanskrit: *Maha-atman*). He contributed a great deal to human rights, and his ideas concerning nonviolent civil disobedience (Sanskrit: *satyagraha*) influenced Martin Luther King Jr. and Nelson Mandela. He managed to synthesize ideas from many religious traditions and stress the fundamental dignity of human beings. He denied the importance of the caste system for Vedic and Brahmanic Hinduism and argued that the so-called untouchables should be thought of as children of God (Sanskrit: *Harijans*, from Hari, one of the names of Krishna-Vishnu). Gandhi was an ecumenical thinker, and he absorbed some of the European Enlightenment values that have become part of the British common law tradition. His success was based in part on following a strategy of forcing the imperial power of Great Britain to aspire universally to the standards it claimed to uphold for its own citizens. The irony was, of course, that in the United Kingdom then (and even today), many aspects of British common law and legislated law were not (and are not) necessarily fully practiced.

In conclusion, the ideas of many thinkers have converged on a fundamental belief in the worth and dignity of all human beings. The idealistic goal of human rights is only now beginning to become somewhat more plausible, and it will take many generations before it is realized for the majority of all inhabitants on earth. Whether we will successfully overcome the problems that natural-resource depletion, global climate weirding, and vastly increased human populations pose before we accomplish human rights at an international level is something no one can predict in advance. The revolution of rising expectations is usually related primarily to consumer wants, but perhaps it will simultaneously also affect the drive toward greater democratic freedoms. One manifestation of that is the recent UN Declaration of the Rights of Indigenous Peoples (2007), which includes Article 9: "Indigenous peoples and individuals have the right to belong to an indigenous community or nation, in accordance with the traditions and customs of the community or nation concerned. No discrimination of any kind may arise from the exercise of such a right." In many parts of the world it will be a very long time before that explicit statement is honored. The fact that it is coming so late, as a third-generation human right, illustrates the evolution of human rights through several stages, including the notion of citizenship in a modern capitalist nation-state versus a "community or nation."

CHAPTER FORTY-TWO

THEORY

Elizabeth A. Gill

> *All political instruction finally should be centered upon the idea that
> Auschwitz should never happen again. This would be possible only
> when it devotes itself openly, without fear of offending any authorities,
> to this most important of problems. To do this education must trans-
> form itself into sociology, that is, it must teach about the societal play
> of forces that operates beneath the surface of political forms.*
> —Theodor Adorno (2003)

Adorno's belief in the discipline's ability to identify the fundamental conditions, processes, and sources of human annihilation has yet to be realized. If the discipline is to live up to its potential, the nature and practice of sociology must change. The discipline's reliance on scientific, rational discourse to further its legitimacy has resulted in a self-imposed moral silence of science. In a sense, sociology is a social construction of the modern society it theorizes, investigates, and uses as a frame for its own discourse. As Bauman stated, "Phrases like 'the sanctity of human life' or 'moral duty' sound as alien in a sociology seminar as they do in the smoke-free, sanitized rooms of a bureaucratic office" (1989, 29).

In order to come to terms with emergent global social and cultural patterns, I believe sociologists ultimately must pay special heed to the issue of human rights. My intention in this chapter is to provide an overview of the challenges and opportunities afforded social theorists in contributing to the nature of the human rights agenda and our ability to practice it.

SOCIOLOGY AND THE NATURE OF HUMAN RIGHTS

In the seventeenth century, Locke (1970 [1689]) developed a theory of "natural rights" stating that all human beings had certain rights that derived from their nature, not from their government or its laws, and the legitimacy of government rested on the respect that it accorded to these rights. During the twentieth century, the human rights framework that became prominent developed out of the societal-rights tradition as shaped by the American and French revolutions. Reflecting a deep and abiding concern with the abuse of power, the Universal Declaration of Human Rights developed against the backdrop of the Holocaust and the increasing efforts by former European colonies to gain independence from the dominance of Western colonial power. Since the close of World War II, we have witnessed a number of practical efforts to implement human rights principles, as well as the development of a growing body of literature on the subject by legal and political scholars. Thus the study and practice of human rights has been dominated by legal positivism, which says that human rights are what human rights law says they are. This perspective removes an important basis for criticizing unjust legal systems by assuming them as a given.

With respect to the development of sociology in relation to human rights, the concept of natural rights of individuals was undermined by the scientific philosophy of the eighteenth and nineteenth centuries and replaced by the science of society (sociology). The founders of the new discipline (e.g., Saint-Simon, Comte, Marx, Weber, and Durkheim) saw rights no longer as fundamental moral ideas to regulate political life but as ideological constructs of social struggle or social morality. In short, social scientists marginalized the concept of rights. Recently, the rising influence of the concept of human rights in international and national politics has made some social scientists aware of the need to apply their distinctive concepts, theories, and methods to the real world of human rights and their violation. Although the social sciences can explain the changing nature of human rights, the social-constructivist approach provides no standard for evaluating these changes. The analytical and explanatory approaches championed by sociology have failed to replace the ethical approach to human rights. The principal challenge of the future will be to reconcile the ethics and social science of human rights.

Although sociology is uniquely poised to address issues of theoretical and empirical import around human rights, the discipline has largely been absent from the discussions. Sociologists neglected human rights until recently based on the aspiration to achieve scientific respectability, which came at the price of ignoring the legal and moral conceptions of human rights. Despite the growing body of sociological knowledge about state behavior, bureaucracy, and ethnic conflict, complex social phenomena such as behavior that violates or upholds human rights remain unexamined. According to Turner (2006), contributions of anthropology and sociology to the study of rights have been negative intellectual contributions emphasizing the cultural relativism of the notion of the human and assuming rights to be Western and individualistic. Because anthropologists and sociologists have typically been either positivists or relativists, both of which orientations preclude the development of an analysis of justice and rights, they have failed to engage in the growth of universal human rights.

Why do we need a sociology of human rights? Taking a disciplinary perspective, it is evident that the problem is particularly sociological, not psychological or philosophical, because our shared human vulnerability forces us into relationships based on social dependency and connectedness. Human vulnerability does not arise in individual isolation, nor can it be addressed apart from collective arrangements, be they social support or legal protections. By its very nature, the sociological imagination (Mills 1959) attempts to understand the constraints on human behavior and the normative opportunities created by the global order. As sociologists, we seek to understand what makes everyday life precarious and what shared values arise from our vulnerabilities. In order to understand the interface between the empirical and the normative, comparative historical research based on the case-study methodology must be combined with an ethical analysis of the human condition (Turner 2006).

THE ETHICIST TRADITION

For the purposes of this chapter, it is important to distinguish the two moral orientations and their principles that undergird sociological thought and inquiry: the ethicist, or social rights, perspective and the human rights perspective. The ethicist or social rights worldview rests on the principle that the acquisition of rights is based on human agents fulfilling their duties to the community or nation-state. In short, duties are a precondition for enhancing one's rights. The human rights tradition, on the other hand, holds to the premise that human agents have rights simply because they are human.

While it is true that sociology became concerned with human rights only recently, some aspect of rights, as expressed in the ethicist tradition, has always been present in sociological thought. A theoretical and empirical analysis of sociological inquiry to date reveals that the discipline is permeated by four major ethical orientations defined as a commitment to value neutrality, relativism, social systems, and utilitarianism (Sjoberg et al. 1995). Utilitarianism in particular contains elements of each of the aforementioned ethical considerations. As noted by Sjoberg and Vaughan, "Utilitarianism is perhaps the dominant ethical commitment of contemporary American Sociologists" (1993, 125). The ethics of utilitarianism are based on the assumption that individual pursuit of self-interests results in the greatest good for the greatest number of people. Thus the individual, the ultimate unit of analysis, pursues his or her self-interest by maximizing his or her preference, resulting in a good society. Utilitarianism, as expressed in exchange theory or rational-choice theory, permeates the discipline. By conceiving of individuals as the unit of analysis, sociologists can apply sampling and statistical-analysis procedures to test hypotheses in the tradition of the national science model.

The discipline's commitment to the aforementioned ethical premises contains serious flaws with respect to formulating a viable human rights orientation. For example, the Holocaust called into question relativism, nation-state categories of morality, ethical commitment to social systems, and the limitations of majoritarianism inherent in utilitarianism by highlighting the discipline's inability to provide a theoretical framework that accommodated the protection of the millions of minorities exterminated as a result of the state-sponsored Final Solution. Contemporary genocidal events in Rwanda, Darfur, and the former Yugoslavia raise serious concerns about the nature of the human rights agenda and our ability to contribute to its practice.

Key Challenges and Possibilities: Toward a Theoretically Viable Sociology of Human Rights

Development of a viable theory of human rights faces many challenges: explaining the meaning of the concept, its justification, its logic and practical implications, the substance of rights, how and if rights give rise to obligations, what these obligations are, who has them, and the relationship between human rights and other values (Donnelly 1985). Human rights, in contrast to legal or civil rights that derive from the laws or customs of a particular society, have been defined as the rights one has simply because one is a human being. Sociologically, human rights are of exceptional importance, designed to protect morally valid and fundamental human interests, particularly against the abuse of political and economic power.

In the process of articulating a disciplinary theoretical orientation that can contribute to furthering the development of a set of universal human rights that can be effectively applied in the contemporary world order, sociologists are confronted with certain key interrelated themes. These themes are proscribed by the discipline's ethical orientations, which must be addressed in order to create a meaningful theoretical contribution to human rights discourse and practice.

In response to human suffering and vulnerability, the call for universal human rights requires that sociologists grapple with moral universalism rather than the cultural particularism inherent in the assumptions of the aforementioned ethicist framework. The development of universal human rights would require an alternative conception of reality that calls for human agents to think in terms of different social contexts, learning to take the roles of divergent others and forge basic understandings of others. One can learn to deal with differences by focusing on commonalities regarding the basic rights of human beings within divergent social, political, and economic realms (Sjoberg, Gill, and Williams 2001, 32). Such an endeavor would also necessitate transcending the ends-driven orientation of formal rationality defined by the system and sustained by the discipline's ethical orientation to the principles of system maintenance and the natural science model. Thus sociology must redefine rationality so as to identify and sustain the basic rights of human beings. By thinking about a form of rationality that encompasses divergent others, we are able to conceive of common elements among social and cultural contexts constructed through the reflective activities of human agents. Thus major differences can be addressed by focusing on commonalities regarding the basic rights of human beings within divergent social, political, and economic contexts (Sjoberg, Gill, and Williams 2001, 32).

The aforementioned human rights–orienting principles of moral universalism, taking the role of divergent others, and redefining rationality and the reflective activities of human agents cannot be considered apart from organized power relationships and the organizational context in which these activities occur. In order to sustain modernity based on the ideal of human dignity for the world's citizenry, sociology is uniquely poised to address the issue of organizations in terms of how they function and how they might be held morally accountable for their activities.

CONTEMPORARY SOCIOLOGY AND THE HUMAN RIGHTS AGENDA

Sociologists and anthropologists have recently begun to contribute to human rights studies (Woodiwiss 1998; Wilson 1997). Sociology, based on its theoretical orientation, can contribute to identifying the "source" of human rights, the impact of the global economy on the protection of human rights (Evans 2001b), and interest in "the human rights movement" as a transnational social movement (Risse, Ropp, and Sikkink 1999).

At the very core of a sociological conceptualization of human rights is the idea of protecting individuals (and perhaps groups) from the abuse of power (Freeman 2002, 167). All societies have power structures, and many of them throughout history have had some conception of the abuse of power. Ultimately, in order to engage with what some consider the most significant institutional revolution of the twentieth and twenty-first centuries, sociology must rethink its commitment to the disciplinary legacies of positivism and relativism by coming up with some legitimate notion of universalism.

UNIVERSAL HUMAN VULNERABILITY

Turner's (2006, 6) contribution to the development of the study of rights is founded upon the sociology of the body, which is based on an idea of embodiment and human vulnerability. His argument for the value of the sociology enterprise in the furtherance of the human rights agenda is twofold: (1) sociology can contribute to the development of a definition of human rights based on the universal principle that humans share a common ontology that is grounded in shared vulnerability, and (2) the discipline is uniquely poised to examine the failures of institutions that exist to protect human vulnerability. The development of such a perspective, according to Turner (2006a), results in the development of a normative sociology. Turner (1993, 1995, 2006a) expands the concept of citizenship and rights associated with particular nation-states to a concept of human rights defined as the need for the protection of vulnerable human beings by social institutions, which could also pose a threat to those human beings. In his view, the institutionalization of human rights through the United Nations and the adoption of the Universal Declaration of Human Rights transformed the philosophical concept of natural rights into the secular concept of human rights in an attempt to protect the vulnerable from institutional precariousness.

INSTITUTIONAL PRECARIOUSNESS

Waters (1996) takes a social-constructionist approach, treating the universality of human rights as a social construction. Thus the institutionalization of rights reflects the prevailing balance of political power and class interests. In the same vein, Stammers (1999) criticizes legalistic nation-state approaches to human rights by arguing that human rights violations occur at the social level in that violations of social and economic rights are often promoted by private economic agencies.

He takes to task those, like Donnelly (2003), who see the state as the solution to human rights issues. The sociological point is not that human rights should never be institutionalized, but rather that institutionalization is a social process involving power, and it should not automatically be assumed to be beneficial (Freeman 2002). This particular line of reasoning is further developed by Turner, who argues that institutions, often the cause of human rights failures, need to be "continuously repaired and redesigned, and human rights need to be constantly reviewed in light of their misapplication, misappropriation, and failures" (1996, 32).

THE NECESSITY OF STRUCTURAL CHANGE

Howard (1985), in her analysis of human rights in Commonwealth Africa, argued that a society's ability to realize human rights was strongly affected by its social structure, where the legitimacy of the state was weakened by its failure to build nations from diverse ethnic groups. Thus ethnic conflict in Africa could not be explained by ethnicity alone; it needed to be contextualized in terms of state power and social inequality. In short, legal reform was insufficient to improve human rights. The restraints on human rights caused by differential access to material resources and political power had to be taken into account, and structural change was necessary in order to address human rights violations.

Woodiwiss (1998, 2003, 2005), whose work centers on the Pacific region, acknowledged the importance of structure in defining and enforcing human rights based on "discourse." For example, he argues that capitalism, based on a set of structural relations and a source of motivations, is intrinsically subversive of respect for human rights. Despite capitalism's structural and cultural barriers to the achievement of equal human rights, he believes that such tendencies can be countered by structural demands for order and/or legitimacy (Woodiwiss 1998). The strength of his orientation is its emphasis on structured obstacles to human rights progress in a global capitalist world characterized by cultural diversity.

HUMAN RIGHTS PRINCIPLES, ORGANIZATIONAL ACCOUNTABILITY, AND BUREAUCRATIC CAPITALISM

Corporate organizations, often multinational in scope, are shaping not only the economic sector of societies but vital aspects of other social spheres as well. Not only are these complex organizations the engines that power modern bureaucratic capitalism, but they also play a central role in fostering inequality, injustice, and other social pathologies in modern life. According to Sjoberg, Gill, and Williams (2001, 33), there are two rather distinct perspectives to be found when relating human rights principles to organizational accountability. The first considers organizational structures as generally moral in nature, although ongoing activities do require monitoring and modification if human rights objectives are to be realized. The second perspective recognizes particular organizations to be fundamentally flawed with respect to human rights principles, thus needing to be reconstituted. Despite the disparity of these approaches, both must be taken into account when

426 ELIZABETH A. GILL

exploring the interrelationship between organizations and human rights principles. In the interest of democratic ideals of social justice, it is important for sociology to investigate how these organizations can be held morally and socially accountable for their activities.

As indicated above, the traditional human rights discourse largely assumes that human beings possess a minimal set of rights simply because they are human (Turner 1993). As a result, the human rights tradition, primarily concerned with violations of human rights principles emphasizing individual responsibility, suffers an individualistic bias that fails to take into account the channeling of power through organized relationships. Although individual responsibility must be taken into account when judging violations of human rights, its inclusion does not excuse a lack of attention to organizational considerations. For the purposes of my analysis, I draw upon Sjoberg, Gill, and Tan's (2003, 25) definition of human rights as claims made by persons in diverse social and cultural systems upon "organized power relationships" in order to advance equal dignity, concern, and respect for all human beings.

Most representative institutions and organizations of modern society have been largely successful in providing for the needs of certain sectors of society by routinizing actions through rule-governed practices and specification of roles and by dehumanizing the objects of these actions. It seems that there is a disjuncture between the substantive rationality of human rights and the instrumental procedures of institutions (Woodiwiss 2005). According to Bauman (1989, 215), social organizations, by their very nature, neutralize the regulatory impact of moral behavior and human rights standards by (1) distancing action and its consequences, (2) obscuring the other as an object of potential moral conduct, and (3) disembodying human "objects"/recipients of action so that each action task can be free from a holistic moral evaluation. Thus social action becomes immeasurable from a moral standpoint that rationalizes the lives of human individuals into abstraction and irrelevance.

Given the removal of accountability from the organization and organizational actors through the fragmentation of tasks and the abstraction and dissemblance of the other, it is essential to reconceptualize organizational actors. They are proactive human agents capable of engaging in complex social calculations and of coping with a myriad of social situations involving systemic moral accountability with respect to human rights. In confronting the moral problems inherent in bureaucratic organizations, it is imperative to construct a moral standard for critical evaluation of the actions of personnel within these organizations and the very nature of the structures themselves. In short, it is not enough to hold individuals morally accountable. It is important to acknowledge the interrelationship between human agents and organizations. Indeed, structures must be held accountable for activities that undermine human dignity (Vaughan and Sjoberg 1984). Sociology can employ a conceptual framework designed to reorient analysis of large-scale, bureaucratic organizations by melding a neo-Weberian framework regarding organizations with the pragmatist theorizing of Mead and Dewey (Sjoberg, Gill, and Tan 2003).

We must understand and enhance the ability of human beings, within the organizational context, to use and manipulate social structures in accordance with moral principles based on human rights. Mead's (1934) concept of the social mind and Dewey's (1922, 1985) concept of social intelligence particularly lend themselves to this task. Mead, in effect, thought of the social mind in terms of reflective consciousness: persons can reflect back on their own actions (as well as those of others) that emerge in the context of social interaction within structured bureaucratic settings. Viewed in this manner, the human agent comes to be more proactive than generally understood in response to the demands and possibilities contained within the organizational context.

Structurally, the organizational actor must be allowed and encouraged to transcend his or her own role perspective in order to reflectively consider the consequences of the formally rational means-ends of organizations. Human agents are capable of challenging and overcoming organizational obstacles by consciously reflecting about the consequences of their actions with respect to the views and experiences of the other. The reflective, proactive human agent offers one strategy for holding powerful organizations accountable by subjecting these organizations to serious social scrutiny that could result in the reconstitution, restructuring, or abolition of existing organizations and the creation of new organizational forms as a means of addressing the human rights agenda.

TAKING MORALITY SERIOUSLY

As indicated above, sociology has shown ambivalence toward the concept of human rights because of its heavily positivistic orientation. It could be argued that social scientists in general have a "trained incapacity" to take morality seriously. In a failed attempt to improve the quality of knowledge produced, sociology's rejection of ethics in the name of positivism has failed to understand itself as a social practice that was and is inescapably ethical. Somehow our analytical commitment to the rigor of science and ethical seriousness surrounding human rights issues has to be reconciled (Hirschman 1983, 30).

It is my view that the study of organizational power lies at the core of modern-day human rights theory and practice. With the rise of large-scale multinational corporations whose structures transcend nation-state boundaries, there is an ever-increasing urgency to reconsider the moral accountability of organizational structures. In the face of these changes, we must rethink the foundations of the question of how democracy can and should function. We stand in need of a minimal set of universal moral standards for evaluating both corporate and state organizations.

Modernity rests upon bureaucracy as the dominant organizational form in what Galbraith (1983) termed "the age of organizations." Although significant segments of the global population have benefited from the advance of bureaucracy, with its ability to mobilize diverse specialists and financial and technical resources, the process of bureaucratization and the centralization of power in the political and economic realms have also created the major moral issues of our times (Vaughan and Sjoberg

1984, 441). The moral problems inherent in the organizational structure require the development of a moral system based on human rights that acknowledges the complex interrelationships between human agents and organizations. Thus one standard for a moral order would depend upon reflective human agents within an organizational structure that overcomes the problems inherent in the means-ends relationship of rationality built into bureaucratic organizations.

Articulating a theoretical framework for understanding the nature of human rights through the lens of social power as wielded through organizational structures seems essential not only to comprehend how these organizations shape the economy, the polity, and other social spheres, but also to explore how human agents might be able to hold these organizations morally and socially accountable and, in the process, reshape them.

CHAPTER FORTY-THREE

EMOTIONS

Ann Branaman

The Universal Declaration of Human Rights proclaims all human beings "free and equal in dignity and rights." The concepts of dignity and rights, the two central concepts in the declaration, are arguably equal in importance. The concept of rights, however, has received far greater attention from both activists and scholars. The general concept of equal rights has been readily translated into lists of specific rights; in turn, activists and scholars have studied trends in respect for or violation of those rights. The concept of dignity, however, has received much less attention, likely because of its relative vagueness. The potential engagement between sociology of emotions and human rights, I argue, lies with the concept of equality in dignity but also with the less tangible emotional dimensions of rights.

This chapter focuses on the topic of dignity, examining the ideal of equality in human dignity as proclaimed in the Universal Declaration of Human Rights in light of what the sociology of emotions tells us about the processes by which human dignity, particularly inequalities in human dignity, are normally maintained. As it has developed since the late 1970s as a distinct subfield in American sociology, the sociology of emotions links better to the concept of dignity than it does to the concept of rights. Consequently, my review of the sociology of emotions focuses on the concept of dignity rather than emotional dimensions of rights. However, in discussing some limitations of the sociology of emotions for human rights concerns, I argue that classical sociologists in the nineteenth century developed analyses of the emotional consequences of macrosocial structures that link better to thinking about emotional dimensions of human rights and that extension of these sorts of analyses will provide a valuable link between the sociological analyses of emotions and human rights.

THE CONCEPT OF DIGNITY IN THE SOCIOLOGY OF EMOTIONS

Although the word "dignity" appears only rarely within the literature of the sociology of emotions, it is arguably central in much of what sociologists of emotion have studied.

429

What is dignity? Several different phenomena are at issue when dignity is the topic. First, dignity entails an emotional experience of a person who could be said to "possess dignity"; this emotional experience involves the feeling of basic self-respect, a sense of emotional security regarding that self-respect, and a positive feeling as a consequence of the positive regard of others. In addition to a set of feelings, at issue is the person's ability to present him- or herself with dignity in social situations. The ability to present oneself with dignity depends on access to a set of basic resources claimed as human rights by the declaration; if dignity is a central but relatively undefined concept in the Universal Declaration of Human Rights, each of its articles names human rights to resources and freedoms that are presumed necessary for the maintenance of dignity. Dignity also involves the worthiness that others attribute to a person and the respect that is shown, control an individual can exert over social circumstances, and the nature of the treatment one receives.

Despite not being centrally concerned with emotions, Erving Goffman was nonetheless an important influence on the establishment of sociology of emotions in late 1970s. Central to the interaction dynamics (in Anglo-American societies) that Goffman (1955, 1956a, 1956b, 1959) detailed throughout his work was the apparent compulsion to affirm the dignity of all human beings in social encounters. At the same time, however, his work powerfully demonstrates the inequalities in human dignity that are pervasive and widely accepted in everyday life (Goffman 1961, 1963). If we define dignity in a "weak" sense, the norm of dignity maintenance (of all people, irrespective of social rank) is not incompatible with treating people with varying levels of respect and regard depending on power, status, or resources. But if we define a "strong" version of dignity, we must conclude that the maintenance of the weaker form of dignity, as depicted not only in Goffman's work but in that of the sociologists of emotion I discuss in this chapter, is dependent on the violation of equality of dignity in the stronger sense.

It is important at the outset, however, to articulate a crucial limitation of the sociology of emotions as considered in relation to the concept of dignity within the Universal Declaration of Human Rights. The sociology of emotions is a relatively young subfield of North American sociology that has focused most of its attention on the emotional experience of the middle classes in North America. Mostly the sociology of emotions assumes, as Goffman did, a tendency in social interaction to maintain the weak version of human dignity in social relationships, emphasizing the importance of emotion norms and regulation to this process. This assumption about the cultural backdrop of interaction cannot be made in contexts where there are intense conflicts between in- and out-groups that cause each to dehumanize the other or in a variety of contexts where deeply institutionalized power and status differences have rendered the dehumanization of particular categories and classes of people routine, taken for granted, or invisible. Furthermore, because of its tendency to focus on social contexts in which norms of politeness prevail, the sociology of emotions has paid relatively little attention to intense negatively charged emotions such as hostility, hatred, or contempt or to relations between people characterized by humiliation, degradation, and abuse. The notable exception is Thomas Scheff's

(1994; Scheff and Retzinger 1991) work on shame, rage, and social conflict. Understanding the nature of the social relationships that produce intense negatively charged emotions and that allow for the unleashing of these emotions in behavior that causes humiliation and degradation is crucially important for bridging the sociology of emotions and the sociology of human rights.

In another sense, however, the North American middle-class bias of most of the sociology of emotions could be regarded as an asset for the purposes of this analysis. In North American middle-class society, all human beings are regarded as "equal in rights and dignity." But within this supposedly egalitarian, human rights–supporting culture, human beings and the emotions of human beings are regarded as unequal in importance and subject to unequal rules and regulation, as the sociology of emotions demonstrates. The unequal treatment and regulation of emotion contributes greatly to legitimating the unequal regard for different categories of human beings. The greatest contribution of the sociology of emotions to thinking about the concept of human dignity is its analysis of the unequal regard, differential expectations, and different responses given to emotions of unequally ranked human beings.

KEY CONTRIBUTIONS OF THE SOCIOLOGY OF EMOTIONS

KEY QUESTIONS

The following five key questions addressed by sociologists of emotion are particularly pertinent to the topic at hand:

1. How do emotion norms and expectations for emotion management and emotional labor vary according to social rank?
2. How does an individual's relative power and status in a social encounter affect emotions? How do emotions affect an individual's relative power and status within social encounters?
3. What is the role of emotions in perpetuating relationships of domination and subordination?
4. How do emotions mark a person's relative power and status in a social encounter? How may emotions be manipulated to alter the balance of power or status in a social encounter?
5. What is "emotional culture"? What are the implications of historical and cultural variations in emotional culture for thinking about the ideal of "equality in dignity"?

METHODOLOGIES

The five questions listed above have been central in the sociology of emotions since its origins in American sociology in the late 1970s. They are, in fact, central questions to five of its central contributors: Arlie Hochschild, Randall Collins, Thomas

Scheff, Candace Clark, and Steven Gordon. These five scholars, the questions they ask, and the methodologies they use hardly represent the entirety of the sociology of emotions, a field that has grown and developed significantly since the late 1970s along paths that diverge significantly from the ones they laid. The thinking about the sociology of emotions of Hochschild, Collins, Scheff, Clark, Gordon, and others has in common a reliance on qualitative methodology, grounded theory, and comparative study of texts across different historical periods. The biggest recent development, however, is expansion of several theoretical research programs already established within sociological social psychology—for example, identity theory, affect control theory, exchange theory, theories of distributive justice, expectation states theory, and others—into the area of emotions (Turner and Stets 2005; Stets and Turner 2007). In contrast to scholars focused on in this chapter, these sociologists of emotion rely most heavily on experimental research; their findings about how people emotionally react to different circumstances (e.g., loss of identity, change in power or status, relative deprivation of resources, receipt of positive or negative evaluation) have relevance to human rights issues. Here I concentrate on work of the founders of the contemporary sociology of emotions in thinking about the emotional dimensions of inequalities of dignity.

Because their methodological orientation is toward qualitative research and grounded theory, these scholars' work does not offer findings based on rigorous scientific testing of hypotheses. The results of their theory and research could be better characterized as a blend of findings (based on qualitative research) and concepts (grounded in both theory and qualitative research).

FINDINGS/CONCEPTS

Emotion Management and Social Rank

Inspired by Erving Goffman's analysis of the norms of social interaction and their importance in maintaining social bonds and the human dignity of participants, Hochschild (1979, 1983) argues that rules govern not only behavior in social interaction but also feeling that motivates emotion management.

People manage their emotions for all sorts of reasons, consciously or not. They observe situational expression rules to show respect, to avoid embarrassment, and to prevent disruption of social situations. They seek to align emotions with their culture's feeling rules so they may feel well-adjusted or avoid the psychological pain of feeling ashamed of "inappropriate" feelings. Sometimes people manage emotions not because of any situational or cultural rules but rather because they find some emotional experiences too difficult to bear. These are but a few examples of reasons people, regardless of their social rank, might manage their emotions. The crucial point for the purposes of this analysis, however, is that a person's social rank—within particular relationships, situations, or society at large—greatly impacts the degree to which emotions are regarded as important (by others and by self), the particular expression rules and feeling rules that apply, the consequences that following (or violating) those rules have for the person's social standing, and the level of autonomy the person may have in setting and enforcing expression and feeling rules for oneself and others.

In *The Managed Heart*, Hochschild (1983) analyzes how occupation, social class, and gender affect emotion norms, expectations for emotion management, and the regard given to a person's feelings. Her study focuses in particular on two middle-class service occupations, flight attendants and bill collectors. Both occupations demand heavy "emotional labor" (defined as emotion work performed for pay), but they differ in how they position the performer relative to the labor's object (i.e., the passenger or the debtor). Flight attendants must emotionally defer, for example, when suppressing anger when a passenger is demeaning. The bill collector, by contrast, must dominate and manipulate debtors' emotions to induce shame and compliance. That these occupations are gendered—the former dominated by women and the latter by men—is not incidental, since qualitative differences in the two occupations' required emotion management parallel differences in emotion norms for men and women. Gendered emotion norms call on men to do emotion work that elevates their own power and status and on women to do emotion work that enhances others' power and status (see also Pierce 1995). At the highest positions in the occupational status hierarchy, a significant amount of emotion management is also required, but with key differences from middle-class service workers. One difference is that the emotion management performed in these occupations is more likely to be perceived as natural and authentic, reflecting the personality and positive attributes of its performer. Second, the emotion management required in high-level positions serves to enhance one's image as powerful, in control, competent, and dignified. Emotional labor is less frequently required in low-level occupations, particularly for male workers, although low-level manual workers are required to manage their emotions sufficiently to avoid disruption of their job performance. They also learn, usually during childhood, the unworthiness of regard for their own emotions (Hochschild 1983).

Some people's feelings matter more than others, as Hochschild's and others' contributions to the sociology of emotions show us. Ironically, it is not the feelings of those who suffer the greatest violations of their rights and dignity that matter the most. Instead, emotions belonging to members of the highest social rank seem to matter most and are considered most worthy of respectful regard and protection. Although the qualitative methodology, rich description, and social-constructionist framework of Hochschild's, Jennifer Pierce's, and other similar work does not explicitly name the emotional dynamics as unjust, it is difficult to come away with any other perception.

Power, Status, and Emotions

Known for his "conflict sociology," Randall Collins (1975) made a strong case for the relevance of the sociology of emotions in addressing sociological questions about social stratification. Emotions, he argues, underlie the legitimacy of the status and power rankings pervasive in everyday life (Collins 1990, 27). "What holds a society together—the 'glue' of solidarity—and what mobilizes conflict—the energy of mobilized groups—are emotions; so is what operates to uphold stratification—hierarchical feelings, whether dominant, subservient, or resentful" (Collins 1990, 27–28).

Because of the tendency toward mutual face maintenance in everyday interaction, as described by Goffman, Collins argues that the most common emotional experience in everyday life is an undramatic feeling of confidence. Depending on a person's power and status relative to others in social situations, he argues, emotional experience takes an "up" or "down" tone. When giving orders (the power dimension), a person's "emotional energy" increases; lower emotional energy is associated with taking orders. When the individual is more central in social interaction (the status dimension), emotional energy increases; lower emotional energy results from marginality. Participants' power and status in social situations, Collins (1990) argues, depends in part on the power and status they have in society, but it is also determined reciprocally by the emotional energy participants demonstrate in these situations.

The emotional energy of participants in social situations, Collins argues, depends not only on how they are treated in any particular situation but also on their overall balance of emotional energy as influenced by a lifetime of social experiences in which they have had varying power or been more central or marginal. Anger, Collins argues, is rarely expressed by the weak. Along the status dimension, similarly, Collins argues that a short-term loss of an individual's status in a social group is more likely to provoke anger, whereas a long-term experience of social marginalization is more likely to produce depression. A high balance of emotional energy stored from prior life experience, Collins argues, serves as powerful protection against emotional debilitation in the face of loss of control or social marginalization.

Collins, like most other sociologists of emotion, did not explicitly speak of dignity. Thought of in terms of emotional energy, the concept of dignity would imply positive emotional energy—a feeling of belonging as well as control over one's own life. Because of the assumptions of his conflict sociology and its analytic rather than critical orientation, Collins assumed a world in which competition for power and status is inevitable, and the high power, status, and emotional energy some enjoy necessitates lower power, status, and emotional energy for others. According to the theory's premises, a person's overall balance of emotional energy determines whether a deprivation of power and status is perceived as a violation of dignity or rights (by that person as well as by others in the situation who "read" the person's level of emotional energy). The ideal of equality of dignity is not easily reconciled with Collins's assumptions, first, of a human drive to maximize power and status and, second, of competition for power and status as a zero-sum game. Only if we impose a critical perspective can we interpret his theory of stratification and emotions from a human rights perspective. On doing so, our perceptions of violation of dignity or rights would lead us not to accept as legitimate subordination that is passively accepted and perceived by all parties within the situation as appropriate. By contrast, precisely those situations of complete and accepted subordination would cause greatest concern, given that they indicate the sustained and systemic nature of dignity or rights violation by one person or group of another.

Emotions and the Maintenance of the Status Quo in Dominant-Subordinate Relationships

Emotions are crucial for understanding people's tendency to act toward one another in ways that affirm inequalities in categories of human worthiness. Scheff's (1988, 1990a, 1990b, 2000) work builds heavily on Goffman's view of fear of embarrassment as motivating conformity to hierarchical social orders. Like Goffman, Scheff views social-bond maintenance as a most crucial human motive, a view that assumes existence of valued social bonds between people or groups (an assumption that cannot necessarily be made in many contexts in which the rights and dignity of human beings are violated). The emotions of pride and shame are most central in Scheff's work as informal sanctions motivating conformity to the social order and, in particular, to maintaining the status quo in dominant-subordinate relationships. Courteous treatment of others (i.e., not commenting on the dynamics of interaction and not "making a scene") is a basic norm of interaction, Scheff argues, a norm that could be considered compatible with the weak concept of dignity. The effect, Scheff suggests, is to maintain social hierarchies while making the act of sustaining social structure invisible to participants. Infusing his microsociology with a psychoanalytic perspective, Scheff (1990a, 187) argues that repression of emotion contributes further to status quo maintenance. Hiding shame associated with being dominated or demeaned renders the nature of the relationship all the more invisible and the hierarchy more easily maintained (Scheff 1990a, 188).

Like Collins's theory, Scheff's theory implies the normalcy of the reproduction of existing social hierarchies. His psychoanalytic perspective, however, leads to a crucial difference. Even if the powerful motivation to avoid embarrassment and shame contributes to sustaining and rendering invisible hierarchical social relationships, Scheff's theory assumes that painful emotions associated with domination are repressed but not vanquished. For this reason, a human rights perspective fits more easily with Scheff's perspective because of the implicit view that strong bonds between people not characterized by hierarchy would do less emotional damage and weaken the latent force of repressed hostilities (between individuals, groups, and nations). Robert W. Fuller and Thomas Scheff (2009) explicitly argue that "rankism" (Fuller 2003) is incompatible with equality in dignity and is harmful to society.

Emotional Micropolitics

Candace Clark's analysis of emotional micropolitics focuses on strategic manipulation of emotions (of self and others) as a way of negotiating "place" in social relationships. (Clark's concept of place seems to encompass both the power and the status dimensions in Collins's theoretical framework.) Emotions, she argues, serve both as "place-markers" and "place-claims." Emotions serve as place-markers when a person's emotional response demonstrates place to self and other. Hurt or shame in response to ridicule lowers the ridiculed; anger or indignation, by contrast, expresses a higher place, a rejection of the demeaning implications of the ridiculer's message (Clark 1990, 310). Emotional numbness in response to abuse or degradation, common among battered women and children, marks inferior standing and provides support for the abuser's assumption of greater entitlement to emotional regard (Clark 1990, 312). Emotions serve as place-claims when they are strategically used as a means of negotiating social place. A strong display of anger or disgust, for example, may be a strategic effort to elevate one's standing while demeaning the target of the anger or disgust. Another use of emotion as a micropolitical strategy involves trying to elevate one's own status at the expense of another by provoking the other's loss of emotional control while maintaining one's own.

To push the analysis of emotional micropolitics more directly into engagement with the human rights' ideal of equality in dignity, Clark's analyses could be usefully employed as a way of drawing attention to emotional expressions and emotional manipulation oriented toward maintaining unjust social hierarchies, demeaning other people or groups, and violating the principle of equality in dignity.

Emotional Culture

Another core emphasis of the sociology of emotions is the idea of emotional culture, a concept developed by sociologist Steven Gordon (1981, 1989a, 1989b). Emotional culture refers to the beliefs about and vocabulary of emotions and the feeling rules that prevail in particular societies, among particular groups in societies, and at different times in history. If human dignity is a universal ideal, the sociology of emotions shows us that the emotional culture of a particular time, place, and social group determines the range of emotional expression and emotional experience that is considered compatible with human dignity. The shamefulness of expressing intense emotion in a culture that links emotional restraint to rationality and rationality to power can, arguably, help us make sense of one of Clark's key points about emotional micropolitics—that the purposeful evocation of intense and uncontrolled emotional response from another is a way of demeaning the target while elevating one's power and status.

A deeper connection between work on emotional culture and human rights, however, has yet to be developed. Mostly the work by sociologists and historians that analyzes historical changes in emotional culture focuses on changing norms about love, anger, fear, grief, jealousy, guilt, or other emotions not obviously related to social hierarchies (beyond those linked to gender and marriage) (e.g., Stearns 1994; Cancian and Gordon 1988; Clanton 1989). I suggest that a deeper engagement between work on emotional culture and human rights would require developing a distinction between rankist or hierarchical emotional culture and a human rights emotional culture that seeks to replace the emotion norms of hierarchical emotional culture with emotion norms that support the equality of rights and dignity of all human beings. This is a shift in emotional culture yet to be realized, although arguments such as Fuller's and Scheff's (and the existence of similar arguments in various contexts over the past several decades) that make a strong case for the strong version of equality in dignity is evidence of its emergence.

HUMAN RIGHTS AND THE SOCIOLOGY OF EMOTIONS

LIMITATIONS OF THE SOCIOLOGY OF EMOTIONS REGARDING THE SOCIOLOGY OF HUMAN RIGHTS

A human rights perspective has been largely absent in the sociology of emotions, at least as it has developed in American sociology in the years since Hochschild's, Collins's, and Scheff's founding work. This absence can largely be explained by development of sociology of emotions since the late 1970s. A debate between social constructionists and positivists has largely disappeared, yet continues to shape approaches to the sociology of emotions. These two approaches differ from one another not so much in their theoretical premises as in their questions, methodologies, and aims of research. On the one hand, theory and research continue to emphasize how culture and society construct emotion norms and vocabularies of emotion that guide how people interpret emotional experience and how they think and feel about emotions they experience. This type of research utilizes qualitative methodologies and grounded theory to understand cultural, historical, and group or category variations in emotion norms and emotional culture. A larger body of theory and research more rooted in positivism and relying heavily on experimental methodologies has sought to develop a science of emotions for predicting a person's emotional response to social stimuli. The dominance of these two theoretical/methodological frameworks has limited the development of a human rights perspective in the sociology of emotions.

Even though a human rights perspective might easily have been developed from Hochschild's work, the main theme that most sociologists have taken from Hochschild is social construction of emotions. This has produced a tendency to focus on identifying differences and changes in emotion norms and avoiding critical judgment of particular emotion norms or emotional cultures. The social-constructionist perspective does not lend itself well to asking questions about emotion norms and emotional cultures that, from a human rights perspective, we would want to address. Are some emotion norms or emotional cultures harmful? Using the language of the declaration, do some emotion norms and emotional cultures violate human dignity or prevent the "full development of the human personality"?

From a wide variety of different theoretical perspectives or theoretical research programs (as sociologists who do this sort of work call them), sociologists have contributed to building a social science of emotions. This research addresses human rights topics, including the effects of power and status on emotions and the role of emotions in determining social arrangements to be just or unjust. It does not, however, take us in a direction that points toward the development of a human rights perspective in the sociology of emotions. Because of its reliance on experiments, most theory and research in the sociology of emotions brackets questions of culture, history, injustice, and systemic power relations.

I noted above the limited cultural backdrop of social interaction assumed by most of the work in the sociology of emotions and questioned whether sociology of emotions provides a framework to analyze the emotional culture of contexts not characterized by norms of politeness and in which dehumanization of entire groups of people is regarded as normal and acceptable. The assumption of the inevitability of power and status differences and their manifestations at the emotional level is a further limitation. Theodore Kemper (1990), Randall Collins (1990), and Kemper and Collins (1990), for example, view power and status as universal dimensions of social interaction and argue that emotions derive from and contribute to defining a person's position within social groups and hierarchies. Mostly, sociologists of emotion have not explicitly argued for the inevitability of power and status hierarchies, but neither have they explicitly questioned the inevitability of power and status hierarchies or their connection to emotion. This is as true of qualitative research that emphasizes the social construction of emotion as it is of experimental research that specifies causal relationships between particular social conditions and emotional responses. Some view power and status hierarchies as intrinsic to human social life; others avoid the assumption of inevitability but nonetheless assume the hierarchical emotional dynamics they describe are pervasive due to the intractability of particular social hierarchies (e.g., class, gender) and the centrality of the principle of hierarchy in how so many people think about human relationships.

POSSIBILITIES FOR A HUMAN RIGHTS PERSPECTIVE IN THE SOCIOLOGY OF EMOTIONS

Up to now this chapter has focused on human rights' concept of "equality in dignity" and suggested how sociologists can further articulate a human rights perspective in the sociology of emotions. In this final section, however, I want to go beyond the concept of equality in dignity to speak more generally about human rights and the potential for building stronger bridges between the sociology of emotions and human rights.

In a sense, Hochschild (1983) implies a human rights perspective in the beginning chapter of *The Managed Heart*, in which she extends Marx's concept of alienation to refer to the additional layer of control employers exercise over their employees, controlling not only the work they perform with their bodies but also their emotions. Insofar as we think of human emotions as more fundamental to individuals' humanity than the physical activities they perform, Hochschild suggests a deeper alienation of humanity caused by the commodification of emotion work. The Universal Declaration of Human Rights proclaims the human right to employment that allows for the "full development of the human personality," a right that is seemingly incompatible with the requirement of workers to follow the prescribed emotional scripts set by employers.

Not only does Hochschild's work suggest the possibility of thinking about human rights regarding emotional experience, but I argue that such questions are implicit in the work of classical sociologists. As a part of their larger project of analyzing modern societies, classical sociologists analyzed the human emotional consequences of macro-level social structures. Classical sociologists assumed a basic human (emotional) nature that would thrive under certain conditions and wither under others. Karl Marx (1978 [1844]) assumed that the core of human nature and highest human satisfaction was the exercise of consciousness and will in labor, but wageworkers were alienated from this fulfillment by the structure of capitalism. Émile Durkheim (1951b) argued that human beings had basic emotional needs for an appropriate balance of liberty and social constraint and individualism and social integration. Max Weber (1978), who rejected the role of social critic as appropriate for the social scientist and viewed the changes he described as largely inevitable, nonetheless suggested that the increasing bureaucratization of modern societies resulted in few opportunities for people to infuse their lives with meaning, passion, sentiment, ethics, and purpose. The important point for our purposes here, however, is that classical sociologists theorized the relationship between macrostructures and emotional aspects of human lives and judged macrostructures to be problematic due to their perceived damaging emotional consequences. Had the sociology of emotions developed more directly out of classical sociology, perhaps the question of human "emotional rights" might have taken a more central place in the sociology of emotions.

CHAPTER FORTY-FOUR

MARXIST SOCIOLOGY

David Fasenfest

It's not the killing that is the problem. It's disposing of the bodies.
—Abby Mann,
Judgment at Nuremberg (1961)

In Rwanda that genocide happened because the international community and the Security Council refused to give, again, another 5000 troops which would have cost, I don't know, maybe fifty, a hundred, million dollars.
—Lakhdar Brahimi, special adviser
to the UN secretary-general

U ndertaking an analysis of Marxism and human rights poses three problems: (1) Marx had almost nothing to say about human rights, (2) there is no clear and consistent view of what constitutes human rights, and, perhaps most critically, (3) Marxism is varied and complex, with no consistency with regard to how it is understood or what is written under its banner. The last point is perhaps overstated, but I return to this later on. Suffice it to say that human rights, as it had come to be understood as a creation of the French and American revolutions at the end of the eighteenth century, was a relatively new and contested concept at the time Marx did most of his important writing. While the notion of human rights, like capitalism itself, was relatively new at the end of that century, it was the emergence of capitalism as the dominant mode of production that propelled both human rights discourse and, as a result of Marx's analysis of capitalism, Marxism itself. And as with the emergence of many forms of capitalist production and the accompanying social relations, there also emerged divergent understandings of what constitutes human rights and varying forms of Marxist analysis.

MARX ON HUMAN RIGHTS

The central argument that Marx was not an advocate of human rights comes in the misinterpretation of his response to Bruno Bauer's assertion that Jews in Germany were misguided in their desire for religious freedom (Bauer argues that no one is free, and Jews should struggle for the political emancipation of the religious person), in which Marx (1843a) appears to reject the notion of individual human rights. For Bauer, universal human emancipation follows political emancipation and is not possible as long as people remain religious. Political emancipation, for Marx, is an illusion and cannot be equated with human emancipation (Brenkert 1986). Indeed, Marx goes on to argue that political emancipation is merely a right to noninterference by the state with an individual, but a politically free state does not ensure that an individual will be free (Engles 2008). Guarantees to religious freedom—guarantees that Marx points out appear in the state constitutions of Pennsylvania and New Hampshire—are implicit in those rights more generally argued: that is, a person has the right to equality, liberty, security, and property.

Marx objects to these four basic rights. First, in his view the right to liberty is an expression of human separation rather than human association. Equality, then, is little more than a right to equal liberty. At the core of a liberal bourgeois notion of the right to property is the expression of self-interest, and security is nothing more than the egoistic assurance that, as disconnected individuals, we can count on all the other rights being inviolate. Human emancipation, according to Marx, cannot come as a result of individualistic and egoistic rights but only as a result of the emergence of a community in which there is not the freedom and right to engage in business but rather the right of freedom from business.

Marx (1843b) conceded that political emancipation has value in that it is the first big step forward; though not in itself a guarantee of human emancipation writ large (Gordon, Swanson, and Buttigieg 2000), it may be the last form of human emancipation possible under the prevailing social and economic system (that is, capitalism). His writings here, as well as his earlier writings on the freedom of the press, reflect at the core a belief in democratic rights and the support for universal suffrage (Kolakowski 1983). Via these, the state can be pressured to grant freedom of association and expression—a precondition to the collective effort at real human emancipation. It is in this sense of collective rights, which did not depend on the benevolent nature of state power, that Marx advocated true human rights. Only as a result of the excesses arising out of the failed revolutions of 1848—in which, for instance, the Paris government brutally killed thousands, and many thousands more were deported—did Marx and Engels (1848) understand the contradictions between the rhetoric of political freedom and the reality of states acting to defend themselves in the face of popular discontent.

Pointing out that the rhetoric of brotherhood and common interests (between the bourgeoisie and the proletariat) lasted only as long as the bourgeoisie needed the proletariat to topple the government, Marx recognized the importance of political as well as economic struggle. Having established a new, postfeudal state, the bourgeoisie had no problem with the use of force against their old "allies" in struggle, and this led Marx and Engels to develop their political ideas for a revolutionary struggle in the interests of the proletariat. Only then can there be the possibility for human emancipation and true human rights. Marx never abandoned democratic rights, since they were the weapon needed by the working masses to build their own political movement. In that regard, human and democratic rights were a relative improvement, providing limited but greater protection within the capitalist system over those found under feudalism.

It is in his later writing, for which Marx is better known, that we find some sense of a social theory of rights, albeit fragmented and not central to his overall agenda—a critique of capitalism. Social relations of production that give rise to the value form of human labor also give rise to modern notions of rights. At first, workers as producers retained the "right" to their product, and this right itself was a revolutionary change relative to precapitalist societies in which no such rights were imparted. This notion of the right of "private" property, absent until the emergence of the capitalist mode of production, allowed individuals to exchange their private property with each other. It is in the loss of control over one's own labor (that is, through labor becoming a commodity) that Marx sees the immiseration and loss of rights of the working class, and all that remains are the rights of property over the rights of the individual. Combined with his political lesson learned earlier, Marx came to believe that only through a revolutionary process that challenges both state power and the social relations of production that sustain it can human rights truly be achieved.

One reason so many feel that Marx does not have a human rights agenda is because the focus of his writing gives the impression that the economic realm (e.g., commodities and capital) is "real," while the noneconomic forms (e.g., religion, law, rights, and the state) are simply manifestations that prop up the economic realm. Others reject Marx's critique (or at least argue it is no longer current) because it is supposedly based on a rejection of human agency in favor of collective agency, and because Marx only views existing rights in the negative (that is, property rights deny rights to others) and not as positive claims (Brown 2003). These are overly materialistic, deterministic, and undialectical understandings of Marx. In that view, agency is lacking and, with it, any true concern for human rights. It is, however, a mistake to reduce Marx in this way. Marx considered his agenda to be a series of critiques—of economy, politics, law, morality—and in the end expected to craft a unifying narrative that brought them all together. An analysis of legal forms under capitalism would, in much the same way as his economic critique did, reveal the true nature of equal rights apart from their illusionary appearance under an unequal set of social relations. In the final analysis, Marx's critique of human rights can be summarized as an assertion that the rights and freedoms they entail are formal and procedural; as such, they are merely illusions of freedom in a bourgeois democracy.

HUMAN RIGHTS DISCOURSE

What, then, are human rights, and from where do they emerge? There is a long tradition of debate between those who see human rights as something imparted by nature and those who see them as the outcome of a social contract. The basis of human rights in philosophy stems first from divine authority, then from natural law, then from some sense of intuition and what can be seen as self-evident, and finally from legal structures or the ratification of conventions (Renteln 1988). It is beyond the brief of this chapter to explore the origins and meaning of human rights, but given that Marx's opposition to the notion of human rights under capitalism is rooted in his rejection of what we now call liberal notions of human rights, some reflection is warranted.

According to Hiskes (2010), the relational notion of human rights originates in the writings of Hobbes, in the proposition that there must be an authority strong enough to guarantee that humans interact civilly one with another. Rejecting nature as a realm capable of assuring this civility, Hobbes argues that people essentially enter into contracts with each other to behave, and from this he derives the need for an external authority to enforce these cooperative relations, that is, the contracts.

A society without cooperation is irrational, and human rights are consequently based both on the capacity to enter into social agreements and on an arbiter who can enforce those agreements. This leads to the notion of a liberal society granting individuals rights and the formulation of human rights as a system of claims on the state. Rights, then, are emergent and only appear in the context of society. Rights are a political and social project, and the state is the point of departure for both identifying and protecting human rights. In the tradition of Weber, the individual is the unit of analysis of society, and human existence is based on a complex system of rights and obligations that, in the end, are secured legally.

There are, of course, eloquent philosophical arguments regarding whether or not individuals have a natural claim on human dignity, and rights thereto. From a practical point of departure, however, it is the form of legal institutions that supports and sustains both the application and the formulation of human rights. We must distinguish between a right—an ideal, moral notion—and a claim—a legal and somewhat informal appeal to justice. Marx clearly argues that all legal and moral rules should be abolished because they reflect a society inherently predicated on inequality, and these rules are designed to perpetuate this inequality and to privilege the beneficiaries of unequal access to political, economic, and social resources. It is precisely the denial of these resources that makes up many human rights claims.

The legal foundation of a rights discourse is well developed (Teitel 1997) and warrants just a casual reference here. In her very detailed review of case law, Stark (1992–1993) outlines the tension between political and economic rights, how and where they are adjudicated, and how US state constitutions effectively leave the boundary between them up to the courts to decide. In the end, she concludes that economic rights are the main concern of the courts, and as a rule courts prohibit rather than proscribe, meaning they do not grant rights but only rule on whether they have been constrained illegally. This is consistent with Bertman's (2004, 90) exploration of the roots and philosophical underpinnings of human rights law, in which he points out that political property rights are determined by the particular laws of a state; yet he does make the claim that laws may end up violating customs and morals, leading to their demise. Once again we are confronted by the fact that political and legal traditions do not necessarily comprise a moral theory (Tabak 2003). Bertman's concern is how theory can lead to practice, and he posits that one should explore how changing material conditions can lead to situations in which natural law can be expressed in terms of custom and civil law.

A liberal reading of human rights, "a specific interpretation and a concrete realization of rights in (Western) societies" (Deflem and Chicoine 2011, 104), hinders the development of a sociology of human rights. Rather, human rights discourse should be recognized as situated within specific contexts. Otherwise, human rights might be reduced to technical legal forms undermining more substantive human rights justice. For example, citizen rights become a proxy for human rights; as a result, the discussion shifts to legal status and migration without regard for how people are treated. It would be better to view the human rights discourse within a sociology tied to a focus on inequality. Hynes et al. (2010), for example, juxtapose social theorizing that argues for human rights with social actions mobilizing to guarantee human rights. The former operates in a rarified frame debating the relative merits of different conceptualizations. The latter is more attuned to the local conditions and historical contexts, which identify and define what is possible. Recognizing we live in an increasingly globalized world (more on that below), where citizenship is eclipsed, Deflem and Chicoine (2011) suggest we should see rights in terms of social movements mobilizing for a better human existence.

Marx rejected the notion of natural law, derived as it was from a Darwinist view of evolution that held that laws, like humans, are accidents of history. His notion of historical materialism led him to the conclusion that material conditions in conflict over who owned and controlled the means of production were behind human progress, not the conflict of ideas or principles. As he and Engels wrote in the *Communist Manifesto*, law and morality are just so many bourgeois instruments to protect bourgeois interests. To paraphrase French Nobel Prize winner for literature Anatole France, the law protects everyone by forbidding the rich as well as the poor from sleeping under bridges, begging on the streets, and stealing bread to feed themselves.

If rights are granted by states through laws, shouldn't we consider the nature of the society and even the legitimacy of the state governments that grant these rights? Indeed, one of the main demands for universal human rights (Penn and Malik 2010) targets some governments that deny these rights to their citizens, often hanging on the claim that those governments have no legitimacy derived from popular support or as a reflection of popular will. But does this lead us, as Renteln (1985) suggests, to be lost in a relativist morass? Anthropologists worry about how we view human rights in the context of cultural practices and pose a problem in considering that we may be imposing one cultural notion of rights on other cultures. As Preis (1996) asks, Are there truly universal rights or only culturally specific formulations? The trend toward postmodern and poststructural analyses of society posits the answer that there may be multiple realities about human rights in place of what Preis calls deterministic, linear, or external views imposed by convention. She calls for more analysis based on a development research model and the inclusion of agency and ongoing life experiences (Preis 1996, 310–311) to validate human rights—though pointing out that human experience is itself the product of prior cultural development (an echo of Marx's well-rehearsed point that while we can make our own history, it occurs in a context not of our own choosing).

Sociology does not escape the cultural relativism problem (Donnelly 2007). Turner (2010) identifies a failure to properly engage in human rights analysis because of its roots in Weber's focus on the individual in society, resulting in more attention paid to citizenship than the normative framework within which the individual in society operates. He leaves us with two problems: How do we account for the role of normative beliefs and values informing social actors, and how does sociology as a science escape its own relative and historically specific knowledge and methodological frame (Turner 2010, 602–603)? Since human rights are as much about values, the traditional fact-value distinction in sociology is a shortcoming and should be relaxed (Sjoberg, Gill, and Williams 2001). That is, we must include normative considerations when proposing human rights legislation, increasingly so in a global context. Furthermore, even as we accept cultural relativism, we must consider morality equally relevant (Donoho 1990–1991).

MARXISM AND HUMAN RIGHTS

Several aspects of human rights derive from a Marxist and socialist agenda (Davidson 2010; Veltmeyer and Rushton 2011). Very few theories about rights challenge the hegemonic liberal (and increasingly neoliberal) logic of markets or the legality of state action on behalf of the rights of private property (Thompson 1978). Profit rates, as Harvey (2008) points out, trump all rights. Harvey posits that by conceptualizing a right to the city, society can attempt to remake itself as a challenge to dominant (i.e., capitalist) social processes by fostering a communal rather than individual notion of rights. The human rights that result will marshal collective power in the form of a common rather than an individual right and more immediately resonate with Marx's desire to promote human emancipation.

Amid the failures, and at times horrors, of socialist rule, mainly in the Soviet Union, we must recognize the contributions made on behalf of the human rights agenda. It is tempting to declare Marxism dead because of the fall of the Soviet Empire, but Marx and Marxism remain the main, if not the only, critical assessment of capitalism in all its workings. A look back at the debates of the time, when socialist states still held sway in many parts of the world, reveals some important contributions to advancing human rights. For example, Scarritt's (1985) study of human rights in Africa points out that a comparison between socialist and nonsocialist states can add to the debate over whether there are universal or relative human rights (Perry 1997). Pointing out that universalists (as he calls them) assert some basic right as a matter of being human, cultural relativists (especially in relation to Africa) argue that the concept is basically derived from Western and European philosophical traditions that do not apply in the African context. Scarritt points out that while at times the rhetoric of human rights in socialist countries seems to promote the rising ruling class, there is a shift from traditional property rights discourse to include broader societal considerations in the formulation of those rights. At the same time, "non-Marxist conceptions of human rights are changing in response to the spread of socialist, and especially Marxist, ideas" (Scarritt 1985, 31).

It is not just in developing countries that socialist and Marxist principles impact our definition and understanding of human rights. As mentioned above, the institutional and structural aspects of Marxist rhetoric and socialist practices gave rise to criticisms among liberal and social democrat human rights activists who saw this as a negation of the individual. Seeking to resurrect and, as she puts it, correct the role of socialism and Marx, Ishay (2004a) undertakes a historical excavation of the contributions of socialist movements to the development of human rights. If, as she posits, liberalism can take the credit for the civil rights movement and be forgiven for the excesses of colonialism, so too must socialism be given credit for its "championing the rights of the hardworking and powerless poor" (Ishay 2004a, 225) and forgiven for the excesses of Stalinism and Maoism in the name of socialism. Revisiting the position of Marx on not wanting to defend bourgeois rights, Ishay goes on to document the efforts on behalf of workers' rights, universal suffrage, and economic rights (not to be hungry, to able to work, to have a home that is adequate and safe, etc.)—all components that later become part of every human rights declaration.

Brad Roth (2004) lays out a case for bringing Marx back into the human rights discussion, pointing out that Marxism offers a normative project that illuminates and unpacks the divergent views of freedom within the rights discourse. He recounts the importance of Marx's writings, revisits the misinterpretations of Marx's position, and supports the idea that equal rights without an analysis of property rights is a contradictory goal. Liberal democrats concede that to provide political rights and sovereign protections without also ensuring the ability to procure food and shelter is a sham, and social democrats advocate socioeconomic reforms to promote more equality. Marx contributes, according to Roth, the suggestion that these neutral and harmonious political efforts at human rights "cannot be realized so long as a society's class antagonisms have not been transcended" (2004, 53). Marxists see contradictory interests and values in a class-based society because, in any class-based society, "the promise of legal protections from arbitrary imposition and of legal implementation of collective empowerment go largely unrealized" (2004, 54).

At the heart of Roth's analysis are the unequal power relationships at the center of any class-based society, relationships that are critical insofar as they either limit the kinds of issues that could be raised in the political arena or privilege the likely outcomes of political engagement. Power inequities have long been recognized as an impediment to promoting the interests of the less powerful (Baxter 1989; Lukes 2005 [1974]), and as Roth notes, "those sectors of society having real weight in political decision-making tend to win the conditions of freedom relevant to those sectors" (2004, 60). Once more we return to Marx's fundamental critique of human rights under capitalism: there can be no human emancipation under a system that inherently privileges one part of society (property holders) over another (those without the means of production).

Globalization poses a serious challenge to, as well as opportunity for, advancing human rights (Langlois 2002; McIntyre 2003). Both an economic and political process, globalization tends to marginalize national efforts at establishing legal frameworks for human rights, albeit based on unequal relationships and the defense of property within each society. Pollis (2004, 343) points out that globalization reveals how inadequate scholars are to conceptualize human rights in that context and that the globalization rhetoric is devoid of the normative principles of justice and humanity. With the end of World War II, an era of increased security and the protection of state sovereignty driven by the atrocities of Germany ushered in a post-Holocaust concern for human rights in the West. Along with this prosperity came a period of "modernization" of non-Western postcolonial and neocolonial societies in Asia, Africa, and Latin America, which did more to export the inequalities of European capitalism than to bring true development. Globalization, along with its neoliberal agenda, subverts all efforts to develop indigenous rights movements and self-rule in the name of the universality of economic growth (Pollis 2004, 354).

More than fifty years separate the atrocities represented by the opening quotes of this chapter: the systematic extermination by the Nazi regime of approximately 9 million people, mainly Jews but also Gypsies, the developmentally disabled and other "social undesirables," and political enemies; and the genocide in Rwanda where, in about one hundred days, Hutu Rwandans massacred upwards of 750,000 Tutsi and some Hutu members of society, in all estimated at about 20 percent of the entire population. The events in Germany from about 1935 to 1945 led to the establishment of a war crimes tribunal at the close of the war (often depicted in film) and then a human rights agenda resulting in the Universal Declaration of Human Rights adopted by the UN General Assembly on December 10, 1948. Yet, half a century later (1994), this same United Nations was unable to prevent the genocide of Tutsis. The failures of the international community to act in defense of a massive human rights violation can be attributed to the problems of implementing world governance in the age of declining states and the assent of neoliberalism (Westra 2011). The formal neutrality of state institutions ends up reinforcing "the structural dynamics of economy and society that maintain the disempowerment of subordinated sectors" (Roth 2004, 66).

TAKING HUMAN RIGHTS FORWARD FROM A MARXIST PERSPECTIVE

If Marxism studies the capitalist system as well as provides proscriptions for the future, how then do we identify a uniquely Marxist agenda for the study of human rights? Clearly, by using a Marxist lens and evaluating the impact of neoliberal policies, we can reflect on forms of resistance (Fasenfest 2009) and speculate on the future of the capitalist state (Jessop 2002). One way of tackling human rights is to ask, What are the various issues facing a globalized world that have an impact on social justice and human emancipation? The fault lines are numerous: immigration, labor, gender, race, and politics are but a few. An examination of globalization and its impact on women, as seen through a feminist lens, offers some insight, especially concerning how these changes both limit human rights and enable social change (Gottfried 2012, especially ch. 12; Walby 2007). A focus on labor and immigration can show how Marx and Marxism can inform our understanding and assessment of the potential for and limits to human emancipation.

Work in this century reflects major changes in both its location (offshoring work, creating foreign manufacturing zones, hiring immigrant labor) and its organization (global command and control, concentration of capital, reliance on finance capital), and it is closely tied to questions of immigration and citizenship. Regulations concerning both are intertwined, as restrictions or special rules governing immigrants also impact how work is performed and how much workers are paid. The threat of moving jobs overseas or hiring low-wage immigrants (documented or not) has a chilling effect on workers' ability to exercise their rights. How should workers rights, then, be viewed (McIntyre 2008)? More important, perhaps, is how we understand the change in work (Brass 2011). In much the same way, immigration entails concerns about citizenship rights (Benhabib and Resnick 2009). The two concerns overlap on the question of protecting the human rights of undocumented workers (Friedman 1986) and the need to combat new and continuing forms of labor exploitation (DeMartino 2010). In an environment of porous borders, shifting location of work, and unenforced or unenforceable labor and immigration laws, how do we coordinate a human rights agenda with immigration and workplace protections?

It is important to recognize that Marxism offers a critique of capitalism and a vision of human emancipation after we overcome a class-based society. Until then, all the laws passed will not ensure human rights. At the same time, Marxists must not adhere to a strictly materialist approach to understanding society and embrace the role human agency plays in challenging and resisting the worst aspects of capitalism. Globalization both creates new challenges and offers opportunities in the struggle to advance a human rights agenda. Marxism offers a way to evaluate how global economies function, provides a language of and mechanisms for resistance to neoliberal agendas that do more to strip human rights than promote them, and promotes common cause with all who struggle to expand human potential. Marxism, with its analysis of the social and political manifestations of capitalism and globalization, can help in the struggle for human rights.

REFERENCES

A., E. 1950a. "Grace Abbot and Hull House 1908-1921. Part 1." *Social Service Review* 24: 374-394.
———. 1950b. "Grace Abbot and Hull House 1908-1921. Part 2." *Social Service Review* 24: 493-518.
Abbot, Andrew. 1988. *The System of Professions: An Essay on the Division of Expert Labor.* Chicago: University of Chicago Press.
———. 2001. "Self-Similar Social Structures." In *Chaos of Disciplines*, 157-196. Chicago: University of Chicago Press.
Abolafia, Mitchell. 2001. *Making Markets: Opportunism and Restraint on Wall Street.* Cambridge, MA: Harvard University Press.
Abraham, David. 2009. "Doing Justice on Two Fronts: The Liberal Dilemma in Immigration." *Ethnic and Racial Studies* 33, no. 6: 968-985.
Abraham, John. 2010. "Pharmaceuticalization of Society in Context: Theoretical, Empirical and Health Dimensions." *Sociology* 44, no. 4: 603-622.
Abramovitz, Mimi. 1998. "Social Work and Social Reform: An Arena of Struggle." *Social Work* 43: 512-526.
Achenbaum, Andrew W. 1978. *Old Age in the New Land: The American Experience since 1790.* Baltimore: Johns Hopkins University Press.
———. 2009. "A Metahistorical Perspective on Theories of Aging." In *Handbook of Theories of Aging*, edited by V. L. Bengston, D. Gans, N. M. Putney, and M. Silverstein. 2nd ed. New York: Springer Publishing.
Acker, Joan. 2006. "Inequality Regimes: Gender, Class and Race in Organizations." *Gender and Society* 20: 441-464.
Ackerly, B. A. 2008. *Universal Human Rights in a World of Difference.* New York: Cambridge University Press.
Ackerly, Brooke A., and Bina D'Costa. 2005. "Transnational Feminism: Political Strategies and Theoretical Resources." Working paper, Australian National University Department of International Relations.
Adam, Barry D. 1998. "Theorizing Homophobia." *Sexualities* 1: 387-404.
Adam, Barry D., Dan Willem Duyvendak, and André Krouwel. 1999. *The Global Emergence of Gay and Lesbian Politics: National Imprints of a Worldwide Movement.* Philadelphia: Temple University Press.
Adams, Carol. 1990. *The Sexual Politics of Meat.* New York: Continuum Press.
Adams, Guy, and Danny Balfour. 1998. *Unmasking Administrative Evil.* Thousand Oaks, CA: Sage.
———. 2004. "Human Rights, the Moral Vacuum of Modern Organizations, and Administrative Evil." In *Human Rights and the Moral Responsibilities of Corporate and Public Sector Organizations*, edited by Tom Campbell and Seamus Miller, 205-221. New York: Kluwer Academic Publishers.
Adams, Vincanne. 1998. "Suffering the Winds of Lhasa: Politicized Bodies, Human Rights, Cultural Difference, and Humanism in Tibet." *Medical Anthropology Quarterly* 12: 74-102.
———. 2010. "Against Global Health? Arbitrating Science, Non-Science, and Nonsense through Health." In *Against Health: How Health Became the New Morality*, edited by Jonathan M. Metzl and Anna Kirkland, 40-58. New York: New York University Press.
Adas, Michael. 2006. *Dominance by Design: Technological Imperatives and America's Civilizing Mission.* Cambridge, MA: Harvard University Press.
Addams, Jane. 1999. *Twenty Years at Hull House.* New York: Signet Classics.
Adelson, Joseph. 2001. "Sex among the Americans." In *Speaking of Sexuality: Interdisciplinary Readings*, edited by J. Kenneth Davidson Sr. and Nelwyn B. Moore, 57-63. Los Angeles: Roxbury Publishing.
Adeola, F. O. 1994. "Environmental Hazards, Health, and Racial Inequity in Hazardous Waste Distribution." *Environment and Behavior* 26: 99-126.
———. 2000a. "Cross-National Environmental Injustice and Human Rights Issues: A Review of Evidence in the Developing World." *American Behavioral Scientist* 43: 686-706.
———. 2000b. "Endangered Community, Enduring People: Toxic Contamination, Health and Adaptive Responses in a Local Context." *Environment and Behavior* 32: 209-249.
———. 2001. "Environmental Injustice and Human Rights Abuse: The States, MNCs, and Repression of Minority Groups in the World System." *Human Ecology Review* 8: 39-59.
———. 2004. "Environmentalism and Risk Perception: Empirical Analysis of Black and White Differentials and Convergence." *Society and Natural Resources* 17: 911-939.

——. 2009. "From Colonialism to Internal Colonialism and Crude Socioenvironmental Injustice: Anatomy of Violent Conflicts in the Niger Delta of Nigeria." In *Environmental Justice in the New Millennium: Global Perspectives on Race, Ethnicity, and Human Rights*, edited by F. C. Steady, 135–163. New York: Palgrave Macmillan.

——. 2011. *Hazardous Wastes, Industrial Disasters, and Environmental Health Risk: Local and Global Environmental Struggles*. New York: Palgrave Macmillan.

Adikari, Y., and J. Yoshitani. 2009. *Global Trends in Water-Related Disasters: An Insight for Policymakers*. Paris: UNESCO.

Adkins, Daniel E., and Stephen Vaisey. 2009. "Toward a Unified Stratification Theory: Structure, Genome, and Status across Human Societies." *Sociological Theory* 27: 99–121.

Adkins, Daniel E., Victor Wang, and Glen H. Elder Jr. 2008. "Stress Processes and Trajectories of Depressive Symptoms in Early Life: Gendered Development." *Advances in Life Course Research* 13: 107–136.

Adkins, W. 2003. "The Social Construction of Disability: A Theoretical Perspective." Paper presented at the annual meeting for the American Sociological Association, Atlanta, Georgia, 1–31.

Adler, Patricia A., and Peter Adler. 2011. *The Tender Cut: Inside the Hidden World of Self-Injury*. New York: New York University Press.

Adorno, T. 2003. "Education after Auschwitz." In *Can One Live after Auschwitz? A Philosophical Reader*, edited by R. Tiedemann, 19–33. Stanford, CA: Stanford University Press.

AFL-CIO. 2005. "The Silent War: The Assault on Workers' Freedom to Choose a Union and Bargain Collectively in the United States." Issue Brief. AFL-CIO. September. http://www.aflcio.org/joinaunion/how/upload/vatw_issuebrief.pdf.

Agyeman, J. 2005. *Sustainable Communities and the Challenge of Environmental Justice*. New York: New York University Press.

Ajrouch, Kristine J. 2007. "Global Contexts and the Veil: Muslim Integration in the United States and France." *Sociology of Religion* 68: 321–325.

Alba, R., and V. Nee. 1997. "Rethinking Assimilation Theory for a New Era of Immigration." *International Migration Review* 31: 826–874.

Albritton, Robert B. 2005. "Thailand in 2004: The 'Crisis in the South.'" *Asian Survey* 45: 166–173.

Aldrich, Howard E. 1999. *Organizations Evolving*. London: Sage.

Alexander, D. 2006. "Globalization of Disaster: Trends, Problems and Dilemmas." *Journal of International Affairs* 59: 1–22.

Alexander, Jeffrey. 2006. *The Civil Sphere*. New York: Oxford University Press.

——. 2010. "Power, Politics, and the Civil Sphere." In *Handbook of Politics: State and Society in Global Perspective*, edited by K. T. Leicht and J. C. Jenkins, 111–126. Heidelberg and New York: Springer Science and Business Media.

Alexander, Jeffrey C. 2004. "On the Social Construction of Moral Universals: The 'Holocaust' from War Crime to Trauma Drama." In *Cultural Trauma and Collective Identity*, edited by J. C. Alexander et al., 196–263. Berkeley: University of California Press.

Alexander, Jeffrey C., Ron Eyerman, Bernard Giesen, Neil J. Smelser, and Piotr Sztompka. 2004. *Cultural Trauma and Collective Identity*. Berkeley: University of California Press.

Alexander, M. Jacqui, and Chandra Talpade Mohanty. 1997. "Introduction." In *Feminist Genealogies, Colonial Legacies, Democratic Future*, edited by M. Jacqui Alexander and Chandra Talpade Mohanty, xiii–xlii. New York: Routledge.

Allegretto, Sylvia A. 2011. "The State of Working America's Wealth, 2011: Through Volatility and Turmoil, the Gap Widens." Economic Policy Institute, State of Working America. http://www.epi.org/page/-/BriefingPaper292.pdf?nocdn=1 (accessed March 23, 2011).

Allen, Beverly. 1996. *Rape Warfare: The Hidden Genocide in Bosnia-Herzegovina and Croatia*. Minneapolis: University of Minnesota Press.

Allman, Paula. 2001. *Critical Education against Global Capitalism: Karl Marx and Revolutionary Critical Education*. Westport, CT: Bergin and Garvey.

——. 2007. *On Marx: An Introduction to the Revolutionary Intellect of Karl Marx*. Rotterdam: Sense Publishers.

Allport, G. W. 1954. *The Nature of Prejudice*. Reading, MA: Addison-Wesley.

Altbach, Philip G., and Patti Peterson. 1971. "Before Berkeley: Historical Perspectives on American Student Activism." *Annals of the American Academy of Political and Social Science* 395: 1–14.

Altenbaugh, Richard J. 1990. *Education for Struggle: The American Labor Colleges of the 1920s and 1930s*. Philadelphia: Temple University Press.

Alvarez-Jimenez, Alberto. 2009. "The WTO Appellate Body's Decision-Making Process." *Journal of International Economics Law* 12, no. 2: 289–331.

Alvesson, Mats, and Hugh Willmott, eds. 1992. *Critical Management Studies*. London: Sage.

——. 2003. *Studying Management Critically*. London: Sage Publications.

Alwin, Duane F., Scott M. Hofer, and Ryan J. McCammon. 2006. "Modeling the Effects of Time: Integrating Demographic and Developmental Perspectives." In *Handbook of Aging and the Social Sciences*, edited by R. H. Binstock and L. K. George, 20–41. 6th ed. Amsterdam: Elsevier.

American Civil Liberties Union (ACLU). 2010. "President Obama Signs Bill Reducing Sentencing Disparities." ACLU. http://www.aclu.org/drug-law-reform/president-obama-signs-bill-reducing-cocaine-sentencing -disparity (accessed October 18, 2011).

American Sociological Association (ASA). 2011. "Animals and Society Section." ASA. www2.asanet.org/ sectionanimals (accessed March 1, 2011).

Amirthalingam, Kumaraligam. 2005. "Women's Rights, International Norms, and Domestic Violence: Asian Perspectives." *Human Rights Quarterly* 27: 683–708.

Amnesty International. 2010. *Amnesty International Report 2010*. London: Amnesty International British Section.

An Na'im, Abdullahi Ahmed. 1992. "Toward a Cross-Cultural Approach to Defining International Standards of Human Rights: The Meaning of Cruel, Inhuman or Degrading Treatment or Punishment." In *Human Rights in Cross-Cultural Perspectives*, edited by Abdullahi Ahmed An-Na'im, 19–43. Philadelphia: University of Pennsylvania Press.

———. 2001. "Human Rights." In *The Blackwell Companion to Sociology*, edited by Judith Blau, 86–99. Malden, MA: Blackwell.

Ancheta, Angelo N. 1998. "Race, Rights, and the Asian American Experience." *Journal of Asian American Studies* 1: 293–297.

Anderson, Benedict. 2006 [1983]. *Imagined Communities: Reflections on the Origin and Spread of Nationalism*. London: Verso, New Left Books.

Anderson, Elijah. 1994. *Code of the Street*. New York: W. W. Norton.

———. 2000. *Code of the Street: Decency, Violence, and the Moral Life of the Inner City*. New York: W. W. Norton.

———. 2011. *The Cosmopolitan Canopy: Race and Civility in Everyday Life*. New York: W. W. Norton.

Anderson, Leon, and David A. Snow. 2001. "Inequality and the Self: Exploring Connections from an Inter-actionist Perspective." *Symbolic Interaction* 24: 395–406.

Anderson, Margo, and Stephen Fienberg. 2001. *Who Counts: The Politics of Census-Taking in Contemporary America*. New York: Russell Sage Foundation.

Andersson, Matthew A., and Colleen S. Conley. 2008. "Expecting to Heal through Self-Expression: A Perceived Control Theory of Writing and Health." *Health Psychology Review* 2: 138–162.

Anghie, Antony. 1970. "On the Measurement of Inequality." *Journal of Economic Theory* 2: 244–263.

———. 2005. *Imperialism, Sovereignty and the Making of International Law*. Cambridge, UK: Cambridge University Press.

Annette, John. 2005. "Character, Civic Renewal and Service Learning for Democratic Citizenship in Higher Education." *British Journal of Educational Studies* 53: 326–340.

Anoushirvani, S. 2010. "The Future of the International Criminal Court: The Long Road to Legitimacy Begins with the Trial of Thomas Lubanga Dyilo." *Pace International Law Review* 22: 213–239.

Antrobus, Peggy. 2004. *The Global Women's Movement: Origins, Issues, and Strategies*. London: Zed Books.

Apocada, C. 2007. "The Whole World Could Be Watching." *Journal of Human Rights* 6: 147–164.

Archibugi, Daniele. 2008. *The Global Commonwealth of Citizens*. Princeton, NJ: Princeton University Press.

Arena, Jay. 2010. "The Contested Terrains of Public Sociology: Theoretical and Practical Lessons from the Movement to Defend Public Housing in Pre- and Post-Katrina New Orleans." *Societies without Borders* 5: 103–125.

Aries, Philippe. 1962. *Centuries of Childhood*. New York: Vintage.

Arington, Michele. 1991. "English Only Laws and Direct Legislation: The Battle in the States over Language Minority Rights." *Journal of Law and Politics* 7: 325–352.

Armstrong, Susan J., and Richard G. Botzler, eds. 2008. *The Animal Ethics Reader*. 2nd ed. London and New York: Routledge.

Aronowitz, Stanley. 1988. *Science as Power: Discourse and Ideology in Modern Society*. Minneapolis: University of Minnesota Press.

Arum, Richard. 2011. *Academically Adrift: Limited Learning on College Campuses*. Chicago: University of Chicago Press.

Arzberger, Peter, Peter Schroeder, Anne Beaulieu, Geof Bowker, Kathleen Casey, Leif Laaksonen, David Moorman, Paul Uhlir, and Paul Wouters. 2004. "An International Framework to Promote Access to Data." *Science* 303, no. 5665: 1777–1778.

Asch, A. 2001. "Disability, Bioethics, and Human Rights." In *Handbook of Disability Studies*, edited by G. L. Albrecht, K. D. Seelman, and M. Bury, 297–326. Thousand Oaks, CA: Sage.

Asencio, Marysol. 2009. *Latina/o Sexualities: Probing Powers, Passions, Practices, and Policies*. New Brunswick, NJ: Rutgers University Press.

Ashar, Sameer. 2003. "Immigration Enforcement and Subordination: The Consequences of Racial Profiling after September 11." *Immigration and National Law Review* 23: 545–560.

Atkin, C. K., K. Neuendorf, and S. McDermott. 1983. "The Role of Alcohol Advertising in Excessive and Hazardous Drinking." *Journal of Drug Education* 13: 313–325.

Atkinson, A. B. 1970. "On the Measurement of Inequality." *Journal of Economic Theory* 2: 244–263.

Atkinson, Anthony B. 1975. *The Economics of Inequality.* London: Oxford.

Atterton, Peter, and Matthew Calarco, eds. 2004. *Animal Philosophy: Ethics and Identity.* New York: Continuum.

Aylward, Carol A. 2010. "Intersectionality: Crossing the Theoretical and Praxis Divide." *Journal of Critical Race Inquiry* 1: 1–48.

Baars, Jan, Dale Dannefer, Chris Philipson, and Alan Walker. 2006. *Aging, Globalization, and Inequality: The New Critical Gerontology.* Amityville, NY: Baywood Publishing Company.

Babugura, Agnes A. 2008. "Vulnerability of Children and Youth in Drought Disasters: A Case Study of Botswana." *Children, Youth, and Environments* 18, no. 1: 126–157.

Baca, Maxine Zinn, and Bonnie Thornton Dill. 1994. "Difference and Domination." In *Women of Color in U.S. Society.* Philadelphia: Temple University Press.

———. 1996. "Theorizing Difference from Multiracial Feminism." *Feminist Studies* 22: 321–331.

Baden, Sally, and Anne Marie Goetz. 1997. "Who Needs [Sex] When You Can Have [Gender]? Conflicting Discourses on Gender at Beijing." In *Women, International Development, and Politics,* edited by Kathleen Staudt, 37–58. Philadelphia: Temple University Press.

Bagemihl, Bruce. 2000. *Biological Exuberance: Animal Homosexuality and Natural Diversity.* New York: St. Martin's Press.

Bailey, Christopher. 2004. "'Informed Choice' to 'Social Hygiene': Government Control of Smoking in the US." *Journal of American Studies* 38, no. 1: 41–65.

Baker, Carrie N. 2007. *The Women's Movement against Sexual Harassment.* New York: Cambridge University Press.

Bakker, J. I. (Hans). 1993. *Toward a Just Civilization: Gandhi.* Toronto: Canadian Scholars' Press.

———. 2010a. "Theory, Role of." In *Encyclopedia of Case Study Research,* edited by Albert J. Mills, Gabrielle Durepos, and Elden Wiebe, 930–932. Los Angeles, CA: Sage.

———. 2010b. "Deference versus Democracy in Traditional and Modern Bureaucracy: A Refinement of Max Weber's Ideal Type Model." In *Society, History and the Global Condition of Humanity,* edited by Zaheer Baber and Joseph M. Bryant, 105–128. Lanham, MD: Lexington Publishers.

Bales, Kevin, and Ron Soodalter. 2009. *The Slave Next Door: Human Trafficking and Slavery in America Today.* Berkeley: University of California Press.

Baltrušaitytė, G. 2010. "Psychiatry and the Mental Patient: An Uneasy Relationship." *Culture and Society* 1. http://culturesociety.vdu.lt/wp-content/uploads/2010/11/G.-Baltrusaityte-Psychiatry-and-the-Mental-Patient-An-Uneasy-Relationship1.pdf (accessed January 22, 2012).

Bandy, Joe, and Jackie Smith. 2005. *Coalitions across Borders: Transnational Protest and the Neoliberal Order.* Lanham, MD: Rowman & Littlefield.

Barak, Gregg, ed. 1991. *Crimes by the Capitalist State: An Introduction to State Criminality.* Albany: State University of New York Press.

Barbalet, J. M. 1995. "Symposium: Human Rights and the Sociological Project (a Social Emotions Theory of Basic Rights)." *Australian and New Zealand Journal of Sociology* 31: 36–42.

Barbotte, E., F. Guillemin, and N. Chau. 2002. "Prevalence of Impairments, Disabilities, Handicaps and Quality of Life in the General Population: A Review of Recent Literature." *Bulletin of the World Health Organization* 79: 1047–1055.

Barham P. 1992. *Closing the Asylum.* London: Penguin Books.

Barnes, C. 1996. "Theories of Disability and the Origins of the Oppression of Disabled People." In *Disability and Society: Emerging Issues and Insights,* edited by L. Barton, 43–60. London: Longman.

Barnes, C., and G. Mercer. 2010. *Exploring Disability.* 2nd ed. Cambridge, UK: Polity Press.

Barnett, H. G. 1948. "On Science and Human Rights." *American Anthropologist* 50, no. 2: 352–355.

Baron, James N. 1984. "Organizational Perspectives on Stratification." *Annual Review of Sociology* 10: 37–69.

Barry, John, and K. Woods. 2009. "The Environment." In *Human Rights: Politics and Practice,* edited by M. Goodhart, 316–333. London: Oxford University Press.

Basch, Linda, Nina Glick Schiller, and Cristina Szanton Blanc. 1994. *Nations Unbound: Transnational Projects, Postcolonial Predicaments, and Deterritorialized Nation-States.* Routledge: London.

Bashford, Alison, and Phillipa Levine, eds. 2010. *The Oxford Handbook of the History of Eugenics.* Oxford: Oxford University Press.

Bass, Gary J. 2000. *Stay the Hand of Vengeance: The Politics of War Crimes Tribunals.* Princeton, NJ: Princeton University Press.

Basu, Amrita, ed. 2010. *Women's Movements in the Global Era: The Power of Local Feminisms.* Boulder, CO: Westview Press.

Batliwala, S. 2007. "Taking the Power Out of Empowerment—an Experiential Account." *Development in Practice* 17: 557–565.

Battersby, P., and J. M. Siracusa. 2009. *Globalization and Human Security.* Lanham, MD: Rowman & Littlefield.

Battle, Juan. 2009. *Black Sexualities: Probing Powers, Passions, Practices, and Policies.* New Brunswick, NJ: Rutgers University Press.

Bauböck, Rainer. 2009. "Global Justice, Freedom of Movement, and Democratic Citizenship." *European Journal of Sociology* 50: 1–31.

Bauman, Zygmunt. 1989. *Modernity and the Holocaust.* Ithaca, NY: New York University Press.

———. 2001. "Wars of the Globalization Era." *European Journal of Social Theory* 4: 11–28.

Baumer, Eric. 1994. "Poverty, Crack and Crime: A Cross-City Analysis." *Journal of Research in Crime and Delinquency* 31: 311–327.

Baumol, William J. 2002. *The Free-Market Innovation Machine: Analyzing the Grown Miracle of Capitalism.* Princeton, NJ: Princeton University Press.

Baxi, Upendra. 2002. *The Future of Human Rights.* New Delhi: Oxford University Press.

Baxter, David. 1989. "Marx, Lukes and Human Rights." *Social Theory and Practice* 15, no. 3: 355–373.

Bearman, Peter S., and Hannah Bruckner. 2001. "Promising the Future: Virginity Pledges and First Intercourse." *American Journal of Sociology* 106: 859–912.

Beating, J. 1993. "Technological Impacts on Human Rights: Models of Development, Science and Technology, and Human Rights." In *The Impact of Technology on Human Rights: Global Case Studies,* edited by C. G. Weeramantry. Tokyo, Japan: United Nations Press. http://unu.edu/unupress/unubooks/uu08ie/uu08ie00.htm (accessed November 12, 2010).

Beaver, Kevin M. 2008. "Nonshared Environmental Influences on Adolescent Delinquent Involvement and Adult Criminal Behavior." *Criminology* 46, no. 2: 341–369.

Beck, Ulrich. 1996. "Risk Society and the Provident State." In *Risk, Environment, and Modernity,* edited by S. Lash, B. Szersynski, and B. Wynne, 27–43. Thousand Oaks, CA: Sage.

———. 1999. *World Risk Society.* Malden, MA: Polity Press.

———. 2007a. *Cosmopolitan Europe.* Cambridge, UK: Polity Press.

———. 2007b. *World at Risk.* Malden, MA: Polity Press.

Beck, Ulrich, and Natan Sznaider. 2006. "Unpacking Cosmopolitanism for the Social Sciences." *British Journal of Sociology* 57, no. 1: 1–23.

Becker, Anne E. 1994. "Nurturing and Negligence: Working on Others' Bodies in Fiji." In *Embodiment and Experience: The Existential Ground of Culture and Self,* edited by Thomas J. Csordas, 100–115. Cambridge, UK: Cambridge University Press.

Becker, Howard S. 1963. *Outsiders: Studies in the Sociology of Deviance.* New York: The Free Press.

———. 1967. "Whose Side Are We On?" *Social Problems* 14: 239–247.

———. 1982. *Art Worlds.* Berkeley: University of California Press.

Beckett, Katherine, and Steve Herbert. 2009. *Banished: The New Social Control in Urban America.* New York: Oxford University Press.

Beckett, Katherine, Kris Nyrop, Lori Pfingst, and Melissa Bowen. 2005. "Drug Use, Drug Possession Arrests, and the Question of Race: Lessons from Seattle." *Social Problems* 52, no. 3: 419–441.

Beckoff, Marc. 2002. *Minding Animals: Awareness, Emotions, and Heart.* New York: Oxford.

Beetham, David. 1995. "What Future for Economic and Social Rights?" *Political Studies* 43: 41–60.

Behar, Ruth. 1997. *The Vulnerable Observer: Anthropology that Breaks Your Heart.* Boston: Beacon Press.

Bell, Daniel. 1978 [1976]. *The Cultural Contradictions of Capitalism.* New York: Basic Books, Harper.

———. 2000. *East Meets West: Human Rights and Democracy in East Asia.* Princeton, NJ: Princeton University Press.

Bell, L. A. 1997. "Theoretical Foundations for Social Justice Education." In *Teaching for Diversity and Social Justice: A Sourcebook,* edited by M. Adams, L. A. Bell, and P. Griffin, 3–15. New York: Routledge.

Beneke, Timothy. 1983. *Men on Rape: What They Have to Say about Sexual Violence.* New York: St. Martin's Press.

Benford, Robert D., and David A. Snow. 2000. "Framing Processes and Social Movements." *Annual Review of Sociology* 26: 611–639.

Bengston, Vern L., Daphna Gans, Norella M. Putney, and Merril Silverstein, eds. 2009a. *Handbook of Theories of Aging.* 2nd ed. New York: Springer Publishing.

———. 2009b. "Theories about Age and Aging." In *Handbook of Theories of Aging,* edited by Vern L. Bengston, Daphna Gans, Norella M. Putney, and Merril Silverstein, 3–24. 2nd ed. New York: Springer Publishing.

Benhabib, Seyla, and Judith Resnick. 2009. "Introduction: Citizenship and Migration Theory Engendered." In *Migrations and Mobilities: Citizenship, Borders, and Gender,* edited by Seyla Benhabib and Judith Resnik, 1–46. New York: New York University Press.

Bennett, Angela. 2006. *The Geneva Convention.* Charleston, SC: History Press.

Bennett, Michael, and Juan Battle. 2001. "'We Can See Them, but We Can't Hear Them': LGBT Members of African American Families." In *Queer Families, Queer Politics: Challenging Culture and the State*, edited by Mary Bernstein and Renate Reimann, 53–67. New York: Columbia University Press.

Benoit, Cecelia, Dena Carroll, and Munaza Chaudhry. 2003. "In Search of a Healing Place: Aboriginal Women in Vancouver's Downtown Eastside." *Social Science and Medicine* 56: 821–833.

Benson, J. Kenneth. 1975. "The Interorganizational Network as a Political Economy." *Administrative Science Quarterly* 20: 229–249.

———. 1977. "Innovation and Crisis in Organizational Analysis." *Sociological Quarterly* 18: 3–16.

———. 1982. "A Framework for Policy Analysis." In *Interorganizational Coordination: Theory, Research, and Implementation*, edited by David L. Rogers and David A. Whetten, 137–176. Ames: Iowa State University Press.

———. 1983. "Paradigm and Praxis in Organizational Analysis." In *Research on Organizational Behavior*, edited by Barry Staw and L. L. Cummings, 33–56. Annual Series 5. Greenwich, CT: JAI Press.

Beresford, P., and A. Wilson. 2002. "Genes Spell Danger: Mental Health Service Users/Survivors, Bioethics and Control." *Disability and Society* 17: 541–553.

Berger, Joseph, Bernard P. Cohen, and Morris Zelditch Jr. 1966. "Status Characteristics and Expectation States." In *Sociological Theories in Progress*, edited by Joseph Berger, Morris Zelditch Jr., and Bo Anderson, 1:29–46. Boston: Houghton Mifflin.

Berger, Peter, and Thomas Luckmann. 1966. *The Social Construction of Reality*. Garden City, NY: Anchor.

Berkovitch, Nitza. 1999. *From Motherhood to Citizenship: Women's Rights and International Organizations*. Baltimore: Johns Hopkins University Press.

Berlant, Lauren, and Michael Warner. 1998. "Sex in Public." *Critical Inquiry* 24: 547–566.

Bernard, L. L. 1945. "The Teaching of Sociology in the United States in the Last Fifty Years." *American Journal of Sociology* 50: 534–548.

Bernerjee, D. 2008. "Environmental Rights." In *The Leading Rogue State: The U.S. and Human Rights*, edited by Judith Blau et al., 163–172. Boulder, CO: Paradigm Publishers.

Bernstein, Basil. 1970. "Education Cannot Compensate for Society." *New Society* 387: 344–347.

———. 1977. *Class, Codes, and Control*. Vol. 3: *Towards a Theory of Educational Transmissions*. London: Routledge and Kegan Paul.

———. 1990. *Class, Codes, and Control*. Vol. 4: *The Structuring of Pedagogic Discourse*. London: Routledge.

———. 1996. *Pedagogy, Symbolic Control, and Identity: Theory, Research, Critique*. London: Taylor and Francis.

Bernstein, Irving. 1960a. *The Lean Years: A History of the American Worker, 1920–1933*. Boston: Houghton Mifflin.

———. 1960b. "Union Growth and Structural Cycles." In *Labor and Trade Unionism*, edited by W. Galenson and S. M. Lipset, 73–89. New York: Wiley.

———. 1970. *The Turbulent Years: A History of the American Worker, 1933–1941*. Boston: Houghton Mifflin.

Bernstein, Mary. 2004. "Paths to Homophobia." *Sexuality Research and Social Policy* 1: 41–55.

———. 2005. "Identity Politics." *Annual Review of Sociology* 31: 47–74.

Bernstein, Mary, and Constance Kostelac. 2002. "Lavender and Blue: Attitudes about Homosexuality and Behavior toward Lesbians and Gay Men among Police Officers." *Journal of Contemporary Criminal Justice* 18: 302–328.

Bernstein, Mary, Constance Kostelac, and Emily Gaarder. 2003. "Understanding 'Heterosexism': Applying Theories of Racial Prejudice to Homophobia Using Data from a Southwestern Police Department." *Race, Gender and Class* 10: 54–74.

Bernstein, Mary, and Renate Reimann, eds. 2001. *Queer Families, Queer Politics: Challenging Culture and the State*. New York: Columbia University Press.

Berry, J. G., and W. H. Jones. 1991. "Situational and Dispositional Components of Reaction towards Persons with Disabilities." *Journal of Social Psychology* 131: 673–684.

Berry, Jason. 1992. *Lead Us Not into Temptation: Catholic Priests and the Sexual Abuse of Children*. New York: Doubleday.

Bertman, Martin. 2004. "The Theoretical Instability and Practical Progress of Human Rights." *International Journal of Human Rights* 8, no. 1: 89–99.

Best, Joel. 2007. *Social Problems*. New York: W. W. Norton and Company.

Best, Steve, and Anthony J. Nocella II. 2004. *Terrorists or Freedom Fighters? Reflections on the Liberation of Animals*. New York: Lantern Books.

Bevc, Christine, Brent K. Marshall, and J. Stephen Picou. 2007. "Environmental Justice and Toxic Exposure: Toward a Spatial Model of Physical Health and Psychological Well-Being." *Social Science Research* 37: 48–67.

Bevington, Douglas, and Chris Dixon. 2005. "Movement-Relevant Theory: Rethinking Social Movement Scholarship and Activism." *Social Movement Studies* 4, no. 3: 185–208.

Beyer, Peter. 2001. *Religion in the Process of Globalization*. Würzburg, Germany: Ergon.

———. 2006. *Religions in Global Society*. London and New York: Routledge.

Beyrer, Chris. 1998. "Burma and Cambodia: Human Rights, Social Disruption, and the Spread of HIV/AIDS." *Health and Human Rights* 2: 84–97.

Bhabha, Homi K. 2004. *RC Series Bundle: The Location of Culture.* 2nd ed. London: Routledge.

Bhattacharji, Preeti. 2009. *Uighurs and China's Xinjiang Region.* Washington, DC: Council on Foreign Relations. http://www.cfr.org/china/uighurs-chinas-xinjiang-region/p16870 (accessed September 30, 2011).

Bhattacharyya, A., P. K. Pattanaik, and Y. Xu. 2011. "Choice, Internal Consistency and Rationality." *Economics and Philosophy* 27, no. 2 (July): 123–149.

Biblarz, Timothy J., and Adrian E. Raftery. 1999. "Family Structure, Educational Attainment, and Socioeconomic Success: Rethinking the 'Pathology of Matriarchy.'" *American Journal of Sociology* 105: 321–365.

Bierne, Piers. 2009. *Confronting Animal Abuse: Law, Criminology, and Human-Animal Relationships.* Lanham, MD: Rowman & Littlefield.

Bigelow, J. 1831. *Elements of Technology.* Boston: Hilliard, Gray, Little and Wilkins.

Bilder, Richard B. 2006. "The Role of Apology in International Law and Diplomacy." *Virginia Journal of International Law* 46: 433–473.

Billson, Janet Mancini. 2008. "Focus Groups in the Context of International Development: In Pursuit of the Millennium Development Goals." In *International Clinical Sociology*, edited by Jan Marie Fritz, 188–207. New York: Springer.

Bilton, C. 2007. *Management and Creativity: From Creative Industries to Creative Management.* Malden, MA: Blackwell.

Binion, Gayle. 1995. "Human Rights: A Feminist Perspective." *Human Rights Quarterly* 17: 509–526.

Binstock, Robert H. 2007. "The Doomsters Are Wrong: What's Needed Are Policies Aimed at Several Generations." *AARP Bulletin* 48, no. 3: 33.

Binstock, Robert H., Linda K. George, Stephen J. Cutler, Jon Hendricks, and James H. Schultz. 2006. *Handbook of Aging and the Social Sciences.* Amsterdam: Elsevier.

———. 2011. *Handbook of Aging and the Social Sciences.* Amsterdam: Elsevier.

Binstock, Robert H., and Stephen G. Post. 1991. *Too Old for Health Care? Controversies in Medicine, Law, Economics, and Ethics.* 6th ed. Baltimore: Johns Hopkins University Press.

Bird, Chloe E., Peter Conrad, and Allen M. Fremont. 2000. "Medical Sociology at the Millennium." In *Handbook of Medical Sociology*, edited by Chloe E. Bird, Peter Conrad, and Allen M. Fremont, 1–10. 5th ed. Upper Saddle River, NJ: Prentice Hall.

Birren, J. E., ed. 1959. *Handbook of Aging and the Individual: Psychological and Biological Aspects.* Chicago: University of Chicago Press.

Black, Donald. 1972. "The Boundaries of Legal Sociology." *Yale Law Journal* 81, no. 6: 1086–1100.

———. 1976. *The Behavior of the Law.* New York: Academic Press.

Black, R. S., and L. Pretes. 2007. "Victims and Victors: Representation of Physical Disability on the Silver Screen." *Research and Practice for Persons with Severe Disabilities* 32: 66–83.

Black, Timothy. 2010. *When a Heart Turns Rock Solid: The Lives of Three Puerto Rican Brothers on and off the Streets.* New York: Vintage.

Blair, T., and M. Minkler. 2009. "Participatory Action Research with Older Adults: Key Principles in Practice." *Gerontologist* 49: 651–662.

Blau, J., and A. Moncada. 2005. *Human Rights: Beyond the Liberal Vision.* Lanham, MD: Rowman & Littlefield.

———. 2006. *Justice in the United States: Human Rights and the U.S. Constitution.* London: Rowman & Littlefield.

———. 2007a. "It Ought to Be a Crime: Criminalizing Human Rights Violations." *Sociological Forum* 22: 364–371.

———. 2007b. "Sociologizing Human Rights: Reply to John Hagan and Ron Levi." *Sociological Forum* 22: 381–384.

———. 2009. *Human Rights: A Primer.* Boulder, CO: Paradigm Publishers.

Blau, Judith. 2005. "Don't Blink Now: It's the Transition to the Second World System." *Contemporary Sociology* 34, no. 1: 7–9.

———. 2006. "Why Should Human Rights Be Important to Sociologists?" Sociologists without Borders. http://www.sociologistswithoutborders.org/president.html (accessed September 5, 2012).

———. 2010. Personal communication with J. M. Fritz. December 24.

———. 2011. "Human Rights Cities: The Transformation of Communities, or Simply Treading Water?" In *Essentials of Community Intervention*, edited by J. M. Fritz and J. Rheaume, draft chapter. The Netherlands: Springer.

Blau, Judith, David Brunsma, Alberto Moncada, and Catherine Zimmer, eds. 2008. *The Leading Rogue State.* Boulder, CO: Paradigm Publishers.

Blau, Judith, and Mark Frezzo, eds. 2011. *Sociology and Human Rights: A Bill of Rights for the Twenty-First Century.* Newbury Park, CA: Pine Forge Press.

Blau, Judith, and Marina Karides. 2008. *The World and US Social Forums: Another World Is Possible and Necessary.* Leiden: Brill Publishers.

Blau, Judith, and Keri Iyall Smith. 2006. *Public Sociologies Reader.* Lanham, MD: Rowman & Littlefield.

Blau, P. M. 1974. "Presidential Address: Parameters of Social Structure." *American Sociological Review* 39: 615-635.

Blau, Peter M., and Richard Schoenherr. 1971. *The Structure of Organizations*. New York: Basic Books.

Blauner, Robert. 1964. *Alienation and Freedom: The Factory Worker and His Industry*. Chicago: University of Chicago Press.

Bloom, Samuel. W. 2000. "The Institutionalization of Medical Sociology in the United States, 1920-1980." In *Handbook of Medical Sociology*, edited by Chloe E. Bird, Peter Conrad, and Allen M. Fremont, 11-31. 5th ed. Upper Saddle River, NJ: Prentice Hall.

Bluestone, Barry, and Bennett Harrison. 1982. *The Deindustrialization of America: Plant Closings, Community Abandonment, and the Dismantling of Basic Industry*. New York: Basic Books.

Blum, T. 1984. "Problem Drinking or Problem Thinking? Patterns of Abuse in Sociological Research." *Journal of Drug Issues* 14: 655-665.

Blumberg, Rae Lesser. 2004. "Extending Lenski's Schema to Hold Up Both Halves of the Sky–a Theory-Guided Way of Conceptualizing Agrarian Societies that Illuminates a Puzzle about Gender Stratification." *Sociological Theory* 22: 278-291.

Blumenson, Eric, and Eva S. Neilsen. 2002. "How to Construct an Underclass, or How the War on Drugs Became a War on Education." NELLCO Legal Scholarship Repository. http://lsr.nellco.org/suffolk_fp/1 (accessed September 2011).

Blute, Marion. 2006. "Gene-Culture Coevolutionary Games." *Social Forces* 85: 145-149.

———. 2010. *Darwinian Sociocultural Evolution: Evolutionary Solutions to Dilemmas in Cultural and Social Theory*. Cambridge, UK: Cambridge University Press.

Boardman, Jason D., Casely L. Blalock, and Fred C. Pampel. 2010. "Trends in the Genetic Influences on Smoking." *Journal of Health and Social Behavior* 51: 108-123.

Bob, Clifford, ed. 2005. *The Marketing of Rebellion: Insurgents, Media, and International Activism*. Cambridge, UK: Cambridge University Press.

———. 2009. *The International Struggle for New Human Rights*. Philadelphia: University of Pennsylvania Press.

Boersema, D. 2011. *Philosophy of Human Rights: Theory and Practice*. Boulder, CO: Westview Press.

Bogason, Peter. 2006. "The Democratic Prospects of Network Governance." *American Review of Public Administration* 36, no. 1: 3-18.

Bogle, Kathleen. 2008. *Hooking Up: Sex, Dating, and Relationships on Campus*. New York: New York University Press.

Boli, John, and George M. Thomas. 1997. "World Culture and the World Polity: A Century of International Non-Governmental Organization." *American Sociological Review* 62, no. 2: 171-190.

———. 1999. *Constructing World Culture: International Nongovernmental Organizations since 1875*. Stanford, CA: Stanford University Press.

Bond, Johanna E. 2003. "International Intersectionality: Theoretical and Pragmatic Exploration of Women's International Human Rights Violations." *Emory Law Journal* 52: 71-187.

Bonilla-Silva, Eduardo. 2003. *Racism without Racists: Color-Blind Racism and the Persistence of Racial Inequality in the United States*. Lanham, MD: Rowman & Littlefield Publishers.

———. 2008. "'Look, a Negro': Reflections on the Human Rights Approach to Racial Inequality." In *Globalization and America*, edited by A. J. Hattery, D. G. Embrick, and E. Smith, 9-22. Lanham, MD: Rowman & Littlefield Publishers.

Bonilla-Silva, Eduardo, and Sarah Mayorga. 2009. "*Si Me Permiter Hablar*: Limitations of the Human Rights Tradition to Address Racial Inequality." *Societies without Borders* 4: 366-382.

Bonnell, Victoria E. 1980. "The Uses of Theory, Concepts and Comparison in Historical Scholarship." *Comparative Study of Society and History* 22: 156-173.

Bonnin, Debbie. 1995. "Road to Beijing." *Agenda* 27: 74-77.

Bookchin, Murray. 1982. *The Ecology of Freedom: The Emergence and Dissolution of Hierarchy*. Palo Alto, CA: Cheshire Books.

Booth, Alan, Douglas A. Granger, and Elizabeth A. Shirtcliff. 2008. "Gender- and Age-Related Differences in the Association between Social Relationship Quality and Trait Levels of Salivary Cortisol." *Journal of Research on Adolescence* 18: 239-260.

Booth, Aland, D. Johnson, and Douglas Granger. 2005. "Testosterone, Marital Quality, and Role Overload." *Journal of Marriage and the Family* 67: 483-498.

Border Network for Human Rights (BNHR). 2003. *Two–US/Mexico Border Reports*. BNHR. http://www.bnhr.org/reports/u-s-mexico-border-reports-2000-2005 (accessed July 17, 2012).

Bordo, Susan. 2004. *Unbearable Weight: Feminism, Western Culture, and the Body*. Berkeley: University of California Press.

Borjas, George. 2004. "Increasing the Supply of Labor through Immigration: Measuring the Impact on Native-Born Workers." Center for Immigration Studies. http://www.cis.org/LaborSupply-ImmigrationEffectsNatives (accessed July 17, 2012).

Bottomore, T. B. 1963. *Karl Marx: Early Writings*. New York: McGraw-Hill.

Bottomore, Tom. 1985. *Theories of Modern Capitalism*. London: Allen & Unwin.

Bouilloud, J.-P. 2010. Personal communication with J. M. Fritz. December 13 and 15.

Bourdieu, Pierre. 1973. "Cultural Reproduction and Social Reproduction." In *Knowledge, Education, and Cultural Change*, edited by Richard Brown, 71–112. London: Tavistock.

———. 1977. *Outline of a Theory of Practice*. Cambridge, UK: Cambridge University Press.

———. 1984. *Distinction: A Social Critique of the Judgment of Taste*. Translated by Richard Nice. London: Routledge and Kegan Paul.

———. 1998. *Acts of Resistance: Against the Tyranny of the Market*. Translated by Richard Nice. New York: The New Press.

Bourdieu, Pierre, and Loic J. D. Wacquant. 1992. *An Invitation to Reflexive Sociology*. Chicago: University of Chicago Press.

Bourgois, Philippe. 1990. "Confronting the Ethics of Ethnography: Lessons from Fieldwork in Central America." In *Ethnographic Fieldwork: An Anthropological Reader*, edited by Antonius C. G. M. Robben and Jeffery A. Sluka. Malden, MA: Blackwell Publishing.

Bourgois, Philippe, and Jeff Schonberg. 2009. *Righteous Dopefiend*. Berkeley: University of California Press.

Bowles, Samuel, and Herbert Gintis. 1976. *Schooling in Capitalist America: Educational Reform and the Contradictions of Economic Life*. London: Routledge and Kegan Paul.

———. 1986. *Democracy and Capitalism: Property, Community, and the Contradictions of Modern Social Thought*. New York: Basic Books.

Boyer, Ernst. 1997. *Scholarship Reconsidered: Priorities of the Professorate*. San Francisco: Jossey-Bass.

Boyle, Elizabeth Heger. 2002. *Female Genital Cutting: Cultural Conflict in the Global Community*. Baltimore: Johns Hopkins University Press.

———. 2007. "Processes of Legislative Globalization." In *Encyclopedia of Law and Society: American and Global Perspectives*, edited by David Scott Clark, 661–665. Thousand Oaks, CA: Sage Publications.

———. 2009. "The Cost of Rights or the Right Cost? The Impact of Global Economic and Human Rights Policies on Child Well-Being since 1989." NSF Grant, Law and Social Science Program.

Boyle, Elizabeth Heger, and Amelia Corl. 2010. "Law and Culture in a Global Context: The Practice of Female Genital Cutting." *Annual Review of Law and Social Science* 6: 195–215.

Brabant, Sarah Callaway. 2008. "Clinical Sociology and Bereavement." In *International Clinical Sociology*, edited by Jan Marie Fritz, 97–114. New York: Springer.

Brabeck, Kalina, and Qingwen Xu. 2010. "The Impact of Detention and Deportation on Latino Immigrant Children and Families: A Quantitative Exploration." *Hispanic Journal of Behavioral Sciences* 32: 341–361.

Brackett, Jeffrey R. 1907. "Contribution to Symposium on How Should Sociology Be Taught—As a College or University Course?" *American Journal of Sociology* 12: 602–603.

Bradshaw, W., D. Roseborough, and M. Armour. 2006. "Recovery from Severe Mental Illness: The Lived Experience of the Initial Phase of Treatment." *International Journal of Psychosocial Rehabilitation* 10: 123–131.

Branch, A. 2007. "Uganda's Civil War and the Politics of ICC Intervention." *Ethics and International Affairs* 21: 179–198.

Branningan, Augustine, and Kelly H. Hardwick. 2003. "Genocide and General Theory." In *Control Theories of Crime and Delinquency*, edited by Chester L. Britt and R. Michael, 109–131. New Brunswick, NJ: Transaction.

Brass, Martin. 2011. *Labour Regime Change in the Twenty-First Century*. Leiden, The Netherlands: Brill.

Braverman, Harry. 1974. *Labor and Monopoly Capital*. New York: Monthly Review Press.

Brenkert, George G. 1986. "Marx and Human Rights." *Journal of the History of Philosophy* 24, no. 1: 55–77.

Brenner, Neil, Peter Marcuse, and Margit Mayer, eds. 2012. *Cities for People, Not for Profit: Critical Urban Theory and the Right to the City*. New York: Routledge.

Brewer, Marilynn. 1997. "The Social Psychology of Intergroup Relations: Can Research Inform Practice?" *Journal of Social Issues* 53: 197–211.

Brewer, Rose. 1993. "Theorizing Race, Class and Gender: The New Scholarship of Black Feminist Intellectuals and Black Women's Labor." In *Theorizing Black Feminisms: The Visionary Pragmatism of Black Women*, edited by Stanlie M. James and Abena P. A. Busia, 13–30. New York: Routledge.

Brewington, David V. 2005. "Late to the Party: Organizing Religious Human Rights." Paper presented at the annual meeting of the American Sociological Association, Philadelphia, Pennsylvania.

———. 2011. "International Associations at the Nexus of Globalization, Religion, and Human Rights." PhD diss., Emory University, Atlanta.

Brewster, Karin L., and Ronald R. Rindfuss. 1990. "Homophobia and Homosociality: An Analysis of Boundary Maintenance." *Sociological Quarterly* 31: 423–439.

——. 2000. "Fertility and Women's Employment in Industrialized Nations." *Annual Review of Sociology* 26: 271–296.

Brice, Arthur. 2010. "Mexico Asks for Probe into Teen's Shooting Death by U.S. Border Agent." CNN News. June 10. http://articles.cnn.com/2010-06-08/us/texas.border.patrol.shooting_1_ciudad-juarez -fbi-agent?_s=PM:US (accessed March 23, 2011).

Briggs, Laura. 1998. "Discourses of 'Forced Sterilization' in Puerto Rico: The Problem with the Speaking Subaltern." *Differences* 10, no. 2: 30–66.

Brinkmann, Svend. 2010. "Human Vulnerabilities: Toward a Theory of Rights for Qualitative Researchers." In *Qualitative Inquiry and Human Rights*, edited by Norman Denzin and Michael Giardina, 82–99. Walnut Creek, CA: Left Coast Press.

Britton, Dana M. 2003. *At Work in the Iron Cage: The Prison as Gendered Organization.* New York: New York University Press.

Brod, H. 1987. *The Making of Masculinities: The New Men's Studies.* Boston, MA: Allen and Unwin.

Brody, David. 1960. *Steelworkers in America: The Nonunion Era.* Cambridge, MA: Harvard University Press.

——. 1965. *Labor in Crisis: The Steel Strike of 1919.* Philadelphia: Lippincott.

——. 1979. "The Old Labor History and the New: In Search of an American Working Class." *Labor History* 20: 111–126.

——. 2001. "Labour Rights as Human Rights: A Reality Check." *British Journal of Industrial Relations* 39: 601–605.

Broido, E. M. 2000. "The Development of Social Justice Allies during College: A Phenomenological Investigation." *Journal of College Student Development* 41: 3–17.

Bronshtein, I. N., and K. A. Semendyayev. 1985. *Handbook of Mathematics.* English translation edited by K. A. Hirsch. Leipzig edition. Based on the original 1945 Russian edition and the 1957 translation into German. New York: Van Nostrand Reinhold.

Brown, B. S. 2011. *Research Handbook on International Criminal Law.* Northampton, MA: Edward Elgar Publishing.

Brown, Lester R. 2009. *Plan B 4.0: Mobilizing to Save Civilization.* New York: W. W. Norton.

Brown, Phil. 2000. "Popular Epidemiology and Toxic Waste Contamination: Lay and Professional Ways of Knowing." In *Perspectives in Medical Sociology*, edited by Phil Brown, 157–181. Prospect Heights, IL: Waveland Press.

Brown, Phil, and Edwin J. Mikkelsen. 1990. *No Safe Place: Toxic Waste, Leukemia, and Community Action.* Berkeley: University of California Press.

Brown, Roger, and Andrew Gilman. 1960. "The Pronouns of Power and Solidarity." In *Style in Language*, edited by Thomas A. Sebeok, 253–276. Cambridge, MA: MIT Press.

Brown, Stephen. 2003. "The Problem with Marx on Rights." *Journal of Human Rights* 2, no. 4: 517–522.

Brown, Tony N., Sherrill L. Sellers, Kendrick T. Brown, and James S. Jackson. 1999. "Race, Ethnicity, and Culture in the Sociology of Mental Health." In *Handbook of the Sociology of Mental Health*, edited by Carol S. Aneshensel and J. C. Phelan, 167–182. New York: Springer.

Brown, Wendy. 1995. *States of Injury.* Princeton, NJ: Princeton University Press.

Browning, Christopher R. 1998. *Ordinary Men: Police Battalion 101 and the Final Solution in Poland.* 2nd ed. New York: HarperCollins.

Brownlie, I. 2008. *Principles of Public International Law.* 7th ed. Oxford: Oxford University Press.

Brubaker, R. 1996. *Nationalism Reframed: Nationhood and the National Question in the New Europe.* Cambridge, UK: Cambridge University Press.

Brubaker, Rogers, Mara Loveman, and Peter Stamatov. 2004. "Ethnicity as Cognition." *Theory and Society* 33: 31–64.

Brubaker, William Rogers. 1990. "Immigration, Citizenship, and the Nation-State in France and Germany: A Comparative Historical Analysis." *International Sociology* 5, no. 4: 379–407.

Brückner, H., and K. U. Mayer. 2005. "De-Standardization of the Life Course: What It Might Mean? And if It Means Anything, whether It Actually Took Place." In *The Structure of the Life Course: Standardized? Individualized? Differentiated?*, edited by R. Macmillan, 27–54. Advances in Life Course Research 9. Amsterdam: JAI Elsevier.

Brunnhölzl, Karl. 2007. "'Introduction' to Nagarjuna." In *In Praise of Dharmadhātu*, edited and translated by Karl Brunnhölzl, 21–55. Ithaca, NY: Snow Lion Publications.

Brunsson, Nils. 1985. *The Irrational Organization.* New York: John Wiley.

Brush, Lisa D. 2002. *Gender and Governance.* Lanham, MD: AltaMira Press.

Bryant, Rachel, and Robin Shura. 2010. "A Life Course of Human Rights? The 'Rising Sun' of Medical Decision-Making over the Life Course." Paper presented at the annual meeting of the American Sociological Association, Atlanta, Georgia, August 16, 2010.

Bucholz, Kathleen, and Lee Robins. 1989. "Sociological Research on Alcohol Use, Problems, and Policy." *Annual Review of Sociology* 15: 163–186.

Bullard, R. D. 1993. *Confronting Environmental Racism: Voices from the Grassroots.* Cambridge, MA: South End Press.

———. 2000. *Dumping in Dixie: Race, Class, and Environmental Quality.* Boulder, CO: Westview Press.

———. 2005. *The Quest for Environmental Justice: Human Rights and the Politics of Pollution.* San Francisco: Sierra Club Books.

Bullard, Robert D., and Beverly Wright, eds. 2009. *Race, Place, and Environmental Justice after Hurricane Katrina.* Boulder, CO: Westview Press.

Bulmer, Martin. 1984. *The Chicago School of Sociology: Institutionalization, Diversity, and the Rise of Sociological Research.* Chicago: University of Chicago Press.

Bumpass, L., and J. Sweet. 1989. *Children's Experience in Single-Parent Families: Implications of Cohabitation and Marital Transitions.* Madison: University of Wisconsin, Center for Demography and Ecology.

Bunch, Charlotte. 1990. "Women's Rights as Human Rights: Toward a Re-Vision of Human Rights." *Human Rights Quarterly* 12: 486–498.

Bunch, Charlotte, and Susana Fried. 1996. "Beijing '95: Moving Women's Human Rights from Margin to Center." *Signs* 22: 200–204.

Bunch, Charlotte, and Niamh Reilly. 1994. *Demanding Accountability: The Global Campaign and Vienna Tribunal for Women's Human Rights.* Rutgers, NJ: Center for Women's Global Leadership and the United Nations Development Fund for Women.

Burawoy, Michael. 1983. "Between the Labor Process and the State: The Changing Face of Factory Regimes under Advanced Capitalism." *American Sociological Review* 48: 587–605.

———. 2004. "Public Sociologies: Contradictions, Dilemmas and Possibilities." *Social Forces* 82, no. 4: 1603–1618.

———. 2005. "For Public Sociology." *American Sociological Review* 70: 4–28.

———. 2006. "A Public Sociology for Human Rights." Introduction to *Public Sociologies Reader,* edited by Judith Blau and Keri Iyall Smith, 1–18. Lanham, MD: Rowman & Littlefield.

———. 2007. "Evaluating 'No Child Left Behind.'" *The Nation.* http://www.thenation.com/doc/20070521/darling-hammond (accessed May 19, 2009).

Burawoy, Michael, and Janos Lukács. 1992. *The Radiant Past: Ideology and Reality in Hungary's Road to Capitalism.* Chicago: University of Chicago Press.

Burchardt, T. 2004. "Capabilities and Disability: The Capabilities Framework and the Social Model of Disability." *Disability and Society* 19: 735–751.

Bureau of Labor Statistics. 2011. "Union Members Summary." Bureau of Labor Statistics, U.S. Department of Labor. http://www.bls.gov/news.release/union2.nr0.htm (accessed January 21, 2011).

Burgers, Jan Herman. 1992. "The Road to San Francisco: The Revival of the Human Rights Idea in the Twentieth Century." *Human Rights Quarterly* 14: 447–477.

Burke, Mary C. 2010. "Transforming Gender: Medicine, Body Politics, and the Transgender Rights Movement." PhD diss., University of Connecticut, Storrs.

Burke, Roland. 2010. *Decolonization and the Evolution of International Human Rights.* Philadelphia: University of Pennsylvania Press.

Burkett, Elinor, and Frank Bruni. 1993. *A Gospel of Shame: Children, Sexual Abuse and the Catholic Church.* New York: Viking.

Burris, Beverly H. 1993. *Technocracy at Work.* Albany: State University of New York Press.

Burton, Linda. 1990. "Teenage Childbearing as an Alternative Life-Course Strategy in Mulit-Generational Black Families." *Human Nature* 1: 58–81.

Burton, Linda, Eduardo Bonilla-Silva, Victor Ray, Rose Buckelew, and Elizabeth H. Freeman. 2010. "Critical Race Theories, Colorism, and the Decade's Research on Families of Color." *Journal of Marriage and Family* 72: 440–459.

Busfield, J. 1996. *Men, Women and Madness: Understanding Gender and Mental Disorder.* London: Macmillan Press.

Bush, Melanie, and Deborah Little. 2009. "Teaching towards Praxis and Political Engagement." In *Engaging Social Justice: Critical Studies of 21st Century Social Transformation,* edited by David Fasenfest, 9–36. Leiden, the Netherlands: Brill.

Bush, Roderick. 2000. *We Are Not What We Seem: Black Nationalism and Class Struggle in the American Century.* New York: New York University Press.

———. 2009. *The End of White World Supremacy: Black Internationalism and the Problem of the Color Line.* Philadelphia: Temple University Press.

Bustamante, Jorge A. 1972. "The Wetback as Deviant: An Application of Labeling Theory." *American Journal of Sociology* 77: 706–718.

Butin, Daniel. 2010. *Service-Learning in Theory and Practice: The Future of Engagement in Higher Education.* New York: Palgrave.

Butler, Judith. 1990. *Gender Trouble: Feminism and the Subversion of Identity.* New York: Routledge.
——. 1993. *Bodies that Matter: On the Discursive Limits of "Sex."* New York: Routledge.
Butler, R. 2002 [1972]. *Why Survive? Being Old in America.* Baltimore: Johns Hopkins.
Button, Graham, ed. 1993. *Technology in Working Order: Studies of Work, Interaction and Technology.* London: Routledge.
Button, Graham, Jeff Coulter, John R. E. Lee, and Wes Sharrock. 1995. *Computers, Minds and Conduct.* Cambridge, UK: Polity Press.
Button, Tanya M. M., Michael C. Stallings, Soo Hyun Rhee, Robin P. Corley, Jason D. Boardman, and John K. Hewitt. 2009. "Perceived Peer Delinquency and the Genetic Predisposition for Substance Dependence Vulnerability." *Drug and Alcohol Dependence* 100: 1–8.
Buvinic, Mayra. 1998. "Women in Poverty: A New Global Underclass." Women in Politics. http://www.onlinewomeninpolitics.org/beijing12/womeninpoverty.pdf (accessed April 11, 2011).
Bynum, Thomas. 2009. "'We Must March Forward!': Juanita Jackson and the Origins of the NAACP Youth Movement." *Journal of African American History* 94: 487–508.
Caetano, R. 1984. "Self-Reported Intoxication among Hispanics in Northern California." *Journal of Studies of Alcohol and Alcoholism* 45: 349–354.
——. 1987. "Acculturation and Attitudes towards Appropriate Drinking among US Hispanics." *Alcohol and Alcoholism* 22: 427–433.
Cagatay, Nilufur. 2001. *Trade, Gender, and Poverty.* New York: United Nations Development Program.
Cahill, Sean. 2009. "The Disproportionate Impact of Antigay Family Policies on Black and Latino Same-Sex Couple Households." *Journal of African American Studies* 13: 219–250.
Caldwell, John C. 2006. *Demographic Transition Theory.* Dordrecht, The Netherlands: Springer.
Calhoun, Craig, ed. 2007. *Sociology in America: A History.* Chicago: University of Chicago Press.
California Legislature. Senate. 1943. *The Report of Joint Fact-Finding Committee on Un-American Activities in California.* Internet Archive. http://www.archive.org/details/reportofjointfac00calirich (accessed December 21, 2011).
Callahan, D. 1987. *Setting Limits: Medical Goals in an Aging Society.* New York: Simon and Schuster.
Callon, Michel. 1986. "Some Elements of a Sociology of Translation: Domestication of Scallops and the Fisherman of St. Brieuc Bay." In *Power, Action, and Belief: A New Sociology of Knowledge?,* edited by J. Law, 196–223. London: Routledge.
Callon, Michel, Pierre Lascoumes, and Yannick Barthe. 2009. *Acting in an Uncertain World: An Essay on Technical Democracy.* Translated by Graham Burchell. Cambridge, MA: MIT Press.
Callon, Michel, and Jean-Pierre Vignolle. 1975. "Breaking Down the Organization: Local Conflicts and Societal Systems of Action." *Social Science Information* 16, no. 2: 147–167.
Campbell, John. 2011. "Neoliberalism in Crisis: Regulatory Roots of the U.S. Financial Meltdown." In *Markets on Trial: The Economic Sociology of the U.S. Financial Crisis,* edited by Michael Lounsbury and Paul M. Hirsch, 65–102. Research in the Sociology of Organizations 30A. London: Emerald Group Publishing.
Campbell-Lendrum, Diarmid, and Majula Lusti-Narasimhan. 2009. "Taking the Heat out of the Population and Climate Change." World Health Organization. http://www.who.int/bulletin/volumes/87/11/09-072652/en/index.html (accessed August 21, 2012).
Cancian, Francesca M., and Steven L. Gordon. 1988. "Changing Emotion Norms in Marriage: Love and Anger in U.S. Women's Magazines since 1900." *Gender and Society* 2: 308–342.
Cantor, Daniel, and Juliet Schor. 1987. *Tunnel Vision: Labor, the World Economy, and Central America.* Boston: South End Press.
Caprioli, Mary. 2001. "Gendered Conflict." *Journal of Peace Research* 37, no. 1: 51–68.
Carlton-Ford, Steve. 2010. "Major Armed Conflicts, Militarization, and Life Chances: A Pooled Time Series Analysis." *Armed Forces and Society* 36: 864–889.
Carpenter, M. 2000. "'It's a Small World': Mental Health Policy under Welfare Capitalism since 1945." *Sociology of Health and Illness* 22: 602–620.
Carson, Rachel. 1962. *Silent Spring.* Boston: Houghton and Mifflin Press.
Casebeer, Kenneth M. 1989. "Drafting Wagner's Act: Leon Keyserling and the Pre-Committee Drafts of the Labor Disputes Act and the National Labor Relations Act." *Industrial Relations Law Journal* 11: 73–131.
Cassese, Antonio A., Guido G. Acquaviva, Mary D. Fan, and Alex A. Whiting. 2011. *International Criminal Law: Cases and Commentary.* Oxford: Oxford University Press.
Castel, R. 1988. *The Regulation of Madness: The Origins of Incarceration in France.* Oxford: Blackwell.
Castells, Manuel. 2000. *The Information Age: Economy, Society and Culture.* Vol. 1: *The Rise of the Network Society.* 2nd ed. Cambridge, UK: Cambridge University Press.
Cavanagh, Shannon E. 2007. "The Social Construction of Romantic Relationships in Adolescence: Examining the Role of Peer Networks, Gender, and Race." *Sociological Inquiry* 77: 572–600.

Centeno, Miguel Angel, and Joseph N. Cohen. 2010. *Global Capitalism: A Sociological Perspective.* Cambridge, MA: Polity.

Centers for Disease Control (CDC). 2011. "Tobacco Use: Targeting the Nation's Leading Killer." CDC. http://www.cdc.gov/chronicdisease/resources/publications/AAG/osh.htm (accessed January 1, 2011).

Cerna, Christina M. 1995. "East Asian Approaches to Human Rights: Proceedings of the Annual Meeting." *American Society of International Law* 89: 152–157.

Cerulo, Karen A. 2007. "The Forum Mailbag." *Sociological Forum* 22: 555–565.

Césaire, Aimé. 2001. *Discourse on Colonialism.* New York: Monthly Review Press.

Chabbott, Collette. 1999. "Development INGOs." In *Constructing World Culture: International Nongovernmental Organizations since 1875*, edited by J. Boli and G. M. Thomas. Stanford, CA: Stanford University Press.

Chambliss, William J. 1964. "A Sociological Analysis of the Law of Vagrancy." *Social Problems* 12, no. 1: 67–77.

———. 1989. "State Organized Crime." *Criminology* 27: 183–208.

Chandler, Alfred D., Jr. 1962. *Strategy and Structure: Chapters in the History of the American Industrial Enterprise.* Cambridge, MA: MIT Press.

———. 1977. *The Visible Hand: The Managerial Revolution in American Business.* Cambridge, MA: Harvard University Press.

Chapel Hill and Carrboro Human Rights Center. 2011. http://www.humanrightscities.org (accessed May 24, 2011).

Chapkis, Wendy. 2000. "Power and Control in the Commercial Sex Trade." In *Sex for Sale: Prostitution, Pornography, and the Sex Industry*, edited by Ronald Weitzer, 181–202. New York: Routledge.

Charlton, Sue Ellen, Jana Everett, and Kathleen Staudt. 1989. *Women, the State, and Development.* Albany: State University of New York Press.

Chase-Dunn, Christopher. 2005. "Social Evolution and the Future of World Society." *Journal of World-Systems Research* 11: 171–192.

Chase-Dunn, Christopher, Robert A. Hanneman, Richard Niemeyer, Christine Petit, and Ellen Reese. 2007. "The Contours of Solidarity and Division among Global Movements." *International Journal of Peace Studies* 12, no. 2: 1–16.

Chaves, Mark. 1994. "Secularization as Declining Religious Authority." *Social Forces* 72: 749–774.

Chavez, Leo R. 2008. *The Latino Threat: Constructing Immigrants, Citizens, and the Nation.* Stanford, CA: Stanford University Press.

Cheng, Shu-Ju Ada, and Lester R. Kurtz. 1998. "Third World Voices Redefining Peace." *Peace Review* 10 (March): 5–12. Available at http://works.bepress.com/lester_kurtz/7 (accessed January 20, 2012).

Cherlin, Andrew. 2008. "Public Display: The Picture-Perfect American Family? These Days, It Doesn't Exist." *Washington Post.* September 7, B1.

Chew, Sing. 1997. "For Nature: Deep Greening World Systems Analysis of the 21st Century." *Journal of World-Systems Research* 3, no. 3: 381–402.

———. 2001. *World Ecological Degradation: Accumulation, Urbanization, and Deforestation: 3000 BC–AD 2000.* New York: Altamira Press.

Child, J. 1972. "Organization Structure, Environment, and Performance: The Role of Strategic Choice." *Sociology* 6: 1–22.

Chiquiar, Daniel, and Gordon H. Hanson. 2005. "International Migration, Self-Selection, and the Distribution of Wages: Evidence from Mexico and the United States." *Journal of Political Economy* 113: 239–281.

Chirayath, Heidi T. 2007. "Difficult, Dysfunctional, and Drug-Dependent: Structure and Agency in Physician Perceptions of Indigent Patients." *Social Theory and Health* 5, no. 1: 30–52.

Chiswick, Barry, and Michael Wenz. 2005. "The Linguistic and Economic Adjustment of Soviet Jewish Immigrants in the United States, 1980 to 2000." IZA DP No. 1726. Institute for the Study of Labor. ftp://repec.iza.org/RePEc/Discussionpaper/dp1238.pdf (accessed July 17, 2012).

Chiswick, Barry R. 1988. "Illegal Immigration and Immigration Control." *Journal of Economic Perspectives* 2, no. 3 (summer): 101–115.

Chomsky, Noam, and Edward S. Herman. 1979. *The Political Economy of Human Rights: The Washington Connection and Third World Fascism.* Boston: South End Press.

Chomsky, Noam, Ralph Nader, Immanuel Wallerstein, Richard C. Lewontin, and Richard Ohmann. 1998. *The Cold War and the University: Toward an Intellectual History of the Postwar Years.* New York: The New Press.

Chow, Esther Ngan-ling. 1996. "Making Waves, Moving Mountains: Reflections on Beijing '95 and Beyond." *Signs* 22: 185–192.

Christakis, Nicholas A., and James H. Fowler. 2009. *Connected: The Surprising Power of Social Networks and How They Shape Our Lives.* New York: Simon and Schuster.

Chudacoff, H. 1989. *How Old Are You? Age Consciousness in America.* Princeton, NJ: Princeton University Press.

Ciganda, Daniel, Alain Gagnon, and Eric Tenkorang. 2010. "Child and Young Adult Headed Households in the Context of the AIDS Epidemic in Zimbabwe, 1988-2006." PSC Discussion Papers Series 24, no. 4: 1-17.

City of Eugene. 2011a. "Equity and Human Rights." City of Eugene. http://www.eugene-or.gov/diversity (accessed May 26, 2011).

———. 2011b. "Sustainable Eugene." City of Eugene. http://www.eugene-or.gov/sustainability (accessed May 26, 2011).

Clanton, Gordon. 1989. "Jealousy in American Culture, 1945-1975: Reflections from Popular Culture." In The Sociology of Emotions: Original Essays and Research Papers, edited by D. D. Franks and E. D. McCarthy, 179-193. Greenwich, CT: JAI Press.

Clapham, Andrew. 2007. Human Rights: A Very Short Introduction. New York: Oxford University Press.

Clapp, J. 2001. Toxic Exports: The Transfer of Hazardous Wastes from Rich to Poor Countries. Ithaca, NY: Cornell University Press.

Clark, Adele E., Laura Mamo, Jennifer R. Fishman, Janet Shim, and Jennifer Fosket. 2003. "Biomedicalization: Technoscientific Transformations of Health, Illness and U.S. Biomedicine." American Sociological Review 68, no. 2: 161-194.

Clark, Candace. 1990. "Emotions and Micropolitics in Everyday Life: Some Patterns and Paradoxes of 'Place.'" In Research Agendas in the Sociology of Emotions, edited by T. D. Kemper, 305-333. Albany: State University of New York Press.

Clark, Cindy Dell. 2010. A Younger Voice: Doing Child-Centered Qualitative Research. New York: Oxford University Press.

Clark-Ibáñez, Marisol. 2007. "Inner-City Children in Sharper Focus: Sociology of Childhood and Photo-Elicitation Interviews." In Visual Research Methods: Image, Society, and Representation, edited by Gregory C. Stanczak, 167-196. Thousand Oaks, CA: Sage Publications.

Clarke, Lee. 2006. Worst Cases: Terror and Catastrophe in the Popular Imagination. Chicago: University of Chicago Press.

Clawson, Dan. 1980. Bureaucracy and the Labor Process. New York: Monthly Review Press.

———. 2003. The Next Upsurge: Labor and the New Social Movements. Ithaca, NY: ILR Press.

Clayton, Mark. 2011. "Fukushima Meltdown Could Be Template for Nuclear Terrorism, Study Says." Christian Science Monitor. June 7.

Clegg, Stewart. 1989. Frameworks of Power. London: Sage.

———. 1990. Modern Organization: Organization Studies in the Postmodern World. London: Sage.

Clegg, Stewart, and Winton Higgins. 1987. "Against the Current: Organizational Sociology and Socialism." Organization Studies 8: 201-221.

Cohany, Sharon, and Emy Sok. 2007. Trends in Labor Force Participation of Married Mothers of Infants. Washington, DC: Bureau of Labor Statistics.

Cohen, Beth. 2007. Case Closed: Holocaust Survivors in Postwar America. New Brunswick, NJ: Rutgers University Press.

Cohen, Carl. 1986. "The Case for the Use of Animals in Biomedical Research." New England Journal of Medicine 315: 865-870.

Cohen, Cathy. 1999. The Boundaries of Blackness: AIDS and the Breakdown of Black Politics. Chicago: University of Chicago Press.

Cohen, Stanley. 2001. States of Denial: Knowing about Atrocities and Suffering. Cambridge, UK: Polity Press.

Cohn, Marjorie. 2001. "The World Trade Organization: Elevating Property Interests above Human Rights." Georgia Journal of International and Comparative Law 29: 427-440.

Cole, W. M. 2005. "Sovereignty Relinquished? Explaining Commitment to the International Human Rights Covenants, 1966-1999." American Sociological Review 70: 472-495.

Coleman, James. 1964. Introduction to Mathematical Sociology. New York: The Free Press.

———. 1990. Foundations of Social Theory. Cambridge, MA: Belknap Press.

———. 2006. The Criminal Elite. New York: Worth Publishers.

Coleman, Matthew. 2007. "Immigration Geopolitics beyond the Mexico-U.S. Border." Antipode 39: 54-76.

Colker, R. 2005. The Disability Pendulum the First Decade of the Americans with Disabilities Act. New York: New York University Press.

Collett, Jessica L., and Omar Lizardo. 2009. "A Power-Control Theory of Gender and Religiosity." Journal for the Scientific Study of Religion 48: 213-231.

Collins, Patricia Hill. 1990. Black Feminist Thought: Knowledge, Consciousness, and the Politics of Empowerment. New York: Routledge, Chapman and Hall.

———. 1993. "Toward a New Vision: Race, Class, and Gender as Categories of Analysis and Connection." Race, Sex and Class 1: 25-45.

———. 1994. "Shifting the Center: Race, Class, and Feminist Theorizing about Motherhood." In Representations of Motherhood, edited by Donna Basin and Margaret Honey, 56-74. New Haven, CT: Yale University Press.

———. 2005. *Black Sexual Politics*. New York: Routledge.

Collins, Randall. 1974. "Three Faces of Cruelty: Towards a Comparative Sociology of Violence." *Theory and Society* 1, no. 4 (winter): 415–440.

———. 1975. *Conflict Sociology: Toward an Explanatory Science*. New York: Academic Press.

———. 1990. "Stratification, Emotional Energy, and the Transient Emotions." In *Research Agendas in the Sociology of Emotions*, edited by T. D. Kemper, 27–57. Albany: State University of New York Press.

———. 1998. *The Sociology of Philosophies: A Global Theory of Intellectual Change*. Cambridge, MA: Belknap Press.

———. 2008. *Violence*. Princeton, NJ: Princeton University Press.

Coltraine, Scott, and Michelle Adams. 2008. *Gender and Families*. Lanham, MD: AltaMira Press.

Columbia Law School Human Rights Institute and International Association of Official Human Rights Agencies (IAOHRA). 2010. *State and Local Human Rights Agencies: Recommendations for Advancing Opportunity and Equality through an International Human Rights Framework*. New York: Columbia Law School Human Rights Institute and IAOHRA.

Comin, Diego, and Bart Hobijn. 2004. "Cross-Country Technology Adoption: Making the Theories Face the Facts." *Journal of Monetary Economics* 51: 39–83.

Committee on Science, Engineering, and Public Policy (COSEPUP). 1995. *On Being a Scientist: Responsible Conduct in Research*. Washington, DC: National Academy Press.

Committee on the Elimination of Racial Discrimination. 2000. "General Recommendation 25, Gender Related Dimensions of Racial Discrimination." University of Minnesota, Human Rights Library. http://www1.umn.edu/humanrts/gencomm/genrexxv.htm (accessed September 6, 2012).

Commons, John, Ulrich Bonnell Phillips, Eugene Allen Gilmore, and John B. Andrews, eds. 1910–1911. *A Documentary History of American Industrial Society*. 11 vols. Cleveland, OH: Arthur Clark Company.

———. 1918–1935. *History of Labor in the United States*. 4 vols. New York: Macmillan.

Compa, Lance. 2000. *Unfair Advantage: Workers' Freedom of Association in the United States under International Human Rights Standards*. Ithaca, NY: ILR Press.

Comte, Auguste. 1970. *Introduction to Positive Philosophy*. Indianapolis: Bobbs Merrill.

Conley, Dalton, Kate W. Strully, and Neil G. Bennett. 2003. *The Starting Gate: Birth Weight and Life Chances*. Berkeley: University of California Press.

Connell, Raeyn. 1987. *Gender and Power: Society, the Person, and Sexual Politics*. Stanford, CA: Stanford University Press.

———. 1995. "Symposium: Human Rights and the Sociological Project (Sociology and Human Rights)." *Australian and New Zealand Journal of Sociology* 31: 25–29.

———. 2005. *Masculinities*. Berkeley: University of California Press.

Conrad, Peter. 2000. "Medicalization, Genetics and Human Problems." In *Handbook of Medical Sociology*, edited by Chloe E. Bird, Peter Conrad, and Allen M. Fremont, 322–333. 5th ed. Upper Saddle River, NJ: Prentice Hall.

———. 2007. *Medicalization of Society: On the Transformation of Human Conditions into Treatable Disorders*. Baltimore: Johns Hopkins University Press.

Conrad, Peter, and Joseph Schneider. 1992. *Deviance and Medicalization: From Badness to Sickness*. Philadelphia: Temple University Press.

Cook, Daniel T., and John Wall, eds. 2011. *Children and Armed Conflict*. Hampshire, UK: Palgrave Macmillan.

Cook, J. A., and E. R. Wright. 1995. "Medical Sociology and the Study of Severe Mental Illness: Reflections on Past Accomplishments and Directions for Future Research." *Journal of Health and Social Behaviour* 35: 95–114.

Cooley, Charles Horton. 1964 [1902]. *Human Nature and the Social Order*. New York: Schocken Books.

Cooney, Mark. 1997. "From Warre to Tyranny: Lethal Conflict and the State." *American Sociological Review* 62: 316–338.

Coontz, S. 1992. *The Way We Never Were: American Families and the Nostalgia Trap*. New York: Basic Books.

———. 1997. *The Way We Really Are: Coming to Terms with America's Changing Families*. New York: Basic Books.

Coosmans, F., F. Grunfeld, and M. T. Kamminga. 2010. "Methods of Human Rights Research: A Primer." *Human Rights Quarterly* 32: 179–186.

Cornfield, Daniel B. 1989. *Becoming a Mighty Voice: Conflict and Change in the United Furniture Workers of America*. New York: Russell Sage.

Corrêa, S., and V. Muntarbhorn. 2007. "The Yogyakarta Principles on the Application of International Human Rights Law in Relation to Sexual Orientation and Gender Identity." The Yogyakarta Principles. http://www.yogyakartaprinciples.org/principles_en.htm (accessed July 21, 2010).

Corsaro, William A. 2005. *The Sociology of Childhood*. Newbury Park, CA: Pine Forge Press.

Corsaro, William A., and Laura Fingerson. 2003. "Development and Socialization in Childhood." In *Handbook of Social Psychology*, edited by John Delamater, 125–156. New York: Kluwer.

Cotterrell, Roger. 2007. "Sociology of Law." In *Encyclopedia of Law and Society: American and Global Perspectives*, edited by David Scott Clark, 1413–1419. Thousand Oaks, CA: Sage Publications.

Coulter, Jeff. 1979. *The Social Construction of Mind: Studies in Ethnomethodology and Linguistic Philosophy.* Totowa, NJ: Rowman & Littlefield.

———. 1982. "Remarks on the Conceptualization of Social Structure." *Philosophy of the Social Sciences* 12: 33–46.

———. 1989. *Mind in Action.* Atlantic Highlands, NJ: Humanities Press International.

Coulter, Jeff, and Wes Sharrock. 2007. *Brain, Mind, and Human Behaviour in Contemporary Cognitive Science: Critical Assessments of the Philosophy of Psychology.* Lewiston, NY: Edwin Mellen.

Council of Europe. 2011. http://www.coe.int (accessed May 24, 2011).

Council of Europe Congress of Local and Regional Authorities. 2010. "The Role of Local and Regional Authorities in the Implementation of Human Rights." Draft Resolution, Congress of Local and Regional Authorities, 18th Session, Strasbourg, France, March 1.

Courant, Richard. 1937 [1934]. *Differential and Integral Calculus.* Translated by E. J. McShane. 2 vols. New York: Wiley.

Courtwright, David. 2001. *Forces of Habit: Drugs and the Making of the Modern World.* Cambridge, MA: Harvard University Press.

Cousins, S. 1989. "Culture and Selfhood in Japan and the U.S." *Journal of Personality and Social Psychology* 56: 124–131.

Cox, Laurence, and Cristina Flesher Fominaya. 2009. "Movement Knowledge: What Do We Know, How Do We Create Knowledge and What Do We Do with It?" *Interface: A Journal for and about Social Movements* 1, no. 1: 1–20.

Cox, Laurence, and Alf Gunvald Nilsen. 2007. "Social Movements Research and the 'Movement of Movements': Studying Resistance to Neoliberal Globalisation." *Sociology Compass* 1, no. 2: 424–442.

Cox, Oliver Cromwell. 1948. *Caste, Class, and Race: A Study in Social Dynamics.* New York: Monthly Review Press.

Crane, Diana. 2005. "Democracy and Globalization in the Global Economy." In *The Blackwell Companion to the Sociology of Culture*, edited by Mark D. Jacobs and Nancy Weiss Hanrahan. 412–427. Malden, MA: Blackwell.

Craven, Matthew C. R. 1995. *The International Covenant on Economic, Social, and Cultural Rights: A Perspective on Its Development.* Oxford: Oxford University Press.

Crenshaw, Kimberlé. 1991. "Mapping the Margins: Intersectionality, Identity Politics, and Violence against Women of Color." *Stanford Law Review* 43: 1241–1299.

Cress, Daniel M., and David A. Snow. 1996. "Mobilization at the Margins: Resources, Benefactors, and the Viability of Homeless Social Movement Organizations." *American Sociological Review* 61: 1089–1109.

———. 2000. "The Outcomes of Homeless Mobilization: The Influence of Organization, Disruption, Political Mediation, and Framing." *American Journal of Sociology* 105: 1063–1104.

Crimmins, Eileen M. 1993. "Demography: The Past 30 Years, the Present, and the Future." *Demography* 30, no. 4: 571–594.

Crocker, Jennifer. 2002. "Contingencies of Self-Worth: Implications for Self-Regulation and Psychological Vulnerability." *Self and Identity* 1: 143–149.

Croissant, Jennifer, and Sal Restivo. 1995. "Technoscience or Tyrannoscience Rex: Science and Progressive Thought." In *Ecologies of Knowledge*, edited by Susan Leigh Star, 39–87. Albany: State University of New York Press.

Crompton, Tom, and Tim Kasser. 2009. *Meeting Environmental Challenges: The Role of Human Identity.* Devon, UK: Green Books (World Wildlife Fund).

Crooms, Lisa. 1997. "Indivisible Rights and Intersectional Identities or 'What Do Women's Rights Have to Do with the Race Convention?'" *Howard Law Journal* 40: 620–640.

Crosnoe, Robert. 2011. *Fitting In, Standing Out: Navigating the Social Challenges of High School to Get an Education.* New York: Cambridge University Press.

Crosnoe, Robert, and Glen H. Elder Jr. 2004. "From Childhood to the Later Years: Pathways of Human Development." *Research on Aging* 26, no. 6: 623–654.

Croteau, David, William Hoynes, and Charlotte Ryan. 2005. *Rhyming Hope and History: Activists, Academics, and Social Movement Scholarship.* Minneapolis: University of Minnesota Press.

Cummins, E. E. 1936. "Workers' Education in the United States." *Social Forces* 14: 597–605.

Cunningham, W. P., and M. A. Cunningham. 2008. *Principles of Environmental Science: Inquiry and Applications.* New York: McGraw-Hill.

Currah, Paisley, Richard M. Juang, and Shannon Price Minter. 2006. *Transgender Rights.* Minneapolis: University of Minnesota Press.

Currie, Elliot. 1994. *Reckoning: Drugs, the Cities, and the American Future.* New York: Hill and Wang.

Cutler, J. Elbert. 1907. "Contribution to Symposium on How Should Sociology Be Taught as a College or University Course." *American Journal of Sociology* 12: 604–606.

Cyert, Richard, and James March. 1963. *A Behavioral Theory of the Firm.* 2nd ed. Malden, MA: Wiley-Blackwell.

Czarniawska, Barbara. 1997. *Narrating the Organization: Dramas of Institutional Identity.* Chicago: University of Chicago Press.

D'Cunha, J. 2005. "Claim and Celebrate Women Migrants' Human Rights through CEDAW: The Case of Women Migrant Workers, a UNIFEM Briefing Paper." United Nations Entity for Gender Equality and the Empowerment of Women. http://www.unwomen-eseasia.org/projects/migrant/mig_pub.htm (accessed July 17, 2012).

Dabbs, J. M., Jr., and M. G. Dabbs. 2000. *Heroes, Rogues, and Lovers: Testosterone and Behavior.* New York: McGraw-Hill.

Dagum, Camilo. 1983. "Income Inequality Measures." In *Encyclopedia of Statistical Sciences,* edited by Samuel Kotz, Norman L. Johnson, and Campbell B. Read, 4:34–40. New York: Wiley.

Dahrendorf, Ralf. 1958. "Out of Utopia: Toward a Reorientation of Sociological Analysis." *American Journal of Sociology* 64, no. 2: 115–127.

Dalai Lama and Paul Eckman. 2008. *Emotional Awareness: Overcoming the Obstacles to Psychological Balance and Compassion.* Foreword by Daniel Goleman. New York: Times Books, Henry Holt and Co.

Dallaire, Bernadette, Michael McCubbin, Paul Morin, and David Cohen. 2000. "Civil Commitment Due to Mental Illness and Dangerousness: The Union of Law and Psychiatry within a Treatment-Control System." *Sociology of Health and Illness* 22: 679–699.

Daniels, Roger. 2004. *Guarding the Golden Door: American Immigration Policy and Immigrants since 1882.* New York: Hill and Wang.

Dannefer, Dale. 1984. "Adult Development and Social Theory: A Paradigmatic Reappraisal." *American Sociological Review* 49: 1.

———. 2010. "Age, the Life Course, and the Sociological Imagination: Prospects for Theory." In *Handbook of Aging and the Social Sciences,* edited by R. Binstock and L. George, 3–16. New York: Academic.

Dannefer, Dale, and P. Uhlenberg. 1999. "Paths of the Life Course: A Typology." In *Handbook of Theories of Aging,* edited by V. Bengtson and K. W. Schaie, 306–327. New York: Springer.

Dannefer, Dale, and Chris Phillipson, eds. 2010. *International Handbook of Social Gerontology.* London: Sage.

Dannefer, Dale, and Robin Shura. 2007. "The Second Demographic Transition, Aging Families, and the Aging of the Institutionalized Life Course." In *Social Structures: Demographic Changes and the Well-Being of Older Persons,* edited by K. Warner Schaie and Peter Uhlenberg, 212–229. New York: Springer.

———. 2009. "Experience, Social Structure and Later Life: Meaning and Old Age in an Aging Society." In *International Handbook of Population Aging,* edited by P. Uhlenberg, 747–755. Dordrecht, the Netherlands: Springer.

Danto, Arthur C. 1967. "Philosophy of Science, Problems of." In *Encyclopedia of Philosophy,* edited by Paul Edwards, 6:296–300. New York: Macmillan.

Davidson, Alastair. 2010. "History, Human Rights and the Left." *Thesis Eleven* 100: 106–116.

Davis, Gerald F., Doug McAdam, W. Richard Scott, and Mayer N. Zald, eds. 2005. *Social Movements and Organization Theory.* Cambridge, UK: Cambridge University Press.

Davis, Jeff, and Daniel Were. 2008. "A Longitudinal Study of the Effects of Uncertainty on Reproductive Behaviors." *Human Nature* 19: 426–452.

Davis, Kingsley, and Wilbert E. Moore. 1945. "Some Principles of Stratification." *American Sociological Review* 10: 242–249.

De Genova, Nicholas. 2005. "In Re: Rodriguez." In *The Oxford Encyclopedia of Latinos and Latinas in the United States,* edited by S. Oboler and D. J. González, 2:380–382. New York: Oxford University Press.

De Haas, H. 2010. "Migration and Development: A Theoretical Perspective." *International Migration Review* 44: 227–264.

De Souza, Roger-Mark, J. S. Williams, and F. A. B. Meyerson. 2003. "Critical Links: Population, Health, and Environment." *Population Bulletin* 58: 1–43.

De Than, C., and E. Shorts. 2003. *International Criminal Law and Human Rights.* London: Sweet and Maxwell.

Deci, Edward L., and Richard M. Ryan. 2000. "The 'What' and 'Why' of Goal Pursuits: Human Needs and the Self-Determination of Behavior." *Psychological Inquiry* 11: 227–268.

Deegan, Mary Jo. 1988. *Jane Addams and the Men of the Chicago School, 1892–1918.* New Brunswick, NJ: Transaction Publishers.

———. 2002. *Race, Hull House, and the University of Chicago: A New Conscience against Ancient Evils.* Westport, CT: Praeger.

Deflem, Mathieu. 2008. *Sociology of Law: Visions of a Scholarly Tradition.* Cambridge, UK: Cambridge University Press.

Deflem, Mathieu, and Stephen Chicoine. 2011. "The Sociological Discourse on Human Rights: Lessons from the Sociology of Human Rights." *Development and Society* 40, no. 1 (June): 101–115.

Delanty, Gerard. 2009. *The Cosmopolitan Imagination.* New York: Cambridge University Press.

Della Porta, Donatella, Massimillano Andretta, Lorenzo Mosca, and Herbert Reiter. 2006. *Globalization from Below: Transnational Activists and Protest Networks.* Minneapolis: University of Minnesota Press.

DeMartino, George. 2010. "On Marxism, Institutionalism and the Problem of Labor Exploitation." *Rethinking Marxism* 22, no. 4: 524-530.

Denning, Michael. 1998. *The Cultural Front: The Laboring of American Culture in the Twentieth Century*. New York: Verso Books.

Denzin, Norman. 1997. *Interpretative Ethnography: Ethnographic Practices for the 21st Century*. Thousand Oaks, CA: Sage.

———. 2010. *The Qualitative Manifesto: A Call to Arms*. Walnut Creek, CA: Left Coast Press.

Denzin, Norman, and Michael D. Giardina. 2010. *Qualitative Inquiry and Human Rights*. Walnut Creek, CA: Left Coast Press.

Department of Homeland Security (DHS). 2009. "Immigration Statistics." DHS. http://www.dhs.gov/files/statistics/immigration.shtm (accessed January 31, 2011).

———. 2010. "Immigration Enforcement Actions: 2009." DHS. http://www.dhs.gov/xlibrary/assets/statistics/publications/enforcement_ar_2009.pdf (accessed October 12, 2010).

Department of Justice. 2010. "Crime in the United States, 2009." Federal Bureau of Investigation. http://www2.fbi.gov/ucr/cius2009/arrests/index.html (accessed January 1, 2011).

Derrida, Jacques. 1978. *Writing and Difference*. London: Routledge and Kegan Paul.

———. 2004. "The Animal that I Am." In *Animal Philosophy: Essential Readings in Continental Thought*, edited by Peter Allerton and Matthew Calarco: 113-128. New York: Continuum.

Desai, Manisha. 2002. "Transnational Solidarity: Women's Agency, Structural Adjustment, and Globalization." In *Women's Activism and Globalization: Linking Local Struggles and Transnational Politics*, edited by N. Naples and M. Desai, 15-33. New York: Routledge.

———. 2005. "Transnationalism: The Face of Feminist Politics Post-Beijing." *International Social Science Journal* 57: 319-330.

DeSouza, Roger-Mark, John S. Williams, and Frederick A. B. Meyerson. 2003. *Critical Links: Population, Health, and the Environment*. Population Resource Bureau. http://www.prb.org/Publications/PopulationBulletins/2003/CriticalLinksPopulationHealthandtheEnvironmentPDF340KB.aspx.

———. 2006. "From Autonomies to Solidarities: Transnational Feminist Practices." In *Handbook of Gender and Women's Studies*, edited by Kathy Davis, Mary Evans, and Judith Lorber, 459-470. Thousand Oaks, CA: Sage Publications.

DeVault, Marjorie. 2007. "Knowledge from the Field." In *Sociology in America: A History*, edited by Craig Calhoun, 155-182. Chicago: University of Chicago Press.

Devinatz, Victor G. 2003. "U.S. Labor and Industrial Relations Historiography: A Review Essay." In *Work in America: An Encyclopedia of History, Policy and Society*, edited by Carl E. Van Horn and Herbert A. Schaffner, xxvii-xxxviii. Santa Barbara, CA: ABC-CLIO.

Devine, Patricia G. 1989. "Stereotypes and Prejudice: Their Automatic and Controlled Components." *Journal of Personality and Social Psychology* 56: 5-18.

Dewey, J. 1922. *Human Nature and Conduct*. New York: Holt.

———. 1980 [1934]. *Art as Experience*. Reprint. New York: Perigree.

———. 1985. *The Later Works, 1925-1953*. Vol. 6. Carbondale: Southern Illinois University Press.

Dhamoon, Rita. 2010. *Identity/Difference Politics: How Difference Is Produced, and Why It Matters*. Vancouver: University of British Columbia.

Diamond, Lisa. 2006. "Careful What You Ask For: Reconsidering Feminist Epistemology and Autobiographical Narrative in Research on Sexual Identity Development." *Signs* 31: 471-491.

Diaz-McConnell, Eileen. 2011. "An 'Incredible Number of Latinos and Asians': Media Representations of Racial and Ethnic Population Change in Atlanta, Georgia." In "Latino/as and the Media," special issue, *Latino Studies* 9, no. 2/3: 177-197.

Dill, Bonnie Thornton. 1983. "Race, Class, and Gender: Prospects for an All-Inclusive Sisterhood." *Feminist Studies* 9: 131-150.

Dillon, Michele. 2005. "Sexuality and Religion: Negotiating Identity Differences." In *The Blackwell Companion to the Sociology of Culture*, edited Mark D. Jacobs and Nancy Weiss Hanrahan, 220-233. Malden, MA: Blackwell.

DiMaggio, Paul, and Walter W. Powell. 1983. "The Iron Cage Revisited: Institutional Isomorphism and Collective Rationality in Organizational Fields." *American Sociological Review* 48: 147-160.

DiMauro, Diane. 1995. *Sexuality Research in the United States: An Assessment of the Social and Behavioral Sciences*. New York: Social Sciences Research Council.

DiPrete, Thomas, and Gregory M. Eirich. 2006. "Cumulative Advantage as a Mechanism for Inequality: A Review of Theoretical and Empirical Developments." *Annual Review of Sociology* 32: 271-297.

Dixit, Raman. 2010. "Naxalite Movement in India: The State's Response." *Journal of Defense Studies* 4, no. 2: http://www.idsa.in/jds/4_2_2010_NaxaliteMovementinIndia_rdixit (accessed July 17, 2012).

Dixon, D., and L. Maher. 2002. "Anh Hai: Policing, Culture, and Social Exclusion in a Street Heroin Market." *Policing and Society* 12, no. 2: 93–110.

Dobbin, Frank. 1994. *Forging Industrial Policy: The United States, Britain, and France in the Railway Age.* Cambridge, UK: Cambridge University Press.

———. 2005. "Comparative and Historical Perspectives in Economic Sociology." In *The Handbook of Economic Sociology*, edited by Neil Smelser and Richard Swedberg, 26–48. 2nd ed. Princeton, NJ: Princeton University Press and Russell Sage Foundation.

Dolgon, Corey, and Chris Baker. 2010. *Social Problems: A Service Learning Approach.* Thousand Oaks, CA: Sage Publications.

Dolgon, Corey, and Mary Chayko. 2010. *Pioneers of Public Sociology: 30 Years of Humanity and Society.* New York: Sloan Publishing.

Dolgon, Corey, Mavis Morton, Tim Maher, and James Pennell. 2012. "Civic Engagement and Public Sociology: Two 'Movements' in Search of a Mission." *Journal of Applied Social Science* 6, no. 1: 5–30.

Domhoff, G. William. 2005. "Power at the Local Level: Growth Coalition Theory." University of Santa Cruz Sociology Department. http://sociology.ucsc.edu/whorulesamerica/local/growth_coalition_theory.html (accessed May 29, 2011).

Donaldson, L. 1987. "Strategy and Structural Adjustment to Regain Fit and Performance: In Defence of Contingency Theory." *Journal of Management Studies* 24, no. 1: 1–24.

Donnelly, Jack. 1982. "Human Rights and Human Dignity: An Analytic Critique of Non-Western Conceptions of Human Rights." *American Political Science Review* 76, no. 2: 303–316.

———. 1985. *The Concept of Human Rights.* London: St. Martin's Press.

———. 2003. *Universal Human Rights in Theory and Practice.* 2nd ed. Ithaca, NY: Cornell University Press.

———. 2006. *International Human Rights.* Boulder, CO: Westview Press.

———. 2007. "The Relative Universality of Human Rights." *Human Rights Quarterly* 28: 281–306.

Donoho, Douglas Lee. 1990–1991. "Relativism versus Universalism in Human Rights: The Search for Meaningful Standards." *Stanford Journal of International Law* 27: 345–391.

Donovan, Josephine, and Carol Adams, eds. 1995. *Animals and Women: Feminist Theoretical Explorations.* Durham, NC: Duke University Press.

———, eds. 2007. *The Feminist Care Tradition in Animal Ethics.* New York: Columbia University Press.

Douglas, Karen Manges, and Rogelio Sáenz. 2010. "The Making of 'Americans': Old Boundaries, New Realities." In *Teaching and Studying the Americas: Cultural Influences from Colonialism to the Present*, edited by A. B. Pinn, C. F. Levander, and M. O. Emerson, 139–156. New York: Palgrave Macmillan.

Douglas, M., and A. Wildavsky. 1982. *Risk and Culture: An Essay on the Selection of Technological and Environmental Dangers.* Berkeley: University of California Press.

Dowd, Jacquelyn Hall. 1993. *Revolt against Chivalry.* New York: Columbia University Press.

Dowse, L. 2001. "Contesting Practices, Challenging Codes: Self Advocacy, Disability Politics and the Social Model." *Disability and Society* 16: 123–141.

Doyal, Lesley. 1995. *What Makes Women Sick: Gender and the Political Economy of Health.* London: Macmillan.

———. 2001. "Sex, Gender, and Health: The Need for a New Approach." *British Medical Journal* (November 3): 323–331.

Dreby, Joanna. 2010. *Divided by Borders.* Berkeley: University of California Press.

Dreier, J. 2004. "Decision Theory and Morality." In *The Oxford Handbook of Rationality*, edited by A. Mele and P. Rawling, 156–181. Oxford: Oxford University Press.

Dreier, Peter, John Mollenkopf, and Todd Swanstrom. 2005. *Place Matters: Metropolitics for the Twenty-First Century.* 2nd ed. Lawrence: University Press of Kansas.

Drew, Paul, and John Heritage, eds. 2006. *Conversation Analysis.* 4 vols. London: Sage.

Drori, Gili, John Meyer, Francisco Ramirez, and Evan Schofer. 2003. *Science in the Modern World Polity: Institutionalization and Globalization.* Palo Alto, CA: Stanford University Press.

Drucker, Peter. 2000. *Different Rainbows.* London: Gay Men's Press.

DuBois, W. E. B. 1983. *Dusk of Dawn: An Essay toward an Autobiography of a Race Concept.* Piscataway, NJ: Transaction Publishers.

———. 2010 [1899]. *The Philadelphia Negro.* New York: Cosimo Classics.

Dudley-Marling, C. 2004. "The Social Construction of Learning Disabilities." *Journal of Learning Disabilities* 37: 482–489.

Dumas, Alex, and Bryan S. Turner. 2007. "The Life-Extension Project: A Sociological Critique." *Health Sociology Review* 16: 5–17.

Dunaway, Wilma A., ed. 2003. *Emerging Issues in the 21st Century World-System.* Vol. 2: *New Theoretical Directions for the 21st Century World System.* Westport, CT: Praeger Publishers.

Duncan-Andrade, Jeffrey, and Ernest Morrell. 2008. *The Art of Critical Pedagogy: Possibilities for Moving from Theory to Practice in Urban Schools.* New York: Peter Lang.

Dunn, Timothy J. 2001. "Border Militarization via Drug and Immigration Enforcement: Human Rights Implications." *Social Justice* 28: 7–30.

———. 2009. *Blockading the Border and Human Rights: The El Paso Operation that Remade Immigration Enforcement.* Austin: University of Texas Press.

Dunn, Timothy J., Ana Maria Aragones, and George Shivers. 2005. "Recent Mexican Migration in the Rural Delmarva Peninsula: Human Rights versus Citizenship Rights in a Local Context." In *New Destinations: Mexican Immigration in the United States,* edited by V. Zúñiga and R. Hernández-León, 155–183. New York: Russell Sage.

Durand, Jorge, William Kandel, Emilio A. Parrado, and Douglas S. Massey. 1996. "International Migration and Development in Mexican Communities." *Demography* 33: 249–264.

Durkheim, Émile. 1915. *L'Allemagne au-desus de tout: la mentalite allemande et la guerre.* Paris: A. Colin.

———. 1951a. *The Division of Labor in Society.* New York: The Free Press.

———. 1951b [1933]. *Suicide.* New York: The Free Press.

———. 1956. *Education and Sociology.* New York: The Free Press.

———. 1962. *Moral Education.* New York: The Free Press.

———. 1964 [1893]. *The Division of Labour in Society.* Translated by George Simpson. New York: The Free Press.

———. 1977. *The Evolution of Educational Thought.* Translated by Peter Collins. London: Routledge and Kegan Paul.

———. 1982. *The Rules of the Sociological Method,* edited by Steven Lukes. New York: The Free Press.

———. 1995. *Elementary Forms of Religious Life.* New York: The Free Press.

Duster, Troy. 1997. "Pattern, Purpose and Race in the Drug War." In *Crack in America: Demon Drugs and Social Justice,* edited by Craig Reinarman and Harry Levine, 260–287. Berkeley: University of California Press.

———. 2003. *Backdoor to Eugenics.* New York: Routledge.

———. 2005. "Race and Reification in Science." *Science* 307: 1050–1051.

Earl, Jennifer, and Katrina Kimport. 2011. *Digitally Enabled Social Change: Activism in the Internet Age.* Cambridge, MA: MIT Press.

Eaton, W. W. 1980. "A Formal Theory of Selection for Schizophrenia." *American Journal of Sociology* 86: 149–158.

Eckel, Jan. 2009. "Utopie der Moral, Kalkül der Macht: Menschenrechte in der globalen Politiknach 1945." *Archiv für Sozialgeschichte* 49: 437–484.

Economic Policy Institute (EPI). 2011. "Income Inequality: It Wasn't Always This Way." EPI. http://www.epi.org/economic_snapshots/entry/income_inequality_it_wasnt_always_this_way (accessed February 9, 2011).

Economist, The. 2006. "Asia: A Specter Haunting India: India's Naxalites." *The Economist* 380, no. 8491: 52.

Edelman, Lauren B. 2004. "Rivers of Law and Contested Terrain: A Law and Society Approach to Economic Rationality." *Law and Society Review* 38, no. 2: 181–198.

Edin, Kathryn, and Maria Kefalas. 2005. *Promises I Can Keep: Why Poor Women Put Motherhood before Marriage.* Berkeley: University of California Press.

Edin, Kathryn, Laura Lein, and Christopher Jencks. 1997. *Making Ends Meet: How Single Mothers Survive Welfare and Low-Wage Work.* New York: Russell Sage Foundation.

Edwards, Bob, and John D. McCarthy. 1992. "Social Movement Schools." *Sociological Forum* 7: 541–550.

Edwards, C., S. Staniszweska, and N. Crichton. 2004. "Investigation of the Ways in Which Patients' Reports of Their Satisfaction with Healthcare Are Constructed." *Sociology of Health and Illness* 26: 159–183.

Edwards, K. E. 2006. "Aspiring Social Justice Ally Identity Development: A Conceptual Model." *NASPA Journal* 43: 39–60.

Edwards, Richard. 1979. *Contested Terrain: The Transformation of the Workplace in the Twentieth Century.* New York: Basic Books.

Egan, Patrick J., and Kenneth Sherrill. 2009. *California's Proposition 8: What Happened, and What Does the Future Hold?* San Francisco: Evelyn and Walter Haas Jr. Fund and the National Gay and Lesbian Task Force Policy Institute.

Ehrenfeld, David. 2002. "The Cow Tipping Point." *Harper's* 305: 13–20.

Eisenstein, Hester. 1983. *Contemporary Feminist Thought.* Boston: G. K. Hall.

Elder, Glen H., Jr. 1999 [1974]. *Children of the Great Depression: Social Change in Life Experience.* 25th anniv. ed. Boulder, CO: Westview Press.

Elder, Glen H., Jr., Elizabeth Colerick Clipp, J. Scott Brown, Leslie R. Martin, and Howard S. Friedman. 2009. "The Life-Long Mortality Risks of World War II Experiences." *Research on Aging* 30, no. 4: 391–412.

Elias, Norbert. 1978. *The Civilizing Process.* New York: Urizen.

Elliott, Michael. 2007. "Human Rights and the Triumph of the Individual in World Culture." *Cultural Sociology* 1: 343–363.

———. 2008. "A Cult of the Individual for a Global Society: The Development and Worldwide Expansion of Human Rights Ideology." PhD diss., Emory University, Atlanta.

Elliott, Richard, Joanne Csete, Evan Wood, and Thomas Kerr. 2005. "Harm Reduction, HIV/AIDS, and the Human Rights Challenge to Global Drug Control Policy." *Health and Human Rights* 8, no. 2: 104–138.

Ellis, Lee. 2001. "The Biosocial Female Choice Theory of Social Stratification." *Social Biology* 48: 298–320.

———. 2004. "Sex, Status, and Criminality: A Theoretical Nexus." *Social Biology* 51: 144–165.

Ellis, Lee, Scott Hershberger, Evelyn Field, and Scott Wersinger. 2008. *Sex Differences: Summarizing More Than a Century of Scientific Research.* London: Psychology Press.

Ellwood, Charles A. 1907. "How Should Sociology Be Taught as a College or University Subject?" *American Journal of Sociology* 12: 588–606.

Elster, J. 1989. *Nuts and Bolts for the Social Sciences.* Cambridge, UK: Cambridge University Press.

———. 1992. *Local Justice: How Institutions Allocate Scarce Goods and Necessary Burdens.* New York: Russell Sage Foundation.

———. 2007. *Explaining Social Behavior: More Nuts and Bolts for the Social Sciences.* Cambridge, UK: Cambridge University Press.

Ely, Richard T. 1886. *The Labor Movement in America.* New York: Thomas Y. Crowell.

Ember, Carol R., and Melvin Ember. 1994. "War, Socialization, and Impersonal Violence: A Cross Cultural Study." *Journal of Conflict Resolution* 38: 620–646.

Emerson, Rupert. 1975. "The Fate of Human Rights in the Third World." *World Politics* 27: 201–226.

End Corporal Punishment. http://www.endcorporalpunishment.org.

Engels, Friedrich. 1847. "The Principles of Communism." Marxists Internet Archive. http://www.marxists .org/archive/marx/works/1847/11/prin-com.htm (accessed July 17, 2012).

England, Paula. 2005. "Gender Inequality in Labor Markets: The Role of Motherhood and Segregation." *Social Politics* 12: 264–288.

Engles, Eric. 2008. "Human Rights According to Marxism." *Guild Practitioner* 65, no. 249: 249–256.

Enloe, Cynthia. 1990. *Bananas, Beaches, and Bases: Making Feminist Sense of International Politics.* Berkeley: University of California Press.

———. 2000. *Maneuvers: The International Politics of Militarizing Women's Lives.* Berkeley: University of California Press.

———. 2007. *Globalization and Militarism: Feminists Make the Link.* Boulder, CO: Rowman & Littlefield.

Epstein, L., and J. Knight. 1998. *The Choices Justices Make.* Washington, DC: Congressional Quarterly.

Epstein, Steven. 1998. *Impure Science: AIDS, Activism, and the Politics of Knowledge.* Berkeley: University of California Press.

Ericksen, Julia A., with Sally A. Steffen. 2001. *Kiss and Tell: Surveying Sex in the Twentieth Century.* Cambridge, MA: Harvard University Press.

Erikson, Kai. 1994. *A New Species of Trouble: Explorations in Disaster, Trauma and Community.* New York: W. W. Norton.

Ermann, M. David, and Richard J. Lundman, eds. 2002. *Corporate and Governmental Deviance: Problems of Organizational Behavior in Contemporary Society.* New York: Oxford University Press.

Ervin-Tripp, Susan. 1972. "On Sociolinguistic Rules: Alternation and Co-Occurrence." In *Directions in Sociolinguistics: The Ethnography of Communication,* edited by John J. Gumperz and Dell Hymes, 213–250. New York: Holt, Rinehart and Winston.

Eschbach, Karl, J. Hagan, N. Rodriguez, R. Hernandez-Leon, and S. Bailey. 1999. "Death at the Border." *International Migration Review* 33: 430–454.

Escober, Arturo. 2006. "Difference and Conflict in the Struggle over Natural Resources: A Political Ecology Framework." *Development* 49: 6–13.

Esping-Andersen, G. 1994. "Welfare States and the Economy." In *The Handbook of Economic Sociology,* edited by N. J. Smelser and R. Swedberg, 711–732. Princeton, NJ: Princeton University Press.

Esping-Andersen, Gøsta. 1999. *Social Foundations of Postindustrial Economies.* Oxford and New York: Oxford University Press.

Esposito, John L., and John O. Voll. 2001. "Islam and Democracy." *Humanities* 22 (November/December). http://www.neh.gov/news/humanities/2001-11/islam.html (accessed January 20, 2012).

Estes, C. L., S. Goldberg, S. Shostack, K. Linkins, and R. Beard. 2006. "Implications of Welfare Reform for the Elderly: A Case Study of Provider, Advocate, and Consumer Perspectives." *Journal of Aging and Social Policy* 19, no. 1: 41–63.

Etzioni, Amatai. 1961. *A Comparative Analysis of Complex Organizations.* Glencoe, IL: Free Press.

———. 1988. *The Moral Dimension: Toward a New Economics.* New York: The Free Press.

———. 2009. "Minorities and the National Ethos." *Politics* 29, no. 2 (June): 100–110.

Etzkowitz, Henry. 2003. "Innovation in Innovation: The Triple Helix of University-Industry-Government Relations." *Social Science Information* 42, no. 3: 293–338.

Eugene Human Rights City Project. 2011. http://www.humanrightscity.com (accessed May 26, 2011).

Eurobarometer. 2010. "Mental Health. Part One: Report." Special Eurobarometer 345/Eurobarometer 73.2. http://ec.europa.eu/health/mental_health/docs/ebs_345_en.pdf (accessed April 20, 2011).

Evans, Derek G. 2007. "Human Rights: Four Generations of Practice and Development." In *Educating for Human Rights and Global Citizenship*, edited by A. Abdi and L. Shultz, 1–12. Albany: State University of New York Press.

Evans, N. J., J. L. Assadi, and T. K. Herriott. 2005. "Encouraging the Development of Disability Allies." *New Directions for Student Services* 110: 67–79.

Evans, Tony. 2001a. "If Democracy, Then Human Rights?" *Third World Quarterly* 22: 623–642.

———. 2001b. *The Politics of Human Rights*. London: Pluto Press.

Ewen, Lynda Ann. 1991. "Coming Home: A Sociological Journey." In *Radical Sociologists and the Movement: Experiences, Lessons, and Legacies*, edited by Martin Oppenheimer, Martin J. Murray, and Rhonda F. Levine, 140–157. Philadelphia: Temple University Press.

Facio, Alda, and Martha I. Morgan. 2009. "Morgan Symposium on the Gender of Constitutional and Human Rights Law: Equity or Equality for Women? Understanding CEDAW's Equality Principles." *Alabama Law Review* 60: 1133.

Fakhoury, W., and S. Priebe. 2002. "The Process of Deinstitutionalization: An International Overview." *Current Opinion in Psychiatry* 15: 187–192.

Fals-Borda, Orlando. 1988. *Knowledge and People's Power*. New Delhi: Indian Social Institute.

Fanon, Frantz. 2005. *The Wretched of the Earth*. New York: Grove Press.

———. 2008. *Black Skin, White Masks*. Revised. New York: Grove Press.

Fantasia, Rick. 1988. *Cultures of Solidarity: Consciousness, Action, and Contemporary American Workers*. Berkeley: University of California Press.

Fararo, Thomas J. 1973. *Mathematical Sociology: An Introduction to Fundamentals*. New York: Wiley.

———. 1989. *The Meaning of General Theoretical Sociology: Tradition and Formalization*. Cambridge, UK: Cambridge University Press.

Farmer, Paul. 2003. *Pathologies of Power: Health, Human Rights, and the New War on the Poor*. Berkeley: University of California Press.

———. 2010. *Partner to the Poor: A Paul Farmer Reader*. Berkeley: University of California Press.

———. 2011. *Haiti after the Earthquake*. New York: Public Affairs.

Farnall, O., and K. A. Smith. 1999. "Reactions to People with Disabilities: Personal Contact versus Viewing of Specific Media Portrayal." *Journalism and Mass Communication Quarterly* 76: 659–672.

Farr, Thomas F., Richard W. Garnett IV, T. Jeremy Gunn, and William L. Saunders. 2009. "Religious Liberties: The International Religious Freedom Act." *Houston Journal of International Law* 31: 469–514.

Fasenfest, David. 2009. *Engaging Social Justice: Critical Studies of 21st Century Social Transformation*. Leiden, the Netherlands: Brill.

Faugeron, C., and M. Kokoreff. 1999. "Les practiques sociales des drogues: elements por una mise en perspective des recherché en France." *Societes Contemporaines* 36: 5–17.

Fausto-Sterling, Anne. 2000a. "The Five Sexes Revisited." *Sciences* 40: 18–23.

———. 2000b. *Sexing the Body: Gender Politics and the Construction of Sexuality*. New York: Basic Books.

Feagin, Joe R. 2006. *Systemic Racism: A Theory of Oppression*. New York: Routledge.

———. 2010. *The White Racial Frame: Centuries of Racial Framing and Counter-Framing*. New York: Routledge.

Feagin, Joe R., and Hernan Vera. 2008. *Liberation Sociology*. 2nd ed. Boulder, CO: Paradigm Publishers.

Feher, Ferenc, Agnes Heller, and Gyorgy Markus. 1986. *Dictatorship over Needs: An Analysis of Soviet Societies*. Oxford: Basil Blackwell.

Fehr, E., and S. Gächter. 2002. "Altruistic Punishment in Humans." *Nature* 415: 137–140.

Fein, Helen. 1979. *Accounting for Genocide*. Chicago: University of Chicago Press.

Fenster, T., ed. 1999. *Gender, Planning and Human Rights*. London and New York: Routledge.

Ferguson, J. 1994. *The Anti-Politics Machine: Development, Depoliticization, and Bureaucratic Power in Lesotho*. Minneapolis: University of Minnesota Press.

Ferguson, Kathy E. 1991. "Interpretation and Genealogy in Feminism." *Signs: Journal of Women in Culture and Society* 16: 322–339.

Ferraris, Maurizio. 1996 [1988]. *History of Hermeneutics*. Translated by Luca Somigli. Atlantic Highlands, NJ: Humanities Press International.

Ferree, Myra Marx, and Tetyana Pudrovska. 2006. "Transnational Feminist NGOs on the Web: Networks and Identities in the Global North and South." In *Global Feminism: Transnational Women's Activism, Organizing, and Human Rights*, edited by Myra Marx Ferree and Aili Mari Tripp, 247–274. New York: New York University Press.

Ferree, Myra Marx, and Aili Mari Tripp. 2006. *Global Feminism: Transnational Women's Activism, Organizing, and Human Rights*. New York: New York University Press.

Fieder, M., and S. Huber. 2007. "The Effects of Sex and Childlessness on the Association between Status and Reproductive Output in Modern Society." *Evolution and Human Behavior* 28: 392–398.

Field, Les W. 1994. "Review: Who Are the Indians? Reconceptualizing Indigenous Identity, Resistance, and the Role of Social Science in Latin America." *Latin American Research Review* 29: 237–248.

Fields, Belden. 2010. "Human Rights Theory, Criteria, Boundaries, and Complexities." In *Qualitative Inquiry and Human Rights*, edited by Norman Denzin and Michael Giardina, 66–81. Walnut Creek, CA: Left Coast Press.

Fillmore, K. M. 1987a. "Prevalence, Incidence and Chronicity of Drinking Patterns and Problems among Men as a Function of Age: A Longitudinal and Cohort Analysis." *British Journal of Addiction* 82: 77–83.

———. 1987b. "Women's Drinking across the Adult Life Course as Compared to Men's: A Longitudinal and Cohort Analysis." *British Journal of Addiction* 82: 801–811.

Fine, Gary Alan. 1993. "The Sad Demise, Mysterious Disappearance, and Glorious Triumph of Symbolic Interactionism." *Annual Review of Sociology* 19: 61–87.

———. 1995. *A Second Chicago School: The Development of a Postwar American Sociology.* Chicago: University of Chicago Press.

Fink, Leon. 2003. *The Mayan of Morganton.* Chapel Hill: University of North Carolina Press.

Finnegan, Amy, Adam R. Saltsman, and Shelley K. White. 2010. "Negotiating Politics and Culture: The Utility of Human Rights for Activist Organizing in the United States." *Journal of Human Rights Practice* 2, no. 3: 307–333.

Finnemore, Martha. 1999. "Rules of War and Wars of Rules: The International Red Cross and the Restraint of State Violence." In *Constructing World Culture: International Nongovernmental Organizations since 1875*, edited by J. Boli and G. M. Thomas, 149–168. Stanford, CA: Stanford University Press.

Firebaugh, Glenn. 1999. "Empirics of World Income Inequality." *American Journal of Sociology* 104: 1597–1630.

Firth, Roderick. 1952. "Ethical Absolutism and the Ideal Observer." *Philosophy and Phenomenological Research* 12: 317–345.

Fish, Stanley. 2008. *Save the World on Your Own Time.* New York: Oxford University Press.

Fitzgerald, Amy, Linda Kalof, and Thomas Dietz. 2009. "Slaughterhouses and Increased Crime Rates: An Empirical Analysis of Spillover from 'The Jungle' into the Surrounding Community." *Organization and Environment* 22: 158–184.

Fitzgerald, John. 2010. "Images of the Desire for Drugs." *Health Sociology Review* 19, no. 2: 205–217.

Fix, Michael, and Wendy Zimmermann. 2001. "All under One Roof: Mixed-Status Families in an Era of Reform." *International Migration Review* 35: 397–419.

Flacks, Richard. 2004. "Knowledge for What? Thoughts on the State of Social Movement Studies." In *Rethinking Social Movements: Structure, Culture, Emotion*, edited by J. Goodwin and J. Jasper, 135–155. Lanham, MD: Rowman & Littlefield.

———. 2005. "The Question of Relevance in Social Movement Studies." In *Rhyming Hope and History: Activists, Academics, and Social Movement Scholarship*, edited by David Croteau, William Hoynes, and Charlotte Ryan, 3–19. Minneapolis: University of Minnesota Press.

Fleischer, D. A., and F. Zames. 2001. *The Disability Rights Movement: From Charity to Confrontation.* Philadelphia: Temple University Press.

Fligstein, Neil. 2001. *The Architecture of Markets: An Economic Sociology of Twentieth Century Capitalist Societies.* Princeton, NJ, and Oxford, UK: Princeton University Press.

Fligstein, Neil, and Adam Goldstein. 2010. "The Anatomy of the Mortgage Securitization Crisis." In *Markets on Trial: The Economic Sociology of the U.S. Financial Crisis*, edited by Michael Lounsbury and Paul M. Hirsch, 20–70. Research in the Sociology of Organizations 30A. London: Emerald Group Publishing.

Flippen, Chenoa Anne. 2004. "Unequal Returns to Housing Investments? A Study of Real Housing Appreciation among Black, White, and Hispanic Households." *Social Forces* 82: 1523–1551.

Florini, Ann, Nihon Kokusai, Koryu Senta, and Carnegie Endowment for International Peace. 2000. *The Third Force: The Rise of Transnational Civil Society.* Tokyo: Japan Center for International Exchange, Washington Carnegie Endowment for International Peace, and Brookings Institution Press.

Fone, Byrne. 2000. *Homophobia: A History.* New York: Metropolitan Books.

Foner, A. 1974. "Age Stratification and Age Conflict in Political Life." *American Sociological Review* 39, no. 2: 187–196.

Foner, Eric. 1984. "Why Is There No Socialism in the United States?" *History Workshop Journal* 17: 57–80.

Forbes, Catherine, Merran Evans, Nicholas Hastings, and Brian Peacock. 2011. *Statistical Distributions.* 4th ed. New York: Wiley.

Fore, Matthew L. 2002. "Shall Weigh Your God and You: Assessing the Imperialistic Implications of the International Religious Freedom Act in Muslim Countries." *Duke Law Journal* 52: 423–453.

Forman, Tyrone A., and Amanda E. Lewis. 2006. "Racial Apathy and Hurricane Katrina: The Social Anatomy of Prejudice in the Post-Civil Rights Era." *Du Bois Review: Social Science Research on Race* 3: 175–202.

Forsythe, David. 2000. *Human Rights in International Relations*. New York: Cambridge University Press.
———. 2007. *The Humanitarians*. New York: Cambridge.
Fortman, Bas de Gaay. 2011. *Political Economy of Human Rights: Rights, Realities and Realization*. London: Routledge.
Foster-Fishman, Pennie, Tiffany Jimenez, Maria Valenti, and Tasha Kelley. 2007. "Building the Next Generation of Leaders in the Disabilities Movement." *Disability and Society* 22: 341–356.
Foucault, Michel. 1978. *The History of Sexuality: An Introduction*. Vol. 1. New York: Vintage Books.
———. 1980. *Power/Knowledge*, edited by Colin Gordon, translated by Colin Gordon, Leo Marshall, John Mephan, and Kate Soper. New York: Pantheon Books.
———. 1995 [1971]. *Madness and Civilization: A History of Insanity in the Age of Reason*. London: Tavistock.
Fox, Mary Frank. 1995. "From the President." *SWS Network News*, 2.
———. 2008. "Institutional Transformation and the Advancement of Women Faculty: The Case of Academic Science and Engineering." In *Higher Education: Handbook of Theory and Research*, edited by John C. Smart, 23: 73–103. New York: Springer.
———. 2010. "Women and Men Faculty in Academic Science and Engineering: Social-Organizational Indicators and Implications." *American Behavioral Scientist* 53, no. 7: 997–1012.
Francis, David, and Stephen Hester. 2004. *An Invitation to Ethnomethodology: Language, Society and Social Interaction*. London: Sage.
Franck, Thomas M. 2001. "Are Human Rights Universal?" *Foreign Affairs* 80: 191–204.
Frank, A. W. 1988. "Garfinkel's Deconstruction of Parsons's Plenum." *Discourse Analysis Research Group Newsletter* 4, no. 1: 5–8.
Frank, Andre G. 1991. *Third World War: A Political Economy of the Gulf War and New World Order*. Róbinson Rojas Archive. http://www.rrojasdatabank.info/agfrank/gulf_war.html (accessed July 17, 2012).
Frankenberg, Ruth. 1993. *White Women, Race Matters: The Social Construction of Whiteness*. London: Taylor and Francis.
Frankl, Viktor E. 1984 [1959]. *Man's Search for Meaning*. New York: Simon and Schuster.
Franklin, James C. 2008. "Shame on You: The Impact of Human Rights Criticism on Political Repression in Latin America." *International Studies Quarterly* 52: 187–211.
Franks, David. 2010. *Neurosociology: The Nexus between Neuroscience and Social Psychology*. New York: Springer.
Franks, David, and Thomas Smith. 2009. "A Neurosociological Perspective on Emotions. A Review Article by David Franks and Thomas Smith: Mind, Brain and Society: Toward a Neurosociology of Emotion." *Sociologie* 5: 244–256.
Fraser, Nancy. 1992. "Rethinking the Public Sphere: A Contribution to the Critique of Actually Existing Democracy." In *Habermas and the Public Sphere*, edited by Craig Calhoun, 109–142. Cambridge, MA: MIT Press.
———. 2009. *Scales of Justice: Reimagining Political Space in a Globalizing World*. New York: Columbia University Press.
Fraser, Nancy, and Axel Honneth. 2003. *Redistribution or Recognition: A Political-Philosophical Exchange*. Translated by Joel Golb, James Ingram, and Christiane Wilke. London: Verso.
Freedman, M. 2007. *Prime Time: How Baby Boomers Will Revolutionize Retirement and Transform America*. Cambridge, MA: Perseus Books.
Freeman, M. 2002. *Human Rights: An Interdisciplinary Approach*. Malden, MA: Blackwell Publishers.
Freeman, Marsha. 1999. "International Institutions and Gendered Justice." *Journal of International Affairs* 52: 513–533.
Freeman, Michael, ed. 2006. *Law and Sociology*. Oxford: Oxford University Press.
Freeman, R. B., and James L. Medoff. 1984. *What Do Unions Do?* New York: Basic Books.
Freese, Jeremy, and Brian Powell. 1999. "Sociobiology, Status, and Parental Investment in Sons and Daughters: Testing the Trivers-Willard Hypothesis." *American Journal of Sociology* 104: 1704–1743.
Freidson, Eliot. 1970. *Professional Dominance: The Social Structure of Medical Care*. New York: Atherton Press.
———. 2001. *Professionalism, the Third Logic*. Chicago: The Third Logic.
Freire, Paulo. 2000. *Pedagogy of the Oppressed*. New York: Continuum International.
Freire, Paulo, and Donald Macedo. 1987. *Literacy: Reading the Word and the World*. New York: Routledge.
Freudenburg, William R., and Robert Gramling. 2010. *Blowout: The BP Oil Disaster and the Future of Energy in America*. Cambridge, MA: MIT Press.
Freudenburg, William R., Robert B. Gramling, Shirley Laska, and Kai Erikson. 2009. *Catastrophe in the Making: The Engineering of Katrina and Disasters of Tomorrow*. Washington, DC: Island Press.
Frezzo, Mark. 2008. "Sociology, Human Rights, and the World Social Forum." *Societies without Borders* 3: 35–47.
———. 2011. "Sociology and Human Rights in the Post Development Era." *Sociology Compass* 5, no. 3: 203–214.
Frickel, Scott, and Kelly Moore, eds. 2006. *The New Political Sociology of Science: Institutions, Networks, and Power*. Madison: University of Wisconsin Press.

Frickel, Scott, and M. Bess Vincent. 2007. "Katrina, Contamination, and the Unintended Organization of Ignorance." *Technology in Society* 29: 181–188.

Friedkin, Noah E. 1998. *A Structural Theory of Social Influence.* Cambridge, UK: Cambridge University Press.

Friedländer, Saul. 2007. *Nazi Germany and the Jews, 1939–1945: The Years of Extermination.* New York: Harper.

Friedman, E. L. 1977. *Industry and Labour: Class Struggle at Work and Monopoly Capitalism,* 18–35. London: Macmillan Press.

Friedman, Elisabeth J. 1995. "Women's Human Rights: The Emergence of a Movement." In *Women's Rights, Human Rights: International Feminist Perspectives,* edited by Julia Peters and Andrea Wolper. New York: Routledge.

———. 2003. "Gendering the Agenda: The Impact of the Transnational Women's Rights Movement at the UN Conferences of the 1990s." *Women's Studies International Forum* 26: 313–331.

Friedman, Lawrence Meir. 2002. *American Law in the 20th Century.* New Haven, CT: Yale University Press.

Friedman, Milton. 1962. *Capitalism and Freedom.* Chicago: University of Chicago Press.

Friedman, Neil A. 1986. "A Human Rights Approach to the Labor Rights of Undocumented Workers." *California Law Review* 74, no. 5: 1715–1745.

Friedman, Thomas L. 2005. *The World Is Flat: A Brief History of the Twenty-First Century.* New York: Farrar, Straus and Giroux.

Friedrichs, David O. 2009. "On Resisting State Crime: Conceptual and Contextual Issues." *Social Justice* 36: 4–27.

Fritz, J. M. 1989. "Dean Winternitz, Clinical Sociology and the Julius Rosenwald Fund." *Clinical Sociology Review* 7: 17–27.

———. 1991. "The Emergency of American Clinical Sociology: The First Courses." *Clinical Sociology Review* 9: 15–26.

———. 2004. "Derriere la magie: models, approaches et theories de mediation [Behind the Magic: Mediation, Models, Approaches and Theories]." *Esprit Critique* 6. http://www.espritcritique.fr/0603/esp0603article01.pdf (accessed September 6, 2012).

———. 2005. "The Scholar-Practitioners: The Development of Clinical Sociology in the United States." In *Diverse Histories of American Sociology,* edited by A. J. Blasi, 40–56. Leiden, the Netherlands: Brill.

———. ed. 2008. *International Clinical Sociology.* New York: Springer.

———. 2010. "Special Education Mediation in the United States." In *People with Health Limitations in Modern Society,* edited by O. Dikova-Favorskaya, 268–285. Zhitomar, Ukraine: DZHIVIES.

Fritz, J. M., P. Bistak, and C. Auffrey. 2000. "The Bumpy Road to a Tobacco-Free Community: Lessons from Well City." *Sociological Practice* 2: 113–126.

Fritz, J. M., S. Doering, and F. Belgin Gumru. 2011. "Women, Peace, Security, and the National Action Plans." *Journal of Applied Social Science* 5, no. 1 (spring): 1–23.

Frost, Jennifer. 2001. *An Interracial Movement of the Poor: Community Organizing and the New Left in the 1960s.* New York: New York University Press.

Fry, C. L. 2007. "Demographic Transitions, Age, and Culture." In *Social Structures: Demographic Changes and the Well-Being of Older Persons,* edited by K. W. Schaie and P. Uhlenberg, 283–300. New York: Springer Publishing Co.

Fukumura, Yoko, and Martha Matsuoka. 2002. "Redefining Security: Okinawa Women's Resistance to U.S. Militarism." In *Women's Activism and Globalization: Linking Local Struggles and Transnational Politics,* edited by Nancy A. Naples and Manisha Desai, 239–263. New York: Routledge.

Fulcomer, David. 1947. "Some Newer Methods of Teaching Sociology." *Journal of Educational Sociology* 21: 154–162.

Fuller, Robert W. 2003. *Somebodies and Nobodies: Overcoming the Abuse of Rank.* Gabriola Island, BC: New Society Publishers.

Fuller, Robert W., and T. Scheff. 2009. "Bleeding Heart Liberals Proven Right: Too Much Inequality Harms a Society." *Huffington Post.* June 18.

Fung, Archon, and Erik Olin Wright. 2003. *Deepening Democracy: Institutional Innovations in Empowered Participatory Governance,* with contributions by Rebecca Neaera Abers et al. London: Verso.

Furstenberg, Frank. 2010. "On a New Schedule: Transitions to Adulthood and Family Change." *Transition to Adulthood* 20, no. 1: 68–87.

Gaer, Felice. 1998. "And Never the Twain Shall Meet? The Struggle to Establish Women's Rights as International Human Rights." In *The International Human Rights of Women: Instruments of Change,* edited by Carol Lockwood et al., 41–69. Washington, DC: American Bar Association Section of International Law and Practice.

Gaines, Atwood D. 2011. "Millennial Medical Anthropology: From There to Here and Beyond, or the Problem of Global Health." *Culture, Medicine and Psychiatry* 35, no. 1: 83–89.

Galbraith, John Kenneth. 1983. *The Anatomy of Power.* Boston: Houghton Mifflin.

Gallahue, Patrick. 2010. "Targeted Killing of Drug Lords: Traffickers as Members of Armed Opposition Groups and/or Direct Participants in Hostilities." *International Yearbook on Human Rights and Drug Policy* 1.

Galtung, Johan. 1996. *Peace by Peaceful Means*. Thousand Oaks, CA: Sage Publications.

Gamson, William A. 1988. "Review: [untitled]." *American Journal of Sociology* 94: 436–438.

———. 1992. *Talking Politics*. Cambridge, UK: Cambridge University Press.

Gamson, William A., and David S. Meyer. 1996. "Framing Political Opportunity." In *Comparative Perspectives in Social Movements: Political Opportunities, Mobilizing Structures, and Cultural Framings*, edited by Doug McAdam, John D. McCarthy, and Mayer N. Zald, 275–290. Cambridge, UK: Cambridge University Press.

Gandhi, Mahatma. 1993a. *The Collected Works of Mahatma Gandhi* (electronic book). New Delhi: Publications Division Government of India.

———. 1993b. *Gandhi and the Gita*, edited by. J. I. (Hans) Bakker. Toronto: Canadian Scholars' Press.

———. 1999. *The Collected Works of Mahatma Gandhi* (electronic book). 98 vols. New Delhi: Publications Division Government of India. http://www.gandhiserve.org/cwmg/cwmg.html (accessed January 20, 2012).

———. 2002. *The Essential Gandhi: An Anthology of His Writings on His Life, Work and Ideas*. New York: Vintage Publishers.

Gans, H. J. 1997. "Toward a Reconciliation of 'Assimilation' and 'Pluralism': The Interplay of Acculturation and Ethnic Retention." *International Migration Review* 31: 875–892.

Gardner, G., and T. Prugh. 2008. "Seeding the Sustainable Economy." In *State of the World: Innovations for Sustainable Economy*, edited by Linda Starke, 3–17. New York: W. W. Norton.

Garey, A. 1999. *Weaving Work and Motherhood*. Philadelphia, PA: Temple University Press.

Garfinkel, Harold. 1967. *Studies in Ethnomethodology*. Englewood Cliffs, NJ: Prentice Hall.

———, ed. 1986. *Ethnomethodological Studies of Work*. London: Routledge and Kegan Paul.

———. 2002. *Ethnomethodology's Program: Working Out Durkheim's Aphorism*, edited and introduced by Anne Warfield Rawls. Lanham, MD: Rowman & Littlefield.

———. 2006. *Seeing Sociologically: The Routine Grounds of Social Action*, edited and introduced by Anne Warfield Rawls. Boulder, CO: Paradigm.

———. 2008. *Toward a Sociological Theory of Information*, edited and introduced by Anne Warfield Rawls. Boulder, CO: Paradigm.

Garfinkel, Harold, and Harvey Sacks. 1970. "On Formal Structures of Practical Action." In *Theoretical Sociology: Perspectives and Developments*, edited by J. C. McKinney and E. A. Tiryakian, 338–366. New York: Appleton-Century-Crofts.

Garfinkel, Harold, and D. Lawrence Wieder. 1992. "Two Incommensurable, Asymmetrically Alternate Technologies of Social Analysis." In *Text in Context: Contributions to Ethnomethodology*, edited by Graham Watson and Robert M. Seiler, 175–206. Newbury Park, CA: Sage.

Gargano, G. 2008. "Art and Science in Italian Clinical Sociology." In *International Clinical Sociology*, edited by J. M. Fritz, 153–169. New York: Springer.

Garland, David. 1990. *Punishment in Modern Society*. Chicago: University of Chicago Press.

Garnett, Richard A. 1988. "The Study of War in American Sociology: An Analysis of Selected Journals, 1936–1988." *American Sociologist* 19: 270–282.

Garrett, William R. 2001. "Religion, Law, and the Human Condition." In *Religion in the Process of Globalization*, edited by Peter Beyer, 289–340. Würzburg: Ergon.

Garroutte, Eva M. 2001. "The Racial Formation of American Indians: Negotiating Legitimate Identities within Tribal and Federal Law." *American Indian Quarterly* 25, no. 2: 224–239.

———. 2003. *Real Indians: Identity and the Survival of Native America*. Los Angeles: University of California Press.

Gaston, Alonso, Noel Anderson, Celina Su, and Jeanne Theoharis. 2009. *Our Schools Suck: Students Talk Back to a Segregated Nation on the Failures of Urban Education*. New York: New York University Press.

Gaulejac, V. de. 2008. "On the Origins of Clinical Sociology in France: Some Milestones." In *International Clinical Sociology*, edited by J. M. Fritz, 54–71. New York: Springer.

———. 2010. Personal communication with J. M. Fritz. December 15.

Gavey, N., K. McPhillips, and M. Doherty. 2001. "'If It's Not On, It's Not On'—or Is It? Discursive Constraints on Women's Condom Use." *Gender and Society* 15: 917–934.

Gecas, Viktor. 1991. "The Self-Concept as a Basis for a Theory of Motivation." In *The Self-Society Dynamic*, edited by Judith A. Howard and Peter L. Callero, 171–185. Cambridge, UK: Cambridge University Press.

Gecas, Viktor, and Peter Burke. 1995. "Self and Identity." In *Sociological Perspectives on Social Psychology*, edited by Karen S. Cook, Gary Alan Fine, and James T. House, 156–173. Boston: Allyn and Bacon.

Geiger, Roger. 1986. *To Advance Relevant Knowledge: The Growth of American Research Universities, 1900–1940*. Oxford: Oxford University Press.

Gendron, Richard, and G. William Domhoff. 2008. *The Leftmost City: Power and Progressive Politics in Santa Cruz*. Boulder, CO: Westview Press.

Gerhardt, U. 1989. *Ideas about Illness: An Intellectual and Political History of Medical Sociology.* New York: New York University Press.

Gerstenfeld, Phylis, Diana Grant, and Chau-Pu Chiang. 2003. "Hate Online: A Content Analysis of Extremist Internet Sites." *Analyses of Social Issues and Public Policy* 3: 29–44.

Ghosh, B. 1992. "Migration-Development Linkages: Some Specific Issues and Practical Policy Measures." *International Migration* 30: 423–452.

GID Reform Advocates. 2008. "GID Reform Advocates." Transgender Forum. http://www.transgender.org/gird (accessed November 11, 2011).

Giddens, Anthony. 1985. *The Nation-State and Violence.* Cambridge, UK: Polity Press.

———. 1998. *The Third Way: The Renewal of Social Democracy.* Cambridge, UK: Polity Press.

———. 1999. *Runaway World.* London: Profile Books.

———. 2009. *The Politics of Climate Change.* Malden, MA: Polity Press.

Giesen, Bernhard. 2004. *Triumph or Trauma.* Boulder, CO: Paradigm.

Gill, Aisha K., and Anitha Sundari. 2011. *Forced Marriage: Introducing a Social Justice and Human Rights Perspective.* Boston: Zed Books.

Gill, Anthony James. 2008. *The Political Origins of Religious Liberty.* Cambridge, UK, and New York: Cambridge University Press.

Gill, D. A., and J. S. Picou. 1998. "Technological Disasters and Chronic Community Stress." *Society and Natural Resources* 11: 795–815.

Gill, E. 2002. "Unlocking the Iron Cage: Human Agency and Social Organization." *Studies in Symbolic Interaction* 25: 109–128.

Gillum, R. F. 2005. "Religiosity and the Validity of Self-Reported Smoking: The Third National Health and Nutritional Examination Survey." *Review of Religious Research* 47, no. 2: 190–196.

Ginsberg, Morris. 1942. "The Individualist Basis of International Law and Morals: The Presidential Address." *Proceedings of the Aristotelian Society* 43: i–xxvi.

Ginsburg, Tom. 2009. "The Clash of Commitments at the International Criminal Court." *Chicago Journal of International Law* 9, no. 2: 499–514.

Giroux, Henry. 1983a. "Theories of Reproduction and Resistance in the New Sociology of Education: A Critical Analysis." *Harvard Educational Review* 55: 257–293.

———. 1983b. *Theories and Resistance in Education.* South Hadley, MA: Bergin and Garvey.

———. 1997. *Pedagogy and the Politics of Hope: Theory, Culture, and Schooling.* Boulder, CO: Westview.

Glazebrook, Susan. 2009. "Human Rights and the Environment." *Victoria University Wellington Law Review* 40: 293–350.

Glazebrook, Trish, and Anthony Kola-Olusanya. 2011. "Justice, Conflict, Capital and Care: Oil in the Niger Delta." *Environmental Ethics* 33, no. 2: 163–184.

Glenn, Evelyn Nakano. 1999. "The Social Construction and Institutionalization of Gender and Race: An Integrative Framework." In *Revisiting Gender,* edited by Myra Marx Ferree, Judith Lorber, and Beth B. Hess, 3–43. New York: Sage.

———. 2002. *Unequal Freedom: How Race and Gender Shaped American Citizenship and Labor.* Cambridge, MA: Harvard University Press.

Gluck, Sherna Berger, with Maylei Blackwell, Sharon Cotrell, and Karen S. Harper. 1997. "Whose Feminism, Whose History? Reflections on Excavating the History of (the) U.S. Women's Movement(s)." In *Community Activism and Feminist Politics: Organizing across Race, Gender, and Class,* edited by Nancy A. Naples, 31–56. New York: Routledge.

Goffman, Erving. 1955. "On Face-Work: An Analysis of Ritual Elements in Social Interaction." *Psychiatry* 18, no. 3: 213–231.

———. 1956a. "The Nature of Deference and Demeanor." *American Anthropologist* 58, no. 3: 473–502.

———. 1956b. "Embarrassment and Social Organization." *American Journal of Sociology* 62, no. 3: 264–271.

———. 1959. *The Presentation of Self in Everyday Life.* 1st ed. Garden City, NY: Anchor.

———. 1961. *Asylums: Essays on the Social Situation of Mental Patients and Other Inmates.* New York: Anchor Books.

———. 1963. *Stigma: Notes on the Management of Spoiled Identity.* Englewood Cliffs, NJ: Prentice Hall.

———. 1979. *Gender Advertisements.* New York: HarperCollins.

———. 1986. *Frame Analysis: An Essay on the Organization of Experience.* Boston: Northeastern University Press.

Golash-Boza, Tanya. 2009. "The Immigration Industrial Complex: Why We Enforce Immigration Policies Destined to Fail." *Sociology Compass* 3: 295–309.

———. 2011. *Immigration Nation: Raids, Detentions, and Deportations in Post-9/11 America.* Boulder, CO: Paradigm Publishers.

Goldberg, David Theo. 1990. *Anatomy of Racism.* Minneapolis: University of Minnesota Press.

Goldberg, Walter. 1986. Personal communication.

Goldfield, Michael. 1987. *The Decline of Organized Labor in the United States*. Chicago: University of Chicago Press.
———. 1989. "Worker Insurgency, Radical Organization, and New Deal Labor Legislation." *American Political Science Review* 83: 1257–1282.
Goldfrank, Walter L. 2000. "Paradigm Regained? The Rules of Wallerstein's World-System Method." *Journal of World-Systems Research* 6, no. 2: 150–195.
Goldfrank, Walter L., David Goodman, and Andrew Szasz. 1999. *Ecology and the World System*. Westport, CT: Greenwood Press.
Goldring, Luin. 1998. "The Power of Status in Transnational Social Fields." In *Transnationalism from Below*, edited by Michael Smith and Luis Guarnizo, 165–195. London: Transaction Publishers.
Goldsmith, Jack, and Stephen D. Krasner. 2003. "The Limits of Idealism." *Daedalus* 132: 47–63.
Goldstein, Joseph, Burke Marshall, and Jack Schwartz. 1976. *The My Lai Massacre and Its Cover-Up: Beyond the Reach of Law? The Peers Commission Report with a Supplement and an Introductory Essay on the Limits of Law*. New York: The Free Press.
Goldstein, Joshua S. 2001. *War and Gender: How Gender Shapes the War System and Vice Versa*. Cambridge, UK: Cambridge University Press.
Goldstone, Jack. 2001. "Towards a Fourth Generation of Revolutionary Theory." *Annual Review of Political Science* 4: 139–187.
Goldthorpe, J. 2007. *On Sociology*. Stanford, CA: Stanford University Press.
Gonzales, Robeto G. 2011. "Learning to Be Illegal." *American Sociological Review* 76: 602–619.
González-López, Gloria. 2005. *Erotic Journeys: Mexican Immigrants and Their Sex Lives*. Berkeley: University of California Press.
Goodale, Mark. 2009. *Surrendering to Utopia: Anthropology of Human Rights*. Stanford, CA: Stanford University Press.
Goode, William J. 1978. *The Celebration of Heroes: Prestige as a Control System*. Berkeley: University of California Press.
Goodhard, Michael. 2003. "Origins and Universality in the Human Rights Debates: Cultural Essentialism and the Challenge of Globalization." *Human Rights Quarterly* 25: 935–964.
Goodwin, Glenn. 1987. "Humanistic Sociology and the Craft of Teaching." *Teaching Sociology* 15, no. 1: 19.
Goodwin, Jeff. 2001. *No Other Way Out*. New York: Cambridge University Press.
Goodwin, Jeff, and James M. Jasper. 2004. *Rethinking Social Movements: Structure, Meaning, and Emotion*. Lanham, MD: Rowman & Littlefield.
Goodyear-Smith, F., and S. Buetow. 2001. "Power Issues in the Doctor-Patient Relationship." *Health Care Analysis* 9: 449–462.
Goonesekere, Savitri. 2000. "Human Rights as a Foundation for Family Law Reform." *International Journal of Children's Rights* 8: 83–99.
Gordon, B. O., and K. E. Rosenblum. 2001. "Bringing Disability into the Sociological Frame: A Comparison of Disability with Race, Sex, and Sexual Orientation Statuses." *Disability and Society* 16: 5–19.
Gordon, Milton. 1964. *Assimilation in American Life*. New York: Oxford University Press.
Gordon, N., J. Swanson, and J. Buttigieg. 2000. "Is the Struggle for Human Rights a Struggle for Emancipation?" *Rethinking Marxism* 12, no. 3: 1–22.
Gordon, Steven L. 1981. "The Sociology of Sentiments and Emotions." In *Social Psychology: Sociological Perspectives*, edited by M. Rosenberg and R. H. Turner, 562–592. New York: Basic Books.
———. 1989a. "Institutions and Impulsive Orientations in Selectively Appropriating Emotions to Self." In *The Sociology of Emotions: Original Essays and Research Papers*, edited by D. D. Franks and E. D. McCarthy, 115–135. Greenwich, CT: JAI Press.
———. 1989b. "The Socialization of Children's Emotions: Emotional Culture, Competence, and Exposure." In *Children's Understanding of Emotion*, edited by C. Saarni and P. L. Harris, 319–349. Cambridge, UK: Cambridge University Press.
———. 1990. "Social Structural Effects on Emotions." In *Research Agendas in the Sociology of Emotions*, edited by T. D. Kemper, 180–203. Albany: State University of New York Press.
Gottfried, Heidi. 2012. *Gender, Work, and Economy: Unpacking the Global Economy*. Cambridge, UK: Polity Press.
Gould, K. A. 2009. "Technological Change and the Environment." In *Twenty Lessons in Environmental Sociology*, edited by K. A. Gould and T. L. Lewis, 95–106. New York: Oxford University Press.
Gould, Stephen Jay. 1981. *The Mismeasure of Man*. New York: Norton.
Gouldner, A. 1955. "Explorations in Applied Social Science." *Social Problems* 3: 169–181.
Government Accountability Office (GAO). 2005. *Denial of Federal Benefits*. GAO-05-238. GAO. http://www.gao.gov/new.items/d05238.pdf (accessed January 1, 2011).
Gramsci, Antonio. 1971. *Selections from the Prison Notebooks*. New York: International Publishers Co.

——. 1982. *Selections from the Prison Notebooks*. London: Lawrence and Wishart.

Gran, Brian K. 2008. "Public or Private Management? A Comparative Analysis of Social Policies in Europe." *Sociology Compass* 2: 1–29.

——. 2010a. "A Comparative-Historical Analysis of Children's Rights." NSF Grant, Law and Social Science Program.

——. 2010b. "Comparing Children's Rights: Introducing the Children's Rights Index." *International Journal of Children's Rights* 18, no. 1: 1–17.

——. 2011. "The Roles of Independent Children's Rights Institutions in Implementing the CRC." In *Children's Rights: From 20th Century Visions to 21st Century Implementation?*, 219–237. Surrey, UK: Ashgate Publishing Group.

Gran, Brian K., and Dawn M. Aliberti. 2003. "The Office of Children's Ombudsperson: Children's Rights and Social-Policy Innovation." *International Journal of the Sociology of Law* 31, no. 2: 89–106.

Grande, Sandy. 2004. *Red Pedagogy: Native American Social and Political Thought*. Lanham, MD: Rowman & Littlefield.

Granovetter, Mark S. 1973. "The Strength of Weak Ties." *American Journal of Sociology* 78: 1360–1380.

Gready, P. 2008. "Rights-Based Approaches to Development: What Is the Value-Added?" *Development in Practice*. http://www.developmentinpractice.org/journals/rights-based-approaches-development-what -value-added (accessed July 17, 2012).

Greenberg, David F. 1988. *The Construction of Homosexuality*. Chicago: University of Chicago Press.

Grewal, Inderpal, and Caren Kaplan, eds. 1994. *Scattered Hegemonies: Postmodernity and Transnational Feminist Practices*. Minneapolis: University of Minnesota Press.

——. 2000. "Postcolonial Studies and Transnational Feminist Practices." *Jouvert: A Journal of Postcolonial Studies* 5. http://social.chass.ncsu.edu/jouvert/v5i1/con51.htm (accessed September 6, 2012).

Griffin, Larry J., Michael Wallace, and Beth A. Rubin. 1986. "Capitalist Resistance to the Organization of Labor before the New Deal: Why? How? Success?" *American Sociological Review* 51: 147–167.

Griswold, Wendy. 1995. *Cultures and Societies in a Changing World*. Los Angeles: Sage Pine Forge.

Grosfoguel, Ramon. 2008. "Transmodernity, Border Thinking, and Global Coloniality." *Eurozine*. http://www.eurozine.com/articles/2008-07-04-grosfoguel-en.html (accessed January 1, 2011).

Gross, James A. 2009. "Takin' It to the Man: Human Rights at the American Workplace." In *Human Rights in Labor and Employment Relations: International and Domestic Perspectives*, edited James A. Gross and Lance Compa, 13–41. Urbana-Champaign, IL: Labor and Employment Relations Association.

Gross, James A., and Lance Compa. 2009. "Introduction." In *Human Rights in Labor and Employment Relations: International and Domestic Perspectives*, edited James A. Gross and Lance Compa, 1–11. Urbana-Champaign, IL: Labor and Employment Relations Association.

Grossberg, Lawrence. 1992. *We Gotta Get Out of This Place: Popular Conservatism and Postmodern Culture*. 1st ed. London: Routledge.

Grouzet, Frederick M. E., Tim Kasser, Aaron Ahuvia, José Miguel Fernandez-Dols, Youngmee Kim, Sing Lau, Richard M. Ryan, Shaun Saunders, Peter Schmuck, and Kennon M. Sheldon. 2005. "The Structure of Goal Contents across 15 Cultures." *Journal of Personality and Social Psychology* 89: 800–816.

Grue, L. 2010. "Eugenics and Euthanasia—Then and Now." *Scandinavian Journal of Disability Research* 12: 33–45.

Grundmann, Reiner, and Nico Stehr. 2012. *Experts: The Knowledge and Power of Expertise*. London: Rutledge.

Guardian. 2010. "Xinjiang Riots: One Year On, Uighur and Han Fears Still Run Deep." *Guardian*, July 4. http://www.guardian.co.uk/world/2010/jul/05/xianjiang-riots-security-uighur-han (accessed September 6, 2012).

Guarnizo, Luis, Alejandro Portes, and William Haller. 2003. "Assimilation and Transnationalism: Determinants of Transnational Political Action among Contemporary Migrants." *American Journal of Sociology* 108: 1211–1248.

Guarnizo, Luis, and Michael Peter Smith. 1998. "The Locations of Transnationalism." In *Transnationalism from Below*, edited by Michael Smith and Luis Guarnizo. London: Transaction Publishers.

Gubrium, Jaber. 1997. *Living and Dying and Murray Manor*. Charlottesville: University Press of Virginia.

Gubrium, Jaber, and James A. Holstein. 2012. "Don't Argue with the Members." *American Sociologist* 43, no. 1 (March): 85–98.

Guillen, M. F. 2001. *The Limits of Convergence: Globalization and Organizational Change in Argentina, South Korea, and Spain*. Princeton, NJ: Princeton University Press.

Gunn, T. Jeremy. 2000. "A Preliminary Response to Criticisms of the International Religious Freedom Act of 1998." *Brigham Young University Education and Law Journal* 841–865.

Guo, Guang, Glen H. Elder, Tianji Cai, and Nathan Hamilton. 2009. "Gene-Environment Interactions: Peers' Alcohol Use Moderates Genetic Contribution to Adolescent Drinking Behavior." *Social Science Research* 38: 213–224.

Guo, Guang, Michael Roettger, and Tianji Cai. 2008. "The Integration of Genetic Propensities into Social

Control Models of Delinquency and Violence among Male Youths." *American Sociological Review* 73: 543–568.

Guo, Guang, and Yuying Tong. 2006. "Age at First Sexual Intercourse, Genes, and Social and Demographic Context: Evidence from Twins and the Dopamine D4 Receptor Gene." *Demography* 43: 747–769.

Guo, Guang, Yuying Tong, and Tianji Cai. 2008. "Gene by Social-Context Interactions for Number of Sexual Partners among White Male Youths: Genetics-Informed Sociology." *American Journal of Sociology* 114: 36–66.

Guskin, Jane, and David Wilson. 2007. *The Politics of Immigration: Questions and Answers.* New York: St. Martin's Press.

Gutman, A., and D. Thompson. 2004. *Why Deliberative Democracy?* Princeton, NJ: Princeton University Press.

Gutman, Herbert G. 1961. "Trouble on the Railroads in 1873–1874: Prelude to the 1877 Crisis?" *Labor History* 2: 215–235.

———. 1962. "Reconstruction in Ohio: Negroes in the Hocking Valley Coal Mines in 1873 and 1874." *Labor History* 3: 243–264.

———. 1976. *Work, Culture, and Society in Industrializing America: Essays in American Working Class and Social History.* New York: Alfred A. Knopf.

Gwangju Metropolitan City, Republic of Korea. 2011. *The Vision of Gwangju as a Human Rights City: The Action Plan and Gwangju Human Rights Index.* Gwangju, Republic of Korea: Gwangju Metropolitan City.

Gwangju World Human Rights Cities Forum. 2011. "Gwangju Declaration." Human Rights Cities. http://humanrightscity.net/eng/subpage.php?pagecode=020301 (accessed July 17, 2012).

Habermas, Jürgen. 1979. *Communication and the Evolution of Society.* Boston: Beacon Press.

———. 1981. *The Theory of Communicative Action.* Vol. 1: *Reason and the Rationalization of Society.* Translated by Thomas McCarthy. Boston: Beacon Press.

———. 1989 [1981]. *The Theory of Communicative Action.* Vol. 2: *Lifeworld and System: A Critique of Functionalist Realism.* Translated by Thomas McCarthy. Boston: Beacon Press.

———. 1995. "Reconciliation through the Public Use of Reason: Remarks on John Rawls' Political Liberalism." *Journal of Philosophy* 92: 109–131.

Hackett, Edward J., Olga Amsterdamska, Michael Lynch, and Judy Wajcman, eds. 2007. *The Handbook of Science and Technology Studies.* 3rd ed. Cambridge, MA: MIT Press.

Hackworth, Jason. 2007. *The Neoliberal City: Governance, Ideology, and Development in American Urbanism.* Ithaca, NY: Cornell University Press.

Haddad, Yvonne Yazbeck. 2007. "The Post-9/11 Hijab as Icon." *Sociology of Religion* 68: 253–267.

Hafner-Burton, Emilie. 2005. "Right or Robust? The Sensitive Nature of Repression to Globalization." *Journal of Peace Research* 42: 679–698.

———. 2008. "'Sticks and Stones': Naming and Shaming the Human Rights Enforcement Problem." *International Organization* 62 (fall): 689–716.

———. 2009. *Forced to Be Good: Why Trade Agreements Boost Human Rights.* Ithaca, NY: Cornell University Press.

Hafner-Burton, Emilie M., and Alexander H. Montgomery. 2008. "Power Positions: International Organizations, Social Networks, and Conflict." *Journal of Conflict Resolution* 54, no. 2: 213–242.

Hafner-Burton, Emilie M., and Kiyoteru Tsutsui. 2005. "Human Rights in a Globalizing World: The Paradox of Empty Promises." *American Journal of Sociology* 110: 1373–1411.

Hafner-Burton, Emilie M., Kiyoteru Tsutsui, and John W. Meyer. 2008. "International Human Rights Law and the Politics of Legitimation: Repressive States and Human Rights Treaties." *International Sociology* 23, no. 1: 115–141.

Hagan, John. 1994. *Crime and Disrepute.* Thousand Oaks, CA: Pine Forge Press.

———. 2003. *Justice in the Balkans.* Chicago: University of Chicago Press.

Hagan, John, and Scott Greer. 2002. "Making War Criminal." *Criminology* 40: 231–264.

Hagan, John, and Sanja Kutnjak. 2006. "War Crimes, Democracy, and the Rule of Law in Belgrade, the Former Yugoslavia, and Beyond." *Annals of the American Academy of Political and Social Science* 605: 130–51.

Hagan, John, and Ron Levi. 2005. "Crimes of War and the Force of Law." *Social Forces* 3: 1499–1534.

———. 2007. "Justiciability as Field Effect: When Sociology Meets Human Rights." *Sociological Forum* 22: 372–384.

Hagan, John, and Ruth Peterson. 1995. "Criminal Inequality in America." In *Crime and Inequality,* edited by John Hagan and Ruth D. Peterson, 14–36. Stanford, CA: Stanford University Press.

Hagan, John, and Wenona Rymond-Richmond. 2008. "The Collective Dynamics of Racial Dehumanization and Genocidal Victimization in Darfur." *American Sociological Review* 6: 875–902.

———. 2009. *Darfur and the Crime of Genocide.* Cambridge, UK: Cambridge University Press.

Hagan, John, Wenona Rymond-Richmond, and Patricia Parker. 2005. "The Criminology of Genocide: The Death and Rape of Darfur." *Criminology* 43: 525–561.

Hagan, John, Heather Schoenfeld, and Alberto Palloni. 2006. "The Science of Human Rights, War Crimes and Humanitarian Emergencies." *Annual Review of Sociology* 32: 329–350.

Hagestad, Gunhild O. 2008. "The Book-Ends: Emerging Perspectives on Children and Old People." In *Families and Social Policy: Intergenerational Solidarity in European Welfare States*, edited by C. Saraceno, 20–37. London: Edward Elgar Publishing.

Hagestad, Gunhild O., and Peter Uhlenberg. 2005. "The Social Separation of Old and Young: A Root of Ageism." *Journal of Social Issues* 61: 343–360.

———. 2006. "Should We Be Concerned about Age Segregation? Some Theoretical and Empirical Explorations." *Research on Aging* 28: 638–653.

———. 2007. "The Impact of Demographic Changes on Relations between Age Groups and Generations: A Comparative Perspective." In *Social Structures: Demographic Changes and the Well-Being of Older Persons*, edited by K. W. Schaie and P. Uhlenberg, 239–261. New York: Springer Publishing Co.

Hagestad, Gunhild O., and Dale Dannefer. 2001. "Concepts and Theories of Aging: Beyond Microfication in Social Science Approaches." In *Handbook of Aging and Social Sciences*, edited by R. Binstock and L. George. 5th ed. San Diego: Academic Press.

Haiken, Elizabeth. 1999. *Venus Envy: A History of Cosmetic Surgery*. Baltimore: Johns Hopkins University Press.

Halbwachs, Maurice. 1992. *On Collective Memory*. Chicago: University of Chicago Press.

Hall, G. B., and G. Nelson. 1996. "Social Networks, Social Support, Personal Empowerment, and the Adaptation of Psychiatric Consumers: Survivors: Path Analytic Models." *Social Science and Medicine* 43: 1743–1754.

Hall, John R. 1987. *Gone from the Promised Land: Jonestown in American Cultural History*. New Brunswick, NJ: Transaction Books.

Hall, John R., Philip Daniel Schuyler, and Sylvaine Trinh. 2000. *Apocalypse Observed: Religious Movements and Violence in North America, Europe, and Japan*. London and New York: Routledge.

Hall, Peter A., and D. Soskice, eds. 2001. *Varieties of Capitalism: The Institutional Foundations of Comparative Advantage*. Oxford: Oxford University Press.

Hall, Peter M. 1987. "Interactionism and the Study of Social Organization." *Sociological Quarterly* 28, no. 1: 1–22.

Hall, Peter M., and Patrick J. W. McGinty. 1997. "Policy as the Transformation of Intentions." *Sociological Quarterly* 38: 439–467.

Hall, S., C. Critcher, T. Jefferson, J. Clarke, and B. Roberts. 1978. *Policing the Crisis: Mugging, the State, and Law and Order*. London: Macmillan.

Hall, Stuart. 1986. "Gramsci's Relevance for the Study of Race and Ethnicity." *Journal of Communication Inquiry* 10: 5–27.

Hall, Stuart, and Paul Du Gay. 1996. *Questions of Cultural Identity*. Thousand Oaks, CA: Sage.

Hall, Thomas. 2002. "World-Systems Analysis and Globalization Directions for the Twenty-First Century." *Research in Political Sociology* 11: 81–22.

Hall, Thomas D., and James V. Fenelon. 2009. *Indigenous Peoples and Globalization: Resistance and Revitalization*. Boulder, CO: Paradigm Publishers.

Haller, B., B. Dorries, and J. Rahn. 2006. "Media Labeling versus the US Disability Community Identity: A Study of Shifting Cultural Language." *Disability and Society* 21: 61–75.

Halliday, Terence C., and Pavel Osinsky. 2006. "Globalization of Law." *Annual Review of Sociology* 32: 447–470.

Hamilton, Laura, Simon Cheng, and Brian Powell. 2007. "Adoptive Parents, Adaptive Parents: Evaluating the Importance of Biological Ties for Parental Investment." *American Sociological Review* 72: 95–116.

Hammond, Michael. 2004. "The Enhancement Imperative and Group Dynamics in the Emergence of Religion and Ascriptive Inequality." *Advances in Group Processes* 21: 167–188.

Haney, Lynn. 2000. "Feminist State Theory: Applications to Jurisprudence, Criminology, and the Welfare State." *Annual Review of Sociology* 26: 641–666.

Hannan, Michael, and John Freeman. 1977. "The Population Ecology of Organizations." *American Journal of Sociology* 82: 929–964.

Hao, Lingxin, and Suet-ling Pong. 2008. "The Role of School in Upward Mobility of Disadvantaged Immigrants' Children." *Annals of the American Academy of Political and Social Sciences* 620, no. 1: 62–89.

Haraway, Donna. 1991. "A Cyborg Manifesto: Science, Technology, and Socialist-Feminism in the Late Twentieth Century." In *Simians, Cyborgs and Women: The Reinvention of Nature*, 149–181. New York; Routledge.

Harding, David J. 2007. "Cultural Context, Sexual Behavior, and Romantic Relationships in Disadvantage." *American Sociological Review* 72: 341–364.

Harding, Sandra. 2003. "How Standpoint Methodology Informs Philosophy of Social Science." In *The Blackwell Guide to the Philosophy of the Social Sciences*, edited by Stephen P. Turner and Paul A. Roth, 291–310. Malden, MA: Blackwell Publishing.

Harding, Sandra, and K. Norberg. 2005. "New Feminist Approaches to Social Science Methodologies: An Introduction." *Signs: Journal of Women in Culture and Society* 30: 2009–2015.

Hardt, Michael, and Antonio Negri. 2000. *Empire*. Cambridge, MA: Harvard University Press.
———. 2009. *Commonwealth*. Cambridge, MA: Belknap Press.
Hare, Richard M. 1981. *Moral Thinking: Its Levels, Method, and Point*. Oxford, UK: Clarendon Press.
Harmon, Katherine. 2009. "Deaths from Avoidable Medical Error More Than Double in Past Decade, Investigation Shows." *Scientific American*. http://www.scientificamerican.com/blog/post.cfm?id=deaths -from-avoidable-medical-error-2009-08-10 (accessed January 1, 2011).
Harper, A. Breeze, ed. 2010. *Sistah Vegan: Black Female Vegans Speak on Food, Identity, Health, and Society*. New York: Lantern Books.
Harris, Angela. 1990. "Race and Essentialism in Feminist Legal Theory." *Stanford Law Review* 42: 581–616.
Harrison, Bennett, and Barry Bluestone. 1988. *The Great U-Turn: Corporate Restructuring and the Polarizing of America*. New York: Basic Books.
Hartman, Chester, and Gregory Squires. 2009. *The Integration Debate: Competing Futures for American Cities*. New York: Routledge.
Harvey, David. 2005. *A Brief History of Neoliberalism*. New York: Oxford University Press.
———. 2008. "The Right to the City." *New Left Review* 53: 23–40.
Hastings, N. A. J., and J. B. Peacock. 1974. *Statistical Distributions*. London: Butterworths.
Hattery, Angela. 2001. *Women, Work, and Family: Balancing and Weaving*. Thousand Oaks, CA: Sage Publications.
———. 2009. *Intimate Partner Violence*. Lanham, MD: Rowman & Littlefield.
Hattery, Angela, and Earl Smith. 2006. "Teaching Public Sociologies." In *Public Sociologies Reader*, edited by Judith Blau and Keri E. Iyall Smith, 265–280. New York: Rowman & Littlefield.
———. 2007. *African American Families*. Thousand Oaks, CA: Sage Publishers.
Haugen, Hans M. 2008. "Human Rights and Technology–a Conflictual Relationship? Assessing Private Research and the Right to Adequate Food." *Journal of Human Rights* 7: 224–244.
Hayden, Tom. 2006. *Radical Nomad: C. Wright Mills and His Times*. Boulder, CO: Paradigm Publishers.
Hayner, Priscilla B. 2001. *Unspeakable Truths: Confronting State Terror and Atrocity*. London: Routledge.
Haynes, J. 2008. *Development Studies*. Malden, MA: Polity.
Hayward, T. 2005. *Constitutional Environmental Rights*. Oxford: Oxford University Press.
Hays, Sharon. 2003. *Flat Broke with Children*. New York: Oxford University Press.
Headrick, D. R. 2010. *Power over Peoples: Technology, Environments, and Western Imperialism, 1400 to the Present*. Princeton, NJ: Princeton University Press.
Heberer, Patricia, and Jürgen Matthäus, eds. 2008. *Atrocities on Trial*. Lincoln: University of Nebraska Press.
Hedström, P., and R. Swedberg. 1998. *Social Mechanisms. An Analytical Approach to Social Theory*. Cambridge, UK: Cambridge University Press.
Heinz, Walter R. 2003. "From Work Trajectories to Negotiated Careers: The Contingent Work Life Course." In *Handbook of the Life Course*, edited by Jeylan T. Mortimer and Michael J. Shanahan, 185–204. New York: Kluwer.
Held, David. 1995. *Democracy and the Global Order: From the Modern State to Cosmopolitan Governance*. Stanford, CA: Stanford University Press.
———. 2004. *Global Covenant: The Social Democratic Alternative to the Washington Consensus*. Cambridge, UK: Polity Press.
———. 2010. *Cosmopolitanism*. Cambridge, UK: Polity Press.
Hendawi, Hamza. 2011. "Egypt: Internet Down, Counterterror Unit Up." *Press-Register*, January 28. http://www.3news.co.nz/Egypt-internet-down-counterterror-unit-up/tabid/417/articleID/196288/Default .aspx (accessed September 6, 2012).
Henderson, Conway W. 1991. "Conditions Affecting the Use of Political Repression." *Journal of Conflict Resolution* 35: 120–142.
———. 1993. "Population Pressures and Political Repression." *Social Science Quarterly* 74: 322–333.
Herd, D. 1985. "Migration, Cultural Transformation, and the Rise of Black Liver Cirrhosis Mortality." *British Journal of Addiction* 80: 397–410.
———. 1988a. "A Review of Drinking Patterns and Alcohol Problems among US Blacks." Report of the Secretary's Task Force on Black and Minority Health. *Chemical Dependency and Diabetes* 7: 7–140. Washington, DC: U.S. Government Printing Office.
———. 1988b. "The Epidemiology of Drinking Patterns and Alcohol Problems among US Blacks." In *Alcohol Use among U.S. Ethnic Minorities*, edited by D. Spiegler, D. Tate, S. Aitken, and C. Christian, 3–51. Rockville, MD: National Institute on Alcohol Abuse and Alcoholism.
Herdt, Gilbert. 1994. *Third Sex, Third Gender*. New York: Zone Books.
———. 1997. *Same Sex, Different Cultures: Exploring Gay and Lesbian Lives*. Oxford: Westview.
Herek, Gregory M., and Kevin T. Berrill. 1992. *Hate Crimes: Confronting Violence against Lesbians and Gay Men*. Newbury Park, CA: Sage Publications.
Herek, Gregory M., and John P. Capitanio. 1996. "'Some of My Best Friends': Intergroup Contact, Concealable

Stigma, and Heterosexuals' Attitudes toward Gay Men and Lesbians." *Personality and Social Psychology Bulletin* 22: 412–424.

Herek, Gregory M., and Eric K. Glunt. 1993. "Interpersonal Contact and Heterosexuals' Attitudes toward Gay Men: Results from a National Survey." *Journal of Sex Research* 30: 239–244.

Herkert, J. R. 2004. "Microethics, Macroethics, and Professional Engineering Societies." In *Emerging Technologies and Ethical Issues in Engineering*, edited by National Academy of Engineering, 107–114. Washington, DC: National Academies Press.

Hernan, R. E. 2010. *This Borrowed Earth: Lessons from the 15 Worst Environmental Disasters around the World.* New York: Palgrave Macmillan.

Hershock, Peter D. 2000. "Dramatic Intervention: Human Rights from a Buddhist Perspective." *Philosophy East and West* 50: 9–33.

Hertel, Shareen, and Kathryn Libal. 2011. *Human Rights in the United States: Beyond Exceptionalism.* New York: Cambridge University Press.

Hess, David J. 1997. *Science Studies: An Advanced Introduction.* New York: New York University Press.

Hesse-Biber, Sharlene Nagy. 2006. *The Cult of Thinness.* New York: Oxford University Press.

Hester, Stephen. 2009. "Ethnomethodology: Respecifying the Problem of Social Order." In *Encountering the Everyday: An Introduction to the Sociologies of the Unnoticed*, edited by Michael Hviid Jacobsen, 234–256. Basingstoke, UK: Palgrave Macmillan.

Hester, Stephen, and Peter Eglin, eds. 1997a. *Culture in Action: Studies in Membership Categorization Analysis.* Washington, DC: International Institute for Ethnomethodology and Conversation Analysis and University Press of America.

——. 1997b. "Membership Categorization Analysis: An Introduction." In *Culture in Action: Studies in Membership Categorization Analysis*, edited by Stephen Hester and Peter Eglin, 1–23. Washington, DC: International Institute for Ethnomethodology and Conversation Analysis and University Press of America.

——. 1997c. "Conclusion: Membership Categorization Analysis and Sociology." In *Culture in Action: Studies in Membership Categorization Analysis*, edited by Stephen Hester and Peter Eglin, 153–163. Washington, DC: International Institute for Ethnomethodology and Conversation Analysis and University Press of America.

Hewitt, Lyndi. 2008. "Feminists and the Forum: Is It Worth the Effort?" *Societies without Borders* 3: 118–135.

——. 2009. *The Politics of Transnational Feminist Discourse: Framing across Differences, Building Solidarities.* PhD diss., Vanderbilt University, Nashville, Tennessee.

Heydebrand, Wolf. 1977. "Organizational Contradictions in Public Bureaucracies, toward a Marxian Theory of Organizations." *Sociological Quarterly* 18, no. 1: 83–107.

——. 1983. "Technocratic Corporatism: Toward a Theory of Occupational and Organizational Transformation." In *Organizational Theory and Public Policy*, edited by Richard Hall and Robert Quinn, 93–114. Beverly Hills, CA: Sage.

Heyman, Josiah. 2002. "U.S. Immigration Officers of Mexican Ancestry as Mexican Americans, Citizens, and Immigration Police." *Current Anthropology* 43: 479–507.

——. 2010. "Human Rights and Social Justice Briefing 1: Arizona's Immigration Law–S.B. 1070." Society for Applied Anthropology. http://www.sfaa.net/committees/humanrights/AZImmigrationLawSB1070 .pdf (accessed July 17, 2012).

Hidalgo, Myra L. 2007. *Sexual Abuse and the Culture of Catholicism: How Priests and Nuns Become Perpetrators.* New York: Haworth Maltreatment and Trauma Press.

Higgins, E. Tory. 1987. "Self-Discrepancy: A Theory Relating Self and Affect." *Psychological Review* 94: 319–340.

Hill, Herman. 1993. "The CIA in National and International Labor Movements. Review of *Compromised Campus: The Collaboration of Universities with the Intelligence Community, 1945–1955*, by Sigmund Diamond." *International Journal of Politics* 6: 405–407.

Hill, Jane H. 2008. *The Everyday Language of White Racism.* Malden, MA: Wiley-Blackwell.

Hinde, Andrew. 1998. *Demographic Methods.* London: Oxford University Press.

Hinton, Alexander L., and Kevin L. O'Neill. 2009. *Genocide: Truth, Memory, and Representation.* Durham, NC: Duke University Press.

Hinze, Susan W., Jielu Lin, and Tanetta Andersson. 2011. "Can We Capture the Intersections? Older Black Women, Education, and Health." *Women's Health Issues* 22, no. 1 (January): e91–e98.

Hinze, Susan W., Noah J. Webster, Heidi T. Chirayath, and Joshua H. Tamayo-Sarver. 2009. "Hurt Running from Police? No Chance of (Pain) Relief: The Social Construction of Deserving Patients in Emergency Departments." *Research in the Sociology of Health Care* 27: 235–261.

Hirschman, A. O. 1983. "Morality and the Social Sciences: A Durable Tension." In *Social Science as Moral Inquiry*, edited by N. Hann et al., 21–32. New York: Columbia University Press.

Hiskes, Richard P. 2010. "The Relational Foundations of Emergent Human Rights: From Thomas Hobbes to the Human Right to Water." *Zeitschrift für Menschenrechte [Journal for Human Rights]* 4, no. 2: 127–146.

Hitlin, Steven, and Jane A. Piliavin. 2004. "Values: A Review of Recent Research and Theory." *Annual Review of Sociology* 30: 359–393.

Hitt, L., ed. 2002. *Human Rights: Great Speeches in History.* San Diego, CA: Greenhaven Press.

Hlaing, Kyaw Y. 2004. "Myanmar in 2003: Frustration and Despair?" *Asian Survey* 44: 87–92.

———. 2005. "Myanmar in 2004: Another Year of Uncertainty." *Asian Survey* 45: 174–179.

Hoang, Nghia. 2009. "The 'Asian Values' Perspective of Human Rights: A Challenge to Universal Human Rights." Social Science Research Network. http://ssrn.com/abstract=1405436 (accessed July 17, 2012).

Hobhouse, L. T. 1922. *The Elements of Social Justice.* London: G. Allen and Unwin.

Hobsbawm, Eric J. 1962. *The Age of Revolution: Europe 1789–1848.* London: Weidenfeld and Nicolson.

———. 1964. *Labouring Men: Studies in the History of Labour.* London: Weidenfeld and Nicolson.

Hochschild, Arlie. 1979. "Emotion Work, Feeling Rules, and Social Structure." *American Journal of Sociology* 85: 551–575.

———. 1983. *The Managed Heart: Commercialization of Human Feeling.* Berkeley: University of California Press.

Hockenberry, J. 1995. *Moving Violations: War Zones, Wheelchairs, and Declarations of Independence.* New York: Hyperion.

Hoffman Plastic Compounds, Inc. v. NLRB. 2002. 122 S. Ct. 1275.

Hoffman, John P. 2006. "Extracurricular Activities, Athletic Participation, and Adolescent Alcohol Use: Gender-Differentiated and School-Contextual Effects." *Journal of Health and Social Behavior* 47, no. 3: 275–290.

Holland, J., C. Ramazanoglu, S. Sharpe, and R. Thomson. 1998. *The Male in the Head: Young People, Heterosexuality and Power.* London: The Tufnell.

Hollingshead, A. B., and F. C. Redlich. 1958. *Social Class and Mental Illness.* New York: Wiley.

Hollingsworth, J. Rogers, Philippe C. Schmitter, and Wolfgang Streeck, eds. 1994. *Governing Capitalist Economies: Performance and Control of Economic Sectors.* New York: Oxford University Press.

Holmes, Malcolm D. 2008. *Race and Police Brutality: Roots of an Urban Dilemma.* Albany: State University of New York Press.

Holstein, James A., and Jaber F. Gubrium. 1999. *The Self We Live By: Narrative Identity in a Postmodern World.* 1st ed. New York: Oxford University Press.

———, eds. 2003. *Inner Lives and Social Worlds: Readings in Social Psychology.* New York: Oxford University Press.

Homans, George C. 1974. *Social Behavior: Its Elementary Forms.* Rev. ed. New York: Harcourt, Brace, Jovanovich.

Hopcroft, Rosemary L. 2005. "Parental Status and Differential Investment in Sons and Daughters: Trivers-Willard Revisited." *Social Forces* 83: 169–193.

———. 2008. "Darwinian Conflict Theory: Alternative Theory or Unifying Paradigm for Sociology?" In *The New Evolutionary Science: Human Nature, Social Behavior and Social Change,* edited by Heinz-Jürgen Niedenzu, Tamás Meleghy, and Peter Meyer. Boulder, CO: Paradigm Publishers.

———. 2009. "Gender Inequality in Interaction: An Evolutionary Account." *Social Forces* 87: 1845–1872.

Hopcroft, Rosemary L., and Dana Burr Bradley. 2007. "The Sex Difference in Depression across 29 Countries." *Social Forces* 85: 1483–1507.

Hopgood, Stephen. 2006. *Keepers of the Flame.* Ithaca, NY: Cornell University Press.

Horkheimer, Max, and Theodor W. Adorno. 1993 [1944]. *Dialectic of Enlightenment.* Translated by John Cumming. New York: Continuum.

Hornburg, Alf. 1998. "Ecosystems and World Systems: Accumulation as an Ecological Process." *Journal of World-Systems Research* 4, no. 2: 169–177.

Horne, Christine. 2004. "Values and Evolutionary Psychology." *Sociological Theory* 22: 477–503.

Horne, Sharon, and Melanie J. Zimmer-Gembeck. 2005. "Female Sexual Subjectivity and Well-Being: Comparing Late Adolescents with Different Sexual Experiences." *Sexuality Research and Social Policy* 2: 25–40.

Horowitz, Louis Irving. 1980. *Taking Lives: Genocide and State Power.* New Brunswick, NJ: Transaction Books.

———. 2002. *Tanking Lives: Genocide and State Power.* 5th ed. New Brunswick, NJ: Transaction.

Horton, Hayward Derrick. 1999. "Critical Demography: The Paradigm of the Future?" *Sociological Forum* 14, no. 3: 363–367.

Hosken, Fran P. 1993. *The Hosken Report: Genital and Sexual Mutilation of Females.* 4th ed. Lexington, MA: Women's International Network News.

House, J. S. 1981. "Social Structure and Personality." In *Social Psychology, Sociological Perspectives,* edited by M. Rosenberg and R. H. Turner, 525–561. New York: Basic Books.

House, James S. 1977. "The Three Faces of Social Psychology." *Sociometry* 40: 161–177.

House, James S., James M. Lepkowski, Ann M. Kinney, Richard P. Mero, Ronald C. Kessler, and A. Regula Herzog. 1994. "The Social Stratification of Aging and Health." *Journal of Health and Social Behavior* 35: 213–234.

Hovenkamp, Herbert. 1991. *Enterprise and American Law, 1836–1937.* Cambridge, MA: Harvard University Press.

Hovey, Michael W. 1997. "Interceding at the United Nations: The Human Right of Conscientious Objection." In *Transnational Social Movements and Global Politics: Solidarity beyond the State*, edited by J. Smith, C. Chatfield, and R. Pagnucco. Syracuse, NY: Syracuse University Press.

Hovil, L., and E. Werker. 2005. "Portrait of a Failed Rebellion: An Account of Rational, Sub-Optimal Violence in Western Uganda." *Rationality and Society* 17: 5–34.

Howard, Jay. 2010. "2009 Hans O. Mauksch Address: Where Are We and How Did We Get Here? A Brief Examination of the Past, Present and Future of the Teaching and Learning Movement in Sociology." *Teaching Sociology* 38: 81–92.

Howard, Judith, and Carolyn Allen. 1996. "Reflections on the Fourth World Conference on Women and NGO Forum '95: Introduction." *Signs* 22: 181–185.

Howard, Rhoda E. 1985. "Legitimacy and Class Rule in Commonwealth Africa: Constitutionalism and the Rule of Law." *Third World Quarterly* 7, no. 2: 323–347.

———. 1995. *Human Rights and the Search for Community*. Boulder, CO: Westview Press.

Howard, Rhoda E., and Jack Donnelly. 1986. "Human Dignity, Human Rights and Political Regimes." *American Political Science Review* 80: 801–817.

Huber, Evelyn, and John Stephens. 2001. *Development and Crisis of the Welfare State*. Chicago: University of Chicago Press.

Huber, Joan. 2007. *On the Origins of Gender Inequality*. Boulder, CO: Paradigm Publishers.

Huda, S. 2006. "Sex Trafficking in South Asia." *International Journal of Gynecology and Obstetrics* 94: 374–381.

Hughes, Everett C. 1963. "Good People and Dirty Work." In *The Other Side*, edited by Howard Becker, 23–36. New York: The Free Press.

———. 1971. *The Sociological Eye: Selected Papers*. Chicago: Aldine-Atherton.

Hughes, Jason. 2003. *Learning to Smoke: Tobacco Use in the West*. Chicago: University of Chicago Press.

Hughes, John A., Peter J. Martin, and W. W. Sharrock. 1995. *Understanding Classical Sociology: Marx, Weber, Durkheim*. London: Sage.

Hughes, John A., and W. W. Sharrock. 2007. *Theory and Methods in Sociology: An Introduction to Sociological Thinking and Practice*. Basingstoke, UK: Palgrave Macmillan.

Hughs, Alex, and Ann Witz. 1997. "Feminism and the Matter of Bodies: From de Beauvoir to Butler." *Body and Society* 3: 47–60.

Huizinga, Johann. 2006 [1919]. *The Autumn of the Middle Ages*. Translated by Rodney J. Payton and Ulrich Mammitzsch. Chicago: University of Chicago Press.

Hulko, Wendy. 2009. "The Time- and Context-Contingent Nature of Intersectionality and Interlocking Oppressions." *Affilia: Journal of Women and Social Work* 24: 44–55.

Human Rights Watch (HRW). 2000. "Racial Disparities in the War on Drugs." HRW. http://www.hrw.org/legacy/reports/2000/usa/Rcedrg00.htm#P54_1086 (accessed January 1, 2011).

———. 2010. *World Report*. New York: HRW.

Hunt, Lynn. 2007. *Inventing Human Rights: A History*. New York: W. W. Norton and Co.

Huntington, Samuel. 1991. *The Third Wave*. Norman: University of Oklahoma Press.

Husak, Douglas. 2003. "The Criminalization of Drug Use." *Sociological Forum* 18, no. 3: 503–513.

Hutchinson, Phil, Rupert Read, and Wes Sharrock. 2008. *There Is No Such Thing as a Social Science: In Defence of Peter Winch*. Aldershot, UK: Ashgate.

Hynes, Patricia, Michele Lamb, Damien Short, and Matthew Waites. 2010. "Sociology and Human Rights: Confrontations, Evasions and New Engagements." *International Journal of Human Rights* 14, no. 6: 811–832.

Hynie, M., and J. E. Lydon. 1995. "Women's Perceptions of Female Contraceptive Behavior: Experimental Evidence of the Sexual Double Standard." *Psychology of Women Quarterly* 19: 563–581.

Ignatiev, N. 1995. *How the Irish Became White*. New York: Routledge.

Ikegami, Eiko. 2005. "Bringing Culture into Macrostructural Analysis in Historical Sociology." *Poetics* 33: 15–32.

Illich, Ivan. 1971. *Deschooling Society*. London: Calder and Boyars.

Inglehart, Ronald. 1977. *The Silent Revolution Changing Values and Political Styles among Western Publics*. Princeton, NJ: Princeton University Press.

Inglehart, Ronald, and Wayne E. Baker. 2000. "Modernization, Cultural Change, and the Persistence of Traditional Values." *American Sociological Review* 65, no. 1: 19–51.

Ingraham, Chrys. 2008. *White Weddings: Romancing Heterosexuality in Popular Culture*. New York: Routledge.

International Criminal Court (ICC). 2011. "Rome Statute." ICC. http://www.icc-cpi.int/Menus/ICC/Legal+Texts+and+Tools/Official+Journal/Rome+Statute.htm (accessed August 15, 2012).

International Federation of Red Cross and Red Crescent Societies. 2004. *World Disaster Report: Focus on Community Resilience*. Bloomfield, CT: Kumarian Press.

International Gay and Lesbian Human Rights Commission (IGLHRC). 2011. "Our Issues." IGLHRC. http://www.iglhrc.org/cgi-bin/iowa/theme/1.html (accessed November 11, 2011).

International Labour Office. 1973. Minimum Age Convention. http://www.ilocarib.org.tt/projects/cariblex/conventions_6.shtml (accessed September 6, 2012).

Irvine, Janice M. 2002. *Talk about Sex: The Battles over Sex Education in the United States*. Berkeley: University of California Press.

Irwin, Alan, and Brian Wynne, eds. 1996. *Misunderstanding Science? The Public Reconstruction of Science and Technology*. Cambridge, UK: Cambridge University Press.

Ishay, Micheline R., ed. 1997. *The Human Rights Reader: Major Political Essays, Speeches, and Documents from the Bible to the Present*. New York: Routledge.

———. 2004a. *The History of Human Rights: From Ancient Times to the Globalization Era*. Berkeley: University of California Press.

———. 2004b. "What Are Human Rights? Six Historical Controversies." *Journal of Human Rights* 3: 359–371.

Israel, Jonathan. 2011. *Democratic Enlightenment: Philosophy, Revolution, and Human Rights*. Oxford: Oxford University Press.

Ito, Mizuko, Sonja Baumer, Matteo Bittanti, Danah Boyd, Rachel Cody, Becky Herr-Stephenson, Heather A. Horst, Patricia G. Lange, Dilan Mahendran, Katynka Z. Martinez, C. J. Pascoe, Dan Perkel, Laura Robinson, Christo Sims, and Lisa Tripp, with Judd Antin, Megan Finn, Arthur Law, Annie Manion, Sarai Mitnick, David Scholssberg, and Sarita Yardi. 2009. *Hanging Out, Messing Around, and Geeking Out*. Cambridge, MA: Massachusetts Institute of Technology Press.

Jacobs, David, Zenchao Qian, Jason T. Carmichael, and Stephanie L. Kent. 2007. "Who Survives on Death Row? An Individual and Contextual Analysis." *American Sociological Review* 72: 610–632.

Jacobs, Mark D. 2012. "Financial Crises as Symbols and Rituals." In *The Oxford Handbook of the Sociology of Finance*, edited by Karin Knorr Cetina and Alex Preda. New York: Oxford University Press.

Jacobs, Mark D., and Nancy Weiss Hanrahan. 2005. Introduction to *The Blackwell Companion to the Sociology of Culture*, edited by Mark D. Jacobs and Nancy Weiss Hanrahan. Malden, MA: Blackwell.

Jacobs, Mark D., and Lyn Spillman. 2005. "Cultural Sociology at the Crossroads of the Discipline." *Poetics* 33: 1–14.

Jaeger, Gertrude, and Philip Selznick. 1964. "A Normative Theory of Culture." *American Sociological Review* 29: 653–669.

Jain, D. 2005. *Women, Development, and the UN: A Sixty-Year Quest for Equality and Justice*. Bloomington: Indiana University Press.

Jalata, Asafa. 2005. "State Terrorism and Globalization: The Cases of Ethiopia and Sudan." *International Journal of Comparative Sociology* 46, no. 1–2: 79–102.

———. 2008. "Struggling for Social Justice in the Capitalist World System: The Cases of African Americans, Oromos, and Southern and Western Sudanese." *Social Identities* 14, no. 3: 363–388.

James, Helen. 2006. "Myanmar in 2005: In a Holding Pattern." *Asian Survey* 46: 162–167.

Jamieson, Dale. 2003. *Morality's Progress: Essays on Humans, Other Animals, and the Rest of Nature*. London: Oxford University Press.

Janoski, Thomas. 1998. *Citizenship and Civil Society*. New York: Cambridge University Press.

Jasper, James. 1997. *The Art of Moral Protest: Culture, Biography, and Creativity in Social Movements*. Chicago: University of Chicago Press.

———. 2004. "A Strategic Approach to Collective Action: Looking for Agency in Social Movement Choices." *Mobilization* 9, no. 1: 1–16.

Jasso, Guillermina. 1978. "On the Justice of Earnings: A New Specification of the Justice Evaluation Function." *American Journal of Sociology* 83: 1398–1419.

———. 1980. "A New Theory of Distributive Justice." *American Sociological Review* 45: 3–32.

———. 1988a. "Distributive-Justice Effects of Employment and Earnings on Marital Cohesiveness: An Empirical Test of Theoretical Predictions." In *Status Generalization: New Theory and Research*, edited by Murray Webster and Martha Foschi, 123–162 (references, 490–493). Stanford, CA: Stanford University Press.

———. 1988b. "Principles of Theoretical Analysis." *Sociological Theory* 6: 1–20.

———. 1990. "Methods for the Theoretical and Empirical Analysis of Comparison Processes." *Sociological Methodology* 20: 369–419.

———. 2001. "Studying Status: An Integrated Framework." *American Sociological Review* 66: 96–124.

———. 2008. "A New Unified Theory of Sociobehavioral Forces." *European Sociological Review* 24: 411–434.

———. 2009. "A New Model of Wage Determination and Wage Inequality." *Rationality and Society* 21: 113–168.

———. 2010. "Linking Individuals and Societies." *Journal of Mathematical Sociology* 34: 1–51.

Jasso, Guillermina, and Samuel Kotz. 2007. "A New Continuous Distribution and Two New Families of Distributions Based on the Exponential." *Statistica Neerlandica* 61: 305–328.

———. 2008. "Two Types of Inequality: Inequality between Persons and Inequality between Subgroups." *Sociological Methods and Research* 37: 31–74.

Jayasree, A. K. 2004. "Searching for Justice for Body and Self in a Coercive Environment: Sex Work in Kerala, India." *Reproductive Health Matters* 12: 58-67.

Jayyusi, Lena. 1984. *Categorization and the Moral Order.* London: Routledge and Kegan Paul.

———. 1991. "Values and Moral Judgment: Communicative Praxis as a Moral Order." In *Ethnomethodology and the Human Sciences,* edited by Graham Button, 227-251. Cambridge, UK: Cambridge University Press.

Jenkins, Alan, and Kevin Shawn Hsu. 2008. "American Ideals and Human Rights: Findings from New Public Opinion Research by the Opportunity Agenda." *Fordham Law Review* 77, no. 2: 439-458.

Jenkins, J. Craig. 1983. "Resource Mobilization Theory and the Study of Social Movements." *Annual Review of Sociology* 9: 527-553.

Jenkins, J. Craig, and Craig Eckert. 1986. "Channeling Black Insurgency: Elite Patronage and the Development of the Civil Rights Movement." *American Sociological Review* 51: 812-830.

Jensen, Gary. 2007. *The Path of the Devil: Early Modern Witch Hunts.* Lanham, MD: Rowman & Littlefield.

Jessop, Robert D. 2002. *The Future of the Capitalist State.* Cambridge, MA: Polity.

Jo, Moon Ho. 1984. "The Putative Political Complacency of Asian Americans." *Political Psychology* 5: 583-605.

Joachim, Jutta. 2003. "Framing Issues and Seizing Opportunities: Women's Rights and the UN." *International Studies Quarterly* 47: 247-274.

Joas, Hans. 2000. *The Genesis of Values.* Cambridge, UK: Polity Press.

———. 2003. *War and Modernity.* Cambridge, UK: Polity Press.

Jochnick, Chris. 1999. "Confronting the Impunity of Non-State Actors: New Fields for the Promotion of Human Rights." *Human Rights Quarterly* 21, no. 1: 56-79.

Johansen, Bruce. 2003. *The Dirty Dozen: Toxic Chemicals in the Earth's Future.* Westport, CT: Praeger.

Johnson, C., and T. Forsyth. 2002. "In the Eyes of the State: Negotiating a 'Rights-Based Approach' to Forest Conservation in Thailand." *World Development* 20: 1591-1605.

Johnson, E. Patrick. 2003. *Appropriating Blackness: Performance and the Politics of Authenticity.* Durham, NC: Duke University Press.

Johnson, Eric A., and Eric H. Monkkonen, eds. 1996. *The Civilization of Crime.* Urbana: University of Illinois Press.

Johnson, Heather Beth. 2006. *The American Dream and the Power of Wealth: Choosing Schools and Inheriting Inequality in the Land of Opportunity.* New York: Routledge.

Johnson, J. 2001. "In-depth Interviewing." In *Handbook of Interview Research: Context and Method,* edited by Jay Gubrium and James Holstein, 103-119. Thousand Oaks, CA: Sage.

Johnson, Jim (aka Bruno Latour). 1988. "Mixing Humans and Nonhumans Together: The Sociology of a Door-Closer." *Social Problems* 35, no. 3: 298-310.

Johnson, Norman L., and Samuel Kotz. 1969-1972. *Distributions in Statistics.* 4 vols. New York: Wiley.

Johnson, Norman L., Samuel Kotz, and N. Balakrishnan. 1994. *Continuous Univariate Distributions.* Vol. 1. 2nd ed. New York: Wiley.

———. 1995. *Continuous Univariate Distributions.* Vol. 2. 2nd ed. New York: Wiley.

Johnson, Victoria. 2011. "Everyday Rituals of the Master Race: Fascism, Stratification, and the Fluidity of 'Animal' Domination." In *Critical Theory and Animal Liberation,* edited by John Sanbonmatsu, 203-218. Lanham, MD: Rowman & Littlefield.

Johnston, Barbara R. 1995. "Human Rights and the Environment." *Human Ecology* 23: 111-123.

Johnston, Hank, and Bert Klandermans, eds. 1995. *Social Movements and Culture.* Minneapolis: University of Minnesota Press.

Johnston, Hank, and John A. Noakes, eds. 2005. *Frames of Protest: Social Movements and the Framing Perspective.* Lanham, MD: Rowman & Littlefield Publishers.

Jordan, Kathleen Casey. 1997. "The Effect of Disclosure on the Professional Life of Lesbian Police Officers." PhD diss., City University of New York.

Jordan-Zachary, Julia S. 2007. "Am I a Black Woman or a Woman Who Is Black? A Few Thoughts on the Meaning of Intersectionality." *Politics and Gender* 3: 254-263.

Jorgensen, Anja, and Dennis Smith. 2009. "The Chicago School of Sociology: Survival in the Urban Jungle." In *Encountering the Everyday: An Introduction to the Sociologies of the Unnoticed,* edited by Michael Hviid Jacobsen, 45-69. New York: Macmillan.

Jorgenson, Andrew. 2003. "Consumption and Environmental Degradation: A Cross-National Analysis of the Ecological Footprint." *Social Problems* 50, no. 3: 374-394.

Joseph, Paul. 1993. *Peace Politics: The United States between the Old and New World Orders.* Philadelphia: Temple University Press.

Jost, Timothy S. 2003. *Disentitlement? The Threats Facing Our Public Health Care Programs and a Rights-Based Response.* Oxford: Oxford University Press.

Jotkowitz, A., S. Glick, and B. Gesundheit. 2008. "A Case against Justified Non-Voluntary Active Euthanasia (The Groningen Protocol)." *American Journal of Bioethics* 8: 23-26.

Juris, Jeffrey. 2008. *Networking Futures.* Durham, NC: Duke University Press.

Kaiser Family Foundation. 2002. *Sex Smarts Survey: Gender Roles.* Menlo Park, CA: Kaiser Family Foundation.

Kalberg, Stephen. 1994. *Max Weber's Comparative-Historical Sociology.* Chicago: University of Chicago Press.

———. 2011. Introduction to *The Protestant Ethic and the Spirit of Capitalism* by Max Weber. Translated by Stephen Kalberg. Rev. 1920 ed. New York: Oxford University Press.

Kaldor, Mary. 1999. *New and Old Wars: Organized Violence in a Global Era.* Stanford, CA: Stanford University Press.

———. 2003. *Global Civil Society: An Answer to War.* Cambridge, UK: Polity Press.

Kang, Miliann. 2003. "The Managed Hand: The Commercialization of Bodies and Emotions in Korean Immigrant-Owned Nail Salons." *Gender and Society* 17: 820–839.

Kant, Immanuel. 1933 [1788]. *Critique of Practical Reason.* Upper Saddle River, NJ: Prentice Hall.

———. 1939. *Perpetual Peace.* New York: Columbia University Press.

Kapur, Ratna. 2002. "The Tragedy of Victimization Rhetoric: Resurrecting the 'Native' Subject in International/Post-Colonial Feminist Legal Politics." *Harvard Law School Human Rights Journal of Law* 15: 1–38.

———. 2005. *Erotic Justice: Law and the New Politics of Postcolonialism.* London: Glasshouse Press.

Kara, Karel. 1968. "On the Marxist Theory of War and Peace." *Journal of Peace Research* 5: 1–27.

Karger, Howard. 1989. "The Common and Conflicting Goals of Labor and Social Work." *Administration in Social Work* 13: 1–17.

Karp, David. 1996. *Speaking of Sadness: Depression, Disconnection, and the Meanings of Illness.* New York: Oxford University Press.

Karpik, Lucien. 1977. "Technological Capitalism." In *Critical Issues in Organizations,* edited by S. Clegg and D. Dunkerley, 41–71. London: Routledge and Kegan Paul.

Karstedt, Susanne. 2007. "Human Rights." In *The Blackwell Encyclopedia of Sociology,* edited by George Ritzer, 2182–2185. Malden, MA: Blackwell Publishing.

———. 2011. "Human Rights." In *The Concise Encyclopedia of Sociology,* edited by George Ritzer and J. Michael Ryan, 294–295. Malden, MA: Wiley-Blackwell.

Kasinitz, Philip, Mary Waters, John H. Mollenkopf, and Jennifer Holdaway. 2009. *Inheriting the City: The Children of Immigrants Come of Age.* New York: Russell Sage Foundation.

Kass, Leon R. 1971. "The New Biology: What Price Relieving Man's Estate?" *Science* 174: 779–788.

Kasser, Tim. 2011. "Cultural Values and the Well-Being of Future Generations: A Cross-National Study." *Journal of Cross-Cultural Psychology* 42, no. 2 (March): 206–215.

Katsui, H., and J. Kumpuvuori. 2008. "Human Rights Based Approach to Disability in Development in Uganda: A Way to Fill the Gap between Political and Social Spaces?" *Scandinavian Journal of Disability Research* 10: 227–236.

Katz, Jonathan. 2007. *The Invention of Heterosexuality.* Chicago: University of Chicago Press.

Kausikan, Bilahari. 1995. "An East Asian Approach to Human Rights." *Buffalo Journal of International Law* 2: 263–283.

Kautsky, Karl. 1931. *Bolshevism at a Deadlock.* London: G. Allen and Unwin.

Keck, Margaret E., and Kathryn Sikkink. 1998. *Activists beyond Borders: Advocacy Networks in International Politics.* Ithaca, NY: Cornell University Press.

Keith, Michael, and Steve Pile. 1993. *Place and the Politics of Identity.* London: Psychology Press.

Keller, C., and M. Siegrist. 2010. "Psychological Resources and Attitudes toward People with Physical Disabilities." *Journal of Applied Social Psychology* 40: 389–401.

Kelman, Herbert C., and V. Lee Hamilton. 2002. "The My Lai Massacre: Crimes of Obedience and Sanctioned Massacres." In *Corporate and Governmental Deviance: Problems of Organizational Behavior in Contemporary Society,* edited by M. David Ermann and Richard J. Lundman, 195–221. Oxford: Oxford University Press.

Kempadoo, Kamala, ed. 2005. *Trafficking and Prostitution Reconsidered: New Perspectives on Migration, Sex Work, and Human Rights.* Boulder, CO: Paradigm Publishers.

Kemper, Theodore D. 1990. "Social Relations and Emotions: A Structural Approach." In *Research Agendas in the Sociology of Emotions,* edited by T. D. Kemper, 207–237. Albany: State University of New York Press.

Kemper, Theodore D., and Randall Collins. 1990. "Dimensions of Microinteraction." *American Journal of Sociology* 93: 32–68.

Kendall, Maurice G. 1943. *The Advanced Theory of Statistics.* Vol. 1: *Distribution Theory.* Original 2-vol. ed. London: Charles Griffin.

Kendall, Maurice G., and Alan Stuart. 1958. *The Advanced Theory of Statistics.* Vol. 1: *Distribution Theory.* First 3-vol. ed. New York: Hafner.

Kendler, Kenneth S., Sara Jaffee, and Dan Romer, eds. 2010. *The Dynamic Genome and Mental Health: The Role of Genes and Environments in Development.* Oxford: Oxford University Press.

Kennedy, David. 2002. "Boundaries in the Field of Human Rights: The International Human Rights Movement: Part of the Problem?" *Harvard Law School Human Rights Journal* 15: 101–25.

Kessler R. C., and J. McLeod. 1984. "Sex Differences in Vulnerability to Undesirable Life Events." *American Sociological Review* 49: 620–631.

Kessler, Suzanne J. 1990. *Lessons from the Intersexed.* New Brunswick, NJ: Rutgers University Press.

Kestnbaum, Meyer. 2009. "The Sociology of War and the Military." *Annual Review of Sociology* 35: 235–254.

Khalili-Borna, C. A. 2007. "Technological Advancement and International Human Rights: Is Science Improving Human Life or Perpetuating Human Rights Violations?" *Michigan Journal of International Law* 29: 95–125.

Kick, Edward, and Andrew Jorgenson. 2003. "Globalization and the Environment." *Journal of World-Systems Research* 9, no. 2: 195–203.

Kikuzawa, Saeko, Sigrun Olafsdottir, and Bernice Pescosolido. 2008. "Similar Pressures, Different Contexts: Public Attitudes toward Government Intervention for Health Care in 21 Nations." *Journal of Health and Social Behavior* 49: 385–399.

Kilbourne, Jean. 1999. *Deadly Persuasion: Why Women and Girls Must Fight the Addictive Power of Advertising.* New York: The Free Press.

Kim, Hyun Sik. 2011. "Consequences of Parental Divorce for Child Development." *American Sociological Review* 76, no. 3: 487–511.

Kimeldorf, Howard. 1991. "Bringing Unions Back In (or Why We Need a New Old Labor History)." *Labor History* 32: 91–103.

Kimeldorf, Howard, and Judith Stepan-Norris. 1992. "Historical Studies of Labor Movements in the United States." *Annual Review of Sociology* 18: 495–517.

Kimmel, Michael S. 2001. "The Kindest Un-Cut: Feminism, Judaism, and My Son's Foreskin." *Tikkun* 16, no. 1. http://www.cirp.org/pages/cultural/kimmel1/ (accessed September 6, 2012).

———. 2005. *Manhood in America: A Cultural History.* New York: Oxford University Press.

Kincaid, Jamaica. 2000. *A Small Place.* 1st ed. New York: Farrar, Straus and Giroux.

Kincheloe, Joe, and Peter McLaren. 1994. "Rethinking Critical Theory and Qualitative Research." In *Handbook of Qualitative Research,* edited by Norman Denzin and Yvonna Lincoln, 138–157. Thousand Oaks, CA: Sage.

Kindleberger, Charles Poor, and Robert Z. Aliber. 2005. *Manias, Panics and Crashes: A History of Financial Crises.* Hoboken, NJ: John Wiley and Sons.

King, Deborah K. 1988. "Multiple Jeopardy, Multiple Consciousnesses: The Context of a Black Feminist Ideology." *Signs: Journal of Women in Culture and Society* 14: 42–72.

King, Martin Luther, Jr. 1986. "If the Negro Wins, Labor Wins." In *A Testament of Hope: The Essential Writings and Speeches of Martin Luther King, Jr.,* edited by James M. Washington. New York: HarperCollins.

Kingsbury, Benedict, Nico Krisch, and Richard Stewart. 2005. "The Emergence of Global Administrative Law." *Law and Contemporary Problems* 68: 15–61.

Kinney, Eleanor D., and Brian Alexander Clark. 2004. "Provisions for Health and Health Care in the Constitutions of the Countries of the World." *Cornell International Law Journal* 37: 285–355.

Kinsey, Alfred, Wardell B. Pomeroy, and Clyde E. Martin. 1948. *Sexual Behavior in the Human Male.* Philadelphia: W. B. Saunders Company.

Kiser, Edgar, and Howard T. Welser. 2010. "The Relationship between Theory and History in Revolutionary Biology: A Model for Historical Sociology?" Unpublished manuscript, University of Washington.

Kitano, Harry H. L. 1988. "Asian Americans and Alcohol: The Chinese, Koreans and Filipinos in Los Angeles." In *Alcohol Use among U.S. Ethnic Minorities,* edited by D. Spiegler, D. Tate, S. Aitken, and C. Christian, 373–382. Rockville, MD: National Institute on Alcohol Abuse and Alcoholism.

Kitschelt, Herbert P. 1986. "Political Opportunity Structures and Political Protest: Anti-Nuclear Movements in Four Democracies." *British Journal of Political Science* 16, no. 1: 57–85.

Klandermans, Bert, and Suzanne Staggenborg, eds. 2002. *Methods of Social Movement Research.* Minneapolis: University of Minnesota Press.

Klare, Karl E. 1978. "Judicial Deradicalization of the Wagner Act and the Origins of Modern Legal Consciousness, 1937–1941." *Minnesota Law Review* 62: 265.

Kleiber, Christian, and Samuel Kotz. 2003. *Statistical Size Distributions in Economics and Actuarial Sciences.* Hoboken, NJ: Wiley.

Knights, David, and Hugh Wilmott, eds. 1990. *Labour Process Theory.* London: Macmillan.

Knoke, D., and E. O. Laumann. 1987. *The Organizational State: Social Choice in National Policy Domains.* Madison: University of Wisconsin Press.

Koch, T. 2004. "The Difference that Difference Makes: Bioethics and the Challenge of 'Disability.'" *Journal of Medicine and Philosophy* 29: 697–716.

Kohler, Hans-Peter, J. L. Rodgers, and Kaare Christensen. 1999. "Is Fertility Behavior in Our Genes? Findings from a Danish Twin Study." *Population and Development Review* 25: 253–288.

———. 2002. "Between Nurture and Nature: The Shifting Determinants of Female Fertility in Danish Twin Cohorts." *Social Biology* 49: 218–248.

Kohli, M., and J. W. Meyer. 1986. "Social Structure and Social Construction of Life Stages." *Human Development* 29, no. 3: 145–149.

Kohli, Martin. 1986. "Social Organization and Subjective Construction of the Life Course." In *Human Development and the Life Course*, edited by A. Sorensen, F. Weinert, and L. Sherrod, 271–292. Cambridge, MA: Harvard University Press.

———. 2007. "The Institutionalization of the Life Course: Looking Back to Look Ahead." *Research in Human Development* 4, no. 3–4: 253–271.

Kohn, Melvin L. 1981. "Social Class and Schizophrenia: A Critical Review and a Reformulation." In *The Sociology of Mental Illness: Basic Studies*, edited by O. Grusky and Pollner M. Holt, 127–143. New York: Rinehart and Winston.

Kohn, Melvin L., and Carmi Schooler. 1983. *Work and Personality: An Inquiry into the Impact of Social Stratification*. Norwood, NJ: Ablex Publishing Corporation.

Kohn, Melvin L., Kazimierz M. Slomczynski, Krystyna Janicka, Valeri Khmelko, Bogdan W. Mach, Vladimir Paniotto, Wojciech Zaborowski, Roberto Gutierrez, and Cory Heyman. 1997. "Social Structure and Personality under Conditions of Radical Social Change: A Comparative Analysis of Poland and Ukraine." *American Sociological Review* 62: 614–638.

Kohn, P. M., and R. G. Smart. 1987. "Wine, Women and Suspiciousness and Advertising." *Journal Studies of Alcohol and Drugs* 48: 161–166.

Kolakowski, Leszek. 1983. "Marxism and Human Rights." *Daedalus* 112, no. 4: 81–92.

Kolben, Kevin. 2010. "Labor Rights as Human Rights?" *Virginia Journal of International Law* 50: 449–484.

Komarovsky, Mirra. 1951. "Editorial: Teaching College Sociology." *Social Forces* 30: 252–256.

Koo, Jeong-Woo, and Francisco O. Ramirez. 2009. "National Incorporation of Global Human Rights: Worldwide Adoptions of National Human Rights Institutions, 1966–2004." *Social Forces* 87: 1321–1354.

Korgen, Kathleen, and Jonathan White. 2010. *The Engaged Sociologist: Connecting the Classroom to the Community*. 3rd ed. Thousand Oaks, CA: Pine Forge.

Kornbluh, Joyce. 1987. *A New Deal for Workers' Education: The Workers' Service Program, 1933–1942*. Urbana: University of Illinois Press.

Korpi, Walter. 1983. *The Democratic Class Struggle*. London: Routledge and Kegan Paul.

Kostecki, Marian, and Krzysztof Mrela. 1984. "Collective Solidarity in Poland's Powdered Society." *Critical Sociology* 12: 131–141.

Koven, Seth, and Sonya Michel, eds. 1993. *Mothers of a New World: Maternalist Politics and the Origins of Welfare States*. New York: Routledge.

Krahe, B., and C. Altwasser. 2006. "Changing Negative Attitudes towards Persons with Physical Disabilities: An Experimental Intervention." *Journal of Community and Applied Social Psychology* 16: 59–69.

Krain, Matthew, and Anne Nurse. 2004. "Teaching Human Rights through Service Learning." *Human Rights Quarterly* 26: 189–207.

Krieger, Nancy. 2000. "Discrimination and Health." In *Social Epidemiology*, edited by L. Berkman and I. Kawachi, 36–75. Oxford: Oxford University Press.

———. 2011. *Epidemiology and the People's Health*. Oxford: Oxford University Press.

Krieger, Nancy, D. L. Rowley, A. A. Herman, B. Avery, and M. T. Philips. 1993. "Racism, Sexism and Social Class: Implications for Studies of Health, Disease, and Well-Being." *American Journal of Preventive Medicine* 9: 82–122.

Krieger, Nancy, and Stephen Sidney. 1997. "Prevalence and Health Implications of Anti-Gay Discrimination: A Study of Black and White Women and Men in the Cardia Cohort." *International Journal of Health Services* 27, no. 1: 157–176.

Krieger, Nancy, Pamela D. Waterman, Cathy Hartman, Lisa M. Bates, Anne M. Stoddard, Margaret M. Quinn, Glorian Sorensen, and Elizabeth M. Barbeau. 2006. "Social Hazards on the Job: Workplace Abuse, Sexual Harassment, and Racial Discrimination—a Study of Black, Latino, and White Low-Income Women and Men Workers in the United States." *International Journal of Health Services* 36: 51–85.

Kriesi, Hanspeter. 2004. "Political Context and Opportunity." In *The Blackwell Companion to Social Movements*, edited by David A. Snow, Sarah A. Soule, and Hanspeter Kreisi, 67–90. Oxford, UK: Blackwell.

Kreisler, Harry. 2005. "Lakhdar Brahimi Interview: Conversations with History; Institute of International Studies. UC Berkeley." Institute of International Studies. April 5. http://globetrotter.berkeley.edu/people5/Brahimi/brahimi-con4.html.

Krippner, Greta. 2010. "Democracy of Credit: Transformations in Economic Citizenship." Paper presented at the annual meeting of the American Sociological Association, Atlanta, Georgia, August.

Kristoff, Nicholas. 2010. "Our Banana Republic." *New York Times*. November 6. http://www.nytimes.com/2010/11/07/opinion/07kristof.html (accessed December 18, 2010).

Krog, Antjie. 2010. "In the Name of Human Rights: I Say (How) You (Should) Speak (before I Listen)." In *Qualitative Inquiry and Human Rights*, edited by Norman Denzin and Michael Giardina, 66–81. Walnut Creek, CA: Left Coast Press.

Krugman, Paul R. 2007. *The Conscience of a Liberal.* New York: W. W. Norton and Co.

Kuhn, Thomas S. 1996. *The Structure of Scientific Revolutions.* Chicago: University of Chicago Press.

Kulick, Don. 1998. *Travesti: Sex, Gender, and Culture among Brazilian Transgendered Prostitutes.* Chicago: University of Chicago Press.

Kunioka, Todd T., and Karen M. McCurdy. 2006. "Relocation and Internment: Civil Rights Lessons from World War II." *PS: Political Science and Politics* 39: 503–511.

Kurashige, Scott. 2002. "Detroit and the Legacy of Vincent Chin." *Amerasia Journal* 28: 51–55.

Kuroiwa, Yoko, and Maykel Verkuyten. 2008. "Narratives and the Constitutions of Common Identity: The Karen in Burma." *Identities: Global Studies in Power and Culture* 15: 391–412.

Kurtz, Lester R. 2008. "Gandhi and His Legacies." *Encyclopedia of Violence, Peace and Conflict,* edited by Lester R. Kurtz, 837–851. 2nd ed. Amsterdam: Elsevier.

———. 2010. "Repression's Paradox in China." OpenDemocracy. November 17. http://www.opendemocracy.net/lester-r-kurtz/repression's-paradox-in-china (accessed January 20, 2012).

———. 2012. *Gods in the Global Village.* Los Angeles: Sage Pine Forge.

Laclau, Ernesto, and Chantal Mouffe. 1985. *Hegemony and Socialist Strategy: Towards a Radical Democratic Politics.* Translated by Winston Moore and Paul Cammack. London: Verso.

Lamb, H. R. 1998. "Mental Hospitals and Deinstitutionalization." In *Encyclopedia of Mental Health,* edited by H. S. Friedman, 2: 665–676. San Diego: Academic Press.

Lamont, Michèle. 2000. *The Dignity of Working Men: Morality and the Boundaries of Race, Class, and Immigration.* Cambridge, MA: Harvard University Press.

Landry, Bart. 2007. *Race, Gender, and Class: Theory and Methods of Analysis.* Upper Saddle River, NJ: Pearson.

Landsman, Stephen. 2005. *Crimes of the Holocaust: The Law Confronts Hard Cases.* Philadelphia: University of Pennsylvania Press.

Langer, Suzanne K. 1953. *Feeling and Form: A Theory of Art.* New York: Scribner.

Langevoort, Donald C. 1996. "Selling Hope, Selling Risk: Some Lessons for Law from Behavioral Economics about Stockbrokers and Sophisticated Customers." *California Law Review* 84: 627.

Langlois, Anthony J. 2002. "Human Rights: The Globalization and Fragmentation of Moral Discourse." *Review of International Studies* 28, no. 3: 479–496.

Lareau, Annette. 2003. *Unequal Childhoods: Class, Race, and Family Life.* Berkeley: University of California Press.

Larson, Heidi. 1999. "Voices of Pacific Youth: Video Research as a Tool for Youth Expression." *Visual Sociology* 14: 163–172.

Laslett, John H. M. 1970. *Labor and the Left: A Study of Socialist and Radical Influences in the American Labor Movement.* New York: Basic Books.

Laslett, John H. M., and Seymour Martin Lipset, eds. 1974. *Failure of a Dream? Essays on the History of American Socialism.* Garden City, NY: Doubleday.

Latour, Bruno. 2007. *Reassembling the Social.* New York: Oxford University Press.

Laumann, Edward O., John H. Gagnon, Robert T. Michael, and Stuart Michaels. 2000. *The Social Organization of Sexuality: Sexual Practices in the United States.*

Lauren, Paul Gordon. 1998. *The Evolution of International Human Rights: Visions Seen.* Philadelphia: University of Pennsylvania Press.

———. 2008. "History and Human Rights: People and Forces in Paradoxical Interaction." *Journal of Human Rights* 7: 91–103.

LaVeist, Thomas A. 2002. "Segregation, Poverty and Empowerment: Health Consequences for African Americans." In *Race, Ethnicity and Health,* edited by Thomas A. LaVeist, 76–96. San Francisco: Jossey-Bass.

Law, Joan, and John Hassard, eds. 1999. *Actor Network Theory and After.* Oxford and Keele, UK: Blackwell and the Sociological Review.

Leary, Virginia A. 1996. "The Paradox of Workers' Rights as Human Rights." In *Human Rights, Labor Rights, and International Trade,* edited by Lance A. Compa and Stephen F. Diamond. Philadelphia: University of Pennsylvania Press.

Leasher, M. K., C. E. Miller, and M. P. Gooden. 2009. "Rater Effects and Attitudinal Barriers Affecting People with Disabilities in Personnel Selection." *Journal of Applied Social Psychology* 39: 2236–2274.

Lebovic, James H., and Erik Voeten. 2006. "The Politics of Shame: The Condemnation of Country Human Rights Practices in the UNHCR." *International Studies Quarterly* 50, no. 4: 861–888.

Lebowitz, Michael. 2010. "Socialism: The Goal, the Paths and the Compass. The Bullet. Socialist Project." *E-Bulletin* 315 (February 20).

Lechner, Frank. 2005. "Religious Rejections of Globalization and Their Directions." In *Religion in Global Civil Society,* edited by M. Juergensmeyer. Oxford: Oxford University Press.

Lechner, Frank, and John Boli. 2005. *World Culture: Origins and Consequences.* Malden, MA: Blackwell Publishing.

Lee, Alfred McClung. 1973. *Toward Humanist Sociology.* Englewood-Cliffs, NJ: Prentice Hall.

———. 1979. "The Services of Clinical Sociology." *American Behavioral Scientist* 22: 487–511.

Lee, Angela Y. 2001. "The Mere Exposure Effect: An Uncertainty Reduction Explanation Revisited." *Personality and Social Psychology Bulletin* 27: 1255–1266.

Lee, Everett S. 1966. "A Theory of Migration." *Demography* 3: 47–57.

Lefebvre, Henri. 1968. *The Sociology of Marx*. Translated by Norbert Guterman. New York: Pantheon Books.

———. 1971. *Everyday Life in the Modern World*. Translated by Sacha Rabinovitch. New York: Harper and Row.

Lefort, Claude. 1986. "Politics and Human Rights." In *The Political Forms of Modern Society* 239. http://www.geocities.com/~johngray/impl13.htm (accessed September 6, 2012).

Leibovitz, Joseph. 2007. "Faultline Citizenship: Ethnonational Politics, Minority Mobilisation, and Governance in the Israeli 'Mixed Cities' of Haifa and Tel Aviv-Jaffa." *Ethnopolitics* 6: 235–263.

Leigh, Gillian, and Robin Gerrish. 1986. "Attitudes toward Alcoholism in Volunteer Therapist Aides: Do They Change?" *Drug and Alcohol Dependence* 17, no. 4: 381–390.

Leik, Robert K., and Barbara F. Meeker. 1975. *Mathematical Sociology*. Englewood Cliffs, NJ: Prentice Hall.

Lekachman, Robert. 1966. *The Age of Keynes*. New York: Random House.

Lembcke, Jerry. 1984. "Labor and Education: Portland Labor College, 1921–1929." *Oregon Historical Quarterly* 85: 117–134.

Lemus, Maria, Kimberly Stanton, and John Walsh. 2005. "Colombia: A Vicious Cycle of Drugs and War." In *Drugs and Democracy in Latin America*, edited by Eileen Rosin and Coletta Youngers, 112–120. Boulder, CO: Lynne Rienner Publishers.

Lengerman, Patricia, and Jill Niebrugge-Brantley. 1998. *The Women Founders: Sociology and Social Theory, 1830–1930*. Boston, MA: McGraw-Hill.

———. 2002. "Back to the Future: Settlement Sociology, 1885–1930." *American Sociologist* 33: 5–20.

———. 2007. "Thrice Told: Narratives of Sociology's Relation to Social Work." In *Sociology in America*, edited by Craig Calhoun, 63–114. Chicago: University of Chicago Press.

Lenin, Vladimir I. 1939. *Imperialism, the Highest Stage of Capitalism*. New York: International Publishers.

———. 2007. *The State and Revolution*. Synergy International of the Americas.

Lenski, Gerhard. 1966. *Power and Privilege: A Theory of Social Stratification*. New York: McGraw-Hill.

———. 2005. *Ecological-Evolutionary Theory: Principles and Applications*. Boulder, CO, and London: Paradigm Publishers.

Lenski, Gerhard, and Patrick Nolan. 2005. "Trajectories of Development among Third World Societies." In *Evolutionary Theory: Principles and Applications*, edited by Gerhard Lenski, 187–201. Boulder, CO: Paradigm Publishers.

Lenzer, Gertrud, and Brian K. Gran. 2011. "Rights and the Role of Family Engagement in Child Welfare: An International Treaties Perspective on Family's Rights, Parents' Rights, and Children's Rights." In "Taking Child and Family Rights Seriously: Family Engagement and Its Evidence in Child Welfare," special issue, *Child Welfare* 90, no. 4: 157–179.

Lerner, S. 2010. *Sacrifice Zones: The Frontlines of Toxic Chemical Exposure in the United States*. Cambridge, MA: MIT Press.

Levels, M., J. Dronkers, and G. Kraaykamp. 2008. "Educational Achievement of Immigrants in Western Countries: Origin, Destination, and Community Effects on Mathematical Performance." *American Sociological Review* 73, no. 5: 835–853.

Levine, Donald Nathan. 1985. "Rationality and Freedom: Inveterate Multivocals." In *The Flight from Ambiguity: Essays in Social and Cultural Theory*, 142–178. Chicago: University of Chicago Press.

Levine, J. 2002. *Harmful to Minors: The Perils of Protecting Children from Sex*. Minneapolis: University of Minnesota Press.

Levine, Judith A., Clifton R. Emery, and Harold Pollack. 2007. "The Well-Being of Children Born to Teen Mothers." *Journal of Marriage and Family* 69 (February): 105–122.

Levit, Nancy. 2002. "Theorizing the Connections among Systems of Subordination." *University of Missouri–Kansas City Law Review* 77: 227–249.

Levitt, Peggy. 2001. *Transnational Villagers*. Berkeley: University of California Press.

———. 2005. "Building Bridges: What Migration Scholarship and Cultural Sociology Have to Say to Each Other." *Poetics* 33: 49–62.

Levitt, Peggy, and Sally Merry. 2009. "Vernacularization on the Ground: Local Uses of Global Women's Rights in Peru, China, India and the United States." *Global Networks* 9, no. 4: 441–461.

Levy, Daniel, and Natan Sznaider. 2006. "Sovereignty Transformed: A Sociology of Human Rights." *British Journal of Sociology* 57: 657–676.

Lewack, Howard. 1953. *Campus Rebels: A Brief History of the Student League for Industrial Democracy*. New York: Student League for Industrial Democracy.

Lewis, L. 2009a. "Introduction: Mental Health and Human Rights: Social Policy and Sociological Perspectives." *Social Policy and Society* 8: 211–214.

——. 2009b. "Politics of Recognition: What Can a Human Rights Perspective Contribute to Understanding Users' Experiences of Involvement in Mental Health Services?" *Social Policy and Society* 8: 257–274.

Lewis, Tammy. 2004. "Service Learning for Social Change? Lessons from a Liberal Arts College." *Teaching Sociology* 32: 94–108.

Leydesdorff, L., and T. Schank. 2008. "Dynamic Animations of Journal Maps: Indicators of Structural Change and Interdisciplinary Developments." *Journal of the American Society for Information Science and Technology* 59, no. 11: 1810–1818.

Liao, Tim Futing. 2006. "Measuring and Analyzing Class Inequality with the Gini Index Informed by Model-Based Clustering." *Sociological Methodology* 36: 201–224.

Lichtenstein, B. 2003. "Stigma as a Barrier to Treatment of Sexually Transmitted Infection in the American Deep South: Issues of Race, Gender, and Poverty." *Social Science & Medicine* 57: 2435–2445.

Liebow, Elliot. 1993. *Tell Them Who I Am: The Lives of Homeless Women*. New York: Penguin.

——. 2003. *Tally's Corner: A Study of Negro Streetcorner Men*. 2nd ed. New York: Rowman & Littlefield.

Liebowitz, Deborah. 2008. *Respect, Protect, and Fulfill: Raising the Bar on Women's Rights in San Francisco*. San Francisco: Women's Institute for Leadership Development for Human Rights.

Light, Donald W. 2001. "Comparative Models of Health Care Systems." In *The Sociology of Health and Illness: Critical Perspectives*, edited by Peter Conrad, 464–479. 6th ed. New York: Worth Publishers.

Lindenberg, S. 2006a. "Rational Choice Theory." In *International Encyclopedia of Economic Sociology*, edited by J. Beckert and M. Zafirovski, 548–552. New York: Routledge.

——. 2006b. "Social Rationality." In *International Encyclopedia of Economic Sociology*, edited by J. Beckert and M. Zafirovski, 16–618. New York: Routledge.

Lindsay, Jo. 2009. "Young Australians and the Staging of Intoxification and Self-Control." *Journal of Youth Studies* 12, no. 4: 371–384.

Link, B. G., B. Dohrenwend, and A. Skodol. 1986. "Socioeconomic Status and Schizophrenia: Noisome Occupational Characteristics as a Risk Factor." *American Sociological Review* 51: 242–258.

Link, B. G., E. L. Struening, M. Rahav, J. C. Phelan, and L. Nuttbrock. 1997. "On Stigma and Its Consequences: Evidence from a Longitudinal Study of Men with Dual Diagnosis of Mental Illness and Substance Abuse." *Journal of Health and Social Behavior* 38: 177–190.

Link, Bruce, and Jo Phelan. 1995. "Social Conditions and Fundamental Causes of Illness." *Journal of Health and Social Behavior* (extra issue) 35: 80–94.

——. 2001. "Conceptualizing Stigma." *Annual Review of Sociology* 27: 363–385.

——. 2010. "Social Conditions as Fundamental Causes of Health Inequalities." In *Handbook of Medical Sociology*, edited by Chloe Bird, Peter Conrad, Allen Fremont, and Stephan Timmermans, 3–17. 6th ed. Nashville, TN: Vanderbilt University Press.

Linzey, Andrew. 2009. *The Link between Animal Abuse and Human Violence*. East Sussex, UK: Sussex Academic Press.

Lippett, R., J. Watson, and B. Westley. 1958. *The Dynamics of Planned Change*. New York: Harcourt, Brace and World.

Lippman, Abby. 1991. "Prenatal Genetic Testing and Screening: Constructing Needs and Reinforcing Tendencies." *American Journal of Law and Society* 17: 15–50.

Lipset, Seymour Martin. 1960. "The Political Process in Trade Unions: A Theoretical Statement." In *Labor and Trade Unionism*, edited by W. Galenson and S. M. Lipset. New York: Wiley.

——. 1981. *Political Man*. Baltimore: John Hopkins University Press.

Lipsitz, George. 2006. *The Possessive Investment in Whiteness: How White People Profit from Identity Politics*. Philadelphia: Temple University Press.

Lipton, M. 1980. "Migration from Rural Areas of Poor Countries: The Impact on Rural Productivity and Income Distribution." *World Development* 8: 1–24.

Lisborg, Russell, S. 1993. "Migrant Remittances and Development." *International Migration* 31: 267–287.

Little, David. 1991. *Varieties of Social Explanation*. Boulder, CO: Westview.

——. 1999. "Review: Rethinking Human Rights: A Review Essay on Religion, Relativism, and Other Matters." *Journal of Religious Ethics* 27: 149–177.

Lo, Clarence Y. H. 2008. "State Capitalism." In *International Encyclopedia of the Social Sciences*, edited by William A. Darity Jr. 2nd ed. Detroit, MI: Macmillan Reference.

——. Forthcoming. *Politics of Justice for Corporate Wrongdoing–Equality, Market Fairness, and Retribution in Enron and Beyond*.

Locke, J. 1970 [1689]. *Two Treatises of Government*. Cambridge, UK: Cambridge University Press.

Lockwood, Elizabeth, Daniel Barstow Magraw, Margaret Faith Spring, and S. I. Strong. 1998. *The International Human Rights of Women: Instruments of Change*. Washington, DC: American Bar Association Section of International Law and Practice.

Loe, Meika. 2006. *The Rise of Viagra: How the Little Blue Pill Changed Sex in America*. New York: New York University Press.

Logan, John R., and Harvey L. Molotch. 2007. *Urban Fortunes: The Political Economy of Place*. 2nd ed. Berkeley: University of California Press.

London, L. 2008. "What Is a Human Rights–Based Approach to Health and Does It Matter?" *Health and Human Rights* 10: 65–80.

Long, A. B. 2008. "Introducing the New and Improved Americans with Disabilities Act: Assessing the ADA Amendments Act of 2008." *Northwestern University Law Review Colloquy* 103: 217–229.

Longmore, P. K. 2003. *Why I Burned My Book and Other Essays on Disability*. Philadelphia: Temple University Press.

López, Ian Haney. 2006. *White by Law: The Legal Construction of Race*. Rev. and updated 10th anniv. ed. New York: New York University Press.

Lopez, Iris. 1993. "Agency and Constraint: Sterilization and Reproductive Freedom among Puerto Rican Women in New York City." *Urban Anthropology* 22: 299–323.

———. 2008. *Matters of Choice: Puerto Rican Women's Struggle for Reproductive Freedom*. New Brunswick, NJ: Rutgers University Press.

Lorber, Judith. 2002. *Gender and the Construction of Illness*. Lanham, MD: AltaMira Press.

Lorber, Judith, and Lisa Jean Moore. 2002. *Gender and the Social Construction of Illness*. Newbury Park, CA: Sage Publications.

———. 2007. *Gendered Bodies: Feminist Perspectives*. New York: Oxford.

Los Angeles Times. 2011. "Mexico under Siege: The Drug War at Our Doorstop." *Los Angeles Times*. http://projects.latimes.com/mexico-drug-war (accessed January 1, 2011).

Lounsbury, Michael, and Paul M. Hirsch, eds. 2010. *Markets on Trial: The Economic Sociology of the U.S. Financial Crisis*. Research in the Sociology of Organizations 30A. London: Emerald Group Publishing.

Low, Petra. 2010. "Devastating Natural Disasters Continue Steady Rise." *Vital Signs: Global Trends that Shape Our Future* (March): 38–41.

Ludvig, Alice. 2006. "'Differences between Women' Intersecting Voices in a Female Narrative." *European Journal of Women's Studies* 13: 245–258.

Lukács, Georg. 1971. *History and Class Consciousness: Studies in Marxist Dialectics*. Translated by Rodney Livingstone. Cambridge, MA: MIT Press.

Luker, Kristin. 2006. *When Sex Goes to School: Warring Views on Sex and Sex Education since the Sixties*. New York: W. W. Norton.

Lukes, Steven. 1972. *Émile Durkheim: His Life and Work*. New York: Harper and Row Publishers.

———. 2005 [1974]. *Power: A Radical View*. Houndsmill, UK: Palgrave Macmillan.

Lupton, D. 1999. *Risk*. New York: Routledge.

Lynch, Michael. 1996. "Ethnomethodology." In *The Social Science Encyclopaedia*, edited by Adam Kuper and Jessica Kuper, 266–267. 2nd ed. London: Routledge.

Lynch, Michael, and Wes Sharrock, eds. 2003. *Harold Garfinkel*. 4 vols. Sage Masters in Modern Social Thought Series. London: Sage.

Lynd, Robert S. 1939. *Knowledge for What? The Place of the Social Sciences in American Culture*. Princeton, NJ: Princeton University Press.

Lynd, Robert S., and Helen Merrell Lynd. 1929. *Middletown: A Study in Modern American Culture*. New York: Harcourt, Brace and World.

Maas, Peter. 2009. *Crude World: The Violent Twilight of Oil*. New York: Alfred Knopf.

Mackelprang, R. W., and R. D. Mackelprang. 2005. "Historical and Contemporary Issues in End-of-Life Decisions: Implications for Social Work." *Social Work* 40: 315–324.

MacKinnon, Catherine. 1993. "On Torture: A Feminist Perspective on Human Rights." In *Human Rights in the Twenty-First Century: A Global Challenge*, edited by Kathleen E. Mahoney and Paul Mahoney. Boston: Springer Publishing.

MacLean, Vicky, and Joyce Williams. 2009. "US Settlement Sociology in the Progressive Era: Neighborhood Guilds, Feminist Pragmatism and the Social Gospel." Paper presented at the annual meeting for the American Sociological Association, San Francisco, California.

Macy, M. W., and A. Flache. 1995. "Beyond Rationality in Models of Choice." *Annual Review of Sociology* 21: 73–91.

Mahler, Sarah. 1998. "Theoretical and Empirical Contributions toward a Research Agenda for Transnationalism." In *Transnationalism from Below*, edited by Michael Smith and Luis Guarnizo. London: Transaction Publishers.

Mahoney, Jack. 2006. *The Challenge of Human Rights: Origin, Development and Significance*. Malden, MA: Wiley-Blackwell.

Maier-Katkin, Daniel, Daniel P. Mears, and Thomas J. Bernard. 2011. "Toward a Criminology of Crimes against Humanity." *Theoretical Criminology* 13: 227–255.

Maira, Sunaina. 2004. "Youth Culture, Citizenship and Globalization: South Asian Muslim Youth in the United States after September 11th." *Comparative Studies of South Asia, Africa and the Middle East* 24: 219–231.

Maldonado-Torres, Nelson. 2007. "On the Coloniality of Being." *Cultural Studies* 21, no. 2–3: 240–270.

Malešević, Siniša. 2010. *The Sociology of War and Violence.* Cambridge, UK: Cambridge University Press.

Mallett, Robin K., Timothy D. Wilson, and Daniel T. Gilbert. 2008. "Expect the Unexpected: Failure to Anticipate Similarities Leads to an Intergroup Forecasting Error." *Journal of Personality and Social Psychology* 94: 265–277.

Mallinder, Louise. 2008. *Amnesties, Human Rights and Political Transitions.* Oxford: Hart.

Mamo, Laura. 2007. *Queering Reproduction: Achieving Pregnancy in the Age of Technoscience.* Durham, NC: Duke University Press.

Maney, Gregory M. 2011. "Of Praxis and Prejudice: Enhancing Scholarship and Empowering Activists through Movement-Based Research." Plenary address, Collective Behavior and Social Movements Workshop, Las Vegas, Nevada.

Mann, Abby. 1961. "Judgment at Nuremberg Script–Dialogue Transcript." Drew's Script-O-Rama. http://www.script-o-rama.com/movie_scripts/j/judgment-at-nuremburg-script-transcript.html (accessed July 20, 2012).

Mann, Jonathan M. 1996. "Health and Human Rights." *British Medical Journal* 312: 924.

Mann, Michael. 1987. "War and Social Theory: Into Battle with Classes, Nations and States." In *Sociology of War and Peace,* edited by Colin Creighton and Martin Shaw. Dobbs Ferry, NY: Sheridan House.

———. 1988. *States, War and Capitalism: Studies in Political Sociology.* Oxford: Blackwell.

Mannheim, Karl. 1936. *Ideology and Utopia.* London: Routledge.

Mansbridge, Jane. 1994. "Feminism and the Forms of Freedom." In *Critical Studies in Organization and Bureaucracy,* edited by Frank Fischer and Carmen Sirianni, 544–543. Rev. ed. Philadelphia: Temple University Press.

Manza, Jeff, and Christopher Uggen. 2006. *Locked Out: Felon Disenfranchisement and American Democracy.* New York: Oxford University Press.

March, James G., and Johan P. Olsen. 1984. "The New Institutionalism: Organizational Factors in Political Life." *American Political Science Review* 78, no. 3: 734–749.

March, James G., and Herbert Simon. 1958. *Organizations.* New York: Wiley.

———. 1976. *Ambiguity and Choice in Organizations.* Bergen, Norway: Universitetsforlaget.

Margolis, Eric. 1999. "Class Pictures: Representations of Race, Gender and Ability in a Century of School Photography." *Visual Sociology* 14, no. 1: 7–38.

Markovic, Mihailo. 1974. *From Affluence to Praxis.* Ann Arbor: University of Michigan Press.

Marks, Stephen P., and Kathleen A. Modrowski. 2008. *Human Rights Cities: Civic Engagement for Societal Development.* New York: UN-HABITAT and PDHRE.

Marmot, Michael G. 2004. *The Status Syndrome: How Your Social Standing Directly Affects Your Health and Life Expectancy.* London: Bloomsbury.

Marriage Project. 2010. *When Marriage Disappears: The New Middle America.* Charlottesville, VA: Institute for American Values.

Marshall, Brent K., and J. Steven Picou. 2008. "Post-Normal Science, Precautionary Principle and Worst Cases: The Challenge of Twenty-First Century Catastrophes." *Sociological Inquiry* 78: 230–247.

Marshall, S. L. A. 1947. *Men against Fire: The Problem of Battle Command.* New York: Morrow.

Marshall, T. H. (Thomas Humphrey). 1964. *Class, Citizenship, and Social Development.* Garden City, NY: Doubleday.

Martin, David. 1978. *A General Theory of Secularization.* New York: Harper and Row.

Martin, Karin A. 1996. *Puberty, Sexuality, and the Self: Boys and Girls at Adolescence.* New York: Routledge.

Martino, George. 2000. *Global Economy, Global Justice: Theoretical Objections and Policy Alternatives to Neo-Liberalism.* New York: Routledge.

Marx Ferree, Myra, and Aili Mari Tripp, eds. 2006. *Global Feminism: Transnational Women's Activism, Organizing, and Human Rights.* New York and London: New York University Press.

Marx, Karl. 1843a. "On the Jewish Question." Marxists Internet Archive. http://www.marxists.org/archive/marx/works/1844/jewish-question (accessed July 18, 2012).

———. 1843b. "Introduction to a Contribution to the Critique of Hegel's Philosophy of Right." Marxists Internet Archive. http://www.marxists.org/archive/marx/works/1843/critique-hpr/intro.htm (accessed July 18, 2012).

———. 1956. *The Holy Family.* Moscow: Foreign Language Publishing House.

——. 1967 [1867]. *Capital: A Critique of Political Economy.* Vol. 1: *The Process of Capitalist Production.* New York: International Publishers.

——. 1978 [1844]. "Economic and Philosophic Manuscripts of 1844." In *The Marx-Engels Reader,* edited by Robert C. Tucker, 56–67. New York: W. W. Norton.

Marx, Karl, and Friedrich Engels. 1848. *The Communist Manifesto.* http://www.anu.edu.au/polsci/marx/classics/manifesto.html (accessed September 5, 2012).

——. 1976 [1846]. *The German Ideology.* Moscow: Progress Publishers.

Mason-Schrock, Douglas. 1996. "Transsexuals' Narrative Construction of the 'True Self.'" *Social Psychology Quarterly* 59: 176–192.

Massey, Douglas S. 1988. "Economic Development and International Migration in Comparative Perspective." *Population and Development Review* 14: 383–413.

——. 2004. "Segregation and Stratification: A Biosocial Perspective." *Du Bois Review: Social Science Research on Race* 1: 7–25.

Massey, Douglas, and Nancy Denton. 1993. *American Apartheid: Segregation and the Making of the Underclass.* Cambridge, MA: Harvard University Press.

Massey, Douglas, Jorge Durand, and Nolan J. Malone. 2002. *Beyond Smoke and Mirrors: Mexican Immigration in an Era of Economic Integration.* New York: Russell Sage Foundation.

Massey, Douglas, and Rene Zenteno. 2000. "A Validation of the Ethnosurvey: The Case of Mexico-U.S. Migration." *International Migration Review* 34: 766–793.

Matcha, Duane A. 2003. *Health Care Systems of the Developed World: How the United States' System Remains an Outlier.* Westport, CT: Praeger.

Matsueda, Ross. 2006. "Differential Social Organization, Collective Action, and Crime." *Crime, Law, and Social Change* 46: 3–33.

Matsueda, Ross, Derek A. Kreager, and David Huizinga. 2006. "Deterring Delinquents: A Rational Choice Model of Theft and Violence." *American Sociological Review* 71: 95–122.

Matthews, N. 2009. "Contesting Representations of Disabled Children in Picture-Books: Visibility, the Body and the Social Model of Disability." *Children's Geographies* 7: 37–49.

Matthus, Jürgen. 2009. *Approaching an Auschwitz Survivor: Holocaust Testimony and Its Transformations.* New York: Oxford University Press.

Mayer, Karl Ulrich, and W. Müller. 1986. "The State and the Structure of the Life Course." In *Human Development and the Life Course: Multidisciplinary Perspectives,* edited by A. B. Sorensen, F. E. Weinert, and L. R. Sherrod, 217–245. Hillsdale, NJ: Lawrence Erlbaum Associates.

Mayer, Karl Ulrich. 2009. "New Directions in Life Course Research." *Annual Review of Sociology* 35: 413–433.

Maynard, Douglas W., and Stephen E. Clayman. 1991. "The Diversity of Ethnomethodology." *Annual Review of Sociology* 17: 385–418.

Mayo, E. 1933. *The Human Problems of an Industrial Civilization.* New York: Macmillan.

Mazower, Mark. 2004. "The Strange Triumph of Human Rights, 1933–1950." *Historical Journal* 47: 379–398.

Mazur, Allan. 2004. *Biosociology of Dominance and Deference.* Lanham, MD: Rowman & Littlefield.

Mazur, Allan, and A. Booth. 1998. "Testosterone and Dominance in Men." *Behavioral and Brain Sciences* 21: 353–363.

McAdam, Doug. 1982. *Political Process and the Development of Black Insurgency, 1930–1970.* Chicago: University of Chicago Press.

——. 1994. "Social Movements and Culture." In *Ideology and Identity in Contemporary Social Movements,* edited by Joseph R. Gusfield, Hank Johnston, and Enrique Laraña, 36–57. Philadelphia: Temple University Press.

——. 1999. *Political Process and Black Insurgency, 1930–1970.* 2nd ed. Chicago: University of Chicago Press.

McAdam, Doug, John D. McCarthy, and Mayer N. Zald. 1996. *Comparative Perspectives on Social Movements: Political Opportunities, Mobilizing Structures, and Cultural Framings.* Cambridge, UK: Cambridge University Press.

McAdoo, Harriette P. 1998. "African-American Families." In *Ethnic Families in America: Patterns and Variations,* edited by Charles H. Mindel, Robert W. Haberstein, and Roosevelt Wright Jr. Upper Saddle River, NJ: Prentice Hall.

McCall, Leslie. 2001. *Complex Inequality: Gender, Class and Race in the New Economy.* New York: Routledge.

——. 2005. "The Complexity of Intersectionality." *Signs* 30: 1771–1800.

McCammon, Holly J. 1990. "Legal Limits on Labor Militancy: U.S. Labor Law and the Right to Strike since the New Deal." *Social Problems* 37: 206–229.

——. 2001. "Stirring Up Suffrage Sentiment: The Formation of the State Woman Suffrage Organizations, 1866–1914." *Social Forces* 80: 449–480.

——. 2012. *A More Just Verdict: The U.S. Women's Jury Movements and Strategic Adaptation.* New York: Cambridge University Press.

McCammon, Holly J., Soma Chaudhuri, Lyndi Hewitt, Courtney Sanders Muse, Harmony D. Newman,

Carrie Lee Smith, and Teresa M. Terrell. 2008. "Becoming Full Citizens: The U.S. Women's Jury Rights Campaigns, the Pace of Reform, and Strategic Adaptation." *American Journal of Sociology* 113: 1104–1148.

McCammon, Holly J., Courtney Sanders Muse, Harmony D. Newman, and Teresa M. Terrell. 2007. "Movement Framing and Discursive Opportunity Structures: The Political Successes of the U.S. Women's Jury Movements." *American Sociological Review* 72: 725–749.

McCarthy, John D., and Mayer N. Zald. 1977. "Resource Mobilization and Social Movements: A Partial Theory." *American Sociological Review* 82: 1212–1241.

McClain, Linda. 1994. "Rights and Responsibilities." *Duke Law Journal* 43, no. 5: 989–1088.

McConnell, Eileen Diaz. 2011. "An 'Incredible Number of Latinos and Asians': Media Representations of Racial and Ethnic Population Change in Atlanta, Georgia." In "Latino/as and the Media," special issue, *Latino Studies* 9 (summer/autumn): 177–197.

McDew, Charles. 1966. "Spiritual and Moral Aspects of the Student Nonviolent Struggle in the South." In *The New Student Left*, edited by Mitchell Cohen and Dennis Hale, 51–57. Boston, MA: Beacon Press.

McFarland, Sam. 2010. "Personality and Support for Human Rights: A Review and Test of a Structural Model." *Journal of Personality* 78: 1–29.

McIntyre, Alice. 1997. *Making Meaning of Whiteness: Exploring Racial Identity with White Teachers*. Albany: State University of New York Press.

McIntyre, Richard P. 2003. "Globalism, Human Rights and the Problem of Individualism." *Human Rights and Human Welfare* 3, no. 1: 1–14.

———. 2008. *Are Worker Rights Human Rights?* Ann Arbor: University of Michigan Press.

McKinlay, John B. 1974. "A Case for Refocusing Upstream: The Political Economy of Illness." Reprinted in *The Sociology of Health and Illness: Critical Perspectives*, edited by Peter Conrad, 519–529. 5th ed. New York: Worth Publishers.

———. 1996. "Some Contributions from the Social System to Gender Inequalities in Heart Disease." *Journal of Health and Social Behavior* 37: 1–26.

McKinney, Kathleen, and Carla Howery. 2006. "Teaching and Learning in Sociology: Past, Present and Future." In *21st Century Sociology: A Reference Handbook*, edited by Clifton D. Bryant and Dennis L. Peck, 2: 379–388. Thousand Oaks, CA: Sage.

McLaren, Peter. 1989. *Life in Schools: An Introduction to Critical Pedagogy in the Foundations of Education*. New York: Longman.

———. 1999. *Schooling as Ritual Performance*. London: Routledge.

———. 2005. *Capitalists and Conquerors: A Critical Pedagogy against Empire*. New York: Rowman & Littlefield.

McLaren, Peter, and Nathalia E. Jaramillo. 1999. "Medicine and Public Health, Ethics and Human Rights." In *Health and Human Rights: A Reader*, edited by Jonathan Mann, Michael A. Grodin, Sofia Gruskin, and George J. Annas, 439–452. New York: Routledge.

———. 2007. *Pedagogy and Praxis in the Age of Empire: Towards a New Humanism*. Rotterdam: Sense Publishers.

McLeod, Jane D., and Kathryn J. Lively. 2003. "Social Structure and Personality." In *Handbook of Social Psychology*, edited by John DeLamater, 77–102. New York: Kluwer.

McNally, David. 2001. *Bodies of Meaning: Studies on Language, Labor and Liberation*. Albany: State University of New York Press.

McWhorter, John. 2011. "How the War on Drugs Is Destroying Black America." *Cato's Letter* 9, no. 1. http://www.cato.org/pubs/catosletter/catosletterv9n1.pdf.

Mead, George Herbert. 1934. *Mind, Self, and Society*. Chicago: University of Chicago Press.

———. 1967. *Mind, Self, and Society: From the Standpoint of a Social Behaviorist*. Chicago: University of Chicago Press.

———. 2008 [1918]. "Immanuel Kant on Peace and Democracy." In *Self, War and Society: George Herbert Mead's Macrosociology*, edited by Mary Jo Deegan, 159–174. New Brunswick, NJ: Transaction Publishers.

Mead, S., and M. E. Copeland. 2001. "What Recovery Means to Us: Consumers' Perspectives." In *The Tragedy of Great Power Politics*, edited by John J. Mearsheimer. New York: Norton.

Mearsheimer, John J. 2001. *The Tragedy of Great Power Politics*. New York: Norton.

Mechanic, David. 1997. "Muddling through Elegantly: Finding the Proper Balance in Rationing." *Health Affairs* 16: 83–92.

Mechanic, David, and Donna D. McAlpine. 2010. "Sociology of Health Care Reform: Building on Research and Analysis to Improve Health Care." *Journal of Health and Social Behavior* 51: S137–S159.

Mele, A., and P. Rawling. 2004. *The Oxford Handbook of Rationality*. Oxford: Oxford University Press.

Melucci, Alberto. 1989. *Nomads of the Present: Social Movements and Individual Needs in Contemporary Society*. Philadelphia: Temple University Press.

Mendez, Jennifer Bickham. 2005. *From the Revolution to the Maquiladoras: Gender, Labor, and Globalization in Nicaragua*. Durham, NC: Duke University Press.

Menjívar, Cecilia, and Leisy Abrego. 2009. "Parents and Children across Borders: Legal Instability and

Intergenerational Relations in Guatemalan and Salvadoran Families." In *Across Generations: Immigrant Families in America*, edited by N. Foner, 160–189. New York: New York University Press.

Menon, Anu. 2010. *Human Rights in Action: San Francisco's Local Implementation of the United Nations' Women's Treaty (CEDAW)*. San Francisco: City and County of San Francisco, Department on the Status of Women.

Mental Health Advisory Team IV. 2006. "Operation Iraqi Freedom 05-07." Final Report of November 17. Office of the Surgeon, Multinational Force–Iraq, and Office of the Surgeon General, United States Army Medical Command.

Merenstein, Beth Frankel. 2008. *Immigrants and Modern Racism: Reproducing Inequality*. Boulder, CO: Lynne Rienner Publishers.

Merry, Sally Engle. 2006. *Human Rights and Gender Violence: Translating International Law into Local Justice*. Chicago: University of Chicago Press.

Merton, Robert K. 1938. "Social Structure and Anomie." *American Sociological Review* 3: 672–682.

———. 1968. *Social Theory and Social Structure*. New York: The Free Press.

———. 1973. *The Sociology of Science: Theoretical and Empirical Investigations*, edited by Norman Storer. Chicago: University of Chicago Press.

Mertus, Julie. 2007. "The Rejection of Human Rights Framings: The Case of LGBT Advocacy in the US." *Human Rights Quarterly* 29: 1036–1064.

Messner, Michael A. 1992. *Power at Play: Sports and the Problem of Masculinity*. Boston: Beacon Press.

Messner, Steven F., and Richard Rosenfeld. 2007. *Crime and the American Dream*. 4th ed. Belmont, CA: Wadsworth.

Mesthene, E. 2000. "The Role of Technology in Society." In *Technology and the Future*, edited by A. H. Teich, 61–70. 8th ed. New York: Bedford/St. Martin's.

Metzger, Barbara. 2007. "Towards an International Human Rights Regime during the Inter-War Years: The League of Nations' Combat of Traffic in Women and Children." In *Beyond Sovereignty: Britain, Empire and Transnationalism, 1880–1950*, edited by Kevin Grant, Philippa Levine, and Frank Trentmann. New York: Palgrave Macmillan.

Meyer, David S. 2004. "Protest and Political Opportunities." *Annual Review of Sociology* 30: 125–145.

Meyer, Jean-Baptiste. 2001. "Network Approach versus Brain Drain: Lessons from the Diaspora." *International Migration* 39: 1468–2435. doi.10.1111/1468-2435.00173.

Meyer, John W., John Boli, George Thomas, and Francisco Ramirez. 1997. "World Society and the Nation-State." *American Journal of Sociology* 103: 144–181.

Meyer, John W. 2010. "World Society, Institutional Theories and the Actor." *Annual Review of Sociology* 36: 1–20.

Meyer, John W., and Brian Rowan. 1977. "Institutionalized Organizations: Formal Structure as Myth and Ceremony." *American Journal of Sociology* 83, no. 2: 340–363.

Meyer, Marshall W., and Lynn G. Zucker. 1989. *Permanently Failing Organizations*. Newbury Park, CA: Sage.

Meyer, William H. 1996. "Human Rights and MNCs: Theory versus Quantitative Analysis." *Human Rights Quarterly* 18: 368–397.

Michels, Robert. 1962 [1915]. *Political Parties*. New York: The Free Press.

Micklin, Michael, and Dudley L. Poston. 1995. *Continuities in Social Human Ecology*. New York: Plenum.

Middelstaedt, Emma. 2008. "Safeguarding the Rights of Sexual Minorities: Incremental and Legal Approaches to Enforcing International Human Rights Obligations." *Chicago Journal of International Law* 9: 353–386.

Midgley, Mary. 1995. *Beast and Man: The Roots of Human Nature*. London: Routledge.

Miech, R. A., A. Caspi, T. E. Moffitt, B. R. E. Wright, and P. A. Silva. 1999. "Low Socioeconomic Status and Mental Disorders: A Longitudinal Study of Selection and Causation during Young Adulthood." *American Journal of Sociology* 104: 1096–1131.

Mignolo, Walter. 2010. "De-Coloniality: Decolonial Thinking and Doing in the Andes: A Conversation by Walter Mignolo with Catherine Walsh." *Reartikulacija* 10–13. http://www.reartikulacija.org/?p=1468 (accessed July 18, 2012).

Milkman, Ruth. 1987. *Gender at Work: The Dynamics of Job Segregation by Sex during World War II*. Urbana: University of Illinois Press.

Miller, Alan S., and Rodney Stark. 2002. "Gender and Religiousness: Can Socialization Explanations Be Saved?" *American Journal of Sociology* 107: 1399–1423.

Miller, Francesca. 1999. "Feminism and Transnationalism." In *Feminisms and Internationalism*, edited by Mrinalini Sinha, Donna Guy, and Angela Woollacott. Oxford, UK: Blackwell Publishers.

Millet, Kris. 2008. "The Naxalite Movement: Exposing Scrapped Segments of India's Democracy." *Culture Magazine*. January 5. http://culturemagazine.ca/politics/the_naxalite_movement_exposing_scrapped_segments_of_indias_democracy.html (accessed July 18, 2012).

Mills, C. Wright. 1948. *The New Men of Power*. New York: Harcourt, Brace.

———. 1956. *The Power Elite*. New York: Oxford University Press.

——. 1959. *The Sociological Imagination.* New York: Oxford University Press.

Mills, Charles W. 1997. *The Racial Contract.* Ithaca, NY: Cornell University Press.

Minh-ha, Trinh T. 2009. *Woman, Native, Other: Writing Postcoloniality and Feminism.* 1st ed. Bloomington: Indiana University Press.

Mink, Gwendolyn. 1986. *Old Labor and New Immigrants in American Political Development: Union, Party, and the State, 1875–1920.* Ithaca, NY: Cornell University Press.

Minkov, Anton. 2009. *Counterinsurgency and Ethnic/Sectarian Rivalry in Comparative Perspective: Soviet Afghanistan and Iraq.* Ottawa, Canada: Centre for Operational Research and Analysis, Defense Research and Development Canada.

Minow, Martha. 1998. *Between Vengeance and Forgiveness: Facing History after Genocide and Mass Violence.* Boston: Beacon Press.

——. 2002. *Breaking the Cycles of Hatred: Memory, Law, and Repair.* Introduced and with commentaries by N. L. Rosenblum. Princeton, NJ: Princeton University Press.

Mirowsky, J., C. E. Ross, and J. R. Reynolds. 2000. "Links between Social Status and Health Status." In *Handbook of Medical Sociology,* edited by Chloe Bird, Peter Conrad, and Alan M. Fremont, 47–67. 5th ed. Upper Saddle River, NJ: Prentice Hall.

Mishel, Lawrence, and Matthew Walters. 2003. "How Unions Help All Workers." Economic Policy Institute Briefing Paper 143. Economic Policy Institute. August. http://www.epi.org/publications/entry/briefingpapers_bp143.

Mishra, Ramesh. 1984. *Welfare State in Crisis.* New York: St. Martin's Press.

Mitchell, Neil, and James McCormick. 1988. "Economic and Political Explanations of Human Rights Violations." *World Politics* 40: 476–498.

Modic, Dolores. 2008. "Stigma of Race." *Raziskave and Razprave/Research and Discussion* 1: 153–185.

Moghadam, Valentine M. 2005. *Globalizing Women: Transnational Feminist Networks.* Baltimore: Johns Hopkins University Press.

Mohanty, Chandra Talpade. 2006. *Feminism without Borders: Decolonizing Theory, Practicing Solidarity.* Durham, NC: Duke University Press.

Mohanty, Chandra Talpade, Ann Russo, and Lourdes Torres, eds. 1991. *Third World Women and the Politics of Feminism.* Bloomington: Indiana University Press.

Mojab, Shahrzad. 2009. "'Post-War Reconstruction,' Imperialism and Kurdish Women's NGOs." In *Women and War in the Middle East,* edited by Nadje Al-Ali and Nicola Pratt, 99–128. London: Zed Books.

Moncada, Alberto, and Judith Blau. 2006. "Human Rights and the Role of Social Scientists." *Societies without Borders* 1: 113–122.

Moody, Kim. 1997. *Workers in a Lean World: Unions in the International Economy.* New York: Verso.

Moore, D. 2003. "A Signaling Theory of Human Rights Compliance." *Northwestern University Law Review* 97: 879–910.

Moore, Jason. 2000. "Sugar and the Expansion of the Early Modern World-Economy." *Review: A Journal of the Fernand Braudel Center* 23, no. 33: 409–433.

Moore, Kelly. 2008. *Disrupting Science: Social Movements, American Scientists, and the Politics of the Military, 1945–1975.* Princeton, NJ: Princeton University Press.

Moore, S. F. 1978. "Law and Social Change: The Semi-Autonomous Social Field as an Appropriate Field of Study." In *Law as Process: An Anthropological Approach,* edited by S. F. Moore, 54–81. London: Routledge.

Moore, Wendy Leo. 2008. *Reproducing Racism: White Space, Elite Law Schools, and Racial Inequality.* Lanham, MD: Rowman & Littlefield.

Morales, Maria Cristina. 2009. "Ethnic-Controlled Economy or Segregation? Exploring Inequality in Latina/o Co-Ethnic Jobsites." *Sociological Forum* 24: 589–610.

Morales, Maria Cristina, and Cynthia Bejarano. 2009. "Transnational Sexual and Gendered Violence: An Application of Border Sexual Conquest at a Mexico-U.S. Border." *Global Networks* 9: 420–439.

Morin, Alain, and James Everett. 1990. "Inner Speech as a Mediator of Self-Awareness, Self-Consciousness, and Self-Knowledge: An Hypothesis." *New Ideas in Psychology* 8: 337–356.

Morrell, Ernest. 2008. *Critical Literacy and Urban Youth: Pedagogies of Access, Dissent, and Liberation.* New York: Routledge.

Morris, Lydia. 2010. *Asylum, Welfare and the Cosmopolitan Ideal.* London: Routledge.

Morse, Janice M., and Linda Niehaus. 2009. *Mixed-Method Design: Principles and Procedures.* Walnut Creek, CA: Left Coast Press.

Morsink, Johannes. 1999. *The Universal Declaration of Human Rights: Origins, Drafting and Intent.* Philadelphia: University of Pennsylvania Press.

Moser, Annalise. 2007. *Gender and Indicators: Overview Report.* Brighton, UK: Institute of Development Studies.

Mossakowski, K. N. 2008. "Dissecting the Influence of Race, Ethnicity, and Socioeconomic Status on Mental Health in Young Adulthood." *Research on Aging* 30: 649–671.

Motley, Susan. 1987. "Burning the South: U.S. Tobacco Companies in the Third World." *Multinational Monitor* 8, no. 7–8: 7–10.

Moulier Boutang, Yann. 1998. *De l'esclavage au salariat: economie histoire du salariat bride*. Paris: Partner University Fund.

Mousin, Craig B. 2003. "Standing with the Persecuted: Adjudicating Religious Asylum Claims after the Enactment of the International Religious Freedom Act of 1998." *Brigham Young University Law Review* 2003: 541–592.

Moyn, Samuel. 2010. *The Last Utopia: Human Rights in History*. Cambridge, MA: Belknap Press.

Mueller, John. 1989. *Retreat from Doomsday: The Obsolescence of Major War*. New York: Basic Books.

Muller, Mike. 1983. "Preventing Tomorrow's Epidemic: The Control of Smoking and Tobacco Production in Developing Countries." *New York State Journal of Medicine* 83, no. 13: 1304–1309.

Mullins, Christopher W., David Kauzlarich, and Dawn L. Rothe. 2004. "The International Criminal Court and the Control of State Crime: Prospects and Problems." *Critical Criminology* 12: 285–308.

Muraven, Mark, Dianne M. Tice, and Roy F. Baumeister. 1998. "Self-Control as Limited Resource: Regulatory Depletion Patterns." *Journal of Personality and Social Psychology* 74: 774–789.

Myers, Kristen, and Laura Raymond. 2010. "Elementary School Girls and Heteronormativity: The Girl Project." *Gender & Society* 24: 167–188.

Nadarajah, Saralees. 2002. "A Conversation with Samuel Kotz." *Statistical Science* 17: 220–233.

Nagarjuna. 2007 [1300]. *In Praise of Dharmadhātu*. With commentary by the Third Karmapa. Translated by Karl Brunnhölzl. Ithaca, NY: Snow Lion Publications.

Nagel, Joane. 2003. *Race, Ethnicity, and Sexuality: Intimate Intersections, Forbidden Frontiers*. New York: Oxford University Press.

Naples, Nancy A. 1991, "Socialist Feminist Analysis of the Family Support Act of 1988." *AFFILIA: Journal of Women and Social Work* 6: 23–38.

———. 1998. *Community Activism and Feminist Politics: Organizing across Race, Gender and Class*. New York: Routledge.

———. 2009. "Teaching Intersectionality Intersectionally." *International Feminist Journal of Politics* 11: 566–577.

———. 2011. "Women's Leadership, Social Capital and Social Change." In *Activist Scholar: Selected Works of Marilyn Gittell*, edited by Kathe Newman and Ross Gittell, 263–278. Thousand Oaks, CA: Sage Publications.

Naples, Nancy A., and Manisha Desai. 2002. *Women's Activism and Globalization: Linking Local Struggles and Transnational Politics*. New York: Routledge.

Narayan, Uma. 1997. *Dislocating Cultures: Identities, Traditions, and Third World Feminism*. New York: Routledge.

———. 1998. "Essence of Culture and a Sense of History: A Feminist Critique of Cultural Essentialism." *Hypatia* 13: 86–106.

Nash, J. C. 2008. "Re-thinking Intersectionality." *Feminist Review* 89: 1–15.

National Center on Addiction and Substance Abuse (CASA) at Columbia University. 2001. "Malignant Neglect: Substance Abuse and America's Schools." CASA. http://www.casacolumbia.org/templates/Publications.aspx?articleid=320&zoneid=52.

National Drug Strategy Network. 1997. "18-Year-Old Texan, Herding Goats, Killed by U.S. Marine Corps Anti-Drug Patrol; Criminal Investigation of Shooting Underway." National Drug Strategy Network News Briefs. July. http://www.ndsn.org/july97/goats.html (accessed March 23, 2011).

Navarro, Vicente. 2004. "The Politics of Health Inequalities Research in the United States." *International Journal of Health Services* 34, no. 1: 87–99.

Neckerman, Kathryn. 2010. *Schools Betrayed: Roots of Failure in Inner-City Education*. Chicago: University of Chicago Press.

Nee, Victor. 2005. "The New Institutionalisms in Economics and Sociology." In *The Handbook of Economic Sociology*, edited by N. J. Smelser and R. Swedberg, 49–74. Princeton, NJ: Princeton University Press and Russell Sage Foundation

Neilson, Brett, and Mohammed Bamyeh. 2009. "Drugs in Motion: Toward a Materialist Tracking of Global Mobilities." *Cultural Critique* 71: 1–12.

Nettle, Daniel, and Thomas V. Pollet. 2008. "Natural Selection on Male Wealth in Humans." *American Naturalist* 172: 658–666.

Nevins, Joseph. 2003. "Thinking Out of Bounds: A Critical Analysis of Academic and Human Rights: Writings on Migrant Deaths in the U.S.-Mexico Border Region." *Migraciones Internacionales* 2: 171–190.

New York City Human Rights Initiative. 2011. http://www.nychri.org (accessed May 25, 2011).

Newman, Katherine S. 2008. *Chutes and Ladders: Navigating the Low-Wage Labor Market*. Cambridge, MA: Harvard University Press.

Ngai, Mae M. 2004. *Impossible Subjects: Illegal Aliens and the Making of Modern America*. Princeton, NJ: Princeton University Press.

Niazi, Tarique. 2002. "The Ecology of Genocide in Rwanda." *International Journal of Contemporary Sociology* 39, no. 2: 219–247.

———. 2005. "Democracy, Development, and Terrorism: The Case of Baluchistan (Pakistan)." *International Journal of Contemporary Sociology* 42, no. 2: 303–337.

———. 2008. "Toxic Waste." In *International Encyclopedia of the Social Sciences*, edited by William A. Darity, 407–409. 2nd ed. Farmington Hills, MI: Gale.

Nibert, David. 2002. *Animal Rights/Human Rights*. Lanham, MD: Rowman & Littlefield.

———. 2006. "The Political Economy of Beef: Oppression of Cows and Other Devalued Groups in Latin America." Paper presented at the annual meeting of the American Sociological Association, Montreal, Quebec, August 11, 2006.

Nichter, Mark, and Elizabeth Cartwright. 1991. "Saving the Children for the Tobacco Industry." *Medical Anthropology Quarterly*, New Series 5, no. 3: 236–256.

Nickel, James. 2010. "Human Rights." Stanford Encyclopedia of Philosophy. http://plato.stanford.edu/entries/rights-human (accessed July 18, 2012).

Nielsen, Francois. 2004. "The Ecological-Evolutionary Typology of Human Societies and the Evolution of Social Inequality." *Sociological Theory* 22: 292–314.

———. 2006. "Achievement and Ascription in Educational Attainment: Genetic and Environmental Influences on Adolescent Schooling." *Social Forces* 85: 193–216.

Nobis, Nathan. 2004. "Carl Cohen's 'Kind' Arguments for Animal Rights and against Human Rights." *Journal of Applied Philosophy* 21: 43–49.

Noguchi, Y. 2008. "Clinical Sociology in Japan." In *International Clinical Sociology*, edited by J. M. Fritz, 72–81. New York: Springer.

Nolan, James. 2001. *Reinventing Justice: The American Drug Court Movement*. Princeton, NJ: Princeton University Press.

Nolan, P., and G. Lenski. 2011. *Human Societies: An Introduction to Macrosociology*. Boulder, CO: Paradigm Publishers.

Nordberg, Camilla. 2006. "Claiming Citizenship: Marginalised Voices on Identity and Belonging." *Citizenship Studies* 10: 523–539.

Nöth, Winfried. 1995. *Handbook of Semiotics*. Bloomington: Indiana University Press.

Nouwen, S., and W. Werner. 2010. "Doing Justice to the Political: The International Criminal Court in Uganda and Sudan." *European Journal of International Law* 21: 941–965.

Núñez, Guillermina, and Josiah McC. Heyman. 2007. "Entrapment Processes and Immigrant Communities in a Time of Heightened Border Vigilance." *Human Organization* 66: 354–365.

Nyland, Chris, and Mark Rix. 2000. "Mary van Kleeck, Lillian Gilbreth and the Women's Bureau Study of Gendered Labor Law." *Journal of Management History* 6: 306–322.

Nystrom, P. C. 1981. "Designing Jobs and Assigning Employees." In *Handbook of Organizational Design*. Vol. 2: *Remodelling Organizations and Their Environments*, edited by P. C. Nystrom and William Starbuck, 272–301. New York: Oxford University Press.

O'Connor, Alice. 2002. *Poverty Knowledge: Social Science, Social Policy and the Poor in Twentieth-Century U.S. History*. Princeton, NJ: Princeton University Press.

O'Connor, Alice, Chris Tilly, and Lawrence D. Bobo. 2001. *Urban Inequality: Evidence from Four Cities*. New York: Russell Sage Foundation.

Offe, Claus. 1984. *Contradictions of the Welfare State*. Cambridge, MA: MIT Press.

———. 1985. *Disorganized Capitalism*. Cambridge, MA: MIT Press.

Office of the High Commissioner for Human Rights (OHCHR). 1998. *Basic Human Rights Instruments*. 3rd ed. Geneva: Office of the High Commissioner for Human Rights.

———. 2010. *2009 OHCHR Report on Activities and Results*. New York: United Nations.

———. 2011. "Human Rights at the Centre of Climate Change Policy." OHCHR. www.ohchr.org/EN/NewsEvents/pages/climate change policy (accessed January 1, 2011).

Ogien, A. 1994. "L'usage de drogues peut-il etre un object de recherché?" In *La Demande sociale de drogues*, edited by A. Ogien and P. Mignon, 7–12. Paris: La Documentation Française.

Okin, Susan Moller. 1989. *Justice, Gender, and the Family*. New York: Basic Books.

Okonta, I., and O. Douglas. 2001. *Where Vultures Feast: Shell, Human Rights, and Oil in the Niger Delta*. San Francisco: Sierra Club Books.

Oliver, Kelly. 2009. *Animal Lessons: How They Teach Us to Be Human*. New York: Columbia University Press.

Olshansky, S. Jay, and A. Brian Ault. 1986. "The Fourth Stage of the Epidemiologic Transition: The Age of Delayed Degenerative Disease." *Milbank Memorial Fund Quarterly* 64: 355–391.

Olson, Mancur. 1982. *The Rise and Decline of Nations: Economic Growth, Stagflation, and Social Rigidities*. New Haven, CT: Yale University Press.

Omi, M., and H. Winant. 1986. *Racial Formation in the United States: From the 1960s to the 1980s*. New York: Routledge.

———. 1994. *Racial Formation in the United States: From the 1960s to the 1980s*. 2nd ed. New York: Routledge.

Omran, Abdel R. 1971. "The Epidemiological Transition." *Milbank Memorial Fund Quarterly* 49: 509–538.

Oneal, John, and Bruce Russett. 2011. *Triangulating Peace: Democracy, Interdependence, and International Organizations*. New York: Norton.

Onken, S. J., and E. Slaten. 2000. "Disability Identity Formation and Affirmation: The Experiences of Persons with Severe Mental Illness." *Sociological Practice: A Journal of Clinical and Applied Sociology* 2: 99–111.

Ontario Human Rights Commission (OHRC). 2001. *An Intersectional Approach to Discrimination, Addressing Multiple Grounds in Human Rights Claims*. OHRC. http://www.ohrc.on.ca/sites/default/files/attachments/An_intersectional_approach_to_discrimination%3A_Addressing_multiple_grounds_in_human_rights_claims.pdf (accessed July 18, 2012).

Oppenheimer, Gerald. 1991. "To Build a Bridge: The Use of Foreign Models by Domestic Critics of US Drug Policy." *Milbank Quarterly* 69, no. 3: 495–526.

Oppenheimer, Martin, Martin Murray, and Rhonda Levine. 1991. *Radical Sociologists and the Movement: Experiences, Legacies, and Lessons*. Philadelphia: Temple University Press.

Orellana, Marjorie Faulstich. 1999. "Space and Place in an Urban Landscape: Learning from Children's Views of Their Social Worlds." *Visual Sociology* 14: 73–89.

Orentlicher, Diane F. 1990. "Bearing Witness: The Art and Science of Human Rights Fact-Finding." *Harvard Law School Human Rights Journal* 3: 83–136.

Orr, David W. 1979. "Catastrophe and Social Order." *Human Ecology* 7: 41–52.

Ortiz, Victor M. 2001. "The Unbearable Ambiguity of the Border." *Social Justice* 28: 96–112.

Osiel, Mark J. 1997. *Mass Atrocities, Collective Memory, and the Law*. New Brunswick, NJ: Transaction Publishers.

Ostrom, Elinor. 1990. *Governing the Commons: The Evolution of Institutions for Collective Action*. Cambridge, UK: Cambridge University Press.

Ouellette-Kuntz, H., P. Burge, H. K. Brown, and E. Arsenault. 2010. "Public Attitudes towards Individuals with Intellectual Disabilities as Measured by the Concept of Social Distance." *Journal of Applied Research in Intellectual Disabilities* 23: 132–142.

Oxtoby, Willard G., and Allan F. Segal, eds. *A Concise Introduction to World Religions*. New York: Oxford University Press.

Page, Charles Hunt. 1982. *Fifty Years in the Sociological Enterprise: A Lucky Journey*. Amherst: University of Massachusetts Press.

Park, Robert E. 1914. "Racial Assimilation in Secondary Groups with Particular Reference to the Negro." *American Journal of Sociology* 19: 606–623.

———. 1928a. "Human Migration and the Marginal Man." *American Journal of Sociology* 33: 881–893.

———. 1928b. "The Bases of Race Prejudice." *Annals of the American Academy of Political and Social Science* 140: 11–20.

Parker, Karen. 2008. *Unequal Crime Decline: Theorizing Race, Urban Inequality, and Criminal Violence*. New York: New York University Press.

Parreñas, Rhacel Salazar. 1998. "The Global Servants: (Im)Migrant Filipina Domestic Workers in Rome and Los Angeles." Unpublished PhD diss., Department of Ethnic Studies, University of California, Berkeley.

Parsons, Talcott. 1951. *The Social System*. New York: The Free Press.

———. 1959. "The School as a Social System." *Harvard Educational Review* 29: 297–318.

Pascal, Celine-Marie. 2007. *Making Sense of Race, Class and Gender: Commonsense, Power and Privilege in the United States*. New York: Routledge.

Pascoe, C. J. 2007. *Dude, You're a Fag: Masculinity and Sexuality in High School*. Berkeley: University of California Press.

Pastor, Eugenia Relaño. 2005. "The Flawed Implementation of the International Religious Freedom Act of 1998: A European Perspective." *Brigham Young University Law Review* 2005: 711–746.

Patai, Raphael. 2002. *The Arab Mind*. New York: Hatherleigh Press.

Patterson, Charles. 2002. *Eternal Treblinka: Our Treatment of Animals and the Holocaust*. New York: Lantern Books.

Pattillo, Mary. 2007. *Black on the Block: The Politics of Race and Class in the City*. Chicago: University of Chicago Press.

Paust, Jordan J. 2004. "Post 9/11 Overreaction and Fallacies Regarding War and Defense, Guantanamo, the Status of Persons, Treatment, Judicial Review of Detention, and Due Process in Military Commissions." *Notre Dame Law Review* 79: 1335–1364.

Payne, Leigh. 2009. "Consequences of Transitional Justice." Paper presented at the Department of Political Science, University of Minnesota, Minneapolis.

PDHRE (People's Movement for Human Rights Learning). 2011. http://www.pdhre.org (accessed May 24, 2011).

Pearlin, L., and C. Schooler. 1978. "The Structure of Coping." *Journal of Health and Social Behavior* 19: 2–21.

Pécoud, Antoine, and Paul de Guchteneire. 2006. "International Migration, Border Controls and Human Rights: Assessing the Relevance of a Right to Mobility." *Journal of Borderlands Studies* 21: 69–86.

Peffley, Mark, and John Hurwitz. 2007. "Persuasion and Resistance: Race and the Death Penalty in America." *American Journal of Political Science* 51: 996–1012.

Pellow, D. N. 2007. *Resisting Global Toxics: Transnational Movements for Environmental Justice.* Cambridge, MA: MIT Press.

Penn, Michael, and Aditi Malik. 2010. "The Protection and Development of the Human Spirit: An Expanded Focus for Human Rights Discourse." *Human Rights Quarterly* 32, no. 3: 665–688.

Penna, David R., and Patricia J. Campbell. 1998. "Human Rights and Culture: Beyond Universality and Relativism." *Third World Quarterly* 19: 7–27.

Pennebaker, James W. 1997. "Writing about Emotional Experiences as a Therapeutic Process." *Psychological Science* 8: 162–166.

Perelman, Michael. 1978. "Karl Marx's Theory of Science." *Journal of Economic Issues* 12, no. 4: 859–870.

Peretti-Watel, Patrick. 2003. "How Does One Become a Cannabis Smoker? A Quantitative Approach." *Revue Française de Sociologie* 44: 3–27.

Peritz, Rudolph J. R. 1996. *Competition Policy in America, 1888–1992: History, Rhetoric, Law.* New York: Oxford University Press.

Perlman, Selig. 1922. *History of Trade Unionism in the United States.* New York: Macmillan.

———. 1928. *A Theory of the Labor Movement.* New York: Macmillan.

Perrin, Andrew J., and Lee Hedwig. 2007. "The Undertheorized Environment: Sociological Theory and the Ontology of Behavioral Genetics." *Sociological Perspectives* 50: 303–322.

Perrow, Charles. 1967. *Complex Organizations: A Critical Essay.* New York: Random House.

———. 1999. *Normal Accidents: Living with High-Risk Technologies.* Princeton, NJ: Princeton University Press.

———. 2002. *Organizing America, Wealth, Power, and the Origins of Corporate Capitalism.* Princeton, NJ, and Oxford, UK: Princeton University Press.

———. 2008. "Complexity, Catastrophe, and Modularity." *Sociological Inquiry* 78: 162–173.

Perrucci, Robert, and Carolyn C. Perrucci. 2009. *America at Risk: The Crisis of Hope, Trust, and Caring.* Lanham, MD: Rowman & Littlefield.

Perry, Michael J. 1997. "Are Human Rights Universal? The Relativist Challenge and Related Matters." *Human Rights Quarterly* 19, no. 3: 461–509.

Pescosolido, Bernice A., Brea L. Perry, J. Scott Long, Jack K. Martin, John I. Nurnberger Jr., and Victor Hesselbrock. 2008. "Under the Influence of Genetics: How Transdisciplinarity Leads Us to Rethink Social Pathways to Illness." *American Journal of Sociology* 114: S171–S201.

Peters, Julie, and Andrea Wolper. 1995. *Women's Rights, Human Rights: International Feminist Perspectives.* New York: Routledge.

Petersen, W. 1978. "International Migration." *Annual Review of Sociology* 4: 533–575.

Peterson, Ruth D., and Lauren J. Krivo. 2010. *Neighborhood Crime and the Racial-Spatial Divide.* New York: Russell Sage Foundation.

Pettigrew, T. F., and L. R. Tropp. 2006. "A Meta-Analytic Test of Intergroup Contact Theory." *Journal of Personality and Social Psychology* 90: 751–783.

PEW Forum on Religion in Public Life. 2009. "Global Restrictions on Religion." PEW Forum on Religion and Public Life, Washington, DC. http://www.pewforum.org/uploadedFiles/Topics/Issues/Government/restrictions-fullreport.pdf (accessed July 18, 2012).

PEW Research Center for the People and the Press. 2010. "Favorability Ratings of Labor Unions Fall Sharply." PEW Research Center for the People and the Press. http://pewresearch.org/pubs/1505/labor-unions-support-falls-public-now-evenly-split-on-purpose-power (accessed February 23, 2010).

Pfeiffer, D. 1993. "Overview of the Disability Movement: History, Legislative Record, and Political Implications." *Policy Studies Journal* 21: 724–734.

———. 2001. "The Conceptualization of Disability." In *Exploring Theories and Expanding Methodologies: Where We Are and Where We Need to Go,* edited by S. N. Barnartt and B. M. Altman, 2:29–52. Oxford: Elsevier Science.

Phemister, A. A., and N. M. Crewe. 2004. "Objective Self-Awareness and Stigma: Implications for Persons with Visible Disabilities." *Journal of Rehabilitation* 70: 33–37.

Picou, J. S., D. A. Gill, and M. J. Cohen, eds. 1997. *The Exxon-Valdez Disaster: Readings on a Modern Social Problem.* Dubuque, IA: Kendall-Hunt Publishers.

Picq, Ardant du. 2006. *Battle Studies.* Charleston, SC: BiblioBazaar.

Pierce, Jennifer L. 1995. *Gender Trials: Emotional Lives in Contemporary Law Firms.* Berkeley and Los Angeles: University of California Press.

Pilgrim, D., and A. A. Rogers. 1999. *A Sociology of Mental Health and Illness.* 2nd ed. Buckingham, UK: Open University Press.

Piven, Frances Fox, and Richard P. Cloward. 1977. *Poor People's Movements: Why They Succeed, How They Fail.* New York: Vintage Books.

Playle, J., and P. Keeley. 1998. "Non-Compliance and Professional Power." *Journal of Advanced Nursing* 27: 304–311.

Poe, Steven C., C. Neal Tate, and Linda Camp Keith. 1999. "Repression of the Human Right to Personal Integrity Revisited: A Global Cross-National Study Covering the Years 1976–1993." *International Studies Quarterly* 43: 291–313.

Polanyi, Karl. 1944. *The Great Transformation.* New York: Farrar and Rinehart.

Polletta, Francesca, and James M. Jasper. 2001. "Collective Identity and Social Movements." *Annual Review of Sociology* 27: 283–305.

Pollis, Adamantia. 2004. "Human Rights and Globalization." *Journal of Human Rights* 3, no. 3: 343–358.

Pollner, Melvin. 1987. *Mundane Reason: Reality in Everyday and Sociological Discourse.* Cambridge, UK: Cambridge University Press.

Ponse, Barbara. 1978. *Identities in the Lesbian World: The Social Construction of Self.* Westport, CT: Greenwood Press.

Poole, Michael. 1975. *Workers' Participation in Industry.* London: Routledge & K. Paul.

Popkin, Eric. 1999. "Guatemalan Mayan Migration to Los Angeles: Constructing Transnational Linkages in the Context of the Settlement Process." *Ethnic and Racial Studies* 22: 267–289.

Popper, Karl R. 1963. *Conjectures and Refutations: The Growth of Scientific Knowledge.* New York: Basic Books.

Population Research Bureau (PRB). 2007. "Is Low Birth Weight a Cause of Problems, or a Symptom of Them?" PBR. http://www.prb.org/Journalists/Webcasts/2007/LowBirthWeight.aspx (accessed January 25, 2012).

Porio, E. 2010. Personal communication with J. M. Fritz. December 12.

Portes, Alejandro, and Rubén Rumbaut. 2001. *Legacies: The Story of the Immigrant Second Generation.* Berkeley: University of California Press.

Poussaint, Alvin F. 1967. "A Negro Psychiatrist Explains the Negro Psyche." *New York Times Magazine.* August 20, 52.

Powell, Walter W., and Paul J. DiMaggio, eds. 1991. *The New Institutionalism in Organizational Analysis.* Chicago: University of Chicago Press.

Power, Samantha. 2002. *A Problem from Hell.* New York: Basic Books.

Prechel, Harland. 2000. *Big Business and the State: Historical Transitions and Corporate Transformation, 1880s–1990s.* Albany: State University of New York Press.

Preeves, Sharon E. 2003. *Intersex and Identity: The Contested Self.* New Brunswick, NJ: Rutgers University Press.

Preis, Ann-Belinda S. 1996. "Human Rights as Cultural Practice: An Anthropological Critique." *Human Rights Quarterly* 18, no. 2: 286–315.

Preston, Julia. 2011. "Risks Seen for Children of Illegal Immigrants." *New York Times.* September 20.

Prew, Paul. 2003. "The 21st Century World-Ecosystem: Dissipation, Chaos, or Transition?" In *Emerging Issues in the 21st Century World-System.* Vol. 2: *New Theoretical Directions for the 21st Century World System,* edited by Wilma A. Dunaway, 203–219. Westport, CT: Praeger Publishers.

Prior, L. 1996. *The Social Organization of Mental Illness.* London: Sage Publications.

Prunier, Gérard. 1997. *The Rwanda Crisis: History of a Genocide.* New York: Columbia University Press.

———. 2005. *Darfur: The Ambiguous Genocide.* Ithaca: Cornell University Press.

Pubantz, Jerry. 2005. "Constructing Reason: Human Rights and the Democratization of the United Nations." *Social Forces* 84: 1291–1302.

Pugh, Allison J. 2009. *Longing and Belonging: Parents, Children, and Consumer Culture.* Berkeley: University of California Press.

Purdy, Laura. 1989. "Surrogate Mothering: Exploitation or Empowerment?" *Bioethics* 3: 18–34.

Putnam, Robert D. 2000. *Bowling Alone: The Collapse and Revival of American Community.* New York: Simon and Schuster.

Quadagno, Jill. 1988. *The Transformation of Old Age Security.* Chicago: University of Chicago Press.

———. 2005. *One Nation, Uninsured: Why the U.S. Has No National Health Insurance.* New York: Oxford University Press.

Quadagno, Jill, and Debra Street, eds. 1995. *Aging for the Twenty-First Century.* New York: St. Martin's Press.

Quataert, Jean H. 2009. *Advocating Dignity: Human Rights Mobilizations in Global Politics.* Philadelphia: University of Pennsylvania Press.

——. 2010. "Women, Development, and Injustice: The Circuitous Origins of the New Gender Perspectives in Human Rights Visions and Practices in the 1970s." Paper presented at a conference titled "A New Global Morality? Human Rights and Humanitarianism in the 1970s," Freiburg Institute for Advanced Studies, Freiburg, Germany, June 10–12.

Queen, Stuart. 1981. "Seventy-Five Years of American Sociology in Relation to Social Work." *American Sociologist* 16: 34–37.

Quesnel-Vallee, Amelie. 2004. "Is It Really Worse to Have Public Health Insurance Than to Have No Insurance at All?" *Journal of Health and Social Behavior* 45, no. 4: 376–392.

Quigley, John. 2009. "The US Withdrawal from the ICJ Jurisdiction in Consular Cases." *Duke Journal of Comparative and International Law* 19, no. 2: 263–305.

Quinney, Richard. 1970. *The Social Reality of Crime*. Boston: Little, Brown and Co.

Rabben, Linda. 2002. *Fierce Legion of Friends: A History of Human Rights Campaigns and Campaigners*. Hyattsville, MD: Quixote Center.

Rainwater, Lee, and Timothy M. Smeeding. 2005. *Poor Kids in a Rich Country*. New York: Russell Sage Foundation.

Raskoff, Sally. 2011. "Welcome Back: Adjusting to Life after Military Service." Everday Sociology Blog. www.everydaysociologyblog.com/2011/12/welcome-back-adjusting-to-civilian-life-after-military-service.html (accessed December 17, 2011).

Ratner, S. R., J. S. Abrams, and J. L. Bischoff. 2009. *Accountability for Human Rights Atrocities in International Law: Beyond the Nuremberg Legacy*. 3rd ed. Oxford: Oxford University Press.

Rawls, A. 2000. "Harold Garfinkel." In *The Blackwell Companion to Major Social Theorists*, edited by George Ritzer, 545–576. Oxford: Blackwell.

——. 2003. "Conflict as a Foundation for Consensus: Contradictions of Industrial Capitalism in Book III of Durkheim's Division of Labor." *Critical Sociology* 29: 195–335.

——. 2006. "Respecifying the Study of Social Order: Garfinkel's Transition from Theoretical Conceptualization to Practices in Details." In *Seeing Sociologically: The Routine Grounds of Social Action* by Harold Garfinkel, 1–97. Boulder, CO: Paradigm.

Rawls, John. 1971. *A Theory of Justice*. Cambridge, MA: Belknap Press.

——. 1995. "Reply to Habermas." *Journal of Philosophy* 92: 132–180. Reprinted in *Political Liberalism*, edited by John Rawls, 372–434. New York: Columbia University Press.

——. 1996. *Political Liberalism*. New York: Columbia University Press.

Ray, Raka, and A. C. Korteweg. 1999. "Women's Movements in the Third World: Identity, Mobilization, and Autonomy." *Annual Review of Sociology* 25: 47–71.

Razack, Sherene. 1998. *Looking White People in the Eye: Gender, Race, and Culture in Courtrooms and Classrooms*. Toronto: University of Toronto Press.

Read, Jen'nan Ghazal. 2007. "Introduction: The Politics of Veiling in Comparative Perspective." *Sociology of Religion* 68: 231–236.

Reading, R., S. Bissell, J. Goldhagen, J. Harwin, J. Masson, S. Moynihan, N. Parton, M. S. Pais, J. Thoburn, and E. Webb. 2009. "Promotion of Children's Rights and Prevention of Child Maltreatment." *The Lancet* 373: 322–343.

Readings, Bill. 1996. *The University in Ruins*. Cambridge, MA: Harvard University Press.

Reardon, Betty. 1985. *Sexism and the War System*. New York: Teachers College Press.

Redwood, Loren K. 2008. "Strong-Arming Exploitable Labor: The State and Immigrant Workers in the Post-Katrina Gulf Coast." *Social Justice* 35: 33–50.

Reed, Michael. 1985. *Redirections in Organizational Analysis*. London: Tavistock.

Regan, Tom. 2004. *The Case for Animal Rights*. Berkeley: University of California Press.

Regnerus, Mark D. 2007. *Forbidden Fruit: Sex and Religion in the Lives of American Teenagers*. New York: Oxford University Press.

Reilly, Niamh. 2007. "Cosmopolitan Feminism and Human Rights." *Hypatia* 22: 180–198.

——. 2009. *Women's Human Rights: Seeking Gender Justice in a Globalizing Age*. Cambridge, MA: Polity Press.

Reimann, Kim. 2006. "A View from the Top: International Politics, Norms and the Worldwide Growth of NGOs." *International Studies Quarterly* 50: 45–67.

Reinarman, Craig, and Harry Levine. 1997. *Crack in America: Demon Drugs and Social Justice*. Berkeley: University of California Press.

Reisch, Michael. 2009. "Social Workers, Unions, and Low Wage Workers: A Historical Perspective." *Journal of Community Practice* 17: 50–72.

Renteln, Alison Dundes. 1985. "The Unanswered Challenge of Relativism and the Consequences for Human Rights." *Human Rights Quarterly* 7, no. 4: 514–540.

——. 1988. "The Concept of Human Rights." *Anthropos* 83: 343–364.

Rheaume, J. 2008. "Clinical Sociology in Quebec: When Europe Meets America." In *International Clinical Sociology*, edited by J. M. Fritz, 36–53. New York: Springer.

——. 2010. Personal communication with J. M. Fritz. December 16.

Rhoades, Lawrence. 1981. "A History of the American Sociological Association, 1905–1980." American Sociological Association. www.asanet.org/about/Rhoades_Chapter3.cfm (accessed December 10, 2011).

Rice, James. 2009. "The Transnational Organization of Production and Uneven Environmental Degradation and Change in the World Economy." *International Journal of Comparative Sociology* 50, no. 3/4: 215–236.

Rich, Adrienne. 1980. "Compulsory Heterosexuality." In *Powers of Desire: The Politics of Sexuality*, edited by Ann Snitow, Christine Stansell, and Sharon Thompson, 177–205. New York: Monthly Review Press.

Rich, Michael, and Richard Chalfen. 1999. "Showing and Telling Asthma: Children Teaching Physicians with Visual Narratives." *Visual Sociology* 14: 51–71.

Richards, Patricia. 2005. "The Politics of Gender, Human Rights, and Being Indigenous in Chile." *Gender and Society* 19: 199–220.

Richardson, L., and T. Brown. 2011. "Intersectionality of Race, Gender and Age in Hypertension Trajectories across the Life Course." Presented at the eighty-first annual meeting of the Eastern Sociological Society, Philadelphia, Pennsylvania, February.

Ridge, D., C. Emslie, and A. White. 2011. "Understanding How Men Experience, Express and Cope with Mental Distress: Where Next?" *Sociology of Health and Illness* 33: 145–159.

Rieker, Patricia P., Chloe E. Bird, and Martha E. Lang. 2010. "Understanding Gender and Health." In *Handbook of Medical Sociology*, edited by Chloe Bird, Peter Conrad, Allen Fremont, and Stephan Timmermans, 52–74. 6th ed. Nashville, TN: Vanderbilt University Press.

Right to the City Alliance. 2011. http://www.righttothecity.org (accessed May 28, 2011).

Riley, J. 2004. "Some Reflections on Gender Mainstreaming and Intersectionality." *Development Bulletin* 64: 82–86.

Riley, M. W., M. E. Johnson, and A. Foner. 1972. *Aging and Society*. Vol. 3: *A Sociology of Age Stratification*. New York: Russell Sage Foundation.

Riley, M. W., R. L. Kahn, and A. Foner. 1994. *Age and Structural Lag: Society's Failure to Provide Meaningful Opportunities in Work, Family, and Leisure*. New York: Wiley.

Riley, M. W., and J. W. Riley Jr. 1994. "Age Integration and the Lives of Older People." *Gerontologist* 3–4, no. 1: 110–115.

Ringelheim, Julie. 2011. "Ethnic Categories and European Human Rights Law." *Ethnic and Racial Studies* 34: 1682–1696.

Rios, Victor M. 2010. "Navigating the Thin Line between Education and Incarceration: An Action Research Case Study on Gang-Associated Latino Youth." *Journal of Education for Students Placed At-Risk* 15, no. 1–2: 200–212.

Risse, Thomas. 2000. "The Power of Norms versus the Norms of Power: Transnational Civil Society and Human Rights." In *The Third Force: The Rise of Transnational Civil Society*, edited by A. Florini, N. Kokusai, K. Senta, and Carnegie Endowment for International Peace. Tokyo: Japan Center for International Exchange, Washington Carnegie Endowment for International Peace, and Brookings Institution Press (distributor).

Risse, Thomas, S. C. Ropp, and K. Sikkink, eds. 1999. *The Power of Human Rights: International Norms and Domestic Change*. Cambridge, UK: Cambridge University Press.

Rist, Ray. 1970. "Student Social Class and Teacher Expectations: The Self-Fulfilling Prophecy in Ghetto Education." *Harvard Educational Review* 40: 411–451.

——. 1973. *The Urban School: Factory for Failure*. Cambridge, MA: MIT Press.

——. 1977. "On Understanding the Processes of Schooling: The Contributions of Labeling Theory." In *Power and Ideology in Education*, edited by Jerome Karabel and A. H. Halsey, 292–305. New York: Oxford University Press.

Rivera Vargas, Maria Isabel. 2010. "Government Influence and Foreign Direct Investment: Organizational Learning in an Electronics Cluster." *Critical Sociology* 36, no. 4: 537–553.

Robert, Stephanie A., and James S. House. 2000. "Socioeconomic Inequalities in Health: An Enduring Sociological Problem." In *Handbook of Medical Sociology*, edited by C. E. Bird, P. Conrad, and A. M. Fremont, 79–97. 5th ed. Upper Saddle River, NJ: Prentice Hall.

Roberts, Christopher N. J. Forthcoming. Untitled Work. Cambridge, UK: Cambridge University Press.

Roberts, Dorothy. 2010. "The Social Immorality of Health in the Gene Age: Race, Disability, and Inequality." In *Against Health: How Health Became the New Morality*, edited by Jonathan M. Metzl and Anna Kirkland, 61–71. New York: New York University Press.

Robertson, Roland. 1992. *Globalization: Social Theory and Global Culture*. London: Sage.

Robinson, Dawn T., Christabel L. Rogalin, and Lynn Smith-Lovin. 2004. "Physiological Measures of

Theoretical Concepts: Some Ideas for Linking Deflection and Emotion to Physical Responses during Interaction." *Advances in Group Processes* 21: 77–115.

Rodan, Garry. 2006. "Singapore in 2005: 'Vibrant and Cosmopolitan' without Political Pluralism." *Asian Survey* 46: 180–186.

Rodríguez, Havidán, Rogelio Sáenz, and Cecilia Menjívar, eds. 2008. *Latina/os in the United States: Changing the Face of América*. New York: Springer.

Rodríguez, Nestor. 2008. "Theoretical and Methodological Issues of Latina/o Research." In *Latina/os in the United States: Changing the Face of América*, edited by H. Rodríguez, R. Sáenz, and C. Menjívar, 3–15. New York: Springer.

Roediger, D. R. 1991. *Wages of Whiteness: Race and the Making of the American Working Class*. London: Verso.

Roethlisberger, F. J., and W. J. Dickson. 1947. *Management and the Worker*. Cambridge, MA: Harvard University Press.

Rogers, Leslie. 1998. *Mind of Their Own: Thinking and Awareness in Animals*. Boulder, CO: Westview Press.

Rogoff, Barbara. 2003. *The Cultural Name of Human Development*. Oxford: Oxford University Press.

Rojas, Fabio. 2007. *From Black Power to Black Studies: How a Radical Social Movement Became an Academic Discipline*. Baltimore: Johns Hopkins University Press.

Rokeach, Milton. 1973. *The Nature of Human Values*. New York: The Free Press.

Romero, Mary. 1988. "Sisterhood and Domestic Service: Race, Class and Gender in the Mistress-Maid Relationship." *Humanity and Society* 12: 318–346.

——. 2006. "Racial Profiling and Immigration Law Enforcement: Rounding Up of Usual Suspects in the Latino Community." *Critical Sociology* 32: 449–475.

——. 2011. "Are Your Papers in Order? Racial Profiling, Vigilantes and 'America's Toughest Sheriff.'" *Harvard Latino Law Review* 14: 337–357.

Romero-Ortuno, Roman. 2004. "Access to Health Care for Illegal Immigrants in the EU: Should We Be Concerned?" *European Journal of Health Law* 11: 245–272.

Roschelle, Anne R., Jennifer Turpin, and Robert Elias. 2000. "Who Learns from Service Learning." *American Behavioral Scientist* 43: 839–847.

Rosenfield, S. 1999. "Gender and Mental Health: Do Women Have More Psychopathology, Men More, or Both the Same (and Why)?" In *Handbook for the Study of Mental Health*, edited by A. Horwitz and T. Scheid, 348–361. Cambridge, UK: Cambridge University Press.

Rosenhan, D. L. 1991. "On Being Sane in Insane Places." In *Down to Earth Sociology*, edited by J. M. Henslin, 294–307. New York: The Free Press.

Ross, J. S. Robert. 1991. "At the Center and the Edge: Notes on a Life in and out of Sociology and the New Left." In *Radical Sociologists and the Movement: Experiences, Lessons, and Legacies*, edited by Martin Oppenheimer, Martin J. Murray, and Rhonda F. Levine, 197–215. Philadelphia: Temple University Press.

Ross, Lauren. 2009. "Contradictions of Power, Sexuality, and Consent: An Institutional Ethnography of the Practice of Male Neonatal Circumcision." PhD diss., University of Connecticut, Storrs.

Rossi, Alice S. 1970. "Status of Women in Graduate Departments of Sociology, 1968–1969." *American Sociologist* (February): 1–12.

——. 1983. "Beyond the Gender Gap: Women's Bid for Political Power." *Social Science Quarterly* 64: 718–733.

——. 1984. "Gender and Parenthood." *American Sociological Review* 49, no. 1: 1–19.

Rossi, Federico M. 2009. "Youth Political Participation: Is This the End of Generational Cleavage?" *International Sociology* 24, no. 4: 467–497.

Roth, Brad. 2004. "Retrieving Marx for the Human Rights Project." *Leiden Journal of International Law* 17: 31–66.

Roth, Wendy D., and Gerhard Sonnert. 2011. "The Costs and Benefits of 'Red-Tape': Anti-Bureaucratic Structure and Gender Inequity in a Science Research Organization." *Social Studies of Science*. January 17. http://sss.sagepub.com/content/early/2011/01/15/0306312710391494 (accessed July 19, 2012).

Rothschild, Joyce. 1979. "The Collectivist Organization: An Alternative to Rational-Bureaucratic Models." *American Sociological Review* 44: 509–527.

Rowe, John, Lisa Berkman, Robert Binstock, Axel Boersch-Supan, John Caciopppo, Laura Carstensen, Linda Fried, Dana Goldman, James Jackson, Matin Kohli, Jay Olshansky, and John Rother. 2010. "Policies and Politics for an Aging America." *Contexts* 9, no. 1: 22–27.

Rowland, Robyn. 1995. "Symposium: Human Rights and the Sociological Project (Human Rights Discourse and Women: Challenging the Rhetoric with Reality)." *Australian and New Zealand Journal of Sociology* 31: 8–25.

Roy, William G. 1997. *Socializing Capital: The Rise of the Large Industrial Corporation in America*. Princeton, NJ: Princeton University Press.

Rubin, Gayle. 1984. "Thinking Sex: Notes for a Radical Theory of the Politics of Sexuality." In *Pleasure and Danger: Exploring Female Sexuality*, edited by Carol Vance, 267–319. London: Pandora Press.

Rumbaut, Rubén. 1994. "Origins and Destinies: Immigration to the United States since World War II." *Sociological Forum* 9: 583–621.

Rumbaut, Rubén, and Walter A. Ewing. 2007. "The Myth of Immigrant Criminality." Border Battles. May 23. http://borderbattles.ssrc.org/Rumbault_Ewing/index.html (accessed November 9, 2010).

Rumbaut, Rubén, and Alejandro Portes. 2001. *Ethnicities: Children of Immigrants in America.* Berkeley: University of California Press.

Rummel, R. J. 1994. *Death by Government.* New Brunswick, NJ: Transaction.

Rupp, Leila J. 1997. *Worlds of Women: The Making of an International Women's Movement.* Princeton, NJ: Princeton University Press.

———. 2009. *Sapphistries: A Global History of Love between Women.* New York: New York University Press.

Ruppel, Oliver C. 2009. "Third Generation Human Rights and the Protection of the Environment in Namibia." Konrad-Adenauer-Stiftung. http://www.kas.de/namibia/en/publications/16045 (accessed December 2, 2010).

Russon, John. 1997. *The Self and Its Body in Hegel's Phenomenology of Spirit.* Toronto: University of Toronto Press.

Rutherford, Markella B. 2011. *Adult Supervision Required.* Piscataway, NJ: Rutgers University Press.

Rytina, Nancy, Michael Hoefer, and Bryan Baker. 2010. "Estimates of the Unauthorized Immigrant Population Residing in the United States: January 2009." Department of Homeland Security. January. http://www.dhs.gov/xlibrary/assets/statistics/publications/ois_ill_pe_2009.pdf (accessed October 12, 2010).

Sabel, Charles, and Jonathan Zeitlin. 1997. *World of Possibilities: Flexibility and Mass Production in Western Industrialization.* Cambridge, UK: Cambridge University Press.

Sachs, A. 1996. "Upholding Human Rights and Environmental Justice." In *State of the World*, edited by Lester Brown, 133–151. New York: W. W. Norton.

Sacks, Harvey. 1972a. "An Initial Investigation of the Usability of Conversational Data for Doing Sociology." In *Studies in Social Interaction*, edited by David Sudnow, 31–74. New York: The Free Press.

———. 1972b. "On the Analyzability of Stories by Children." In *Directions in Sociolinguistics: The Ethnography of Communication*, edited by John J. Gumperz and Dell Hymes, 325–345. New York: Holt, Rinehart and Winston.

———. 1984. "Notes on Methodology." In *Structures of Social Action: Studies in Conversation Analysis*, edited by J. Maxwell Atkinson and John Heritage, 21–27. Cambridge, UK: Cambridge University Press; Paris: Les Éditions de la Maison des Sciences de l'Homme.

———. 1992. *Lectures on Conversation*, edited by Gail Jefferson with introductions by Emanuel A. Schegloff. 2 vols. Oxford: Basil Blackwell.

Sacks, Harvey, Emanuel A. Schegloff, and Gail Jefferson. 1974. "A Simplest Systematics for the Organization of Turn Taking for Conversation." *Language* 50, no. 4: 696–735.

Sadovnik, A. R., ed. 2007. *Sociology of Education: A Critical Reader.* New York: Routledge.

Sáenz, Rogelio. 2010a. "Latinos in the United States 2010." Population Reference Bureau. http://www.prb.org/pdf10/latinos-update2010.pdf (accessed July 19, 2012).

———. 2010b. "Latinos, Whites, and the Shifting Demography of Arizona." Population Reference Bureau. http://www.prb.org/Articles/2010/usarizonalatinos.aspx (accessed March 24, 2011).

Sáenz, Rogelio, Cynthia M. Cready, and Maria Cristina Morales. 2007. "Adios Aztlan: Mexican American Outmigration from the Southwest." In *The Sociology of Spatial Inequality*, edited by L. Lobao, G. Hooks, and A. Tickamyer, 189–214. Albany: State University of New York Press.

Sáenz, Rogelio, Cecilia Menjívar, and San Juanita Edilia Garcia. 2011. "Arizona's SB 1070: Setting Conditions for Violations of Human Rights Here and Beyond." In *Sociology and Human Rights: A Bill of Rights for the Twenty-First Century*, edited by J. Blau and M. Frezzo. Newbury Park, CA: Pine Forge Press.

Sáenz, Rogelio, Maria Cristina Morales, and Maria Isabel Ayala. 2004. "United States: Immigration to the Melting Pot of the Americas." In *Migration and Immigration: A Global View*, edited by M. I. Toro-Morn and M. Alicea, 211–232. Westport, CT: Greenwood Press.

Sáenz, Rogelio, and Lorena Murga. 2011. *Latino Issues: A Reference Handbook.* Santa Barbara, CA: ABC-CLIO.

Safran, S. P. 2001. "Movie Images of Disability and War: Framing History and Political Ideology." *Remedial and Special Education* 22: 223–232.

Said, Edward W. 1979. *Orientalism.* 1st ed. Vintage.

Saito, Leland T. 1998. *Race and Politics: Asian Americans, Latinos, and Whites in a Los Angeles Suburb.* Chicago: University of Illinois Press.

———. 2009. *The Politics of Exclusion: The Failure of Race-Neutral Policies in Urban America.* Palo Alto, CA: Stanford University Press.

Salvo, J. J., M. G. Powers, and R. S. Cooney. 1992. "Contraceptive Use and Sterilization among Puerto Rican Women." *Family Planning Perspectives* 24, no. 5: 219–223.

Salzinger, Leslie. 2005. *Genders in Production: Making Workers in Mexico's Global Factories.* Berkeley: University of California Press.

Sampson, Robert J., and Stephen W. Raudenbush. 1999. "Systematic Social Observation of Public Spaces: A New Look at Disorder in Urban Neighborhoods." *American Journal of Sociology* 105: 603-651.

Sampson, Robert J., Patrick Sharkey, and Stephen W. Raudenbush. 2008. "Durable Effects of Concentrated Disadvantage on Verbal Ability among African-American Children." *Proceedings of the National Academy of Sciences of the United States of America* 105, no. 3: 845-852.

Sampson, Robert J., and William J. Wilson. 1995. "Toward a Theory of Race, Crime, and Urban Inequality." In *Crime and Inequality*, edited by John Hagan and Ruth D. Peterson, 37-54. Stanford, CA: Stanford University Press.

San Miguel, Guadalupe. 2005. *Brown, Not White: School Integration and the Chicano Movement in Houston*. College Station: Texas A&M University Press.

Sanbonmatsu, John, ed. 2011. *Critical Theory and Animal Liberation*. Lanham, MD: Rowman & Littlefield.

Sanchez-Jankowski, Martin. 2008. *Cracks in the Pavement: Social Change and Resilience in Poor Neighborhoods*. Berkeley: University of California Press.

Sanders, Joseph. 1990. "The Interplay of Micro and Macro Processes in the Longitudinal Study of Courts: Beyond the Durkheimian Tradition." *Law and Society Review* 24, no. 2: 241-256.

Sanderson, Matthew R., and Jeffrey D. Kentor. 2008. "Foreign Direct Investment and International Migration: A Cross-National Analysis of Less-Developed Countries, 1985-2000." *International Sociology* 23, no. 4: 514-539.

Sanderson, Stephen K. 2001. *The Evolution of Human Sociality*. Lanham, MD: Rowman & Littlefield.

———. 2007. "Marvin Harris, Meet Charles Darwin: A Critical Evaluation and Theoretical Extension of Cultural Materialism." In *Studying Societies and Cultures: Marvin Harris's Cultural Materialism and Its Legacy*, edited by Lawrence A. Kuznar and Stephen K. Sanderson, 194-228. Boulder, CO: Paradigm Publishers.

———. 2008. "Adaptation, Evolution, and Religion." *Religion* 38: 141-156.

Sanford, Victoria. 2003. *Buried Secrets: Truth and Human Rights in Guatemala*. New York: Palgrave Macmillan.

Santos, B. S. 2009. "A Non-Occidentalist West? Learned Ignorance and Ecology of Knowledge." *Theory, Culture and Society* 26, no. 7-8: 103-125.

Sarbin, T. R., and E. Keen. 1998. "Classifying Mental Disorders: Nontraditional Approaches." In *Encyclopedia of Mental Health*, edited by H. S. Friedman, 2:461-473. San Diego: Academic Press.

Sarver, Joshua H., Susan W. Hinze, Rita K. Cydulka, and David W. Baker. 2003. "Racial/Ethnic Disparities in Emergency Department Analgesic Prescription." *American Journal of Public Health* 93, no. 12: 2067-2073.

Sassen, Saskia, ed. 1989. "America's 'Immigration Problem.'" *World Policy* 6: 811-832.

———. 1999. *Globalization and Its Discontents: Essays on the New Mobility of People and Money*. New York: The New Press.

———. 2001. *The Global City: New York, London, Tokyo*. Updated ed. Princeton, NJ: Princeton University Press.

———. 2006a. *Cities in a World Economy*. 3rd ed. Boulder, CO: Pine Forge Press.

———. 2006b. *Territory, Authority, Rights: From Medieval to Global Assemblages*. Princeton, NJ: Princeton University Press.

———, ed. 2007. *Deciphering the Global: Its Spaces, Scales and Subjects*. New York: Routledge.

Satterthwaite, Margaret L. 2005. "Crossing Borders, Claiming Rights: Using Human Rights Law to Empower Women Migrant Workers." *Yale Human Rights and Development Law Journal* 8: 1-66.

Savage, Joanne, and Bryan J. Vila. 2003. "Human Ecology, Crime, and Crime Control: Linking Individual Behavior and Aggregate Crime." *Social Biology* 50: 77-101.

Savelsberg, Joachim J. 2010. *Crime and Human Rights: Criminology of Genocide and Atrocities*. London: Sage.

Savelsberg, Joachim J., and Ryan D. King. 2007. "Law and Collective Memory." *Annual Review of Law and Social Science* 3: 189-211.

———. 2011. *American Memories: Atrocities and the Law*. New York: Russell Sage.

Scambler, Graham. 2004. *Medical Sociology, Major Themes in Health and Social Welfare*. New York: Taylor and Francis.

Scarritt, James R. 1985. "Socialist States and Human Rights Measurement in Africa." *Africa Today* 32, no. 1/2: 25-36.

Scheff, Thomas J. 1988. "Shame and Conformity: The Deference-Emotion System." *American Sociological Review* 53: 395-406.

———. 1990a. *Microsociology: Discourse, Emotion, and Social Structure*. Chicago: University of Chicago Press.

———. 1990b. "Socialization of Emotions: Pride and Shame as Causal Agents." In *Research Agendas in the Sociology of Emotions*, edited by T. D. Kemper, 281-304. Albany: State University of New York Press.

———. 1994. *Bloody Revenge: Emotions, Nationalism, and War*. Boulder, CO: Westview.

———. 1999. *Being Mentally Ill: A Sociological Theory*. 3rd ed. New York: Aldine De Gruyter.

———. 2000. "Shame and the Social Bond: A Sociological Theory." *Sociological Theory* 18, no. 1: 84-99.

Scheff, Thomas J., and Suzanne M. Retzinger. 1991. *Emotions and Violence: Shame and Rage in Destructive Conflicts*. Lexington, MA: Lexington Books.

Schegloff, Emanuel A. 2007a. "A Tutorial on Membership Categorization." *Journal of Pragmatics* 39: 462–482.

———. 2007b. "Categories in Action: Person-Reference and Membership Categorization." *Discourse Studies* 9: 433–461.

———. 2007c. *Sequence Organization in Interaction: A Primer in Sequential Analysis.* Vol. 1. Cambridge, UK: Cambridge University Press.

Schegloff, Emanuel A., Gail Jefferson, and Harvey Sacks. 1977. "The Preference for Self-Correction in the Organization of Repair in Conversation." *Language* 53, no. 2: 361–382.

Scheid, T. L. 2005. "Stigma as a Barrier to Employment: Mental Disability and the Americans with Disabilities Act." *International Journal of Law and Psychiatry* 28: 670–690.

Schenkein, Jim. 1978. "Sketch of an Analytic Mentality for the Study of Conversational Interaction." In *Studies in the Organization of Conversational Interaction,* edited by Jim Schenkein, 1–6. New York: Academic.

Schnittker, Jason. 2008. "Happiness and Success: Genes, Families, and the Psychological Effects of Socioeconomic Position and Social Support." *American Journal of Sociology* 114: S233–S259.

Schofer, Evan, and John W. Meyer. 2005. "The Worldwide Expansion of Higher Education in the Twentieth Century." *American Sociological Review* 70: 898–920.

Schrag, Peter. 2002. "A Quagmire for Our Time: The War on Drugs." *Journal of Public Health Policy* 23, no. 3: 286–298.

Schrecker, Ellen. 1986. *No Ivory Tower: McCarthyism and the Universities.* Oxford: Oxford University Press.

Schulz, William F. 2009. *Power of Justice: Applying International Human Rights Standards to American Domestic Practices.* Washington, DC: Center for American Progress.

Schulze, B., and M. C. Angermeyer. 2003. "Subjective Experiences of Stigma: Schizophrenic Patients, Their Relatives and Mental Health Professionals." *Social Science and Medicine* 56: 299–312.

Schwalbe, Michael L., and Douglas Mason-Schrock. 1996. "Identity Work as Group Process." In *Advances in Group Processes,* edited by Barry Markovsky, Michael J. Lovaglia, and Robin Simon, 13:113–147. Greenwich, CT: JAI Press.

Schwartz, Pepper, and Virginia Rutter. 1998. *The Gender of Sexuality.* Lanham, MD: AltaMira Press.

Schwartz, Shalom H. 1992. "Universals in the Content and Structure of Values: Theoretical Advances and Empirical Tests in 20 Countries." In *Advances in Experimental Social Psychology,* edited by Mark P. Zanna, 24: 1–65. San Diego: Academic Press.

———. 2006. "Basic Human Values: Theory, Measurement, and Applications." *Revue Française de Sociologie* 47: 249–288.

Schwartz, Shalom H., and Galit Sagie. 2000. "Value Consensus and Importance: A Cross-National Study." *Journal of Cross-Cultural Psychology* 31, no. 4: 465–497.

Schwed, Uri, and Peter Bearman. 2010. "The Temporal Structure of Scientific Consensus Formation." *American Sociological Review* 75: 817–840.

Schwerner, Cassie. 2005. "Building the Movement for Education Equity." In *Rhyming Hope and History: Activists, Academics, and Social Movement Scholarship,* edited by David Croteau, William Hoynes, and Charlotte Ryan, 157–175. Minneapolis: University of Minnesota Press.

Scimecca, Joseph A. 1976. "Paying Homage to the Father: C. Wright Mills and Radical Sociology." *Sociological Quarterly* 17: 180–196.

Scott, J. 2000. "Rational Choice Theory." In *Understanding Contemporary Society: Theories of the Present,* edited by G. Browning, A. Halcli, and F. Webster, 126–138. London: Sage.

Scott, W. Richard. 1998. *Organizations: Rational, Natural and Open Systems.* 4th ed. New Brunswick, NJ: Prentice Hall.

———. 2001. *Institutions and Organizations.* 2nd ed. Thousand Oaks, CA: Sage.

Scott, Tony. 2004. "Teaching the Ideology of Assessment." *Radical Teacher* 71: 30–37.

Scruton, Roger. 2000. *Animal Rights and Wrongs.* London: Claridge Press.

Scull, A. T. 1984. *Decarceration: Community Treatment and the Deviant–a Radical View.* Cambridge, UK: Polity Press.

Segura, Denise. 1989. "Chicana and Mexican Immigrant Women at Work: The Impact of Class, Race, and Gender on Occupational Mobility." *Gender and Society* 3: 37–52.

Seiwert, Hubert. 1999. "The German Enquete Commission on Sects: Political Conflicts and Compromises." *Social Justice Research* 12: 323–340.

———. 2003. "Freedom and Control in the Unified Germany: Governmental Approaches to Alternative Religions since 1989." *Sociology of Religion* 64: 367–375.

Sekulic, D., G. Massey, and R. Hodson. 2006. "Ethnic Intolerance and Ethnic Conflict in the Dissolution of Yugoslavia." *Ethnic and Racial Studies* 29: 797–827.

Selmi, Patrick, and Richard Hunter. 2001. "Beyond the Rank and File Movement: Mary Van Kleeck and Social Work Radicalism in the Great Depression, 1931–1942." *Journal of Sociology and Social Welfare* 28: 75–100.

Seltzer, William, and Margo Anderson. 2002. "Using Population Data Systems to Target Vulnerable Population Subgroups and Individuals: Issues and Incidents." In *Statistical Methods for Human Rights*, edited by Jana Asher, David Banks, and Fritz J. Scheuren, 273ff. New York: Springer.

Selznick, Philip. 1947. *TVA and the Grass Roots*. Berkeley and Los Angeles: University of California Press.

———. 1957. *Leadership in Administration: A Sociological Interpretation*. New York: Harper and Row.

———. 1959. "The Sociology of the Law." In *Sociology Today: Problems and Prospects*, edited by Robert K. Merton, Leonard Broom, and Leonard Cottrell Jr., 115–127. New York: Basic Books.

Sen, Amartya. 1981. *Poverty and Famines: An Essay on Entitlement and Deprivation*. New York: Oxford University Press.

———. 1992. *Inequality Reexamined*. New York: Russell Sage Foundation.

———. 1999a. "Democracy as a Universal Value." *Journal of Democracy* 10: 3–17.

———. 1999b. *Development as Freedom*. New York: Knopf.

———. 2006. *Identity and Violence: The Illusion of Destiny*. New York: W. W. Norton and Co.

Sengupta, Amit. 2003. "Health in the Age of Globalization." *Social Scientist* 31, no. 11–12: 66–85.

Serrano, P. A., and L. Magnusson, eds. 2007. *Reshaping Welfare States and Activation Regimes in Europe*. Brussels and New York: PIE–Peter Lang.

Serrano, Susan K., and Dale Minami. 2003. "*Korematsu vs. United States*: A 'Constant Caution' in a Time of Crisis." *Asian Law Journal* 10: 37–50.

Settersten, R. A., Jr. 2005. "Linking the Two Ends of Life: What Gerontology Can Learn from Childhood Studies." *Journals of Gerontology, Series B: Psychological Sciences* 60B, no. 4: 173–180.

Settersten, R. A., Jr., and J. L. Angel, eds. 2011. *Handbook of Sociology of Aging*. New York: Springer.

Settersten, R. A., Jr., and G. Hagestad. 1996a. "What's the Latest? Cultural Age Deadlines for Family Transitions." *Gerontologist* 36, no. 2: 178–188.

———. 1996b. "What's the Latest II: Cultural Age Deadlines for Educational and Work Transitions." *Gerontologist* 36, no. 5: 602–613.

Settersten, Richard, and Barbara E. Ray. 2010. *Not Quite Adults: Why 20-Somethings Are Choosing a Slower Path to Adulthood, and Why It's Good for Everyone*. New York: Bantam.

Sevigny, R. 2010. Personal communication with J. M. Fritz. December 14.

Shah, Natubhai. 1998. *Jainism: The World of Conquerors*. Sussex, UK: Sussex Academic Press.

Shakespeare, T., and N. Watson. 2001. "The Social Model of Disability: An Outdated Ideology?" In *Exploring Theories and Expanding Methodologies: Where We Are and Where We Need to Go*, edited by S. N. Barnartt and B. M. Altman, 2:9–28. Oxford, UK: Elsevier Science.

Shakespeare, Tom. 2006. *Disability Rights and Wrongs*. New York: Routledge.

Shanahan, Michael J., Shawn Bauldry, and Jason Freeman. 2010. "Beyond Mendel's Ghost." *Contexts* 9: 34–39.

Shanahan, Michael J., Stephen Vaisey, Lance D. Erickson, and Andrew Smolen. 2008. "Environmental Contingencies and Genetic Propensities: Social Capital, Educational Continuation, and Dopamine Receptor Gene DRD2." *American Journal of Sociology* 114: S260–S286.

Shanks, Cheryl, Harold K. Jacobson, and Jeffrey H. Kaplan. 1996. "Inertia and Change in the Constellation of International Governmental Organizations, 1981–1992." *International Organization* 50: 593–627.

Sharrock, W. W. 1980. "The Possibility of Social Change." In *The Ignorance of Social Intervention*, edited by D. C. Anderson, 117–133. London: Croom Helm.

———. 2001. "Fundamentals of Ethnomethodology." In *Handbook of Social Theory*, edited by George Ritzer and Barry Smart, 250–259. London: Sage.

Sharrock, W. W., and D. R. Watson. 1988. "Autonomy among Social Theories: The Incarnation of Social Structures." In *Actions and Structure: Research Methods and Social Theory*, edited by Nigel Fielding, 56–77. London: Sage.

Sharrock, Wes, and Bob Anderson. 1991. "Epistemology: Professional Skepticism." In *Ethnomethodology and the Human Sciences*, edited by Graham Button, 51–76. Cambridge, UK: Cambridge University Press.

Sharrock, Wes, and Graham Button. 1991. "The Social Actor: Social Action in Real Time." In *Ethnomethodology and the Human Sciences*, edited by Graham Button, 137–175. Cambridge, UK: Cambridge University Press.

Shaw, Martin. 2000. *The Theory of the Global State: Globality as Unfinished Revolution*. Oxford: Cambridge University Press.

Shell-Duncan, B. 2008. "From Health to Human Rights: Female Genital Cutting and the Politics of Intervention." *American Anthropologist* 110: 225–236.

Shergill, S. S., D. Barker, and M. Greenberg. 1998. "Communication of Psychiatric Diagnosis." *Social Psychiatry and Psychiatric Epidemiology* 33: 32–38.

Shevelow, Kathryn. 2008. *For the Love of Animals: The Rise of the Animal Protection Movement*. New York: Henry Holt and Co.

Shields, Joseph, Kirk M. Broome, Peter J. Delany, Bennett W. Fletcher, and Patrick M. Flynn. 2007. "Religion and Substance Abuse Treatment: Individual and Program Effects." *Journal for the Scientific Study of Religion* 46, no. 3: 355-371.

Shils, Edward. 1968. "Deference." In *Social Stratification*, edited by John A. Jackson, 104-132. Cambridge, UK: Cambridge University Press.

———. 1975. *Center and Periphery: Essays in Macrosociology.* Chicago: University of Chicago Press.

Shin, Y., and S. Raudenbush. 2011. "The Causal Effect of Class Size on Academic Achievement: Multivariate Instrumental Variable Estimators with Data Missing at Random." *Journal of Educational and Behavioral Statistics* 34, no. 2: 154-185.

Shirazi, Farid, Ojelanki Ngwenyama, and Olga Morawczynski. 2010. "ICT Expansion and the Digital Divide in Democratic Freedoms: An Analysis of the Impact of ICT Expansion, Education and ICT Filtering on Democracy." *Telematics and Informatics* 27: 21-31.

Shiva, Vandana. 1997. *Biopiracy: The Plunder of Nature and Knowledge.* Cambridge, MA: South End Press.

Shor, Eran. 2008. "Conflict, Terrorism, and the Socialization of Human Rights Norms: The Spiral Model Revisited." *Social Problems* 55, no. 1: 117-138.

Shor, Ira. 1992. *Empowering Education: Critical Teaching for Social Change.* Portsmouth, NH: Heinemann.

Shorter, Edward. 1977. *The Making of the Modern Family.* New York: Basic Books.

Shostak, Sara, and Jeremy Freese. 2010. "Gene-Environment Interaction and Medical Sociology." In *Handbook of Medical Sociology*, edited by Chloe Bird, Peter Conrad, Allen Fremont, and Stephan Timmermans, 418-434. 6th ed. Nashville, TN: Vanderbilt University Press.

Shukin, Sharon. 2009. *Animal Capital: Rendering Life in Biopolitical Times.* Minneapolis: University of Minnesota Press.

Shupe, Anson D. 1998. *Wolves within the Fold: Religious Leadership and Abuses of Power.* New Brunswick, NJ: Rutgers University Press.

———. 2007. *Spoils of the Kingdom: Clergy Misconduct and Religious Community.* Urbana: University of Illinois Press.

Shura, Robin, Rebecca A. Siders, and Dale Dannefer. 2010. "Culture Change in Long-Term Care: Participatory Action Research and the Role of the Resident." *Gerontologist* 51, no. 2: 212-225.

Shuval, Judith T. 2001. "Migration, Health and Stress." In *The Blackwell Companion to Medical Sociology*, edited by W. Cockerham, 126-143. Oxford, UK: Blackwell.

Shwed, U., and Peter Bearman. 2010. "The Temporal Structure of Scientific Consensus Formation." *American Sociological Review* 75, no. 6: 817-840.

Sibley, David. 1995a. "Gender, Science, Politics and Geographies of the City." *Gender, Place and Culture: A Journal of Feminist Geography* 2: 37-50.

———. 1995b. "Women's Research on Chicago in the Early 20th Century." *Women and Environments* 14, no. 2: 6-8.

SIECUS. 1917. *Der Krieg und die Geistigen Entscheidungen.* Munich: Duncker and Humblot.

———. 1950. *The Sociology of Georg Simmel.* Translated by Kurt H. Wolff. New York: The Free Press.

———. 1955. *Conflict and the Web of Group Affiliations.* Glencoe, IL: The Free Press.

———. 2010. "Fact Sheet: State by State Decisions: The Personal Responsibility Education Program and Title V Abstinence-Only Program." http://www.siecus.org/index.cfm?fuseaction=Page.ViewPage&PageID=1272 (accessed September 5, 2012).

Sienkiewicz, Dorota. 2010. "Access to Health Services in Europe." *European Social Watch Report* 2010: 17-20.

Sigmon, Robert. 1990. "Service Learning: Three Principles." In *Combining Service and Learning: A Resource Book for Community and Public Service*, edited by Jane Kendall and Associates, 1: 56-64. Raleigh, NC: National Society for Internships and Experiential Education.

Sikkink, Kathryn. 2011. *Justice Cascade.* New York: Knopf.

Sikkink, Kathryn, and Hunjoon Kim. 2009. "Explaining the Deterrence Effect of Human Rights Prosecutions in Transitional Countries." *International Studies Quarterly.*

Silbey, Susan. 2005. "Everyday Life and the Constitution of Legality." In *The Blackwell Companion to the Sociology of Culture*, edited by Mark D. Jacobs and Nancy Weiss Hanrahan, 332-345. Malden, MA: Blackwell.

Silvers, A. 1998a. "Formal Justice." In *Disability, Difference, Discrimination: Perspectives on Justice in Bioethics and Public Policy*, edited by A. Silvers, D. Wasserman, and M. B. Mahowald, 13-145. Lanham, MD: Rowman & Littlefield.

———. 1998b. "Introduction." In *Disability, Difference, Discrimination: Perspectives on Justice in Bioethics and Public Policy*, edited by A. Silvers, D. Wasserman, and M. B. Mahowald, 1-12. Lanham, MD: Rowman & Littlefield.

Simmel, Georg. 1968. "The Conflict in Modern Culture." In *The Conflict in Modern Culture and Other Essays*, edited and translated by K. Peter Etzkorn. New York: Teachers College Press.

———. 1990. *The Philosophy of Money.* London: Routledge.

Simon, H. 1957. *Models of Man, Social and Rational: Mathematical Essays on Rational Human Behavior in a Social Setting.* New York: Wiley.

Simon, Herbert Alexander. 1947. *Administrative Behavior: A Study of Decision-Making Processes in Administrative Organization.* New York: Macmillan.

Simon, Karla W. 2010. "International Non-Governmental Organizations and Non-Profit Organizations." *International Lawyer* 44: 399–414.

Sims, Beth. 1992. *Workers of the World Undermined: American Labor's Role in U.S. Foreign Policy.* Boston: South End Press.

Singer, Peter. 1993. *Practical Ethics.* 2nd ed. Cambridge, UK: Cambridge University Press.

———. 2005. *Animal Liberation.* New York: Harper Perennial.

———. 2009. *The Life You Can Save.* New York: Random House.

Sinha, Mrinalini, Donna Guy, and Angela Woollacott, eds. 1999. *Feminisms and Internationalism.* Oxford, UK: Blackwell Publishers.

Sjoberg, Gideon. 1999. "Some Observations on Bureaucratic Capitalism: Knowledge about What and Why?" In *Sociology for the Twenty-First Century: Continuities and Cutting Edges,* edited by Janet Abu-Lughod, 43–64. Chicago: University of Chicago Press.

Sjoberg, Gideon., E. A. Gill, B. Littrell, and N. Williams. 1997. "The Reemergence of John Dewey and American Pragmatism." *Studies in Symbolic Interaction* 23: 73–92.

Sjoberg, Gideon., E. A. Gill, and J. E. Tan. 2003. "Social Organization." In *Handbook of Symbolic Interactionism,* edited by Larry T. Reynolds and Nancy J. Herman-Kinney, 411–432. New York: AltaMira Press.

Sjoberg, Gideon., E. A. Gill, N. Williams, and K. E. Kuhn. 1995. "Ethics, Human Rights and Sociological Inquiry: Genocide, Politicide and Other Issues of Organizational Power." *American Sociologist* 26: 8–19.

Sjoberg, Gideon., and T. R. Vaughan. 1993. "The Ethical Foundations of Sociology and the Necessity for a Human Rights Alternative." In *A Critique of Contemporary American Sociology,* edited by T. R. Vaughan, G. Sjoberg, and L. T. Reynolds, 114–159. Dix Hills, NY: General Hall.

Sjoberg, Gideon, Elizabeth A. Gill, and Leonard Cain. 2003. "Counter System Analysis and the Construction of Alternative Futures." *Sociological Theory* 21, no. 3: 214–235.

Sjoberg, Gideon, Elizabeth A. Gill, and Norma Williams. 2001. "A Sociology of Human Rights." *Social Problems* 48, no. 1: 11–47.

Sklar, Martin J. 1988. *The Corporate Reconstruction of American Capitalism, 1890–1916: The Market, the Law, and Politics.* New York: Cambridge University Press.

Skocpol, Theda. 1979. *States and Social Revolutions: A Comparative Analysis of France, Russia, and China.* Cambridge, UK: Cambridge University Press.

———. 1984. "Sociology's Historical Imagination." In *Vision and Method in Historical Sociology,* edited by Theda Skocpol. New York and Cambridge, UK: Cambridge University Press.

———. 1992. *Protecting Soldiers and Mothers: The Political Origins of Social Policy in the United States.* Cambridge, MA: Belknap Press.

Skrentny, John D. 2002. *The Minority Rights Revolution.* Cambridge, MA: Harvard University Press.

Slovic, Paul. 2000. *The Perception of Risk.* London: Routledge.

Smaje, Chris. 2000. *Natural Hierarchies: The Historical Sociology of Race and Caste.* Malden, MA: Blackwell.

Small, Mario Luis. 2009. *Unanticipated Gains: Origins of Network Inequality in Everyday Life.* New York: Oxford University Press.

Smith, Adam. 2002 [1759]. *The Theory of Moral Sentiments,* edited by Knud Haakonssen. New York: Cambridge University Press.

Smith, Christian. 2010. *What Is a Person?* Chicago: University of Chicago Press.

Smith, Dorothy E. 1987. *The Everyday World as Problematic: A Feminist Sociology.* Toronto: University of Toronto Press.

———. 1990. *Texts, Facts, and Femininity: Exploring the Relations of Ruling.* New York: Routledge.

———. 1999. *Writing the Social: Critique, Theory, and Investigations.* Toronto: University of Toronto Press.

Smith, Jackie. 1999. "Human Rights and the Global Economy: A Response to Meyer." *Human Rights Quarterly* 21, no. 1: 80–92.

———. 2004. "Exploring Connections between Global Integration and Political Mobilization." *Journal of World-Systems Research* 10, no. 1: 255–285.

———. 2005. "Response to Wallerstein: The Struggle for Global Society in a World System." *Social Forces* 83, no. 3: 1279–1285.

———. 2008. *Social Movements and Global Democracy.* Baltimore: Johns Hopkins University Press.

Smith, Jackie, Melissa Bolyard, and Anna Ippolito. 1999. "Human Rights and the Global Economy: A Response to Meyer." *Human Rights Quarterly* 21, no. 1: 207–219.

Smith, Jackie, and Hank Johnston, eds. 2002. *Globalization and Resistance: Transnational Dimensions of Social Movements.* Lanham, MD: Rowman & Littlefield.

Smith, Jackie, Marina Karides, Marc Becker, Christopher Chase Dunn, Dorval Brunelle, Donnatella Della

Porta, Rosalba Icaza, Jeffrey Juris, Lorenzo Mosca, Ellen Reese, Jay Smith, and Rolando Vasquez. 2008. *The World Social Forums and the Challenges for Global Democracy*. Boulder, CO: Paradigm Publishers.

Smith, Jackie, Ron Pagnucco, and George A. López. 1998. "Globalizing Human Rights: The Work of Transnational Human Rights NGOs in the 1990s." *Human Rights Quarterly* 20, no. 2: 379–412.

Smith, Jackie, and Dawn Wiest. 2005. "The Uneven Geography of Global Civil Society: National and Global Influences on Transnational Association." *Social Forces* 84, no. 2: 621–652.

Smith, Linda Tuhiwai. 1999. *Decolonizing Methodologies: Research and Indigenous Peoples*. New York: Zed Books.

———. 2005. "On Tricky Ground: Researching the Native in an Age of Uncertainty." In *Handbook of Qualitative Research*, edited by Norman Denzin and Yvonna Lincoln, 18–108. Beverly Hills, CA: Sage Publications.

Smith, Philip. 2008. *Punishment and Culture*. Chicago: University of Chicago Press.

Smith, Robert. 2005. *Mexican New York: Transnational Lives of New Immigrants*. Berkeley: University of California Press.

Smith, Sylvia. 2005. "The $100 Laptop—Is It a Wind-Up?" CNN.com. http://edition.cnn.com/2005/WORLD/africa/12/01/laptop (accessed January 23, 2010).

Smith, Thomas Spence. 2004. "Where Sociability Comes From: Neurosociological Foundations of Social Interaction." In *The Dialogical Turn: New Roles for Sociology in the Postdisciplinary Age*, edited by Charles Camic and Hans Joas, 199–220. Lanham, MD: Rowman & Littlefield.

Smith, Tom W. 2009. "National Pride in Comparative Perspective." In *The International Social Survey Programme, 1984–2009: Charting the Globe*, edited by Max Haller, Roger Jowell, and Tim W. Smith, 197–221. New York: Routledge.

Smith-Doerr, Laurel. 2004. *Women's Work: Gender Equality vs. Hierarchy in the Life Sciences*. Boulder, CO: Lynne Rienner Publishers.

Snipp, C. Matthew. 2003. "Racial Measurement in the American Census: Past Practices and Implications for the Future." *Annual Review of Sociology* 29: 563–588.

Snow, David A. 2004. "Framing Processes, Ideology, and Discursive Fields." In *The Blackwell Companion to Social Movements*, edited by David A. Snow, Sarah A. Soule, and Hanspeter Kreisi, 380–412. Oxford: Blackwell.

Snow, David A., and Leon Anderson. 1987. "Identity Work among the Homeless: The Verbal Construction and Avowal of Personal Identities." *American Journal of Sociology* 92: 1336–1371.

Snow, David, E. Burke Rochford Jr., Steven K. Worden, and Robert D. Benford. 1986. "Frame Alignment Processes, Micro-Mobilization and Movement Participation." *American Sociological Review* 51: 464–481.

Snyder, Howard. 2011. "Arrest in the United States: 1980–2009." Bureau of Justice Statistics. http://bjs.ojp.usdoj.gov/content/pub/pdf/aus8009.pdf (accessed October 2011).

Snyder, Jack, and Leslie Vinjamuri. 2003/2004. "Trials and Errors: Principle and Pragmatism in Strategies of International Justice." *International Security* 28: 5–44.

Sobell, L. C., M. B. Sobell, D. M. Riley, F. Klajner, G. I. Leo, G. Pavan, and A. Cancill. 1986. "Effect of Television Programming and Advertising on Alcohol Consumption in Normal Drinkers." *Journal Studies of Alcohol and Drugs* 47: 333–340.

Sok, Chivy, and Kenneth Neubeck. Forthcoming. "Building U.S. Human Rights Culture from the Ground Up: International Human Rights Implementation at the Local Level." In *In Our Own Backyard: Human Rights, Injustice, and Resistance in the United States*, edited by Bill Armaline, Bandana Purkayastha, and Davita Silfen Glasberg, 231–243. Philadelphia: University of Pennsylvania Press.

Soley, Lawrence. 1999. *Leasing the Ivory Tower: The Corporate Takeover of Academia*. Boston: South End Press.

Sombart, Werner. 1913. *Krieg und Kapitalismus*. Munich: Duncker and Humblot.

Somers, Margaret R. 2008. *Genealogies of Citizenship: Markets, Statelessness, and the Right to Have Rights*. New York: Cambridge University Press.

Somers, Margaret R., and Christopher Roberts. 2008. "Towards a New Sociology of Rights: A Genealogy of 'Buried Bodies' of Citizenship and Human Rights." *Annual Review of Law and Social Science* 4: 385–425.

Soohoo, Cynthia, Catherine Albisa, and Martha F. Davis, eds. 2008. *Bringing Human Rights Home: Portraits of the Movement*. Vol. 3. Westport, CT: Praeger.

Sorenson, John. 2011. "Constructing Extremists, Rejecting Compassion: Ideological Attacks on Animal Advocacy from Right and Left." In *Critical Theory and Animal Liberation*, edited by John Sanbonmatsu, 219–238. Lanham, MD: Rowman & Littlefield.

Sørensen, Aage B. 1979. "A Model and a Metric for the Analysis of the Intragenerational Status Attainment Process." *American Journal of Sociology* 85: 361–84.

South African Human Rights Commission (SAHRC). 1998. *My Rights, Your Rights: Respect, Responsibilities and the SAHRC*. English ed. Pretoria: Government of South Africa.

Soysal, Yasemin. 1994. *Limits of Citizenship: Migrants and Postnational Membership in Europe*. Chicago: University of Chicago Press.

Speier, Matthew. 1973. *How to Observe Face-to-Face Communication: A Sociological Introduction*. Pacific Palisades, CA: Goodyear.

Spencer, Herbert. 1967. *Evolution of Society*. Chicago: University of Chicago Press.

Spirer, Herbert F. 1990. "Violations of Human Rights: How Many? The Statistical Problems of Measuring Such Infractions Are Tough, but Statistical Science Is Equal to It." *American Journal of Economics and Sociology* 49: 199–210.

Spring, Joel. 2000. *The Universal Right to Education*. Mahwah, NJ: Lawrence Erlbaum Associates.

———. 2007. *A New Paradigm for Global School Systems*. New York: Routledge.

Squires, Gregory, and Charis B. Kubrin. 2006. *Privileged Places: Race, Residence, and the Structure of Opportunity*. Boulder, CO: Lynne Rienner Publishers.

St. Jean, Peter K. B. 2007. *Pockets of Crime: Broken Windows, Collective Efficacy, and the Criminal Point of View*. Chicago: University of Chicago Press.

Stacey, Judith. 1988. "Can There Be a Feminist Ethnography?" *Women's Studies International Forum* 11: 21–27.

———. 1991. "Can There Be a Feminist Ethnography?" In *Women's Words*, edited by Sherna B. Gluck and Daphne Patai, 111–119. New York: Routledge.

Stack, Carol. 1974. *All Our Kin: Strategies for Survival in a Black Community*. New York: Harper and Row.

Stacy, Helen. 2009. *Human Rights in the 21st Century*. Stanford, CA: Stanford University Press.

Staggenborg, Suzanne. 1988. "The Consequences of Professionalization and Formalization in the Pro-Choice Movement." *American Sociological Review* 53, no. 4: 585–605.

Stammers, Neil. 1999. "Social Movements and the Social Construction of Human Rights." *Human Rights Quarterly* 21: 980–1008.

———. 2009. *Human Rights and Social Movements*. New York: Pluto Press.

Stamp Dawkins, Marian. 2006. "The Scientific Basis for Assessing Suffering of Animals." In *In Defense of Animals: The Second Wave*, edited by Peter Singer. Cambridge, MA: Blackwell Publishers.

Stanton, Timothy, Dwight Giles, and Nadine Cruz. 1999. *Service Learning: A Movement's Pioneers Reflect on Its Origins, Practice, and Future*. San Francisco, CA: Jossey-Bass.

Stark, Barbara. 1992–1993. "Economic Rights in the United States and International Law: Towards an Entirely New Strategy." *Hastings Law Journal* 44: 79–130.

Staudt, Kathleen. 1990. *Women, International Development, and Politics: The Bureaucratic Mire*. Philadelphia: Temple University Press.

———. 1997. "Gender Politics in Bureaucracy: Theoretical Issues in Comparative Perspective." In *Women, International Development, and Politics*, edited by Kathleen Staudt, 3–36. Philadelphia: Temple University Press.

Stearns, Peter N. 1994. *American Cool: Constructing a Twentieth-Century Emotional Style*. New York: New York University Press.

Stein, Dorothy. 1988. "Burning Widows, Burning Brides: The Perils of Daughterhood in India." *Pacific Affairs* 61: 465–485.

Steiner, Gary. 2010. *Anthropocentrism and Its Discontents: The Moral Status of Animals in the History of Western Philosophy*. Pittsburgh, PA: University of Pittsburgh Press.

Steiner, Henry J., Phillip Alston, and Ryan Goodman. 2008. *International Human Rights in Context: Law, Politics, Morals*. Oxford: Oxford University Press.

Steinmetz, George. 2007. *The Devil's Handwriting: Precoloniality and the German Colonial State in Qingdao, Samoa, and Southwest Africa*. Chicago: University of Chicago Press.

Steinmo, Sven, Kathleen Thelen, and Frank Longstreth, eds. 1992. *Structuring Politics: Historical Institutionalism in Comparative Analysis*. New York: Cambridge University Press.

Stephan, W. G., C. W. Stephan, and W. B. Gudykunst. 1999. "Anxiety in Intercultural Relations: A Comparison of Anxiety/Uncertainty Management Theory and Integrated Threat Theory." *International Journal of Intercultural Relations* 23: 613–628.

Stephens, Lowndes. 1979. "The Goebbels Touch." *Journal of Communication* 29: 2205–2206.

Stets, Jan E., and Emily K. Asencio. 2008. "Consistency and Enhancement Processes in Understanding Emotions." *Social Forces* 86: 1055–1078.

Stets, Jan E., and Jonathan H. Turner, eds. 2007. *Handbook of the Sociology of Emotions*. New York: Springer.

Stevens, Fred. 2001. "The Convergence and Divergence of Modern Health Care Systems." In *The Blackwell Companion to Medical Sociology*, edited by William Cockerham, 159–176. Malden, MA: Blackwell Publishing.

Stevenson, Betsey, and Justin Wolfers. 2007. "Marriage and Divorce: Changes and Their Driving Forces." *Journal of Economic Perspectives* 21, no. 2: 27–52.

Stinchcombe, Arthur L. 1997. "On the Virtues of the Old Institutionalism." *Annual Review of Sociology* 23: 1–18.

Stolleis, Michael. 2007. "Law and Lawyers Preparing the Holocaust." *Annual Review of Law and Social Science* 3: 213–232.

Stover, Eric. 2005. *The Witnesses: War Crimes and the Promise of Justice in The Hague*. Philadelphia: University of Pennsylvania Press.

Straus, Scott, and Robert Lyons. 2006. *Intimate Enemy: Images and Voices of the Rwandan Genocide*. Cambridge, MA: MIT Press.

Strauss, Anselm L. 1978. *Negotiations*. New York: Wiley.

———. 1993. *Continual Permutations of Action*. New York: Aldine De Gruyter.

Streeck, Wolfgang. 1992. *Social Institutions and Economic Performance: Studies of Industrial Relations in Advanced Capitalist Economies*. London: Sage Publications.

Streeter, Sonya, Jhamirah Howard, Rachel Licata, and Rachel Garfield. 2011. "The Uninsured, a Primer: Facts about Americans without Health Insurance." Kaiser Family Foundation. http://www.kff.org/uninsured/upload/7451.pdf (accessed July 19, 2012).

Strickland, D. E. 1983. "Advertising Exposure, Alcohol Consumption and Misuse of Alcohol." In *Economics and Alcohol: Consumption and Controls*, edited by M. Grant, M. Plant, and A. Williams, 201–222. New York: Gardner.

Strom, Elizabeth A., and John H. Mollenkopf, eds. 2006. *The Urban Politics Reader*. New York: Routledge.

Stryker, Sheldon. 1980. *Symbolic Interactionism: A Social Structural Version*. Menlo Park, CA: Benjamin Cummings.

Stryker, Sheldon, and Kevin D. Vryan. 2003. "The Symbolic Interactionist Frame." In *Handbook of Social Psychology*, edited by John DeLamater, 3–28. New York: Kluwer.

Stuart, Alan, and J. Keith Ord. 1987. *Kendall's Advanced Theory of Statistics*. Vol. 1: *Distribution Theory*. 5th ed. Originally by Sir Maurice Kendall. New York: Oxford University Press.

Stuart, Tristram. 2006. *The Bloodless Revolution: A Cultural History of Vegetarianism from 1600 to Modern Times*. New York: W. W. Norton and Co.

Stuhr, John J. 2010. *100 Years of Pragmatism: William James's Revolutionary Philosophy*. Bloomington: Indiana University Press.

Substance Abuse and Mental Health Services Administration (SAMHSA). 2010. *Results from the 2009 National Survey on Drug Use and Health*. SAMHSA. http://oas.samhsa.gov/NSDUH/2k9NSDUH/2k9Results.htm#7.3.1 (accessed January 1, 2011).

Sunder, Madhavi. 2003. "Piercing the Veil." *Yale Law Journal* 112: 1401–1472.

Sutter, Molly Hazel. 2006. "Mixed-Status Families and Broken Homes: The Clash between the U.S. Hardship Standard in Cancellation of Removal Proceedings and International Law." *Transnational Law and Contemporary Problems* 783: 1–28.

Swedberg, Richard. 2010. "The Structure of Confidence and the Collapse of Lehman Brothers." In *Markets on Trial: The Economic Sociology of the U.S. Financial Crisis*, edited by Michael Lounsbury and Paul M. Hirsch, 71–114. Research in the Sociology of Organizations 30A. London: Emerald Group Publishing.

Swidler, Anne. 1986. "Culture in Action: Symbols and Strategies." *American Sociological Review* 51: 273–286.

Switzer, J. V. 2003. *Disabled Rights: American Disability Policy and the Fight for Equality*. Washington, DC: Georgetown University Press.

Symington, Alison. 2004. "Intersectionality: A Tool for Gender and Economic Justice." Association for Women's Rights in Development. http://www.awid.org/content/download/48805/537521/file/intersectionality_en.pdf (accessed September 17, 2012).

Szell, G. 1994. "Technology, Production, Consumption and the Environment." *International Social Science Journal* 140: 213–225.

Tabak, Mehmet. 2003. "Marxian Considerations on Morality, Justice, and Rights." *Rethinking Marxism* 15, no. 4: 523–540.

Tajfel, H. 1970. "Experiments in Intergroup Discrimination." *Scientific American* 223: 96–102.

Takacs-Santa, A. 2004. "The Major Transitions in the History of Human Transformation of the Biosphere." *Human Ecology Review* 11, no. 1: 51–66.

Takagi, Dana. 1994. "Maiden Voyage: Excursion into Sexuality and Identity Politics in Asian America." *Amerasia Journal* 20, no. 1: 1–17.

Takeuchi, David T., Emily Walton, and ManChui Leung. 2010. "Race, Social Contexts and Health: Examining Geographic Spaces and Places." In *Handbook of Medical Sociology*, edited by Chloe Bird, Peter Conrad, Allen Fremont, and Stephan Timmermans, 92–105. 6th ed. Nashville, TN: Vanderbilt University Press.

Takeuti, N. 2010. Personal communication with J. M. Fritz. December 14.

Tarnas, Richard. 1991. *The Passion of the Western Mind: Understanding the Ideas that Have Shaped Our World View*. New York: Ballantine Books.

Tarrow, Sidney G. 1998. *Power in Movement: Social Movements and Contentious Politics*. New York and Cambridge, UK: Cambridge University Press.

———. 2005. *The New Transnational Activism*. New York: Cambridge University Press.

Tatum, Beverly Daniel. 2003. *"Why Are All the Black Kids Sitting Together in the Cafeteria?" and Other Conversations about Race.* New York: Basic Books.

Taylor, Frederick W. 1910. *The Principles of Scientific Management.* New York: Harper and Brothers.

Taylor, Greg. 2003. "Scientology in the German Courts." *Journal of Law and Religion* 19: 153–198.

Taylor, J. 1999. "The New Economics of Labour Migration and the Role of Remittances in the Migration Process." *International Migration* 37, no. 1: 63–68.

Tazreiter, Claudia. 2010. "Local to Global Activism: The Movement to Protect the Rights of Refugees and Asylum Seekers." *Social Movement Studies* 9, no. 2: 201–214.

Teitel, Ruti. 1997. "Human Rights Genealogy (Symposium: Human Rights on the Eve of the Next Century)." *Fordham Law Review* 66: 301–317.

———. 2000. *Transitional Justice.* Oxford: Oxford University Press.

TenHouten, Warren D. 2005. "Primary Emotions and Social Relations: A First Report." *Free Inquiry in Creative Sociology* 33, no. 2: 79–92.

Terl, Allan H. 2000. "An Essay on the History of Lesbian and Gay Rights in Florida." *Nova Law Review* 24 (spring): 793–853.

Thayer, Carlyle A. 2004. "Laos in 2003: Counterrevolution Fails to Ignite." *Asian Survey* 44, no. 1: 110–114.

Thayer-Bacon, Barbara. 2004. "An Exploration of Myles Horton's Democratic Praxis: Highlander Folk School." *Educational Foundation* 18, no. 2, 5–23.

Theil, Henri. 1967. *Economics and Information Theory.* Amsterdam: North-Holland.

Therborn, G. 1980. *The Ideology of Power and the Power of Ideology.* London: Verso.

Thomas, George. 2004. "Constructing World Civil Society through Contentions over Religious Rights." *Journal of Human Rights* 3: 239–251.

Thomas, George M. 1987. *Institutional Structure: Constituting State, Society, and the Individual.* Newbury Park, CA: Sage Publications.

———. 2001. "Religions in Global Civil Society." *Sociology of Religion* 62: 515–533.

Thomas, James. 2010. "The Racial Formation of Medieval Jews: A Challenge to the Field." *Ethnic and Racial Studies* 33: 1737–1755.

Thomas, James, and David Brunsma. 2008. "Bringing Down the House: Reparations, Universal Morality, and Social Justice." In *Globalization and America: Race, Human Rights, and Inequality,* edited by Angela Hattery, David G. Embrick, and Earl Smith, 65–81. Lanham, MD: Rowman & Littlefield.

Thomas, John, John W. Meyer, Francisco O. Ramirez, and John Boli. 1987. *Institutional Structure: Constituting State, Society, and the Individual.* Newbury Park, CA: Sage.

Thomas, Nigel, Brian K. Gran, and Karl Hansen. 2011. "An Independent Voice for Children's Rights in Europe? The Role of Independent Children's Rights Institutions in the EU." *International Journal of Children's Rights* 19, no. 3: 429–449.

Thomas, Robert J. 1994. *What Machines Can't Do: Politics and Technology in the Industrial Enterprise.* Berkeley: University of California Press.

Thomas, W. H. 2004. *What Are Old People For? How Elders Will Save the World.* Acton, MA: VanderWky and Burnham.

Thompson, E. P. 1963. *The Making of the English Working Class.* London: V. Gollancz.

———. 1978. *The Poverty of Theory.* London: Merlin Press.

Thompson, Silvanus P. 1946 [1910]. *Calculus Made Easy.* 3rd ed. New York: St. Martin's Press.

Thorne, B. 1993. *Gender Play: Boys and Girls in School.* Piscataway, NJ: Rutgers University Press.

Thorne, S., B. Paterson, S. Acorn, C. Canam, G. Joachim, and C. Jillings. 2002. "Chronic Illness Experience: Insights from a Metastudy." *Qualitative Health Research* 12, no. 4: 437–452.

Tiefer, Lenore. 2004. *Sex Is Not a Natural Act and Other Essays.* Boulder, CO: Westview Press.

Tilly, Charles. 1978. *From Mobilization to Revolution.* New York: McGraw-Hill Companies.

———. 1992. *Coercion, Capital and European States.* Oxford: Blackwell.

Timasheff, N. S. 1941. "Fundamental Problems of the Sociology of Law." *American Catholic Sociological Review* 2, no. 4: 233–248.

Timmermans, S. 2001. "Social Death as Self-Fulfilling Prophecy." In *Sociology of Health and Illness: Critical Perspectives,* edited by P. Conrad, 305–321. New York: Worth.

Tinkler, Penny. 1995. *Constructing Girlhood.* Oxfordshire, UK: Taylor and Francis.

Tisdall, E. K. M. 2008. "Is the Honeymoon Over? Children and Young People's Participation in Public Decision-Making." *International Journal of Children's Rights* 16, no. 3: 343–354.

Tocqueville, Alexis de. 1960 [1835]. *Democracy in America.* New York: Alfred A. Knopf.

Tolman, Deborah L. 1994. "Doing Desire: Adolescent Girls' Struggles for/with Sexuality." *Gender and Society* 8, no. 3: 324–342.

Tomasevski, Katerina. 1995. *Women and Human Rights.* London: Zed Books.

Toney, Jeffery H., H. Kaplowitz, R. Pu, F. Qi, and G. Chang. 2010. "Science and Human Rights: A Bridge towards Benefiting Humanity." *Human Rights Quarterly* 32, no. 4: 1008–1017.

Tonry, Michael H. 1995. *Malign Neglect–Race, Crime, and Punishment in America*. New York: Oxford University Press.

Torres, Bob. 2007. *Making a Killing: The Political Economy of Animal Rights*. Oakland, CA: AK Press.

Toulmin, Stephen. 1953. *The Philosophy of Science: An Introduction*. London: Hutchinson.

———. 1978. "Science, Philosophy of." In *The New Encyclopaedia Britannica, Macropaedia* 16: 375–393. 15th ed. Chicago: Britannica.

Touraine, Alain. 1981. *The Voice and the Eye*. Cambridge, UK: Cambridge University Press.

———. 1983. *Solidarity: The Analysis of a Social Movement, Poland 1980–1981*. Cambridge, UK: Cambridge University Press.

Townsend, Peter. 2006. "Policies for the Aged in the 21st Century: More 'Structured Dependency' or the Realisation of Human Rights?" *Aging and Society* 26: 161–179.

Traer, Robert. 1991. *Faith in Human Rights: Support in Religious Traditions for a Global Struggle*. Washington, DC: Georgetown University Press.

Trevino, Javier A. 1996. *The Sociology of Law: Classical and Contemporary Perspectives*. New York: St. Martin's Press.

———. 1998. "The Influence of C. Wright Mills on Students for a Democratic Society: An Interview with Bob Ross." *Humanity and Society* 22: 260–277.

Tripp, Aili, and Myra Marx Ferree, eds. 2006. *Global Feminism: Transnational Women's Activism, Organizing, and Human Rights*. New York: New York University Press.

Trucios-Haynes, Inid. 2001. "Why 'Race Matters': LatCrit Theory and Latina/o Racial Identity." *La Raza Law Journal* 12, no. 1: 1–42.

Tsutsui, Kiyoteru. 2004. "Global Civil Society and Ethnic Social Movements in the Contemporary World." *Sociological Forum* 19, no. 1: 63–87.

Tuan, Mia. 1999. *Forever Foreigners or Honorary Whites? The Asian Ethnic Experience Today*. New Brunswick, NJ: Rutgers University Press.

Tuchman, Gaye. 2011. *Wannabe U: Inside the Corporate University*. Chicago: University of Chicago Press.

Turk, Austin. 1969. *Criminality and Legal Order*. Chicago: Rand McNally.

———. 1982. *Political Criminology*. Thousand Oaks: Sage.

Turmel, André. 2008. *A Historical Sociology of Childhood*. New York: Cambridge University Press.

Turner, Bryan S. 1993. "Outline of the Theory of Human Rights." In *Citizenship and Social Theory*, edited by Bryan S. Turner, 162–190. London: Sage.

———. 1995. "Symposium: Human Rights and the Sociological Project (Introduction)." *Australian and New Zealand Journal of Sociology* 31: 1–8.

———. 1996. *Vulnerability and Human Rights: Essays on Human Rights*. University Park: Penn State University Press.

———. 2002. "The Problem of Cultural Relativism for the Sociology of Human Rights: Weber, Schmitt and Strauss." *Journal of Human Rights* 1, no. 4: 587–605.

———. 2006. "Global Sociology and the Nature of Rights." *Societies without Borders* 1: 41–52.

———. 2010. "The Problem of Cultural Relativism for the Sociology of Human Rights: Weber, Schmitt and Straus." *Journal of Human Rights* 1, no. 4: 587–605.

Turner, Jonathan H. 2007. *Human Emotions: A Sociological Theory*. New York: Routledge.

Turner, Jonathan H., and Alexandra Maryanski. 2005. *Incest: The Origin of the Taboo*. Boulder, CO: Paradigm Publishers.

———. 2008. *On the Origins of Societies by Natural Selection*. Boulder, CO: Paradigm Publishers.

Turner, Jonathan H., and Jan E. Stets. 2005. *The Sociology of Emotions*. Cambridge, UK: Cambridge University Press.

———. 2006. "Sociological Theories of Human Emotions." *Annual Review of Sociology* 32: 25–52.

Turner, R. J., B. Wheaton, and D. A. Lloyd. 1995. "The Epidemiology of Social Stress." *American Sociological Review* 60: 104–125.

Turner, Ralph. 1976. "The Real Self: From Institution to Impulse." *American Journal of Sociology* 81: 989–1016.

Turner, Ralph H., and Steven Gordon. 1981. "The Boundaries of the Self: The Relationship of Authenticity in the Self-Conception." In *Self-Concept: Advances in Theory and Research*, edited by Mervin D. Lynch, Ardyth A. Norem-Hebeisen, and Kenneth J. Gergen, 39–57. Cambridge, MA: Ballinger.

Turner, Stephanie S. 1999. "Intersex Identities: Locating New Intersections of Sex and Gender." *Gender and Society* 13, no. 4: 457–479.

Turner, Stephen. 1977. "Blau's Theory of Differentiation: Is It Explanatory?" *Sociological Quarterly* 18: 17–32.

———. 2007. "A Life in the First Half-Century of Sociology: Charles Ellwood and the Division of Sociology." In *Sociology in America: A History*, edited by Craig Calhoun, 115–154. Chicago: University of Chicago Press.

Udehn, L. 2001. *Methodological Individualism. Background, History, and Meaning*. London: Routledge.

Udry, J. Richard. 2000. "Biological Limits of Gender Construction." *American Sociological Review* 65, no. 3: 443–457.

Uhlenberg, Peter. 2009a. "Children in an Aging Society." *Journals of Gerontology, Series B: Psychological Sciences* 64B: 489–496.

———, ed. 2009b. *International Handbook of Population Aging.* Dordrecht, The Netherlands: Springer.

Uhlenberg, Peter, and Michelle Cheuk. 2010. "The Significance of Grandparents to Grandchildren: An International Perspective." In *Sage Handbook of Social Gerontology*, edited by D. Dannefer and C. Phillipson, 447–458. London: Sage.

Uhlenberg, Peter, and Jenny de Jong Gierveld. 2004. "Age-Segregation in Later Life: An Examination of Personal Networks." *Ageing and Society* 24: 5–28.

Underhill, Kristen, Paul Montgomery, and Don Operario. 2007. "Systematic Review of Abstinence-Only Programmes Aiming to Prevent HIV Infection in High-Income Countries." *British Medical Journal* 335: 248.

United Nations. 1948. "The Universal Declaration of Human Rights." United Nations. www.un.org/en/documents/udhr/index.shtml (accessed December 10, 2010).

———. 1991. "The Protection of Persons with Mental Illness and the Improvement of Mental Health Care." United Nations. http://www.un.org/documents/ga/res/46/a46r119.htm (accessed November 10, 2010).

———. 1992. *Rio Declaration on Environment and Development.* 31 ILM874. United Nations. www.un-documents.net/rio-dec.htm (accessed January 20, 2012).

———. 1993. "Vienna Declaration and Programme of Action." Office of the United Nations High Commissioner for Human Rights. http://www.unhchr.ch/huridocda/huridoca.nsf/(symbol)/a.conf.157.23.en (accessed July 20, 2012).

———. 1995. *UN Report of the Fourth World Conference on Women.* New York: United Nations.

———. 2000. "Gender and Racial Discrimination Report of the Expert Group Meeting." United Nations. http://www.un.org/womenwatch/daw/csw/genrac/report.htm (accessed January 11, 2012).

———. 2001. "Background Briefing on Intersectionality, Working Group on Women and Human Rights, 45th Session of the UN CSW." Center for Women's Global Leadership. http://www.cwgl.rutgers.edu/csw01/background.htm (accessed March 31, 2011).

———. 2002. "Johannesburg Declaration on Sustainable Development." United Nations. http://www.un.org/esa/sustdev/documents/WSSD_POI_PD/English/POI_PD.htm (accessed July 20, 2012).

———. 2007. "United Nations Declaration on the Rights of Indigenous Peoples." New York: Official Records of the General Assembly, Sixty-First Session, Supplement No. 53 (A/61/53), Pt. One, Ch. 2, Sect. A, and 107th Plenary Meeting, September 13.

———. 2008. "International Migrant Stock: The 2008 Revision." United Nations. http://esa.un.org/migration/index.asp?panel=1 (accessed October 12, 2010).

———. 2009. *15 Years of the United Nations Special Rapporteur on Violence against Women, Its Causes and Consequences.* Office of the High Commissioner for Human Rights. http://www2.ohchr.org/english/issues/women/rapporteur/docs/15YearReviewofVAWMandate.pdf (accessed January 11, 2012).

———. 2010. "Gender Dimensions of Agricultural and Rural Employment: Differentiated Pathways out of Poverty." UN Food and Agriculture Organization. http://www.fao.org/docrep/013/i1638e/i1638e00.htm (accessed January 21, 2011).

United Nations Development Program (UNDP). 1987. *Brundtland Report.* New York: UNDP.

United Nations Educational Scientific and Cultural Organization (UNESCO). 1990. "Meeting Basic Learning Needs: A Vision for the 1990s." UNESCO. http://www.unesco.org/en/efa/the-efa-movement/jomtien-1990.

United Nations Food and Agriculture Organization (UNFAO). 2006. "Livestock's Long Shadow: Environmental Issues and Options." UNFAO. http://www.fao.org/docrep/010/a0701e/a0701e00.htm (accessed July 20, 2012).

———. 2010. *Gender Dimensions of Agricultural and Rural Employment: Differential Pathways out of Poverty.* Rome: UNFAO, International Fund for Agricultural Development, and International Labour Office.

United Nations High Commissioner for Refugees (UNHCR). 1966. "International Covenant on Economic, Social, and Cultural Rights." UNHCR. http://www2.ohchr.org/english/law/cescr.htm (accessed January 11, 2012).

———. 2010. "UNHCR Refugee Figures." UNHCR. http://www.unhcr.org/pages/49c3646c1d.html (accessed on January 11, 2012).

United Nations Human Development Reports. 2010. "The Real Wealth of Nations: Pathways to Human Development." UN Human Development Reports. http://hdr.undp.org/en/reports/global/hdr2010 (accessed July 20, 2012).

United Nations Human Rights Council. 2008. "Human Rights and Climate Change." UN Human Rights Council Resolution 7/23, March 28.

United Nations Office on Drugs and Crime (UNODC). 2010. *Drug Control, Crime and Prevention: A Human Rights Perspective.* International Centre on Human Rights and Drug Policy. http://www.humanrightsanddrugs.org/wp-content/uploads/2010/03/UNODC-Human-Rights-Conference-Paper.pdf (accessed January 1, 2011).

United States 111th Congress. 2009. *Afghan's Narco War: Breaking the Link between Drug Traffickers and Insurgents.* Government Printing Office. http://www.gpoaccess.gov/congress/index.html (accessed January 1, 2011).

United States Census Bureau. 2008. "U.S. Population Projections." US Census Bureau. http://www.census.gov/population/www/projections/summarytables.html (accessed January 29, 2012).

United States Department of Defense. 2003. *An Abrupt Climate Change Scenario and Its Implications for United States National Security.* Washington, DC: US Department of Defense.

United States Department of Health and Human Services. 2010. "Fact Sheet: Sex Trafficking." Administration for Children and Families. http://www.acf.hhs.gov/trafficking/about/fact_sex.html (accessed December 21, 2010).

United States Department of State. 2009. "2009 Human Rights Report: Singapore." US Department of State. http://www.state.gov/g/drl/rls/hrrpt/2009/eap/136008.htm (accessed October 1, 2011).

———. 2010a. "2010 Human Rights Report: Saudi Arabia." US Department of State. http://www.state.gov/documents/organization/160475.pdf (accessed October 1, 2012).

———. 2010b. "2010 Human Rights Report: China (Includes Tibet, Hong Kong, and Macau)." US Department of State. http://www.state.gov/g/drl/rls/hrrpt/2010/eap/154382.htm (accessed October 20, 2011).

United States Government Accountability Office (GAO). 2005. "Drug Offenders: Various Factors May Limit the Impacts of Federal Laws that Provide for Denial of Selected Benefits." GAO-05-238. GAO. http://www.gao.gov/new.items/d05238.pdf (accessed September 2011).

United States Human Rights Fund. 2010. *Perfecting Our Union: Human Rights Success Stories from across the United States.* New York: US Human Rights Fund.

United States Human Rights Network. 2011. http://www.ushrnetwork.org (accessed May 26, 2011).

United States National Institute of Standards and Technology (NIST). 2003. *Engineering Statistics Handbook.* NIST. http://www.itl.nist.gov/div898/handbook (accessed January 20, 2012).

University of Warwick, Sociology Department. n.d. "The Module in 10 Points." University of Warwick. http://www2.warwick.ac.uk/fac/soc/sociology/staff/emeritus/robertfine/home/teachingmaterial/humanrights/tenpoints (accessed January 1, 2011).

Unno, Mark T. 1999. "Review: Questions in the Making: A Review Essay on Zen Buddhist Ethics in the Context of Buddhist and Comparative Ethics." *Journal of Religious Ethics* 27, no. 3: 507–536.

Updegraff, K., A. Booth, and Shawna Thayer. 2006. "The Role of Family Relationship Quality and Testosterone Levels in Adolescents' Peer Experience: A Biosocial Analysis." *Family Psychology* 20: 21–29.

US Constitution Online. "U.S. Constitution—Amendment 1." 1791. US Constitution Online. http://www.usconstitution.net/xconst_Am1.html (accessed July 20, 2012).

Vaillancourt, Jean-Guy. 2010. "From Environmental Sociology to Global Ecosociology: The Dunlap-Buttel Debates." In *The International Handbook of Environmental Sociology,* edited by Michael R. Redclift and Graham Woodgate, 48–62. Northampton, MA: Edward Elgar Publishing.

Valentine, David. 2007. *Imagining Transgender: An Ethnography of a Category.* Durham, NC: Duke University Press.

Valenzuela, Angela. 1999. *Subtractive Schooling.* Albany: State University of New York.

Valliant, George E. 1983. *The Natural History of Alcoholism.* Cambridge, MA: Harvard University Press.

Van Aelst, Peter, and Stefaan Walgrave. 2002. "New Media, New Movements? The Role of the Internet in Shaping the 'Anti-Globalization' Movement." *Information, Communication, & Society* 5, no. 4: 465–493.

Van Bockstaele, J., M. Van Bockstaele, J. Malbos, M. Godard-Plasman, and N. Van Bockstaele. 2008. "Socioanalysis and Clinical Intervention." In *International Clinical Sociology,* edited by J. M. Fritz, 170–187. New York: Springer.

Van den Berghe, Pierre L. 1979. *Human Family Systems.* New York: Elsevier.

———. 1981. *The Ethnic Phenomenon.* New York: Elsevier.

Van der Kroef, Justus M. 1976. "Indonesia's Political Prisoners." *Pacific Affairs* 49, no. 4: 625–647.

Van Krieken, Robert. 1999. "The 'Stolen Generations': On the Removal of Australian Indigenous Children from Their Families and Its Implications for the Sociology of Childhood." *Childhood* 6, no. 3: 297–311.

Vanwesenbeeck, I. 1997. "The Context of Women's Power(lessness) in Heterosexual Interactions." In *New Sexual Agendas,* edited by L. Segal. New York: New York University Press.

Vaughan, Diane. 1999. "The Dark Side of Organizations: Mistake, Misconduct, and Disaster." *Annual Review of Sociology* 25: 271–305.

———. 2002. "Criminology and the Sociology of Organizations." *Crime, Law, and Social Change* 37: 117–136.

Vaughan, T. R., and G. Sjoberg. 1984. "The Individual and Bureaucracy: An Alternative Meadian Interpretation." *Journal of Applied Behavioral Science* 20: 57–69.

Vaughn, Michael G, Matt Delisi, Kevin M. Beaver, and John Paul Wright. 2009. "DAT1 and 5HTT Are Associated with Pathological Criminal Behavior in a Nationally Representative Sample of Youth." *Criminal Justice and Behavior* 36, no. 11: 1103–1114.

Vaughn, Ted R., Gideon Sjoberg, and Larry Reynolds, eds. 1993. *A Critique of Contemporary American Sociology.* Dix Hills, NY: General Hall.

Veblen, Thorstein. 1991. *The Theory of the Leisure Class.* Fairfield, CT: A. M. Kelley.

———. 1998. *The Nature of Peace.* New Brunswick, NJ: Transaction Publishers.

Vegans of Color. 2011. "Liberation Veganism." Vegans of Color. http://vegansofcolor.wordpress.com/tag/animal-rights (accessed March 28, 2011).

Velez, Veronica, Lindsay Perez Huber, Corina Benavides López, Ariana de la Luz, and Daniel G. Solorzano. 2008. "Battling for Human Rights and Social Justice: A Latina/o Critical Race Media Analysis of Latina/o Student Youth Activism in the Wake of 2006 Anti-Immigrant Sentiment." *Social Justice* 35, no. 1: 7–27.

Veltmeyer, Henry, and Mark Rushton. 2011. *The Cuban Revolution as Socialist Human Development.* Leiden, the Netherlands: Brill.

Venetis, Penny M. 2012. "Making Human Rights Treaty Law Actionable in the United States." *Alabama Law Review* 63, no. 1: 97–160.

Venkatesh, Sudhir Alladi. 2009. *Off the Books: The Underground Economy of the Urban Poor.* Cambridge, MA: Harvard University Press.

Verkutyten, Maykel, Jochem Thijs, and Hidde Bekhuis. 2010. "Intergroup Contact and Ingroup Reappraisal: Examining the Deprovincialization Thesis." *Social Psychology Quarterly* 73, no. 4: 358–379.

Vermeersch, Peter. 2003. "Ethnic Minority Identity and Movement Politics: The Case of the Roma in the Czech Republic and Slovakia." *Ethnic and Racial Studies* 26: 879–901.

Verrijn, Stuart, H. 2008. "The ICC in Trouble." *Journal of International Criminal Justice* 6: 409–417.

Vialles, Noelie. 1994. *Animal to Edible.* Translated by J. A. Underwood. Cambridge, UK: Cambridge University Press.

Vinck, Patrick, Phuong N. Pham, Laurel E. Fletcher, and Eric Stover. 2009. "Inequalities and Prospects: Ethnicity and Legal Status in the Construction Labor Force after Hurricane Katrina." *Organization and Environment* 22, no. 4: 470–478.

Virchow, R. 1848. *Die Medizinische Reform.* Berlin: Druck und Verlag von G. Reimer.

Viscusi, Kip W. 1998. "Constructive Cigarette Regulation." *Duke Law Journal* 47, no. 6: 1095–1131.

Volti, R. 1995. *Society and Technological Change.* New York: St. Martin's Press.

Voss, Kim. 1992. "Disposition Is Not Action: The Rise and Demise of the Knights of Labor." *Studies in American Political Development* 6: 272–321.

Wagner, David, and Joseph Berger. 1985. "Do Sociological Theories Grow?" *American Journal of Sociology* 90: 697–728.

Wagner, Jon. 1999a. "Beyond the Body in a Box: Visualizing Contexts of Children's Action." *Visual Sociology* 14: 143–160.

———. 1999b. "Visual Sociology and Seeing Kids' Worlds." *Visual Sociology* 14.

Waites, Matthew. 2009. "Critique of 'Sexual Orientation' and 'Gender Identity' in Human Rights Discourse: Global Queer Politics beyond the Yogyakarta Principles." *Contemporary Politics* 15, no. 1: 137–156.

Waitzkin, H. 1981. "The Social Origins of Illness: A Neglected History." *International Journal of Health Services* 11: 77–103.

Wakefield, Sara E. L., and J. Baxter. 2010. "Linking Health Inequality and Environmental Justice: Articulating a Precautionary Framework for Research and Action." *Environmental Justice* 3, no. 3: 95–102.

Walby, Sylvia. 2007. "Introduction: Theorizing the Gendering of the Knowledge Economy: Comparative Approaches." In *Gendering the Knowledge Economy: Comparative Perspectives,* edited by Heidi Gottfried, Karin Gottschall, Mari Osawa, and Sylvia Walby, 3–50. Houndsmill, UK: Palgrave.

———. 2009. *Globalization and Inequalities: Complexity and Contested Modernities.* Los Angeles and London: Sage.

Wales, Steven. 2002. "Remembering the Persecuted: An Analysis of the International Religious Freedom Act." *Houston Journal of International Law* 24: 579–648.

Wallace, John, Ryoko Yamaguchi, Jerald G. Bachman, Patrick M. O'Malley, John E. Schulenberg, and Lloyd D. Johnston. 2007. "Religiosity and Adolescent Substance Use: The Role of Individual and Contextual Influences." *Social Problems* 54, no. 2: 308–327.

Wallace, Michael, Beth A. Rubin, and Brian T. Smith. 1988. "American Labor Law: Its Impact on Working-Class Militancy, 1901–1980." *Social Science History* 12: 1–29.

Wallerstein, Immanuel. 1974. *The Modern World System I: Capitalist Agriculture and the Origins of the European World-Economy in the Sixteenth Century.* New York: Academic Press.

———. 1979. *The Capitalist World System.* Cambridge, UK: Cambridge University Press.

———. 1980. *The Modern World System II: Mercantilism and the Consolidation of the European World Economy, 1600–1750.* New York: Academic Press.

———. 1983. *Historical Capitalism.* London: Verso.

———. 1984. *The Politics of the World-Economy: The States, the Movements, and the Civilizations.* Cambridge, UK: Cambridge University Press.

———. 2002. "The Itinerary of World Systems Analysis: or, How to Resist Becoming a Theory." In *New Directions in Contemporary Sociological Theory*, edited by Joseph Berger and Morris Zelditch, 358–376. Lanham, MD: Rowman & Littlefield.

———. 2005a. "After Development and Globalization, What?" *Social Forces* 83, no. 3: 1263–1278.

———. 2005b. "Render unto Caesar? The Dilemmas of a Multicultural World." *Sociology of Religion* 66: 121–133.

Walsh, Catherine. 2010. "De-Coloniality, Decolonial Thinking and Doing in the Andes: A Conversation by Walther Mignolo with Catherine Walsh." *Reartikulacija* 10–13. http://www.reartikulacija.org/?p=1468 (accessed February 25, 2011).

Walters, Kerry S., and Lisa Portness, eds. 1999. *Ethical Vegetarianism: From Pythagoras to Peter Singer.* Albany: State University of New York Press.

Walters, Suzanna Danuta. 2001. "Take My Domestic Partner, Please: Gays and Marriage in the Era of the Visible." In *Queer Families, Queer Politics: Challenging Culture and the State*, edited by Mary Bernstein and Renate Reimann, 338–357. New York: Columbia University Press.

Waltz, Kenneth N. 1979. *Theory of International Politics.* New York: Random House.

Wang, Guang-zhen, and Vijayan K. Pillai. 2001. "Women's Reproductive Health: A Gender-Sensitive Human Rights Approach." *Acta Sociologica* 44, no. 3: 231–242.

Wardell, Mark L., and Stephen P. Turner, eds. 1986. *Sociological Theory in Transition.* Boston: Allen and Unwin.

Waring, Marilyn. 2003. "Counting for Something! Recognising Women's Contributions to the Global Economy through Alternative Accounting Systems." *Gender and Development* 11, no. 1: 35–43.

Warner, R. 1994. *Recovery from Schizophrenia.* Routledge: London.

Warner, Michael. 2000. *The Trouble with Normal: Sex, Politics and the Ethics of Queer Life.* Cambridge, MA: Harvard University Press.

Warner-Smith, Penny, Lois Bryson, and Julie Ellen Byles. 2004. "The Big Picture: The Health and Well-Being of Women in Three Generations in Rural and Remote Areas of Australia." *Health Sociology Review* 13, no. 1: 15–26.

Warren, John T. 2001. "Doing Whiteness: On the Performative Dimensions of Race in the Classroom." *Communication Education* 50, no. 2: 91–108.

Washington, DC, City Council. 2008. "Washington D.C. Human Rights City Resolution." American Friends Service Committee. December 10. http://afsc.org/resource/washington-dc-human-rights-city-resolution (accessed May 24, 2011).

Washington, Silvia H. 2010. "Birth of a Sustainable Nation: The Environmental Justice and Environmental Health Movements in the United States." *Environmental Justice* 3, no. 2: 55–60.

Waters, Malcolm. 1995. "Globalisation and the Social Construction of Human Rights." Symposium: "Human Rights and the Sociological Project." *Australian and New Zealand Journal of Sociology* 31: 29–36.

———. 1996. "Human Rights and the Universalization of Interests: Towards a Social Constructionist Approach." *Sociology* 30, no. 3: 593–600.

Watkins-Hayes, Celeste. 2009. "Two-Faced Racism: Whites in the Backstage and Frontstage (review)." *Social Forces* 87: 2183–2185.

Watson, D. R. 1981. "Conversational and Organisational Uses of Proper Names: An Aspect of Counselor-Client Interaction." In *Medical Work: Realities and Routines*, edited by Paul Atkinson and Christian Heath, 91–106. Farnborough, UK: Gower.

———. 1983. "The Presentation of Victim and Motive in Discourse: The Case of Police Interrogations and Interviews." *Victimology* 8: 31–52.

———. 1984. "Racial and Ethnic Relations." In *Applied Sociological Perspectives*, edited by R. J. Anderson and W. W. Sharrock, 43–65. London: George Allen and Unwin.

———. 1997. "Some General Reflections on 'Categorization' and 'Sequence' in the Analysis of Conversation." In *Culture in Action: Studies in Membership Categorization Analysis*, edited by Stephen Hester and Peter Eglin, 49–75. Washington, DC: International Institute for Ethnomethodology and Conversation Analysis and University Press of America.

Weber, Bruce. 2011. "Harold Garfinkel, a Common-Sense Sociologist, Dies at 93." *New York Times.* May 3.

Weber, Max. 1946. "Religious Rejections of the World and Their Direction." In *From Max Weber*, edited by H. H. Gerth and C. Wright Mills, 24–26. New York: Oxford University Press.

———. 1948a. "Class, Status, Party." In *Max Weber: Essays in Sociology*, edited by H. H. Gerth and C. Wright Mills, 180–195. Oxford: Oxford University Press.

——. 1948b. "Politics as a Vocation." In *Max Weber: Essays in Sociology*, edited by H. H. Gerth and C. Wright Mills, 77–128. New York: Oxford: Oxford University Press.

——. 1949. *The Methodology of the Social Sciences*. New York: The Free Press.

——. 1968 [1920]. *Economy and Society*. Translated by Guenther Roth and Claus Wittich. 3 vols. Berkeley: University of California Press.

——. 1978. *Economy and Society*, edited by Guenther Roth and Claus Wittich. Berkeley: University of California Press.

——. 2002. *The Protestant Ethic and the Spirit of Capitalism*. London: Penguin Books.

——. 2007 [1914]. "Basic Sociological Terms." In *Classical Sociological Theory*, edited by Craig Calhoun et al., 211–227. New York: Blackwell.

——. 2011. *The Protestant Ethic and the Spirit of Capitalism*. Rev. 1920 ed. USA: Intercultural Publishing.

Weeramantry, C. G., ed. 1993. *The Impact of Technology on Human Rights: Global Case Studies*. Tokyo: United Nations University Press.

Weglyn, Michi Nishiura. 1976. *Years of Infamy: The Untold Story of America's Concentration Camps*. Seattle: University of Washington Press.

Weibel-Orlando, Joan C. 1989. "Pass the Bottle, Bro!: A Comparison of Urban and Rural Indian Drinking Patterns." In *Alcohol Use among U.S. Ethnic Minorities*, edited by D. Spiegler, D. Tate, S. Aitken, and C. Christian, 269–289. Rockville, MD: National Institute on Alcohol Abuse and Alcoholism.

Weinstein, J. 2010. *Social Change*. 3rd ed. Lanham, MD: Rowman & Littlefield.

Weir, Margaret. 1992. *Politics and Jobs: The Boundaries of Employment Policy in the United States*. Princeton, NJ: Princeton University Press.

Weis, L., ed. 2008. *The Way Class Works: Readings on School, Family, and the Economy*. New York: Routledge.

Weissbrodt, David S., and Clay Collins. 2006. "The Human Rights of Stateless Persons." *Human Rights Quarterly* 28, no. 1: 245–276.

Weitz, Eric D. 2003. *A Century of Genocide: Utopias of Race and Nation*. Princeton, NJ: Princeton University Press.

——. 2008. "From the Vienna to the Paris System: International Politics and the Entangled Histories of Human Rights, Forced Deportations, and Civilizing Missions." *American Historical Review* 113, no. 5: 1313–1343.

Weitzer, Ronald, ed. 2000. *Sex for Sale: Prostitution, Pornography, and the Sex Industry*. New York: Routledge.

Wejnert, Barbara. 2005. "Diffusion, Development, and Democracy, 1800–1999." *American Sociological Review* 70: 53–81.

Wendt, Alexander. 1999. *Social Theory of International Politics*. Cambridge, UK: Cambridge University Press.

West, Nathaniel. 1841. "A Coppie of the Liberties of the Massachusetts Colonie in New England." In *American History Leaflets 25*, edited by Albert Bushnell Hart and Edward Channing. New York: A. Lovell and Co., 1896. http://www.lonang.com/exlibris/organic/1641-mbl.htm (accessed September 4, 2012).

Westra, Laura. 2011. *Globalization, Violence and World Governance*. Leiden, the Netherlands: Brill.

Whitbeck, Les B. 2009. *Mental Health and Emerging Adulthood among Homeless Young People*. New York: Psychology Press.

White, Geoffry D., ed. 2000. *Campus, Inc.: Corporate Power in the Ivory Tower*. New York: Prometheus Books.

White, Orion. 1974. "The Dialectical Organization: An Alternative to Bureaucracy." *Public Administration Review* 29, no. 1: 32–42.

Whitmeyer, Joseph M. 1997. "Endogamy as a Basis for Ethnic Behavior." *Sociological Theory* 15, no. 2: 162–178.

Whyte, William Foote. 1943. *Street Corner Society*. Chicago: University of Chicago Press.

Wieder, D. Lawrence. 1974. *Language and Social Reality: The Case of Telling the Convict Code*. The Hague: Mouton.

Wieviorka, Michael. 2005. "From Marx to Braudel and Wallerstein." *Contemporary Sociology* 34, no. 1: 1–7.

WILD for Human Rights. 2006. *Making Rights Real: A Workbook on the Local Implementation of Human Rights*. San Francisco: Women's Institute for Leadership Development for Human Rights.

Wilentz, Sean. 1984. "Against Exceptionalism: Class Consciousness and the American Labor Movement, 1790–1920." *International Labor and Working-Class History* 26: 1–24.

Wiley, Norbert. 1994. *The Semiotic Self*. Chicago: University of Chicago Press.

Wilkinson, Lindsey, and Jennifer Pearson. 2009. "School Culture and the Well-Being of Same-Sex-Attracted Youth." *Gender and Society* 23, no. 4: 542–568.

Wilkinson, Richard. 1992. "National Mortality Rates: The Impact of Inequality?" *American Journal of Public Health* 82: 1082–1084.

——. 1996. *Unhealthy Societies: The Afflictions of Inequality*. New York: Routledge.

Wilkinson, Richard, and Michael Marmot, eds. 2003. *Social Determinants of Health: The Solid Facts*. Geneva: World Health Organization.

William, Archbishop of Tyre. 1943. *A History of Deeds Done beyond the Sea*. Translated and annotated by Emily Atwater Babcock and A. C. Krey. New York: Columbia University Press.

Williams, B. 1994. "Patient Satisfaction—a Valid Concept?" *Social Science and Medicine* 38, no. 4: 509–516.

Williams, D. R., Y. Yu, J. S. Jackson, and N. B. Anderson. 1997. "Racial Differences in Physical and Mental Health: Socio-Economic Status, Stress and Discrimination." *Journal of Health Psychology* 2, no. 3: 335-351.

Williams, David R., and Michelle Sternthal. 2010. "Understanding Racial-Ethnic Disparities in Health: Sociological Contributions." *Journal of Health and Social Behavior* 51, no. 1: S15-S27.

Williams, William Appleman. 1962. *The Tragedy of American Diplomacy*. New York: Dell.

Williamson, Oliver E. 1985. *The Economic Institutions of Capitalism, Firms, Markets, Relational Contracting*. New York: The Free Press.

Willmott, Hugh, Todd Bridgman, and Mats Alvesson, eds. 2009. *The Oxford Handbook of Critical Management Studies*. New York: Oxford University Press.

Wilsnack, R. W., and R. Cheloha. 1987. "Women's Roles and Problem Drinking across the Lifespan." *Social Problems* 34: 231-248.

Wilson, Edward O. 1978. *On Human Nature*. Cambridge, MA: Harvard University Press.

Wilson, R. A. 1997. *Human Rights, Culture and Context: Anthropological Perspectives*. London: Pluto Press.

Wilson, William Julius. 1987. *The Truly Disadvantaged: The Inner City, the Underclass and Public Policy*. Chicago: University of Chicago Press.

———. 2009. *More Than Just Race: Being Black and Poor in the Inner City*. New York: W. W. Norton.

Winant, Howard. 2006. "Race and Racism: Towards a Global Future." *Ethnic and Racial Studies* 29, no. 5: 986-1003.

Winch, Peter. 2008. *The Idea of a Social Science and Its Relation to Philosophy*. 3rd ed. London: Routledge Classics.

Wines, Michael. 2011. "Deadly Violence Strikes Chinese City Racked by Ethnic Tensions." *New York Times*. July 31. http://www.nytimes.com/2011/08/01/world/asia/01china.html (accessed September 4, 2012).

Winter, Bronwyn. 2006. "Religion, Culture, and Women's Human Rights: Some General and Theoretical Considerations." *Women's Studies International Forum* 29, no. 4: 381-394.

Wirth, L. 1931a. "Clinical Sociology." *American Journal of Sociology* 37: 49-66.

———. 1931b. *Sociology: Vocations for Those Interested in It*. Vocational Guidance Series 1. Chicago: University of Chicago, Department of Special Collections. Louis Wirth Collection. Box LVI, Folder 6.

Wise, Steven. 2005. *Rattling the Cage: Toward Legal Rights for Animals*. New York: Perseus Press.

Wisner, Ben, Piers Blaikie, Terry Cannon, and Ian Davis. 2004. *At Risk: Natural Hazards, People's Vulnerability and Disasters*. New York: Routledge.

Witz, Ann. 2000. "Whose Body Matters? Feminist Sociology and the Corporeal Turn in Sociology and Feminism." *Body and Society* 6, no. 2: 1-24.

Wodak, Alex. 1998. "Health, HIV Infection, Human Rights, and Injecting Drug Use." *Health and Human Rights* 2, no. 4: 24-41.

Woddiwiss, A. 1998. *Globalisation, Human Rights, and Labour Law in Pacific Asia*. Cambridge, UK: Cambridge University Press.

———. 2003. *Making Human Rights Work Globally*. London: The Glass House Press.

———. 2005. *Human Rights*. London: Routledge.

Woehrle, Lynne M., Patrick G. Coy, and Gregory M. Maney. 2008. *Contesting Patriotism: Culture, Power and Strategy in the Peace Movement*. Lanham, MD: Rowman & Littlefield.

Wolf, Diane L., ed. 1996. *Feminist Dilemmas in Fieldwork*. Boulder, CO: Westview.

Wolf, Kurt. 1950. "Introduction." In *The Sociology of Georg Simmel*, edited and translated by Kurt H. Wolff, xvii-xiv. New York: The Free Press.

Women's Refugee Commission. 2011. *The Living Ain't Easy: Urban Refugees in Kampala*. New York: Women's Refugee Commission.

Wood, Charles. 1999. "Losing Control of America's Future: The Census, Birthright Citizenship, and Illegal Aliens." *Harvard Journal of Law and Public Policy* 22, no. 2: 465-522.

Woolford, Andrew. 2006. "Making Genocide Unthinkable: Three Guidelines for a Critical Criminology of Genocide." *Critical Criminology* 14: 87-106.

World Conference against Racism. 2001. "World Conference against Racism, Racial Discrimination, Xenophobia and Related Intolerance: Declaration." United Nations. http://www.un.org/durbanreview2009/pdf/DDPA_full_text.pdf (accessed July 20, 2012).

World Health Organization (WHO). 1948. *Constitution of the World Health Organization*. Geneva: WHO.

———. 2000. *Maternal Mortality in 2000: Estimates Developed by WHO, UNICEF, and UNFPA*. Relief Web. http://www.reliefweb.int/library/documents/2003/who-saf-22oct.pdf (accessed January 20, 2012).

———. 2001. *The World Health Report 2001: Mental Health: New Understanding, New Hope*. WHO. http://www.who.int/whr/2001/en (accessed July 20, 2012).

———. 2007. "Community Mental Health Services Will Lessen Social Exclusion, Says WHO." WHO. http://www.who.int/mediacentre/news/notes/2007/np25/en/index.html (accessed January 20, 2012).

———. 2010. *Global Strategies for Women's and Children's Health*. New York: Partnership for Maternal, Newborn, and Child Health.

World People's Conference on Climate Change and the Rights of Mother Earth. 2010. "Draft Universal Declaration of the Rights of Mother Earth." Global Alliance for the Rights of Nature. http:// therightsofnature.org/wp-content/uploads/pdfs/FINAL-UNIVERSAL-DECLARATION-OF-THE -RIGHTS-OF-MOTHER-EARTH-APRIL-22-2010.pdf (accessed March 20 2011).

World Resources Institute's Earth Trends. 2008. World Resources Institute. http://earthtrends.wri.org/ pdf_library/data_tables/food_water_2008.pdf (accessed January 22, 2011).

Wotipka, Christine Min, and Kiyoteru Tsutsui. 2008. "Global Human Rights and State Sovereignty: State Ratification of International Human Rights Treaties 1965–2001." *Sociological Forum* 23, no. 4: 724–754.

Wrench, John. 2011. "Data on Discrimination in EU Countries: Statistics, Research and the Drive for Comparability." *Ethnic and Racial Studies* 34: 1715–1730.

Wright, Eric R., and Brea L. Perry. 2010. "Medical Sociology and Health Services Research: Past Accomplishments and Future Policy Challenges." *Journal of Health and Social Behavior* 51: S107–S119.

Wright, James D. 2009. *Address Unknown: The Homeless in America*. Piscataway, NJ: Transaction Publishers.

Wright, Quincy. 1948. "Relationship between Different Categories of Human Rights." In *Human Rights: Comments and Interpretations*, edited by United Nations Educational Scientific and Cultural Organization (UNESCO). Paris: UNESCO.

Wronka, J. 1998. *Human Rights and Social Policy in the 21st Century*. Lanham, MD: University Press of America.

Yang, Alan S. 1998. *From Wrongs to Rights: Public Opinion on Gay and Lesbian American's Moves toward Equality*. Washington, DC: National Gay and Lesbian Task Force Policy Institute.

Yates, Michael D. 2009. *Why Unions Matter*. New York: Monthly Review Press.

Yeung, W. J., and D. Conley. 2008. "Black-White Achievement Gap and Family Wealth." *Child Development* 79: 303–324.

Yosso, T., M. Ceja, W. Smith, and D. Solorzano. 2009. "Critical Race Theory, Racial Microaggressions, and Campus Racial Climate for Latina/o Undergraduates." *Harvard Educational Review* 79: 659–690.

Young, Iris. 1990. *Justice and Politics of Difference*. Princeton, NJ: Princeton University Press.

Youngers, Coletta. 2005. "The Collateral Damage of the U.S. War on Drugs: Conclusions and Recommendations." In *Drugs and Democracy in Latin America*, edited by Eileen Rosin and Coletta Youngers. Boulder, CO: Lynne Rienner Publishers.

Youngers, Coletta, and Eileen Rosin. 2005. *Drugs and Democracy in Latin America: The Impact of U.S. Policy*. Boulder, CO: Lynne Rienner Publishers.

Yuker, H. E. 1994. "Variables that Influence Attitudes toward People with Disabilities: Conclusions from the Data." *Journal of Social Behavior and Personality* 9, no. 5: 3–22.

Yuval-Davis, N. 2006a. "Intersectionality and Feminist Politics." *European Journal of Women's Studies* 13, no. 3: 193–209.

——. 2006b. "Women, Citizenship and Difference." *Feminist Review* 57: 4–27.

Zajdow, Grazyna. 2005. "What Are We Scared Of? The Absence of Sociology in Current Debates about Drug Treatments and Policies." *Journal of Sociology* 41, no. 2: 185–199.

Zajdow, Grazyna, and Jo M. Lindsay. 2010. "Editorial: Sociology, Recreational Drugs and Alcohol." *Health Sociology Review* 19, no. 2: 146–150.

Zakaria, Fareed, and Kuan Yew Lee. 1994. "Culture Is Destiny: A Conversation with Lee Kuan Yew." *Foreign Affairs* 73, no. 2: 109–126.

Zald, Mayer N. 1992. "Looking Backward to Look Forward: Reflections on the Past and Future of the Resource Mobilization Research Program." In *Frontiers in Social Movement Theory*, edited by Aldon D. Morris and Carol McClurg Mueller, 326–348. New Haven, CT: Yale University Press.

Zeitlin, Irving M. 2000. *Ideology and the Development of Sociological Theory*. 7th ed. Englewood Cliffs, NJ: Prentice Hall.

——. 2009. "Education for Democracy in Peirce, James, Dewey and Mead: The North Central Sociological Association's Ruth and John Unseem Plenary Address." *Sociological Focus* 43, no. 4: 317–329.

Zellner, Robert, et al. 2008. "Brandeis in the Sixties." A panel presented at the annual meeting of the Association for Humanist Sociology, Boston, Massachusetts.

Zheng, Tiantian. 2010. *Sex Trafficking, Human Rights, and Social Justice*. New York: Routledge.

Zimmerman, Don H. 1970. "The Practicalities of Rule Use." In *Understanding Everyday Life: Toward the Reconstruction of Sociological Knowledge*, edited by Jack D. Douglas, 221–238. Chicago: Aldine.

Zinn, Maxine Baca, Lynn Weber Cannon, Elizabeth Higginbotham, and Bonnie Thornton Dill. 1986. "The Costs of Exclusionary Practices in Women's Studies." *Signs: Journal of Women in Culture and Society* 11: 290–303.

Zitzelsberger, Hilde. 2005. "(In)visibility: Accounts of Embodiment of Women in Physical Disabilities and Differences." *Disability and Society* 20, no. 4: 389–403.

Žižek, Slavoj. 2005. "Against Human Rights." *New Left Review* 34 (May–June): 115–131.

Zolberg, Aristide. 1986. "How Many Exceptionalisms?" In *Working-Class Formation: Nineteenth-Century Patterns in Western Europe and the United States,* edited by I. Katznelson and A. Zolberg, 397–455. Princeton, NJ: Princeton University Press.

Zou, M., and Zwart, T. 2011. "Rethinking Human Rights in China: Towards a Receptor Approach." In *Human Rights in the Asia-Pacific Region: Towards Institution Building,* edited by H. Nasu and B. Saul, 249–263. London: Routledge.

Zuberi, Tukufu, and Eduardo Bonilla-Silva. 2008. *White Logic, White Methods: Racism and Methodology.* Lanham, MD: Rowman & Littlefield.

Zukin, Sharon. 2011. *Naked City: The Death and Life of Authentic Urban Places.* New York: Oxford University Press.

Zuo, J., and Robert D. Benford. 1995. "Mobilization Processes and the 1989 Chinese Democracy Movement." *Sociological Quarterly* 36: 131–156.

Zweigenhaft, R., and G. Domhoff. 2006. *Diversity in the Power Elite.* Lanham, MD: Rowman & Littlefield.

INDEX

Francis O. Adeola is professor of sociology at the University of New Orleans. He is author of *Hazardous Wastes, Industrial Disasters, and Environmental Health Risks: Local and Global Environmental Struggles* (2011) and several peer-reviewed articles published in *American Behavioral Scientist, Armed Forces and Society, Environment and Behavior, Human Ecology Review, Community Development Society Journal, Society and Natural Resources,* and *Sociological Spectrum.*

Matthew Andersson is a doctoral student in sociology at the University of Iowa. His interests include human capital, culture in action, and social structure and personality.

J. I. (Hans) Bakker is professor of sociology at the University of Guelph in Guelph, Ontario, Canada. He was born in the Netherlands, grew up in Ohio and Alabama, and moved to Canada in 1971. He received an International Development Research Center fellowship to study in Indonesia and a Ford Foundation internship grant to study Mahatma Gandhi and human rights in India. Having published more than forty articles and edited three books, he is author of *Toward a Just Civilization*, a book about Gandhi's social theory. He has spent three years doing rural development research in Indonesia. He speaks the Indonesian language, Bahasa Indonesia, at an advanced-intermediate level and has done anthropological ethnographic fieldwork with the sea nomads of Sulawesi (Bajo Laut). He is very interested in Indic civilization, especially in Bali, where he is currently doing tourism research.

Giedrė Baltrušaitytė is a professor and researcher in the Department of Sociology at Vytautas Magnus University in Lithuania. Her teaching and research areas include sociology of health, illness, and health care. Her doctoral dissertation focused on psychiatric care from the mental patient's perspective. Currently she is working on a research project examining medically unexplained symptoms in primary health care.

J. Kenneth Benson is professor emeritus of sociology at the University of Missouri, Columbia, where he has served two terms as department chair and also chaired campus committees on peace studies and minority affairs. He worked one year at the University of Gothenburg, Sweden, as a Fulbright fellow. His work has been published in *Administrative Science Quarterly, Sociological Quarterly, Journal for the Scientific Study of Religion, Review of Religious Research,* and other journals and edited volumes. He has written on ethics in social research, religious organizations, interorganizational networks, coordination of human services, bureaucratic-professional conflict, dialectical theory, multiorganizational policy sectors, industrial policy, and religion and the professions. His paper "The Interorganizational Network as a Political Economy" (1975) was designated a Citation Classic in *Current Contents*. He continues to work on a dialectical approach to the study of organizations, occupations, networks, and policy sectors.

Mary Bernstein is professor of sociology at the University of Connecticut (UConn). Her scholarship seeks to understand the role of identity in social movements and how movement actors interact with the state and the law. Her recent publications include "What Are You? Explaining Identity as a Goal of the Multiracial Hapa Movement" (coauthored with Marcie De La Cruz), "Identity Politics," "Paths to Homophobia," "Nothing Ventured, Nothing Gained? Conceptualizing Social Movement 'Success' in the Lesbian and Gay Movement," and "Culture, Power, and Institutions: A Multi-Institutional Politics Approach to Social Movements" (coauthored with Elizabeth Armstrong). She is also coeditor of *Queer Families, Queer Politics: Challenging Culture and the State* (2001) and *Queer Mobilizations: LGBT Activists Confront the Law* (2009).

Ann Branaman is associate professor of sociology at Florida Atlantic University. She is author of several chapters and articles on Erving Goffman and on feminist social thought; she also coedited *The Goffman Reader* and edited *Self and Society*. Her current work focuses on the interface between social theory and social psychology.

David V. Brewington's dissertation, "International Associations at the Nexus of Globalization, Human Rights, and Religion," was completed in summer 2011. He currently evaluates community- and state-based preventative health policy advocacy for a large US NGO and continues his research efforts on international NGOs and the changing role of religion in the era of globalization. He lives in Chicago with his wife.

Jennifer Bronson is a doctoral student studying sociology at Howard University, with concentrations in medical sociology and social inequality. She has worked as a research associate in the field of substance abuse and served as program coordinator for Amnesty International's Human Rights Education Service Corps. Her dissertation utilizes a human rights framework to address maternal mortality in the United States.

David L. Brunsma is professor of sociology at Virginia Tech. His areas of research include sociologies of human rights and human rights sociologies, racial identity and racism, cognitive sociology and epistemologies, and multiraciality and whiteness. He is currently working on a major textbook about the social construction of difference. He is currently coeditor of *Societies without Borders: Human Rights and the Social Sciences* and section editor of the Race and Ethnicity Section of *Sociology Compass*. He lives and loves with his family in Blacksburg, Virginia.

Rachel Bryant is director of the International Children's Rights Index project at Case Western Reserve University. Her research areas include children's rights as well as a focus on public and private actors responsible for human rights implementation. Recent publications include "Children's Rights" with Brian Gran in *Sociology and Human Rights*, edited by J. Blau and M. Frezzo.

Jennifer L. Croissant is associate professor in gender and women's studies at the University of Arizona. Trained in science and technology studies, she has projects studying collaboration and climate in chemistry with colleague Laurel Smith-Doerr; she also has interests in pain measurement as well as agnotology and absences.

Mary Yu Danico is vice-chair and professor at CalPoly Pomona. Her areas of expertise are in race relations and family, and she has vested interests in Asian American studies; Korean American family and community formation; ethnic identity, 1.5- and second-generation issues; immigration; diaspora and reverse migration; and LGBT communities. She developed and runs the department Peer Mentor Program and advises students in the Four-Year Pledge program and students who want to be engaged in university life. She was a Fulbright senior scholar in Seoul, Korea (2005–2006), formerly chaired the Asia/Asia America Section of the American Sociological Association (ASA), and is the incoming president of the Association for Asian American Studies (2012–2014). She is author of many journal articles and *The 1.5 Generation: Becoming Korean American in Hawaii* (2004), *Asian American Issues* (2004), and *Transforming the Ivory Tower: Challenging Racism, Sexism, and Homophobia in Higher Education* (2012).

Héctor L. Delgado is professor of sociology at the University of La Verne and executive officer of the Society for the Study of Social Problems (SSSP). He is author of *New Immigrants, Old Unions: Organizing Undocumented Workers in Los Angeles* (1993) and numerous articles on labor, immigrants, and race and ethnicity.

Corey Dolgon received his doctorate in American culture from the University of Michigan in 1994. Since then he has taught at the Friends World Program at Southampton College, Worcester State College, and Harvard and Clark universities; he is now inaugural director of Stonehill College's Office of Community-Based Learning. He has published three books, including the award-winning *The End of the Hamptons: Scenes from the Class Struggle in America's Paradise* (2005 Humanist Sociology book award and 2007 Marxist Sociology Section award) and the textbook *Social Problems: A Service-Learning Approach* (2010). Dolgon is past editor of *Humanity and Society: The Journal of the Association for Humanist Sociology* and is currently coeditor of *Teaching Matters*, the ASA Section on Teaching and Learning's newsletter, and assistant editor of *Theory in Action*. Dolgon lives near Boston with his wife, Deborah, and two incredible daughters, Bailey and Ruby.

Karen Manges Douglas is associate professor of sociology at Sam Houston State University. Her areas of concentration include race/ethnic inequality, social stratification, and poverty. She has authored or coauthored articles and book chapters in these areas, including "U.S.-Mexican Border Families' Responses to U.S. Poverty Programs: Making a Living on the U.S. Side of the Border" (with Laura Lein and Kathleen Murphy), "An Account of a Life Lived: Herbert Blumer Revisited," and "No Phone, No Vehicle, No English and No Citizenship: The Vulnerability of Mexican Immigrants in the United States" (with Rogelio Sáenz). Manges Douglas is a past president of the Southwestern Sociological Association. She received her PhD in sociology from the University of Texas, Austin.

Peter Eglin is professor of sociology at Wilfrid Laurier University in Waterloo, where he has taught since 1976. He is author, coauthor, or coeditor of five books, including *The Montreal Massacre: A Story of Membership Categorization Analysis* (with Stephen Hester, 2003) and *Intellectual Citizenship and the Problem of Incarnation* (2012). As a student of ethnomethodology and conversation analysis, he investigates the use of categories, most recently gender categories and the category "feminist," for describing persons in practical reasoning in talk and texts in various settings. He is currently engaged in a study of what about the activities going on in universities makes these institutions observably universities. He is also exercised by the question of the responsibility of intellectuals for violations of human rights and has published studies on the complicity of Canadian government, business, media, universities, and intellectuals in state terrorism in El Salvador and the Indonesian near-genocide in East Timor. He has also carried out studies, given talks, and otherwise spoken out about the complicity of Canadian institutions in Israeli state terrorism, war crimes, and general oppression of the Palestinians. He has become increasingly concerned about the growing virulence of attacks on organizations and persons who speak out in defense of the human rights of Palestinians, particularly on university campuses.

David Fasenfest is associate professor of sociology and urban affairs in the College of Liberal Arts and Sciences at Wayne State University. As an economist and sociologist, he has written numerous articles on regional and urban economic development, labor market analysis and workforce development, and income inequality. His work has appeared in *Economic Development Quarterly, Urban Affairs Review, International Journal of Urban and Regional Review,* and *International Journal of Sociology.* He is editor of *Community Economic Development: Policy Formation in the U.S. and U.K.* (1993), *Critical Perspectives on Local Development Policy Evaluation* (2004), *Engaging Social Justice: Critical Studies of 21st Century Social Transformation* (2009), and *Social Change, Resistance and Social Practice* (2010). In addition, he edits the journal *Critical Sociology* and is editor of the book series Studies in Critical Social Science published by Brill Academic Press.

Jan Fritz is a professor at the University of Cincinnati in Ohio. She is also a senior research fellow at the Centre for Sociological Research at the University of Johannesburg (South Africa), a Woodrow Wilson Fellow (2012–2013), the Fulbright Distinguished Chair in Human Rights and International Studies at the Danish

Institute for Human Rights (Denmark, 2011–2012), and a special education mediator for the state of Kentucky in the United States. She is president of the clinical sociology division of the International Sociological Association (ISA) and also a member of the ISA's executive committee. In 2010, she received the ASA's Distinguished Career Award for the Practice of Sociology and, in 2011, the annual award (the Better World Award) of the Ohio Mediation Association. She is author and editor of numerous publications, including *International Clinical Sociology*. Her e-mail address is jan.fritz@uc.edu.

Elizabeth A. Gill received her MA from Yale University and her PhD from the University of Texas, Austin. Currently, she is a professor of sociology at Randolph-Macon College in Ashland, Virginia, where she holds the Potts Professorship of Social Sciences. She has authored and coauthored more than twenty-five articles and numerous presentations on death and dying, the family, human rights, mindfulness and social justice, and pragmatism, all of which examine the effects of the organizational context upon an individual's existence through empirical specification and the development of theoretical frameworks designed to bridge the agency/structure divide. More specifically, her research interests focus on comparative studies between existing bureaucratic organizations and effective alternatives to problems facing individuals embedded within these organizations. Presently, she is working on a book examining suicide as a human rights issue through a comprehensive examination of social and cultural factors deemed consequential to the current suicide and mental health crisis within the military, including the telling, framing, and analysis of war-related events in the media; the structural and social isolation of veterans; the decommunalization and deritualization of veterans' experiences of violence and death; and the medicalization of emotion associated with war-related traumatic experiences.

Tanya Golash-Boza is author of *Yo Soy Negro: Blackness in Peru* (2011), *Immigration Nation: Raids Detentions and Deportations in Post-9/11 America* (2012), and *Due Process Denied: Detention and Deportation in the United States* (2012), in addition to more than a dozen peer-reviewed articles and book chapters. Her scholarship recently earned the Distinguished Early Career Award of the Racial and Ethnic Minorities Studies Section of the ASA.

Brian K. Gran is a former lawyer whose sociological research focuses on human rights and institutions that support and hinder their enforcement, with a particular interest in whether law can intervene in private spheres. A cofounder of the ASA Human Rights Section, Gran is directing a project funded by the National Science Foundation (NSF) to develop an international Children's Rights Index. He serves on the Council of the Science and Human Rights Project of the American Association for the Advancement of Science. Gran was recently elected president of the ISA Thematic Group on Human Rights and Global Justice (TG03). For his research on independent children's rights institutions, he was a visiting fellow of the Swiss National Science Foundation. Gran recently learned he has been awarded a

Fulbright grant to research and teach at the School of Law at Reykjavik University in Iceland.

Barbara Gurr's research highlights the intersections of race, class, gender, sexuality, citizenship, and the body. Her dissertation utilized a reproductive justice frame-work to examine the consequences of locating Native American women's health care in a federal agency, the Indian Health Service. Her current research considers family-identity tasks for cisgender parents with young transgender children. She is currently assistant professor in residence in the Women's, Gender, and Sexuality Studies Program at the University of Connecticut, and her work has been published in *International Journal of Sociology of the Family*, *Sociology Compass*, *Journal of the Association for Research on Mothering*, and elsewhere.

Angela J. Hattery is professor of sociology at George Mason University and serves as the associate director of the Women and Gender Studies Program there. Her research focuses on social stratification, gender, family, and race. She is author of numerous articles, book chapters, and books, including *The Social Dynamics of Family Violence* (2012), *Prisoner Reentry and Social Capital* (2010), *Interracial Intimacies* (2009), *Interracial Relationships* (2009), *Intimate Partner Violence* (2008), *African American Families* (2007), and *Women, Work, and Family* (2001).

Jeremy Hein is professor of sociology at the University of Wisconsin, Eau Claire. His research is on forced migration in Asia and the impact of racism on immigrants in the United States. His publications include *Ethnic Origins: The Adaptation of Cambodian and Hmong Refugees in Four American Cities* (2006).

Lyndi Hewitt is assistant professor of sociology at the University of North Carolina, Asheville. Her scholarship has appeared in journals such as *American Journal of Sociology*, *Mobilization*, *Societies without Borders*, and *Interface*. She has written about framing and mobilization in US state women's suffrage movements, strategic adaptation among US state women's jury movements, the utility of the World Social Forum as a space for transnational women's activism, and organizational influences on counterhegemonic framing among transnational feminist organizations. Her current research, a collaborative project with the Global Fund for Women, draws upon literature from the fields of social movements, advocacy evaluation, and development to investigate the influence of different sources and models of funding on the strategic action and outcomes of women's rights organizations.

Susan W. Hinze is associate professor of sociology and director of women's and gender studies at Case Western Reserve University. She earned her doctorate in sociology from Vanderbilt University. Her substantive interests lie primarily in medical sociology, gender, social inequality, and the emerging work/family or work/life nexus. Her research interests include the influence of patient race/ethnicity, social class, and gender on physician decision-making, and the gendered career and family paths of physicians. Her current project explores the rapid growth of workplace coaching as a profession. Her work appears in *Research in the Sociology of Health Care*; *Health: An Interdisciplinary Journal for the Social Study of Health and Medicine*; *Research in the Sociology of Work*; *American Journal of Public Health*, *Work and Occupations*; *Academic Emergency Medicine*; *Annals of Internal Medicine*; *Sociological Quarterly*; *Social Forces*; and *Women's Health Issues*.

Steven Hitlin is associate professor of sociology at the University of Iowa. His research areas largely fall under the domains of social psychology and the life course, and he is involved in a number of collaborations intended to build a more explicit subfield around the sociological study of morality. He is author of *Moral Selves, Evil Selves: The Social Psychology of Conscience* (2008).

Rosemary L. Hopcroft is professor of sociology at the University of North Carolina, Charlotte. Her research and teaching focus on the intersection of biology and social science. Her work can be found in journals that include the *American Journal of Sociology*, *American Sociological Review*, and *Social Forces*. She has also authored numerous book chapters, one book, and the text *Sociology: A Biosocial Introduction* (2010).

Keri E. Iyall Smith's research explores the intersections between human rights doctrine, the state, and indigenous peoples in the context of a globalizing society. She has published articles on hybridity and world society, human rights, indigenous peoples, and teaching sociology. She is author of *States and Indigenous Movements* (2006), editor of *Sociology of Globalization* (2012), and coeditor of *Public Sociologies Reader* (with Judith R. Blau, 2006) and *Hybrid Identities: Theoretical and Empirical Examinations* (with Patricia Leavy, 2008). She is assistant professor of sociology at Suffolk University in Boston, Massachusetts, where she teaches courses on globalization, sociological theory, Native Americans, and introductory sociology. She is a former vice president of Sociologists without Borders.

Mark Jacobs is professor of sociology at George Mason University, where from 1992 to 1999 he was founding director of the first interdisciplinary PhD program in cultural studies in the United States. He is a past chair of the Section on the Sociology of Culture of the ASA; since September 2011 he has been vice-chair of the Research Network on Culture of the European Sociological Association, and he was the 2010–2011 Robin M. Williams Distinguished Lecturer of the Eastern Sociological Society. He wrote *Screwing the System and Making It Work: Juvenile Justice in the No-Fault Society* (1990); collaborated with Gerald D. Suttles on *Front-Page Economics* (2010); and coedited a special issue of *Poetics* titled "Cultural Sociology and Sociological Publics" (2005) and *The Blackwell Companion to the Sociology of Culture* (2005).

Thomas Janoski is professor of sociology at the University of Kentucky, Lexington. His research focuses on the intersection of work and politics, especially the development of citizenship rights and obligations in the eighteen countries of the

Organization for Economic Cooperation and Development. Recent books include *The Ironies of Citizenship: Naturalization and Integration in Industrialized Countries* (2010), *Diversity at Kaizen Motors: Gender, Race, Age and Insecurity in a Japanese Auto Transplant* (with Darina Lepadatu, 2011), and *The Handbook of Political Sociology: States, Civil Society and Globalization* (coedited with Robert Alford, Alexander Hicks, and Mildred Schwartz, 2005). His article "The Spirit of the Civil Sphere" in *Comparative Social Research* won the 2010 Outstanding Author Contribution Award from the Emerald Literati Network. His research on citizenship, social policy, employment, immigration, and political sociology has been published in numerous journals and edited books. His current NSF project is *The Vortex of Labor: The Causes of Structural Unemployment*, which continues his earlier work on the political economy of work and the new forms of corporate organization. He teaches political sociology, the sociology of work, and comparative/historical methodology to graduate students; to undergraduates, he teaches work and organizations, the sociology of immigration, and political sociology.

Nathalia E. Jaramillo is a senior lecturer in the Faculty of Education, School of Critical Studies in Education, University of Auckland, New Zealand. She is author of *Immigration and the Challenge of Education* (2012) and coeditor of *Epistemologies of Ignorance in Education* (with Erik Malewski, 2011). She writes in the fields of decolonial thought, critical pedagogy, and the politics of education.

Guillermina Jasso is Silver Professor and professor of sociology at New York University. Her main research interests are basic theory and international migration, together with inequality, probability distributions, and factorial survey methods, topics on which she has published widely, including such papers as "How Much Injustice Is There in the World?" (1999), "A New Unified Theory of Sociobehavioral Forces" (2008), "Two Types of Inequality" (2008), and "Migration and Stratification" (2011). Her contributions (some with coauthors) include a mathematical formula for the sense of justice, a justice index with poverty and inequality components, two new distributions, and methods for estimating the family-reunification multiplier, the number of persons waiting for high-skill permanent visas, and the previous illegal experience of new legal immigrants, as well as for deriving an empirically based point system for immigrant selection. She is currently co–principal investigator of The New Immigrant Survey, president of the International Sociological Association's Research Committee on Social Psychology (RC42), chair of the ASA's Methodology Section, and chair of the Census Scientific Advisory Committee. She was a fellow at the Center for Advanced Study in the Behavioral Sciences and is an elected member/fellow of the Johns Hopkins Society of Scholars, the Sociological Research Association, and the American Association for the Advancement of Science. Two recent papers won awards. Her Erdös number is 3.

Victoria Johnson is associate professor of sociology at the University of Missouri, Columbia. She received her BA from San Francisco State University and her PhD from the University of California, Davis, with a designated emphasis on social theory and comparative history. Her areas of emphasis include social movements and collective behavior, historical and comparative methods, political and cultural sociology, sociology of media, and animal and society studies. She is author of *How Many Machine Guns Does It Take to Cook One Meal? The Seattle and San Francisco General Strikes* (2008), the coedited anthology *Waves of Protest: Social Movements since the Sixties* (1999), and numerous articles.

Valeska P. Korff is a postdoctoral fellow at the Center on Philanthropy and Civil Society at Stanford University. Her research focuses on the study of organizations, particularly nonprofits and nongovernmental organizations, and the dynamics and effects of professionalization processes.

Lester R. Kurtz is professor of public sociology at George Mason University, where he teaches courses on violence and nonviolence, social movements, peace and conflict, globalization, comparative sociology of religion, and social theory. He also lectures regularly at the European Peace University. Kurtz holds an MA in religion from Yale University and a PhD in sociology from the University of Chicago and was previously director of religious studies at the University of Texas. He is editor of the three-volume *Encyclopedia of Violence, Peace and Conflict* (2008) and coeditor of *Nonviolent Social Movements* (1999) and *The Web of Violence* (1996). He is author of many books and articles, including *Gods in the Global Village* (2011), *The Nuclear Cage* (1994), and *The Politics of Heresy* (1986), which received the Society for the Scientific Study of Religion's Distinguished Book Award. He is currently working on books titled *Gandhi's Paradox* and *Gods and Bombs*. Kurtz is a past chair of the Peace and Justice Studies Association as well as the Peace, War, and Social Conflict Section of the ASA, which awarded him its Robin Williams Distinguished Career Award in 2005. He has lectured in Europe, Asia, Africa, and North America and taught at the University of Chicago, Northwestern University, Delhi University in India, and Tunghai University in Taiwan.

Clarence Y. H. Lo is author of *Small Property versus Big Government* and coeditor of *Social Policy and the Conservative Agenda*. He is director of graduate studies in sociology at the University of Missouri, Columbia, and director of the Peace Studies Program there.

Jean M. Lynch received her PhD from Brown University and is professor in and chair of the Department of Sociology and Gerontology at Miami University in Oxford, Ohio. Her areas of expertise include LGBT issues, applied research, and disability scholarship. She has published extensively on lesbian and gay relationships and has particularly been involved in scholarship concerning lesbian and gay stepfamilies. In her research on the latter, she has developed models of identity transformation that occur for the biological parents and the stepparents who enter these stepfamily relationships. More recently, her scholarship focuses on the disability community. In this work, she particularly emphasizes the perceptions developed by the able-bodied toward those with disability and the subsequent treatment afforded those with disabilities.

Amir B. Marvasti is associate professor of sociology at Pennsylvania State University, Altoona. His research focuses on the social construction of deviant identities in everyday life. He is author of *Being Homeless: Textual and Narrative Constructions* (2003), *Qualitative Research in Sociology* (2003), *Middle Eastern Lives in America* (with Karyn McKinney, 2004), and *Doing Qualitative Research: A Comprehensive Guide* (with David Silverman, 2008). He is coeditor of *SAGE Handbook of Interview Research: The Complexity of the Craft* (with Jaber Gubrium, Jim Holstein, and Karyn McKinney, 2012). His articles have been published in *Journal of Contemporary Ethnography, Qualitative Inquiry, Symbolic Interaction,* and *Critical Sociology.*

Karyn D. McKinney is associate professor of sociology and women's studies at Pennsylvania State University, Altoona. Her research has focused on the role of race and racism in identity and experience. Her publications include *Being White: Stories of Race and Racism* (2005), *Middle Eastern Lives in America* (with Amir Marvasti, 2004), and *The Many Costs of Racism* (with Joe Feagin, 2003). She is coeditor of *SAGE Handbook of Interview Research: The Complexity of the Craft* (with Jaber Gubrium, Jim Holstein, and Amir Marvasti, 2012). In addition, she has published articles in journals such as *Race and Society, Social Identities,* and *Critical Sociology.*

Peter McLaren is professor of education in the Graduate School of Education and Information Studies, University of California, Los Angeles, and part-time faculty member of Critical Studies in Education, Te Kura o te Kotuinga Akoranga Matauranga, Faculty of Education, University of Auckland, Te Kura Akoranga o Tamaki Makarau, New Zealand. He is also the founding professor of the Instituto McLaren de Pedagogia Critica y Educacion Popular Enseñada, Baja California, Mexico. He is author, editor, or coeditor of more than forty-five books, has won numerous book awards, and lectures widely worldwide. His writings have been translated into twenty languages. He is a fellow of the Royal Society of Arts and Letters and the American Education Research Association.

Maria Cristina Morales received a PhD from Texas A&M University and is currently assistant professor of sociology at the University of Texas, El Paso. She has written several articles on labor market inequality among Latina/o workers, including how masculinity operates to mask discriminatory practices in the construction industry. Moreover, she coined the term "citizenship-divide" to describe how ethnicity is formed along citizenship/nativity lines and used the concept to examine the ethnic resources of workers, wage returns, and political perceptions. She also coined the term "border sexual conquest" (BSC) to describe the processes that exacerbate sexual/gendered violence in marginalized places. Thus far, BSC has been used to examine the feminicides in Júarez and women laborers on both sides of the México-US border, the erasure of victimization, and migration. Lastly, she has written on the role that academics play in the immigration movement at the border.

Nancy A. Naples is professor of sociology and women's studies at the University of Connecticut. Prior to joining the UConn faculty in 2001, she was associate professor of sociology and women's studies at the University of California, Irvine, where she also served as director and associate director of the Women's Studies Program. She was president of Sociologists for Women in Society in 2004 and of the SSSP from 2007 to 2008. She is currently president-elect of the Eastern Sociological Society. Her research on citizenship, social policy, immigration, and community activism has been published in numerous journals and edited books. Her scholarship includes publication of two solo-authored books, four edited volumes, twenty-five journal articles, twenty-seven book chapters, and many book reviews and other publications. Her first book, *Grassroots Warriors: Activist Mothering, Community Work and the War on Poverty* (1998), received honorable mention from the Section on Race, Gender and Class of the ASA and was a finalist for the C. Wright Mills Award, sponsored by the SSSP. Her most recent book, *The Sexuality of Migration: Border Crossing and Mexican Immigrant Men* by Lionel Cantú (2009), coedited with Salvador Vidal-Ortiz, received the 2010 Best Book Award from the Sexualities Section of the ASA and honorable mention from the Latino Studies Section of the Latin American Studies Association. She has received numerous grants for her research, including funding from the National Institute of Mental Health, the Center for US Mexican Studies, UC Mexus, and the ASA's Spivack Program on Applied Social Research, as well as from the ASA's Fund for the Advancement of the Discipline and the NSF. She received the 2008 Faculty Excellence Award in Research (Humanities/Social Sciences), given by UConn's Alumni Association, and the 2011 Excellence in Research Award for Social Sciences from UConn's College of Liberal Arts and Sciences. She also received the 2010 Distinguished Feminist Lecturer Award and the 2011 Feminist Mentor Award from Sociologists for Women in Society.

Kenneth Neubeck is vice-chair of the City of Eugene (Oregon) Human Rights Commission, which is exploring ways to implement international human rights principles and standards across Eugene at the local community level (see www.humanrightscity.com). Neubeck is a founder and co-coordinator of the Community Coalition for Advancement of Human Rights, an informal network of social justice groups and their allies in the Eugene area, and serves on the board of directors of Amigos Multicultural Services Center, which advocates for immigrant rights as human rights. He is emeritus professor of sociology at the University of Connecticut, where he served as director of the interdisciplinary undergraduate human rights minor. He is author of *When Welfare Disappears: The Case for Economic Human Rights* (2006), which addresses poverty in the United States as a human rights violation. In *Welfare Racism: Playing the Race Card against America's Poor* (2001), Neubeck and coauthor Noel Cazenave analyze racism's negative impact on US welfare policy. Neubeck's current scholarship focuses on efforts to implement the human rights framework at the local community level.

Tarique Niazi is associate professor at the University of Wisconsin, Eau Claire. He has a PhD in environmental studies from the University of Wisconsin, Madison. He teaches environmental sociology, sociology of the Middle East, and contemporary social problems. His research interests include environmental security, sustainable development, and ethnonational movements. He specializes in resource-based conflicts. He has written numerous articles and book chapters. His work has appeared in *Journal of Environment and Development, International Journal of Contemporary Sociology, Journal of Peasant Studies, Economic and Political Weekly,* and *China and Eurasia Forum,* among other publications.

J. Steven Picou is professor of sociology at the University of South Alabama, Mobile. He is coeditor and contributor (with D. Brunsma and D. Overfelt) to *The Sociology of Katrina: Perspectives on a Modern Catastrophe* (2010). For more information, visit his website at www.stevenpicou.com.

Jean H. Quataert is professor of history at Binghamton University (State University of New York, Binghamton) and coeditor of *Journal of Women's History.* A historian of nineteenth-century Germany by training, she has written extensively on socialism and feminism in German social democracy, protoindustry, and philanthropy and dynastic nationalism in German history; she has also authored a well-received textbook on European women's history. More recently she has turned to transnational and global themes and has published a book on human rights history titled *Advocating Dignity: Human Rights Mobilizations in Global Politics* (2009). Currently, she is working on women's human rights and the challenge to transnational feminism.

Christopher N. J. Roberts is associate professor at the University of Minnesota Law School. He studies human rights and international law from an interdisciplinary perspective rooted in sociology, law, and public policy. His forthcoming book, *The Epoch of Struggle,* looks at the historical development of the modern international human rights regime.

Mary Romero is professor of justice studies and social inquiry at Arizona State University. She is author of *The Maid's Daughter: Living Inside and Outside the American Dream* (2011) and *Maid in the U.S.A.* (1992; 10th anniv. ed., 2002) and coeditor of numerous collections. She received the ASA Section on Racial and Ethnic Minorities' 2009 Founder's Award, recognizing career excellence in scholarship and service. In 2004, she received the SSSP's 2004 Lee Founders Award, the highest award made by the society for a career in activist scholarship.

Benita Roth is associate professor of sociology, history, and women's studies at Binghamton University. Her work focuses on the intersections of gender, social protest, race/ethnicity, and sexuality. Her book *Separate Roads to Feminism: Black, Chicana, and White Feminist Movements in America's Second Wave* (2003) won the Distinguished Book Award from the Sex and Gender Section of the ASA and is in its fourth printing. She is also associate editor for *Journal of Women's History* and coeditor, with Jean Quataert, of a special issue of the journal on the impact of UN-sponsored global meetings of women for transnational feminism and human rights organizing. She is currently working on a book about anti-AIDS organizing in Los Angeles in the 1980s and 1990s.

Jean J. Ryoo is a doctoral candidate in the Graduate School of Education and Information Studies at the University of California, Los Angeles. She currently works closely with Los Angeles Unified School District high school teachers and high school students in the Exploring Computer Science project funded by the NSF. Her research interests in revolutionary critical pedagogy, cultural-historical activity theories of learning, and educational civil rights stem from her previous work as a middle and high school teacher in public schools.

Rogelio Sáenz is dean of the College of Public Policy and Peter Flawn Professor of Demography at the University of Texas, San Antonio. He is also a Carsey policy fellow at the Carsey Institute at the University of New Hampshire. Sáenz received his PhD in sociology from Iowa State University. He has written extensively in the areas of demography, Latina/os, race and ethnic relations, inequality, and immigration. Sáenz is coeditor of *Latina/os in the United States: Changing the Face of América* and coauthor of *Latino Issues: A Reference Handbook.* He also writes regularly for the Population Reference Bureau on ongoing demographic trends and authored the bureau's Population Bulletin Updated titled *Latinos in the United States 2010.* Sáenz is currently vice president of the Southwestern Social Science Association and is also chair of the Council of the Inter-University Consortium for Political and Social Research (ICPSR).

Nader Saiedi, born in Tehran, Iran, received an MS in economics from Pahlavi University in Shiraz, Iran (1978) and a PhD in sociology from the University of Wisconsin, Madison (2003). Has taught sociology at the University of California, Los Angeles; Vanderbilt; the University of Virginia; and Carleton College. He is currently professor of sociology at Carleton College. His books include *The Birth of Social Theory* (1993), *Logos and Civilization* (2000), and *Gate of the Heart* (2008).

John Sanbonmatsu is associate professor of philosophy at Worcester Polytechnic Institute. Sanbonmatsu received his PhD in the history of consciousness from the University of California, Santa Cruz. He is author of *The Postmodern Prince* (2004) and editor of *Critical Theory and Animal Liberation* (2011). His academic writing has appeared in, among other publications, *Social Theory and Practice, American Journal of Economics and Sociology, Socialist Register,* and *Theory and Society.* Among his current research interests are critical social theory (Frankfurt School, Marxism, feminism, ecology, and animal liberation theory), as well as Continental philosophy and the sociology of knowledge.

Jenniffer M. Santos-Hernández is a PhD candidate in sociology at the University of Delaware. As a graduate student, she worked for the Disaster Research Center, one of the world's leading research centers, as well as its oldest, devoted to studying the social aspects of disasters. Santos-Hernández also worked as a research fellow for Oak Ridge National Laboratory. Her interests include population studies, disasters, emergency management, risk communication, collective behavior, race and ethnicity, stratification, development, environmental sociology, and geographic information sciences.

Joachim J. Savelsberg is professor of sociology at the University of Minnesota. Recent writings address legal responses to hate crime, genocide, and atrocities and their impact on nonpublic representations and collective memories. Publications include *American Memories: Atrocities and the Law* (with Ryan D. King, 2011), *Crime and Human Rights: Criminology of Genocide and Atrocities* (2010), "Law and Collective Memory" (with King, 2007), and "Institutionalizing Collective Memories of Hate: Law and Law Enforcement in Germany and the United States" (with King, 2005). Current research, funded by the NSF, is titled "Collective Representations and Memories of Atrocities after Judicial Intervention: The Case of Darfur in International Comparison." "Discourses on Darfur: Science, Law, Media" (with John Hagan and Jens Meierhenrich) is also in progress, supported by the Rockefeller Foundation. Savelsberg has held fellowships and visiting professorships at Johns Hopkins University, Harvard University, University of Graz, University of Munich, the Rockefeller Center at Bellagio, and Humboldt University, Berlin. He is a past chair of the ASA Section for Sociology of Law and the SSSP's Theory Division. See also http://www.soc.umn.edu/people/savelsberg_j.html.

Robin Shura is assistant professor of sociology at Hiram College. Her research within the sociology of age includes long-term care, ageism, intergenerational family relationships, and life-course research. She has also done research on intercountry adoption. She teaches courses on sociological theory, sociology of age, long-term care, sociology of youth, medical sociology, and social problems. Her recent publications include "Culture Change in Long-Term Care: Participatory Action Research and the Role of the Resident" (2010).

Earl Smith is professor of sociology and the Rubin Distinguished Professor of American Ethnic Studies at Wake Forest University, where he is director of the American Ethnic Studies Program. He chaired the Department of Sociology from 1997 to 2005 and has numerous publications (books, articles, chapters, etc.) in the areas of professions, social stratification, family, and urban sociology; he has also published extensively on the sociology of sport. His most recent books include *African American Families Today: Myths and Realities* (with Angela J. Hattery, 2007), *The Social Dynamics of Family Violence* (with Angela J. Hattery, 2011), *Sociology of Sport and Social Theory* (2010), *Prisoner Reentry and Social Capital: The Long Road to Reintegration* (with Angela J. Hattery, 2010), and *Race, Sport and the American Dream* (2nd ed., 2009).

Phi Hong Su is a second-year PhD student in the Department of Sociology at the University of California, Los Angeles. She is pursuing research on international migration, politics, ethnic communities, and diaspora/transnationalism.

James Michael Thomas received his PhD from the University of Missouri in 2011. His dissertation, a comparative ethnography, examines how stand-up comedy, as a cultural and affectual mechanism, aids and constrains the diffusion of contentious political ideas and expressions among audiences. His published works have spanned a variety of topics, including the Black Reparations Movement in the United States, prototypes of racial formations among medieval Jews, and the impact of Richard Pryor's stand-up comedy on the facilitation of contentious racial politics in the American context. He is currently on the job market.

Rafael Wittek is professor of sociology at the University of Groningen, the Netherlands, and scientific director of the Interuniversity Center for Social Science Theory and Methodology. His research interests include the sociology of organizations, social-network analysis, the sociology of aging, and sociological theory. He is coeditor of *Handbook of Rational Choice Social Research* (with Tom Snijders and Victor Nee, forthcoming).

Mimi Zou is a doctoral student at the Faculty of Law and junior dean at St. John's College, University of Oxford. She is also a lawyer qualified in Australia, England, and Wales and specializes in human rights, employment, and administrative/public law. She was formerly a research fellow at the Netherlands School of Human Rights Research. Her research interests focus on human rights implementation and judicial developments in Asia, particularly China.

Tom Zwart is professor of human rights at the Faculty of Law, Economics and Governance of Utrecht University. He is also director of the Netherlands School of Human Rights Research, established by the five leading Dutch universities. He has developed the so-called receptor approach to human rights, which aims to uncover social institutions other than law and legally enforceable rights through which international human rights obligations are being implemented in Asian and African societies. This includes research into the relation between international criminal law and local peace and justice initiatives, as well as traditional values. Zwart has been a visiting scholar at a number of universities around the world, including Cambridge University, Sciences-Po (Paris), Sydney University, Tsinghua University, Washington University (St. Louis), and Zhejiang University. He has advised national and international governmental bodies, including the European Union, the Council of Europe, and the UN Human Rights Council, on human rights. Prior to taking up his position at Utrecht, Zwart served as head of the European and Legal Affairs Department of the Dutch Home Office and as senior counsel to the Dutch deputy prime minister.